OLD FAMILIAR FACES

OLD FAMILIAR FACES

The Great Character Actors and Actresses of Hollywood's Golden Era

ROBERT A. JURAN

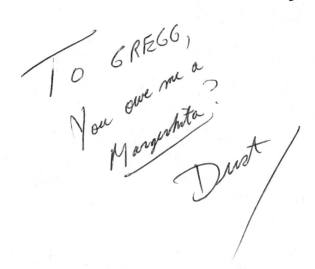

To GREGG,
You owe me a
Margherita?
Dust

MOVIE MEMORIES
PUBLISHING
SARASOTA, FLORIDA

Publisher's Cataloging-in-Publication Data

Juran, Robert A.
    Old Familiar Faces: The Great Character Actors
and Actresses of Hollywood's Golden Era.
        p. cm.
        Includes filmographies, bibliography, and index.
        Preassigned LCCN: 95-76418.

        1. Motion picture actors and actresses—
Biography. I. Title.
PN1998.2.J87 1995   791.43'028'0922
ISBN 0-9646340-0-7
                        QBI95-20122

First American Edition, 1995
10 9 8 7 6 5 4 3 2 1

DEDICATION

To my wife, Margaret, who loves old movies as much as I do.

ACKNOWLEDGMENTS

Several fellow old-movie buffs contributed their time, knowledge, and other resources to producing this book. The author would like to thank eminent film historian James Robert Parish, himself the author of many books on Hollywood's Golden Era; Fred Santon and Terry Porter, both of whom have written articles on old movies. For the photos, credit goes to Howard Mandelbaum of Photofest, New York City. Typesetting was by Golding Publications, Canyon Lake, Calif.

ABOUT THE AUTHOR

Robert A. Juran, a longtime fan of Hollywood movies of the Thirties, retired in 1992 after a long career as a newspaper editor. He has on many occasions been a state and national award winner for editorial writing and in other categories. In 1968 he won the national first prize in the Sigma Delta Chi Foundation Writing Awards. His interest in old movies led him to serve as the publisher and editor of the magazine Los Angeles Film Calendar from 1975 to 1977, and he is the author of articles on Spencer Tracy and director Frank Borzage. In the past he founded, published and edited two other magazines, Overset (a journalism review) and Antiquarian Bookseller (for dealers in used and rare books). He is also the author of a privately published book, "The Comprehensive Guide to Collectable Authors," and several other publications and monographs: "Rating the Newspaper Chains," "A Manual of Antiquarian Bookselling" and "How to Start a Used-Book Store." With his wife, Margaret, he lives in Sarasota, Florida.

NOTE TO THE READER

The first thing we would like to point out to the reader is that he or she will find far fewer errors in this book than in other movie reference books. The mistakes (not to mention misspellings of actors' names) that can be found in books on film is absolutely appalling. We have found and corrected hundreds, maybe thousands of errors.

Of course, we do not profess omniscience—merely a good strong knowledge of Hollywood films in the Thirties. And lacking omniscience, we find some situations where reference sources disagree and we do not know the answer ourselves. In those instances, we have taken the trouble to point out that the sources differ. (Very few movie books have ever taken that approach.)

As to the filmographies (the list of the actor's credits at the end of each chapter): It's difficult to find two movie reference books that agree on the credits of just about any performer. What we have tried to do is to make the filmographies in this book complete by incorporating credits from many reference books. As the final authority (at least for the Twenties and Thirties), we have used the reliably definitive American Film Institute Catalog. Unfortunately for earlier film historians, the Catalog's three-volume set on the Thirties was not published until 1993. In preparing our filmographies, each actor's credits were rigorously checked against the Catalog. Where even the Catalog had to point out that it is uncertain whether a given actor appeared in a given film, we have used the notation "Credit uncertain" for that film's listing in the filmography.

Another thing to note about the filmographies is this: It would have been a massive undertaking to check the official release dates for some five thousand films and thus list the films in precise order of release date within each year. What we have done is to simply group the films year by year, but not in precise order of release date. Generally we have started off each year with the most important films the actor appeared in, or that offered his best roles.

Within the main text, the same thing applies: Within each year, the films are not discussed in precise order of release date. And it should also be noted that, for the most part, the first film cited for a given year is followed by the last two digits of the year in parentheses, rather than the full four digits, thus: "In **Sadie McKee** (34) he was convincing as an unstable alcoholic millionaire..." The "34" of course means 1934.

In a work of this scope, the reader will still find some errors. We welcome corrections from readers. Some sort of documentation of the error should be provided if possible. Our address: Movie Memories Publishing, 6205 Crestwood Ave., Sarasota, FL 34231-3832; phone (941) 922-5633.

TABLE OF CONTENTS

x

INTRODUCTION

The film's nattily attired hero closes the door to his 1935 Art Deco apartment and sets out for the day's adventures. He can be William Powell, Spencer Tracy, Cary Grant, Edward G. Robinson, take your pick.

He may visit his girlfriend. At her home, he is greeted by her cheerful, comical black maid, and shortly thereafter by the young lady's sympathetic mother (or maybe she's an aristocratic dowager, or possibly a scatterbrained, social-climbing society matron). If they're really rich, the unctuous butler makes his appearance. Also on hand might be the girlfriend's grandmother, a crusty but basically kindly old lady.

Later on we'll meet the hero's male friend (beaming, not too bright) and the heroine's female friend (blonde, sassy, wisecracking). Now the plot gets more complicated. A scheming "other woman" is putting the make on our hero, while a suave Continental seducer has designs on the girlfriend. All this is of considerable interest to the prying town gossip.

The girlfriend's pal is a showgirl. The musical she's in is being backed financially by a lecherous "sugar daddy," who in turn is being worked by a cynical blonde gold-digger. And the showgirl is being wooed by a rich, not overly bright hayseed from the sticks.

Before the movie is half an hour old, there is a murder. Somebody did in an irascible millionaire, or maybe the victim was a pompous banker or a crusty old man with a (concealed) heart of gold. It happened in a hotel room, and the prissy, flustered hotel manager is going out of his mind. A brash, wisecracking reporter is bombarding the minions of the law with questions; we see the tough-talking police sergeant and his associate, the dumb detective. A crotchety old doctor has just pronounced the victim dead.

We'll find out—about five minutes before the end of the picture—that the foul deed was done by a vicious, cold-blooded gangster. Meanwhile, though, we'll be treated to a parade of "red herrings," making it tough for us to guess the murderer's identity. Each of them had a motive for bumping off the deceased. They are: a crooked politician, a shyster lawyer, an avuncular theatrical producer with several young actress "protégées," and two foreign noblemen, one a stuffy, bumbling Englishman, the other an eccentric, language-mangling Russian.

Before the film is finally over, though, we'll meet still more characters. There's the kindly priest. The mad scientist. The stern judge. The fanatical foreign spy. The blowsy, good-hearted hooker. The street-smart cab driver with a Brooklyn accent. The genial drunk. The toothless, cackling deputy sheriff in a rural town.

A week after seeing the movie you might very well have forgotten about Powell, Tracy, Grant or Robinson. But you would still recall the sharply etched portrayals of the unctuous butler, the treacherous "other woman," the prissy hotel functionary, the murderous gangster, the tough cop and the wise-guy cabbie. Because *these were people you were likely to encounter in real life.* (At least in 1935.) And because they were more nearly like us ordinary mortals (rather than the godlike stars whose fantasies we lived out), these supporting players, or character actors, who enacted the roles we recognized from real life, were the people who really held together the make-believe world up there on the screen.

To understand the importance of the character actor or actress, it is necessary first to examine the incredible hold the movies had on the America of the 1930s. In that decade the typical adult went to a film *more often than once a week* in those Depression times. (In the Thirties, the typical moviegoer was an adult—not a teen-ager like today.) Whereas today the average moviegoer attends about once every two months—and most adults hardly ever attend!

Much of America virtually *lived* in the world of the cinema during the Thirties, or at least was constantly turning to it. As Andrew Bergman notes in his book "We're in the Money," a study of the effect of movies on America in the Depression: "...As economic paralysis spread [and] the number of unemployed moved toward 15 million...it was evident that the total of...moviegoers included many people who could scarcely afford to be there...Americans needed their movies, [which] had come to play too important a role in their lives to be considered just another luxury item...[They] did not escape into a void each week; escapism is hardly a useful concept. People do not escape into something they cannot relate to. The movies were meaningful because they depicted things lost or things desired."

Historian Arthur Schlesinger Jr. has pointed out that American films of the Thirties had "a vital connection with American emotions—more, I think, than [they] ever had before...The movies were near the operative center of the nation's consciousness."

In other words, America's political, economic and social problems were frequently reflected in the movies. The film became the vehicle that could give the viewer what one writer has called "revenge, adjustment, repair of self-esteem, reconciliation, acceptance." In those trying times, little wonder that audiences found themselves so deeply stirred by what was happening on the screen. For 90 minutes or so the troubles of everyday living could be forgotten. In the darkened movie palace, the film, and the characters in it, reflected the problems and psyches of the viewers. For 25 cents, they got the equivalent of a cheap visit to a psychotherapist.

Possibly even more than they identified with the stars of those movies, the audience identified with the character actors who personified a certain mood, an emotion, an attribute. Those performers provided a continuity, week after week and year after year. The character actor usually appeared regularly in a certain kind of role. When his or her face flashed on the screen, your brain registered "haughty butler" or "scheming other woman" or "irascible millionaire" or "murderous gangster." Your mind formed a bridge to what was coming. Explanations were unnecessary. You felt in familiar surroundings; you knew where things stood. And these professional actors produced for you a matrix of your own living experience—reached out of the darkened theater into your own home, your job, your life, to recapture and re-create them with their character portrayals.

But what precisely *is* a character actor? A character role is not that of a star, a romantic lead or an ingenue, but a distinctive type, usually a mature type, characterized by occupation, mentality, emotional makeup, or attitudes toward life—or a combination of all of these.

And the great character actors of Hollywood's Golden Era were, many of them, one of a kind. While in many roles you could have replaced James Cagney with Humphrey Bogart or Edward G. Robinson, or substituted Barbara Stanwyck or Bette Davis for Joan Crawford, it would have been difficult to find performers who could play the roles usually taken by Franklin Pangborn, Margaret Hamilton, Mischa Auer, Walter Brennan, Eric Blore, May Robson, Donald Meek or Akim Tamiroff—to name a few examples. For each of these actors had perfected a type to such a degree that virtually no one could successfully imitate it.

While some character actors cornered the market on a narrowly defined type of role, others were performers of astonishing range and versatility. The greatest character actors—people such as Walter Huston, Claude Rains and Thomas Mitchell—could literally take any part ever written and breathe life into it. The character could be a noble, virtuous hero or a slimy, treacherous villain—it made little difference. No matter what the role, you believed in the performance, and were caught up in it.

Whether they were distinct "types" or performers of great versatility, their faces became almost as familiar to you as those of your family and friends. You might not have known their names, but you sure knew the faces. And in time they became a part of your consciousness—just as much as Clark Gable and Greta Garbo did.

These character actors, with their ability to play supporting roles that urgently needed to be filled in the approximately 5,000 films made by the Hollywood studios in the Thirties—some 3,580 by the eight major studios or releasing organizations alone—had the opportunity to chalk up enviable totals in their career filmographies. For example, J. Carrol Naish made 168 movies, Andy Devine 142, Alan Hale 186, Barton MacLane 142, Eugene Pallette 173, Lewis Stone 147—and John Carradine an incredible 220 or so.

Meanwhile, the major stars of the period typically appeared in 60 to 80 films over their careers. In fact, John Wayne and Myrna Loy were probably the only stars to make 100 or more—and Miss Loy was able to do so mainly because she was really a *character* actress for her first seven years on the screen, making an amazing 70 movies in that short time, playing campy vamps and Oriental menaces. After she became a star and portrayed noble heroines, she made only 53 films in the next half-century!

Another significant difference between the character actors and the stars comes in the areas of age and experience. Most stars of the Golden Era were performers in their twenties and thirties, with little, if any, stage experience—or much of any other kind of life experience. Many—such as Robert Taylor and Loretta Young—weren't even skilled dramatic actors and had little to recommend them other than physical beauty or handsomeness.

The character actors, on the other hand, generally tended to be in their forties, fifties and sixties, or even older, and most of them were veterans of the stage before coming to films. The truth is that, by and large, they could act rings around the stars they supported. That's why they stole so many scenes from them.

But in addition, the life experiences of character actors often were formidable. Donald Crisp had been a major film director in the silent era. Maria Ouspenskaya, a member of the famed Moscow Art Theater under

Konstantin Stanislavsky, ran her own acting school. Sig Rumann was a bacteriologist between acting assignments. Victor McLaglen had been a prizefighter and once fought a six-round bout against the great heavyweight champion Jack Johnson. Billie Burke, a major Broadway stage star of the World War I era, was married to impresario Florenz Ziegfeld. Brian Donlevy served in both Gen. Pershing's border expedition against Pancho Villa and in France's Lafayette Flying Corps during World War I, and later was an "Arrow Collar Man" model for artist J.F. Leyendecker. Sir C. Aubrey Smith had been a member of England's national cricket team in world competition. Joseph Calleia and Eduardo Ciannelli had been opera singers. Alan Hale was a successful inventor, Gene Lockhart a songwriter, Thomas Mitchell a playwright, and Lionel Barrymore an artist, composer, novelist, and film director.

Some character actors, throughout Hollywood's history, actually became movie stars. Several of those in this book were stars for a time during their careers, but settled into character roles later. At the same time, some character actors were so good at their craft that they won Academy Awards not in supporting roles but as *best actor* (Lionel Barrymore, Victor McLaglen and Paul Lukas). And besides those who won supporting Oscars, an impressive number got nominations as *best actor or actress* (Lewis Stone, Adolphe Menjou, May Robson, Frank Morgan, Walter Huston [twice] and Fay Bainter).

But for most character actors, stardom and/or an Oscar were forever beyond reach. They were like the sidemen in an orchestra or the linemen in football—skilled professionals who did their jobs well, who made the stars look good, who won the respect and admiration of their colleagues, and who had to be content to see their names appear below the title.

But what would the films of the Golden Era have been without them? They were the potatoes, gravy, vegetables, salad, and condiments that accompanied the roast beef—and they were the dessert, too.

Critic Gilbert Seldes has said of character actors that they "are alike in this: You recognize something concrete, a human character, in them…The minor players are allowed certain human qualities that the major ones forgo. They are rude, violent, ironic, mean, brutal and mocking. They say what the audience often feels, pricking the great bubble of pretensions that floats through the morals of every movie. They are disruptive elements. And they are very good company."

And now, let us meet them.

Don't trust a man who laughs like that:
EDWARD ARNOLD

It was that laugh of his. Always that laugh.

It was too facile, too jovial, while his eyes remained cool and wary. His screen adversaries didn't see through it, and made the mistake of trusting him too quickly.

Often he didn't merely laugh, he literally *shook* with laughter, his portly frame rocking with mirth. But in any case there was the air of bonhomie, the lilt to the voice, the conspiratorial gleam in the eye. It wasn't just that he wanted to be your pal; he *wanted* something from you—and it was strongly hinted that you'd better deliver.

Director Frank Capra knew that laugh well: "Arnold had the power and presence of a J.P. Morgan. He could be as unctuous as a funeral director or as cold and ruthless as a Cosa Nostra chief. He had a laugh as unique and as phony as a $3 bill. It would wind up in pitch like the flywheel starter of a fighter plane, then explode in choked-up pops like its motor. Arnold was anathema to directors. In take after take he would blow his lines and shrug it off with that phony laugh."

With that J.P. Morgan-like power, Arnold specialized in playing figures of authority. He could be an uncompromising or apoplectic businessman, a senator, a rich plutocrat, a press lord, a crooked financier, a corrupt politician. Yet he also played many detectives and, later in life, kindly fathers—not to mention Daniel Webster, Johann Sutter, Jim Fisk and Diamond Jim Brady. Still, you remember him as a scoundrel, sometimes amiable, sometimes nasty. And always with that laugh.

He was solidly built, with strong and unmistakable features and a decidedly persuasive manner. And like the fastest gun in the West, his facile smile could turn instantly to an unpleasant scowl if you crossed him.

Guenther Edward Arnold Schneider was born February 18, 1890, to impoverished German immigrants on New York City's Lower East Side. Orphaned during a miserable childhood, forced to quit school in the sixth grade, he worked in his youth as a newsboy, bellhop, butcher's helper, and errand boy, and at 14 oiled engines in a basement at Columbia University, then later was a stoker. At age 17 he made his stage debut as Lorenzo in a settlement-house production of Shakespeare's **The Merchant of Venice** (he would entitle his 1940 autobiography "Lorenzo

Goes to Hollywood"); another source says the debut came in **A Midsummer Night's Dream.** Later he appeared on stage with Ethel Barrymore.

By age 25 he was a strapping young hero type with some stock-company experience, and so the Essanay film studio in Chicago signed him up as a cowboy star, in which capacity he made more than 50 one- and two-reel shorts before returning to the stage in 1919, the year he co-starred on Broadway in **The Storm.** Meanwhile, he also made 10 Hollywood feature films during the period 1916-20.

Arnold married Harriet Marshall in 1917, and they had three children, Elizabeth, Dorothy Jane and William (some sources give the son's name as Edward Jr.). He and Harriet would divorce in 1927; he would marry Olive Emerson in 1929, with a divorce in 1948, and then marry Cleo McClain in 1951.

More than a decade on the stage polished the actor's skills, and he went from husky young cowboy star to forceful Broadway actor. But as silent films turned to talkies, Hollywood was scouring New York cast lists for performers with resonant voices. One of those on the lookout was film director Tay Garnett, who was looking for someone to play a villain role in his 1932 film **Okay America.** He recalled later: "The script called for an improbable heavy, a ruthless but polished gang leader—sort of an erudite Al Capone…We had leafed fruitlessly through the Casting Directory before I remembered a guy I had seen on Broadway in the legit comedy **Whistling in the Dark,** a gent with a deep, infectious laugh…His name was Edward Arnold."

Within a year, Arnold had established himself as a character actor of the first magnitude in Hollywood, where he would stay for a quarter of a century.

In **Okay America,** he played a racketeer who is double-crossed by radio columnist Lew Ayres and later shot to death by him. And he stole the show as a gangster chieftain in **Afraid to Talk.** But the following year, in **The White Sister,** he was a kindly Italian priest, and in **Jennie Gerhardt** he played the oily seducer of Sylvia Sidney, also appearing in **The Barbarian** as an Egyptian pasha lusting after Myrna Loy and in **Secret of the Blue Room** as a police commissioner (the first of many roles as a police official or detective).

He was now winning major roles opposite established stars. In **Sadie McKee** (34) he was convincing as an unstable alcoholic millionaire whom Joan Crawford marries out of pity, rehabilitates, and later leaves. He was a ruthless detective chief in **The President Vanishes,** played a German intelligence officer in **Madame Spy,** was a police lieutenant on the trail of racketeer Robert Montgomery in **Hide-Out,** and was outstanding as a racketeer himself in **Million Dollar Ransom;** in the latter film, the New York Times called him "an actor of extraordinary conviction."

In the 1935 version of **The Glass Key,** Arnold was a ward heeler who becomes a political boss, trying to go in for clean politics but finding himself framed for the murder of a colleague's son (Ray Milland). In **Cardinal Richelieu** he was well cast as Louis XIII. **Crime and Punishment** saw him cast as the relentless Inspector Porfiry, on the trail of Peter Lorre as the murderer Raskolnikov, and he also played a detective in **Remember Last Night?** That same year saw one of his biographical films, **Diamond Jim,** become a hit as he played the definitive Diamond Jim Brady (which he was to do again in **Lillian Russell** in 1940).

Arnold was virtually a star at this point. In fact, in all three of his 1936 films he was top-cast. The best one was **Come and Get It,** a big hit in which he

stole most of the scenes even from that master scene-stealer Walter Brennan, who that year won the first of his three Academy Awards for the film. Arnold was brilliant in what was possibly his greatest role, as Barney Glasgow, the ruthless paper-mill baron who fights and schemes his way to the top. The love interest was that tragic and doomed actress Frances Farmer. He also played the sedentary detective in the title role of **Meet Nero Wolfe,** and appeared in **Sutter's Gold** as Sutter, a part in which he was badly miscast.

Critics and public alike hailed him in **The Toast of New York** (37), with a lavish and exact portrayal of the 19th-century financier Jim Fisk, a role he was born to play. He was also in his element in **Easy Living** as the miserly, irascible tycoon (one of America's biggest bankers) who throws his wife's expensive new fur coat from a penthouse roof, only to have it land in the lap of Jean Arthur, riding in an open-topped bus below. Ray Milland played his son.

But fate conspired to rob Edward Arnold of stardom. **The Toast of New York** was a big-budget picture (Cary Grant played the actor's partner), but Arnold didn't have enough star power at the box office to carry it. The film racked up a big loss for RKO, and from that time on he would be strictly a character actor in other stars' movies. (Still, he was highly regarded enough to be elected president of the Screen Actors Guild.)

You Can't Take It With You (38) saw the quintessential Arnold, black-coated and beetle-browed as the evil industrialist (whose reformation at the end, typical of director Frank Capra's films, rings all too false). But his nastiest tycoon role came the next year in **Mr. Smith Goes to Washington** (again for Capra), as the newspaper magnate and state political boss who is out to ruin young senator James Stewart. In **Let Freedom Ring** he was a ruthless, land-grabbing railroad tycoon, and in **Slightly Honorable** he tried to frame Pat O'Brien for murder. He had a major role in **Idiot's Delight,** with Norma Shearer cast as his mistress (he's a munitions tycoon); he deserts her and she ends up back in the arms of old flame Clark Gable. He was murdered by Robert Montgomery in **The Earl of Chicago** (40), and played Tyrone Power's father, an imprisoned embezzler, in **Johnny Apollo.**

In 1941 Arnold again appeared for Capra as the fascistic political boss fighting Gary Cooper in **Meet John Doe.** He was more convincingly real than the rest of the cast, and press and public alike found him to be superb as the pitiless, pince-nez-wearing menace with his army of black-clad storm troopers. It was his last really great role, at age 51, but he had another 15 years of movies to go. Also in that year, he was the gangster who bankrolls reporter Edward G. Robinson, who wants to publish his own newspaper, in **Unholy Partners;** later Robinson wants to expose Arnold's rackets, and ends up killing the gangster in self-defense. In **All That Money Can Buy** (later retitled **The Devil and Daniel Webster**) he was good as Webster, but the film was stolen by Walter Huston as the Devil.

From then on the actor's parts grew more routine, with the exception of his blind detective in **Eyes in the Night** (42) and **The Hidden Eye** (45). He was lost in the crowd in films such as **Mrs. Parkington** (44), **Weekend at the Waldorf** (45), **The Hucksters** (47) and **Command Decision** (48). And for the final decade of filmmaking, it was strictly routine parts in movies that not many people seem to remember.

In the final years, Arnold—who during the Forties at one time considered running for the U.S. Senate—also appeared on television, in "The Edward Arnold Theatre" and "Strange Stories." But when he died in 1956 at age 66 he was still in harness, having made three films that year.

His was a career that had climaxed a generation earlier when he had portrayed powerful and memorable villains and heroes with great skill and authority.

And that laugh…

THE FILMS OF EDWARD ARNOLD

1916: When the Man Speaks; The Primitive Strain; The Misleading Lady; The Vultures of Society; The Return of Eve.

1917: The Slacker's Heart; The Wrong Way.

1919: A Broadway Saint; Phil-for-Short.

1920: The Cost.

1932: Okay America; Three on a Match; Afraid to Talk; I Am a Fugitive from a Chain Gang.

1933: The White Sister; Jennie Gerhardt; Whistling in the Dark; Her Bodyguard; I'm No Angel; The Barbarian; Secret of the Blue Room; Lawyer Man; Roman Scandals; Rasputin and the Empress.

1934: Sadie McKee; Hide-Out; The President Vanishes; Madame Spy; Million Dollar Ransom; Thirty Day Princess; Unknown Blonde; Wednesday's Child.

1935: Diamond Jim; Cardinal Richelieu; The Glass Key; Crime and Punishment; Remember Last Night?; Biography of a Bachelor Girl.

1936: Come and Get It; Meet Nero Wolfe; Sutter's Gold.

1937: Easy Living; The Toast of New York; John Meade's Woman; Blossoms on Broadway.

1938: You Can't Take It With You; The Crowd Roars.

1939: Mr. Smith Goes to Washington; Idiot's Delight; Man About Town; Let Freedom Ring; Slightly Honorable.

1940: The Earl of Chicago; Johnny Apollo; Lillian Russell.

1941: Meet John Doe; All That Money Can Buy (later retitled The Devil and Daniel Webster); The Penalty; The Lady from Cheyenne; Nothing but the Truth; Unholy Partners; Johnny Eager; Design for Scandal.

1942: The War Against Mrs. Hadley; Eyes in the Night.

1943: The Youngest Profession.

1944: Mrs. Parkington; Kismet; Janie; Standing Room Only.

1945: Main Street After Dark; Weekend at the Waldorf; The Hidden Eye.

1946: Three Wise Fools; Janie Gets Married; The Mighty McGurk; No Leave, No Love; Ziegfeld Follies; My Brother Talks to Horses.

1947: Dear Ruth; The Hucksters.

1948: Big City; Three Daring Daughters; Wallflower; Command Decision.

1949: John Loves Mary; Take Me Out to the Ball Game; Dear Wife; Big Jack.

1950: The Yellow Cab Man; The Skipper Surprised His Wife; Annie Get Your Gun.

1951: Dear Brat.

1952: Belles on Their Toes.

1953: The City That Never Sleeps; Man of Conflict.

1954: Living It Up.

1956: The Ambassador's Daughter; The Houston Story; Miami Expose.

Is there a mad doctor in the house?:
LIONEL ATWILL

"Mad? I, who have solved the secret of life—you call me mad?"

Yes, Lionel Atwill actually had that line of dialogue in one of his films, and yes, he virtually cornered the market on dark, brooding mad doctors and staring-eyed scientists in some of Hollywood's most wonderfully campy horror films.

Stolid, starchy, suave, with clipped speech and a suspicious mustache to match, with a fierce face and sly eyeballs, with impeccable diction and an air of seedy sophistication, he oozed corruption under an imposing façade.

Besides malicious-eyed mad scientists, he had a neat line in Mittel-European police inspectors, Teutonic villains, burgomasters, arrogant generals, lecherous seducers, crooked lawyers, Nazi spies, and wealthy protectors of pretty young courtesans. And he was a memorably malevolent Professor Moriarty to Basil Rathbone's Sherlock Holmes.

At his peak, Atwill was one of Hollywood's most reliable and prolific character actors. Although his style was flamboyant, he could be a good actor when given good material—but he all too seldom got it. Nonetheless, it's nice that he was around when they needed to cast those mad doctors.

Born March 1, 1885, in Croydon, Surrey, a suburb of London, he made his stage debut at 19 in **The Walls of Jericho** after a brief fling at studying architecture. He spent many years on the London stage, in the beginning primarily in the plays of Henrik Ibsen. In 1915 he came to the United States and quickly became a major Broadway leading man. He gained a reputation as the "perfect lover" opposite such leading ladies as Alla Nazimova (with whom he appeared in three major Ibsen plays in 1918), the up-and-coming star Katharine Cornell, and the young Helen Hayes (he won critical acclaim as Caesar to her Cleopatra in George Bernard Shaw's **Caesar and Cleopatra** in 1925). He also toured the country playing opposite Lily Langtry in **Mrs. Thompson**.

The actor had his first crack at the movies during the period 1918-21, when he appeared in five of them, mainly "society dramas," but otherwise concentrated on the stage for many more years, appearing in starring roles on Broadway all through the 1920s and also directing plays. Not counting one quickie film in 1928, he finally re-entered the movies in 1932, to stay for 14 unforgettable years.

Atwill was married at least four times and divorced at least three. He married actress Phyllis Ralph (or Relph) in 1917 and they were divorced in 1919. He then wed Elsie Mackay the same year and they had a child, John, but were divorced in 1928. His third marriage, in 1930, was to Louise Cromwell Stotesbury, who was divorced from Gen. Douglas MacArthur; this union ended in divorce in 1943. By his fourth wife, Mary Shelstone (married 1943), he had another son, Lionel Jr., born very shortly before Atwill died. (Another source lists one more wife, writer Paula Pruter, but several sources make no mention of her.)

After his sound-film debut at age 47 as an innocent nobleman on trial for murder in **Silent Witness,** Atwill scored strongly in **Doctor X** (32), which was also his horror-film debut. He was a clubfooted, evil-looking red herring who seemed the most obvious murder suspect at first.

But 1933 was to be his *annus mirabilis.* In **The

Mystery of the Wax Museum, made in crude two-color Technicolor (blue-green and orange), he was a mad genius, an apparently benevolent museum owner confined to a wheelchair, who kidnaps people who resemble historical characters, dips them in boiling wax and displays them à la Mme. Tussaud's. A classic of the horror genre, it is best remembered for the great scene in which Fay Wray, slated to become the next waxen victim (Marie Antoinette), slaps Atwill's face, which then cracks to pieces and reveals the horribly burned, gnarled flesh beneath. His fine performance transcended the horror genre and was top-notch acting by any standard.

Even better (but today half forgotten) was **Murders in the Zoo,** in which Atwill, as a big-game hunter, pushes his faithless wife into a crocodile pool, but not before sewing up the lips of one of her lovers (in the manner of head-shrinkers) and leaving him tied up in the jungle to die, and exposing another to a snake's poisonous fangs. At the end, he himself ends up being killed by a boa constrictor.

Film historian William K. Everson says of **Murders in the Zoo:** "It is a showcase for the bravura nastiness of…Atwill, who, apart from relishing every line and nuance, also managed to suggest general tendencies toward unspecified depravities that his scripts never intended. The gleam that came into [his] eye, the sneer on his lips, his quick dismissal of unspeakable things that had happened off-screen before the story got under way—all these little acting ploys somehow turned him into an unwholesome killer as well as an illegal one."

If the truth be told, some of the actor's horror roles were not well chosen, but the genre gained respect from his presence; he had the talent and voice of a classic actor.

Another 1933 entry was **The Song of Songs,** in which he gave a memorable performance as the lecherous, evil old baron whom Marlene Dietrich is forced to marry but later leaves. In this one, he nearly stole the show from the star. And there was another horror film, **The Vampire Bat,** in which he was a mad doctor who drains the lifeblood from peasants in a Teutonic village.

In **Nana** (34) Atwill was the haughty colonel to whom Anna Sten surrenders after she believes his young brother dead (of course he isn't). Once again he was the best thing in the film. **One More River** saw him as the sneering attorney for Colin Clive, bringing a divorce action against his wife, and in **The Age of Innocence** he was an unscrupulous banker. In **The Man Who Reclaimed His Head** he played a corrupt newspaper publisher to whom writer Claude Rains sells his talents; he later betrays Rains and sells out to the munitions makers who will profit by a war, so Rains goes mad and kills him. But he had a sympathetic role in **Beggars in Ermine** as a steel-mill owner who loses his legs in an accident. In **Stanboul Quest** he was the head of the German secret service.

Writer Danny Peary has said of Atwill, "His sinister characters were highly intelligent and deadly serious, without even the hint of warmth that marked [Boris] Karloff. Completely unhuggable, he seemed to make the screen grow dark around him."

Only one of his 1935 films had a good part for the actor. In director Josef von Sternberg's **The Devil Is a Woman** he was again mad for Marlene Dietrich, this time as a military officer infatuated with her. Oddly, in the end she gives up Cesar Romero to return to Atwill—but some critics and filmgoers noticed that Atwill was made up to look remarkably like Sternberg, whose protegée Dietrich was (this was the last of the seven Dietrich-Sternberg collaborations). Also that year, he was a police captain in **Murder Man,** and Olivia de Havilland's father, a sadistic plantation owner, in **Captain Blood,** Errol Flynn's first starring film.

Now, for several years (1936-38), the actor was submerged in a succession of movies that offered him no good parts (one exception was a role as the playwright Beaumarchais in **The Great Garrick** [37]). He re-emerged in 1939 to begin his final descent into grade "B" horror films, most of which would be utterly forgotten today were it not for his splendidly campy performances as assorted madmen.

But several passable dramatic roles intervened. In **Son of Frankenstein** (39) he was the police chief with an artificial arm, the original one having been torn off by the monster many years before. In **The Hound of the Baskervilles** he was a fine red herring, bearded and wearing thick eyeglasses so sinister-looking that you knew instantly he could *not* be the guilty party. **The Sun Never Sets** found him in a role that presaged what was to come for the next seven years: He played a would-be African dictator who from his jungle hideaway spreads revolts, strikes, arson, bomb plots and war fever by means of his secret radio station. The viewer could be forgiven for thinking he was watching an episode of **Flash Gordon.**

In 1940 he had his last good part, as the top criminal lawyer who tries unsuccessfully to keep Edward Arnold out of prison in **Johnny Apollo.**

For film fans and others, Atwill's private life after 1939 (when he separated from his wife) was to become considerably more interesting than any of his screen appearances—and that private life also provided the main reason why his screen career went to ruin. A whole chapter is devoted to it in Kenneth Anger's book "Hollywood Babylon II." According to Anger, this is the story:

"Left alone with a lonely libido," the actor maintained a busy work schedule at the film studios but used his home freely as the setting for sex-oriented weekend parties, attended by many movie notables and lesser lights. Inevitably, someone spilled the beans to the authorities and told them that Atwill was presiding over frequent large-scale sex orgies at his home.

A 16-year-old girl who attended his 1940 Christmas party had the actor brought to trial, Anger relates, on charges of corrupting the morals of a minor. However, he was cleared on this occasion. A year later he was recalled for trial on a perjury charge stemming from the same case. He changed his plea from not guilty to guilty on that charge, and was given five years' probation. He was obliged to report weekly to a probation officer, and was without work for seven months, until the judge freed him from the probation sentence.

But, Anger continues, the legal troubles that had made Atwill *persona non grata* at the studios caused him to leave Hollywood for Broadway, where there were no offers for the 58-year-old actor in 1943. He went back to the film capital, and although he was never again offered a major role by a major studio, Universal did agree to give him small parts in two features and a few serials. Atwill then found himself an employee of the most poverty-stricken of all the Poverty Row studios—PRC, or Producers Releasing Corp. He was reduced to quickie features that were shot in five days.

Meanwhile, to backtrack slightly, he had begun in 1941, during his legal troubles, to work for Universal in horror films. He might well have become another Boris Karloff, but as a mad scientist his career did not have the integrity of Karloff's. As one writer has put it, "Soon he was off on harebrained schemes to raise armies of electrical supermen with which to rule the world."

In **Man-Made Monster** (41), for example, he was a mad doctor who seeks to create a race of superwomen run by electricity, but is killed off by Lon Chaney Jr. This was more or less the beginning of Universal's World War II horror cycle featuring the same old names again and again—Atwill, Chaney, Bela Lugosi, John Carradine, Evelyn Ankers, George Zucco, J. Carrol Naish and Sir Cedric Hardwicke, to name some of them. In these, Atwill efficiently played assorted Germanic types who were generally up to no good.

In **The Ghost of Frankenstein** he was the assistant to Hardwicke, who played the scion of the Frankensteins. Atwill was the evil soul-mate to Ygor (Lugosi), who revives the monster (Chaney); the monster goes blind and later hurls Atwill into an electrical generator. In such films the actor delivered his gloriously campy lines with a relish and bravura that few of his contemporaries could have matched.

After all this, audiences could be pardoned for correctly guessing who would play the title role in **The Mad Doctor of Market Street** (42). It was (as it had been for a decade) typecasting pure and simple. Still, he could handle other roles; he was one of Jack Benny's acting troupe in **To Be or Not to Be** (also 42).

Time was running out. There was another Sherlock Holmes outing, two more Frankensteins, a Dracula, and then the ultimate nadir, a spate of serials. Imagine starring in serials called **Junior G-Men of the Air, Captain America, and Raiders of Ghost City**…if you can. But Atwill was born to play these roles.

While working on his last film, the serial **Lost City of the Jungle** (46), Lionel Atwill suddenly died at 61 of pneumonia (his remaining scenes were completed by a double). In it he was an evil warmonger, Sir Eric Hazarias. Still stolid, still clipped of speech, still oozing corruption.

And still magnificently mad.

THE FILMS OF LIONEL ATWILL

1918: Eve's Daughter; For Sale.
1919: The Marriage Price.
1921: Indiscretion; The Highest Bidder.
1928: The White-Faced Fool.
1932: Silent Witness; Doctor X.
1933: The Mystery of the Wax Museum; Murders in the Zoo; The Song of Songs; The Vampire Bat; The Secret of Madame Blanche; The Sphinx; Solitaire Man; The Secret of the Blue Room.
1934: The Man Who Reclaimed His Head; Nana; The Age of Innocence; One More River; Stamboul Quest; The Firebird; Beggars in Ermine.

1935: The Devil Is a Woman; Captain Blood; Murder Man; Rendezvous; Mark of the Vampire.
1936: Lady of Secrets; Absolute Quiet; Till We Meet Again.
1937: The Great Garrick; The Road Back; Last Train from Madrid; Lancer Spy; The Wrong Road.
1938: Three Comrades; The Great Waltz.
1939: Son of Frankenstein; The Three Musketeers; The Hound of the Baskervilles; The Mad Empress; The Gorilla; The Sun Never Sets; Mr. Moto Takes a Vacation; The Secret of Dr. Kildare; Balalaika.
1940: Johnny Apollo; The Great Profile; Boom Town; The Girl in 313;

Charlie Chan in Panama; Charlie Chan's Murder Cruise.

1941: Man-Made Monster.

1942: The Ghost of Frankenstein; To Be or Not to Be; The Strange Case of Doctor Rx; Pardon My Sarong; Cairo; Night Monster; Sherlock Holmes and the Secret Weapon; The Mad Doctor of Market Street; Junior G-Men of the Air (serial).

1943: Frankenstein Meets the Wolf Man.

1944: Lady in the Death House; Secrets of Scotland Yard; Captain America (serial); Raiders of Ghost City (serial).

1945: House of Frankenstein; House of Dracula; Fog Island; Crime, Inc.

1946: Genius at Work; Lost City of the Jungle (serial).

Who is that crazy Russian?:
MISCHA AUER

In the stereotyped Hollywood of the Thirties, each ethnic group or nationality had its clichéd characteristics. In the case of Russians, they were often seen as comically zany idiots. Mischa Auer virtually cornered the market on this type of role and made a nice living at it.

With a long, sad face, prominent eyes, wild gestures and a droll accent, the lanky actor played many a mournful or manic Russian. He could also be a nasty villain, a cocky butler or a mad scientist. But it is as a madcap that he is best remembered, for he was a virtuoso of madcaps, his foolish characters stealing countless scenes and leaving audiences laughing helplessly.

He was born as Mischa Ounskowsky on November 17, 1905, in Russia's imperial city of St. Petersburg (later Leningrad). Either during or after the Russian revolution of 1917 he was brought to the United States by Leopold Auer, the eminent violinist who was his maternal grandfather and from whom he took a new surname for stage work.

He made his stage debut in 1925 in a Broadway production, at age 19, after studying at the Ethical Culture School. Three years later he was appearing in **Magda** when film director Frank Tuttle gave him his first movie break with a role in **Something Always Happens.** It was the start of a 38-year film career.

For several years Auer grabbed at bit parts and walk-ons in mostly minor Hollywood productions, playing either swarthy villains or comic roles. Some of these films were made by such Poverty Row cheapie studios as Tiffany, Chesterfield, Monogram and Majestic. But he also worked for Paramount, Fox and other major studios.

Typical of his roles in those early days were the sinister valet, a red herring who sure *looked* guilty, in **The Benson Murder Case** and the treacherous Hindu in league with the Germans in World War I in **Inside the Lines** (both 1930). He was an unsavory Russian prince in **The Unholy Garden** (31), Una Merkel's unsuccessful suitor in **Command Performance,** and a lecherous man who accosts Elissa Landi in **The Yellow Ticket** (she is saved by Laurence Olivier).

In 1931 the actor married for the first of four times; his first wife was Norma Tillman, by whom he had two children, Anthony and Zoe, the latter

adopted, and the couple divorced in 1940. He married Joyce Hunter in 1941 and they split up in 1950. His next wife was Susanne Kalish, whom he married that same year; they had a daughter and ultimately were divorced. Near the end of his life, in 1965, he married Elise Souls.

Auer continued to appear in numerous major and minor films in the early Thirties, but you'd be hard put to remember any of his small roles in nearly all of them. He played a half-witted homicidal maniac in **The Monster Walks** (32), a mad, murderous Russian spy in **Murder at Dawn,** a deaf-mute convict in **The Midnight Patrol,** a spy who is executed in the Greta Garbo starrer **Mata Hari,** an "agitator in restaurant" in **Call Her Savage,** a guide in the Louvre in **Arsene Lupin,** a rabbi in **No Greater Love,** and a saloon owner who forges a will in **The Western Code.** All told, he was in 15 movies that year.

In 1933 he was the high priest in the Buster Crabbe outing **Tarzan the Fearless,** a phony crystal-ball gazer in **Sucker Money,** a counterspy in **After Tonight,** a priest in **Cradle Song,** a half-insane radical scientist who commits all the murders in **Corruption,** a South Seas native chieftain in **The Flaming Signal,** and an Arab leader in **Clear All Wires.** In **Storm at Daybreak** he played Gavrilo Prinzip, whose 1914 assassination at Sarajevo of the archduke of Austria-Hungary plunged the world into war. In **Viva Villa** (34) he was a military attaché, in **Wharf Angel** a seaman, in **Bulldog Drummond Strikes Back** a thug menacing Ronald Colman, and in **Beyond the Law** a gangster killed by Tim McCoy.

By 1935, if his parts weren't getting much bigger, at least Auer was appearing in plenty of outstanding films. He was seen in the Greta Garbo outing **Anna Karenina,** was a Hindu in **Clive of India,** played a monk in **The Crusades,** was yet another Hindu in **The Lives of a Bengal Lancer,** and portrayed a pianist in **I Dream Too Much** and an Oriental consul in **Murder in the Fleet.** He was cast as a radical in **Winterset** (36), a detective in **The Princess Comes Across,** a German spy in **Sons o' Guns** and a gangster in **Tough Guy.**

But in that same year, 1936, the actor suddenly hit the big time, and hit it with a vengeance. In the classic screwball comedy **My Man Godfrey** he practically stole the show with his hilarious performance as Alice Brady's protégé, a language-mangling Russian zany who does gorilla imitations and is constantly bursting into song with "Otchi tchorniya." Auer was nominated for an Academy Award for best supporting actor in the first year of that award, but Walter Brennan was the winner.

Mischa Auer's future was now secure, at the age of 30. He would, most of the time, play noble idiots with wild gestures and ridiculously broken English. A narrow niche, to be sure, but it kept him busy.

He stole the picture as a temperamental European movie star in **Pick a Star** (37), and was an impecunious nobleman with a taste for liquor and none for gainful employment in Deanna Durbin's debut film, **Three Smart Girls,** also being featured in the teen-age star's **One Hundred Men and a Girl.** Third-billed, he was a captain in the French secret police in **We Have Our Moments,** and did a comic turn as Hamlet in **Top of the Town.** He played an impoverished Hungarian count in **Prescription for Romance,** a newspaper artist in **Marry the Girl,** and a Russian prince who operates a swanky fashion-design salon in **Walter Wanger's Vogues of 1938.** He was a fortune-hunting French baron in pursuit of Madeleine Carroll's millions in **It's All Yours.**

Auer scored another hit in director Frank Capra's comedy **You Can't Take It with You** as the ballet teacher who says of student Ann Miller, "Confidentially, she steenks!" The film was one of the top box-office hits of 1938. He was the musical librettist for Jeanette MacDonald and Nelson Eddy in **Sweethearts.** Again third-billed, he was a waiter who helps Danielle Darrieux find romance with Douglas Fairbanks Jr. in **The Rage of Paris,** and he played a Russian prince working as a chef in **Service de Luxe,** Vincent Price's debut film.

In **East Side of Heaven** (39) he was Bing Crosby's best pal, and **Destry Rides Again** cast him as the husband of Una Merkel; Miss Merkel engages in a memorable saloon brawl with Marlene Dietrich in this classic comedy that also starred James Stewart. In **Seven Sinners** (40) he was a part-time magician and part-time pickpocket with kleptomaniac tendencies, and in **Alias the Deacon** a fastidious barber. Third-billed again, he had a key role in the Deanna Durbin starrer **Spring Parade.** He was the Communist butler to a rich family in **Elsa Maxwell's Public Deb No. 1**.

The actor was well attuned to French director René Clair's subtle comedic material in **Flame of New Orleans** (41), again with Miss Dietrich. **Hellzapoppin** found him being pursued by Martha Raye. As late as 1942 he could still walk off with the picture, as he did in **Twin Beds** (Miss Merkel was once again his spouse), but Joan Bennett and George Brent were hardly stiff competition.

The end of the era of screwball comedy marked a downward turning point in Auer's career. Because from that time on it is difficult to name a really good role he played. Nonetheless, he still had more than 20 years to go in the movies.

Eccentric Russians having worn thin in Hollywood, he returned in the late Forties to Europe, where he made most of the rest of his films. Many of them were French productions. One interesting movie in which he appeared was director/star Orson Welles' **Mr. Arkadin** (55); he was a flea-circus proprietor, and gave the part all his old *joie de vivre.*

Auer died in 1967 at 61, having made the impressive total of 139 films. His star burned brightly but all too briefly in the late Thirties, when any time the script called for a zany Russian, the call went out, "Get me Mischa Auer!"

THE FILMS OF MISCHA AUER

1928: Something Always Happens.
1929: The Studio Murder Mystery; Marquis Preferred; The Mighty; Fame and the Devil.
1930: The Benson Murder Case; Paramount on Parade; Inside the Lines; Just Imagine.
1931: No Limit; The Unholy Garden; Delicious; The Yellow Ticket; Working Girls; Command Performance; Drums of Jeopardy; Women Love Once; The Lady from Nowhere; The Spy.
1932: Mata Hari; The Midnight Patrol; Arsene Lupin; Call Her Savage; Rasputin and the Empress; Sinister Hands; Drifting Souls; The Monster Walks; Beauty Parlor; Murder at Dawn; No Greater Love; Scarlet Dawn; The Unwritten Law; The Western Code; The Intruder.
1933: The Infernal Machine; Sucker Money; Corruption; Tarzan the Fearless; After Tonight; Cradle Song; Storm at Daybreak; Girl Without a Room; Dangerously Yours; The Flaming Signal; Clear All Wires; Gabriel over the White House.
1934: The Crosby Case; Student Tour; Viva Villa; Wharf Angel; Bulldog Drummond Strikes Back; Stamboul Quest; Woman Condemned; Beyond the Law. *Credit uncertain:* Change of Heart.
1935: Anna Karenina; Condemned to Live; The Lives of a Bengal Lancer; The Crusades; Clive of India; Mystery Woman; Murder in the Fleet; I Dream Too Much; The Adventures of Rex and Rinty (serial).
1936: My Man Godfrey; Winterset; The Princess Comes Across; One Rainy Afternoon; The Gay Desperado; Here Comes Trouble; Tough Guy; The House of a Thousand Candles; Sons o' Guns; We're Only Human.
1937: Three Smart Girls; One Hundred Men and a Girl; We Have Our Moments; Top of the Town; Merry-Go-Round of 1938; Prescription for Romance; Pick a Star; Marry the Girl; That Girl from Paris; It's All Yours; Walter Wanger's Vogues of 1938.
1938: The Rage of Paris; Service de Luxe; Sweethearts; You Can't Take It with You; Little Tough Guys in Society.
1939: Destry Rides Again; East Side of Heaven; Unexpected Father.
1940: Alias the Deacon; Sandy Is a Lady; Margie; Spring Parade; Seven Sinners; Trail of the Vigilantes; Elsa Maxwell's Public Deb No. 1.
1941: Flame of New Orleans; Cracked Nuts; Hold That Ghost; Sing Another Chorus; Moonlight in Hawaii; Hellzapoppin.
1942: Twin Beds; Don't Get Personal.
1943: Around the World.
1944: Lady in the Dark; Up in Mabel's Room.
1945: And Then There Were None; A Royal Scandal; Brewster's Millions.
1946: Sentimental Journey; She Wrote the Book.
1947: For You I Die.
1948: Sofia.
1950: Fame and the Devil.
1952: The Sky Is Red; Song of Paris.
1955: Frou-Frou; Escalier de service; Mr. Arkadin; Treize à table; L'impossible M. Pipelet.
1956: Mannequins de Paris; La polka des menottes; En effeuillant la Marguerite.
1957: The Monte Carlo Story; Le tombeur.
1958: Mam'zelle Pigalle; The Foxiest Girl in Paris; Tabarin; Sacrée jeunesse.
1959: Futures vedettes.
1960: A Dog, a Mouse and a Sputnik.
1962: We Joined the Navy.
1963: Ladies First; Dynamite Girl.
1964: Whatever Happened to Baby Toto?; Queste pazze, pazze, pazze donne.
1966: The Christmas That Almost Wasn't; Arrivederci, Baby; Per amore…per magia…

Tea and sympathy:
FAY BAINTER

There was a part for a mother—sometimes several mothers—in most Hollywood films of the Golden Era. There were dithery, scatterbrained mothers; harsh, bitter matriarchs; empty-headed society matrons; stern mothers, selfish mothers, devoted mothers.

One of the more common types was the sympathetic mother, and hardly anyone ever played that part quite so well as Fay Bainter, a former Broadway star with considerable stage experience who came to Hollywood in middle age and for more than a decade had sympathy by the carload to offer her movie children, who included some of filmdom's most famous stars.

Sympathetic these mothers were, yes, but stalwart too. And long-suffering. Miss Bainter, with sensitive, darting eyes and a husky, ingratiating voice, interpreted them with great intelligence. She could be warm—or icily cold, on occasion. Besides mothers, she also played martyr-like wives and wise aunts, and once was a particularly nasty villainess. And three Oscar nominations (one as *best actress*) testified to her skill at her profession.

Fay Bainter, born December 7, 1892 (one source says 1891), in Los Angeles, first appeared on stage at age five in a stock company, playing a role in **The Little Jewess** with Nance O'Neil. At eight, she was with the Belasco Stock Company, out of Los Angeles. She became a regular member of the Morosco Stock Company, and made her Broadway debut in 1912 in **The Rose of Panama,** later moving toward stardom in **The Willow Tree** in 1917, and scoring her first big success as Ming Toy in **East Is West** in 1918, at age 26. From that point on she was a Broadway star.

Miss Bainter in 1922 married naval officer Reginald Venable, who would die in 1964. They had a son, Reginald Jr. (1926-74), who had a few small supporting roles in films in the sound era.

The actress continued for many years on the Broadway stage, her starring vehicles including **The Enemy** (25), **She Stoops to Conquer** (28) and **The Admirable Crichton** (31). In 1933 she played Topsy in blackface in **Uncle Tom's Cabin.** She scored a triumph in 1934 as Fran Dodsworth in **Dodsworth,** opposite Walter Huston. Although that role in the 1936 film was taken by Ruth Chatterton, Miss Bainter was called to Hollywood in 1934 to play Lionel

Barrymore's wife in **This Side of Heaven.** In the film, she has just sold her novel to Hollywood.

But this brief excursion into the movies was not immediately a launching into a film career. The actress remained on the stage until 1937, then returned permanently to Hollywood. In **Quality Street** (37) she was Katharine Hepburn's fluttery old-maid sister, and in **The Soldier and the Lady** she had a stabbing vignette as the hero's tortured mother. In **Make Way for Tomorrow** she was the hoity-toity, frosty, nervous wife of Thomas Mitchell, the latter playing one of the thoughtless children who refuse to find a way for their aging parents (Beulah Bondi and Victor Moore) to live together in one of their homes.

In 1938 Miss Bainter had one of her best roles, as Bette Davis' aunt in **Jezebel,** sternly denouncing the star: "I'm thinking about a woman called Jezebel, who did wrong in the sight of God," but also saying of her later, "I love her most when she's the meanest,

11

'cause that's when I know she's lovin' the most." Miss Davis later recalled: "Her performance in **Jezebel** was an enormous contributing factor to the believability of the picture as a whole and to my performance in particular."

In that same year she played a Mary Worth-type role in **White Banners** as the patient wife of Claude Rains, a small-town professor who tries to make it as an inventor. And it was this seemingly innocuous wife role that caused Fay Bainter to make Academy Award history. For she was nominated for *two* different Oscars that year—as best actress for **White Banners** and as best supporting actress for **Jezebel.** She won the Oscar for **Jezebel.**

Even those two fine parts were not the end of Miss Bainter's outstanding screen work in 1938. She also played, in **The Shining Hour,** the neurotic spinster sister of Melvyn Douglas and Robert Young, a woman who resents Douglas' new bride Joan Crawford so much that she sets fire to their newly completed house, almost killing, in the process, Margaret Sullavan, playing Young's wife.

In **Yes, My Darling Daughter** (39) she was a sedate Connecticut matron, keeping from daughter Priscilla Lane her past (circa World War I) as a militant feminist and advocate of free love as practiced in Greenwich Village. When Miss Lane learns the truth, including a well documented love affair, her mother is in no position to act highly moral when the daughter announces she plans to spend the weekend with her boyfriend.

In **Daughters Courageous** the actress was once again the wife of Claude Rains; deserted by him 20 years before, she is about to marry Donald Crisp when the husband suddenly materializes again. And in **The Lady and the Mob** she was excellent as an eccentric, aristocratic dowager who establishes her own gang of colorful mobsters in an effort to rid her town of protection racketeers.

Now began a long siege of mothers. She was Mickey Rooney's mom in **Young Tom Edison** (40) and Maureen O'Hara's in the remake of **A Bill of Divorcement** (trying to deal with husband Adolphe Menjou, an escaped mental patient). In **Our Town** she was the sympathetic mother of young William Holden.

In 1942 she played Katharine Hepburn's crusading aunt (who is involved in a bittersweet middle-aged romance) in **Woman of the Year,** played the title role in the remake of **Mrs. Wiggs of the Cabbage Patch,** and scored a personal triumph in the title role of **The War Against Mrs. Hadley,** as a Washington, D.C., society matron who finds the demands of the war effort disrupting her secure and placid life but finally sees the error of her ways.

In **The Human Comedy** (43) Miss Bainter mothered Van Johnson and (again) Mickey Rooney, and in the grim war drama **Cry Havoc** she was the eldest of the nurses. She played Van Heflin's mother in **Presenting Lily Mars,** and Wallace Beery's wife in **Salute to the Marines.** But in **Dark Waters,** cast against type, she was fine in a villainous role, conspiring with Thomas Mitchell to drive heiress Merle Oberon insane; John Qualen played Miss Bainter's husband in this 1944 outing.

Of her ensuing mother roles, the only one that stands out in the viewer's memory is that in **Deep Valley** (47), as the mother of Ida Lupino. Miss Bainter and Henry Hull are a husband and wife who haven't spoken to each other in seven years. This grim and powerful drama, directed by Jean Negulesco, is one of Hollywood's most interesting and most neglected films.

After 1948 the actress made only two films in 10 years (one each in 1951 and 1953). But in 1961, at the age of 68, she returned triumphantly for one last film and one more Oscar nomination as best supporting actress. This was **The Children's Hour**—the original title of Lillian Hellman's play about a possible lesbian relationship between two schoolteachers, first filmed in 1936 as **These Three** with the lesbian angle scissored out by censors. William Wyler directed both the 1936 and 1961 versions. Miss Bainter played the wise and knowing grandmother of the vicious young girl who accuses the teachers (taking the part originally played by Alma Kruger).

With a final Academy Award nomination for the part—one of the oldest performers ever to receive a nomination—Fay Bainter retired from the screen. She died in 1968 at 78, leaving an impressive mark as an actress and surely also leaving fond memories in the hearts of all her screen "children."

THE FILMS OF FAY BAINTER

1934: This Side of Heaven.

1937: Make Way for Tomorrow; Quality Street; The Soldier and the Lady.

1938: Jezebel; White Banners; The Shining Hour; Mother Carey's Chickens; The Arkansas Traveler.

1939: Daughters Courageous; Yes, My Darling Daughter; The Lady and the Mob; Our Neighbors the Carters.

1940: Young Tom Edison; A Bill of Divorcement; Our Town; Maryland.

1941: Babes on Broadway.

1942: Woman of the Year; The War Against Mrs. Hadley; Journey for Margaret; Mrs. Wiggs of the Cabbage Patch.

1943: The Human Comedy; Cry Havoc; Presenting Lily Mars; Salute to the Marines; The Heavenly Body.

1944: Dark Waters; Three Is a Family.

1945: State Fair.

1946: The Kid from Brooklyn; The Virginian.

1947: Deep Valley; The Secret Life of Walter Mitty.

1948: Give my Regards to Broadway; June Bride.

1951: Close to My Heart.

1953: The President's Lady.

1961: The Children's Hour.

Chewing up the scenery:
LIONEL BARRYMORE

There were really two Lionel Barrymores.

Up to the mid-1930s he was one of Hollywood's most respected character actors, a forceful performer with considerable range, virtually a star, and the winner of a best-actor Academy Award. But from the mid-Thirties on something changed. He became a bored and lethargic older man (and ultimately an *old* man), going through the motions, with only one performance to give—a crude and mannered caricature of himself. As one writer has put it, "He fought off boredom by grunting."

Sometimes he played kindly gentlemen, and occasionally villains, but far more often he was a grumpy, crusty, irascible father or grandfather (usually with a well concealed heart of gold), overacting and chewing up the scenery with great relish. His voice was something between a snarl and a drawl, and his facial expression was invariably a grimace. Little wonder that the young doctor came on the run when Barrymore bawled out, "Doc...tor Kildare...!", as he did in fully 15 films.

A longtime member of the MGM galaxy, he was under contract to that studio for more than a quarter of a century (1926-53); in fact, after 1938 he made no films for any other studio.

The eldest of the three Barrymores, he made far more movies than John and Ethel combined. His total was 143 feature-length films (which doesn't count the many shorts he made under director D.W. Griffith from 1911 [some sources say 1909] to 1913)—and the last 40 of them were all acted from a wheelchair.

Barrymore was born Lionel Blythe on April 28, 1878, in Philadelphia, to the actors Maurice and Georgie Drew Barrymore (their real name was Blythe). Maurice was the son of equally famous actors John Drew and Louisa Lane. (Drews and Barrymores have been on the stage since the 18th century, and are still acting today.)

As is typical with the clan, Lionel made his stage debut at age five, with his parents, but he did not act professionally on a regular basis until he was in his late teens. By 1900 he was a leading performer on the Broadway stage, often appearing with his uncle, also named John Drew, and also with brother John, and traveling worldwide in plays.

Lionel decided at this point that he wanted to be an artist, and went to Paris to study. But about 1908, shortly after Ethel's marriage, he said he was tired of

being a "remittance man," as he put it, returned to the United States, worked for a year as an illustrator, then resumed acting, largely because of persuasion from brother John. During the stay in Paris he had married actress Doris Rankin in 1904. (They were to have a daughter, Ethel, and would be divorced in 1923. In that same year he married another actress, Irene Fenwick, despite the fact that John had once had an affair with her. Rumor had it that Irene married Lionel to punish him for breaking off her affair with John. Director George Cukor once said, "Irene treated Lionel with cruelty, almost sadistically, [but] Lionel worshiped her, then her memory [she died in 1936], until the day he died.")

After some more time on Broadway, the actor was induced by pioneer film director D.W. Griffith to come to Hollywood and join the fledgling film industry; this probably occurred in 1909. Director Raoul Walsh, himself a pioneer actor with Griffith, later said of Barrymore: "[He] cracked the space barrier between the legitimate stage and motion pictures. Before him, no theater actor would have been found dead in a movie. He led the way, and many another great name followed."

The actor may have made his first screen appearance in 1911 in **Fighting Blood,** although some sources say it was in 1909 in **Friends.** In any case, all his films until 1913 were shorts, the feature-length film not making its first U.S. appearance until that year. He filmed regularly with Griffith for several years, later expanding his work to other studios. One of the key Griffith films was **The New York Hat** (12), in which he was a clergyman suspected of immorality because he innocently bought Mary Pickford a hat (he was entrusted with disbursing her legacy). In 1913 he appeared (in six bit parts) in Griffith's first (40-minute) feature, **Judith of Bethulia.** In 1915 he was the villain in the Pearl White serials **The Romance of Elaine** and **The Exploits of Elaine.**

Barrymore had not, however, abandoned the Broadway stage completely at this point. He was a sensation as the star of **The Copperhead** in 1918, in which he co-starred with first wife Doris Rankin. He repeated the role in the 1920 Paramount film version (along with Doris), and again received acclaim. It was the story of a man who enrages his fellow Illinois small-towners by voicing pro-Southern sympathies and becoming a conscientious objector in the Civil War. Forty years later he reveals that he had been appointed by Abraham Lincoln to infiltrate the Copperheads (Southern conspirators in the North) and sworn to lifelong secrecy.

He continued to act on the boards and also in films for another six years. On stage, he starred in **Macbeth** in 1921, and in that same year co-starred with brother John in the smash hit **The Jest.** In 1923 he and John (and both first wife Doris and second wife Irene) were in **The Claw,** and he was in **Laugh, Clown, Laugh.**

The actor was primarily a villain in his films of the early Twenties, although he played one of the first incarnations of Boston Blackie in **The Face in the Fog** (22). In **The Eternal City** (23) he was an unscrupulous politician who seeks to be the dictator of Italy, and in D.W. Griffith's **America** (24) he portrayed the wicked Capt. Walter Butler, a real-life figure from Colonial history, an Indian agent for the British who led the Iroquois on savage raids against settlers loyal to the Revolutionary cause; he played him as a lip-smacking, sneering, hunchbacked sadist.

Barrymore's stage career, meanwhile, was resulting in an ever-increasing number of flops. During the period 1921-25, while **The Claw** and **Laugh, Clown, Laugh** were moderately successful, three

others were catastrophes at the box office—**The Piker, Taps,** and **Man or Devil.** In the fall of 1925 the actor followed his brother John, by now a major film star, to a permanent residence in Hollywood. In 1926, at age 48, he signed the contract with MGM that would lead to a 27-year connection with the studio, one that terminated only with his death. (Only Lewis Stone, who started with MGM in 1924, worked longer for the studio.)

As a master portrayer of offbeat and villainous roles, often in heavy makeup, Barrymore was beginning at this point to rival Lon Chaney. In **The Thirteenth Hour** (27), for example, he played a professor whose house is full of sliding panels operated from a secret switchboard, and who goes out nightly on murderous prowls, coming home to put on a wig and a pleasant smile. In **Body and Soul** he was a disgraced doctor who lusts after Aileen Pringle and, in a jealous rage, brands her.

In 1928 silent films began to give way to talkies, and Barrymore, with his superb speaking voice and heavy stage experience, quickly became a top character star. His first part-talkie, **The Lion and the Mouse** (28), set off a wave of critical applause for his skill. While the film's other actors, lacking trained voices, floundered helplessly, Barrymore, starring as a ruthless financier, took sound in his stride and even changed the dialogue to suit his portrayal. One critic said, "Little question [but] that Barrymore's voice holds this one up."

In that same year the actor was a sensation in one of Hollywood's last silent films, portraying the tyrannical, reform-minded clergyman who pursues (in more ways than one) Gloria Swanson, playing the South Seas tart in the title role of **Sadie Thompson,** adapted from Somerset Maugham's story "Rain." The director, Raoul Walsh, later said that Barrymore "came on camera like an inquisitor hunting heretics…he was only a few weeks from his 50th birthday, and the years had sharpened his facial angles to a semblance of asceticism. With equal conviction he could have played Savonarola or a hanging judge after the battle of Culloden."

Miss Swanson was equally impressed with her co-star. In her memoirs she said: "He had been acting too long with the greats ever to doubt how this or that role should be tackled. One of those perfect chameleons of the profession, he would, without any visible effort, turn into [Rev.] Davidson the minute Raoul started calling out directions…A mild, distant, unkempt man, Lionel…could shake off his customary lethargy and disorder in an instant and be a half-mad zealot with eyes ablaze, roaring at Sadie Thompson in a voice big enough for the biggest theater that she would be punished for her wickedness."

Additionally, that year he stole the show as the humpbacked cuckolded husband in D.W. Griffith's **Drums of Love.**

At this point, besides acting, Barrymore also directed six films (1929-31), mostly quite forgettable. For one of them, **Madame X**, however, he was Oscar-nominated for best director. Another, **His Glorious Night,** turns up as a footnote in Hollywood history because MGM allegedly ordered Barrymore to sabotage star John Gilbert's career by making him overact horrendously (the studio had grown weary of Gilbert's demands for ever-higher salaries). No one, however, has ever proved that the director either received or carried out any such orders.

And now, in 1931, the time had arrived for the greatest triumph in the career of Lionel Barrymore.

In **A Free Soul,** he was a brilliant, alcoholic criminal lawyer whose daughter (Norma Shearer) turns from her stuffy fiancé (Leslie Howard) to the arms of a ruthless gangster (Clark Gable, not yet a star). Howard shoots Gable dead and Barrymore defends him in a sensational courtroom scene that was the high point and climax of the film. His 14-minute speech to the jury set a record that still stands for the longest monologue in any film and also for the longest take in a commercially made feature-length movie; since a reel of camera film lasts only 10 minutes, the take was accomplished by using six cameras, since sound editing had yet to be perfected.

At the end of the passionate peroration, the lawyer drops dead in front of judge and jurors. This performance (done on the very first take for director Clarence Brown) stole the picture and, what was far more important, won for Barrymore the Academy Award as *best actor.*

In another film he made that year, **Guilty Hands,** the plot is remarkably similar. Again he is a lawyer, and again his daughter (Madge Evans) is in love with a bounder (Alan Mowbray). Barrymore murders Mowbray and places the gun in the dead man's hands to simulate a suicide. However, the corpse's stiffening fingers tighten on the trigger and Barrymore is shot dead. In **The Yellow Ticket,** he played a Russian police chief harassing Elissa Landi, who is saved by Laurence Olivier.

The actor was now at his peak. In 1932 he appeared for the only time with both brother John and sister Ethel, in **Rasputin and the Empress,** wildly sinister as the mad monk Rasputin and chewing up the scenery in one of his most flamboyant performances. He was fine in **Grand Hotel,** both humorous and pathetic as Kringelein, a downtrodden wage

slave hoping for one worldly fling in his short remaining time to live; at least he gets to dance with Joan Crawford. Brother John was one of the co-stars. In **Arsene Lupin** he was the clubfooted Paris police chief, matching wits with John as the thief of the title role. **Mata Hari** cast him as a spymaster killed by Greta Garbo, his ex-lover and ex-accomplice.

Collapsing and dying on screen seemed to be Barrymore's specialty. In **Washington Masquerade** he was a righteous senator corrupted and trapped into marriage by a scheming blonde (Karen Morley) who gets him to take a bribe from lobbyists. There is an investigation, he admits the truth, and at the conclusion of his testimony keels over and dies. And he was in director Ernst Lubitsch's drama **Broken Lullaby (The Man I Killed)** as the father of the slain soldier.

In **One Man's Journey** (33) the actor played a selfless rural doctor, and in **The Stranger's Return** he was an 85-year-old grandfather running an Iowa farm, in one of his best performances; at the end, he triumphs in a sanity hearing set up by scheming relatives who are after his property. **Looking Forward** cast him as an old bookkeeper who saves a centuries-old London department store, and in **Sweepings** he *owned* a department store, in which his ungrateful children showed no interest. In the classic comedy-drama **Dinner at Eight** he was a shipping magnate and the husband of Billie Burke, around whose dinner party the film revolves. He co-starred with his brother for the last time in **Night Flight,** playing an airline inspector.

But it's a long road that has no turning. In **The Girl from Missouri** (34) he put on display the other side of his acting ability—the bad side. As Franchot Tone's father, looking with extreme disapproval on Jean Harlow, his performance was ponderous, his crustiness phony, his heartiness fake, his contempt not believable. It was a harbinger of performances to come. Also that year, he played Billy Bones in **Treasure Island,** was a Southern patriarch who commits suicide in **Carolina,** and appeared in **This Side of Heaven** as an accountant, wrongly suspected of embezzling, who *attempts* suicide; Fay Bainter, in her screen debut, played his wife.

Barrymore had the opportunity at this point to star in two interesting and offbeat films, both directed by that master of the macabre, Tod Browning. In **Mark of the Vampire** (35) he was a professor of demonology(!), delving into the occult, and in **The Devil Doll** (36) he was a vengeful man (wrongly imprisoned for 20 years) who disguises himself as a little old lady shopkeeper and works with a scientist who has mastered the technique of reducing humans to the size of tiny dolls, whom Barrymore uses to commit crimes.

Also in 1935, he was Dan Peggotty in the classic **David Copperfield,** appeared as the head of the family in **Ah, Wilderness** (with Spring Byington as his wife and Mickey Rooney as his son), and fell afoul of child star Shirley Temple on the set of **The Little Colonel.** In her memoirs, Miss Temple recalls that Barrymore, playing an old Southern colonel, had to have his cues and lines written out for him on a large blackboard. At one point the seven-year-old Shirley, wanting to be helpful, prompted the veteran actor. "Dammit!" he exploded. "I'm 30 years in this business!" Later Shirley went to his dressing room and apologized.

Another 1936 film was the classic Greta Garbo starrer **Camille,** in which he was Robert Taylor's father. Even under a director of the caliber of George Cukor, he gave an unforgivably hammy performance, which looked even worse since he played most of his scenes with Garbo. In **The Gorgeous Hussy,** starring Joan Crawford, he was Andrew Jackson, with Beulah Bondi as his pitiful wife. He portrayed an old infantry soldier in **The Road to Glory.**

In 1937 the actor was fine as the captain of the fishing smack in **Captains Courageous,** and played the father in **A Family Affair,** the first in the Hardy Family series; he was replaced by Lewis Stone for the balance of the long-running series.

A 1938 accident that broke a hip and a kneecap, combined with arthritis, crippled Barrymore severely. In constant pain, he walked for a time on crutches and then was ordered by his doctors into a wheelchair. In all his remaining 40 films he appeared in that wheelchair, which failed to diminish his considerable activity as an actor. How did he stand the ongoing pain? He once said of MGM studio head Louis B. Mayer: "L.B. gets me $400 worth of cocaine a day to ease my pain. I don't know where he gets it. And I don't care. But I bless him every time it puts me to sleep."

You Can't Take It with You (38) cast him for director Frank Capra as the crusty, philosophical, income tax-defying Grandpa Vanderhof, who has quit the business world many years earlier to enjoy life. And in that same year Barrymore made a significant debut as Dr. Gillespie in the second Dr. Kildare film, **Young Dr. Kildare**—a role he would fill in the incredible total of 15 movies. Dr. Gillespie was the grumpy old head doctor at Blair General Hospital, and Lew Ayres was—until 1942—Dr. Kildare. The older physician bullied the young doctor and everyone else in sight.

Barrymore had a good role in 1939 in **On Borrowed Time** as a stubborn old man who entraps Death (Sir Cedric Hardwicke) in a magical apple tree because he (Barrymore) is set on not dying until he can secure the future of his little grandson. But he also did two Dr. Kildares, which were strictly program fillers. In 1940, for the first time, *all* his films were Kildares—three of them. The following year he made two more Kildares and three other films that no one but the studio accountants remembers.

Off the screen, the actor was a remarkably talented man, and he had some success as a painter and etcher, composed orchestral music (several of his pieces were performed by orchestras), wrote a novel, "Mr. Cantonwine," and in 1951 published his memoirs, "We Barrymores."

In 1942 Lew Ayres disappeared from the Kildare scene after announcing that as a conscientious objector he would refuse combat duty during the war. Quickly MGM made the 64-year-old Barrymore the star of the series, and the next three films were entitled **Calling Dr. Gillespie, Dr. Gillespie's New Assistant,** and **Dr. Gillespie's Criminal Case.**

But other than those, the actor was playing strictly routine supporting roles, and sometimes not very skillfully. It's difficult now to recall more than a tiny handful of his performances from the Forties—although good ones from the Thirties are legion. Still, he was good as the vindictive abolitionist Thaddeus Stevens in **Tennessee Johnson** (43), and wonderfully malevolent in director Frank Capra's classic **It's a Wonderful Life** (46), as the hard-hearted old banker who refuses to help James Stewart. He had a good role that same year in **Duel in the Sun** as the rancher fighting the incursion of the railroad; playing his wife was Lillian Gish, who had appeared with him in some D.W. Griffith films 30-odd years earlier. In 1948 he won good notices in **Key Largo** as Lauren Bacall's father, spouting defiance to gangster Edward G. Robinson.

Meanwhile, in **Dark Delusion** (47) he had finally wound down the Kildare series after 10 years and 15 films, and in **Down to the Sea in Ships** (49) he gave one last memorable performance, as a grizzled sea captain. There were a few more films, concluding with **Main Street to Broadway** in 1953.

Lionel Barrymore died in 1954 at age 76, leaving an imperishable memory of the time when he had been one of the finest character actors the screen has ever seen.

THE FILMS OF LIONEL BARRYMORE

NOTE: Only feature-length films are listed, which means that the early D.W. Griffith shorts, 1909-13 (or possibly 1911-13) have been eliminated, as have several later shorts. Also not included here are the six films he directed, but did not appear in, in the period 1929-31.

1913: Judith of Bethulia (four reels, about 40 minutes).

1914: The Woman in Black; The Seats of the Mighty; The Span of Life. *Credit uncertain:* Men and Women; Strongheart; Under the Gaslight; Classmates; The Power of the Press; The Massacre; Brute Force.

1915: Wildfire; A Modern Magdalen; The Curious Life of Judge Legarde (or The Curious Conduct of Judge Legarde); The Flaming Sword; Dora Thorne; A Yellow Streak; The Romance of Elaine, The Exploits of Elaine (serials).

1916: Dorian's Divorce; The Quitter; The Upheaval; The Brand of Cowardice.

1917: The End of the Tour; His Father's Son; The Millionaire's Double.

1918: *Credit uncertain:* The Yellow Ticket.

1919: *Credit uncertain:* The Valley of Night.

1920: The Copperhead; The Master Mind; The Devil's Garden.

1921: The Great Adventure; Jim the Penman.

1922: Boomerang Bill; The Face in the Fog.

1923: Enemies of Women; Unseeing Eyes; The Eternal City.

1924: Decameron Nights; America; Meddling Women; I Am the Man.

1925: The Iron Man; Children of the Whirlwind; The Girl Who Wouldn't Work; The Wrongdoers; Fifty-Fifty; The Splendid Road. *Credit uncertain:* Die Frau mit dem schlechten Ruf.

1926: Paris at Midnight; The Bells; The Temptress; The Barrier; Brooding Eyes; The Lucky Lady.

1927: The Show; Women Love Diamonds; Body and Soul; The Thirteenth Hour. *Credit uncertain:* Love.

1928: Sadie Thompson; Drums of Love; West of Zanzibar; The Lion and the Mouse; Road House; River Woman.

1929: Alias Jimmy Valentine; The Mysterious Island; The Hollywood Revue of 1929.

1930: Free and Easy (cameo, as himself).

1931: A Free Soul; The Yellow Ticket; Guilty Hands.

1932: Rasputin and the Empress; Mata Hari; Arsene Lupin; Broken Lullaby (The Man I Killed); Grand Hotel; Washington Masquerade.

1933: Sweepings; Looking Forward; Dinner at Eight; The Stranger's Return; Night Flight; One Man's Journey; Should Ladies Behave?; Christopher Bean (The Late Christopher Bean).

1934: This Side of Heaven; Carolina; Treasure Island; The Girl from Missouri.

1935: Mark of the Vampire; The Little Colonel; David Copperfield; Ah, Wilderness; Public Hero Number One; The Return of Peter Grimm.

1936: Camille; The Gorgeous Hussy; The Devil Doll; The Road to Glory; The Voice of Bugle Ann.

1937: Captains Courageous; A Family Affair; Saratoga; Navy Blue and Gold.

1938: You Can't Take It with You; Test Pilot; A Yank at Oxford; Young Dr. Kildare.

1939: Let Freedom Ring; On Borrowed Time; Calling Dr. Kildare; The Secret of Dr. Kildare.

1940: Dr. Kildare's Strange Case; Dr. Kildare Goes Home; Dr. Kildare's Crisis.

1941: The Bad Man; The Penalty; Lady Be Good; The People vs. Dr. Kildare; Dr. Kildare's Wedding Day.

1942: Tennessee Johnson; Dr. Kildare's Victory; Calling Dr. Gillespie; Dr. Gillespie's New Assistant.

1943: Thousands Cheer; A Guy Named Joe; Dr. Gillespie's Criminal Case.

1944: Since You Went Away; Three Men in White; Dragon Seed (narrator only).

1945: The Valley of Decision; Between Two Women.

1946: It's a Wonderful Life; Duel in the Sun; Three Wise Fools; The Secret Heart.

1947: Dark Delusion.

1948: Key Largo.

1949: Down to the Sea in Ships; Malaya.

1950: Right Cross.

1951: Bannerline.

1952: Lone Star.

1953: Main Street to Broadway.

Sometimes he even got the girl:

RALPH BELLAMY

Talk about typecasting! In Hollywood in the Thirties there was a characterization that became known as "the Ralph Bellamy role," because that actor played it so often. Simply put, the Ralph Bellamy role was the rich, simple-minded hayseed who never got the girl. (Who got her? Well, somebody like Cary Grant.)

While Bellamy spent much of his screen career chasing and losing his leading ladies, this fair-haired, soft-voiced, serious-looking actor also played pipe-smoking detectives, villainous murderers, and friends of the family. But almost always he portrayed someone who was dull and dependable. Hollywood never really assessed his true worth, and he all too seldom got the parts his genuine talent demanded. It took the Broadway stage in the postwar era to prove he could out-act most film stars.

Being a good foil isn't always easy. In truth, his seeming dullness on the screen enabled his co-stars to shine. And as critic Molly Haskell has written, "As the alternative whereby women learned their original choice wasn't so bad, he could have started a one-man liberation movement."

Bellamy was born June 17, 1904, in Chicago, the son of an advertising executive who lived in suburban Winnetka. In his younger days he worked as a soda jerk, an office clerk, a sheep-pelt sorter(!) and a fruit picker. His father fired him from a position at his Chicago advertising firm. The young man then began intensive training for a stage career—not just acting, but also directing, producing, designing sets and handling props, working with 15 assorted stock companies, including a Shakespearean troupe, for four years, touring the Midwest and playing an incredible 375 parts. He had the difficult leading role in **The Servant in the House,** and also enacted the parts of Old Matt and Wash Gibbs in **The Shepherd of the Hills,** among many others. He once said, "I lived for a week at a time on a daily ration of a pound of peanuts, including the shells, and huge quantities of tap water."

In 1925, at the age of 21, he started his own company, the North Shore Players, in Evanston, another Chicago suburb. For two seasons they played the Midwest, with Bellamy as the tyrannical Rev. Davidson in **Rain** and also in the title role of **Rip Van Winkle.** (He was good at playing older men.) Then for a while he ran his own troupes in Des Moines, Iowa, and Nashville.

Meanwhile, in 1922 he had married Alice Delbridge, from whom he was divorced in 1930. From 1931 to 1945 he was wed to actress Catherine Willard, with two children, Catherine and Willard. In 1945 he married organist Ethel Smith; they divorced in 1949, and his fourth marriage was to Alice Murphy.

Bellamy came to New York around 1927, but didn't make it onto the Broadway stage until 1929, in **Town Boy.** Unfortunately, the show closed after opening night. After this inauspicious debut, he toured in **Holiday** and then with Helen Hayes in **Coquette,** returning to Broadway in **Roadside,** for which he won critical acclaim that mentioned his "pipe-organ voice." **Roadside** lasted only 11 performances, but in Hollywood, where talkies had just taken over, producers were looking for pipe-organ voices.

The actor made his screen debut in 1931 in **The Secret Six,** as a murderous gangster who is killed off fairly early. He co-starred with Ruth Chatterton in

The Magnificent Lie, as a blinded ex-World War I soldier who falls in love with a café singer. This performance won critical plaudits, and studios were clamoring for his services. In a change of pace, he now played a ruthless German captain in charge of a World War I prison camp in **Surrender.**

He was Barbara Stanwyck's bellicose newspaperman husband in director Frank Capra's fine drama **Forbidden** (32), murdered by her when he threatens to reveal her past liaison with politician Adolphe Menjou. In **Disorderly Conduct** he played an upright police captain, in **Young America** a sympathetic juvenile-court judge, in **The Woman in Room 13** the villainous, scheming, philandering husband of Elissa Landi, in **Wild Girl** a gambler in the old West, in **Rebecca of Sunnybrook Farm** the doctor, and in director John Ford's **Air Mail** a levelheaded airport superintendent clashing with stunt flier Pat O'Brien.

Bellamy scored a hit in **Destination Unknown** (33) as the mysterious, Christ-like stowaway who saves a stranded ship. In **Picture Snatcher** he was James Cagney's alcoholic city editor, in **Second Hand Wife** a business executive married to faithless Helen Vinson, in **Blind Adventure** the leader of an extortionist gang, and in **Below the Sea** a gruff deep-sea diver who grapples with a giant octopus and romances Fay Wray. **Parole Girl** cast him as a store manager who, when Mae Clarke pulls a scam on the store, gets her sent to prison, and she plans revenge, but then falls in love with him (although he is married to Marie Prevost). Most of these films were made for Columbia Pictures, for which the actor did much of his work in the Thirties. Columbia was at that time close to being a Poverty Row studio. Many of Bellamy's roles in those days were strictly routine, and some of them were as standard heavies, the "bad guy," such as the murderous cuckolded husband, owner of a flying circus, in **Flying Devils.**

But there was one significant development in 1933. It occurred in a minor and long-forgotten film called **Headline Shooter.** This movie provided the actor with his first "Ralph Bellamy role"—as a "sober banker from the South" who loses Frances Dee to newsreel cameraman William Gargan.

In 1934, Bellamy sometimes even got the girl, by golly. In **This Man Is Mine** he was a bovine playboy happily married to Irene Dunne but temporarily distracted by old flame Constance Cummings. And in **Spitfire,** playing a construction boss, it is strongly hinted at the finale that he will wind up with Katharine Hepburn, no less (she played a hillbilly tomboy type). Also that year, he was good as Inspector Trent in two films, **Girl in Danger** and **One Is Guilty.** He also played detectives in **Before Midnight** and **The**

Crime of Helen Stanley, and was a surgeon in **Once to Every Woman.**

But at this point he started "not getting the girl" in spades. In director King Vidor's fine drama **The Wedding Night** (35) he was a Polish lout engaged to Anna Sten. On their wedding night, enraged by her coldness, he sets out to murder Gary Cooper, with whom she is really in love, but Miss Sten is killed in a fall down a staircase. He had another good role as the wealthy, kindly cripple in love with manicurist Carole Lombard in **Hands Across the Table,** an excellent, neglected film by director Mitchell Leisen. Alas, he loses her to the impoverished Fred MacMurray. And he starred in **Air Hawks** and others.

In **Dangerous Intrigue** (36) he was a celebrated surgeon, rejected by his snobbish fiancée; he suffers an attack of amnesia and while in that condition aids injured workers in a steel mill. He starred as a dashing aviator opposite Fay Wray in **Roaming Lady.**

In 1937 he played his greatest "Ralph Bellamy role" and won an Oscar nomination as best supporting actor for it. The film was **The Awful Truth,** and he portrayed the dull, rich, bashful Oklahoma farmer engaged to Irene Dunne—until she decides to return to ex-husband Cary Grant. Under Leo McCarey's expert direction, the entire cast turned in sparkling performances, and the screwball comedy was one of the standouts of the year.

Meanwhile, in a totally different kind of part, the versatile actor starred in **The Man Who Lived Twice,** playing virtually a dual role as an eminent doctor and a vicious criminal. As the fugitive killer, he undergoes brain surgery as a human guinea pig in return for a new face, emerging with no memory of his past. In 10 years he becomes an eminent medical scientist, but his unchanged voice allows a relentless detective to find him. He stands trial for the murderer's crimes and is found guilty, but gets a last-minute reprieve. Also that year, he was a weatherman who wins Ida Lupino in **Let's Get Married.**

In **Carefree** (38) Bellamy was the stuffy fiancé of Ginger Rogers—and of course he loses her to Fred Astaire, as if you couldn't guess. In **Boy Meets Girl** he was featured as the head of a Hollywood studio. **Trade Winds** found him playing a rather dumb detective on the trail of Joan Bennett; critics remarked that he was simply reprising his **Awful Truth** persona. He also starred in **The Crime of Doctor Hallet** as a dedicated doctor working in the jungle to develop a vaccine for fever.

Bellamy's best film in 1939 was **Blind Alley,** in which he portrayed a psychoanalyst helping vicious killer Chester Morris sort out the cause of his recurrent nightmares. He lost Frances Dee—again—this time to Randolph Scott in **Coast Guard,** and starred as a government spy-catcher in **Smashing the Spy Ring.** In **Let Us Live** he was a police lieutenant who helps find the evidence that frees Henry Fonda from a murder charge.

In 1940 the actor was once more a big loser, this time yielding up Rosalind Russell in director Howard Hawks' rapid-fire comedy **His Girl Friday.** As usual, he was a boring hick, the dull fiancé hoping to spirit newspaper reporter Russell off to domestic bliss in Albany, New York, where he is an insurance salesman. Guess who gets the girl? Right—Cary Grant.

He also played a hardboiled naval officer in **Flight Angels,** starred as an FBI agent in **Queen of the Mob,** and was a hick Western rancher in **Brother Orchid,** engaged to Ann Sothern and helping Edward G. Robinson fight a gang of racketeers (in the film, Miss Sothern is Robinson's girl before taking up with Bellamy). Robinson was one of many who deplored the waste of Bellamy's very real talent in the screen roles he got. He would say in his memoirs: "When you need an actor to play *anything,* get Ralph Bellamy. His range is limitless; his abilities unparalleled; his ego, barely ever ruffled. He is the kind of star who makes it possible to make pictures. Never getting the girl is a difficult role; it enables an actor to grow old gracefully."

In that year he also starred as detective Ellery Queen for the first of several times, and was featured in **Dance, Girl, Dance** as a ballet impresario involved with Maureen O'Hara.

Off the screen, Bellamy developed various business interests, and he and actor Charles Farrell cofounded the Palm Springs Racquet Club.

At this point the actor started a siege of pictures totally unworthy of his acting abilities. In them he was generally either a detective or the "surprise" murderer. The quotation marks around "surprise" are appropriate, because audiences quickly caught on that when Bellamy was *not* the detective, an actor of his caliber in a "B" movie must be...the killer. So when his face appeared on the screen, they promptly labeled him the murderer. A typical example was **Footsteps in the Dark** (41), in which he played a dentist for whom oral surgery is merely a cover-up for murder; he ends up being nabbed by Errol Flynn.

Also in 1941, he reverted to type in **Affectionately Yours** as a wealthy, dumb hayseed chasing Merle Oberon—and of course losing her to Dennis Morgan. Now he even got into some horror films. In **The Wolf Man** he played a non-horror part, and in **The Ghost of Frankenstein** (42) he and Evelyn

Ankers were the romantic leads. He also scored in **The Great Impersonation,** once again in a dual role in this double-spy outing.

Bellamy was by now growing tired of the obvious waste of his talents. He later recalled, "For me, Hollywood had become just a chore. I had to get out." Broadway producers were offering him good parts. And so in 1943 he returned to the New York stage in **Tomorrow the World,** playing a troubled American college professor unnerved by the presence of a 12-year-old Nazi youth (Skippy Homeier) in his home. When the smash-hit play was brought to the screen, Bellamy's part was taken by Fredric March, a bigger box-office name.

In 1944, at age 40, he was back in Hollywood, filming **Guest in the House,** as a magazine illustrator forced to deal with a neurotic, scheming Anne Baxter (she's the guest in his house). The following year he was again the "surprise" (uh-huh) murderer in the Deanna Durbin starrer **Lady on a Train.** And then he returned to the stage; in the next 21 years he would appear in only two films.

In 1945 he starred on Broadway in another smash hit, **State of the Union,** as a presidential hopeful; Spencer Tracy appeared in the film version. The play ran for two years, and then he turned for a while to that new medium television, starring in the detective series "Man Against Crime." In 1949 he once again became the star of a smash Broadway hit, **Detective Story,** as a police detective obsessed with incarcerating criminals. This play also ran for two years. The movie version? Kirk Douglas got the part.

In 1952 Bellamy was elected president of Actors' Equity, the union for stage performers, and he served four terms, through 1964.

He returned briefly to Hollywood in 1955 for a small part in **The Court-Martial of Billy Mitchell,** and then was back on the boards again. In 1958 he once again starred in a hit Broadway play, portraying future president Franklin D. Roosevelt in **Sunrise at Campobello,** for which he won a Tony award. This time Hollywood producers realized that no other actor could possibly do justice to the role, and so for the first and only time he re-created his stage part on the screen, in 1960, with Greer Garson as Eleanor. Oddly enough, she won an Oscar nomination as best supporting actress, while the fine performance that had won Bellamy the Tony as best actor of the year garnered no such honors in Tinseltown.

He was now a craggy and redoubtable character actor in his late fifties. He turned to television at this point for his primary source of work and income, and in 1964 replaced the ailing Wendell Corey as a psychiatrist in the series "The Eleventh Hour." In 1966 he was briefly back on the screen as the aging husband of nubile young Claudia Cardinale in **The Professionals,** and returned in 1968 for **Rosemary's Baby,** as the treacherous doctor who helps the coven of witches in their plot against the unfortunate Mia Farrow.

The following year he was in one of TV's biggest flops, "The Survivors," as Lana Turner's father; the series quickly folded. In 1971 he made another film, **Doctors' Wives,** as the millionaire father of the murdered Dyan Cannon, and also was in **Cancel My Reservation** (72). His TV work continued apace, including a good role as Adlai Stevenson, U.S. ambassador to the United Nations, in "The Missiles of October" in 1975. Now in his seventies, he had a small part in the film **Oh, God!** (77) and also appeared in **The Millionaire** (78). In 1979 he penned his autobiography, "When the Smoke Hit the Fan." He appeared in the hit film **Trading Places** in 1983. In his eight-ies, Bellamy continued to appear in films. In **The Disorderlies** (87) he was a Palm Beach millionaire whose nephew and valet contrive unsuccessfully to murder him for his estate. He was in several hit movies: **Coming to America** and **The Good Mother** (both 88) and **Pretty Woman** (90).

Meanwhile, in 1986 he was presented with an honorary Academy Award for "his unique artistry and his distinguished service to the profession of acting." Before he died at 87 in 1991, Ralph Bellamy could look back on an acting career of more than six decades, in which his fine talents, too often wasted by Hollywood on silly "other man" roles, were ultimately better appreciated by the Broadway stage, with a record of four smash hits out of four wartime or postwar plays. And as for Irene Dunne, Rosalind Russell, Carole Lombard, and all those other fickle females—ladies, how could you say no to Ralph? Oh, well— Cary Grant *did* have his good points.

THE FILMS OF RALPH BELLAMY

1931: The Secret Six; The Magnificent Lie; Surrender.
1932: Forbidden; West of Broadway; Disorderly Conduct; Young America; Rebecca of Sunnybrook Farm; The Woman in Room 13; Wild Girl; Air Mail; Almost Married.
1933: Second Hand Wife; Parole Girl; Destination Unknown; Picture Snatcher; The Narrow Corner; Below the Sea; Headline Shooter; Flying Devils; Blind Adventure; Ace of Aces; Ever in My Heart.
1934: This Man Is Mine; Once to Every Woman; Spitfire; One Is Guilty; Before Midnight; The Crime of Helen Stanley; Girl in Danger; Woman in the Dark.
1935: Hands Across the Table; The Wedding Night; Helldorado; Rendezvous at Midnight; Air Hawks; Eight Bells; The Healer; Gigolette; Navy Wife.
1936: Dangerous Intrigue; The Final Hour; Roaming Lady; Straight from the Shoulder; Wild Brian Kent.
1937: The Awful Truth; The Man Who Lived Twice; Counterfeit Lady; Let's Get Married; It Can't Last Forever.
1938: Carefree; Trade Winds; Boy Meets Girl; The Crime of Doctor Hallet; Fools for Scandal; Girls' School.
1939: Let Us Live; Blind Alley; Coast Guard; Smashing the Spy Ring.
1940: His Girl Friday; Brother Orchid; Queen of the Mob; Dance, Girl, Dance; Flight Angels; Meet the Wildcat; Ellery Queen, Master Detective; Elsa Maxwell's Public Deb No. 1.
1941: The Wolf Man; Footsteps in the Dark; Affectionately Yours; Dive Bomber; Ellery Queen's Penthouse Mystery; Ellery Queen and the Perfect Crime; Ellery Queen and the Murder Ring.
1942: The Ghost of Frankenstein; The Great Impersonation; Lady in a Jam; Men of Texas.
1943: Stage Door Canteen.
1944: Guest in the House.
1945: Lady on a Train; Delightfully Dangerous.
1955: The Court-Martial of Billy Mitchell.
1960: Sunrise at Campobello.
1966: The Professionals.
1968: Rosemary's Baby.
1971: Doctors' Wives.
1972: Cancel My Reservation.
1977: Oh, God!
1978: The Millionaire.
1983: Trading Places.
1987: The Disorderlies; Amazon Women on the Moon.
1988: Coming to America; The Good Mother.
1990: Pretty Woman.

Rebel with a cause:
CHARLES BICKFORD

The year was 1930, and the film called **The Sea Bat** was turning into a disaster, with location shooting scrapped, the director replaced, and the rushes engendering howls of laughter over some of the acting. MGM czar Louis B. Mayer had ordered the company back to the studio to reshoot it at night, and now one of the stars, Charles Bickford, was complaining about working evening hours. Nothing unusual there; Bickford was well known as the actor who was always telling producers and others where to get off.

"Mr. Mayer, I will not spend my evenings working on this silly fiasco, and that is that!" he declaimed.

The powerful studio boss turned several shades of purple. "Why, you redheaded son of a bitch..."

"I'm redheaded all right, and I may be a son of a bitch, but I'm outraged to be called one by a venomous little junk peddler like you," said Bickford. "To hell with you, you posturing little ignoramus!"

Mayer, who in his early days had been a junk dealer, was shaking with rage. "One day you'll come crawling on your knees to apologize for that!" he screamed.

Charles Bickford looked at him contemptuously. "Get back to your junkyard, little man," he snapped.

Bickford's attitude toward Hollywood and its mighty moguls was, to put it charitably, condescending. He was the possessor of some very strong opinions, and these certainly included views on acting and the movie industry. He never hesitated to express these views to all and sundry.

"I have been an independent spirit since I was that high," he said in his later years. "It's a characteristic of mine and there's nothing I can do about it, even if I wanted to. I have never been unreasonable at any time—merely firm."

For Bickford was Hollywood's foremost rebel of the Thirties. Frequently defiant and uncooperative, he was an iconoclast, but an intelligent and supremely realistic one, the epitome of integrity, forever exposing fakery and sycophancy. His attitude toward the studio hierarchy removed him from the ranks of the stars and reduced him to playing character parts—but the amazing thing is that he was allowed to keep on acting in Hollywood at all. The answer is that as a screen performer he was virtually unique: rugged, dependable, good at playing equally well a hero or a

villain; an actor who could be stubborn or unscrupulous but could also be warm and sincere.

In fact, he was a great standby actor, able to take on almost any kind of role and give it a feeling of absolute reality. His performances were consistently good, characteristically intense, often projecting a rugged and thoughtful sincerity, and he won three Academy Award nominations as best supporting actor—and probably would have won an Oscar had he had more friends among the powers that be in Hollywood.

Bickford was born January 1, 1889, in Cambridge, Massachusetts, and originally studied engineering at MIT. His combative nature was shaped by some early rugged experiences: In addition to working for a time as a civil engineer, he reportedly worked as a logger, a carnival barker, a seaman, a wheat harvester, a brewery-truck driver, and possibly some other jobs—and he is said to have spent time in a hobo jungle. For a time he was a sparring partner for a professional boxer—but it could hardly have been James J. Corbett, as one source has it, because his reign as heavyweight champion ended when Bickford was eight years old.

At age 25 he entered show business via burlesque. The show folded and he went to Boston, where he joined the Castle Square Theatre stock company, and within a year was playing Tybalt, Laertes, and other Shakespearean roles. He tried repertory on tour, and was also the star on an Ohio River showboat.

After naval service in World War I he turned to the legitimate stage, and made his Broadway debut in David Belasco's **Dark Rosaleen,** with Thomas Mitchell and Beryl Mercer in the cast. For a while he haunted booking offices, then was selected to replace George Abbott in **Zander the Great** in Detroit. He drew raves from Chicago critics when the play went to that city. Then he signed with the star of **Dark Rosaleen,** Alice Brady, for a season of vaudeville, playing in a condensed version of her hit play **Drifting.**

Bickford's big break came in 1925 when he starred in Maxwell Anderson's **Outside Looking In,** as the tough hobo Oklahoma Red (James Cagney was in the supporting cast). The play was a smash hit, and now the actor could write his own ticket to success.

Meanwhile, in 1919 he had married actress Beatrice Loring. They became the parents of two children, Doris and Rex.

The actor turned down an offer by Hollywood director Herbert Brenon to co-star with Ronald Colman in the silent film version of **Beau Geste,** but the movies were in fact his destiny, and that destiny was drawing nearer.

He opened in 1928 in the Broadway play **The Gods of the Lightning,** also by Maxwell Anderson, in a cast that included Sylvia Sidney and Barton MacLane. This version of the Sacco-Vanzetti case featured Bickford as the bold, outspoken anarchist Macready, and he scored a hit, especially in the courtroom scenes. The performance caught the attention of one of Hollywood's biggest names: Cecil B. DeMille. Little did the producer/director know what he was letting himself in for.

Bickford, at age 40, was co-starred with Kay Johnson and Conrad Nagel in DeMille's 1929 film **Dynamite** for his movie debut, with young Joel McCrea as the juvenile lead. On the first day on the set, the rebel made his presence felt: "Understand me, Mr. DeMille, I am not criticizing the construction of this story. I don't know enough about screenwriting for that. But I've been writing and acting in stage plays for many more years than you've been produc-

ing motion pictures [actually that wasn't the case], and this dialogue stinks!"

Later, when Miss Johnson stumbled over one of her lines and DeMille sarcastically told her to get her act together, Bickford said to her, "Why do you take it? Tell the son of a bitch to go to hell." Oddly enough, actor and producer patched up their differences, and DeMille later used him in four other films.

Bickford's next feud—one that would flare up again nearly 30 years later—was with the young director William Wyler on **Hell's Heroes** (also 29), an early version of the story later filmed twice as **Three Godfathers.** But this was quickly forgotten as he was cast opposite Greta Garbo in her first talkie, **Anna Christie,** as her lover, Matt Burke. He was impressive, the critics thought after viewing the MGM release. But a vengeful Louis B. Mayer was not about to make Bickford a star. Instead, he got good but non-showy parts and frequently had to appear in second-string features.

In the aforementioned **The Sea Bat** he was an escaped convict posing as a clergyman, and in DeMille's **The Squaw Man** (31) a ruthless murderer, ultimately killed by Lupe Velez to save Warner Baxter's life. In **Panama Flo** (32), opposite Helen Twelvetrees, he started out as the disagreeable villain and was converted into the romantic hero. **Scandal for Sale** cast him as a ruthless newspaper editor who, to win a cash prize, sends star reporter Pat O'Brien to his death in an attempted trans-ocean flight, pockets the money, but then quits in disgust. In **Thunder Below** he was an egotistical oil rigger married to Tallulah Bankhead, not suspecting that she is in love with his best friend (Paul Lukas); Bickford goes blind, Tallulah goes off with yet a third man and finally throws herself off a cliff. He played a rough, violent Suez roustabout who is actually an English detective in **The Last Man,** and a two-fisted, heart-of-gold policeman in **Vanity Street,** in which he rescues down-and-out Helen Chandler from ruin, sets her up as a Follies girl, then, after arresting her for a murder she didn't really commit, clears her name and marries her.

In DeMille's **This Day and Age** (33) he was a murderous gangster who is kidnapped by a mob of teen-agers and forced to confess to a killing, and in **A Wicked Woman** (34), as a newspaperman, he falls in love with confessed murderer Mady Christians. The Shirley Temple film **Little Miss Marker** found him playing the villain who reforms and arranges a blood transfusion that saves the little girl's life.

In most of these films of the early and mid-Thirties Bickford was cast (probably by hostile producers) as a villain of deepest dye. For example, in the 1933 film **Song of the Eagle** he was a liquor-truck driver who becomes a bootlegger and kills his former boss, Jean Hersholt. In **The Farmer Takes a Wife** (35) he was the nasty who gives a hard time to young canal-boat man Henry Fonda, making his film debut. And in **A Notorious Gentleman** that same year he was seen as a ruthless mouthpiece who almost gets away with killing a rival lawyer because a jury disagrees—but a relentless district attorney falls back on a frame-up to see that justice is served. Still, he also played such roles as the boss of a crew of sandhogs, tangling with rival crew boss Victor McLaglen, in **Under Pressure** (also 35).

But Bickford sometimes managed to get co-starring parts opposite top female stars. In the 1933 film **No Other Woman,** for example, he was a steelworker married to Irene Dunne; becoming rich on a dye formula he invented, he falls for a temptress and frames his wife by bribing witnesses in order to get a divorce, but finally comes to his senses and returns to her.

During the late Thirties the actor's career was definitely in the doldrums. Typically, in those days he was a brutish, avaricious lumberman or land-grabber who ends up bested in a fistfight by someone like Randolph Scott or Wayne Morris. All too often his films were strictly programmers, and when he got into a major production it was in a supporting role of only modest size, as in **Of Mice and Men** (39), where he played Slim, the tough but fair-minded ranch foreman. But as time passed he was playing fewer villains and an increasing number of kindly men, such as the heroic prison chaplain who puts down a riot in **Mutiny in the Big House** (also 39). Still, he got in some last villainous licks as a brutal smuggler of Chinese aliens in **Daughter of Shanghai** (37) and as a bitter, vengeful ex-convict in **Street of Missing Men** (39).

The actor played a clergyman in **Thou Shalt Not Kill** (also 39), and in 1941 was actually reduced to appearing in a serial, **Riders of Death Valley.** His other films of the period bore such now-forgotten titles as **Queen of the Yukon, Burma Convoy** and **The Girl from God's Country.** In 1942 he had a small but good part as the mate of the vessel Tyfib in his last film for DeMille, **Reap the Wild Wind.** And now, at the age of 53, Charles Bickford had good reason to believe that his career was badly stalled.

All that came to an end in 1943, the beginning of a mighty sea-change that put him in the front ranks of Hollywood's character actors and brought him three Academy Award nominations in six years.

The film that turned the tide was **The Song of Bernadette** (43), in which he played Peyremale, the understanding Dean of Lourdes who helps Jennifer Jones realize her dream. For this performance he won the first of his Oscar nominations as best supporting actor. (However, he never won the award.)

He had now begun playing fathers—for example, Fred MacMurray's in **Captain Eddie** (45). But the Oscar nomination was paying off in better roles. Playing a tough police detective in **Fallen Angel,** he turned out to be the surprise murderer of Linda Darnell, trying to pin the crime on Dana Andrews. And in the Western epic **Duel in the Sun** (46) he was excellent as Sam, the aging ranch foreman who wins the hand of Jennifer Jones but is murdered by Gregory Peck.

It could probably be said that 1947 was Bickford's *annus mirabilis*. In all three of his films that year he had good parts, and he won a second Oscar nomination. In **Brute Force** he was the grimly realistic convict Gallagher, who agrees to help Burt Lancaster in his doomed attempt at a prison break. In director Jean Renoir's taut melodrama **Woman on the Beach** he was somewhat on the hammy side as the blind artist husband of Joan Bennett, holding her in a sadistic relationship and even encouraging her to have a love affair with Robert Ryan; finally Bickford burns down the house and all his paintings to exorcise the sick relationship. (Interestingly, in real life the actor took up oil painting as a hobby the following year.)

His 1947 Oscar nomination came for the role of Joseph Cotten's worldly-wise and outspoken butler in **The Farmer's Daughter.** And in 1948 he won yet another Oscar nomination as Jane Wyman's rough-hewn father in **Johnny Belinda,** an intense and excellent portrayal. He was also a no-nonsense newspaper correspondent in **Command Decision,** a relentless lawman (called Sheriff Pat Garrett!) in **Four Faces West,** and a priest in **The Babe Ruth Story.**

One curious aspect of Bickford's unsuccessful Oscar nominations was that in all three films the female stars—Jennifer Jones, Loretta Young and Jane Wyman—won the Academy Award as best actress for *their* performances. Bickford at the very least may have been a good-luck charm for them.

The actor portrayed Cardinal Josef Mindszenty, the Hungarian primate imprisoned by the Communists, in **Guilty of Treason** (49), but then didn't have a strong role in a major film for another five years. The 1954 remake of **A Star Is Born** saw him as the understanding studio head helping Judy Garland, and in **Not as a Stranger** (55) he played the gruff, wise older doctor accidentally killed during an operation by Robert Mitchum. In **The Court-Martial of Billy Mitchell** he was the reactionary general who headed the tribunal that convicted Gary Cooper.

In 1958 Bickford was cast as the patriarch of one of two feuding cattle-ranching families in **The Big Country.** The director was William Wyler, and now *their* 30-year-old feud blazed up anew. One day the actor returned to the set an hour late from lunch.

"Charlie, you're late," said Wyler.

"Yes, I am. What are you going to do about it?"

"Well, I guess you've got me there. I can't fire you, because you're in half the picture."

"So let's cut the bullshit and get to work," the actor rejoined. At age 69, clearly, some things about Charles Bickford had never changed.

In the film, there is a final bloody shootout between the two ranching families, and the two patriarchs, Bickford and Burl Ives, kill each other. Wyler, of course, was a painstaking perfectionist, shooting retake after retake, and one wonders how many times the elderly actor had to drop dead before Wyler finally liked it.

At this point Bickford's career moved largely into television, although he still continued to film. In 1958 he scored in the TV production of "Days of Wine and Roses," as the father of alcoholic Piper Laurie, and in 1962 he repeated the role in the film version, with Lee Remick as the daughter, married to Jack Lemmon. Also on TV, he appeared in "Winterset" and "The Cradle Song." After one final Hollywood film, **A Big Hand for the Little Lady** (66), he replaced Lee J. Cobb as the head of Shiloh Ranch in the TV series "The Virginian." Meanwhile, in 1965, at age 76, he had written his memoirs, "Bulls, Balls, Bicycles and Actors"—as outspoken as he himself had always been. It concluded with this advice to actors: "Protect yourself in the clinches," and signed off with the words "Up the rebels."

Charles Bickford died at 78 in 1967. For 37 years he had been one of the movies' finest actors—and, always, Hollywood's most defiant rebel.

THE FILMS OF CHARLES BICKFORD

1929: Dynamite; Hell's Heroes; South Sea Rose.
1930: Anna Christie; Passion Flower; The Sea Bat; The River's End.
1931: The Squaw Man; East of Borneo; Pagan Lady; The Men in Her Life.
1932: Panama Flo; Thunder Below; Scandal for Sale; The Last Man; Vanity Street.
1933: No Other Woman; Song of the Eagle; This Day and Age; White Woman.
1934: Little Miss Marker; A Wicked Woman.
1935: A Notorious Gentleman; Under Pressure; The Farmer Takes a Wife; East of Java.
1936: The Plainsman; Rose of the Rancho; Pride of the Marines.
1937: Night Club Scandal; Thunder Trail; Daughter of Shanghai; High, Wide and Handsome.
1938: Gangs of New York; Valley of the Giants; The Storm; Stand Up and Fight.
1939: Street of Missing Men; Of Mice and Men; Romance of the Redwoods; Our Leading Citizen; One Hour to Live; Mutiny in the Big House; Thou Shalt Not Kill.
1940: The Girl from God's Country; Queen of the Yukon; South to Karanga.
1941: Burma Convoy; Riders of Death Valley (serial).

1942: Reap the Wild Wind; Tarzan's New York Adventure.
1943: The Song of Bernadette; Mr. Lucky.
1944: Wing and a Prayer.
1945: Fallen Angel; Captain Eddie.
1946: Duel in the Sun.
1947: Brute Force; The Farmer's Daughter; Woman on the Beach.
1948: Johnny Belinda; Command Decision; Four Faces West; The Babe Ruth Story.
1949: Guilty of Treason; Whirlpool; Roseanna McCoy.
1950: Branded; Riding High.
1951: The Raging Tide; Elopement; Jim Thorpe-All-American.
1953: The Last Posse.
1954: A Star Is Born.
1955: Not as a Stranger; Prince of Players; The Court-Martial of Billy Mitchell.
1956: You Can't Run Away from It.
1957: Mister Cory; Dark Wave (listed by one source, but this film cannot be found in several standard checklists of films).
1958: The Big Country.
1960: The Unforgiven.
1962: Days of Wine and Roses.
1966: A Big Hand for the Little Lady.

If looks could kill... :
ERIC BLORE

The adjectives tumble over one another when one attempts to describe the mannerisms and facial contortions of Eric Blore.

Petulant...scornful...supercilious...sniveling...haughty...smug...unctuous...insulting...contemptuous.

No Fred Astaire-Ginger Rogers film of the mid-Thirties (he was in five of them) seemed complete without this archetypal gentleman's gentleman, who was one of the movies' two best-known butlers (the other was Arthur Treacher). Actually, he played other functionaries in some Astaire-Rogers films, but he portrayed so many Hollywood butlers that it's hard to imagine him without a serving tray or clothes brush in hand.

His utterly proper and subservient manner scarcely concealed his contempt for lesser mortals, whom he viewed with pained tolerance. He commented on their behavior in acid tones, delivered with a distinctive lisp. He was excited but unflappable, and his look could kill across a crowded room. With eyebrows raised and keen eyes squinting, he pouted in an exasperated way, and his grin could expand into a full-faced grimace. All these mannerisms blended into a persona so inimitable that it might be compared in that respect to Peter Lorre's. The New York Times has called him a "constant source of delight."

Eric Blore was born in London on December 23, 1887, and after working as an insurance agent he gained stage experience touring Australia, followed by appearances in numerous plays and revues in England. In 1923 he came to the United States to take a role in an Irene Bordoni stage vehicle, and continued on the New York stage in scores of character parts. He co-starred on Broadway in 1926 in **The Ghost Train,** among other appearances.

The actor was married twice, but sources seem confused about which order his wives appeared in. Some sources say he was wed to actress Clara Mackin and that after she died he married Viola Winter; others assert that he was first the widower of Miss Winter and then married Miss Mackin, with whom he had a child and whom he later divorced. In any case, Miss Mackin was in the cast of some films in the period 1938-40.

In 1926 Blore had a brief Hollywood fling, playing Lord Digby in the first of the three film versions of **The Great Gatsby,** this one starring Warner

Baxter. He then went back to the stage, not to return for at least four years.

The frequent uncertainty of pinpointing actors' screen credits in small parts or "bits," especially in the early days of the sound era, makes it difficult to say with certainty whether Blore next filmed in 1930 or in 1933. Some sources say he had a small part in **Laughter** (30) and also in two Tallulah Bankhead vehicles of 1931, **My Sin** and **Tarnished Lady.** But other sources do not indicate his participation in those movies.

It is certain, however, that he drew laughs in his first Astaire-Rogers picture, **Flying Down to Rio,** in 1933, playing the assistant to hotel manager Franklin Pangborn. In the following year he was an unctuous waiter in another of the dancing duo's films, **The Gay Divorcee.** Critics liked his incomparable expression of stunned amazement, and sang his praises. That year he also had parts in **Limehouse Blues** and **Behold My Wife.**

For a while, every year he was in a new Astaire-Rogers film. He played the petulant butler in **Top Hat** (35), the huffy dance-school manager in **Swing Time** (36), and yet another assistant hotel manager in **Shall We Dance** (37). He was also Edward Arnold's sidekick in 1935's **Diamond Jim,** and Joe E. Brown's comic butler (and later his top sergeant) in **Sons o' Guns** (36). Other 1937 roles included the recruiting sergeant in **Quality Street,** the harried war correspondent in **The Soldier and the Lady,** and Leslie Howard's irrepressible valet in **It's Love I'm After.**

One writer has commented, "His hotel managers, dancing-school managers, waiters, valets and butlers were men who don't have lofty positions, but rule their domains. They are energetic, erudite, fussy, interfering, argumentative, critical, and have an air of superiority."

Blore usually stole the scenes from the stars he appeared with, for he could give as good as he got in the wisecrack department, and he zestfully wrapped his tongue around his every utterance. This resulted in a spate of comic-butler roles in the late Thirties, but few of the films were memorable. Then, in 1941, he was sized up by director Preston Sturges as the ideal actor to play the fake English baronet, "Sir Alfred McGlennan Keith," in **The Lady Eve.** The beady-eyed Blore was a card shark preying on the suburban Connecticut contract-bridge circuit. When informed that Henry Fonda is the scion of an ale-brewing family, he remarks, "I positively *swill* in his ale."

Also that year, besides Joel McCrea's valet in Sturges' **Sullivan's Travels,** he played a shrill, limping bookkeeper in the gambling casino in director Josef von Sternberg's peculiar, heavy-breathing drama **The Shanghai Gesture.** Clearly, when cast by a top director he could give a performance that made people talk.

Every Hollywood detective needed a comic sidekick, and Warren William, star of the Lone Wolf series, was no exception. In five films during 1940-41 Blore played the Lone Wolf's valet Jamison, usually getting involved in the plot. (In 1946 and 1947 he would appear in three more Lone Wolf entries, with Gerald Mohr in the title role.) But alas, being a detective's sidekick in "B" movies was hardly up to the Astaire-Rogers level.

One of his best films was one in which he was never seen. Walt Disney's animated feature **The Adventures of Ichabod and Mr. Toad** (49) featured Blore's unctuous voice as Mr. Toad in this version of "The Wind in the Willows." It is hard to think of an actor whose voice would have been better for the part.

He wound down his career with one film each in 1950, 1952 and 1954. Oddly, the last two both bore the name "Bagdad" in their titles—**Babes in Bagdad** and **Bowery to Bagdad.** The latter, his swan song, was a sorry end to a fine comic career, for it was a Bowery Boys outing. He was fatuous and asinine as a hammy genie.

Eric Blore died in 1959 at 71, still unchallenged as Hollywood's greatest comic butler. But if the truth be known, he would have made a sensational Uriah Heep.

THE FILMS OF ERIC BLORE

1926: The Great Gatsby.
1930: *Credit uncertain:* Laughter.
1931: *Credit uncertain:* My Sin; Tarnished Lady.
1933: Flying Down to Rio.
1934: The Gay Divorcee; Limehouse Blues; Behold My Wife.
1935: Top Hat; Folies Bergere; To Beat the Band; The Good Fairy; Diamond Jim; Old Man Rhythm; The Casino Murder Case; I Live My Life; I Dream Too Much; Seven Keys to Baldpate. *Credit uncertain*: Enchanted April.
1936: Swing Time; Two in the Dark; The Ex-Mrs. Bradford; The Smartest Girl in Town; Sons o' Guns; Piccadilly Jim.
1937: Shall We Dance; Quality Street; The Soldier and the Lady; Breakfast for Two; Hitting a New High; It's Love I'm After.
1938: Joy of Living; Swiss Miss; A Desperate Adventure.
1939: Island of Lost Men; $1,000 a Touchdown.
1940: Music in My Heart; The Man Who Wouldn't Talk; Till We Meet Again; South of Suez; The Boys from Syracuse; The Earl of Puddlestone; The Lone Wolf Strikes; The Lone Wolf Meets a Lady; The Lone Wolf Keeps a Date.

1941: The Lady Eve; Sullivan's Travels; The Shanghai Gesture; Road to Zanzibar; Red Head; Lady Scarface; New York Town; Three Girls About Town; The Lone Wolf Takes a Chance; Secrets of the Lone Wolf.
1942: The Moon and Sixpence; Confirm or Deny; Counter Espionage.
1943: Happy Go Lucky; The Sky's the Limit; Forever and a Day; Holy Matrimony; Submarine Base; Passport to Suez; One Dangerous Night.
1944: San Diego, I Love You.
1945: Kitty; Penthouse Rhythm; Men in Her Diary; Easy to Look at.
1946: Two Sisters from Boston; Abie's Irish Rose; The Notorious Lone Wolf.
1947: Winter Wonderland; The Lone Wolf in London; The Lone Wolf in Mexico.
1948: Romance on the High Seas.
1949: Love Happy; The Adventures of Ichabod and Mr. Toad (voice only).
1950: Fancy Pants.
1952: Babes in Bagdad.
1954: Bowery to Bagdad.

The glory of triumphant daffiness:
MARY BOLAND

Mary Boland and Charlie Ruggles: They went together like ham and eggs.

Mary and Charlie made more films together (12) than did William Powell and Myrna Loy (11), Fred Astaire and Ginger Rogers (10), or any other co-starring pair. And this despite the fact that they were not really stars but character actors.

The Ruggles-Boland outings were, of course, strictly second-feature fare for moviegoers of the Thirties. In them, typically, Mary and Charlie portrayed a middle-class, middle-aged couple, frequently with a marriageable daughter. Mary was the genteel but dominant wife, Charlie the agitated, timid husband. Their teamwork was polished and professional, and audiences loved them in these domestic comedies.

Beyond that, Miss Boland for a decade, in her fifties, played madcap wives and scatterbrained mothers in many another Thirties film, usually in supporting roles. Few in the audience, watching the wonderful daffiness on screen, had any idea that many years earlier she had been a great tragedienne and one of the most beautiful young actresses on the Broadway stage.

Mary Boland was born January 28, 1880 (some sources say 1882), in Philadelphia and was educated in a Detroit convent. Following the example of her actor father, she began acting in stock while in her teens. In 1905 she made her Broadway debut as the female lead in **Strongheart,** and for several seasons (1908-13) was the leading lady of John Drew, the uncle of the three Barrymores. She was a success in tragic dramas, and during the period 1915-18 starred in seven movies in tragic roles while continuing her stage work. (In one of these, **The Prodigal Wife,** she was a surgeon's wife who leaves him because he is too poor.) She would not be seen on the screen again until the sound era.

It was in 1919, at age 39, that she first displayed her talent as a stately scatterbrain, playing opposite Alfred Lunt (Helen Hayes also co-starred) in Booth Tarkington's play **Clarence.** She was liked so well in this role that she became typecast in it, and from that point on she was no longer a tragedienne but a leading Broadway comedienne. Her biggest stage hits in the Twenties included **The Torch Bearers** (22), **Meet the Wife,** with Clifton Webb (23), and **Cradle Snatchers** (25), the latter's cast including Edna May

Oliver and a young Humphrey Bogart. In 1930 she and Billie Burke were in **The Vinegar Tree.**

In 1931 the actress, now in her fifties, returned to films for a Hollywood career that would last two decades, inevitably playing a daffy wife or mother. **The Night of June 13th** (32) was the first of her dozen films with Charlie Ruggles. These would include such hilarious programmers as **Mama Loves Papa, Six of a Kind, Melody in Spring, People Will Talk, Early to Bed, Wives Never Know** and **Night Work.**

Three-Cornered Moon (33) launched the seemingly interminable cycle of Thirties films about peculiar screwball families. Miss Boland played a scatterbrained widow who bought worthless mining stock, wiping out the Rimplegar family fortune and leaving them with only their large and unsalable Brooklyn house. In **Down to Their Last Yacht** (34) she was the daffy queen of a South Seas island where the yacht of now-impoverished socialites, chartered by a newly rich family, is beached. Meanwhile, she continued to work on the Broadway stage; in 1935 she got rave reviews as the star of **Jubilee.**

She was a hit—along with the entire cast—in the film **Ruggles of Red Gap** (35), as the social climber who, with husband Ruggles, comes back from Europe to her Western tank town, bringing with her an impeccable butler, Charles Laughton. In **Two for Tonight** she was Bing Crosby's mother. In the following year she essayed a tragic role in the maudlin mother-love drama **A Son Comes Home,** as a restaurant owner who continually sacrifices for son Donald Woods, who ultimately becomes a murderer. But audiences did not respond favorably, and so it was back to screwball comedies for Miss Boland. The outings with Ruggles continued for the next several years.

In 1939 she stole scene after scene from the big-name stars (Joan Crawford, Norma Shearer, Rosalind Russell) in **The Women,** as the ribald, oft-married dowager countess staying at a Reno divorce ranch, ordering incessant "wee drinkies" and engaged in an unceasing quest for "l'amour," as she put it. She has been swept off her feet once too often, but takes her marriage failures philosophically: "Oh, l'amour, l'amour, how it can let you down!"

She was ideally cast as Greer Garson's overpowering mother, Mrs. Bennet, the silly, determined mother hen to a brood of female chicks, in **Pride and Prejudice** (40), giving one of her best performances as she turned 60. After a four-year hiatus, during which she starred on Broadway as Mrs. Malaprop in Sheridan's **The Rivals,** she returned to appear in minor roles in four 1944 films, and then there was another four-year gap before she made **Julia Misbehaves** in 1948.

The actress appeared in her final movie, **Guilty Bystander,** in 1950, at the age of 70. The role she played in this *film noir* was totally unlike anything she had done before, for she was in fact the principal villain, albeit a relatively sympathetic one. She played a hotel proprietor with underworld connections, double-crossing the smugglers so that she might live out her old age in comfort. Miss Boland, who had put on considerable weight, brought pathos to the role and certainly was of considerably more interest than the star, Zachary Scott.

She continued to appear on the Broadway stage. In her last play, **Lullaby** (54), she was an awesome, possessive mother. Critic Walter Kerr was moved to comment, "She has not lost an ounce of that brazen, badgering and triumphant witlessness which was always her fiercest glory."

Mary Boland spent her last years living quietly in her suite at New York's Essex House, sometimes journeying to Hollywood to visit old friends. She lived alone, for she had never married. In 1965 she died at the age of 85, having spent half a century as an actress, one of the few ever to achieve notable success both in tragic and in comic roles.

THE FILMS OF MARY BOLAND

1915: The Edge of the Abyss.
1916: The Stepping Stone; The Price of Happiness; Big Jim Garrity.
1918: His Temporary Wife; The Prodigal Wife; A Woman's Experience.
1931: Personal Maid; Secrets of a Secretary.
1932: If I Had a Million; The Night of June 13th; Evenings for Sale.
1933: Mama Loves Papa; Three-Cornered Moon; The Solitaire Man.
1934: Four Frightened People; Six of a Kind; Melody in Spring; Stingaree; Here Comes the Groom; Down to Their Last Yacht; The Pursuit of Happiness.
1935: Ruggles of Red Gap; People Will Talk; Two for Tonight; The Big Broadcast of 1936.
1936: Early to Bed; A Son Comes Home; College Holiday.
1937: Marry the Girl; There Goes the Groom; Danger—Love at Work; Mama Runs Wild.
1938: Wives Never Know; Artists and Models Abroad; Little Tough Guys in Society.
1939: The Women; The Magnificent Fraud; Boy Trouble; Night Work.
1940: Pride and Prejudice; He Married His Wife; New Moon; One Night in the Tropics; Hit Parade of 1941.
1944: In Our Time; Forever Yours; Nothing But Trouble; They Shall Have Faith.
1948: Julia Misbehaves.
1950: Guilty Bystander.

You don't have to be old to be an old lady:
BEULAH BONDI

You could call Beulah Bondi the female equivalent of Walter Brennan. At age 27, as a member of a stock company, she played an old lady in a stage production. By her early forties she was portraying elderly women on the screen. And she continued to do so until finally she herself was an old lady, with half a century of experience in the role.

Like Brennan's characters, her old ladies tended basically to be rural types, sometimes even backwoods types. They could be either kindly or cantankerous, but whatever they were, audiences and critics alike fell in love with her. She received two Academy Award nominations (as best supporting actress) and deserved far more. And the dedication of film historian John Springer's book about screen actresses of the Thirties, "They Had Faces Then," reads simply, "To our beloved Beulah Bondi."

She played mothers, grandmothers, widowers, dowagers, harridans, aristocrats and religious psalm-singers. A superlative actress, with distinctively sharp features and a penetrating manner, she actually gave a wide variety of mature characterizations. But you remember her best as James Stewart's loving mother.

Miss Bondi was born (as Beulah Bondy) May 3, 1892, in Chicago (some sources give an 1888 birthdate), and grew up in Valparaiso, Indiana. She first appeared on stage at age seven in a small-town production of **Little Lord Fauntleroy,** and continued to do some acting while getting her education. After receiving a degree at a Catholic college in Montreal and taking a master's degree in oratory at hometown Valparaiso University, she directed school and club dramatics at the latter school, but decided to make a professional stage career.

She made her debut in 1919, at age 27, in the Stuart Walker stock company in Indianapolis, her first role being, of course, that of an elderly lady. (Walker later became a Hollywood film director for a short time in the early Thirties.) From the beginning she played only character roles, and did it so well that she drew the attention of New York producers.

In 1925, at 33, she made her Broadway debut as Maggie, the 70-year-old servant, in **One of the Family.** She had good roles in such plays as **Saturday's Children, Cock Robin** and **Distant Drums.** Then she got a superb part—the nosy gossip Emma Jones, adder-tongued archetype of all tenement slatterns, in Elmer Rice's hit play **Street Scene.** Critics were lav-

ish in their praise, and when Hollywood decided to film the play in 1931, there was no question but that Beulah Bondi would make her screen debut in the role.

In that same year she played Helen Hayes' mother—actually a very small part—in director John Ford's **Arrowsmith,** and in 1932 was good as the pince-nez-wearing, self-righteous wife of tyrannical clergyman Walter Huston in the Joan Crawford starrer **Rain.** In **The Stranger's Return** (33) she played Lionel Barrymore's embittered, acid-tongued spinster stepdaughter, and in **Christopher Bean (The Late Christopher Bean)** she was the same actor's tactless, avaricious wife. The following year the actress portrayed the ultra-snobbish headmistress in **Finishing School.**

She was cast as Greta Garbo's mother (and Jean Hersholt's wife) in the 1934 drama **The Painted Veil,** but some of the earlier portions of the film were reshot to tighten up the action, and for some reason

Miss Bondi was replaced in the retakes by Bodil Rosing. Some reviews listed Miss Bondi in the cast, and some film reference books still include the film with her credits (and even show her in stills from it); nonetheless, the mother on screen is clearly Miss Rosing, and the New York Times review credited that actress.

Miss Bondi's first Oscar nomination as best supporting actress came in the first year of that award, 1936, for her role as the pathetic, pipe-smoking Rachel Jackson, wife of Andrew Jackson (Lionel Barrymore) in **The Gorgeous Hussy;** many felt she walked off with the acting honors in a film that starred Joan Crawford and Robert Taylor. She also gave a beautiful portrayal of Melissa Tolliver, the backwoods mother crying out against the bloodshed of mountain feuds, in **The Trail of the Lonesome Pine,** the first outdoor film in full Technicolor. She was Madeleine Carroll's unfeeling mother-in-law in **The Case Against Mrs. Ames,** and played Margaret Sullavan's companion in **The Moon's Our Home.**

In **Maid of Salem** (37), a historical drama, she was a half-crazed crone trying to regain her youth. And in that same year came her most magnificent portrayal, one for which she should rightfully have been Oscar-nominated as best actress—Lucy Cooper in director Leo McCarey's superb drama about the problems of aged parents, **Make Way for Tomorrow.**

Miss Bondi and Victor Moore (normally a comedian) played an elderly couple who lose the family home and hope that their four children will help them buy a smaller one. But the children (one was played by Thomas Mitchell, married to Fay Bainter) find that this will be impossible, and the old couple—while pretending to each other that this is not the case—realize that they will spend their final years *apart,* with Lucy going to an "old ladies' home." This poignant drama—praised by the New York Times for its "humanity, honesty and warmth"—is one of the great all-time Hollywood tearjerkers.

Fondly remembered by movie buffs is the devastating scene in which Miss Bondi receives a long-distance phone call from Moore, talking to him while the guests at a bridge party listen, pouring out her love and loneliness. If you ever get a chance to see the movie, bring along several handkerchiefs for *that* scene.

Another of her great achievements was the unsentimental but deeply felt portrayal of a sacrificing rural mother during the Civil War era in **Of Human Hearts** (38), for which she again won an Oscar nomination. Once again she was the wife of Walter Huston (who was once again a clergyman), and James Stew-

art played their son—the first of four times she would play his mother on screen. In that same year she was Stewart's mother again (and Charles Coburn's wife) in **Vivacious Lady,** and played Bette Davis' mother in **The Sisters.**

Miss Bondi was the beautiful old lady who willingly goes with Death (Sir Cedric Hardwicke) in **On Borrowed Time** (39), and in that year also played Stewart's mother for the third time in **Mr. Smith Goes to Washington,** director Frank Capra's fine populist drama. She was good as Martha Scott's mother in **Our Town** (40), and outstanding as Fred MacMurray's mother in **Remember the Night,** being nice to the guest her prosecuting-attorney son has brought home for the Christmas holidays—a jewel thief played by Barbara Stanwyck. She was also considered for the part of Ma Joad in **The Grapes of Wrath,** but Jane Darwell got the nod.

The actress was a villainous backwoods woman practicing witchcraft in **The Shepherd of the Hills** (41), played the orphanage matron in **Penny Serenade** (starring Cary Grant and Irene Dunne), and had a small role as a servant in **Watch on the Rhine** (43), also portraying Lee J. Cobb's peasant wife and Annabella's mother in **Tonight We Raid Calais.** Her next memorable role came in 1945, as the senile grandmother of Zachary Scott in director Jean Renoir's **The Southerner,** a superb and now half-forgotten rural drama. In 1946 she played James Stewart's mother for the fourth and last time on screen in Frank Capra's classic tearjerker **It's a Wonderful Life.**

In **The Snake Pit** (48) she was a standout as a crazed elderly inmate of the mental hospital, and in 1950 sharply slowed down her film-making pace, usually appearing in only one a year henceforward. In 1954 she dominated the movie as the harsh, bitter matriarch in **Track of the Cat.**

Miss Bondi was now in her sixties, and had finally reached the point where she was actually as old as the old ladies she had been playing for so many years. But the parts she got in her remaining films were nothing special. She closed out her film career in 1963 with **Tammy and the Doctor.**

The actress, who had never married, thereupon retired for eight years, took two world tours, and then turned to the stage and television in the early 1970s, with a handful of impressive guest roles marking her appearances on the tube. And an incredible 33 years after she had first done so, she portrayed James Stewart's mother once again in his 1971 TV series; she was now 79 and he was 63. In 1977, at the remarkable age of 85, she won a TV Emmy award for her performances in the series "The

Waltons"—very likely the oldest performer to win such an award.

In 1981 Beulah Bondi died at the age of 89. Turn on your TV set late at night, and you can still see her—that wonderful actress playing those wonderful old ladies.

THE FILMS OF BEULAH BONDI

1931: Street Scene; Arrowsmith.

1932: Rain.

1933: The Stranger's Return; Christopher Bean (The Late Christopher Bean).

1934: Finishing School; Two Alone; Registered Nurse; Ready for Love.

1935: The Good Fairy; Bad Boy.

1936: The Trail of the Lonesome Pine; The Gorgeous Hussy; The Moon's Our Home; The Case Against Mrs. Ames; The Invisible Ray; Hearts Divided.

1937: Make Way for Tomorrow; Maid of Salem.

1938: Of Human Hearts; Vivacious Lady; The Sisters; The Buccaneer.

1939: On Borrowed Time; Mr. Smith Goes to Washington; The Underpup.

1940: Our Town; Remember the Night; The Captain Is a Lady.

1941: The Shepherd of the Hills; One Foot in Heaven; Penny Serenade.

1943: Watch on the Rhine; Tonight We Raid Calais.

1944: And Now Tomorrow; I Love a Soldier; Our Hearts Were Young and Gay; The Very Thought of You; She's a Soldier Too.

1945: The Southerner; Back to Bataan.

1946: It's a Wonderful Life; Sister Kenny; Breakfast in Hollywood.

1947: High Conquest.

1948: The Snake Pit; So Dear to My Heart; The Sainted Sisters.

1949: Reign of Terror; Mr. Soft Touch; The Life of Riley.

1950: The Furies; The Baron of Arizona.

1952: Lone Star.

1953: Latin Lovers.

1954: Track of the Cat.

1956: Back from Eternity.

1957: The Unholy Wife.

1959: The Big Fisherman; A Summer Place.

1961: Tammy Tell Me True.

1962: The Wonderful World of the Brothers Grimm.

1963: Tammy and the Doctor.

NOTE: Miss Bondi was originally cast in the 1934 film **The Painted Veil,** but her scenes were re-shot with another actress. See the text for details.

From scatterbrains to Mother Courage:

ALICE BRADY

The screen career of Alice Brady was split into two distinct halves.

In the first half, 1914-23, she was a young leading lady starring in romantic dramas filmed in New York City studios. There followed a 10-year hiatus during which she appeared exclusively on the stage and ultimately won plaudits in one of the great dramatic roles of the American theater. And the second half of her movie career, 1933-39, saw her undergo a sea-change to play fluttery society matrons, culminating—in yet another change—with two final great dramatic performances and an Academy Award before her untimely death.

Miss Brady was born November 2, 1892, in New York City, the daughter of prominent stage producer (and later film producer) William A. Brady; her mother was dancer Rose Marie René. She studied voice and began her career as a singer and actress in operettas, beginning with **The Balkan Princess** (11) and also including Gilbert and Sullivan. Bored with the limitations of singing roles, she turned to drama on the stage (starring in **Little Women** in 1912) and also began to play romantic roles in films. Her Broadway debut was in **Sinners** (15); meanwhile, she had made her first movie, **As Ye Sow** (14).

Through World War I and the immediate postwar era, she alternated with great success between the stage and the screen; some of her movies were adaptations of her stage hits. (One of these was **The Maid of Belgium** [17], in which she was a young Belgian wife who loses her memory from the shock of seeing wartime atrocities.) All told, she appeared in 52 films in 10 years. One source says she was the highest-paid actress in movies until Mary Pickford hit her stride.

In 1919 the actress married one of her stage leading men, James Lyon Crane. They had a son, Donald, but Crane soon became an alcoholic; she obtained a divorce and never remarried. However, during the Twenties she reportedly was one of the actresses who had brief affairs with the young Clark Gable, then an unknown bit player.

Miss Brady was a romantic star on the screen but a powerful dramatic star on stage, typically playing, during the Twenties, "lush ladies—women good enough but also faintly bad," as one critic put it, in plays that usually had short runs. Late in the decade she turned to the heavy-breathing dramas of Eugene

O'Neill, and was scheduled to star in **Strange Interlude,** but a few weeks before opening night she collapsed, and was replaced by Lynn Fontanne.

She was determined to star in an O'Neill drama, however, and in 1931 appeared as Lavinia in **Mourning Becomes Electra,** with Alla Nazimova as her mother. This critically acclaimed stage hit established her as a top dramatic actress of emotional power, but for some reason she turned her back on Broadway and accepted an offer to return to the movies, buying a home in Beverly Hills and settling in to the life of the film capital.

Her movie comeback had been timed to perfection. The era of screwball comedy had just been launched, and one part that always needed to be filled was the fluttery, scatterbrained mother or society woman. Some of its great practitioners were Billie Burke and Mary Boland, and Miss Brady quickly became another one, beginning in 1933 as the chattering, tactless hostess in **When Ladies Meet,** which virtually typecast her in such roles. Brittle and brilliant, she nearly stole the film from Ann Harding, Robert Montgomery and Myrna Loy. If the truth be told, she stole scenes so easily that stars dreaded working with her.

In that same year she was also fine in the title role of **Stage Mother,** as a selfish, conscienceless woman who drives her daughter, Maureen O'Sullivan, to break away from her, and was typically scatterbrained as a not-overly bright socialite in **Should Ladies Behave?** She also had a good role as Frank Morgan's wife in **Broadway to Hollywood.** They played an old vaudeville team who visit Hollywood to watch their film-star grandson as he plays a scene before the cameras. While observing the scene Morgan dies, and Miss Brady watches, afraid to cry out for fear of spoiling the take. Her stricken eyes and expression of horror live on in the memory.

In 1934 she had a supporting role as Ginger Rogers' aunt in **The Gay Divorcee,** and was notable in the now-forgotten film **Miss Fane's Baby Is Stolen.** In that movie, a screen star (Dorothea Wieck) finds that her child (Baby LeRoy) has been kidnapped. A friendly, inquisitive neighbor (Miss Brady) happens to go into the isolated shack where the baby is being held. She inadvertently brushes some shoe-polish dye off the child's blond hair, suddenly sees the light, grabs the baby and roars away in her old car with the gang in frantic pursuit.

Miss Brady also developed a reputation as an off-screen Hollywood playgirl, and was an irrepressible presence on the social scene, ultimately leading producers to cast her on the screen in the role she played in real life. In movie stills from 1934 on she is usually seen with cocktail in hand. In private life she was chic but outré, always wore black, and had her Beverly Hills mansion decorated entirely in red and white.

The actress played, in **Metropolitan** (35), a gloriously demented, capricious and temperamental operatic prima donna who walks out on the Met and forms her own company, later walking out on that one too. In **Lady Tubbs** she was a railroad-camp cook who inherits a fortune and schools herself to enter society. She also had a comic supporting role in **Gold Diggers of 1935.**

Her first Academy Award nomination as best supporting actress came in 1936 in **My Man Godfrey,** as the fluttery wife of Eugene Pallette and mother of Carole Lombard and Gail Patrick, driving her family to distraction with her latest protégé, a weirdo played by Mischa Auer. It was the first year of the supporting-actor Oscars. She also was good in **Mind Your Own Business,** perfectly cast as a gossip columnist,

and starred as the scheming mother in **The Harvester.** In the latter film, her poignant portrayal of a hard-worked, ignorant farm woman—along with other roles like it—amazed filmgoers and critics by their contrast to her parts in scatterbrained comedies.

She played the conniving mother of gold-digger Binnie Barnes in 1937's **Three Smart Girls,** Deanna Durbin's screen debut; starred in **Mama Steps Out** in her patented role of dizzy matron; and drew laughs in the Durbin starrer **100 Men and a Girl** (as Eugene Pallette's wife again). All told, she was in six films in 1937, her busiest year on the screen in the sound era.

Relatively few filmgoers—unless they had happened earlier to see her star on Broadway in **Mourning Becomes Electra**—could possibly have been prepared for what happened next. Alice Brady won the best-supporting-actress Oscar for her powerful performance in the dramatic role of Mrs. O'Leary in **In Old Chicago.**

A pet project of 20th Century-Fox studio boss Darryl F. Zanuck and one of the most expensive films of its day, **In Old Chicago,** directed by Henry King, centers around a superb re-creation of the great fire of 1871, supposedly caused by Mrs. O'Leary's cow kicking over a lantern. It also features her two fictional sons (Tyrone Power and Don Ameche, feuding over Alice Faye). But the nominal stars were forgotten as critics fell over themselves to praise Miss Brady's performance as a sort of Mother Courage, projecting patient endurance.

Time magazine said: "She is by all odds the most convincing performer. She reduces the whole caboodle of headline stars to the ranks of supporting players." **In Old Chicago,** nominally a 1938 release, was allowed to screen at a few theaters the previous Christmas to qualify for the 1937 Academy Awards. Miss Brady's Oscar was the only one won by the film.

Shortly after the Academy ceremonies, Alice Brady visited her doctor. He told her she had terminal cancer.

The actress did not indulge in any orgy of self-pity. Instead, she went back to work, first appearing as a snobbish dowager in **Zenobia** (39), and, in that same year, in her final role delivering her greatest screen performance, made while she was virtually on her deathbed.

In director John Ford's outstanding drama **Young Mr. Lincoln,** Henry Fonda starred as the young lawyer and future president. Miss Brady was an anguished frontier mother whose two sons Lincoln saves from a murder charge in a trial. This performance was in fact even more moving than her Oscar role, but she wasn't even nominated for it. (However, 1939, the year of **Gone With the Wind,** was an outstanding year for performances by supporting actresses, while 1937 had been a relatively weak one.)

In that year, 1939, cancer claimed the life of Alice Brady. She was 46 years old.

THE FILMS OF ALICE BRADY

1914: As Ye Sow.

1915: The Boss; The Cup of Chance; The Lure of Woman.

1916: The Rack; The Ballet Girl; The Woman in 47; Then I'll Come Back to You; Tangled Fates; La Vie de Boheme; Miss Petticoats; The Gilded Cage; Bought and Paid For.

1917: A Woman Alone; A Hungry Heart; The Dancer's Peril; Darkest Russia; The Divorce Game; Maternity; A Self-Made Widow; Betsy Ross; A Maid of Belgium.

1918: Her Silent Sacrifice; Woman and Wife; The Knife; The Spurs of Sybil; At the Mercy of Men; The Trap; The Whirlpool; The Death Dance; The Ordeal of Rosetta; The Better Half; In the Hollow of Her Hand; Her Great Chance.

1919: The Indestructible Wife; The World to Live In; Marie, Ltd.; The Redhead; His Bridal Night.

1920: The Bear Market; Sinners; A Dark Lantern; The New York Idea.

1921: Out of the Chorus; The Land of Hope; Little Italy; Dawn of the East; Hush Money.

1922: Anna Ascends; Missing Millions.

1923: The Leopardess; The Snow Bride.

1933: When Ladies Meet; Broadway to Hollywood; Beauty for Sale; Stage Mother; Should Ladies Behave?

1934: The Gay Divorcee; Miss Fane's Baby Is Stolen.

1935: Gold Diggers of 1935; Let 'em Have It; Lady Tubbs; Metropolitan.

1936: My Man Godfrey; Go West, Young Man; Mind Your Own Business; The Harvester.

1937: Three Smart Girls; Call It a Day; Mama Steps Out; Mr. Dodd Takes the Air; One Hundred Men and a Girl; Merry-Go-Round of 1938.

1938: In Old Chicago; Joy of Living; Goodbye Broadway.

1939: Young Mr. Lincoln; Zenobia.

NOTE: The film **In Old Chicago** was basically a 1938 release. However, it was screened at a few theaters during Christmas week of 1937 in order to qualify for the 1937 Academy Awards.

Amazing what you can do with false teeth:
WALTER BRENNAN

"What's your acting technique?" someone once asked Walter Brennan.

"Hell, sonny, my only acting technique's whether or not I use my false teeth!"

Whatever the technique, Brennan is the all-time Oscar-winning champion among character actors and actresses: three victories in four tries for the best-supporting-actor statuette. (No one had ever won more than three in *any* acting category until Katharine Hepburn finally topped Brennan with her fourth Academy Award in 1981; but he won his three in the first five years the supporting awards were handed out, never being beaten until his fourth try.)

Brennan in his thirties was playing toothless old men, and his distinctive voice sounded as though it were emerging from a wad of chewing tobacco. He was usually seen on screen in battered old clothes that matched his face. With all this, it was only logical that he would play backwoodsmen, countrified wits, cracker-barrel philosophers and seedy old swamp denizens. But in his 44-year film career he was also to be found as a villain, a comedian, a college professor, sometimes even a city slicker.

Actually, false teeth were not his only acting technique. He was pensive, he cackled, he limped, he employed dialects. But gimmickry was not his sole stock in trade; he was an exceptionally versatile actor, and he was still a popular character star 30 years after he had won his last Oscar.

Brennan was born July 25, 1894, in Swampscott, Massachusetts, an upper-middle-class suburb of Boston. He is said to have left home at age 11. Originally trained as an engineer, he chose acting as a career and appeared in vaudeville and stock, supporting himself also as a lumberjack and bank clerk, then served in the field artillery in World War I. In 1920 he married his childhood sweetheart, Ruth Wells, and they had three children, Arthur, Walter Jr. and Ruth.

The actor next was a ditchdigger, a bank messenger, tried raising pineapples in Guatemala, and was a real-estate salesman and speculator in Los Angeles before turning finally to the stage. Sometime around 1923 he arrived in Hollywood, where he began work as an extra and stunt man in films, the first one being **Lorraine of the Lions** (25). (This extra and stunt work is not indicated in the filmography that follows this chapter; the filmography shows only those roles where his name appears in the credits or where pub-

lished sources identify his appearance on screen.) During this period he became the good friend of another actor who was at that time also working as an extra; that friend, Gary Cooper, later made seven movies with Brennan.

That this obscure bit player might some day become the screen's Academy Award champion would have mystified filmmakers in the late silent era. But Brennan was on his way. Meanwhile, what seemed like some bad luck would later turn out to be fortuitous—while working as a stunt man the actor's teeth were knocked out in falls from horses.

His first screen credit came in **The Ridin' Rowdy** (27), one of half a dozen Westerns he appeared in from 1927 to 1929; he was a ranch foreman in **Smilin' Guns** (29). He then moved into mainstream films, and appeared as an inmate of an insane asylum in **One Hysterical Night.** He was prominently featured as the star of a comedy skit in the musical revue **The King of Jazz** (30).

Brennan's films of the early sound era showed little indication of what was to come. From 1932 to 1935 he definitely appeared in 49 movies and possibly in 18 more—a busy schedule. But in most of them he was so far down the cast list that he didn't appear in the credits. His big break, however, was drawing nearer.

Even during the busy year of 1934, in which he appeared in at least 19 films and possibly four more, he was usually found in such roles as "waiter," "bus driver" or "hot-dog vendor." He did have a good part in **The Life of Vergie Winters** as a gossipy barfly who helps ruin Ann Harding's reputation.

In 1935, in a major film such as **Bride of Frankenstein**, he was still so little known that he was billed 27th in the cast, virtually at the bottom, playing a "neighbor." And you hardly noticed him as one of the burglars breaking into W.C. Fields' basement in **The Man on the Flying Trapeze.** But in that same year Walter Brennan got the break he had been waiting for.

Getting his first big chance in director Howard Hawks' **Barbary Coast,** starring Miriam Hopkins, Edward G. Robinson and Joel McCrea, he virtually walked off with the film as he portrayed a treacherous, toothless barfly called Old Atrocity. Nothing quite like him had been seen on the screen before, and audiences and critics loved him in the role. At the same time, this portrayal typecast the actor for many a performance to come.

He won his first Oscar in 1936 for **Come and Get It,** as Swan Bostrom, the lumberjack who marries Frances Farmer. Actually, his performance—featuring a heavy Swedish accent—wasn't even as good as that of the star, Edward Arnold, and—in this first year that supporting-actor Oscars were handed out—he should by rights have lost the award to Akim Tamiroff (**The General Died at Dawn**). But his rural rustic had become a popular type at that moment in time.

That year he also played a loose-mouthed rural deputy sheriff in Fury, and was one of the three outlaws in **Three Godfathers,** along with Lewis Stone and Chester Morris. He played other rustic types in **Banjo on My Knee, These Three,** and **The Moon's Our Home** (as the justice of the peace who marries Margaret Sullavan and Henry Fonda).

After a spate of weak films in 1937, Brennan won his second Oscar in 1938 for an extremely routine—and very hammy—"old Kentucky colonel" part in **Kentucky.** This time *all* of the four other contenders for the supporting Oscar gave stronger performances than his. (For the record, they were John Garfield in **Four Daughters,** Gene Lockhart in **Algiers,** Robert

Morley in **Marie Antoinette** and Basil Rathbone in **If I Were King.**)

That year he also played the village drunkard Muff Potter in **The Adventures of Tom Sawyer** and backwoodsman Ezra Peavey in **The Buccaneer.** In 1939 he was Spencer Tracy's sidekick in **Stanley and Livingstone** and the devoted family retainer to Fred Astaire and Ginger Rogers in **The Story of Vernon and Irene Castle.**

In 1940 he had an excellent role as one of Tracy's rangers in **Northwest Passage,** and also won his third Oscar, playing Judge Roy Bean in director William Wyler's fine film **The Westerner.** Bean was a real-life historical figure who idolized the actress Lily Langtry and named the Texas town he lived in Langtry (which it remains to this day). Virtually every film critic, in rave reviews, insisted that Brennan had stolen the picture from its star, Gary Cooper. Life magazine said he was "a paradoxical renegade, big-hearted and cruel, weak and indomitable." And he had a good death scene (a boon to any actor) after being shot by Cooper.

This time Brennan deserved the Oscar, and it was just as well that his competition that year was weak. And now the actor was pretty well fixed for life; as a character player, he could write his own ticket. He was still only 46 years old.

He received his final Oscar nomination (and this time lost, to Donald Crisp for **How Green Was My Valley**) for his rural clergyman in **Sergeant York** (with Cooper), and also played Cooper's pal in **Meet John Doe.** But his best role that year was for the momentarily expatriate French director Jean Renoir in **Swamp Water;** he was fine as the innocent man hiding out in Georgia's huge Okefenokee swamp, on the run for a crime he didn't commit. He also played a lovelorn postman in **Nice Girl?** and a sea captain in **This Woman Is Mine.**

In **Hangmen Also Die** (43) he showed his versatility by playing a Czech professor, and he was a Russian in **The North Star,** also portraying a foolish millionaire who thinks Lana Turner is his long-lost daughter in **Slightly Dangerous.** In 1944 he clearly enjoyed his banter with Humphrey Bogart, playing Bogie's pathetic alcoholic sidekick Eddie in **To Have and Have Not.**

Villainy was not a hallmark of the Brennan *oeuvre,* but he was excellent as the murderous Old Man Clanton in director John Ford's **My Darling Clementine** (46), a scabby old desert rattlesnake who murders Wyatt Earp's (Henry Fonda's) brother; at the end, Fonda, Victor Mature and their aides shoot down the Clantons in the famous gunfight at the O.K. Corral.

In that year he also had a good role in **Nobody Lives Forever** as a mentor and father-figure to John Garfield. Brennan and George Coulouris are aging con men with opposing attitudes toward life: Brennan is mellow and relaxed, Coulouris a vicious and desperate swindler who in the climactic scene kills Brennan.

And in yet another good 1946 role, he was the lighthouse keeper in the Bette Davis starrer **A Stolen Life.** Miss Davis later commented: "Walter Brennan...had a phenomenally successful career due to his great talent. How lucky any of us were to have him in our films...What a joy he was to play scenes with. What a joy to have known Walter Brennan as a person."

In 1948 he was a rustic cowpoke in the superb Western **Red River,** but then played mostly forgettable (and stereotyped) parts for a while to come. In 1952 he replayed his old **Swamp Water** part in a remake, **Lure of the Wilderness.** And audiences loved him in the 1954 Spencer Tracy starrer **Bad Day at Black Rock,** cryptic and caustic as the spunky local mortician in the desert town with a guilty secret. In that year he turned 60.

He played James Stewart's cattle-driving partner, shot by a claim-jumper, in the fine Western **The Far Country** (55), and an old man sharing his love of a dog with a young boy (Brandon DeWilde) in **Goodbye, My Lady** (56). In **God Is My Partner** (57) he starred as a respected surgeon who, upon re-

tiring, begins to give away much of his money to religious causes; after his family sues him, declaring him incapable, he is victorious in a trial.

Brennan now began to act on television while continuing his film work. He was hugely successful as the star of the series 'The Real McCoys" (1957-63), but less so in "Tycoon" and "The Guns of Will Sonnett." Meanwhile, he had become a wealthy man, and owned two large Oregon ranches. In 1959 the actor brought back fond memories as he played the drunken deputy sheriff in **Rio Bravo,** using his fabled false teeth to good advantage. He was now, at 65, down to appearing in about one film a year, sometimes none at all (as in 1958, 1960, 1961 and 1965). He played the murderous old river pirate killed by James Stewart in **How The West Was Won** (63). In 1966 he had a small part in the appropriately named **The Oscar,** and in the following year starred in Walt Disney's **The Gnome-Mobile,** as a crusty old businessman trying to protect the gnomes he has found in a redwood forest.

In his seventies, he was finally *starring* in at least a few films. **The One and Only Genuine Original Family Band** (68) saw him as the founder of the band. But Walter Brennan's screen work, and his life, were drawing to a close. After three more films, the last one in 1971, he died in 1974 at age 80, still the undisputed all-time champion Academy Award winner among Hollywood's character actors.

THE FILMS OF WALTER BRENNAN

NOTE: Films in which he appeared during the period 1925-27 as an uncredited extra or stunt man are not indicated here.

1927: The Ridin' Rowdy.
1928: Tearin' into Trouble; The Ballyhoo Buster; Silks and Saddles.
1929: Smilin' Guns; The Lariat Kid; The Long, Long Trail; One Hysterical Night; The Shannons of Broadway.
1930: The King of Jazz.
1931: Dancing Dynamite; Neck and Neck; Is There Justice?
1932: Law and Order; Texas Cyclone; Two-Fisted Law; The All-American; The Airmail Mystery (serial); Hello Trouble; Honeymoon Lane; Speed Madness. *Credit uncertain:* Miss Pinkerton; The Fourth Horseman.
1933: Man of Action; Fighting for Justice; Sing, Sinner, Sing; One Year Later; My Woman; The Phantom of the Air (serial); Sensation Hunters; Silent Men. *Credit uncertain:* The Invisible Man; The Keyhole; Lilly Turner; Baby Face; The Kiss Before the Mirror; Saturday's Millions; Female; From Headquarters; Parachute Jumper; Strange People.
1934: Half a Sinner; Riptide; Beloved; Cheating Cheaters; Fugitive Lovers; Helldorado; Good Dame; The Life of Vergie Winters; Whom the Gods Destroy; Death on the Diamond; Rustlers' Roundup; I'll Tell the World; Murder in the Clouds; Murder in the Private Car; The Prescott Kid; There's Always Tomorrow; Uncertain Lady; A Wicked Woman; You Can't Buy Everything. *Credit uncertain:* The Painted Veil; Housewife; Desirable; Stamboul Quest.

1935: Barbary Coast; Bride of Frankenstein; The Man on the Flying Trapeze; Seven Keys to Baldpate; Metropolitan; Lady Tubbs; The Wedding Night; Party Wire; Spring Tonic; Welcome Home; Northern Frontier; Law Beyond the Range; The Mystery of Edwin Drood; Public Hero No. 1. *Credit uncertain:* Alice Adams; We're in the Money.
1936: Come and Get It; Fury; These Three; Banjo on My Knee; Three Godfathers; The Moon's Our Home; Paradise Valley.
1937: When Love Is Young; Wild and Woolly; She's Dangerous; The Affairs of Cappy Ricks.
1938: Kentucky; The Buccaneer; The Texans; The Adventures of Tom Sawyer; The Cowboy and the Lady; Mother Carey's Chickens.
1939: Stanley and Livingstone; The Story of Vernon and Irene Castle; They Shall Have Music; Joe and Ethel Turp Call on the President.
1940: The Westerner; Northwest Passage; Maryland.
1941: Sergeant York; Swamp Water; Meet John Doe; Rise and Shine; Nice Girl?; This Woman Is Mine.
1942: The Pride of the Yankees; Stand By for Action.
1943: Hangmen Also Die; The North Star; Slightly Dangerous.
1944: To Have and Have Not; The Princess and the Pirate; Home in Indiana.
1945: Dakota.
1946: My Darling Clementine; Nobody Lives Forever; A Stolen Life; Centennial Summer.
1947: Driftwood.
1948: Red River; Blood on the Moon; Scudda Hoo! Scudda Hay!

1949: The Green Promise; Brimstone; Task Force.
1950: Curtain Call at Cactus Creek; A Ticket to Tomahawk; Singing Guns; Surrender; The Showdown.
1951: Along the Great Divide; The Wild Blue Yonder; Best of the Bad Men.
1952: Lure of the Wilderness; Return of the Texan.
1953: Sea of Lost Ships.
1954: Bad Day at Black Rock; Drums Across the River; Four Guns to the Border.
1955: The Far Country; At Gunpoint.
1956: The Proud Ones; Glory; Come Next Spring; Goodbye, My Lady.
1957: The Way to the Gold; God Is My Partner; Tammy and the Bachelor.
1959: Rio Bravo.
1962: How the West Was Won.
1963: Shootout at Big Sag.
1964: Those Calloways.
1966: The Oscar.
1967: Who's Minding the Mint?; The Gnome-Mobile.
1968: The One and Only Genuine Original Family Band.
1969: Support Your Local Sheriff.
1970: The Young Country.
1971: Smoke in the Wind.

Doctor Watson, I presume:
NIGEL BRUCE

Perhaps the most typical Englishman, to American eyes at least, is the bumbling upper-class buffoon. In the Anglophile Hollywood of the Thirties, the actor who best exemplified that stereotype was thickset Nigel Bruce, who could always be counted on to mumble, tweak his mustache and shuffle his feet in a convincing show of amiable incompetence.

He made a fairly substantial career out of being a stuffy bumbler—essentially, a Colonel Blimp. He had a narrow range, playing characters who were simply variations of himself, but within those limits no one could play them better. These characters were upper-class gentlemen (usually former military officers) who love to hear themselves talk, especially at dinner parties, who quickly jump to wrong conclusions, and who huff and puff if anyone does anything that defies English social convention.

Within this career, the actor carved out a mini-career of playing Dr. Watson to Basil Rathbone's Sherlock Holmes, in 14 films in eight years. His Watson was the definitive screen Watson—just as Rathbone's Holmes was the definitive Holmes—and it is also just about the only thing for which one remembers Nigel Bruce today.

William Nigel Bruce was born February 4, 1895 (one source says September 4), in Ensenada, Mexico, while his parents were visiting there (his father was an English baronet, a role the actor played many times). He received the usual education of upper-class Britishers, and was a crackerjack cricket player. Serving with the British army in World War I, he was severely wounded in the leg by German machine-gun fire at the battle of Cambrai in 1917. (Interestingly, the military career of the fictional Dr. Watson ended in similar fashion.)

Recovering from his injuries, he became an actor and went on the London stage in 1920. He also married Violet Campbell (some sources give her surname as Shelton), with whom he had two daughters, Jennifer and Pauline. After a decade on the stage, including appearances in such plays as **Bulldog Drummond,** he started to include movies in his acting schedule, beginning with the British film **Red Aces** in 1929.

Seven movies and five years later Bruce joined the mass exodus of trained English stage actors to Hollywood, beginning a 20-year career as a character actor in American films by appearing as a butler

in the auspiciously titled **Coming Out Party** (34). In that year he also was cast as the garrulous Squire Trelawney in the hit picture **Treasure Island,** was good as a detective in **Murder in Trinidad,** and played a stuffy Englishman named Dinwiddie in the Shirley Temple starrer **Stand Up and Cheer.** (Meanwhile he had also starred on Broadway in **Springtime for Henry** in 1931.)

The Scarlet Pimpernel (35) saw him as the Prince Regent, and in **Becky Sharp** he was third in the cast as Joseph Sedley in this version of Thackeray's "Vanity Fair," the first feature-length film in full Technicolor. In **She** he was British scientist Archibald Holly, leading an expedition to search for the secret of eternal life. He played Maurice Vaughn, whose illegitimate daughter Pheasant is the source of the principal conflict, in **Jalna,** and was Ronald Colman's valet in **The Man Who Broke the Bank at Monte Carlo.**

Bruce had now carved out a corner for himself

as a well-meaning bumbler or a cuckolded husband. In real life, however, he was one of the keenest minds and most popular hosts in the film colony, and was active in the Hollywood Cricket Club.

His stereotypical roles were nothing to challenge an actor's skill, but they went on and on. He played Sir Benjamin Warrenton in **The Charge of the Light Brigade** (36), with Spring Byington as his wife, and Captain Menzies in **Under Two Flags.** Similar parts came his way in **The Last of Mrs. Cheyney** (37) and in **Suez** and **Kidnapped** (both 38). In **The Rains Came** (39) he was positively nasty as the cuckolded husband of Myrna Loy (she preferred Tyrone Power).

Fortunately, this situation did not last forever. In 1939, by some genius of casting, the lean, saturnine Basil Rathbone and the rotund, bumbling Bruce were given the roles of Sherlock Holmes and Dr. Watson in **The Hound of the Baskervilles,** a fine version of Sir Arthur Conan Doyle's novel. The teaming was such a success that they repeated it that same year in **The Adventures of Sherlock Holmes,** and the series was off and running.

Bruce's major function as Watson was to provide amusement for Holmes and the audience, to represent the staunch, patriotic Britisher, and to make the audience see how clever Holmes was. Rathbone and Bruce were hardly the first actors to portray the noted duo. In fact, Holmes is the fictional character who has most often been played on the screen (175 films up through 1980, far more than the 133 credited for the runner-up, Count Dracula). But the Rathbone-Bruce combination clicked with film fans, and they demanded more movies; producers were glad to oblige. (Incidentally, the two actors were good friends offscreen.)

Not only did the popularity of the Sherlock Holmes series assure Bruce of steady work through 1946, but it also immediately resulted in better parts in non-Holmes films. He played Major Giles Lacy in director Alfred Hitchcock's **Rebecca** (40), and that year also had roles in such major productions as **The Blue Bird, Lillian Russell** (as lyricist W.S. Gilbert), **Susan and God, A Dispatch from Reuters** and **Hudson's Bay.**

In Hitchcock's **Suspicion** (41) he delivered the only performance that ever caused critics to call him a superior actor. Some said he stole the film from Cary Grant and the Oscar-winning Joan Fontaine. Bruce played Grant's friend Beaky, who Miss Fontaine erroneously believes has been murdered by her husband, Grant, leading her to think that she will become the next victim. The actor built up his part out of very little; still, it was the usual Bruce stereotype.

In **This Above All** (42) he was positively Dickensian as Mr. Ramsbottom, the proprietor of the quaint old inn where Tyrone Power and Joan Fontaine stay. And in that year the Holmes series resumed, to continue at the rate of two or three films a year through 1946.

Ultimately, filmmakers began to see Bruce as a comedian. One result was that his performances as Watson were now declining into caricature, which weakened the films. And in other roles he was becoming positively campy, as with his High Sheriff in the absurd Maria Montez starrer **Gypsy Wildcat** (44). But in the Bette Davis picture **The Corn Is Green** (45) he was good as the Squire.

All too often he was asked to play a comic, stuffy Englishman visiting at the home of the film's star (as in **The Two Mrs. Carrolls** [47], with Humphrey Bogart and Barbara Stanwyck). And roles of that caliber were just about all that remained, now that the Holmes series had come to an end, sunk by progressively weaker scripts and lower budgets.

The remaining films in which Bruce appeared constitute a weird mishmash. **Vendetta** (50) was Howard Hughes' misbegotten attempt to make a star of the no-talent Faith Domergue, and **Hong Kong** (51) was a bunch of nothing starring an over-the-hill Ronald Reagan. There were parts in Charlie Chaplin's **Limelight** (52) and in **Bwana Devil,** the first commercial feature made in the 3-D process.

The last movie he made was a *film noir,* **World for Ransom,** starring Dan Duryea. Bruce played the governor in this 1954 outing, set in Singapore. It was released the year after he died, 1953; he was only 58 years old.

Rereading the Sherlock Holmes stories today, one can instantly see Nigel Bruce as Dr. Watson, tweaking his mustache and mumbling. In fact, on the screen he was always a variation of Watson. And if he made the good doctor something of a buffoon—well, moviegoers liked it that way.

THE FILMS OF NIGEL BRUCE

1929: Red Aces.
1931: The Squeaker; Escape; The Perfect Alibi (Birds of Prey); The Calendar (Bachelor's Folly).
1932: Lord Camber's Ladies; The Midshipmaid.
1933: I Was a Spy.
1934: Treasure Island; Springtime for Henry; Coming Out Party; Channel Crossing; Stand Up and Cheer; Murder in Trinidad; The Lady Is Willing. *Credit uncertain:* The World Moves On.
1935: The Scarlet Pimpernel; Becky Sharp; She; Jalna; The Man Who Broke the Bank at Monte Carlo.
1936: The Charge of the Light Brigade; Under Two Flags; The Trail of the Lonesome Pine; The White Angel; The Man I Marry; Follow Your Heart. *Credit uncertain:* Make Way for a Lady.
1937: The Last of Mrs. Cheyney.
1938: Suez; Kidnapped; The Baroness and the Butler.
1939: The Hound of the Baskervilles; The Adventures of Sherlock Holmes; The Rains Came.
1940: Rebecca; The Blue Bird; Lillian Russell; Hudson's Bay; Susan and God; A Dispatch from Reuters; Adventure in Diamonds.

1941: Suspicion; The Chocolate Soldier; This Woman Is Mine; Free and Easy.
1942: This Above All; Journey for Margaret; Roxie Hart; Eagle Squadron; Sherlock Holmes and the Voice of Terror; Sherlock Holmes and the Secret Weapon.
1943: Forever and a Day; Lassie Come Home; Crazy House; Sherlock Holmes in Washington; Sherlock Holmes Faces Death.
1944: Frenchman's Creek; Gypsy Wildcat; Follow the Boys; Pearl of Death; The Spider Woman; The Scarlet Claw.
1945: The Corn Is Green; Son of Lassie; House of Fear; Pursuit to Algiers; The Woman in Green.
1946: Dragonwyck; Terror by Night; Dressed to Kill.
1947: The Two Mrs. Carrolls; The Exile.
1948: Julia Misbehaves.
1950: Vendetta.
1951: Hong Kong.
1952: Limelight; Bwana Devil.
1954: World for Ransom.

A birdbrain fluttering, a birdlike voice twittering:
BILLIE BURKE

In the 1970s, on the TV show "Laugh-In," a young actress dressed up in a beautiful ballroom gown and with a tiara on her head did an imitation-and a very good one—of a middle-aged lady with a twittering, birdlike voice, ending the impersonation with the words "And Toto, too!" Audiences instantly recognized the character of Glinda the Good Witch from the movie **The Wizard of Oz.** Chances are, however, that most of them could not have named the actress being imitated.

Audiences of the Thirties would have had no such problem. She was instantly identifiable as Billie Burke.

Miss Burke's unique chirping voice helped make her probably the best-known of that ubiquitous species of actress to be found in Thirties films, the fluttery, empty-headed society matron. Eternally, she was a lady whose lack of logic brought the rest of the cast to despair, and the audience to helpless laughter.

In addition to that, she played the mother of many of the female stars of her time, including Bette Davis, Katharine Hepburn and Joan Crawford; was the real-life wife of the great showman Florenz Ziegfeld; and will probably always be unique as the only *character* actress to have part of her own life portrayed on the screen by a *star* (Myrna Loy in **The Great Ziegfeld**). All in all, quite a life and quite a career for one lady.

Mary William Ethelbert Appleton Burke was born August 7, 1885, in Washington, D.C., the only child of William (Billy) Burke, an internationally renowned singing clown in the Barnum & Bailey circus and one of a family of entertainers. As a child she toured with him throughout Europe, singing "coon songs" and doing pantomime. Following an education in England, she took her father's nickname before making her legitimate stage debut at age 18 in London in 1903 in **The School Girl,** singing "Mamie, I Have a Little Canoe." Before that, she had appeared in music halls.

The play was a hit, and she appeared on the London stage for four years. She then came to Broadway, making her debut opposite John Drew, the uncle of the three Barrymores, in **My Wife** in 1907. She continued to play opposite him for several years, in such plays as **Love Watches** (which made her a star), Somerset Maugham's **Mrs. Dot** and **The Land of Promise,** and Sir Arthur Wing Pinero's **The Ama-**

zons and **The Mind-the-Paint Girl.** A delicate beauty with a sparkling personality, she was soon the toast of Broadway, her backstage admirers including Mark Twain, Enrico Caruso and Sir James Barrie.

In 1913 Somerset Maugham escorted Miss Burke to a New Year's Eve party at the Hotel Astor, where she was introduced to Florenz Ziegfeld, then at the height of his fame as the creator and producer of the annual **Ziegfeld Follies.** The following year they eloped. They lived until his death in 1932 on a Westchester County, New York, estate, surrounded by a menagerie that included an elephant, bears, lion cubs, a herd of deer, and 15 dogs. She and Ziegfeld had a daughter, Patricia. The couple's marriage was a tempestuous one, due to his many flings with other actresses.

In 1915, the year the actress turned 30, producer Thomas H. Ince of Triangle Pictures offered her $10,000 a week—a royally fabulous sum of money then—to appear in her first film, **Peggy,** co-starring as a Scottish miss opposite William Desmond. (This record salary would soon be topped by Mary Pickford and Charlie Chaplin.) Ince also offered her a five-year contract, but she said no, realizing the difficulty of being both a movie star and Mrs. Flo Ziegfeld.

Nevertheless, she appeared in another movie in 1916, this one a 20-part serial, **Gloria's Romance**; it was a box-office failure (although she was paid $300,000 for it). But producers remained insistent, and in the next five years, while still appearing on the Broadway stage, she made 15 films, with Ziegfeld acting as her agent. Most of them were flops. She was a scatterbrain mistaken for a German spy in **In Pursuit of Polly** (18) and a mischievous American girl who rescues engineer Thomas Meighan from execution by the Huns in **Arms and the Girl** (17). In 1921 she returned to the New York stage.

Miss Burke starred in a number of plays in the Twenties, including Booth Tarkington's **Intimate Strangers** with Alfred Lunt in 1921 and Noel Coward's **The Marquise** in 1927, but was also kept preoccupied running the Ziegfeld household and raising her daughter. Then the Wall Street crash of 1929 wiped Ziegfeld out, and in an effort to help him financially she returned to full-time acting, starting with her first character role, in Ivor Novello's **The Truth Game.** This led to an offer to appear in the Los Angeles production of Paul Osborne's **The Vinegar Tree** in 1931.

As fate would have it, the role typecast her for 30 years to come. She was to say later in her autobiography, "These characters, these bird-witted ladies...derive from my part in **The Vinegar Tree.**"

At age 47, Miss Burke accepted Hollywood's offer to make movies again. Her sound-film debut was auspicious, as the youthful, radiant mother of Katharine Hepburn and the wife of mentally ill John Barrymore in director George Cukor's **A Bill of Divorcement** (32). She followed this with **Christopher Strong** (33), as the wife of Colin Clive, who, in the title role, falls in love with Miss Hepburn. And in **Only Yesterday** she was good as the cheerful, broad-minded aunt of Margaret Sullavan.

In that same year she had one of her finest roles, as the vapid, anxious hostess in director Cukor's **Dinner at Eight.** Even today, more than 60 years after the film was made, revival audiences break into applause at her hysterical tirade dismissing the serious problems of her husband (Lionel Barrymore) and daughter as trifles compared to the impending ruin of her dinner party.

She was a standout as Frances Dee's selfish mother in **Finishing School** (34), and in **Society Doctor** (35) played the rich hospital patroness who offers to set Chester Morris up in private practice, nearly stealing the film from him and Robert Taylor. In **Doubting Thomas** she was Will Rogers' silly wife, with stage aspirations, employing Alison Skipworth as a drama coach, and **Becky Sharp** cast her as a gurgling duchess. She was Joan Bennett's mother, married to Walter Connolly, in **She Couldn't Take It.** In 1936 she played Ann Sothern's doting mother in **My American Wife.**

Producer Hal Roach had the brilliant inspiration to cast Miss Burke and Roland Young as the married couple in **Topper** (37), a film that became both a smash hit and an enduring comedy classic. Although Cary Grant and Constance Bennett were the nominal stars, audiences found themselves far more interested in the antics of the Toppers. They were an irresistible combination; he bumbled, she dithered. But the actress, who longed for serious parts, was still playing a feather-brained, twittery comedienne, typecast against her will.

In 1938 she and Young were again husband and wife in the delicious comedy-drama **The Young in Heart,** as the parents of Janet Gaynor and Douglas Fairbanks Jr., with the entire family operating as con artists who attempt to fleece—but are reformed by—an old lady named Miss Fortune. She also played Judy Garland's mother in **Everybody Sing.** In that year Miss Burke received her only Academy Award nomination as best supporting actress, for **Merrily We Live,** one of the ubiquitous crazy-family screwball comedies, in which she hires a fake tramp (Brian Aherne) as a chauffeur so he can tame her spoiled daughter (Constance Bennett). The British periodical New Statesman said her performance "attains (like **Parsifal**) to a foolishness so pure that it verges on beauty."

It was true: Her bird-witted lady was a perfect characterization in an imperfect world. The actress, now in her mid-fifties, still pretty and fluffy, was doomed to play variations on dithery matrons. That was what audiences—and producers—wanted.

In 1939 there came a **Topper** sequel, **Topper Takes a Trip,** but it was all but forgotten in the excitement over another movie she made that year, providing her with her most famous role—Glinda the Good Witch in **The Wizard of Oz.** This was inspired casting. She adopted a deliciously eccentric, girlish look for the part, and a somewhat zany smile that blended curiously with the corny "goodness" of her dialogue. In any event, if you have seen **The Wizard of Oz** you will never forget Billie Burke in it.

After she played Oliver Hardy's wife that same year in **Zenobia,** she and Roland Young were back together again in **Topper Returns** (41); they had also been married in **Dulcy** (40). In **The Man Who Came to Dinner** (41) she was the Ohio matron in whose home Monty Woolley is forced by an accident to hole up. She did have a good dramatic part, and was deeply touching, in In **This Our Life** (42), as the downtrodden, defeated, neurotic and bedridden mother of Bette Davis and Olivia de Havilland; it was the kind of thing she wished she had always been able to do on the screen. She also played Joan Crawford's mother in **They All Kissed the Bride.**

Interspersed with her film work at this time, she tried Broadway again, starring in two comedies, **This Rock** in 1943 and **Mrs. January and Mr. X** in 1944; neither play was successful. She returned to the screen to play a straight dramatic role in **The Cheaters** (45) as a selfish, spoiled, unthinking mother. But now audiences were laughing even at her serious portrayals, because her voice had become even more like the twittering of birds. So for the remainder of her career it would be strictly comedy roles.

Her film activity decreased sharply now, as she entered her sixties. In 1947 and 1948 she did not film at all. In 1950 she played bridegroom Don Taylor's mother in **Father of the Bride,** which starred Spencer Tracy and Elizabeth Taylor, and was in the sequel, **Father's Little Dividend,** the next year. From 1954 to 1958 she made no movies at all, returning to play a scatty multi-millionairess in **The Young Philadelphians** (59), at age 74. The following year she made her last movies, playing small parts in **Pepe** and in director John Ford's **Sergeant Rutledge.** Meanwhile, she had written two volumes of memoirs, "With a Feather on My Nose" in 1949 and "With Powder on My Nose" in 1959.

Toward the end of her life, now aged and destitute, the actress called for help on an old friend—director George Cukor, who had guided her to two memorable performances some 30 years before. She asked for any kind of job at all—holding script, coaching young actors. Cukor made sure she was provided for.

Billie Burke died in 1970 at the age of 85. But grateful film buffs will always remember, among many other roles, her delicious twittering as Glinda the Good Witch in **The Wizard of Oz.** And Toto, too.

THE FILMS OF BILLIE BURKE

1915: Peggy.
1916: Gloria's Romance (serial).
1917: The Land of Promise; The Mysterious Miss Terry; Arms and the Girl; The Runaway.
1918: Eve's Daughter; In Pursuit of Polly; The Make Believe Wife; Let's Get a Divorce.
1919: Good Gracious, Annabelle; The Misleading Widow; Sadie Love; Wanted-a Husband.
1920: Away Goes Prudence.
1921: The Education of Elizabeth; The Frisky Mrs. Johnson.
1932: A Bill of Divorcement.
1933: Dinner at Eight; Christopher Strong; Only Yesterday.
1934: Finishing School; Where Sinners Meet; We're Rich Again; Forsaking All Others.
1935: Society Doctor; After Office Hours; Doubting Thomas; Becky Sharp; She Couldn't Take It; Splendor; A Feather in Her Hat.
1936: Piccadilly Jim; My American Wife; Craig's Wife.
1937: Topper; Parnell; The Bride Wore Red; Navy Blue and Gold.
1938: The Young in Heart; Everybody Sing; Merrily We Live.

1939: The Wizard of Oz; Topper Takes a Trip; Bridal Suite; Eternally Yours; Remember?; Zenobia.
1940: Irene; And One Was Beautiful; The Captain Is a Lady; Dulcy; Hullabaloo; The Ghost Comes Home.
1941: Topper Returns; The Man Who Came to Dinner; The Wild Man of Borneo; One Night in Lisbon.
1942: In This Our Life; They All Kissed the Bride; What's Cookin'?; Girl Trouble.
1943: Hi Diddle Diddle; Gildersleeve on Broadway; So's Your Uncle; You're a Lucky Fellow, Mr. Smith.
1944: *Credit uncertain:* Laramie Trail.
1945: The Cheaters; Sing Out, Sister.
1946: Breakfast in Hollywood; The Bachelor's Daughters.
1949: The Barkleys of Broadway.
1950: Father of the Bride; And Baby Makes Three; The Boy from Indiana; Three Husbands.
1951: Father's Little Dividend.
1953: Small Town Girl.
1959: The Young Philadelphians.
1960: Sergeant Rutledge; Pepe.

Hi, Mom!:
SPRING BYINGTON

We've all got mothers. Most of us have *nice* mothers. When it came to playing pleasant, loving moms on screen in the Thirties and Forties, the undisputed champion was Spring Byington.

These mothers, besides being nice, were often addlepated or scatty, but they were always young in spirit. Miss Byington was also good at playing small-town gossips, and even gossip columnists. This attractive and polished actress, who had appeared on stage for a quarter of a century before turning to movies, had a bewitching sense of comedy that brought her roles in nearly 100 films.

She was born October 17, 1893 (one source says 1886), in Colorado Springs, Colorado. Her father was an English instructor at Colorado College and her mother was one of the first woman doctors in the West. But Spring was orphaned as a small girl. At the age of 14 she made her stage debut with the stock company at Elitch's Gardens, a popular Denver amusement park.

For about a decade, before and during World War I, she toured the United States in stock and repertory, typically in one-night appearances. Sometime during this period she was married to Roy Chandler. They had two daughters, Phyllis and Lois, and were divorced; she never remarried. At this point the actress went on the Broadway stage, making her New York debut in 1924 in **Beggar on Horseback,** with Roland Young in one of the leads.

For the next decade Miss Byington was seen regularly on Broadway, appearing in about 30 plays. Many of them were hits, but her parts were not normally starring roles; she was a supporting player. Still, she did have major roles in **Once in a Lifetime** in 1930 and **When Ladies Meet** in 1932. Stage-trained performers were increasingly in demand by Hollywood in the early sound era, and she was summoned. It was her good fortune to make her movie debut in one of the greatest of screen classics; it pretty well made her career.

Under George Cukor's direction, she played "Marmee," the loving mother of the four girls, in **Little Women** (33), a film that still enchants audiences more than 60 years later. Her daughters were Katharine Hepburn, Joan Bennett, Frances Dee and Jean Parker; the cast was also enhanced by Paul Lukas and Edna May Oliver. Miss Byington had barely turned 40 when the film was released, but her screen future as a mother was secure.

Cheerfulness was the hallmark of her movie mothers. Regarding her film image, the actress once said, "It's very simple—Lady Macbeth and I aren't friends."

In 1934 she was back on Broadway fulfilling some final promises to appear in stage productions, but in 1935 she returned to Hollywood for good. In that year she made eight movies, launching a heavy schedule that lasted to the beginning of World War II. She played her now-typecast loving-mother role, married to Lionel Barrymore and bringing up sons Eric Linden and Mickey Rooney, in **Ah, Wilderness.** She was Henry Fonda's mom, a gossiping troublemaker, in **Way Down East,** and a lady in distress in the horror film **Werewolf of London.** She played Franchot Tone's mother in **Mutiny on the Bounty,** and had a key role in **Love Me Forever.**

In 1936 Miss Byington played gossips in both **Dodsworth** and **Theodora Goes Wild** (in the latter, a malicious busybody); was married to Nigel Bruce in **The Charge of the Light Brigade;** and played Dick Powell's mother in **Stage Struck.** But her hopes of continuing to have good parts in major productions took a downward turn that year when she had the misfortune to be cast in **Every Saturday Night,** the first of the interminable 15-picture Jones Family series, a collection of dreary rural comedies that one might charitably call "B" pictures; they were roughly comparable to the worst TV sitcoms of the Fifties. Jed Prouty, a now-forgotten comedian, was the father and Miss Byington the mother. These awful programmers, evidently popular in such places as rural Arkansas, made money for 20th Century-Fox up through 1940.

The actress played Anita Louise's mother in **Green Light** (37), an adaptation of the Lloyd C. Douglas novel, and was Mickey Rooney's mother again in the first Hardy Family movie, **A Family Affair,** with Lionel Barrymore again her husband. (Fay Holden and Lewis Stone took over the parental roles for the rest of the series.)

Spring Byington's greatest screen triumph came in 1938 when she played Penny Sycamore, the scatterbrained mother of Jean Arthur, in director Frank Capra's smash-hit comedy **You Can't Take it with You.** The actress received her only Academy Award nomination as best supporting actress for her deliciously comic portrayal of the novel-typing mother (she is writing the book because someone left a typewriter at the house), using a cat for a paperweight. She had a small role as a New Orleans society matron in **Jezebel,** played the Widow Douglas in **The Adventures of Tom Sawyer,** and had a good part as Dolley Madison in **The Buccaneer.** In **The Story of Alexander Graham Bell** (39) she was Loretta Young's mother and Charles Coburn's wife.

The youthful-looking actress played Shirley Temple's mom in **The Blue Bird** (40); in real life she was just about old enough to be Shirley's grandmother. But the best news that year was the end of the Jones Family series. In 1941 she was good as the store clerk wooed by the elderly Coburn in **The Devil and Miss Jones,** played Barbara Stanwyck's sympathetic mother in **Meet John Doe,** and was the hostess, a silly, tactless gossip, in **When Ladies Meet.** But she was also a charwoman falsely accused of theft in a wretched Republic Pictures programmer, **Arkansas Judge.**

Miss Byington played nosy gossip columnist Mary Sunshine in the hilarious Ginger Rogers comedy **Roxie Hart (42),** and was a standout in **Rings on Her Fingers,** playing the partner of confidence man Laird Cregar and trying to marry off Gene Tierney to millionaire Henry Fonda. In director Ernst Lubitsch's superb comedy-drama **Heaven Can Wait** (43) she was the mother of the child who grows up to be Don Ameche, and Judy Garland was her daughter in **Presenting Lily Mars.** Maternal love held sway for **I'll Be Seeing You** (44), in which her daughters were Miss Rogers and Shirley Temple.

The actress was a somewhat less than nice mom in **The Enchanted Cottage** (45), as the unthinkingly insensitive mother of war-disfigured Robert Young. Then began a long siege of routine parts in routine films. In **In the Good Old Summertime** (49) she was reduced to being wooed by S.Z. (Cuddles) Sakall, and she played Mickey Rooney's mother once again in **The Big Wheel.** But she had a good role in **Louisa** (50), moving in with son Ronald Reagan and becoming the object of the geriatric affections of both Charles Coburn (once again) and Edmund Gwenn. She was in six films that year, but her schedule then rapidly declined, and in 1954 she turned to television, starring for four years in the series "December Bride" as a widow who draws the attentions of elderly men. (She was now in her sixties.)

In 1960 she made her last film, **Please Don't Eat the Daisies,** playing David Niven's mother, and appeared in another TV series, "Laramie," which lasted until 1962; she was the surrogate mother of a family of ranchers. Then she retired. In 1971 Spring Byington died at the age of 77, leaving an empty place in the hearts of her many screen "children."

THE FILMS OF SPRING BYINGTON

1933: Little Women.
1935: Ah, Wilderness; Mutiny on the Bounty; Werewolf of London; The Great Impersonation; Love Me Forever; Orchids to You; Way Down East; Broadway Hostess.
1936: Dodsworth; Theodora Goes Wild; The Charge of the Light Brigade; Every Saturday Night; Educating Father; Back to Nature; The Voice of Bugle Ann; Palm Springs; Stage Struck; The Girl on the Front Page.
1937: Green Light; The Road Back; Penrod and Sam; Off to the Races; Big Business (The Jones Family in Big Business); Hot

Water; Borrowing Trouble; Hotel Haywire; It's Love I'm After; Clarence; A Family Affair.
1938: You Can't Take It with You; Jezebel; The Adventures of Tom Sawyer; The Buccaneer; Love on a Budget; A Trip to Paris; Safety in Numbers; Penrod and His Twin Brother; Down on the Farm.
1939: The Story of Alexander Graham Bell; The Jones Family in Hollywood; Everybody's Baby; Quick Millions (The Jones Family in Quick Millions); Chicken Wagon Family; Too Busy to Work.
1940: The Blue Bird; My Love Came Back; Lucky Partners; A Child

Is Born; On Their Own; Laddie; Young as You Feel.

1941: The Devil and Miss Jones; Meet John Doe; When Ladies Meet; The Vanishing Virginian; Arkansas Judge; Ellery Queen and the Perfect Crime.

1942: Roxie Hart; Rings on Her Fingers; The War Against Mrs. Hadley; The Affairs of Martha.

1943: Heaven Can Wait; Presenting Lily Mars; The Heavenly Body.

1944: I'll Be Seeing You.

1945: The Enchanted Cottage; Thrill of a Romance; Captain Eddie; A Letter for Evie; Salty O'Rourke.

1946: Dragonwyck; Meet Me on Broadway; Little Mr. Jim; Faithful in My Fashion; My Brother Talks to Horses.

1947: Cynthia; Living in a Big Way; Singapore; It Had to Be You.

1948: B.F.'s Daughter.

1949: In the Good Old Summertime; The Big Wheel.

1950: Louisa; Please Believe Me; Devil's Doorway; Walk Softly, Stranger; The Skipper Surprised His Wife; The Reformer and the Redhead (voice only).

1951: Angels in the Outfield; Bannerline; According to Mrs. Hoyle.

1952: No Room for the Groom; Because You're Mine.

1954: The Rocket Man.

1960: Please Don't Eat the Daisies.

The merchant of menace:
JOSEPH CALLEIA

In Hollywood's Golden Era, when you wanted to cast a sinister, swarthy, Latinate hoodlum—a role that was far from uncommon—you invariably thought of Joseph Calleia.

His characters generally dripped with menace—in fact, they were positively frightening. He could be a vicious murderer, a threatening mobster, a white slaver, or almost any other kind of villain. On the other hand, he was also versatile enough to play a kindly priest, a police detective, or a gypsy. But for the most part, he scared the hell out of you. The Godfather would have loved to have him as a hit man.

The actor also had an uncanny knack of seeming to be aware of what everybody else on the screen was thinking. This unnerving facility riveted an audience's attention on his piercing dark eyes.

Joseph Spurin-Calleja (one source gives the name as Joseph Alexander Herstall Vincent Calleja) was born August 14, 1897, in Rebat, Malta, the only well-known Hollywood performer ever to come from that country, a small island in the Mediterranean. Sent by his parents to London to study engineering, he found he liked performing on the music-hall stage better. There he did impressions of the Scottish star Sir Harry Lauder—hardly an easy feat for a Maltese. He became a successful, but not very well paid, music-hall singer, and also branched out to the concert stage, meanwhile getting some serious voice training that finally turned him into an operatic singer.

Several successful years in opera, performing in Italy, England and New York, followed, and Calleia then turned to composing music, finally settling on being a stage actor. He appeared in London and on Broadway during the Twenties, to increasingly good notices, and in 1931 made his film debut in a small part as a maritime agent in **His Woman,** a boring film starring Gary Cooper and Claudette Colbert. The demand for his services was not exactly deafening, and after playing small roles in two more 1931-32 films he went back to Broadway for three more years. Among other roles there, he had a part in the original cast of **The Front Page.**

In 1935 he scored a hit as the menacing hoodlum Trock Estrella in Maxwell Anderson's play **Winterset** (in the part originally played by Eduardo Ciannelli, who later took the role in the film version), and this time producers were falling over themselves in an effort to bring him back to Hollywood. He was memorable as the bitter, sad-eyed gang leader, a cold-blooded killer, in the film **Public Hero No. 1** (35), tracked down by G-man Chester Morris with the help of Lionel Barrymore (although Morris is in love with Calleia's sister, Jean Arthur). The actor also played the slippery fish-cannery boss in **Riffraff,** bringing in scabs to break a strike and giving a better performance than the stars, Spencer Tracy and Jean Harlow.

Earlier, Calleia had married Eleonore Vassallo in 1929. Theirs was an enduring marriage that would end only with her death in 1968.

In **His Brother's Wife** (36) he was menacing as the gambler Fish-eye, and in **Exclusive Story** he stole the show as the vicious lieutenant of the king of the numbers racket. He played a blackmailing, murderous nightclub owner in **After the Thin Man.** But in **Tough Guy** he was a gang leader who turns out to be a pushover for a little boy and his dog when runaway rich boy Jackie Cooper falls into the gang's hands.

He played a protection racketeer in **Sworn Enemy,** and a cabaret tycoon in **Sinner Take All.**

The actor had a good role in 1937's **Man of the People,** as an immigrant who works his way to a high political post with racketeers, but then repents and turns the tables on them. He acted the part with skill and intensity.

He was now among the screen's more prominent character actors, and was getting good notices from critics and finding favor with audiences. They observed that the dark-haired, mustached actor had a smile that instantly turned into a vicious scowl when he was crossed—which was frequently. But Hollywood being Hollywood, he always got his comeuppance, as often as not being led away by the cops at the finale.

Demonstrating his versatility, Calleia in **Algiers** (38) played the patient, determined Inspector Slimane, the police detective who finally captures Charles Boyer after he comes out of the Casbah in pursuit of Hedy Lamarr. In **Marie Antoinette** he had a small but telling part as Drouet, who detects the queen (Norma Shearer) attempting to flee in disguise and is the cause of her being taken back for her ultimate execution.

One of his best vicious mobsters was his role in **Golden Boy** (39) as Fuseli, who insists that manager Adolphe Menjou force prizefighter William Holden to take a dive in the big bout (Holden doesn't). In **Full Confession** he was a priest who has heard the confession of murderer Victor McLaglen but is bound by his vows not to break the seal of silence even to save the life of an innocent man. The New York Times, remembering his mobster roles, commented: "We were on tenterhooks all through his mass, lest he reach under his vestments and pull out a blunt-nosed automatic."

He was also good in **Five Came Back** as Vasquez, the political assassin in the custody of lawman John Carradine, demonstrating his innate decency after the plane on which they are flying crashes in the South American jungle, while Carradine becomes a parasitic drunkard.

Calleia's most unusual role came in **My Little Chickadee** (40), as a corrupt saloonkeeper who at night turns into an amorous masked rider and courts a willing Mae West. In **The Monster and the Girl** (41) he was involved in the white-slavery racket, his

only appearance in a horror film. He was another stereotypical mobster in **The Glass Key** (42), and was Sabu's villainous stepfather in **The Jungle Book.** In 1943 he was one of the few Latins to play a Spaniard in **For Whom the Bell Tolls;** most of the other character actors in that film were of Slavic extraction, which didn't work well on the screen. He was also good in **The Cross of Lorraine** as one of the French soldiers in a World War II German prison camp, tormented by Nazi sergeant Peter Lorre.

He was a police inspector again in **Gilda** (46), one of his better roles, but in **Lured** (47) he was once again a white slaver, menacing Lucille Ball. **The Beginning or the End** cast him as atomic scientist Enrico Fermi. He had a good role as the compassionate saloon owner who befriends fugitive Joel McCrea in **Four Faces West** (48), and then it was back to a mobster part in an Abbott and Costello outing, **The Noose Hangs High.** In **Branded** (50) he was an outlaw forcing Alan Ladd to impersonate Charles Bickford's long-missing son.

He had a small part in **Valentino** (51) as a helpful friend of the doomed actor (played by Anthony Dexter), and in 1955 was to be found as a Mexican in both **The Littlest Outlaw** and **The Treasure of Pancho Villa.** The following year he was Mario Lanza's singing teacher in **Serenade,** and played Jane Russell's conniving gypsy father in **Hot Blood,** betrothing her to any willing clansman, then pocketing the dowry money and skipping town.

In 1958, at the age of 61, Calleia got his finest film role, in Orson Welles' masterpiece **Touch of Evil.** Welles (who also directed) was a crooked, murderous detective and Calleia his loyal, devoted partner, suffering mental agony as he receives from Charlton Heston the secretly tape-recorded confession of Welles to murder that Calleia will use to bring his boss to justice. At the climactic finale, Calleia and Welles shoot it out and kill each other.

It was back to the old gang again as he played a mobster in **Cry Tough** (59). In director-star John Wayne's **The Alamo** (60) he was a Mexican again, and then he had his final film role in **Johnny Cool** (63), playing—what else?—a vicious gangster.

Joseph Calleia died in 1975 (some sources say 1976) at age 77 in Malta, his birthplace. But his menacing mobsters still glower and glare from the TV tube in the wee small hours of the morning.

THE FILMS OF JOSEPH CALLEIA

1931: His Woman; My Sin.
1932: The Divorce Racket.
1935: Public Hero No. 1; Riffraff.
1936: After the Thin Man; His Brother's Wife; Exclusive Story; Tough Guy; Sworn Enemy; Sinner Take All.
1937: Man of the People; Bad Man of Brimstone.
1938: Algiers; Marie Antoinette. *Credit uncertain:* Four's a Crowd.
1939: Golden Boy; Juarez; Full Confession; Five Came Back; The Gorilla.
1940: My Little Chickadee; Wyoming.
1941: The Monster and the Girl; Sundown.
1942: The Glass Key; The Jungle Book.
1943: For Whom the Bell Tolls; The Cross of Lorraine.
1944: The Conspirators.
1946: Gilda; Deadline at Dawn.

1947: Lured; The Beginning or the End.
1948: Four Faces West; The Noose Hangs High.
1950: Captain Carey, U.S.A.; Vendetta; Branded.
1951: Valentine.
1952: The Iron Mistress; Yankee Buccaneer; When in Rome; The Light Touch.
1953: The Caddy.
1955: Underwater!; The Treasure of Pancho Villa; The Littlest Outlaw.
1956: Serenade; Hot Blood.
1957: Wild Is the Wind.
1958: Touch of Evil; The Light in the Forest.
1959: Cry Tough.
1960: The Alamo.
1963: Johnny Cool.

The road goes ever on:
JOHN CARRADINE

The story of John Carradine's screen career encompasses more than half a century of American films in the sound era. He began filming in 1930, only months after the Wall Street crash, and was still vigorously active up to his death 58 years later. He was in more than 220 movies—more than almost any actor of his time.

He played Lincoln, Dracula, Bret Harte, Bluebeard, the biblical Aaron, and Nazi hangman Reinhard Heydrich, among others. A splendid villain, he was also cast in sympathetic roles in some memorable movies. Although he had a tendency toward hammy overacting, he worked again and again for some of Hollywood's best directors, notably John Ford. "Directors never direct me, they just turn me loose," he once said. That was often a mistake.

Tall, gaunt, cadaverous and saturnine, with a deep, cultured, vibrant voice that could drip with menace, he was one of the best and most prolific character actors on the screen during the decade 1935-45. In later years he allowed himself to play mad doctors, sinister butlers or evil henchmen in some incredibly cheap horror films, but to Carradine acting was a business that paid the rent and put food on the table. He once said, "I don't care how mean or despicable I am as long as the roles keep coming."

John Carradine was born (as Richmond Reed Carradine) on February 5, 1906, in New York City's Greenwich Village. His father was a lawyer, poet and painter (one source says newspaperman), and his mother was a doctor. As a young man he tried painting and sculpture, and at one point set off to make a living touring the South sketching portraits in office-building lobbies. While in New Orleans he decided on an acting career, and in 1925, at age 19, made his stage debut in a local production of **Camille.** Later he joined a Shakespearean stock company, beginning a lifelong association with the plays of the Bard.

In 1927 he hitchhiked to California, again supporting himself by sketching portraits. He tried to crash the movies in that year, but was unsuccessful, and turned to local stage productions for several years, also working as a dishwasher when his funds were low. During this period he became known as the "Bard of the Boulevards" for his habit of reciting Shakespeare in a booming voice while walking the streets of the film capital. If nothing else, this certainly brought him to the attention of movie produc-

ers. (It also gained him a reputation as an eccentric ham.)

Carradine (filming under the name John Peter Richmond) appeared in his first movie in 1930. This was the forgettable remake of **Tol'able David** starring Richard Cromwell; Carradine played one of the hillbillies, far down the cast list. He was still unnoticed in one and possibly two 1931 films. (In the early Thirties, it is difficult to pin down his screen credits with any precision.) The following year he made the first of several movies for producer-director Cecil B. DeMille, who had seen him as the "Bard of the Boulevards." This was **The Sign of the Cross,** in which he finally got screen credit, playing two small roles, "Leader of Gladiators" and "Christian." However, in several DeMille films his compelling voice was used off-camera to lead mob cries and read oratorical statements or proclamations. (Film historians aren't completely sure in every case just which movies this occurred in.)

He was lost in the crowd as a Cockney villager in **The Invisible Man** (33), and played "A Roman" in DeMille's **Cleopatra** (34), also taking a small part as a devil-worshiper in director Edgar G. Ulmer's **The Black Cat.** Then, in 1935, he began a hectic schedule that involved him in from nine to 14 films a year for five straight years, mainly for 20th Century-Fox, with which he signed a contract at this point. He was far down the cast list in DeMille's **The Crusades** that year, again playing two parts, "A King" and "A Wise Man." He was a hunter in **Bride of Frankenstein,** "A Drunken-Faced Clerk" in **Clive of India,** and "A Customer" in a ZaSu Pitts programmer, also getting small roles in such major productions as **Les Miserables** and **Cardinal Richelieu.**

In 1936 he started work under his 20th Century-Fox contract and began using the name John Carradine on screen. For a while he was to be a one-man stock company for 20th, appearing on screen far more often than, say, MGM's all-purpose character actor Reginald Owen. And in that year he finally got a part he could sink his teeth into, cast by director John Ford as the sadistic prison guard who torments Warner Baxter in **The Prisoner of Shark Island,** a performance that virtually stole the film and drew plaudits from critics. He also played David Rizzio, the elegant Italian secretary to Mary, Queen of Scots (Katharine Hepburn) in Ford's **Mary of Scotland;** in the film, the terrified Rizzio is pursued through the castle and stabbed to death by Mary's antagonists.

Additionally in 1936, Carradine had a role in **Under Two Flags** as a member of the French Foreign Legion, and scowled maliciously as the renegade Simon Girty in **Daniel Boone.** He was excellent in the opening scenes of **Winterset** as the wrongfully executed Romagna, a kindly and idealistic man who was poles apart from **Shark Island's** vicious prison guard. He was good as a villainous claim jumper in **White Fang;** played a foreboding sand diviner, or clairvoyant, in **The Garden of Allah;** and was in **Ramona** and two Shirley Temple vehicles, **Captain January** and **Dimples.**

Carradine had come out of nowhere to become one of the screen's top character actors, with at least six fine performances in one year. Producers and directors sat up and took notice: Who *was* this remarkably versatile actor, anyway?

He had also become a family man. He had married Ardanelle Cosner in 1935, a union that was to result in two sons, Bruce and John Jr. (later to call himself David); Bruce was adopted. The marriage ended in divorce in 1944. Sonia Sorel, whom he wed in 1945, gave him three more sons, Christopher, Rob-

ert and Keith; this marriage ended in divorce in 1957. That year he married Doris Rich, and was widowed in 1973 when their California home burned. The actor married Emily Cisneros in 1975. Sons David, Robert and Keith have followed in their father's footsteps and are now well-known screen actors.

In **Danger—Love at Work** (37) Carradine was cast as an oddball artist who does surrealistic paintings on windowpanes, and in **Captains Courageous** he was the seaman Long Jack. He played yet another sadistic prison guard in John Ford's **The Hurricane** (altogether he would appear in 11 of Ford's films, through 1964), and portrayed assorted villainous types in such films as **This Is My Affair, The Last Gangster, Nancy Steele Is Missing,** and **Thank You, Mr. Moto.** Hidden behind a beard, he was not recognizable playing Abraham Lincoln in the Civil War drama **Of Human Hearts** (38), in a cameo appearance, admonishing soldier James Stewart for not writing to his mother (Beulah Bondi), but alert filmgoers could have detected his vibrant voice. In **I'll Give a Million** he and Peter Lorre were fine as a pair of oddball hoboes.

Offscreen, Carradine was part of the hard-drinking, high-spirited gang that included John Barrymore, Errol Flynn, Anthony Quinn, and artist John Decker. The actor also owned and sailed a yacht, played the piano, and could sing many operas by heart.

The year 1939 saw him in two of his most famous roles, as the chivalrous Southern gambler Hatfield in John Ford's **Stagecoach** and as "that dirty little coward" Bob Ford in **Jesse James,** treacherously murdering Tyrone Power as Jesse. He was a dissolute, alcoholic detective in **Five Came Back** and also had a key villainous part in Ford's **Drums Along the Mohawk.**

In Ford's classic drama **The Grapes of Wrath** (40) he was memorable and distinctive as Preacher Casy, shot down by a deputy sheriff. But in **The Return of Frank James** he got what was coming to him for shooting Jesse when Frank (Henry Fonda) caught up with him. He also played a fiery Mormon scout in **Brigham Young—Frontiersman,** and was excellent in a cameo as a circus' advance agent in **Chad Hanna.** In **Blood and Sand** (41) he was a friend of matador Power, and both of them end up gored to death by bulls. **Man Hunt** cast him as a sinister Nazi agent in London. But, ominously, he also had a small part in a Poverty Row horror film, Monogram Studios' **King of the Zombies.**

During World War II Carradine moved fairly rapidly into the horror genre. In **Captive Wild Woman** (43) he was a mad scientist who turns a circus ape into a woman—who ultimately kills him. **Revenge** of the Zombies was a low-budget Monogram horror film in which he was a mad doctor experimenting on humans and building a zombie army for Hitler. This was unfortunate typecasting—except for the fact that Carradine liked the paychecks and didn't really mind the assignments. He also played more Nazis—notably Reinhard Heydrich in the title role of **Hitler's Madman,** overacting outrageously, especially in a deathbed scene; a Nazi official in the Joan Crawford-John Wayne starrer **Reunion in France,** an evil Nazi general in **Black Parachute,** and a murderous Nazi agent in **Waterfront.** (These were released during the period 1942-44.)

One of his most remarkable performances came in director Edgar G. Ulmer's **Bluebeard** (44), in the title role. This was a Faustian story in which the actor, playing a Parisian puppeteer, finds himself irresistibly drawn to kill the women he loves; he ends by falling from a rooftop and drowning in the Seine. In that year he also was ideally cast as author Bret Harte in **The Adventures of Mark Twain;** the physical resemblance was striking. He continued in mediocre horror films, playing Count Dracula in **House of Frankenstein** (he would repeat the role the next year in **House of Dracula**) and also having key roles in **The Mummy's Ghost** and **The Invisible Man's Revenge.** In **Return of the Ape Man** his brain was transplanted by Bela Lugosi into the Missing Link.

Carradine appeared in very few films in the immediate postwar era, and from 1950 through 1953 made none at all. He went back on the stage to do a number of plays, including Shakespeare—he starred as Hamlet, Shylock, Othello, and the like—and other classics, and also did more of his one-man Shakespearean readings. He also started to take television roles; his TV credits would ultimately include the series "Trapped" (as the host), "My Friend Irma" and "The Munsters."

Back on the screen, he had a small part in director Nicholas Ray's unusual Western **Johnny Guitar** (54) and also appeared for Ray in 1957 in **The True Story of Jesse James,** reprising, naturally, his role as killer Bob Ford. In **The Egyptian** (also 54) he was cast as a grave robber. He was an evil Arab sheik in **Desert Sands** (55), and a corrupt lawyer turned prosecutor in **Stranger on Horseback.** He played Aaron

in **The Ten Commandments** (56) and also had a key role in **Around the World in 80 Days.** In John Ford's **The Last Hurrah** (58) he was good as newspaper publisher Amos Force, one of Spencer Tracy's chief antagonists.

In the late Fifties and early Sixties there was a spate of science-fiction cheapies, films with such titles as **The Cosmic Man, Invisible Invaders, The Incredible Petrified World** and **Invasion of the Animal People.** Carradine, now in late middle age, had begun his inexorable slide into schlock and junk. By the late Sixties the science-fiction cheapies had turned to horror cheapies, in which he camped it up outrageously. They bore such titles as **Blood of Dracula's Castle, Horror of the Blood Monsters** and **Blood of Ghastly Horror.** An astonishing number of them—all from 1969 through 1975—had "Blood" in the title.

Occasionally he would still be offered a role in a major production (he was the greedy undertaker in the 1976 film **The Shootist,** starring John Wayne), but as the years rolled by he just took any part at all in just about any kind of film. (He also did dramatic readings in the horror genre on tape cassettes.) **House of the Seven Corpses...Satan's Cheerleaders... Vampire Hookers...The Monster Club.** It had been a long ride since the glory days working for John Ford, a long journey from **The Prisoner of Shark Island, Stagecoach** and **The Grapes of Wrath.**

He was in his seventies now, and camping it up unmercifully in an ongoing procession of unredeemable junk. Even in his 80th year he was in something called **Monster in the Closet.** But 1986 marked the end of film work for the actor.

In 1988 he was invited to a film festival in Milan, Italy, to be the guest of honor at a showing of **Stagecoach,** just short of its 50th anniversary. And while in Milan John Carradine died at the age of 82. He was an actor who didn't know how to stop acting. But he should have known how, so that instead of the horror junk in the latter part of his career, we could know him only by his distinguished performances in those John Ford classics of the late Thirties. The two vicious, sadistic prison guards...the chivalrous gambler...the unforgettable Preacher Casy. Just remember those performances, and let them be what we remember about John Carradine.

THE FILMS OF JOHN CARRADINE

NOTE: From 1930 to 1935 inclusive he was credited on screen as John Peter Richmond, or sometimes as Peter Richmond. Beginning in 1936, he was credited as John Carradine.

1930: Tol'able David.

1931: Heaven on Earth. *Credit uncertain:* Bright Lights.

1932: The Sign of the Cross; Forgotten Commandments.

1933: The Invisible Man; Morning Glory; To the Last Man. *Credit uncertain:* This Day and Age; The Story of Temple Drake.

1934: Cleopatra; The Black Cat. *Credit uncertain:* Of Human Bondage; The Meanest Gal in Town.

1935: Les Miserables; The Crusades; Bride of Frankenstein; Clive of India; Cardinal Richelieu; The Man Who Broke the Bank at Monte Carlo; Alias Mary Dow; Bad Boy; She Gets Her Man; Transient Lady.

1936: Mary of Scotland; Winterset; The Prisoner of Shark Island; Under Two Flags; Captain January; Ramona; Anything Goes; Laughing at Trouble; White Fang; Dimples; The Garden of Allah; Daniel Boone; A Message to Garcia (voice only). *Credit uncertain:* Half Angel.

1937: The Hurricane; Captains Courageous; This Is My Affair; Love Under Fire; The Last Gangster; Nancy Steele Is Missing; Danger—Love at Work; Thank You, Mr. Moto; Laughing at Trouble; Ali Baba Goes to Town. *Credit uncertain:* Charlie Chan at the Olympics.

1938: Of Human Hearts; Submarine Patrol; Four Men and a Prayer; International Settlement; Alexander's Ragtime Band; Gateway; Kidnapped; I'll Give a Million; Kentucky Moonshine.

1939: Stagecoach; Jesse James; The Hound of the Baskervilles; Drums Along the Mohawk; Frontier Marshal; The Three Musketeers; Five Came Back; Captain Fury; Mr. Moto's Last Warning.

1940: The Grapes of Wrath; The Return of Frank James; Chad Hanna; Brigham Young—Frontiersman.

1941: Blood and Sand; Man Hunt; Western Union; Swamp Water; King of the Zombies.

1942: Reunion in France; Son of Fury; Northwest Rangers; Whispering Ghosts.

1943: Hitler's Madman; Isle of Forgotten Sins; Captive Wild Woman; Gangway for Tomorrow; I Escaped from the Gestapo; Revenge of the Zombies; Silver Spurs.

1944: Bluebeard; The Adventures of Mark Twain; House of Frankenstein; The Mummy's Ghost; Barbary Coast Gent; Black Parachute; The Invisible Man's Revenge; Return of the Ape Man; Voodoo Man; Alaska; Waterfront.

1945: Fallen Angel; Captain Kidd; House of Dracula; It's in the Bag.

1946: Down Missouri Way; Face of Marble.

1947: The Private Affairs of Bel Ami.

1949: C-Man.

1954: Johnny Guitar; The Egyptian; Casanova's Big Night; Thunder Pass.

1955: Stranger on Horseback; The Kentuckian; Desert Sands; Dark Venture.

1956: Around the World in 80 Days; The Ten Commandments; The Court Jester; The Female Jungle; The Black Sleep; Hidden Guns.

1957: The True Story of Jesse James; The Story of Mankind; The Unearthly; Half Human; Hellship Mutiny.

1958: The Last Hurrah; The Proud Rebel; Showdown at Boot Hill.

1959: The Oregon Trail; The Cosmic Man; Invisible Invaders.

1960: The Adventures of Huckleberry Finn; Tarzan the Magnificent; Sex Kittens Go to College; The Incredible Petrified World.

1962: The Man Who Shot Liberty Valance; Invasion of the Animal People.

1964: Cheyenne Autumn; The Patsy; The Wizard of Mars; Curse of the Stone Hand.

1965: House of the Black Death.

1966: Billy the Kid vs. Dracula; Munster, Go Home; The Hostage; Dr. Terror's Gallery of Horrors; Night Train to Mundo Fine.

1967: Hillbillys [sic] in the Haunted House; Creatures of the Red Planet; The Astro-Zombies; La Senora Muerte (Mrs. Death); The Electronic Brain; Lonely Man.

1968: They Ran for Their Lives; Autopsy of a Ghost; Pacto Diabolico (Pact with the Devil); The Hostage; Genesis (narrator only).

1969: The Trouble with Girls; The Good Guys and the Bad Guys; Blood of Dracula's Castle; The Man with the Synthetic Brain; Cain's Way; Vampire Men of the Lost Planet; Las Vampiras.

1970: Myra Breckinridge; The McMasters; Shock Waves; Hell's Bloody Devils; Blood of Frankenstein.

1971: Five Bloody Graves; Blood of the Iron Maiden; The Seven Minutes; Bigfoot; Horror of the Blood Monsters; Threshold; Decisions! Decisions!; Legacy of Blood; Shinbone Alley (voice only).

1972: Richard; Boxcar Bertha; Everything You Always Wanted to Know About Sex But Were Afraid to Ask; The Gatling Gun; Portnoy's Complaint; Blood of Ghastly Horror; Night of the Dark Full Moon; Shadow House; House of the Seven Corpses.

1973: Silent Night, Bloody Night; Terror in the Wax Museum; Bad Charleston Charlie; Hex; Superchick; Legacy of Blood; House of Dracula's Daughter; 1,000,000 A.D.; Smashing the Crime Syndicate.

1974: Moonchild.

1975: Mary, Mary, Bloody Mary.

1976: The Shootist; The Last Tycoon; Won Ton Ton, the Dog Who Saved Hollywood; The Killer Inside Me; Crash.

1977: The Sentinel; Shock Waves; The White Buffalo; Golden Rendezvous; Satan's Cheerleaders; The Mouse and His Child (voice only); Journey into the Beyond (narrator only).

1978: Vampire Hookers; Sunset Cove; The Bees; Missile X; Nocturna; The Mandate of Heaven.

1979: Teheran Incident; Monster; Americathon; The Nesting.

1980: The Boogey Man; The Long Riders; Carradines in Concert; Phobia; The Monster Club.

1981: The Howling; Zorro the Gay Blade; The Scarecrow; Dark Eyes.

1982: The Secret of NIMH (voice only).

1983: House of the Long Shadows; Klynham Summer; Boogey Man II; Evils of the Night.

1984: The Ice Pirates.

1985: The Tomb; Prison Ship 2005 (Star Slammer).

1986: Monster in the Closet; Peggy Sue Got Married.

Hey, Ceesco:
LEO CARRILLO

Many of Hollywood's character players of the Thirties were ethnic specialists, almost invariably called on when the role was someone of their race or nationality. And when the part was a humorous Hispanic or Italian, the one they always sent for was Leo Carrillo.

He enjoyed a successful career as an amiably garrulous Latin, usually talking in fractured English, as when he said to Buddy Ebsen in **Girl of the Golden West,** "Hey, who *say* the West she don' be wild some more?"

He could be a lovable, not-so-bad gangster, but usually he was a comic *bandido,* plump, dark-haired and mustached—a performance that almost never changed throughout his quarter-century screen career.

And, like Ralph Bellamy, he almost never seemed to get the girl.

Carrillo looked much younger on screen than in real life. In the Thirties, he looked like a man about 40 years old, when in fact he was in his fifties. He was born (as Leo Antonio Carrillo) on August 6, 1881, in Los Angeles, the scion of a wealthy Spanish-Californian land-owning family (some sources give an 1880 birthdate).

After graduation from St. Vincent of Loyola College, he was a journalist and cartoonist before becoming an Italian-dialect comedian in vaudeville and later on the legitimate stage, including Broadway appearances. At the age of 47 he entered films, making his Hollywood debut in a small part in the 1928 Norma Talmadge picture **The Dove,** a silent. The following year he was the star in **Mr. Antonio,** a tale about an Italian florist and street musician.

Resuming screen work in 1931, he played a well-meaning Italian mobster regenerated by his love for a singer (Lola Lane) in **Hell Bound,** a Poverty Row outing made by Tiffany Studios. His longtime typecasting as a good-hearted Latin gangster probably resulted from that performance. Then he starred as a gangster who helps his son go straight in **Homicide Squad,** and was yet another mobster in **Guilty Generation,** hoping his daughter (Constance Cummings) will be accepted by society. When she marries the son (Robert Young) of his hated rival (Boris Karloff, not yet a star), Carrillo goes gunning for Karloff, but is shot dead by his own aged mother.

In **Broken Wing** (32) Carrillo played an ingratiating but murderous Mexican official courting Lupe

Velez, but losing her to Melvyn Douglas. **Girl of the Rio** saw him as a sneering Mexican *caballero,* a villain of interesting moods, making advances to Dolores Del Rio. (He would play the same role in the 1939 remake, **The Girl and the Gambler.**)

Often he was called on to portray an Italian-American in some blue-collar occupation. He was fine as an immigrant barber in **Obey the Law** (33), and also played a barber who fights a corrupt tenement boss out to control the local vote in **The Winning Ticket** (35). He was a laborer in **Men Are Such Fools** (32), a ditchdigger in **It Had to Happen** (36), and a fisherman in **Fisherman's Wharf** (39).

Meanwhile, his gangster roles went on and on. In **Parachute Jumper** (33) he played a racketeer who employs Bette Davis and Douglas Fairbanks Jr., but they turn him over to the police. In **Moonlight and Pretzels** he was cast as a genial mobster who backs a stage musical. But in **Deception** he was merely a scoundrely wrestling promoter, and in **Racetrack** a gambler. He was excellent as Pancho Villa's (Wallace Beery's) trigger-happy chief henchman in **Viva Villa** (34), and in **Manhattan Melodrama** he was a priest. In **Four Frightened People** he played an English-speaking jungle native named Montague.

One of his best roles came in 1935 in **Love Me Forever,** co-starring with Grace Moore and giving one of the year's best performances as the illiterate, sentimental little racketeer and nightclub owner ruined by his obsessive love for the singer. In **If You Could Only Cook** he was the genial gourmet ex-gangster who hires Jean Arthur and Herbert Marshall as his cook and butler.

The part for which Carrillo probably is best remembered is his comic-opera *bandido* with a heart of gold in the fine musical spoof **The Gay Desperado** (36). He holds the film together with a wonderfully funny performance as the badman who has learned how to be bad by watching American gangster films. He kidnaps eloping heiress Ida Lupino and a ridiculous tenor played by Nino Martini; before the film ends Miss Lupino falls for the tenor. Also that year, he was a murdered opera star in **Moonlight Murder.**

He was in fine comic form as a chef, Charles Boyer's best pal, in the 1937 film **History Is Made at Night,** portrayed an accordion-playing street minstrel in **52nd Street,** and was loony astrologer Zodiac Z. Zippe in **Hotel Haywire.** He now ran into a long string of forgettable parts in mostly forgettable films. He was passable as newsreel cameraman Clark Gable's assistant in **Too Hot to Handle** (38), and appeared in **City Streets** as the benefactor of an orphan girl, fighting the child-welfare authorities. He played restaurateur Tony Pastor in **Lillian Russell** (40), giving the singer (Alice Faye) her first big break. But by World War II he was appearing in low-budget programmers, a situation that continued to the end of his career.

In 1940, at age 59, Carrillo finally married; his bride was Edith Haeselbarth. They had a daughter, Antoinette, but the actor was widowed in 1953.

In 1944 he played a gypsy leader in the wildly campy Maria Montez starrer **Gypsy Wildcat,** and in 1947 he had a fairly substantial role as the chief of police in director John Ford's **The Fugitive,** starring Henry Fonda.

The next five films he made (1948-50) were all Cisco Kid outings in which he played Pancho, the sidekick to Cisco (Duncan Renaldo). In 20th Century-Fox' earlier Cisco Kid series in the late Thirties, Cisco and Pancho had been played by Cesar Romero and Chris-Pin Martin. Carrillo was born to portray Pancho, and after one last film (the Mexican production **Pancho Villa Returns,** in which he starred as Villa, in 1952) he turned to television, along with Renaldo, to continue the series in that medium. The actor was now in his seventies, and still looking far from his real age on the tube.

Leo Carrillo died at 79 in 1961. His characterizations died with him, for any actor essaying a comic Latin *bandido* role today would be hooted off the screen by Hispanics proud of their heritage. But for a moment in time, he *was* the comic Latin for two decades of filmgoers in a far simpler era.

THE FILMS OF LEO CARRILLO

1928: The Dove.
1929: Mr. Antonio.
1931: Hell Bound; Guilty Generation; Homicide Squad; Lasca of the Rio Grande.
1932: Broken Wing; Girl of the Rio; Deception; Men Are Such Fools.
1933: Parachute Jumper; Moonlight and Pretzels; Racetrack; Obey the Law; Before Morning.
1934: Viva Villa; Manhattan Melodrama; Four Frightened People; The Gay Bride; The Band Plays On.
1935: Love Me Forever; If You Could Only Cook; The Winning Ticket; In Caliente.
1936: The Gay Desperado; It Had to Happen; Moonlight Murder.
1937: History Is Made at Night; I Promise to Pay; 52nd Street; Hotel Haywire; The Barrier; Manhattan Merry-Go-Round.
1938: Too Hot to Handle; Blockade; Girl of the Golden West; Arizona Wildcat; City Streets; Flirting with Fate; Little Miss Roughneck.
1939: Society Lawyer; Chicken Wagon Family; Rio; The Girl and the Gambler; Fisherman's Wharf.
1940: Lillian Russell; Captain Caution; One Night in the Tropics; Wyoming; Twenty-Mule Team.
1941: Barnacle Bill; Horror Island; Tight Shoes; The Kid from Kansas; Road Agent; Riders of Death Valley (serial).
1942: What's Cookin'?; Unseen Enemy; Escape from Hong Kong; Men of Texas; Top Sergeant; Sin Town; Timber; American Empire; Danger in the Pacific.
1943: The Phantom of the Opera; Follow the Band; Crazy House; Frontier Bad Men; Larceny with Music.
1944: Gypsy Wildcat; Moonlight and Cactus; Merrily We Sing; Babes on Swing Street; Bowery to Broadway; The Ghost Catchers.
1945: Under Western Skies; Crime, Inc.; Mexicana.
1947: The Fugitive.
1948: Valiant Hombre.
1949: The Gay Amigo; Satan's Cradle; The Daring Caballero.
1950: The Girl from San Lorenzo.
1952: Pancho Villa Returns.

A face etched in stone:
EDUARDO CIANNELLI

He had a face like a death's-head, and it was his fortune.

Eduardo Ciannelli's craggy features, seemingly etched in granite, went well with his malevolent eyes, suave manner, and incisive, grating speech to produce a portrayal that could thoroughly frighten impressionable moviegoers. He was one of Hollywood's most menacing and expert villains, usually playing manic criminal masterminds and gang bosses. Yet he could also handle sympathetic parts.

Ciannelli was born July 30, 1887 (some sources say 1884, 1888 or 1889), on the island of Ischia, not far from Capri, off the Italian coast near Naples. He originally planned to be a doctor, and took his medical degree at the University of Naples. But he turned to music, and more specifically to grand opera, as a baritone, performing at La Scala in Milan and touring Italy and the Continent.

He served in the Italian army in World War I, and when the war ended he married Alma Wolfe in 1918; they had two sons, Eduardo and Lewis, and the actor would be widowed in 1968.

Soon he emigrated to the United States, and began performing in operettas and plays on Broadway. He appeared in, among others, **Rose Marie** (his Broadway debut, in 1925), **Yellow Jack, The Front Page,** and the Katharine Cornell version of Shaw's **St. Joan.** (He also wrote a play, **Foolscap,** which had a moderate success in 1933.)

Ciannelli made his movie debut in 1933 in **Reunion in Vienna,** in a featured role, but continued to work on the Broadway stage, not filming again until 1935, when he appeared in **The Scoundrel.** In that year he also scored a sensational triumph as the evil gangster Trock Estrella in Maxwell Anderson's play **Winterset;** he reprised the role in the movie version the following year. Now he was in such demand on the screen that his career would henceforth be devoted solely to movies.

No one who has seen **Winterset** can ever forget Ciannelli as Trock Estrella. He riveted audiences in a performance filled with unmitigated malevolence, yet he was fear-ridden even though assured, cringing even though ruthless. It was one of the best acting performances of 1936, but since **Winterset** was a "little" film he was nominated for no awards.

He delivered a chilling portrait of yet another racketeer, Johnny Vanning, in **Marked Woman** (37),

ordering his stooges to beat and facially disfigure Bette Davis (hence the title) when she threatens to expose his nefarious activities. (Vanning was based on Lucky Luciano, who lived off the income of prostitutes; in the film, made at the height of the Production Code's sway, they were called "nightclub hostesses.") Vanning ultimately is convicted when Miss Davis enlists the aid of district attorney Humphrey Bogart.

In the same year, Ciannelli played the arch-villain, "The Poison Pen," captured by comic detective Jack Oakie in **Super Sleuth,** and was the mysterious madman with a "destruction ray" tracked down by Karen Morley in **The Girl from Scotland Yard.** In 1938 he was a sneering mobster in **Law of the Underworld.**

In 1939 he darkened his skin to play the fanatical high priest Guru (yes, that was his name), leader of the Thuggees, in **Gunga Din,** one of Hollywood's finest adventure films, in which he is bested by Cary

Grant, Victor McLaglen and Douglas Fairbanks Jr.—not to forget Sam Jaffe in the title role of Kipling's famous poem. He was also the villain brought to justice by Walter Pidgeon in **Society Lawyer,** a menacing hoodlum in **Risky Business,** and played assorted dirty rats in **Angels Wash Their Faces** and **Bulldog Drummond's Bride.**

In **Strange Cargo** (40) he was a religious fanatic, one of the eight convicts (including Clark Gable and Paul Lukas) escaping from Devil's Island, and was one of the baddies in director Alfred Hitchcock's **Foreign Correspondent,** but had a sympathetic role as the thoughtful bartender in **Kitty Foyle.** In **The Mummy's Hand** he was the ancient High Priest of Karnak, shaking and quivering splendidly and indoctrinating acolyte George Zucco in a quavering voice. In the serial **Mysterious Dr. Satan** he was the deranged doctor of the title, busily creating robots. He played the hotel manager in the Gable starrer **They Met in Bombay** (41) and was a villainous doctor in **I Was a Prisoner on Devil's Island.**

Ciannelli inevitably appeared in several spy epics during World War II, at one point playing an Axis agent menacing Bob Hope in **They Got Me Covered** (43). **Flight for Freedom** cast him as a restaurateur. He was the chief engineer of the freighter in the Humphrey Bogart starrer **Passage to Marseille** (44), and the mayor of an Italian town in **A Bell for Adano** (45). In **Heartbeat** (46), starring Ginger Rogers, he was an aristocrat, Baron Dvorak, and he played a priest in **The Lost Moment** (47), the year he turned 60.

Good roles were becoming fewer in the postwar era, and beginning in 1948 he commuted between the United States and Italy, filming in both countries. He was now more likely to play benevolent gentlemen than to portray villainous types. He was on screen far less frequently now, and from 1959 through 1961, for example, and again from 1965 through 1967, made no films at all.

In his last two years in movies (1968-69), besides appearing as an American Indian named Prairie Dog in **MacKenna's Gold,** he showed them that at the age of 81, just before he died in Rome in 1969, he could still play a menacing Mafioso, which he did in **The Brotherhood, Stiletto** and **The Syndicate: A Death in the Family,** as aging mobsters in all three. Right to the last, Eduardo Ciannelli's death's-head face and evil eyes could still be impressively frightening.

THE FILMS OF EDUARDO CIANNELLI

1933: Reunion in Vienna.
1935: The Scoundrel.
1936: Winterset.
1937: Marked Woman; Hitting a New High; On Such a Night; Super-Sleuth; The Girl from Scotland Yard; Criminal Lawyer; The League of Frightened Men.
1938: Law of the Underworld; Blind Alibi. *Credit uncertain:* The Saint in New York.
1939: Gunga Din; Society Lawyer; Angels Wash Their Faces; Risky Business; Bulldog Drummond's Bride.
1940: Strange Cargo; Foreign Correspondent; Kitty Foyle; Zanzibar; Forgotten Girls; The Mummy's Hand; Outside the Three-Mile Limit; Mysterious Dr. Satan (serial; some sources indicate that it was also released in a feature length-version titled Dr. Satan's Robots).
1941: They Met in Bombay; I Was a Prisoner on Devil's Island; Ellery Queen's Penthouse Mystery; Paris Calling; Sky Raiders (serial).
1942: Dr. Broadway; Cairo; You Can't Escape Forever.
1943: The Constant Nymph; They Got Me Covered; Flight for Freedom.

1944: Passage to Marseille; The Mask of Dimitrios; The Conspirators; Storm over Lisbon.
1945: A Bell for Adano; Dillinger; Incendiary Blonde.
1946: Heartbeat; California; Perilous Holiday; The Crime Doctor's Warning; The Wife of Monte Cristo; Joe Palooka—Champ.
1947: The Lost Moment; Seven Keys to Baldpate; The Crime Doctor's Gamble; Rose of Santa Rosa.
1948: On Our Merry Way (A Miracle Can Happen); To the Victor; I Love Trouble; The Creeper.
1950: Rapture.
1951: The People Against O'Hara; Fugitive Lady.
1953: Volcano.
1954: The City Stands Trial; Voice of Silence.
1955: Mambo; Helen of Troy; The Stranger's Hand.
1957: Love Slaves of the Amazon; The Monster from Green Hell.
1958: Houseboat; Attila.
1962: Forty Pounds of Trouble.
1964: The Visit.
1968: The Brotherhood.
1969: The Secret of Santa Vittoria; MacKenna's Gold; Stiletto; Boot Hill; Syndicate: A Death in the Family.

The benevolent scene-stealer:
CHARLES COBURN

"Acting for the movies requires no great effort if you're just naturally good," Charles Coburn once said.

Coburn was as good as they come. Arriving in Hollywood late in life, he quickly became the movies' leading portrayer of crusty but benevolent senior gentlemen, stealing scene after scene from major stars and winning an Academy Award for his acting. Film historian James Harvey has praised his "breathtaking comic timing and intelligence."

He could be a gruff businessman, an irate politician, a kindly father, a haughty aristocrat. He was outstanding in comedy roles, and several times also played villains of the deepest dye. With a flabby face, thick lips and a paunch, his voice rasping, often smoking a cigar and sometimes sporting a monocle, he delighted moviegoers for a quarter of a century.

Charles Douville Coburn was born June 19, 1877, in Savannah, Georgia. At age 17 he became the manager of a Savannah theater where he had started as a program boy three years earlier. It was inevitable that he would become an actor. In 1901 he made his Broadway debut, and in 1906 he organized the Coburn Shakespeare Players, touring the nation. Joining him in that enterprise was his wife, the former Ivah Wills, whom he married that same year. (She died in 1937, and late in life, in 1959, he would marry Winifred Natzka.)

It wasn't long before the Coburns were together on Broadway, co-starring in a string of hits and always billed as Mr. and Mrs. Charles Coburn. Soon he began to receive offers to appear in films, but he resisted them for years, since they did not include parts for his wife. Finally, in 1933, at age 56, he starred in the title role of **Boss Tweed,** an utterly forgotten short film for Columbia. (One source lists this as a 1935 film.)

The actor appeared in a 1934 British film, **Say It with Flowers,** and in 1935 returned to Hollywood and, according to some sources, had a small, uncredited part in **The People's Enemy.** Then he went back to the stage for three years, during which period his wife died.

He made an impressive return to the screen in 1938, starting with his role as the rural doctor, a friend of the family, in the James Stewart starrer **Of Human Hearts.** He was also good as Stewart's father, a dignified college president, in **Vivacious Lady,** try-

ing to cope with the fact that his son has on the spur of the moment married nightclub entertainer Ginger Rogers; in this film Coburn was married to Beulah Bondi.

He was liked so well by audiences in these films that he was instantly, at age 61, catapulted into the front rank of Hollywood character actors, where he would remain for more than 20 years.

Coburn's subtlety and versatility charmed moviegoers and critics alike. Critic Otis Ferguson once said, "He always seems to me as though the part were made for him, as though he were there and not even thinking about acting—which of course demands the best and only true thinking about acting."

In 1939 he was Cary Grant's father in **In Name Only,** deceived by daughter-in-law Kay Francis and realizing only at the *dénouement* that Carole Lombard is the woman Grant should marry. In **Made for Each Other** he was James Stewart's stern boss, with Miss Lombard again the co-star. **Bachelor Mother** cast him as a department-store owner watching romance bloom between his son, David Niven, and shopgirl Ginger Rogers. He played a research scientist in **Idiot's Delight,** and in **The Story of Alexander Graham Bell** was Loretta Young's father and Spring Byington's husband, helping Don Ameche invent the telephone.

The Captain Is a Lady (40) was a comedy in which he disguises himself as a woman to accompany wife Beulah Bondi to an old folks' home, already populated by the likes of Billie Burke and Helen Broderick. In **Three Faces West** he was a Viennese refugee doctor whose daughter falls in love with John Wayne. And he played Bing Crosby's stern tycoon father in **The Road to Singapore.**

In 1941 Charles Coburn had his *annus mirabilis.* A supporting actor in one year rarely gets parts such as he played in **Kings Row, The Devil and Miss Jones** and **The Lady Eve;** had he not been in his mid-sixties by this time, they would have made him a star.

In **Kings Row** he gave his greatest dramatic performance, as the sadistic small-town surgeon, Dr. Gordon, unnecessarily amputating Ronald Reagan's legs because of attentions paid to the doctor's daughter, calling the operation a punishment for "wickedness." The benevolent paterfamilias had suddenly turned into an actor of great dramatic power—but never again would he be given a role to match this one.

His other two outstanding roles that year were both in comedies. In **The Devil and Miss Jones** (for which he received the first of his three Oscar nominations as best supporting actor) he was once again a department-store owner, the world's richest man, who learns a lesson in humanity from employee Jean Arthur, while at the same time getting involved in a senior-citizen romance with Spring Byington. **The Lady Eve** gave him one of his finest comedic roles, as "Handsome Harry," a crooked card sharp, joining forces with his daughter, Barbara Stanwyck, to fleece Henry Fonda in this superb comedy classic directed by Preston Sturges. He also played Robert Young's father in **H.M. Pulham, Esq.,** and in **Unexpected Uncle** was a former steel tycoon who gives away $40 million and preaches the gospel of happiness as an itinerant horseshoe pitcher.

Coburn's one good role in 1942, under John Huston's direction, was as Bette Davis' lecherous old uncle in the overheated drama **In This Our Life,** inviting her to come and live with him (she declines). The bullying, arrogant uncle has cheated Miss Davis' father in business, and now he has no scruples about feeling an incestuous passion for her. But that pas-

sion is pathetically quenched when a doctor tells him he has only weeks left to live.

He was back in stride in a hit comedy in 1943, winning the Oscar as best supporting actor for his performance in **The More the Merrier,** revolving around the apartment shortage in wartime Washington; he and Joel McCrea are sharing Jean Arthur's digs. He simply walked off with the movie. **Heaven Can Wait** cast him as Don Ameche's plain-speaking grandfather; the New York Times called him "a curmudgeon full of venom and gleeful naughtiness." In **Together Again** (44) he was Irene Dunne's father, and in the historical epic **Wilson** he played a Princeton professor.

As a widower, the aging Coburn (now in his late sixties) was quite the gay blade in wartime Hollywood, and was frequently seen at Sunset Strip nightclubs doing a torrid tango with some lovely young starlet.

He was grandly elegant as the star of **Colonel Effingham's Raid** (45), playing a retired Army colonel living in a small Georgia town and fighting to keep its traditions alive, and in **Shady Lady** he was once again a professional card sharp. His final Oscar nomination came for his superb performance as little Dean Stockwell's grandfather in **The Green Years** (46), portraying the rascally old gentleman with a splendidly old-fashioned air but blending much sentiment into the frequently comical proceedings. In director Alfred Hitchcock's **The Paradine Case** (47) he was an elderly lawyer who tries to help Gregory Peck, and in **Lured** he was a police inspector assisting a frightened Lucille Ball.

Coburn played Barbara Stanwyck's father once again, a strong-willed business tycoon, in **B.F.'s Daughter** (48), and in **Louisa** (50) he was once again courting Spring Byington, this time with Edmund Gwenn for a rival. In **Monkey Business** (52) he was the elderly scientist ogling Marilyn Monroe and helping Cary Grant experiment with chimpanzees. In **Has Anybody Seen My Gal?** he shamelessly stole every scene he was in, as a millionaire who returns after many years to see whether the family of the girl who once jilted him is worthy of inheriting his fortune.

In **Gentlemen Prefer Blondes** (53) he was a rich old playboy who now went after Marilyn Monroe much more seriously (to little effect). There was, finally, another good villainous role in the *film noir* **The Long Wait** (54), as Anthony Quinn's former employer, the financier behind the mob. And he walked off with the film again in **How to Be Very, Very Popular** (55) as a college president who will graduate anyone with money.

At age 80 the actor had a cameo as Hippocrates

in the absurd farce-drama **The Story of Mankind** (57), and in **How to Murder a Rich Uncle** he was, of course, the uncle, fending off a batch of murderous relatives. He was the perfect choice to do a cameo as Benjamin Franklin in **John Paul Jones** (59), and ended his film career in 1960 with **Pepe.**

Charles Coburn died in 1961 at the age of 84, but he lives on whenever you turn the TV dial late at night and watch one of the wonderful comedies or fine dramas in which, with practiced ease, he brazenly stole so many scenes from some of Hollywood's greatest stars.

THE FILMS OF CHARLES COBURN

1934: Say It with Flowers.

1935: *Credit uncertain:* The People's Enemy.

1938: Of Human Hearts, Vivacious Lady; Yellow Jack; Lord Jeff.

1939: Made for Each Other; In Name Only; Stanley and Livingstone; The Story of Alexander Graham Bell; Bachelor Mother; Idiot's Delight.

1940: Edison, the Man; The Road to Singapore; The Captain Is a Lady; Florian; Three Faces West.

1941: Kings Row; The Devil and Miss Jones; The Lady Eve; H.M. Pulham, Esq.; Our Wife; Unexpected Uncle.

1942: In This Our Life; George Washington Slept Here.

1943: The More the Merrier; Heaven Can Wait; The Constant Nymph; Princess O'Rourke; My Kingdom for a Cook.

1944: Wilson; Together Again; The Impatient Years; Knickerbocker Holiday.

1945: Colonel Effingham's Raid; A Royal Scandal; Rhapsody in Blue; Over 21; Shady Lady.

1946: The Green Years.

1947: The Paradine Case; Lured.

1948: B.F.'s Daughter; Green Grass of Wyoming.

1949: Everybody Does It; The Doctor and the Girl; Yes Sir, That's My Baby; The Gal Who Took the West; Peggy; Impact.

1950: Louisa; Mr. Music.

1951: The Highwayman.

1952: Monkey Business; Has Anybody Seen My Gal?

1953: Gentlemen Prefer Blondes; Trouble Along the Way.

1954: The Long Wait; The Rocket Man.

1955: How to Be Very, Very Popular.

1956: Around the World in 80 Days; The Power and the Prize.

1957: Town on Trial; The Story of Mankind.

1958: How to Murder a Rich Uncle.

1959: Stranger in My Arms; John Paul Jones; The Remarkable Mr. Pennypacker.

1960: Pepe.

Behold the angry millionaire:
WALTER CONNOLLY

Walter Connolly had a specialty. It was playing the irate, choleric millionaire father of the female star of the movie (usually a screwball comedy), holding himself responsible for spoiling his bratty daughter. Lucky for him that there were so many parts like that in Hollywood films of the Thirties.

Actually, his range was wider than that. He could be an impatient newspaper editor, a senile night watchman, a small-town doctor, an elderly senator or judge, a beer-loving Graustarkian duke, or a famous detective (he played both Nero Wolfe and Father Brown). But he was at his best in angry roles—blustering, irascible or apoplectic, often going into a towering rage.

Heavy-set and flabby, with a thick black mustache, a squeaky voice and a spluttery speech pattern, he is instantly recognizable to film buffs, although he had but a short hour in the sun, making only 46 films in a career almost precisely spanning the decade of the Thirties and dying at an all-too-early age.

Connolly was born April 8, 1887, in Cincinnati, and educated at St. Xavier College there and also at the University of Dublin (Ireland). He first worked as a bank clerk, but then decided on an acting career. "Bankers' hours" allowed him time to study acting, and before long he had left the teller's cage for the theater. Soon he was appearing on the Broadway stage, which he continued to do for many years before finally being persuaded to enter the movies by Columbia Pictures czar Harry Cohn. (Among those Broadway roles, he appeared with Lillian Gish in 1930's **Uncle Vanya.**)

The actor married stage actress Nedda Harrigan in 1923, and they had a daughter, Ann. Miss Harrigan appeared in about a dozen films in the sound era.

Connolly made his first movie appearance in 1932. In **Washington Merry-Go-Round** he was an elderly senator who wins a lot of money at poker because an ambitious lobbyist allows him to, and in **No More Orchids** he was the best thing in the picture as Carole Lombard's self-sacrificing banker father, deliberately crashing his own plane to give her the benefits of his insurance policy. Back on the Broadway stage, he co-starred opposite Pauline Lord in **The Late Christopher Bean** (he wasn't cast in the movie version).

In director Frank Capra's strikingly offbeat film

The Bitter Tea of General Yen (33) he played Mr. Jones, the adviser and financier to the Chinese general (Nils Asther), and he was a self-styled shanty-town preacher in **Man's Castle.** In Capra's **Lady for a Day** he sported a goatee as Count Romero, the future father-in-law of the ingenue. **Paddy, the Next Best Thing** gave him a good part as the father of Irish tomboy Janet Gaynor. In **East of Fifth Avenue** he was an elderly man who, with his wife, decides to take his own life.

It was Claudette Colbert's turn to be his daughter in Capra's smash hit **It Happened One Night** (34); he was frustrated and enraged as he tried to keep her from marrying a playboy, and—at first—equally upset when she fell for reporter Clark Gable. The actor was the theatrical backer of John Barrymore in the comedy classic **Twentieth Century,** the irascible captain in **The Captain Hates the Sea** (the last film of the declining star John Gilbert), Myrna Loy's and Helen Vinson's wealthy father in Capra's **Broadway**

Bill, Janet Gaynor's Scandinavian financier father in **Servants' Entrance,** a night-court judge in **Lady by Choice,** and an aging hospital head clashing with assistant Ralph Bellamy in **Once to Every Woman.**

But his best role that year was one that Emil Jannings in his prime might have played. In **Whom the Gods Destroy** Connolly had a fine dramatic part as a theatrical producer caught in a Titanic-like shipwreck; panic-stricken after heroically saving a number of lives, he saves himself by donning a woman's coat so he can get into a lifeboat. He returns home to find himself idolized as a dead hero, and so goes on for years concealing his identity from his wife and family.

In 1935 he became the screen's first portrayer of G.K. Chesterton's clergyman detective in **Father Brown, Detective,** and he looked bored as Margaret Sullavan's drunken, aristocratic father in the soppy Civil War drama **So Red the Rose.** In **She Couldn't Take It** he played a man nailed for tax evasion and sent to prison, where he makes fellow inmate George Raft the executor of his will and then drops dead; Raft later tames Connolly's daughter, Joan Bennett (Billie Burke played Connolly's wife). And he was a prison warden in **One Way Ticket.** In that year he also took time out to star on Broadway in **The Bishop Misbehaves.**

Back on screen, he was in his element as Myrna Loy's angry millionaire father in the comedy classic **Libeled Lady** (36). He was excellent as the beer-swilling Duke Max of Bavaria, father of Grace Moore, in **The King Steps Out;** his wife calls him "a grease-spot on the pages of history." In **Soak the Rich** he once again played a choleric tycoon, with his daughter falling in love with a radical.

The part for which Connolly is probably best remembered is his irate, dyspeptic newspaper editor in the fine comedy-drama **Nothing Sacred** (37), threatening reporter Fredric March, "I'll take your heart out and stuff it like an olive!" He was the gambling uncle, an ingratiating old rascal, in **The Good Earth,** an elderly and henpecked Supreme Court justice in **First Lady,** a munitions tycoon whose daughter is kidnapped by Victor McLaglen in **Nancy Steele Is Missing,** and Rex Stout's corpulent detective Nero Wolfe in **The League of Frightened Men,** his performance suffering by comparison with that of Edward Arnold, who had played the part previously and whose personality was more suited to it.

It was back to angry millionaires again in **Four's a Crowd** (38), as the blustering, eccentric father of Olivia de Havilland, and one of the most hated men in the country. He stayed angry as the boss of newsreel cameraman Clark Gable in **Too Hot to Handle,** and played a district attorney turned prison warden in **Penitentiary;** his daughter (Jean Parker) falls in love with a convict Connolly has sent to prison.

In **Fifth Avenue Girl** (39) he turned benevolent as an industrialist neglected by his social-climbing family and then meeting jobless Ginger Rogers, who straightens everything out. **Those High Gray Walls** cast him as a small-town doctor imprisoned for shielding an outlaw whose family he knew; the prison physician at first scorns Connolly's humane philosophy, but is eventually won over. In the title role of the biographical musical **The Great Victor Herbert** he looked very much like the famed composer. He played a dyspeptic tycoon in **Good Girls Go to Paris.** In his last film, **The Adventures of Huckleberry Finn,** he played the comic role of the King, a hobo who befriends Mickey Rooney. (At some unspecified time the actor had also played Charlie Chan on the radio.)

Walter Connolly was only 53 when he died in 1940. Had he lived on, his career might have suffered. In the postwar era, how many films had parts for choleric millionaires with spoiled daughters?

THE FILMS OF WALTER CONNOLLY

1932: Washington Merry-Go-Round; No More Orchids; Man Against Woman.
1933: The Bitter Tea of General Yen; Lady for a Day; Man's Castle; Paddy, the Next Best Thing; East of Fifth Avenue; Master of Men.
1934: It Happened One Night; Twentieth Century; Broadway Bill; Lady by Choice; The Captain Hates the Sea; Servants' Entrance; Whom the Gods Destroy; Eight Girls in a Boat; Once to Every Woman; White Lies. *Credit uncertain:* Many Happy Returns.
1935: Father Brown, Detective; So Red the Rose; She Couldn't Take It; One Way Ticket.
1936: Libeled Lady; The King Steps Out; Soak the Rich; The Music Goes 'Round.
1937: Nothing Sacred; The Good Earth; Nancy Steele Is Missing; Let's Get Married; First Lady; The League of Frightened Men.
1938: Too Hot to Handle; Four's a Crowd; Penitentiary; Start Cheering.
1939: The Great Victor Herbert; Fifth Avenue Girl; The Adventures of Huckleberry Finn; Those High Gray Walls; The Girl Downstairs; Good Girls Go to Paris; Bridal Suite; Coast Guard.

Flutter, flutter:
LAURA HOPE CREWS

"Flibbertigibbet" might be the perfect word to describe Laura Hope Crews. She fidgeted, fussed and fluttered in comic-hysteric roles.

Her typical part was a sweetly poisonous mother or society matron, trying to conceal her nasty thoughts with lovable manners. One writer has called her "a snappish pudding of a woman." She was round, rumpled, pillow-like, with glittering eyes and a pie-shaped face.

In three major films the actress was either a procuress or the madam of a brothel. She was definitely not easy to love, but throughout the Thirties she gave skillful portrayals of a certain type of woman you might have encountered in real life.

Miss Crews was born December 12, 1879, in San Francisco, the daughter of a carpenter and a stage actress. She made her debut in stock at age four, "retiring" three years later to attend school. She returned to the boards at 19 as an ingenue with San Francisco's Alcazar Stock Company, and three years later, in 1901, made it to Broadway as a leading lady, playing opposite John Drew (the uncle of the three Barrymores) and Sir Herbert Beerbohm Tree, and touring with them. In 1906 she was the leading lady in **Brown of Harvard** on Broadway. She appeared with Mary Boland in 1913 in Shakespeare's **Much Ado About Nothing.** Then she made a quick side trip to films, starring in **The Fighting Hope** (15).

Back on Broadway, she was in **Peter Ibbetson** in 1917, and co-starred with Alfred Lunt in **Romance and Arabella.** In 1921 she was the star in A.A. Milne's **Mr. Pim Passes By.** In her forties now, she had hit her stride as a character star, appearing in such plays as **Ariadne,** Noel Coward's **Hay Fever** (25) and Sidney Howard's **The Silver Cord** (26), in which she scored a triumph as a monstrous mother. In 1928 she co-starred in Ferenc Mólnar's **Olympia.** During this period she also reportedly was one of the older actresses who had affairs with the young Clark Gable.

In 1928, as the director of the summer-stock version of **Mr. Pim Passes By** at the Cape Playhouse in Dennis, Massachusetts, Miss Crews gave a young, inexperienced actress a break by casting her in a small part. The 20-year-old, with some coaching from Miss Crews, proved successful, and Bette Davis was on her way to fame. At a later date she would have an opportunity to show her gratitude.

Miss Crews then went to Hollywood, arriving

during the transition to sound films to work as a speech coach. Her first assignment was with the star Norma Talmadge, but she could do little for that lady's emphatic Brooklyn accent, and sadly watched her retire from the screen. Colleen Moore was another of her students. She also served as an associate producer whose primary function was to find suitable stage plays for filming and to train actors for the talkies.

With her considerable stage experience, it was inevitable that she would start acting in films herself, and in 1929 she appeared in **Charming Sinners,** in a supporting role. That year she also wrote the screenplay for the Gloria Swanson starrer **The Trespasser,** according to some sources, although others credit the screenplay to the director, Edmund Goulding. For three more years, though, she continued to work primarily as a speech coach and associate producer.

In 1932 Miss Crews returned to screen acting,

appearing in **New Morals for Old** and getting good notices as Robert Young's prudish, Victorian mother (and Lewis Stone's wife), sniffing her disapproval of her son's romance with vamp Myrna Loy. She went through part of the filming of director George Cukor's **Rockabye,** as Constance Bennett's mother, but producer David O. Selznick scrapped her footage and that of Phillips Holmes, and began shooting again with Jobyna Howland and Joel McCrea in the parts.

In 1933 the actress reprised her 1926 stage success as the poisonous, clinging mother in the film of **The Silver Cord.** It was a devastating portrait of the kind of mom that most of us are glad we don't have. Skillfully directed by John Cromwell, she played the possessive mother of Joel McCrea (married to Irene Dunne) and Eric Linden (engaged to Frances Dee). Hating all men because of her own failed marriage, Mrs. Phelps tries to possess her sons and keep them from marrying. In the end, Miss Dunne tells off the selfish woman and gives McCrea an ultimatum to choose between them; fortunately, he gives Mom the heave-ho. Meanwhile, Miss Dee nearly kills herself after Linden jilts her.

Film historian Jerry Vermilye was to say years later that in this film the actress "delivers an awe-inspiring performance in a long and verbose part that requires effusive speech, subtle charm, thinly veiled self-pity, snobbishness and cutting insults. Mrs. Phelps is often not what she seems, and it's the fascination of watching such an incredible monster in action that holds our interest, especially when the part is spun out with the wealth of detail that [she] invests in it."

That year she also played Clive Brook's mother in **If I Were Free** (Miss Dunne was again the star) and, going from the sublime to the ridiculous, was the overprotecting mother of comedian Slim Summerville in **Out All Night,** trying to break up his marriage to ZaSu Pitts. But she hadn't yet given up the New York stage; she co-starred with Roland Young in the play **Her Master's Voice.** (Three years later she repeated the role in the movie version.)

Miss Crews had a good part in the screen version of Edith Wharton's novel **The Age of Innocence** (34) as the mother of Julie Haydon, the wife with whom John Boles is stuck even though he really loves Irene Dunne. In **Behold My Wife,** she and H.B. Warner were Gene Raymond's parents, shocked because he has married an American Indian (Sylvia Sidney). She played the mother superior of a convent in **The Melody Lingers On** (35).

One of her best roles came in the classic drama **Camille** (36), under George Cukor's direction, in a bravura performance as the cigar-smoking procuress, the stout and flighty Prudence, passing dirty jokes (unheard on the screen) around the dinner table to Greta Garbo and other friends. In **Her Master's Voice** she unwisely advised son-in-law Edward Everett Horton to ask for a raise; he lost his job instead.

The actress was excellent as a grand duchess of Russian extraction who purports to run a high-class haven for sophisticated ladies in the 1937 Marlene Dietrich starrer **Angel;** actually, the place is a fancy brothel. In **The Road Back** she played the aunt of a German soldier. In 1938 Miss Crews supported Bette Davis, now a superstar, in **The Sisters,** running a thinly disguised house of ill fame where Miss Davis finds shelter for a while after losing her child by Errol Flynn. She also supported both Bing Crosby and Bob Hope, but separately (in **Dr. Rhythm** and **Thanks for the Memory** respectively).

Undoubtedly her most famous role—but definitely not her best one—was as Aunt Pittypat, the fluttery flower of Southern aristocracy, in **Gone With the Wind** (39). Pittypat is seen as idiotic, constantly revealing her folly; critics tended to dislike the actress' performance. She was also a supercilious dowager in **The Rains Came,** played a singer named Carlotta Salvini in the Bing Crosby film **The Star Maker,** and had a cameo as an alcoholic phony clairvoyant assisted by Clark Gable in **Idiot's Delight.** The following year she was Miriam Hopkins' mother in **The Lady with Red Hair,** and played Mrs. Luxury, the wife of Nigel Bruce, in the Shirley Temple starrer **The Blue Bird.**

Miss Crews, now in her sixties, was excellent in **The Flame of New Orleans** (41) as a worldly-wise dowager imparting the facts of life to Marlene Dietrich on the eve of the latter's wedding. In her last film, **One Foot in Heaven,** she and husband Gene Lockhart are the town's wealthy leading citizens who maliciously spread lies about clergyman Fredric March's son because the minister ousted all the middle-aged singers from the choir and substituted children.

The actress was then to have appeared in **The Man Who Came to Dinner;** she had largely been reduced to coaching actors in speech and taking small parts where she could find them. One of the film's stars, Bette Davis, remembering the older woman's kindness of the past, went out of her way to be nice to her, and in return Miss Crews gave her a jewel-encrusted watch that the star always cherished. Unfortunately, before the film was sent out to theaters all of Miss Crews' scenes were cut from the release print.

In 1942 she briefly succeeded Josephine Hull as

one of the murderous little old ladies in the Broadway play **Arsenic and Old Lace,** with Erich von Stroheim substituting for Boris Karloff in the villain's role. It was the last acting she would ever do. The actress, who had never married, died that year at 62.

But film buffs can still find ways to see, on the big or small screen, the doings of fluttery Aunt Pittypat, the lewd procuress Patience, or, best of all, that absolutely horrible mother Mrs. Phelps, played by that wonderful actress Laura Hope Crews.

THE FILMS OF LAURA HOPE CREWS

1915: The Fighting Hope.
1929: Charming Sinners.
1932: New Morals for Old.
1933: The Silver Cord; I Loved You Wednesday; If I Were Free; Blind Adventure; Ever in My Heart; Female; Out All Night.
1934: The Age of Innocence; Behold My Wife; Rafter Romance; Lightning Strikes Twice.
1935: Escapade; The Melody Lingers On.
1936: Camille; Her Master's Voice.
1937: Angel; The Road Back; Confession.
1938: The Sisters; Doctor Rhythm; Thanks for the Memory.

1939: Gone With the Wind; The Rains Came; Idiot's Delight; Remember?; Reno; The Star Maker; The Hunchback of Notre Dame.
1940: The Blue Bird; Lady with Red Hair; The Girl from Avenue A; I'm Nobody's Sweetheart Now.
1941: The Flame of New Orleans; One Foot in Heaven.

NOTE: Miss Crews was replaced part way through the filming of the 1932 movie **Rockabye** and all her scenes were reshot with another actress. Additionally, all of her scenes were deleted from the release print of the 1941 film **The Man Who Came to Dinner.**

The patriarch:
DONALD CRISP

He was one of the pioneers.

Donald Crisp started as a film actor in 1910, working for director D.W. Griffith when movies were still in their infancy. After playing one of the most obnoxious villains in screen history in a famous film of the silent era, he later became Hollywood's grand old man, portraying mostly lovable fathers and grandfathers until he was in his eighties, chalking up more than half a century on the screen and winning an Academy Award in the process. He was also a prolific film director in the silent era; in fact, of all the actors who became directors while they continued to fill acting roles, he directed the most movies.

He could be stern, genial or ruthless, but always with the Scottish burr that he never lost in his 93 years.

Crisp was born July 27, 1880, in Aberfeldy, Scotland, and educated at Oxford. He fought and was wounded in the Boer War in South Africa. Arriving in the United States in 1906, he appeared in stage plays, worked as a stage manager, and also sang in operas before going to Hollywood in 1910, at age 30, to work for director Griffith, who had just moved his film operations there from New York City. (Griffith had begun directing in 1908.)

Hollywood's output in 1910 consisted entirely of shorts, the feature-length film in the United States still being three years away. Crisp's first film for Griffith was **The Two Paths** (10). He was soon appearing regularly in Griffith's productions, and before long was an assistant director for him as well. He served in the latter capacity on **The Birth of a Nation** in 1915, directing some battle scenes and also playing General Grant. He also may have played a small part in **Intolerance** (16).

Crisp directed **Ramona** (16), beginning a 15-year career behind the megaphone during which he would appear as an actor but rarely, only to abandon directing permanently at the beginning of the sound era and take up acting again with a vengeance.

His most famous acting role in the silent era, however, came in 1919, in Griffith's **Broken Blossoms,** in which, overacting horrendously, he played one of the screen's most despicable villains, the prizefighter Battling Burrows, viciously beating to death his daughter (Lillian Gish).

In 1919 Crisp was divorced from his first wife, Marie Stark. In 1932 he married screenwriter Jane Murfin, a union that ended in divorce in 1944; Miss

Murfin wrote the screenplays for many notable films, especially works directed by George Cukor and John Cromwell.

The actor directed a total of 46 films during the period 1916-30 (while at the same time acting in 14 movies). Few could be called classics; mostly they were routine dramas and comedies, then, in the middle and late Twenties, historical costume dramas. They seldom featured major stars, but among the stars he did direct were Joseph Schildkraut, Leatrice Joy, Charles Ray, Rod La Rocque, Lupe Velez, William Boyd, Bessie Love and Mary Astor. He handled just two really top productions during this period: **Don Q, Son of Zorro** (25), starring Douglas Fairbanks, in which the director also played the villain, Don Sebastiani, and **The Navigator** (24), starring Buster Keaton (who co-directed), in which Crisp did a cameo as a hideous face grinning through a porthole. The director also starred in his own **The Bonnie Brier Bush,** as the stern deacon of a Scottish church.

Working as an actor under other directors, he played a faithful old Scot in the Fairbanks starrer **The Black Pirate** (26) and starred as Leif Ericsson in **The Viking** (28). In **Trent's Last Case** (29), director Howard Hawks' version of E.C. Bentley's classic detective whodunit, he starred in a fine performance as the villainous victim, Sigsbee Manderson, apparently murdered but who turns out to have committed suicide; he was vicious and lunatic enough to shoot himself in such a way as to have his death blamed on his secretary because of circumstantial evidence. In **The Pagan** he was the no-good South Seas trader trying to steal Renee Adoree from Ramon Novarro, and in **The Return of Sherlock Holmes** he played the villain, Col. Sebastian Moran.

Crisp, now entering his fifties, played a vicious blackmailer in **Scotland Yard** (30), and was one of the rubber-plantation employees in the Clark Gable-Jean Harlow starrer **Red Dust** (32). He was the ideal choice to play stern Scottish elders in **The Little Minister** and **What Every Woman Knows,** both 1934 films adapted from Sir James M. Barrie's plays, and in **The Key** he was an Irish freedom fighter captured by the British and just barely saved from hanging. **The Crime Doctor** cast him as the district attorney, and in **The Life of Vergie Winters** he was an unpleasant tavern owner who destroys Ann Harding's reputation. He had a key role as one of the mutineers in the classic **Mutiny on the Bounty** (35).

He was stern as a colonel in **The Charge of the Light Brigade** (36), and no less so as Huntley in director John Ford's **Mary of Scotland.** In **A Woman Rebels** he played Katharine Hepburn's icy Victorian father. **Beloved Enemy** cast him once again as a die-hard Irish rebel. He played a lawyer helping Emile Zola (Paul Muni) defend Alfred Dreyfus (Joseph Schildkraut) in the biographical classic **The Life of Emile Zola** (37), and was Henry Fonda's domineering father in **That Certain Woman,** trying to keep Bette Davis from seeing her child by Fonda. He was also a police captain in **The Great O'Malley** and the presiding judge in **Confession.**

The actor was a senior officer in **The Dawn Patrol** (38) and had a key role as a family friend in the Bette Davis-Errol Flynn starrer **The Sisters.** He was prominent as a doctor in Miss Davis' **Jezebel,** and gave a fine performance as a relentless police inspector in **The Amazing Dr. Clitterhouse.** Continuing to work in top-of-the-line film classics, he played Dr. Kenneth in **Wuthering Heights** (39) and Marechal Bazaine in **Juarez.** He kept busy in Bette Davis vehicles: He was admirable as the understanding, compassionate family doctor in **The Old Maid** and played Sir Francis Bacon in **The Private Lives of Elizabeth and Essex. In Daughters Courageous** Fay Bainter was planning to marry him until her ex-husband, Claude Rains, reappeared on the scene.

Crisp portrayed the stern Minister Althoff in **Dr. Ehrlich's Magic Bullet** (40) and the kindly Brother Superior of the monastery in **Brother Orchid,** supporting Edward G. Robinson in both cases. Continuing to display his versatility, he was James Cagney's boxing trainer, Scotty McPherson, in **City for Conquest,** was one of the noblemen of Queen Elizabeth I's court (once again) in **The Sea Hawk,** and played a priest in **Knute Rockne—All-American.** In the following year he was Lana Turner's father in the Spencer Tracy version of **Dr. Jekyll and Mr. Hyde.**

Through all these years the actor had been good, dependable, and relatively dull, delivering performances that filmgoers would not remember a week later. All that changed in 1941 with director John Ford's **How Green Was My Valley.** Surely there was no actor who could have brought more strength and character to the difficult role of the aging coal miner, Mr. Morgan, patriarch of a large Welsh family. It was an affecting portrait of strength, goodness and idiosyncrasy, and it won him a deserved Academy Award as best supporting actor—the only time anyone ever defeated Walter Brennan for that honor out of the four times he competed for it.

Donald Crisp at age 61 was now typecast as a stern but good-hearted patriarch, and he would play that role on screen for another generation to come. He was a bit long in the tooth to be playing the fathers of Roddy McDowall and Elizabeth Taylor (in **Lassie Come Home** and **National Velvet** respectively)—after all, Lillian Gish, whose father he had once portrayed, was old enough to be little Miss Taylor's *grandmother*—but he fitted in well with the animal-lover ambiance, well enough so that in 1945 he was the father again in **Son of Lassie.** He also played Gregory Peck's father in **The Valley of Decision.** He did another Lassie in 1948, and in the following year there was one final one. In all these films the actor got the opportunity to roll his R's with great skill, since they had Scottish settings.

In private life, Crisp was one of Hollywood's wealthiest actors. A director of the Bank of America, he was responsible for approving most of the loans by that bank, California's biggest financial institution, to would-be film producers. This was occasionally embarrassing to his acting career, because sometimes he had to turn down prospective employers.

The Lassie series having come to an end, he got an excellent part as Gary Cooper's rival tobacco tycoon in **Bright Leaf** (50), dispossessing the star of his land. But then Cooper becomes wealthier and more powerful, and ends up marrying Crisp's daughter (Patricia Neal), which drives the older man to suicide. He was off the screen for a couple of years, and returned to play Tyrone Power's old Irish father in John Ford's **The Long Gray Line** in 1955. In that same year he was excellent as James Stewart's enemy in the fine Western **The Man from Laramie,** as a megalomaniacal land baron, ruling an entire county. He is an almost Shakespearean character, going blind, thrown off course by his love for his wayward son, and who in the end tries to partly atone for his sins by finally telling the truth. In one scene he tries to tell Stewart about his nightmares; it was a memorable piece of acting.

In 1958 he had the role of the Cardinal, head of the Boston archdiocese, in Ford's **The Last Hurrah,** and also played a powerful land owner in the Robert Taylor Western **Saddle the Wind.** Crisp was now turning 80. He played one of the misanthropes reformed by young Hayley Mills in the remake of **Pollyanna** (60), and it was back to doggie doings in **A Dog of Flanders** (59) and **Greyfriars Bobby** (61), two more children's classics. His final film was **Spencer's Mountain** (63), in which at age 82 he played Henry Fonda's father, as he had done a quarter of a century earlier.

Donald Crisp died in 1974 at the age of 93. He had been a part of American movies from their infancy through the glory years into the period of decline—more than half a century working for the industry. Truly, few persons better deserved to be called a film pioneer.

THE FILMS OF DONALD CRISP

NOTE: Only feature-length films are listed, which means that his films up through 1913, all of which were shorts, are omitted. This filmography lists only the films in which he had an *acting* role, so the many movies he *directed* are not included unless he also acted in them.

1914: The Battle of the Sexes; The Great Leap; The Escape; Home Sweet Home; The Avenging Conscience.
1915: The Birth of a Nation; The Love Route; The Blue or the Gray; The Girl of Yesterday; The Foundling; The Commanding Officer; May Blossom; Such a Little Queen; Bred in the Bone.
1916: Ramona. *Credit uncertain:* Intolerance.
1917: Joan the Woman; The Countess Charming.
1918: One More American.
1919: Broken Blossoms.
1921: The Bonnie Brier Bush.
1924: The Navigator.
1925: Don Q, Son of Zorro.
1926: The Black Pirate.
1928: The Viking; The River Pirate.
1929: Trent's Last Case; The Pagan; The Return of Sherlock Holmes.
1930: Scotland Yard.
1931: Svengali; Kick In.
1932: Red Dust; A Passport to Hell.
1933: Broadway Bad.
1934: What Every Woman Knows; The Little Minister; British Agent; The Life of Vergie Winters; The Key; Crime Doctor.
1935: Mutiny on the Bounty; Oil for the Lamps of China; Vanessa, Her Love Story; Laddie.
1936: The Charge of the Light Brigade; Mary of Scotland; A Woman Rebels; Beloved Enemy; The White Angel.
1937: The Life of Emila Zola; Parnell; Confession; That Certain Woman; The Great O'Malley.
1938: Jezebel; The Sisters; The Dawn Patrol; The Amazing Dr. Clitterhouse; Valley of the Giants; Comet over Broadway; Sergeant Murphy; The Beloved Brat.
1939: Wuthering Heights; Juarez; The Old Maid; The Private Lives of Elizabeth and Essex; Daughters Courageous; The Oklahoma Kid.
1940: Dr. Ehrlich's Magic Bullet; The Sea Hawk; Brother Orchid; City for Conquest; Knute Rockne—All-American.
1941: How Green Was My Valley; Dr. Jekyll and Mr. Hyde; Shining Victory.
1942: The Gay Sisters; The Battle of Midway (narrator only; documentary).
1943: Forever and a Day; Lassie Come Home.
1944: National Velvet; The Adventures of Mark Twain; The Uninvited.
1945: The Valley of Decision; Son of Lassie.
1947: Ramrod.
1948: Hills of Home; Whispering Smith.
1949: Challenge to Lassie.
1950: Bright Leaf.
1951: Home Town Story.
1954: Prince Valiant.
1955: The Man from Laramie; The Long Gray Line.
1957: Drango.
1958: The Last Hurrah; Saddle the Wind.
1959: A Dog of Flanders.
1960: Pollyanna.
1961: Greyfriars Bobby.
1963: Spencer's Mountain.

Suave, unsmiling villainy:

HENRY DANIELL

He was a superb villain. Incisive, austere and calculating, with cold eyes, a hard unsmiling face, thin lips and a rat-trap mouth, Henry Daniell could be suave or cold-blooded, and was usually splendidly malicious, although he sometimes was sympathetic in offbeat roles. In many films, he was more interesting than the stars.

He adroitly played doctors, lawyers, society gentlemen, and several crazed scientists; he also portrayed Sherlock Holmes' mortal enemy Professor Moriarty, the Nazi leader Von Ribbentrop, William III of England, and Franz Liszt, not to mention Greta Garbo's cynical lover. All in all, while he was a character actor of great range, he is best remembered as one of the screen's great nasties.

His unfriendly face and snide, conceited voice warned audiences not to trust him, yet he usually got away with his treachery until the hero finally did him in at the end. He was best cast as evil advisers in costume dramas, deceiving and manipulating powerful figures.

Charles Henry Daniell was born March 5, 1894 (one source gives May 5 as the date), in London. After completing his schooling he chose acting as a career, and was given a starring role, his first big break, at age 20 in a play that opened in London; as bad luck would have it, opening night was the day England went to war in that summer of 1914. But he persevered, gained a stage reputation, and ultimately ended up in the United States, winning a niche for himself on Broadway in the Twenties. Among other plays, he co-starred with Ethel Barrymore in **The Second Mrs. Tanqueray** in 1924.

Daniell was among the many stage-trained performers called to Hollywood as the sound era began. He played an innocent murder suspect in **Jealousy** (29), starring Fredric March and the doomed, drug-addicted actress Jeanne Eagels; it was Miss Eagels' last film. He also co-starred with Ina Claire in the marital drama **The Awful Truth,** which went unnoticed and was remade to far better effect in 1937 as a screwball comedy classic starring Cary Grant and Irene Dunne. In 1930 he was far down the cast list as a nobleman in **The Last of the Lone Wolf.**

Having made little impression on film audiences, the actor returned to the stage for several years. In 1934 he appeared in an English movie, **Path of Glory,** and in 1935 starred on Broadway as the murderous

villain in **Kind Lady,** a part that Basil Rathbone later played on the screen. He came back to Hollywood in 1936. This time the impression he made in films would be very different.

He scored a triumph in the important role of the Baron de Varville, sometime lover of Greta Garbo, in director George Cukor's superb romantic drama **Camille** (36). Garbo amuses herself with Daniell to discourage her new lover, impetuous young Robert Taylor, who is not so easily dissuaded. Of the two actors, Daniell was by far the superior performer, winning accolades from critics for his suavely perfect, coolly vicious Varville. He gave a richly cynical interpretation of a man so sarcastic that he cannot alter his character even to demonstrate his affection for his mistress.

The actor's future in Hollywood was assured. In that same year he played an unpleasant blackmailer harassing Franchot Tone in **The Unguarded Hour** (it was far from the last time he would be a blackmailer). He was now securely set to play an ongoing variety of tight-mouthed, hard-eyed villains, men you love to hate.

Daniell was married to English writer Ann Knox. Their son, Henry Jr., also became an actor.

The actor's screen nastiness reached new heights in **Under Cover of Night** (37); he was in fine sneering form as a crazed scientist, the cold-blooded killer of five persons, who finally kills himself. In **The Thirteenth Chair** he was the murder victim. He had a small part in **Holiday** (38) as Katharine Hepburn's cousin, an obnoxious right-winger, and he was far down the cast list as La Motte in **Marie Antoinette.** In **The Private Lives of Elizabeth and Essex** (39) he was a noble lord of Elizabeth I's court.

He played a Basil Rathbone-like role in the historical costume-drama **The Sea Hawk** (40), as spy-villain Lord Wolfingham, dueling to the death with Errol Flynn in a set-to that takes them through virtually every room in the palace. Charlie Chaplin chose him for the role of propaganda minister Garbisch (i.e., Joseph Goebbels) in **The Great Dictator,** and in the classic **The Philadelphia Story** he played Sidney Kidd, the malicious editor of Spy magazine who blackmails Cary Grant (by means of withholding a story) into easing journalists James Stewart and Ruth Hussey into Katharine Hepburn's home.

Daniell was the public prosecutor in the Joan Crawford starrer **A Woman's Face** (41). He and John Carradine played sneering Nazi officers in another Crawford outing, **Reunion in France** (42), and he was a saboteur in **Sherlock Holmes and the Voice of Terror,** also appearing as Diana Barrymore's father in **Nightmare.** He was yet another Nazi in the fine drama **Watch on the Rhine** (43), and one of the ultimate Nazis, Hitler's henchman Joachim von Ribbentrop, in **Mission to Moscow.** He played a spy in **Sherlock Holmes in Washington.**

The actor was reprieved from these penny-dreadful roles in 1944 with two fine parts in which he delivered outstanding performances. In **Jane Eyre,** which starred Orson Welles and Joan Fontaine, he gave a malevolently edgy interpretation of Brocklehurst, the sadistic religious fanatic who runs the Lowood School for orphans. And in **The Suspect** he was intense and brilliant as the nosy neighbor who tries to blackmail wife-murderer Charles Laughton, only to end up as the second murder victim.

There were two equally good roles in 1945. In **The Woman in Green** he played the sinister Professor Moriarty to Basil Rathbone's Sherlock Holmes (Rathbone was to call him "the best Moriarty of all"). And he gave one of his greatest performances in pro-

ducer Val Lewton's horror classic **The Body Snatcher,** as a dedicated, brilliant scientist who ends up as a wonderfully malevolent ghoul, a doomed, tortured, hollow-eyed doctor who employs Boris Karloff as a grave robber to furnish corpses for medical experiments. (Later he experiences guilty pangs of conscience.) No one who has seen this movie will ever forget the horrifying final scene in which Daniell, now a haunted murderer, driving a horse-drawn hearse with Karloff's corpse beside him, suddenly sees the shroud fall open and is encircled by the dead man's arms while Karloff's voice seems to intone, "Never get rid of me, never get rid of me." The terrified Daniell loses control of the reins and the hearse crashes, killing him. This is definitely not a film to see just before walking home through a graveyard late at night.

In another 1945 role, he played England's King William III in **Captain Kidd,** and he was the villain in **The Bandit of Sherwood Forest** (46), also taking a good part as composer Franz Liszt in the 1947 film **Song of Love,** although the New York Times thought him "reminiscent of the Phantom of the Opera on a night out." He was also seen again on Broadway, co-starring in **Lady Windermere's Fan** and Shakespeare's **The Winter's Tale,** both in 1946. In the film **Wake of the Red Witch** (48), starring John Wayne, he played co-star Gail Russell's father. The mediocre Yvonne De Carlo outing **Buccaneer's Girl** (50) had him ninth on the cast list as a pirate captain, and at this juncture Daniell decided he wanted out for a while.

The actor returned to the screen four years later, but was wasted in a nothing part in **The Egyptian** (54). **The Prodigal** (55) was more of the same. He had a better role as the father of painter Vincent Van Gogh (Kirk Douglas) in **Lust for Life** (56), and was a businessman in **The Man in the Gray Flannel Suit.** Now in his sixties, he had the cameo role of the Bishop of Beauvais, chief antagonist to Joan of Arc (Hedy Lamarr), in the absurd farce-drama **The Story of Mankind** (57), and played a lawyer in **Witness for the Prosecution,** a doctor in **The Sun Also Rises,** and the judge in **Les Girls.**

In the mediocre horror outing **The Four Skulls of Jonathan Drake** (59) he was involved with a voodoo curse, and in **Voyage to the Bottom of the Sea** (61) he played someone with the real-life surname of another well-known character actor—Dr. Zucco(!). **Five Weeks in a Balloon** (62) found him as an elderly desert sheik, and he was a ruthless advertising tycoon in **Madison Avenue.**

His final role was a very small one, virtually a bit part, as someone called Prince Gregor of

Transylvania in director George Cukor's big hit **My Fair Lady** (64). He collapsed and died on the set in 1963, shortly after completing this minuscule role for the director who had given him such a major role opposite the great Garbo 28 years earlier. According to one source, he had been in more of Cukor's films (five) than anyone except Katharine Hepburn.

Henry Daniell was under-used and often misused by Hollywood. But he remains one of the screen's greatest masters of the art of villainy.

THE FILMS OF HENRY DANIELL

1929: Jealousy; The Awful Truth.
1930: The Last of the Lone Wolf.
1934: Path of Glory.
1936: Camille; The Unguarded Hour.
1937: Madame X; Under Cover of Night; The Thirteenth Chair; The Firefly.
1938: Marie Antoinette; Holiday.
1939: The Private Lives of Elizabeth and Essex; We Are Not Alone.
1940: The Philadelphia Story; The Great Dictator; All This and Heaven, Too; The Sea Hawk.
1941: A Woman's Face; The Feminine Touch; Dressed to Kill; Four Jacks and a Jill.
1942: Random Harvest; Reunion in France; The Great Impersonation; Nightmare; Castle in the Desert; Sherlock Holmes and the Voice of Terror.
1943: Watch on the Rhine; Mission to Moscow; Sherlock Holmes in Washington.
1944: Jane Eyre; The Suspect.

1945: The Body Snatcher; Hotel Berlin; The Woman in Green; Captain Kidd; The Chicago Kid.
1946: The Bandit of Sherwood Forest.
1947: Song of Love; The Exile.
1948: Wake of the Red Witch; Siren of Atlantis.
1949: The Secret of St. Ives.
1950: Buccaneer's Girl.
1954: The Egyptian.
1955: The Prodigal; Diane.
1956: Lust for Life; The Man in the Gray Flannel Suit.
1957: Witness for the Prosecution; The Sun Also Rises; Les Girls; The Story of Mankind; Mr. Cory.
1958: From the Earth to the Moon.
1959: The Four Skulls of Jonathan Drake.
1961: Voyage to the Bottom of the Sea; The Comancheros.
1962: The Chapman Report; The Notorious Landlady; Five Weeks in a Balloon; Madison Avenue.
1964: My Fair Lady.

With a croak and a joke:
ANDY DEVINE

With many actors, their trademark is their voice. And so it was with Andy Devine. His voice was a raucous, high-pitched croak, husky and raspy. To go along with it, he was roly-poly and jolly, which made him ideal for country bumpkins and, later, as the comic sidekick to many a screen cowboy.

This gravely voice and droll persona kept him busy in more than 150 films over a period of half a century. He is said to have made more movies for Universal Studios than any performer in its history, the total being 79.

Devine was born as Jeremiah Schwartz on October 7, 1905, in Flagstaff, Arizona, the son of a hotel owner. A husky (but not yet fat) young man, he was a football star at the University of Santa Clara in California, after attending two other colleges. He arrived in Hollywood in 1926 hoping to become an actor. After a number of unrecorded bit parts in a variety of light silent films, he began to get supporting roles, including parts in "The Collegians" series of shorts.

He played "a sophomore" in the college film **Red Lips** (28) and was a soldier in **We Americans.** In **Hot Stuff** (29) he was back on campus again. He had a very small part as a convict in **The Criminal Code** (31). In **The Spirit of Notre Dame** he had one of the leading roles, as a football player, and in **Law and Order** (32) he played his first Western role, an accidental killer hanged by lawmen. He was back on the gridiron, amusing and dull-witted, in **The All-American** (the first of many films in which he appeared with Richard Arlen), and also had good parts in **The Man from Yesterday** (as Clive Brook's friend), **The Impatient Maiden** (as Una Merkel's boyfriend), and **Tom Brown of Culver** (as one of the cadets). **Three Wise Girls** cast him as a chauffeur, gazing longingly at Jean Harlow but ending up with her roommate, Marie Prevost.

Saturday's Millions (33) was another football epic; the New York Times praised Devine's "good thick-skulled humor." He also had good parts in **Doctor Bull** (as a hypochondriacal soda jerk), **Midnight Mary, Chance at Heaven** and **The Big Cage.** His increasing girth and his squeaky voice had become assets in comedy, and he was kept busy filming.

In 1933 Devine married actress Dorothy House, to whom he had been introduced by Will Rogers. They had two sons, Denny and Tad (both of whom later appeared with him in the 1946 film **Canyon Pas-**

sage). Miss House had one credited film role, in 1932, as a "bathing beauty."

The comedic quality of the actor's parts at this point in time was reflected in the names of his screen characters. In 1934, for example, three of them were called Egghead," "Careful" and "Gravel"—that being the way they were listed in the screen credits, rather than any first and last names. That year he was a chauffeur again in **Upper World,** a World War I pilot in **Hell in the Heavens,** and also had good parts in **The President Vanishes** (as a grocery delivery boy), **Stingaree** (as Richard Dix' valet) and **Wake Up and Dream.**

He played rustic bumpkins in **Way Down East** (35) and in Henry Fonda's debut film, **The Farmer Takes a Wife.** In **Fighting Youth** he was back on the college campus, but in **Hold 'em Yale** he at least got a change of pace as "Liverlips," a small-time Broadway ticket scalper.

Devine was now considered good enough to be

cast as comic relief in the part of Peter in the big-budget production of **Romeo and Juliet** (36)—and he proved himself a true Elizabethan clown. He was the sympathetic boarding-house dweller who is helpful to Janet Gaynor in **A Star Is Born** (37). But **The Road Back** was fatally flawed by the casting of him and Slim Summerville as German soldiers, two of the leading players, in this sequel to **All Quiet on the Western Front.**

The actor began sliding downward into grade "B" programmer pictures. Sometimes he would have a small part in a major film, such as the Irish cop in **Doctor Rhythm** and Fred MacMurray's aircraft mechanic in **Men with Wings** (both 38) and Buck, the stagecoach driver, in the classic **Stagecoach** (39); he also had a key role in 1938's **In Old Chicago.** But in 1939 he began a long string of films as the comic sidekick of Richard Arlen—mediocre, low-budget adventure movies, involving an enormous amount of stock footage and featuring the pair as oilfield workers, miners, lumberjacks or similar blue-collar occupations. These 14 films kept him extremely busy through 1941. After the Arlen films stopped, he frequently partnered Leo Carrillo in a number of "B" Westerns. And Roy Rogers and other screen cowboys benefited from his assistance.

Still, the Arlen-Devine films had their moments. One of the best of these occurred in **Raiders of the Desert** (41) when the tubby comedian, accompanying himself on the ukulele, tried to romance a singularly unimpressed Maria Montez by singing "I'm a Big Bad Bagdad Daddy."

The immediate postwar years brought a spate of second-rate formula Westerns, mainly for Republic,

a Poverty Row studio that specialized in that genre. But there was the occasional first-rank film. Devine, now in his forties, was one of the soldiers in director John Huston's **The Red Badge of Courage** (51) and had a good part in **Island in the Sky** (53). But he was now making only about one film a year. He was the first mate of the ship in **Around the World in 80 Days** (56) and then left the screen for four years, turning his full attention to television, where he had already begun work as Guy Madison's sidekick, Jingles, in the series "Wild Bill Hickok." He also later starred in his own series, "Andy's Gang."

He also worked on the stage, playing Captain Andy in **Show Boat** and, later, the father in **Never Too Late.** But as a veteran of movie Westerns, he would come back to the screen when a good part called. Director John Ford gave him roles in three superior Westerns in 1961 and 1962: **Two Rode Together, How the West Was Won** and **The Man Who Shot Liberty Valance;** in the latter, he played the cowardly sheriff. And he was again a sheriff, this time comical, in **It's a Mad, Mad, Mad, Mad World** (63). He played a judge in **The Ballad of Josie** (67).

Devine, now 65, had the misfortune to be caught in that disaster **Myra Breckinridge** (70), playing a character called Coyote Bill, and was one of the many actors playing cameos in **Won Ton Ton, the Dog Who Saved Hollywood** (76). Meanwhile, only his unique voice was heard in Walt Disney's cartoon features **Robin Hood** (73) and **The Mouse and His Child** (77).

In 1977 Andy Devine died at 71, leaving half a century of movie memories. Who could forget his girth, his mirth, and that inimitable voice?

THE FILMS OF ANDY DEVINE

1928: Lonesome; We Americans; Red Lips.
1929: Naughty Baby; Hot Stuff.
1930: The Criminal Code.
1931: Spirit of Notre Dame; Danger Island (serial).
1932: Law and Order; The Impatient Maiden; The Man from Yesterday; Man Wanted; Tom Brown of Culver; Radio Patrol; Three Wise Girls; Fireman Save My Child; Fast Companions; Destry Rides Again; The All-American.
1933: Doctor Bull; Chance at Heaven; Song of the Eagle; Midnight Mary; Saturday's Millions; The Big Cage; Horseplay; The Cohens and Kellys in Trouble.
1934: The President Vanishes; Upper World; Stingaree; Wake Up and Dream; The Gift of Gab; Hell in the Heavens; Million Dollar Ransom; The Poor Rich; Let's Talk It Over.
1935: Way Down East; The Farmer Takes a Wife; Straight from the Heart; Hold 'em Yale; Fighting Youth; Coronado; Chinatown Squad.
1936: Romeo and Juliet; Small Town Girl; Flying Hostess; The Big Game; Mysterious Crossing; Yellowstone.
1937: A Star Is Born; The Road Back; Double or Nothing; You're a Sweetheart.

1938: In Old Chicago; Men with Wings; Yellow Jack; Doctor Rhythm; The Storm; Strange Faces; Personal Secretary; Swing That Cheer.
1939: Stagecoach; Geronimo; The Spirit of Culver; Tropic Fury; Never Say Die; Mutiny on the Blackhawk; Legion of Lost Flyers.
1940: Torrid Zone; Little Old New York; Trail of the Vigilantes; Buck Benny Rides Again; Hot Steel; Black Diamonds; The Man from Montreal; Margie; Danger on Wheels; When the Daltons Rode; The Leatherpushers; The Devil's Pipeline.
1941: Flame of New Orleans; Mutiny in the Arctic; Lucky Devils; Raiders of the Desert; Badlands of Dakota; A Dangerous Game; South of Tahiti; Road Agent; The Kid from Kansas; Men of the Timberland.
1942: Top Sergeant; Timber; North to the Klondike; Unseen Enemy; Escape from Hong Kong; Between us Girls; Danger in the Pacific; Sin Town.
1943: Corvette K-225; Crazy House; Rhythm of the Islands; Frontier Badmen.
1944: Ali Baba and the Forty Thieves; The Ghost Catchers; Follow the Boys; Babes on Swing Street; Bowery to Broadway.

1945: Sudan; Frontier Gal; That's the Spirit; Frisco Sal.
1946: Canyon Passage.
1947: The Michigan Kid; The Vigilantes Return; Bells of San Angelo; Springtime in the Sierras; The Fabulous Texan; The Marauders; Slave Girl; On the Old Spanish Trail.
1948: The Gallant Legion; The Gay Ranchero; Old Los Angeles; Under California Stars; Eyes of Texas; Grand Canyon Trail; Night-time in Nevada; The Far Frontier.
1949: The Last Bandit.
1950: Never a Dull Moment; The Traveling Saleswoman.
1951: The Red Badge of Courage; New Mexico; Slaughter Trail.
1952: Montana Belle.
1953: Island in the Sky.
1954: Thunder Pass.
1955: Pete Kelly's Blues.
1956: Around the World in 80 Days.
1960: The Adventures of Huckleberry Finn.
1961: Two Rode Together.
1962: How the West Was Won; The Man Who Shot Liberty Valance.
1963: It's a Mad, Mad, Mad, Mad World.
1965: Zebra in the Kitchen.
1967: The Ballad of Josie.
1968: The Road Hustlers.
1970: Myra Breckinridge; The Phynx.
1973: Robin Hood (voice only).
1976: Won Ton Ton, the Dog Who Saved Hollywood; A Whale of a Tale.
1977: The Mouse and His Child (voice only).

The 'Other Woman':
CLAIRE DODD

While middle-aged and elderly actresses were kept very busy in Hollywood films of the Thirties, there were also plenty of roles for attractive young actresses, but these usually were either star turns—glamorous, dramatic or both—or else conventional "leading lady" or "ingenue" parts that demanded little in the way of acting ability, requiring only a pretty face.

For a select few of the younger actresses, typecasting as "The Other Woman" proved beneficial to their careers. "The Other Woman" was an untrustworthy (and usually socially prominent) seductress who schemed to steal the male star from the nominal heroine. Ultimately, of course, the hero woke up to find that she was a no-good two-timer, and returned to the heroine, but in the meantime audiences were treated to a delightful display of bitchery from "The Other Woman."

One of the best of these was Claire Dodd, a chic and dimple-cheeked blonde whose appearance on screen almost invariably sent the message, "Don't trust this woman." Dazzling and deliciously nasty, she could be a seductress, a murdered mistress, a scheming blonde or a treacherous blackmailer. And occasionally she could even be nice—for example, as detective Perry Mason's secretary.

Miss Dodd was born December 29, 1908, in New York City, and as a child studied under tutors. While still in her teens she was signed by impresario Florenz Ziegfeld as a showgirl in his Broadway musical extravaganzas. In 1928 she appeared in his show **Whoopee!,** starring Eddie Cantor, and in 1930 was in the Marilyn Miller musical **Smiles.** That year she made her film debut as one of the "mannequins," as the screen credits put it, in a department store in the Joan Crawford outing **Our Blushing Brides,** and also appeared in the screen version of **Whoopee!** as one of the "Goldwyn Girls" (i.e., the singing and dancing chorus), who also included two other then-unknowns, Betty Grable and Virginia Bruce.

Somewhere along the line the actress was married to Jack M. Strauss. Later came another marriage, to H. Brand Cooper.

She was busy working for Paramount in 1931, appearing, to little notice, as a gold-digger in **Girls About Town** and in small parts in at least two (and possibly as many as six) other films. (Screen credits for some performers at this point in time are often

difficult to authenticate.) In **The Broken Wing** (32) she had her first important role, as a rich society girl who almost wins Melvyn Douglas away from Mexican señorita Lupe Velez. It was her first "Other Woman" part.

The performance caught the attention of Warner Bros., which saw her potential, wooed her away from Paramount and gave her an excellent part in **Lawyer Man,** in which, as a potential breach-of-promise client, she almost destroys attorney William Powell when she tries to frame him on a blackmail charge. She also played a murder victim in **Guilty as Hell.** But her other performances during 1932 were not so noticeable, in films such as **The Match King, Crooner** and **Alias the Doctor,** although in a couple of them she was billed fourth or fifth in the cast.

Miss Dodd could fully appreciate, in 1933, her switch to the Warners lot. In the musical classic **Footlight Parade** she was the society temptress who almost wins over James Cagney from loyal secretary

Joan Blondell, and she also tried to seduce him in **Hard to Handle,** in which she was a promiscuous debutante who loses him to Mary Brian. In **Parachute Jumper,** as racketeer Leo Carrillo's mistress, she hires Douglas Fairbanks Jr. as a chauffeur and all too soon is caught with him in a compromising situation by Carrillo. (Also on hand is Bette Davis, who is hired by the racketeer as a secretary but is secretly in league with Fairbanks and turns Carrillo in to the law.)

Miss Dodd was good in **Ann Carver's Profession** as a dipsomaniac philanderer who steals lawyer Fay Wray's husband, Gene Raymond; Miss Dodd dies accidentally and Raymond is accused of killing her, but is cleared by his wife. She was a blonde Park Avenue menace stealing Helen Twelvetrees' husband in **My Woman,** a villainous actress in **Elmer the Great,** the wife of Frank McHugh in the Bette Davis starrer **Ex-Lady,** and appeared in **Blondie Johnson.**

In **Journal of a Crime** (34) she was the mistress of Adolphe Menjou and was killed by his wife, Ruth Chatterton, after the wife saw the two kissing. **Babbitt** cast her as a designing woman trying to blackmail Guy Kibbee (in the title role) into going along with a crooked real-estate deal. Her best role that year was in **Gambling Lady,** as an ex-girlfriend of Joel McCrea who blackmails his wife, Barbara Stanwyck, into divorcing him. (There was one effective scene in which Miss Dodd keeps losing at the card game "21" and is forced to give up all her jewelry.) A newspaper reviewer wrote, "Miss Dodd...is...invariably assigned to the role of a shallow and discomfited villainess, and again she handled it with a vividness worthy of better things. I suspect that she is one of the most unappreciated of the screen's potentially important figures."

Also that year, she was the white girlfriend of American Indian Richard Barthelmess in **Massacre,** losing him to Ann Dvorak, another Indian. She worked her seductive wiles on Pat O'Brien in **The Personality Kid** (he was married to Glenda Farrell) and also tried to charm him in **I Sell Anything.** She cozied up to Warren William in **Smarty,** and failed to win him away from wife Joan Blondell, but she must have impressed him, for as detective Perry Mason he employed her as his secretary (Della Street) in **The Case of the Curious Bride** (35) and again in **The Case of the Velvet Claws** the following year.

Also in 1935, the actress was a jewel thief in **The Goose and the Gander,** played the love interest of political boss Edward Arnold in **The Glass Key,** and was at her acrid, vindictive best in **The Payoff,** involved with gangsters and proving the undoing of husband James Dunn. In **Don't Bet on Blondes** she was an actress who ultimately succumbs to Warren William; playing a small role as one of her admirers was Errol Flynn in his brief pre-stardom days. In **Roberta,** she temporarily stole Randolph Scott from Irene Dunne.

But 1936 was a weak year for Miss Dodd. She was far down the cast list in the mediocre Humphrey Bogart vehicle **Two Against the World,** and also worked for a Poverty Row studio, Republic, in **Navy Born.** The only good part came in **Murder by an Aristocrat,** as one of the victim's family. In her only 1937 release, **Women Men Marry,** she co-starred as George Murphy's two-timing wife.

There was a good part in **Romance in the Dark** (38). It seems that Miss Dodd, a countess, is loved by John Barrymore and also by tenor John Boles. Well, Boles transforms Gladys Swarthout (an opera star in real life, briefly trying her luck in the movies that year) into a singing celebrity to lure Barrymore away from Miss Dodd—but wouldn't you just know it, Boles falls in love with Miss Swarthout instead. Miss Dodd was a seductive blonde menace again in **Fast Company,** in league with crook Louis Calhern, and was a murder victim in **Charlie Chan in Honolulu.** In **Three Loves Has Nancy** she was an actress who hopes to marry Robert Montgomery but loses him to Janet Gaynor.

There was only one film in 1939, **Woman Doctor,** in which she was still putting the make on somebody, only this time it was Henry Wilcoxon, married to Frieda Inescort in the title role. Let's face it— Wilcoxon was a long way downhill from Cagney. Her 1940 roles, in the Bing Crosby starrer **If I Had My Way** and in **Slightly Honorable,** were nothing special, although in the latter she played Edward Arnold's murdered mistress. She was far down the cast list in **The Black Cat** (41), and also was reduced to appearing in an Abbott and Costello vehicle, **In the Navy.** Maybe it was time to bid farewell to the movies.

Her last year on screen, at age 33, was 1942. In the absurd **The Mad Doctor of Market Street** she was one of several persons shipwrecked on a tropical island where the natives worship—you guessed it, a mad doctor, played by Lionel Atwill. She was then reduced to appearing in a serial, **Don Winslow of the Navy,** as the hero's girlfriend. And the actress went out in style, playing someone named Gladys LaVerne and *singing a song,* of all things, in **Mississippi Gambler,** a weak programmer starring Kent Taylor and Frances Langford (Miss Langford got to sing *two* songs and was billed much higher). For the record, Miss Dodd's song was "I'm Hitting the Hot Spots." You remember *that* one, don't you?

Well, even if you don't, Claire Dodd—who died in 1973 at age 64—is worth remembering. In her heyday she was a wonderfully bitchy seductress, and if it weren't for the fact that the script insisted on the hero's ultimately winding up with some insipid ingenue, one wonders...would he possibly have really preferred the tempting allure of Miss Dodd?

THE FILMS OF CLAIRE DODD

1930: Our Blushing Brides; Whoopee!

1931: The Secret Call; Working Girls; Girls About Town. *Credit uncertain:* An American Tragedy; Up Pops the Devil; The Lawyer's Secret; The Road to Reno.

1932: Lawyer Man; The Broken Wing; The Match King; Crooner; Under 18; Two Kinds of Women; Alias the Doctor; Man Wanted; Guilty as Hell; This Is the Night. *Credit uncertain:* Dancers in the Dark.

1933: Footlight Parade; Parachute Jumper; Hard to Handle; Ex-Lady; Blondie Johnson; Ann Carver's Profession; Elmer the Great; My Woman.

1934: Massacre; Gambling Lady; Babbitt; Journal of a Crime; The Personality Kid; I Sell Anything; Smarty.

1935: Roberta; The Case of the Curious Bride; The Glass Key; Don't Bet on Blondes; The Goose and the Gander; The Payoff; The Secret of the Chateau.

1936: The Singing Kid; Murder by an Aristocrat; The Case of the Velvet Claws; Navy Born; Two Against the World.

1937: Women Men Marry.

1938: Romance in the Dark; Fast Company; Three Loves Has Nancy; Charlie Chan in Honolulu.

1939: Woman Doctor.

1940: If I Had My Way; Slightly Honorable.

1941: The Black Cat; In the Navy.

1942: The Mad Doctor of Market Street; Mississippi Gambler; Don Winslow of the Navy (serial).

Oh, a tough guy, huh?:
BRIAN DONLEVY

Brian Donlevy started out in films of the sound era as a tough, brusque villain, but moved on to become a leading man and near-star of rugged action films and thrillers. In his decline, he ended up playing villains again, in cheap Westerns.

Strong, heavy-set and handsome, he was known for his fast, terse delivery of dialogue, which tended to type him as a politician, crook, racketeer, newspaperman, Western outlaw, frontiersman, military officer or cop. He also tended to move stiffly, which caused one unkind critic to say he looked as though he couldn't act until someone wound the clockwork to start him moving.

Grosson Brian Boru Donlevy (named for a 10th century king of Ireland, Brian Boru, he later changed it to Waldo Brian Donlevy) was born February 9, 1899 (some sources say 1901 or 1903), in Portadown, County Armagh, Northern Ireland, the son of a whiskey distiller. When he was still an infant the family emigrated to the United States, settling in Sheboygan Falls, Wisconsin. Donlevy attended a military academy, then, at 17, enlisted in the Army and served as a bugler in General John J. Pershing's border expedition against Mexican bandit Pancho Villa in 1916.

The following year he became a sergeant and pilot in the Lafayette Flying Corps, the American offshoot of France's Lafayette Escadrille, serving under the French flag and flying missions against the Germans in World War I. Also a member of the flying corps was future film director William A. Wellman, who a generation later would direct Donlevy in his greatest screen role. Donlevy, who wrote poetry during this war service, was twice wounded, and returned to receive an appointment to the U.S. Naval Academy at Annapolis, but resigned in 1922 after learning that graduation would mean three years of sea duty.

The broad-shouldered, barrel-chested young man went to New York City and found work modeling shirts. He came to the attention of artist J.F. Leyendecker, who added him to his roster of models for the "Arrow Collar Man." He began meeting theatrical people, and in 1923 made his screen debut in a small part in a low-budget historical drama, **Jamestown.** The following year he had another small role in a New York-made film, **Damaged Hearts,** and an infinitesimally tiny bit part in the Rudolph Valentino starrer **Monsieur Beaucaire.** Actor Louis Wolheim got him a small role in the hit Broadway play **What Price**

Glory in 1924; it ran 435 performances, but during the run the actor shuttled to Vitagraph's Brooklyn studios for a supporting role in the movie **School for Wives** (25). During this period his stage roles frequently were as comic drunks.

In 1926 he won his first notice as an actor, and also played his first villain, in the film **A Man of Quality,** as the head of a gang of silk smugglers who also abducts the heroine. He played a sailor in the 1927 stage musical **Hit the Deck** on Broadway and on tour, and then returned for a short-lived play, **Ringside,** and an equally short-lived musical, **Rainbow,** both in 1928; in the latter, he and actress Louise Brown sang the song "Virginia." He played Morton Downey's brother in the musical film **Mother's Boy** (29) and was far down the cast list in **Gentlemen of the Press.** This was to be almost his last screen work for six years.

Donlevy married Ziegfeld showgirl Yvonne Grey in 1928. They were divorced in 1936, and that year he married singer Marjorie Lane. Miss Lane was a "voice double," providing the singing voice on the soundtrack for Eleanor Powell in at least three Thirties films and also reportedly for Jean Harlow and other actresses in unidentified films. The couple had a daughter, Judith Ann, but were divorced in 1947. In 1966 the actor married Lillian Lugosi, the ex-wife of screen menace Bela Lugosi.

Late in 1929 he appeared in the play **Queen Bee** on Broadway, and continued to keep busy on the stage in the next few years. (He popped back to the screen briefly in 1932 for a two-reel short subject.) In 1934 he suddenly got a spate of major roles, in the plays **No Questions Asked, The Perfumed Lady** and **The Milky Way** (in the latter, as a prizefighter). Then came a long-run musical, the revue **Life Begins at 8:40.** When this show took to the road, so did Donlevy—to Hollywood. This time screen success lay before him.

He began with a run of glowering villains. He was Edward G. Robinson's murderous hired gunman in **Barbary Coast** (35), ending up hanged by vigilantes, and a relentless killer in **Mary Burns, Fugitive.** In **Another Face** he played a gangster who gets plastic surgery, kills the doctor, and goes to Hollywood to start over as a movie actor, but is caught.

Donlevy signed a contract with 20th Century-Fox in 1936; that studio (at least initially) didn't see him as a villain. In **Human Cargo** (36) he and Claire Trevor were rival newspaper reporters who uncover a smuggling ring, and he was also a newsman in **Half Angel,** clearing Frances Dee of murder charges. **Thirteen Hours by Air** cast him as a federal agent posing as a doctor, and in **High Tension** he was a cable layer in love with magazine writer Glenda Farrell. **Crack-Up** found him as a test pilot foiling foreign spy Peter Lorre, and in **36 Hours to Kill** he was a G-man bringing a gangster to justice and falling in love with reporter Gloria Stuart. But in **Strike Me Pink** he played a racketeer menacing Eddie Cantor.

He was another bad guy, Barbara Stanwyck's brother and one of a gang of bank robbers, in **This Is My Affair** (37), a turn-of-the-century historical drama. But his two other parts that year were both as good-guy cab drivers. In **Born Reckless** he played an auto-racing champ who, in need of a job, drives a taxi and ends the harassment of cabbies by protection racketeer Barton MacLane. And in **Midnight Taxi** he wasn't an honest-to-goodness cab driver, just a federal agent posing as one to break up a counterfeiting ring.

Audiences seemed to find Donlevy more interesting as a villain than as a nice guy, and producers quickly got wise. In **In Old Chicago** (38) he was the vicious political boss who shoots Don Ameche in the back but ends up killed himself, trampled to death by a herd of stampeding cattle during the famous fire.

But in **Battle of Broadway** he played Victor McLaglen's bickering buddy, and he was the same actor's rival in the oilfield-boom story **We're Going to Be Rich.** In **Sharpshooters** he was an ace newsreel cameraman.

Now, in 1939, full-scale villainy was to be Donlevy's hallmark. He surprised all of Hollywood that year by winning an Academy Award nomination as best supporting actor for his film-stealing performance as the sadistic Sergeant Markoff in director William A. Wellman's Foreign Legion epic, **Beau Geste,** one of the year's biggest box-office hits. As the crazed, bullying noncom, he gave an astonishingly strong display of acting that pushed him into virtual stardom and almost made audiences forget about the film's stars, Gary Cooper and Ray Milland. (Still, he lost the Oscar to Thomas Mitchell, for **Stagecoach.**)

But that was not the actor's only fine villainous part in what was to be his *annus mirabilis.* In **Jesse James** he played the brutal Barshee, one of whose mob kills Jane Darwell (the mother of Tyrone Power and Henry Fonda, playing Jesse and Frank). In **Union Pacific** he was the thug hired to block the advance of the railroad by luring laborers with gambling, liquor and women. And he was the nasty town boss giving James Stewart a hard time in **Destry Rides Again.** Back on the good side of the law, he starred in **Behind Prison Gates** as an agent of the state's attorney's office posing as a convict to find out about stolen loot hidden by cop-killers.

In 1940, for director Preston Sturges, the actor had what was probably his second-best role of all time, as the title figure in **The Great McGinty,** giving a surprisingly good performance as a man who rises from hungry tramp to ward heeler to mayor to reform governor, only to meet his downfall on a graft charge and wind up as a bartender in a banana republic. Sharing acting honors was Akim Tamiroff as his crooked mentor. That year he also played a rival to Mormon leader Brigham Young (Dean Jagger) in **Brigham Young—Frontiersman.**

Donlevy was the tough training officer in **I Wanted Wings** (41), and in **Billy the Kid** played Billy's (Robert Taylor's) boyhood pal who as the town marshal (a thinly disguised Sheriff Pat Garrett) ends up killing the outlaw. Now in his forties, he played the tough political boss in **The Glass Key** (42) and was excellent as the ghost of Andrew Jackson, aiding modern-day politician William Holden, in **The Remarkable Andrew.** He was ideally cast as the commanding officer in **Wake Island.** In **A Gentleman After Dark** he escaped prison to redeem the honor of his daughter by killing his blackmailing wife (Miriam Hopkins). In 1943 he was a Czech patriot fighting the Nazis and killing one of their leaders in director Fritz Lang's **Hangmen Also Die.**

One of his most interesting films was director King Vidor's **An American Romance** (44), in which he portrayed an immigrant steelworker who rises to wealth and power. But it would have worked better with Vidor's original choice, the more charismatic Spencer Tracy, who was unavailable. In 1946 the actor played writer Richard Henry Dana in **Two Years Before the Mast,** crusading to expose the mistreatment of sailors by a brutal captain (however, Alan Ladd was the film's star). He was also the villain Trampas in the remake of **The Virginian** (to whom Joel McCrea says, "Smile when you call me that"), and a semi-bad guy in **Canyon Passage.**

He was an assistant district attorney in **Kiss of Death** (47) and a big-time gambler in **Killer McCoy.** Critics found him artificial as a "Pentagon commando" in **Command Decision** (48), and at this point Brian Donlevy's career started skidding downhill. By 1950 he was playing villains in formula Westerns and giving routine support in programmer crime thrillers. He also began to turn to television; for a while, beginning in 1952, he starred as an investigator of espionage in the series "Dangerous Assignment."

Now making only one or two films a year, he also began working on the stage again. He played the Bing Crosby role as the drunken, washed-up actor in **The Country Girl** (in real life Donlevy had his own problems with alcohol), and went on tour in the comedy **King of Hearts.** Again on TV, he appeared in the series "Crossroads."

He had a passably good film role in **The Big Combo** (55) as a mobster ultimately killed off by the mob's financier (Richard Conte), and also was fine as the star of two British science-fiction films, playing the tetchy scientist Quatermass in **The Quatermass Experiment (The Creeping Unknown)** (56) and **Enemy from Space (Quatermass II)** (57). In **Cowboy** (58) he was a retired gunman whose idiosyncrasies were most realistic. But for the most part the actor was now lost in a welter of cheap programmers, films with such titles as **Juke Box Rhythm, The Curse of the Fly** and **How to Stuff a Wild Bikini.**

He was now wealthy, semi-retired to his Palm Springs home, and involved to a considerable extent with Mojave Desert tungsten mines he had bought in the late Thirties. In 1969, at age 70, he made his last film, **Pit Stop,** in the lead role in this very low-budget action movie about a racing-car organization that will stop at nothing to win. In 1972 he entered the Motion Picture Country House and Hospital, near Los Angeles, following a throat operation, and died there a few days later. His wealth had dwindled, and he left an estate of only $8,000.

Brian Donlevy had an erratic and spasmodic career, but he gave us some unforgettable moments. Oh, for a time machine to take us all back to 1939, to see again the sadistic Sergeant Markoff of **Beau Geste,** the brutal Barshee of **Jesse James,** the railroad-busting thug of **Union Pacific,** and the swaggering villain of **Destry Rides Again.** Let's face it—those guys were *mean.*

THE FILMS OF BRIAN DONLEVY

1923: Jamestown.
1924: Monsieur Beaucaire; Damaged Hearts.
1925: School for Wives.
1926: A Man of Quality.
1929: Mother's Boy; Gentlemen of the Press.
1935: Barbary Coast; Mary Burns, Fugitive; Another Face.
1936: Human Cargo; Thirteen Hours by Air; High Tension; Crack-Up; 36 Hours to Kill; Half Angel; Strike Me Pink.
1937: Midnight Taxi; This Is My Affair; Born Reckless.
1938: In Old Chicago; Battle of Broadway; We're Going to Be Rich; Sharpshooters.
1939: Beau Geste; Jesse James; Union Pacific; Destry Rides Again; Allegheny Uprising; Behind Prison Gates.
1940: The Great McGinty; Brigham Young—Frontiersman; When the Daltons Rode.
1941: I Wanted Wings; Hold Back the Dawn; Billy the Kid; Birth of the Blues; South of Tahiti.
1942: The Glass Key; Wake Island; A Gentleman After Dark; The Remarkable Andrew; The Great Man's Lady; Stand By for Action; Two Yanks in Trinidad; Nightmare.
1943: Hangmen Also Die.
1944: An American Romance; The Miracle of Morgan's Creek.
1945: Duffy's Tavern.

1946: Two Years Before the Mast; The Virginian; Canyon Passage; Our Hearts Were Growing Up.
1947: Kiss of Death; The Beginning or the End; Song of Scheherazade; The Trouble with Women; Killer McCoy; Heaven Only Knows.
1948: Command Decision; A Southern Yankee.
1949: Impact; The Lucky Stiff.
1950: Shakedown; Kansas Raiders.
1951: Slaughter Trail; Fighting Coast Guard.
1952: Hoodlum Empire; Ride the Man Down.
1953: The Woman They Almost Lynched.
1955: The Big Combo.
1956: A Cry in the Night; The Quatermass Experiment (The Creeping Unknown).
1957: Enemy from Space (Quatermass II).
1958: Cowboy; Escape from Red Rock.
1959: Never So Few; Juke Box Rhythm.
1961: The Errand Boy.
1962: The Pigeon That Took Rome.
1965: The Curse of the Fly; How to Stuff a Wild Bikini.
1966: Waco; The Fat Spy.
1967: Hostile Guns; Gammera, the Invincible.
1968: Rogue's Gallery; Arizona Bushwhackers.
1969: Pit Stop.

Nastiness is a paying commodity:
DOUGLASS DUMBRILLE

Villainy on the screen almost invariably pays off in regular employment and financial security. For Douglass Dumbrille, it meant steady work for 34 years in the sound era and an impressive career total of about 150 films.

"We have ways of making men talk," he said in threatening Gary Cooper and Franchot Tone in **The Lives of a Bengal Lancer**. "Little bamboo slivers...but when they're driven under the fingernails and *lighted,* we find them very effective." He was eternally a smooth, suave villain.

Eagle-eyed, stern-faced and saturnine, with a sharply etched speech pattern, he made nastiness pay. Besides suave menaces, he also played unsavory lawyers, mobsters, corrupt tycoons, crooked politicians, shifty businessmen and unscrupulous swindlers, and frequently was the antagonist for "B"-movie detectives. His stuffy screen personality also made him an ideal foil for comedians; he was matched against the Marx Brothers, Bob Hope, and Abbott and Costello, in each case on more than one occasion. In fact, he menaced every major comedy team in pictures except Laurel and Hardy.

Dumbrille was born October 13, 1890 (some sources say 1888), in Hamilton, Ontario. He started out in the banking field, but left his clerical job to join a stock company of actors. He appeared in one 1916 film, **What 80 Million Women Want.** Following his Broadway debut as Banquo in **Macbeth,** in 1924, he sold his Ontario onion farm and devoted himself to a stage career. In the next seven years he appeared in numerous Broadway plays before being summoned by Hollywood in 1931, at age 40.

The actor made his sound-film debut (as did Joseph Calleia) that year in **His Woman.** In 1932 he registered strongly as the district attorney in the classic drama **I Am a Fugitive from a Chain Gang,** which so impressed casting directors that in 1933 he appeared in a total of 16 movies. In **Lady Killer** he replaced James Cagney as the leader of a gang of burglars, only to have Cagney bring the gang to justice. In **The World Changes** he was, incredibly, cast as Buffalo Bill, advising Paul Muni to go into the cattle business. He played an Oriental king in **Voltaire,** and was one of a parade of businessmen seduced by Barbara Stanwyck in **Baby Face.** He was once again a district attorney in the Cagney vehicle **Hard to Handle,** one of many parts he played in this busy year.

The actor was one of the evil pirates in **Treasure Island** (34), and a mobster (whose gang murders Bette Davis) in **Fog over Frisco.** In **Massacre** he was a crooked official of the government bureau supervising Indian reservations, and **Hi Nellie!** cast him as the temporary substitute for Paul Muni as a newspaper's managing editor when Muni is demoted to advice-to-the-lovelorn columnist. He played Confederate general Jeb Stuart, being spied on by Marion Davies, in the Gary Cooper starrer **Operator 13,** and was a bookie bribing a jockey to throw a race in **Broadway Bill.**

Dumbrille was evil incarnate as the Indian mogul Mohammed Khan in **The Lives of a Bengal Lancer** (35), with his "ways of making men talk," and in **Naughty Marietta** he was a stuffy nobleman hoping to marry Jeanette MacDonald and extremely irked when she runs off with Nelson Eddy instead. In **Cardinal Richelieu** he was the villain trying to usurp the throne of Louis XIII (Edward Arnold), and he played the mastermind of a jewel-theft ring in **The Lone Wolf Returns.** In **Crime and Punishment** he tried first to seduce and then to blackmail Peter Lorre's sister (Tala Birell), and in **Love Me Forever** he was a gambling-house proprietor harassing Leo Carrillo over a debt. He played Gary Cooper's stern uncle in **Peter Ibbetson.**

Audiences cheered in 1936 when he got his comeuppance in director Frank Capra's hit comedy-drama **Mr. Deeds Goes to Town;** he was the crooked lawyer Cedar, trying to cheat Cooper out of his inheritance, and at the climax of the courtroom scene Cooper floors the villainous attorney with a blow to the jaw. In **The Princess Comes Across** he was a French detective who turns out to be the murderer, and **The Calling of Dan Matthews** found him up to no good as the evil proprietor of a red-light district, routed by crusading clergyman Richard Arlen. In **You May Be Next** he was the villain jamming radio stations with high-frequency transmitters, and not content with that, engaged in blackmailing. He played Ann Harding's dastardly employer in **The Witness Chair,** conniving to make a false embezzlement charge against business associate Walter Abel but ending up accidentally killed by Miss Harding.

The actor was the crooked horse-race gambler foiled by the Marx Brothers in **A Day at the Races** (37), and played an espionage chieftain in **The Emperor's Candlesticks,** as well as the villain bested by Allan Jones in **The Firefly.** He portrayed Governor Claiborne in **The Buccaneer** (38), and was a Union officer in the Civil War in **Kentucky.** Jewel thievery was his game in **Stolen Heaven,** and in **Storm over Bengal** he played yet another Hindu khan, similar to the one in **The Lives of a Bengal Lancer.** But he had an unusual sympathetic role in **The Mysterious Rider.** In the Ritz Brothers vehicle **The Three Musketeers** (39) he played Athos. He also played stock villains in two Charlie Chan outings and one Mr. Moto.

Dumbrille was one of the pirates stealing the natives' pearls in **South of Pago Pago** (40), and was bested by Lloyd Nolan in **Michael Shayne, Private Detective.** The Marx Brothers got the better of him again in **The Big Store** (41); he was the crooked manager of the department store, plotting to kill Tony Martin and get control of the store by marrying Margaret Dumont (what a pair *they* would have made!). Ralph Bellamy was the next detective to foil his machinations, in **Ellery Queen and the Perfect Crime,** and he was the villain bested by Abbott and Costello in **Ride 'em Cowboy.**

The actor was cast as General William Henry Harrison (the future U.S. president) in **Ten Gentle-man from West Point** (42), and was back as a villain again (and foiled by Charlie Chan again) in **Castle in the Desert.** He played a convict of Italian ancestry in **A Gentleman After Dark.** He had a key role in **Du Barry Was a Lady** (43), and was the police commissioner hunting escaped murderer Errol Flynn in **Uncertain Glory** (44). He was not only villainous but also lecherous in **Gypsy Wildcat,** as a wicked baron who imprisons the object of his attentions, Maria Montez, in his castle. **Lost in a Harem** had him in yet another losing battle with Abbott and Costello.

Bing Crosby and Bob Hope outwitted him in **Road to Utopia** (45); by now the 55-year-old actor had a reputation as the best comic villain in films. But in **The Frozen Ghost** he was a police inspector, and in **Flame of the West** he was, amazingly, cast in a heroic role. He appeared in his first serial, **Jungle Queen.** Bob Hope proved his undoing in **Monsieur Beaucaire** (46). He was merely one of three "High Priests" in the absurd desert epic **A Night in Paradise,** and he was starting to appear farther down cast lists now. Also, half of his 1946 releases were for Poverty Row studios, Republic and Monogram.

Douglass Dumbrille still had many years of filming ahead of him, but he had pretty well run out of good parts. He could still be bested by the detective The Lone Wolf, but by this time the star of the series was being played by an actor nobody now remembers. And he could still fall victim to Bob Hope (**Son of Paleface,** 1952) and Guess Who (**Abbott and Costello in the Foreign Legion** in 1950). But now, when there was a villain in the film, he was usually played by somebody else, with Dumbrille in a smaller part.

Occasionally he would get a role in a major film: **Julius Caesar** (53) cast him as Lepidus, but he was billed 21st. And now and then he would get better billing, such as his appearance as a Singapore police inspector in **World for Ransom** (54). He had a small part in **The Ten Commandments** (56).

The actor at this point was the widower of his first wife, stage actress Jessie Lawson; their marriage lasted from 1911 to her death in 1958. He must have surprised many people when in 1960, at the age of 69, he married 28-year-old Patricia Mowbray, the daughter of his friend, character actor Alan Mowbray.

In the latter stages of his career he also appeared on television, as a regular in the series "You'll Never Get Rich" and "China Smith," plus appearances in "Petticoat Junction," "The Life of Riley" and "Grand Jury," among others.

Dumbrille was still up to villainy in his seventies, involved in a robbery of art treasures in **Air**

Patrol (62). But he was far down the cast list in his last two pictures, both made in 1964, **Shock Treatment** and the appropriately named **What a Way to Go!**

In his last years he entered the Motion Picture Country House and Hospital near Los Angeles, where he died in 1974 at age 83. It had been a long time since he was one of the screen's suavest and nastiest menaces. But even at the end, one surmises, Douglass Dumbrille still knew ways of making men talk...

THE FILMS OF DOUGLASS DUMBRILLE

1916: What 80 Million Women Want.
1931: His Woman.
1932: I Am a Fugitive from a Chain Gang; Laughter in Hell; The Wiser Sex; Blondie of the Follies; That's My Boy; The Pride of the Legion.
1933: Lady Killer; Heroes for Sale; The World Changes; Voltaire; Baby Face; Elmer the Great; Female; Hard to Handle; The Silk Express; Convention City; King of the Jungle; Smoke Lightning; Rustlers' Roundup; The Big Brain; The Man Who Dared; The Way to Love.
1934: Treasure Island; Fog over Frisco; Massacre; Broadway Bill; Hi Nellie!; Journal of a Crime; Operator 13; Stamboul Quest; Harold Teen.
1935: The Lives of a Bengal Lancer; Naughty Marietta; Love Me Forever; Crime and Punishment; Peter Ibbetson; Cardinal Richelieu; The Secret Bride; The Lone Wolf Returns; The Public Menace; Air Hawks; Unknown Woman.
1936: Mr. Deeds Goes to Town; The Princess Comes Across; The Calling of Dan Matthews; The Music Goes 'Round; You May Be Next; End of the Trail; The Witness Chair; M'liss; Counterfeit Lady.
1937: A Day at the Races; The Emperor's Candlesticks; The Firefly; Ali Baba Goes to Town; Woman in Distress.
1938: The Buccaneer; Kentucky; Stolen Heaven; The Mysterious Rider; Storm over Bengal; Crime Takes a Holiday; Fast Company; Sharpshooters.
1939: The Three Musketeers; Thunder Afloat; Captain Fury; Tell No Tales; Rovin' Tumbleweeds; Charlie Chan at Treasure Island; Mr. Moto in Danger Island; City in Darkness.
1940: Slightly Honorable; Virginia City; South of Pago Pago; Michael Shayne, Private Detective.
1941: The Big Store; Washington Melodrama; The Roundup; Murder Among Friends; Ellery Queen and the Perfect Crime.
1942: Ten Gentlemen from West Point; I Married an Angel; Stand By for Action; Castle in the Desert; A Gentleman After Dark; Ride 'em Cowboy.
1943: Du Barry Was a Lady; False Colors.
1944: Uncertain Glory; Gypsy Wildcat; Lost in a Harem; Forty Thieves; Jungle Woman; Lumberjack.
1945: A Medal for Benny; Road to Utopia; The Frozen Ghost; Flame of the West; The Daltons Ride Again; Jungle Queen (serial).
1946: Monsieur Beaucaire; A Night in Paradise; Pardon My Past; The Cat Creeps; Spook Busters; Under Nevada Skies; The Catman of Paris.
1947: Dishonored Lady; Dragnet; Christmas Eve; The Fabulous Texan; It's a Joke, Son!
1948: Blonde Savage; Last of the Wild Horses.
1949: Dynamite; Alimony; Tell It to the Judge; The Lone Wolf and His Lady; Riders of the Whistling Pines; Joe Palooka in the Counterpunch.
1950: Riding High; Buccaneer's Girl; Rapture; The Savage Horde; Abbott and Costello in the Foreign Legion.
1951: A Millionaire for Christy.
1952: Son of Paleface; Apache War Smoke; Sky Full of Moon.
1953: Julius Caesar; Plunder of the Sun; Captain John Smith and Pocahontas.
1954: World for Ransom; Lawless Rider.
1955: Jupiter's Darling.
1956: The Ten Commandments; Shake, Rattle and Rock.
1958: The Buccaneer.
1960: High Time.
1962: Air Patrol.
1964: Shock Treatment; What a Way to Go!

She didn't understand the jokes:
MARGARET DUMONT

Call her Mrs. Rittenhouse. Or Mrs. Teasdale. Or Mrs. Claypool, or Mrs. Dukesbury. Just don't ask her to wash out a pair of socks for you.

Margaret Dumont, the perfect comic foil, played in seven films the stately, smiling, and bewildered society matron who was the target for assorted inanities wrought upon her by the Marx Brothers, notably Groucho, who inflicted on her again and again a combination of insults and amorous advances.

Film critic Cecelia Ager once said, "There ought to be a statue erected, or a Congressional Medal awarded, or a national holiday proclaimed, to honor that great woman, Margaret Dumont, the dame who takes the raps from the Marx Brothers...a lady of epic ability to take it...her fortitude is nothing human. It's godlike."

And to top it off, Groucho always insisted that she didn't understand the jokes. Maybe that's why she was able to keep a straight face in those films.

As a number of easily duped, rich, philanthropic widows, she was Groucho's entrée into high society, the political arena, and the opera. Her stuffy dowagers are charmed by his outrageous characters because, unlike every other male in her polite, pompous circle, they throw propriety to the winds and make passionate overtures to her. She is so taken by his brazen advances that she can't tell the difference between his insults and his flirtations.

But she was more than just a fine comic foil. She personified in her statuesque dowager-duchess figure exactly what made her the perfect target for the Marxes—the pomp and pretension of high society. What is amazing is that in real life she *was* in fact a wealthy society matron, the widow of the heir to a fortune, a genuine blueblood living in a Pasadena mansion.

While agreeing that Miss Dumont was born October 20, 1889, sources differ as to some of the other facts, with some saying she was born as Margaret (or Marguerite) Baker in Brooklyn, New York, and some asserting it was Daisy Baker in Atlanta, Georgia (and the latter sources saying she was the goddaughter of "Uncle Remus" author Joel Chandler Harris and that he raised her). In any case, she started out in her teens as a singer, touring Europe (as Daisy Dumont) in ingenue roles in revues in London, Paris, Vienna and Berlin. Making her Broadway debut in a George M. Cohan play, she then appeared with comedian Lew

Fields in **The Girl Behind the Counter,** and after that was in two more shows with him.

In 1910, at the age of 20, the actress became the wife of John Moller Jr., heir to a sugar fortune, and retired from the stage for several years. She is also said to have appeared in a 1917 film, an early version of **A Tale of Two Cities** starring William Farnum. When Moller died in 1918, she resumed her career. She returned to Broadway in 1922, appeared in two shows with Cohan, and played several blue-blooded dowagers in those and other plays. She had the part of a social climber in **The Four Flusher** (25), where she was seen by producer Sam Harris, who cast her in a similar role in a new comedy, **The Cocoanuts,** starring four knockabout farceurs—the Marx Brothers.

The Cocoanuts was a huge success, and Miss Dumont and the brothers then appeared in a similar farce, **Animal Crackers.** In 1929, at the beginning of the sound era, they all journeyed to Hollywood to make the film version of **The Cocoanuts.** The actress repeated her stage role as wealthy, snooty Mrs. Potter, in lace dress and wide-brimmed, floppy hat. Groucho wastes no time in establishing the format of what is to be their 12-year courtship: "Did anyone ever tell you you look like the Prince of Wales? I don't mean the present Prince of Wales. One of the *old* Wales. And believe me, when I say whales, I mean whales. I know a whale when I see one."

Animal Crackers was the next film, in 1930. Here the actress was Mrs. Rittenhouse, holding a party at her mansion to celebrate the return of "Captain Spaulding, the African explorer," and no prizes for guessing who plays him. The courtship continues. Groucho: "You've got beauty, charm, money. You *have* got money, haven't you? Because if you haven't, we can quit right now...Would you wash out a pair of socks for me?" Naturally, Mrs. Rittenhouse is won over.

Miss Dumont, now in her early forties, was not in the cast of the next two Marx films (neither of whose scripts called for a wealthy dowager), and in the interim she was in one movie, **The Girl Habit** (31). But in 1933 she was summoned back to co-star with the brothers as Mrs. Teasdale in **Duck Soup.** Mrs. Teasdale is the multimillionairess who controls the government of the bankrupt kingdom of Freedonia with the power of her purse. The country needs a new president, so she chooses...you guessed it. Groucho's courtship soon gets into a dialogue about her late husband; she says, "I was with him to the end." Groucho: "No wonder he passed away." Mrs. Teasdale: "I held him in my arms and kissed him." Groucho: "So it was murder, eh?" Mrs. Teasdale: "He left me his entire fortune." Groucho: "Can't you see what I'm trying to tell you? I love you!" Mrs. Teasdale: "Oh, Your Excellency!" Groucho: "You're not so bad yourself."

Through all this—and far worse—the actress serenely maintains her poise, eternally beaming tolerantly on Groucho, turning to jelly when he flirts with her, and tolerating such comments as "I'm fighting for this woman's honor, which is more than *she* ever did." (Off camera, she asked Groucho what that line of dialogue meant.) And it was this one-sided love affair that soon made Miss Dumont into a cult figure—what film historian Ethan Mordden has called "the supernova of dowagers."

When Zeppo Marx left the brothers' act after **Duck Soup,** she became established in the public's mind as "the fourth Marx Brother," the only one to play it straight. She once remarked, "I'm not a stooge; I'm the best straight woman in Hollywood. There's an art to playing straight. You must build up your

man, but never top him, never steal the laughs from him." Fat chance of that...

During their switch from Paramount to MGM, the brothers were off the screen in 1934, and the actress appeared in three films without them. In 1935 she was reunited with Groucho, Chico and Harpo in **A Night at the Opera,** as the millionairess Mrs. Claypool, seeking to make her place in high society. Sporting a tiara and wielding a lorgnette, a tightly girdled pillar of rectitude, she also attracts a rival to Groucho for her affections: opera impresario Sig Rumann. No prizes for guessing who wins.

There was no Marx Brothers outing in 1936, and Miss Dumont was featured as a dowager in the Bing Crosby starrer **Anything Goes** and also made another movie. **A Day at the Races** (37), her next Marx film, saw the actress at her finest. As the millionaire Mrs. Upjohn—again with a lorgnette—she is fretfully haughty and still stoically maintaining her aplomb in the face of the usual harassment. The film's highlight occurs when she is visited with unspeakable indignities while undergoing a Marxian medical examination. While the actress never won an Academy Award nomination, for this film she won an honor nearly as good—the Screen Actors Guild, which conferred its own awards, named her as best supporting actress.

This was her busiest year on the screen; she was also in four other releases, none of them noteworthy (except possibly for the fact that **High Flyers** was the last movie the fading comedy team of Wheeler and Woolsey ever made); one was the Miriam Hopkins vehicle **Wise Girl.**

She was fortunate in having been omitted from the cast of the Marx Brothers' worst movie, **Room Service,** a box-office failure. In the year it was released, 1938, she appeared in a much better film, **Dramatic School,** perfectly cast as the teacher of pantomime to Luise Rainer, Paulette Goddard and others; her genuine comic talent was well displayed here.

The public still demanded Margaret Dumont along with its Marx Brothers movies, though, and she returned to the ranks in **At the Circus** (39), as Mrs. Dukesbury. Are you surprised to hear that she was a millionaire dowager? In this one, she is shot from a cannon and catapulted right into the middle of a bizarre trapeze act. Performed by doubles? Hardly. Miss Dumont later reported, "Most people accuse me of using a stand-in. But I hung head down while the Marx boys clutched my legs. I had to see it through."

That year she also had a small part in director George Cukor's **The Women,** with an all-female cast, in which she played a dowager named Mrs. Wagstaff (possibly an in-joke, since Groucho's character in **Horse Feathers**—a non-Dumont film—was named Professor Wagstaff). Cukor later commented, "Her elegance was so perfectly bogus."

When the actress was omitted from the cast of the brothers' next film, **Go West** (40), there was a public outcry; letters of protest poured in to MGM. People genuinely missed the great dowager, with her aristocratic bearing, wonderful sense of timing, and unlimited patience and good humor. They wanted her back. And so in 1941 she returned for what was to be her last Marx Brothers film, **The Big Store.** She was department-store heiress Mrs. Phelps, whom villain Douglass Dumbrille hopes to marry and thus take control of the store. The brothers quickly put a stop to that.

Miss Dumont also had a romp in another release that year, **Never Give a Sucker an Even Break,** starring W.C. Fields (who obviously thought up the name of her character, Mrs. Hemoglobin). She is a mountain-dwelling Amazon with an attractive daughter; Fields courts first the daughter and then the mother, since *she* has the money. In 1942 the actress appeared in some forgettable musicals in which (if the titles are any indication) nothing is more important than singing: **Born to Sing, Rhythm Parade, Sing Your Worries Away.**

In 1943 she supported Laurel and Hardy in one of their last and weakest films, **The Dancing Masters,** and in 1944, Danny Kaye in **Up in Arms** and Red Skelton in **Bathing Beauty.** The following year it was Jack Benny in **The Horn Blows at Midnight;** she was also in a cheap Republic Western. In 1946 Abbott and Costello joined the list of comedians she had assisted, in **Little Giant.**

Miss Dumont was now in her late fifties. At this point there was a sharp cutback in her screen activity; she would make only six movies in the next 18 years. The next one wasn't until 1952: **Three for Bedroom C,** starring Gloria Swanson; she was also in another film that year. The actress also moved into television, often appearing with such comedians as Bob Hope and Dean Martin.

In 1956 she had a part in something called **Shake, Rattle and Rock,** and in 1958 a virtual bit role in **Auntie Mame.** Now in her seventies and in failing health, she appeared in **Zotz!** in 1962, and her final film, **What a Way to Go!,** in 1964, as Shirley MacLaine's shrewish mother.

Only a few days before her death at 75 in 1965, she did a TV sketch with Groucho. Talk about memories! They could look back across 40 years to those knockabout days doing **The Cocoanuts** on Broadway. The old gleam came back to the elderly comedian's eye as he glanced at Margaret Dumont. Maybe, just maybe, she could wash out another pair of socks for him...

THE FILMS OF MARGARET DUMONT

1917: *Credit uncertain:* A Tale of Two Cities.
1929: The Cocoanuts.
1930: Animal Crackers.
1931: The Girl Habit.
1933: Duck Soup.
1934: Kentucky Kernels; Fifteen Wives; Gridiron Flash.
1935: A Night at the Opera; Orchids to You. *Credit uncertain:* Rendezvous.
1936: Anything Goes; Song and Dance Man.
1937: A Day at the Races; The Life of the Party; Wise Girl; Youth on Parole; High Flyers.
1938: Dramatic School.
1939: At the Circus; The Women.
1941: The Big Store; Never Give a Sucker an Even Break; For

Beauty's Sake.
1942: About Face; Born to Sing; Rhythm Parade; Sing Your Worries Away.
1943: The Dancing Masters.
1944: Up in Arms; Bathing Beauty; Seven Days Ashore.
1945: The Horn Blows at Midnight; (Billy Rose's) Diamond Horseshoe; Sunset in Eldorado.
1946: Little Giant; Susie Steps Out.
1952: Three for Bedroom C; Stop, You're Killing Me.
1956: Shake, Rattle and Rock.
1958: Auntie Mame.
1962: Zotz!
1964: What a Way to Go!

The wisecracking blonde:
GLENDA FARRELL

If any single character type absolutely epitomized American movies of the Thirties, that type was probably the breezy, cynical, wisecracking, gold-digging blonde, snapping her chewing gum and casting a steely eye on some rich sucker. And the actress who was perfectly cast in such roles was Glenda Farrell.

Buoyant and witty, with long, penciled eyebrows, she had an I've-been-around look that went well not only with gold-diggers but also with the newspaper reporters, floozies, chorines, and gangsters' molls she also played. And you could frequently find her as Joan Blondell's pal. Self-reliant, vivacious, funny, resourceful and independent, she was well known for her trademark jutting lower lip (as one writer has put it, "She dropped many a caustic quip from a curled lip"). And she was also known for an exciting, rapid-fire delivery of dialogue—sort of the female equivalent to Lee Tracy. She was, in short, a lot of fun to have around.

Miss Farrell was born June 30, 1904, in Enid, Oklahoma. At age seven she was playing Little Eva in **Uncle Tom's Cabin** with Virginia Brissac's stock company (Miss Brissac later played small parts in Hollywood films), and after her schooling (in a convent) she appeared in **Rebecca of Sunnybrook Farm** with a San Diego stock company.

In the early 1920s she married war veteran Thomas Richards, and they had a son, Tommy, but after a tour with a mediocre vaudeville act with her husband that paid starvation wages, the marriage broke up. (She returned to live with her parents for a while, and her son, who later became an actor, grew up as Tommy Farrell.) Although Miss Farrell later had a romance with screenwriter Robert Riskin (who ended up marrying Fay Wray), in 1941 she wed Dr. Henry Ross, a West Point graduate and New York surgeon who was at one time an Army colonel.

The actress reached Broadway in the mid-Twenties, and was a hit in several successful plays, including **Skidding** in 1928. She made her screen debut in 1929 in a bit part in **Lucky Boy**, and in 1930 had her first major role, as Douglas Fairbanks Jr.'s girlfriend and dancing partner, sneered at by gangster Edward G. Robinson, in **Little Caesar.** (She was badly miscast in this part, as in her early career she was simply inept in a straight dramatic role.) Meanwhile, she was continuing her stage work. Prior to **Little Caesar** she was on Broadway in **Recapture, On the Spot, Di-**

vided Honor, and with Clark Gable, George Brent and Alice Brady in **Love, Honor and Betray;** following the gangster film she co-starred with Cesar Romero in the play **Strictly Dishonorable** and then appeared with Romero, Judith Anderson and Ralph Morgan in **Cobra.**

She is said by some sources to have had a small part in the Barbara Stanwyck film **Night Nurse** (31), and then opened on Broadway in the play **Life Begins,** as one of several new mothers in a hospital maternity ward; she was a hard-as-nails showgirl who doesn't want her child. She was called back to Hollywood to repeat the role in the 1932 film version, and her notices were so good that Warner Bros. signed her to a contract.

Also that year, Miss Farrell was good in the classic melodrama **I Am a Fugitive from a Chain Gang,** as the scheming, slatternly landlady who discovers Paul Muni's secret (as expressed in the film's title) and blackmails him into marrying her; when he asks for a divorce, she tips off the police. She was billed third in the cast of **The Match King,** as Warren William's abandoned girlfriend, and was in support in **Scandal for Sale** and **Three on a Match.**

Warner Bros. was something like a factory with a busy production line in the early Thirties, and the actress, along with others, had little time to rest in 1933, appearing in 11 films. She played the first of her many breezy newspaper reporters in **Mystery of the Wax Museum,** and was the cynical, wisecracking estranged wife of Pat O'Brien in **Bureau of Missing Persons,** dropping in periodically to ensure getting her alimony payments and ending up getting spanked(!) by him; later it turns out that she is a bigamist and they aren't even married. She was a chorus girl in **Girl Missing,** vied unsuccessfully for Cary Grant's affections in **Gambling Ship,** and played a brassy, Texas Guinan-like nightclub owner, Missouri Martin, in **Lady for a Day.** She was a wisecracking nurse in **Mary Stevens, M.D.,** and **Havana Widows** found her digging gold with Joan Blondell for the first time. (She was also a gold-digger in **The Keyhole.**) In **Man's Castle** she was showgirl Fay LaRue, willing to support out-of-work Spencer Tracy—but he leaves her for the appealing Loretta Young. The actress also had roles in **Grand Slam** and **Central Airport.**

She and Miss Blondell were digging gold together again in **Kansas City Princess** and **I've Got Your Number** (both 34); in the latter, Miss Farrell was a phony fortune-teller. She played a newspaper's advice-to-the-lovelorn columnist, succeeded in that job by Paul Muni, in **Hi Nellie!,** and was hardboiled as Edward G. Robinson's (temporarily) discarded mistress in **Dark Hazard.** She had good parts in **The Big Shakedown** (as crook Ricardo Cortez' jealous ex-girlfriend), **Heat Lightning** and **The Personality Kid** (as boxer Pat O'Brien's pregnant wife), and was Hugh Herbert's wife in **Merry Wives of Reno.**

There was seemingly no end to the actress' ability to dig the gold in partnership with Joan Blondell, for they were doing it again in **We're in the Money** and **Traveling Saleslady** (both 35); in the former, they set their sights on the potential defendant in a breach-of-promise suit. But Miss Farrell could do just as well as a solo gold-digger; in **Gold Diggers of 1935** she was up to her elbows in chicanery as a stenographer transforming eccentric millionaire Herbert's song lyric into an incriminating love letter and suing him for breach of promise. (In 1935, it seems, one just didn't go around breaking such promises.) She played Al Jolson's sister in **Go into Your Dance,** was with Miss Blondell again in **Miss Pacific Fleet** (as a showgirl), and had key parts in **The**

Secret Bride (third-billed, as district attorney Warren William's secretary), **Little Big Shot** (as a hatcheck girl who helps a little girl) and **In Caliente** (as a gold-digger pursuing Pat O'Brien but ending up with Edward Everett Horton instead).

Somebody at the Warners studio then had the bright idea to cast Glenda Farrell as the star of a series of snappy little "B" pictures about the adventures of a newspaper reporter named Torchy Blane, "The Adventurous Blonde." These predictable programmers, co-starring Barton MacLane as her boyfriend, Lieutenant Steve McBride of the police homicide division, kicked off in 1936 with **Smart Blonde.**

The Torchy Blane films were only passably good, but they were popular, thanks primarily to the actress' performance as the brassy reporter, who often scoops her male colleagues. Torchy is clever enough to solve a mystery under McBride's nose, but not smart enough to lead him to the altar. A sensational murder or similar big story always pops up to postpone the wedding bells.

Miss Farrell said later that she had found the typical cinematic newspaper sob sisters to be "caricatures of newspaperwomen as I knew them. So before I undertook to do the first Torchy, I determined to create a real human being and not an exaggerated comedy type. I met [newspaperwomen] who visited Hollywood and watched them work on visits to New York. They were generally young, intelligent, refined and attractive. By making Torchy true to life, I tried to create a character practically unique in movies."

Another gold-digger role came along, naturally enough, in **Gold Diggers of 1937.** In this 1936 film, the actress, hired by killers to "love [Victor Moore] to death," utters the immortal line beloved of gold-diggers everywhere: "It's so hard to be good under the capitalistic system." In **High Tension** she was a magazine writer involved in a romance with cable layer Brian Donlevy, and she played a secretary in **Here Comes Carter.** She also had a major role in **Nobody's Fool** (as a con artist who falls in love with Edward Everett Horton), and co-starred as a lawyer in **The Law in Her Hands.**

In 1937 it was a Torchy Blane year. She did **Torchy Blane, the Adventurous Blonde; Blondes at Work** and **Flyaway Baby.** These were all murder mysteries which the irrepressible Torchy managed to solve. In **Breakfast for Two** she played a gold-digging actress romancing Herbert Marshall until Barbara Stanwyck breaks it up. The following year brought **Torchy Gets Her Man,** the fifth in the series. She portrayed a jewel thief in **Stolen Heaven.** Winding up her Warners contract, she was now freelancing. In **Prison Break** she was the romantic interest for unjustly imprisoned (for a murder he didn't commit) tuna fisherman Barton MacLane, and **Exposed** cast her as a magazine photographer exposing crooked district attorney Otto Kruger.

The Torchy series ended in 1939 with her only releases for that year, **Torchy Blane in Chinatown and Torchy Runs for Mayor.** (While the series was winding down, Jane Wyman and Lola Lane each had one crack at the part.) And at this point Miss Farrell's screen activity started to decline noticeably, following her 1941 marriage to Dr. Henry Ross. But she also returned frequently to the stage (in 1939, for example, she had the Greta Garbo starring role in Eugene O'Neill's **Anna Christie** in summer stock).

She had a small supporting role in **Johnny Eager** (41), and also played modest-sized parts in **The Talk of the Town** and **Twin Beds** (both 42), meanwhile selling her Hollywood home to Gabby Hayes and settling in New York. In 1943 and 1944 she appeared in a few forgettable programmers, and then stayed off the screen for three years, sometimes appearing on the Broadway stage. Her three films in 1947 and 1948 weren't much better, and a four-year absence from movies ensued, during which she returned to the stage and also became active in television.

In her late forties, Miss Farrell was now content to appear sporadically in films as a character actress, spending most of her time on the stage and in TV.

Apache War Smoke (52) was a tired Western. In **Girls in the Night** (53) she was the mother of a pair of juvenile delinquents. There was another mother role in **Susan Slept Here** (54), and a part in **Secret of the Incas.** After 1955's **The Girl in the Red Velvet Swing** (as Joan Collins' mother), she was again absent from Hollywood for four years, returning in 1959 for a genuinely good part as Kim Novak's mother in **Middle of the Night.**

In 1963 the actress won a TV Emmy award as best supporting actress for an appearance in the "Ben Casey" series. The following year she played Elvis Presley's mother in **Kissin' Cousins,** and was billed directly under star Jerry Lewis in **The Disorderly Orderly.** Her last two films, in fairly small parts, were **Dead Heat on a Merry-Go-Round** (66) and **Tiger by the Tail** (68).

In 1968, now in her mid-sixties, she was engaged to play Julie Harris' sophisticated mother in the Broadway play **Forty Carats,** but after two months of the run she was forced by illness to leave the cast. It was then found that she had terminal lung cancer. She died in 1971, and as the wife of an Army officer is the only actress to be buried in the cemetery of the U.S. Military Academy at West Point.

The wisecracking blonde gold-digger as a character type is with us no more; she existed for but a brief moment in time, as history goes. But late-night TV viewers are fortunate in that they can still see her epitomized in the screen portrayals of the brassy and self-reliant Glenda Farrell.

THE FILMS OF GLENDA FARRELL

1929: Lucky Boy.
1930: Little Caesar.
1931: *Credit uncertain:* Night Nurse.
1932: I Am a Fugitive from a Chain Gang; Life Begins; Three on a Match; Scandal for Sale; The Match King.
1933: Mystery of the Wax Museum; Grand Slam; Central Airport; Girl Missing; The Keyhole; Gambling Ship; Lady for a Day; Mary Stevens, M.D.; Bureau of Missing Persons; Havana Widows; Man's Castle.
1934: Kansas City Princess; The Big Shakedown; Hi Nellie!; I've Got Your Number; Dark Hazard; Heat Lightning; Merry Wives of Reno; The Personality Kid.
1935: Gold Diggers of 1935; the Secret Bride; Traveling Saleslady; Go into Your Dance; In Caliente; We're in the Money; Little Big Shot; Miss Pacific Fleet.
1936: Smart Blonde; Gold Diggers of 1937; Nobody's Fool; High Tension; Snowed Under; The Law in Her Hands; Here Comes Carter.
1937: Torchy Blane, the Adventurous Blonde; Hollywood Hotel;

Blondes at Work; Breakfast for Two; Flyaway Baby; Dance Charlie Dance.
1938: Torchy Gets Her Man; Stolen Heaven; The Road to Reno; Prison Break; Exposed.
1939: Torchy Blane in Chinatown; Torchy Runs for Mayor.
1941: Johnny Eager.
1942: The Talk of the Town; Twin Beds; A Night for Crime.
1943: City Without Men; Klondike Kate.
1944: Ever Since Venus.
1947: I Love Trouble; Heading for Heaven.
1948: Lulu Belle.
1952: Apache War Smoke.
1953: Girls in the Night.
1954: Susan Slept Here; Secret of the Incas.
1955: The Girl in the Red Velvet Swing.
1959: Middle of the Night.
1964: Kissin' Cousins; The Disorderly Orderly.
1966: Dead Heat on a Merry-Go-Round.
1968: Tiger by the Tail.

Tough dame with a heart of gold:
WYNNE GIBSON

She was as tough as they come—a hard-boiled dame.

With her mouth set in a tight line and her green eyes blazing, Wynne Gibson was best at personifying gangsters' jealous molls or venomous tramps. But many of her characters had a heart of gold—even the tough ones—and a few times she was even cast in **Madame X**-like mother roles that cried out for Helen Hayes or Gladys George.

Winifred Gibson was born July 3, 1903 (some sources say 1899 or 1905), in New York City. At about age 15 she ran away from home to join a road show over her parents' objections. She appeared in vaudeville and as a chorus girl in numerous musicals in stock companies and on Broadway, including Lew Fields' production **Snapshots of 1921, June Love,** the Shuberts' **Poor Little Ritz Girl** (in which she played 13 bit parts), and **Snapshots of 1923,** in which she did a dance number with a young performer named James Cagney.

She and her vaudeville partner, Ray Raymond (who was presumably also her lover at this time), were together in a musical, **When You Smile,** and then she was in the smash hit musical **Sunny,** followed by a national tour with **The City Chap** and a role with the West Coast company of **Castles in the Air.** During the latter show's run in San Francisco, director Erich von Stroheim offered her a part in his film **The Wedding March,** but her schedule did not allow her to accept. When Raymond was killed in a fight with screen actor Paul Kelly over Raymond's wife, actress Dorothy Mackaye (Kelly served a two-year prison term for manslaughter), Miss Gibson returned to Broadway and had a good part in **Jarnegan** in 1928 with Richard Bennett and his daughter Joan.

A short-lived marriage to actor John Gallaudet (who appeared in small parts in a number of "B" films from the mid-Thirties through the Fifties) broke up around 1929, and in that year the actress made her first movie, **Nothing but the Truth,** as Helen Kane's twin sister (actually, her screen debut had been in a Vitaphone short, **Sympathy**). In **Children of Pleasure** (30) she was an heiress who insists on her right to continue, after her prospective marriage, the affair she is having with the understudy of her fiancé, a singer; the fiancé walks out on her. In **The Fall Guy** she was Jack Mulhall's inquisitive wife. She turned down a part in Cecil B. DeMille's **Madam Satan,**

and then signed a contract with Paramount; that studio kept her busy with 13 films in the next two years.

In **City Streets** (31), starring Gary Cooper and Sylvia Sidney, she was a malicious tramp, the discarded moll of gangster Paul Lukas; finally she kills him. She played blackmailer William Powell's confederate in **Man of the World,** threatening to betray him to the police if he leaves her, and in **Ladies of the Big House** she was a hard-bitten convict, giving Miss Sidney a rough time. She played a gangster's moll again in **The Gang Buster,** and a crook's girlfriend (ending up a suicide) in **Kick In.** Revealing that drama was not her only skill, she virtually stole the comedy **June Moon** from Jack Oakie (she played a composer's avaricious, unfaithful wife).

Miss Gibson was into heavy drama in **The Strange Case of Clara Deane** (32), a story of sacrificial mother love. She is a dress designer who marries crook Pat O'Brien and is sentenced to 15 years as his accomplice, although innocent, ending up by killing him to protect their daughter (Frances Dee); any attempt at a good performance was defeated by the soap-opera plot. In **Night After Night** she was George Raft's venomous rejected mistress, and she tries unsuccessfully to kill him, as she had done to Paul Lukas the previous year. She gave a fine performance in **Lady and Gent,** a rowdy romance with George Bancroft, keeping the sloppy sentimentality to a minimum as a tough nightclub hostess who gives it up for motherhood in the country. In **Two Kinds of Women** she is married to Phillips Holmes but refuses to give him up so he can marry Miriam Hopkins; ultimately she kills herself by plunging from a window.

But as good as these roles were, her best-remembered performance in 1932 came in her segment of the eight-episode film **If I Had a Million,** revolving around the reactions of eight widely assorted persons who each receive a philanthropist's gift of a million dollars. She played a waterfront prostitute who, after obtaining the largesse, rents an expensive suite in a plush hotel and goes to sleep in a satin-sheeted bed— *alone.* All this was, of course, before the advent of the Production Code; in most prints of the movie now available this segment has, lamentably, been scissored out.

In the strange drama **Aggie Appleby, Maker of Men** (33) the actress portrayed another soft-hearted tough dame, turning sissy Charles Farrell into a tough guy and tough guy William Gargan into a sissy (don't ask why). She was a hard-boiled gold-digger in **Her Bodyguard,** falling in love with Edmund Lowe (in the title role) and singing "Where Have I Heard That Melody?" She played a cynical nurse in **Emergency Call,** and co-starred with Jean Hersholt—making a somewhat odd wife for that actor—in **Crime of the Century;** she has a lover on the side, and ends up murdered.

I Give My Love (34) was yet another soppy mother-love drama, in which Miss Gibson kills her husband (doing in Paul Lukas once again), serves 10 years in prison, becomes a combination flower seller and artist's model in Paris, and poses for her son (Eric Linden), who thinks she's dead. She was freelancing now, and her career started to decline, with appearances in some dismal programmers. As one of the suspects, she helped solve a murder in **The Crosby Case,** and she appeared in **The Captain Hates the Sea** as a former prostitute, now respectably married, who attempts suicide when her past is exposed by newsman John Gilbert (the former superstar was making his last film). She was a gold-digger in **Gam-** **bling,** starring George M. Cohan, and was top-billed in **Sleepers East** as a paroled convict.

The following year, 1935, the actress went to England and made just two films, playing a movie star kidnapped by pirates in **Admirals All** and a newspaperwoman captured by an evil Arab in **The Crouching Beast.** Her only 1936 film was a weak programmer, **Come Closer, Folks,** and in 1937 there was a string of four "B" pictures, two of them for Republic, on Poverty Row; in one of the latter, **Michael O'Halloran,** she was good as a frivolous woman adopting two orphans. **Trapped by G-Men** cast her as G-man Jack Holt's partner and love interest. These programmers continued apace right on through 1941. Who today can remember **Racketeers in Exile, Flirting with Fate, Cafe Hostess** or **Forgotten Girls**? Things finally came to an end in 1943, when she was a murder suspect, seventh on the cast list, in **The Falcon Strikes Back,** and then made her last movie, a Republic cheapie called **Mystery Broadcast.** In the **Falcon** film, at age 40, she looked 50; life hadn't been kind to her, and that's how the director (Edward Dmytryk, then just beginning to make a name for himself) played it—art imitating life.

The actress was not through with her profession yet, though. She continued to appear on stage, but was even more successful on the radio, being heard in "My True Story," "Thanks for Tomorrow," "When a Girl Marries," "Modern Romances" and "Whispering Streets," among others. She later turned to television, and appeared in such shows as "Studio One," "Martin Kane," "Valiant Lady" and "Three Houses."

For a while Miss Gibson appeared in summer stock on the East Coast, and then became an actors' agent in partnership with Beverly Roberts, another retired Thirties actress, who had appeared with her in a 1938 film, **Flirting with Fate.** They had an office in Manhattan, and lived together in West Babylon, Long Island, New York. In the early 1980s a report said their home was at that time in nearby Westchester County; other, more recent sources say they later moved to California.

Interestingly, even in very recent years the elderly actress, in her seventies, was still listing herself in New York and Hollywood actors' directories as being available for work. She died in 1987 at age 84. But if you turn on your TV late at night, you can sometimes see Wynne Gibson in action once again. There she is—still throwing a good scare into George Raft or Paul Lukas. That dame was *tough!*

THE FILMS OF WYNNE GIBSON

1929: Nothing but the Truth.

1930: Children of Pleasure; The Fall Guy.

1931: City Streets; Ladies of the Big House; Man of the World; Kick In; The Gang Buster; June Moon; The Road to Reno; Touchdown! (extra, in one scene).

1932: If I Had a Million; Two Kinds of Women; The Strange Case of Clara Deane; Lady and Gent; Night After Night; The Devil Is Driving.

1933: Aggie Appleby, Maker of Men; Crime of the Century; Her Bodyguard; Emergency Call; The Sign of the Cross (bit or extra, in one scene).

1934: I Give My Love; The Captain Hates the Sea; The Crosby Case; Gambling; Sleepers East.

1935: Admirals All; The Crouching Beast.

1936: Come Closer, Folks!

1937: Racketeers in Exile; Trapped by G-Men; Michael O'Halloran.

1938: Flirting with Fate; Gangs of New York.

1939: My Son Is Guilty; Cafe Hostess; A Miracle on Main Street.

1940: Forgotten Girls.

1941: Double Cross.

1942: A Man's World.

1943: The Falcon Strikes Back; Mystery Broadcast.

Oh, yeah? Sez who? Is zat so?:
JAMES GLEASON

Director Frank Capra minced no words about him: "My favorite character actor." There are many who would agree.

A little tough guy with a heart of gold, talking out of the side of his mouth in a Brooklynese accent, James Gleason played acidic, pugnacious and exasperated characters—typically, policemen, editors, detectives, boxing managers, cab drivers, Army or Marine sergeants, or somebody's best friend. Wiry, thin-faced and with a pencil mustache, he always built a character who was instantly identifiable and usually likable, and he made the stars look good in some 125 movies.

He usually concealed his niceness beneath an ill-tempered façade—and when he lost that temper, watch out! Director Tay Garnett has said, "There has never been a comic to equal Jimmy at pantomiming fury. His sharp-honed Irish pan would writhe, his eyes would take fire, and his sinewy body would draw itself into an exclamation point of rage." Someone else put it more succinctly, tagging the actor as "140 pounds of Irish dynamite." When he opened his mouth on screen, the odds were that he would say at least one of three things: "Oh, yeah?" "Sez who?" "Is zat so?"

Gleason was born May 23, 1886 (some sources say 1882), in a theatrical boarding house in New York City, to parents who were actors. He was on stage from infancy, and toured with his mother and father in family productions, so his education was intermittent. In 1905 he married Lucille Webster, who was to appear with him in many a stage show and movie. She died in 1947. Their son Russell, born in 1908, appeared in a number of films in the sound era (sometimes with his parents); he died in 1945 in a fall from a hotel window.

After long service in his parents' stock company, James Gleason served in the military in World War I, returning to play roles in Broadway productions, both straight plays and musicals. He simultaneously became active as a director and playwright, authoring a number of light dramas and musicals and acting in many of them himself. Some of these were later made into films, including **Is Zat So?, The Shannons of Broadway, Mammy, The Fall Guy** and **Rain or Shine.** Meanwhile, in 1922 he appeared in a small part in a film, **Polly of the Follies.** In 1928 he moved to Hollywood permanently, launching 30 years of

steady movie work at age 42 with a role in **The Count of Ten;** he was the best thing in this late silent, as prizefighter Charles Ray's tough, no-nonsense, misogynistic manager.

He and his wife co-starred in **The Shannons of Broadway** (29), the screen version of his 1928 play, as a vaudeville couple. Also that year, he was busy as a screenwriter or dialogue specialist on four films. He appeared in **Her Man** (30) as one of a bunch of sailors visiting a dance hall, and was Lilyan Tashman's husband in **The Matrimonial Bed. In Oh, Yeah?** he and Robert Armstrong were a pair of hoboes, and Gleason romanced ZaSu Pitts; he was also the film's dialogue director. **Dumbbells in Ermine** cast Armstrong as a prizefighter and Gleason as his manager, and he was a sports writer in **The Swellhead.**

He had a supporting role in **A Free Soul** (31), the film that made Clark Gable a star, and was jockey Eddie Quillan's loyal pal in **Sweepstakes.** In **Sui-**

cide Fleet he, Armstrong and William Boyd were sailors vying for the affections of Ginger Rogers (at that time an obscure starlet). He played an insurance investigator posing as a gangster in **The Big Gamble,** and was a World War I soldier (married to ZaSu Pitts) in **Beyond Victory.**

His most auspicious role in 1932 came in **The Penguin Pool Murder,** the first of a six-film series in which he played a wisecracking, know-it-all police detective, Inspector Oscar Piper, who keeps finding that he is not as smart as an amateur detective, spinster schoolteacher Hildegarde Withers, who was played in the first three films by the inimitable Edna May Oliver. He also played Marion Davies' plebeian old father in **Blondie of the Follies** and was outstanding as a habitually gloomy football coach in **The All American.** Once again he was a boxing manager in **Lady and Gent,** and played a garage owner in **The Devil Is Driving,** a crooked horse-race gambler in **Fast Companions,** and a motorcycle cop in **The Crooked Circle.**

Gleason supported Lee Tracy in **Clear All Wires** (33), and had a good part in Clara Bow's last film, **Hoopla.** He played a pickpocket in **Billion Dollar Scandal.** The second Hildegarde Withers outing with Miss Oliver was **Murder on the Blackboard** (34), and he was a shady promoter in **Search for Beauty** and a barber in **The Meanest Gal in Town.** He played a movie director on the screen in **Orders Is Orders,** and then did so in real life when he co-directed **Hot Tip** (35), also co-starring in it as a horse-race gambler, once again wed to ZaSu Pitts. **West Point of the Air** cast him as an Army airplane mechanic, and **Murder on a Honeymoon** was the third Hildegarde Withers film and the last with Edna May Oliver. That series took a downward turn with her replacement by Helen Broderick in **Murder on a Bridle Path** (36).

Also in 1936, the actor played a policeman who believes in doing things "by the book" in **We're Only Human,** trying to tame Preston Foster as a cop who thinks he can eliminate crime singlehanded. ZaSu Pitts became the third and last Hildegarde Withers in **The Plot Thickens.** He played a police inspector in **The Ex-Mrs. Bradford** and a tough cop in **Don't Turn 'Em Loose,** also portraying a sports gambler in **The Big Game** and a pal of casino owner George Raft in **Yours for the Asking.**

Miss Pitts wound up the Hildegarde Withers series with **Forty Naughty Girls** in 1937, and then Gleason worked almost exclusively for Republic, a Poverty Row studio, through 1940, including the five-film Higgins Family series (starting with **The Higgins Family** in 1938), featuring his wife Lucille and son

Russell in all five. The critics roasted these dreary programmers.

But if anybody thought that James Gleason's career was washed up at this point, he was very much mistaken. In 1941 he bounced back with an Academy Award-nominated supporting performance as boxing manager Max Corkle in the fine fantasy-comedy **Here Comes Mr. Jordan.** He did the film's best acting (in competition with Robert Montgomery and Claude Rains) and was poignantly splendid as a man with cosmic premonitions, reacting in amazement at each "return" of Montgomery, playing a dead man who has come back to life in someone else's body.

In that same year he played a newspaper editor in **Meet John Doe,** supported Ronald Reagan in **Nine Lives Are Not Enough,** and was a police inspector again in **A Date with the Falcon,** in support of George Sanders. In 1942 he ran a mission flophouse in **Tales of Manhattan,** did another Falcon, **The Falcon Takes Over** (with Sanders again), and was busy in other films. He had a major featured role as an explosive old Army Air Corps colonel in **A Guy Named Joe** (43), and in **Crash Dive** played a Navy chief petty officer with a serious heart condition who sacrifices his life to hold off the Germans during an American commando raid.

The actor was the skeptical police officer, Lieutenant Rooney, in **Arsenic and Old Lace** (44), and played a missionary doctor in China in **The Keys of the Kingdom.** He had a fine cameo as a milkman in **The Clock** (45), and had top featured roles in **A Tree Grows in Brooklyn** and **Captain Eddie.** Gleason was now playing fairly routine supporting roles, but at least he was continuing to support major stars. Entering his sixties, he was appearing in four films a year, including a good part as a cab driver assisting Cary Grant, Loretta Young and David Niven in **The Bishop's Wife** in 1947.

At this point Gleason frequently appeared in films in which he was an old character connected in some way with horses, racetracks and stables, as in **The Homestretch** (47), **The Return of October** (48) and **Riding High** (50). He was James Stewart's reporter pal in **The Jackpot** (50), and had a fine part as the recovering alcoholic who tries to help James Cagney overcome his drinking problem in **Come Fill the Cup** (51). He played a general in **What Price Glory** (52).

The actor supported Ginger Rogers in his only 1953 outing, **Forever Female,** and the following year his sole appearance was in **Suddenly,** a weird and now-forgotten film starring Frank Sinatra as a vicious would-be presidential assassin. In 1955 Gleason demonstrated his dramatic skill again as the senile, drunken riverboat captain in **The Night**

of the Hunter, the only film directed by Charles Laughton.

He was in a cheap Western, **Star in the Dust** (56), and in 1957 supported such diverse talents as Orson Welles (**Man in the Shadow**) and Elvis Presley (**Loving You**). In 1958, his last year on the screen (at age 72), he was suddenly busy again, appearing in six movies, but the only really good part was in di-rector John Ford's **The Last Hurrah,** as one of Spencer Tracy's aides. The other films were routine or worse.

James Gleason died the following year, 1959. It would be nice if he could be reincarnated to confront someone who insists that today's movies are better than those of Hollywood's Golden Era. His reply is predictable: "Oh, yeah? Sez who? Is zat so?"

THE FILMS OF JAMES GLEASON

NOTE: Gleason did not appear, contrary to some sources, in the 1929 films **High Voltage, The Flying Fool, The Broadway Melody** and **His First Command;** the 1930 film **What a Widow!;** or the 1934 film **Change of Heart;** rather, he wrote or co-wrote the scripts. Some sources also erroneously credit him with appearances in the 1942 films **All Through the Night** and **Tramp, Tramp, Tramp;** the actor involved was Jackie Gleason.

1922: Polly of the Follies.
1928: The Count of Ten.
1929: The Shannons of Broadway.
1930: Her Man; The Matrimonial Bed; Big Money; Oh, Yeah?; Putting On the Ritz; Dumbbells in Ermine; The Swellhead.
1931: A Free Soul; It's a Wise Child; Sweepstakes; The Big Gamble; Suicide Fleet; Beyond Victory.
1932: Lady and Gent; Blondie of the Follies; The Penguin Pool Murder; The Devil Is Driving; The All American; Fast Companions; The Crooked Circle.
1933: Clear All Wires; Hoopla; Billion Dollar Scandal.
1934: Orders Is Orders; Search for Beauty; Murder on the Blackboard; The Meanest Gal in Town.
1935: West Point of the Air; Murder on a Honeymoon; Helldorado; Hot Tip (also co-directed).
1936: The Ex-Mrs. Bradford; We're Only Human; Murder on a Bridle Path; Don't Turn 'em Loose; The Big Game; The Plot Thickens; Yours for the Asking.
1937: Forty Naughty Girls; Manhattan Merry-Go-Round.
1938: Army Girl; The Higgins Family.
1939: On Your Toes; The Covered Trailer; Should Husbands Work?; My Wife's Relatives.

1940: Money to Burn; Grandpa Goes to Town; The Earl of Puddlestone.
1941: Here Comes Mr. Jordan; Meet John Doe; Affectionately Yours; Nine Lives Are Not Enough; Babes on Broadway; A Date with the Falcon; Tanks a Million; Safe at Home.
1942: Tales of Manhattan; Footlight Serenade; My Gal Sal; Manila Calling; The Falcon Takes Over; Hayfoot.
1943: A Guy Named Joe; Crash Dive.
1944: Arsenic and Old Lace; The Keys of the Kingdom; Once Upon a Time.
1945: A Tree Grows in Brooklyn; The Clock; Captain Eddie; This Man's Navy.
1946: Home Sweet Homicide; the Hoodlum Saint; Lady Luck; The Well-Groomed Bride.
1947: The Bishop's Wife; Down to Earth; The Homestretch; Tycoon.
1948: When My Baby Smiles at Me; The Return of October; Smart Woman; The Dude Goes West.
1949: Take One False Step; The Life of Riley; Miss Grant Takes Richmond; Bad Boy.
1950: Key to the City; Riding High; The Yellow Cab Man; The Jackpot.
1951: Come Fill the Cup; I'll See You in My Dreams; Two Gals and a Guy; Joe Palooka in the Triple Cross.
1952: What Price Glory; We're Not Married; The Will Rogers Story.
1953: Forever Female.
1954: Suddenly.
1955: The Night of the Hunter; Girl Rush.
1956: A Star in the Dust.
1957: Spring Reunion; Man in the Shadow; Loving You.
1958: The Last Hurrah; The Female Animal; Once Upon a Horse; Rockabye Baby; Money, Women and Guns; Man or Gun.

Hale and hearty:
ALAN HALE

Alan Hale had a prodigious career, appearing in at least 180 films over 39 years. Had he not died at the untimely age of 57, he might have set an incredible record.

He started out in movies well before World War I as a handsome young hero, but through most of the Twenties played villains of the deepest dye. Then, in the sound era, he soon became a jovial, back-slapping (but often untrustworthy) type, frequently appearing later on as Errol Flynn's gregarious buddy. All told, three entirely different personas in one film career.

Tall and burly, with wavy blond hair, he was garrulous, rough-hewn, bluff and hearty, with a loud and raucous laugh. His was one of the most familiar faces ever to flash on the screen, and he had 114 movies to his credit in the sound era alone.

Hale was born as Rufus Alan McKahan on February 10, 1892, in Washington, D.C., the son of a manufacturer of patent medicines. He studied at the University of Pennsylvania to be an osteopath, but decided to give it up for the stage after a brief spell writing obituaries for a Philadelphia newspaper. He tried to make it as an opera singer, but that didn't work out, and he briefly took to the legitimate stage, then, at 19, entered the fledgling film industry with the Lubin studio. From the first he played handsome heroes, his initial appearance being in **The Cowboy and the Lady** (11); in those early days all films were shorts, the feature-length movie being still a couple of years away.

The young actor's first feature-length film was **The Power of the Press** (14). He was an admirable hero that year in **Martin Chuzzlewit** (in the title role), **The Cricket on the Hearth** and **Masks and Faces,** the first two based on Dickens novels. In 1915 he starred as Rochester in **Jane Eyre,** and was in **Under Two Flags.** Freelancing now, he appeared in films for many studios, including Biograph, Metro, Fox, World, Paramount, Selznick, Universal, Graphic, Select and Hodkinson. He co-starred with such prominent female stars as Clara Kimball Young and Pauline Frederick.

In 1914 Hale married actress Gretchen Hartman. They had three children, Alan Jr., Karen and Jeanne. Alan Jr., the physical image of his father, became a film and television actor and later a restaurateur. There was a second marriage, to Betty Reed Doer, in 1943.

About 1920 Hale made a change from playing leading men to working as a character actor, primarily in villainous roles. In **The Four Horsemen of the Apocalypse** (21), the first film to give Rudolph Valentino a starring role, he was Valentino's German cousin, Karl von Hartrott; at the conclusion, they meet in combat on a battlefield and are killed by an exploding shell. **A Voice in the Dark** was a murder mystery in which, playing a doctor, he is killed off at the outset; the murderer turns out to be a nurse he has seduced. In **The Fox,** as a crooked banker in league with outlaws, he is undone by the hero, Harry Carey.

One Glorious Day (22) cast him as the villain, with designs on Lila Lee, but forced to flee after a sound thrashing by Will Rogers. In **The Trap** he cheats French-Canadian trapper Lon Chaney (in a sympathetic role) out of a mining claim and also steals his girlfriend, but loses the mine in a landslide. Alla Nazimova, starring in and producing a screen version of Henrik Ibsen's play **A Doll's House,** chose him to play her stolid husband, Torvald Helmer, an overbearing male chauvinist. He also played Little John to Douglas Fairbanks' **Robin Hood**—the first of three times he would enact the role.

Hale portrayed one of his best silent-screen villains in the classic **The Covered Wagon** (23), as Sam Woodhull, a scoundrel without a single redeeming feature, initially engaged to heroine Lois Wilson but losing her to the hero, J. Warren Kerrigan, whom he tries to kill. In **Quicksands,** as the head of a narcotics-smuggling ring, he is bested by Richard Dix. The film version of Sinclair Lewis' novel **Main Street** found him as town handyman Miles Bjornstam, engaged in a comic romance with Louise Fazenda; Florence Vidor was the star. In the Buck Jones vehicle **The Eleventh Hour** he played the mad Prince Stefan, plotting to take over the world as soon as he can acquire a new explosive being developed. And in director John Ford's **Cameo Kirby** he is killed in a duel with the hero, John Gilbert.

In **One Night in Rome** (24) the actor played Duke Mareno, apparently committing suicide at the outset in remorse for his wartime treachery and leaving a note accusing his wife (Laurette Taylor) of infidelity; it later turns out he was murdered by a gardener to revenge a wronged woman. He played a safecracker abducting the heroine in **Troubles of a Bride.** A non-villainous role came up in **Dick Turpin** (25), in which he helped his friend, Tom Mix, as the highwayman, to escape the scaffold. In **The Crimson Runner** he was a Viennese janitor who assaults heroine Priscilla Dean and later, remarkably, becomes the chief of police, but is killed by the hero in a duel. **Hearts and Fists** (26) cast him as a lumberman who hires thugs to foil his rival, but is ultimately defeated and loses his fiancée to the rival as well.

At this point in time Hale also worked briefly as a director, for Cecil B. DeMille's producing company, turning out seven films in the period 1925-27; none was particularly memorable. In his spare time the actor was also an inventor; he is credited with either inventing or financing the invention of the sliding theater seat, improved automobile brakes, the hand fire extinguisher, and greaseless potato chips.

Continuing his siege of villainy, he was a bully who tries to seduce Leatrice Joy in **Vanity** (27), only to be killed by the ship's cook. In **The Spieler** (28) he was a con man, falling in love with carnival owner Renee Adoree; later he kills villain Fred Kohler. In **The Leopard Lady** he was back as the villain again, as a Cossack working in a circus with a vicious ape he has trained as a killer.

In that same year he began a four-film series with William Boyd (the future Hopalong Cassidy) in which they were buddies working in dangerous occupations. The first, **Skyscraper,** cast them as high steel workers; Boyd is injured while rescuing Hale, the latter pretends to be interested in Sue Carol, and this causes Boyd to recover—just as Hale had planned. In **The Cop** the two actors were of course policemen, and in **Power** they played dam builders. The absurd part-talkie melodrama **Sal of Singapore** cast Hale as a sea captain who finds a baby abandoned on his ship and abducts a waterfront prostitute (Phyllis Haver) to care for it; later he marries her. Fred Kohler was the villain again.

The Leatherneck (29), also a part-talkie, was the last of the films with Boyd; the pair are Marines, serving in China, Hale is driven insane by "water torture," and once more Kohler was the bad guy. The actor played a songwriter in **Red Hot Rhythm,** his first all-sound film, and was involved in misappropriating bank funds along with Edward Everett Horton and Franklin Pangborn in **The Sap.** In **She Got What She Wanted** (30) he was a gambler who marries Betty Compson (with Lee Tracy as another suitor) and later becomes involved in a murder case.

The actor was still up to no good in 1931, attempting to rape Greta Garbo in **Susan Lenox: Her Fall and Rise.** In **The Night Angel** he was the brutish nightclub bouncer infatuated with Nancy Carroll and killed by Fredric March in self-defense. His part in **The Sin of Madelon Claudet** was small as a potential suitor who rejects Helen Hayes. In the screen version of Edna Ferber's novel **So Big** (32) he played Klaus Poole, taking in Selina (Barbara Stanwyck) as a boarder; George Brent was his son. **Union Depot** cast him as a phony baron with a fortune in bank notes stashed in a violin case, and he was the town atheist, living in sin with a woman but later reforming, in **Rebecca of Sunnybrook Farm.**

He had a top villainous role in **Destination Unknown** (33), as the bosun of a disabled ship drifting helplessly on the ocean, and was a rapist and murderer in **Picture Brides,** also portraying villains of the deepest dye in two other films. Three of his four releases that year were for cheapie Poverty Row studios, and the movies were of execrable quality.

Hale appeared in 13 movies in 1934, and more than half of them were to become enduring Hollywood classics. In **It Happened One Night** he was the motorist who gives Clark Gable and Claudette Colbert a lift and then makes off with their luggage. **Of Human Bondage** cast him as the loutish salesman who deserts the pregnant Bette Davis. He was one of the soldiers killed off early in the action in director John Ford's **The Lost Patrol,** and played the good-hearted crook who befriends Margaret Sullavan and Douglass Montgomery in **Little Man, What Now?,** getting the latter a job before being taken off to prison. In Universal's weak version of Dickens' **Great Expectations** he was Joe Gargery, Pip's uncle, and he played the furniture man in **Imitation of Life,** the contrite village drunkard in **The Little Minister,** the police chief in **Fog Over Frisco,** and one of the kidnappers in **Miss Fane's Baby Is Stolen.**

He was in costume for the key role of Blondel in **The Crusades** (35), and likewise for **The Last Days of Pompeii,** as a friend of the star of the film, Preston Foster. As her employer, he cast lecherous eyes on Margaret Sullavan in **The Good Fairy,** and he was a gambling-hall operator who ultimately reforms in **Grand Old Girl.** He played a film producer in **Another Face.** He was one of the chief villains, a top international spy, in **A Message to Garcia** (36), and supported Laurel and Hardy in **Our Relations,** as a waiter. He played a police inspector in **Two in the Dark,** a fur smuggler in **The Country Beyond,** a detective in **Yellowstone,** and the sidekick to a crooked politician in **Parole!**

The actor was in top form in **Stella Dallas** (37), as the uncouth lout Ed Munn, involved for a while with Barbara Stanwyck (Jean Hersholt had played the part in the silent version). In **The Prince and the Pauper,** the first of his numerous films with Errol Flynn, the latter ran the villainous Hale through with a sword; their later on-screen encounters would be less unpleasant. He was a thug in **High, Wide and Handsome,** a detective in **Music for Madame,** and an underworld figure, a bootlegger, in **When Thief Meets Thief (Jump for Glory),** trying to blackmail Douglas Fairbanks Jr. and ending up killed in a fight with him.

The Hale-Errol Flynn combination really got going in 1938 with the fine adventure classic **The Adventures of Robin Hood,** in which (for the second time) he played Little John, engaging Flynn in the famous bout with quarterstaves on a log spanning a stream and later joining Robin's merry men in Sherwood Forest. The actor, now in his mid-forties, was a member of Charles Boyer's Casbah gang in **Algiers,** and in **The Sisters** he played the middle-aged millionaire who is married to Anita Louise although she does not love him. In director John Ford's **Four Men and a Prayer** he was the villain, a wealthy arms dealer who is revealed as the murderer of Sir C. Aubrey Smith. He played Kaidu, leader of the Mongols, in **The Adventures of Marco Polo,** and was a nice guy, a Mr. Fix-It type, helping

Judy Garland and Freddie Bartholomew in **Listen, Darling.**

Hale was Flynn's sidekick again in the historical Western **Dodge City** (39), but in **The Private Lives of Elizabeth and Essex** he played the Earl of Tyrone, the Irish rebel who defeats Flynn on the battlefield. In **Dust Be My Destiny** he was a city editor, and he was ideally cast as the bluff Porthos, one of the Three Musketeers, in **The Man in the Iron Mask.** He portrayed a ballet impresario in **On Your Toes.**

There were three films with Flynn in 1940. He was a comic sidekick to the star in **The Sea Hawk** and **Virginia City,** and generally provided comic relief in **Santa Fe Trail.** In **They Drive by Night** he was murdered by wife Ida Lupino, who is on the make for George Raft. He was a sergeant in **The Fighting 69th,** keeping an eye on James Cagney. He and Marjorie Rambeau tried to recreate the chemistry between Wallace Beery and Marie Dressler seven years earlier in **Tugboat Annie Sails Again,** but it didn't work very well.

Hale now was getting father roles: He was Cagney's dad in **The Strawberry Blonde** (41) and Flynn's in **Gentleman Jim** (42). Also in 1941, he was an unlikely police inspector in **Footsteps in the Dark** and a too-raucous, too-comic power lineman in **Manpower.** Other 1942 films included **Desperate Journey,** in which he and Ronald Reagan were Flynn's sidekicks (they were all pilots battling the Germans). In 1943 it was a naval year, and he was perfectly cast as Cookie, the ship's cook, in **Destination Tokyo,** with Cary Grant, and as "Boats" O'Hara, the bosun, in **Action in the North Atlantic,** with Humphrey Bogart.

He was comic relief in **The Adventures of Mark Twain** (44), and actually played a Nazi in **Hotel Berlin** (45). He was now playing fairly routine parts, although still supporting top stars. Villainy was still in the picture now and then, as when he portrayed a counterfeiter who murders Ruth Warrick's father in **Perilous Holiday** (46). He was Flynn's comic sidekick for the last time in **The Adventures of Don Juan** (48), and for the third and last time he played Little John, crossing quarterstaves with Robin Hood, in **Rogues of Sherwood Forest** (50)—but John Derek was no Errol Flynn.

The actor's last film was the superior drama **Stars in My Crown,** but the part was not a big one in this 1950 release. By the time it came out, he was dead at the early age of 57. But Alan Hale still lives on the TV or movie screen, sharing many a chuckle with his pal Errol Flynn.

THE FILMS OF ALAN HALE

NOTE: This filmography includes only feature-length films, so it omits all of Hale's appearances from 1911 through 1913, since they were not feature-length.

1914: The Power of the Press; Martin Chuzzlewit; Masks and Faces; Strongheart; Men and Women; Adam Bede; The Cricket on the Hearth. *Credit uncertain:* The Woman in Black.

1915: Dora Thorne; East Lynne; Jane Eyre; Under Two Flags. *Credit uncertain:* After the Storm; The Americano.

1916: The Purple Lady; The Love Thief; Rolling Stones; The Scarlet Oath; Pudd'nhead Wilson.

1917: The Woman in the Case; The Price She Paid; Life's Whirlpool; The Eternal Temptress; One Hour.

1918: Masks and Faces (possibly a remake of the 1914 film, or an error?); Moral Suicide; The Whirlpool.

1919: Love Hunger; The Trap; The Blue Bonnet.

1921: The Four Horsemen of the Apocalypse; A Voice in the Dark; The Barbarian; A Wise Fool; Over the Wire; The Great Impersonation; The Fox.

1922: Robin Hood; One Glorious Day; A Doll's House; The Trap; The Dictator; Shirley of the Circus.

1923: The Covered Wagon; Quicksands; Main Street; The Eleventh Hour; Hollywood; Cameo Kirby; Long Live the King; Black Oxen.

1924: Code of the Wilderness; Girls Men Forget; One Night in Rome; For Another Woman; Troubles of a Bride.

1925: Dick Turpin; The Crimson Runner; Flattery; Ranger of the Big Pines.

1926: Hearts and Fists; Redheads Preferred.

1927: Vanity; The Wreck of the Hesperus.

1928: The Spieler; The Leopard Lady; Skyscraper; Oh, Kay!; The Cop; Power; Sal of Singapore.

1929: The Leatherneck; Sailor's Holiday; Red Hot Rhythm; The Sap.

1930: She Got What She Wanted.

1931: Susan Lenox: Her Fall and Rise; The Sin of Madelon Claudet; The Night Angel; Aloha; The Sea Ghost.

1932: So Big; Union Depot; The Match King; Rebecca of Sunnybrook Farm.

1933: Destination Unknown; Picture Brides; The Eleventh Commandment; What Price Decency.

1934: It Happened One Night; Of Human Bondage; Imitation of Life; The Little Minister; The Lost Patrol; Fog Over Frisco; Babbitt; Little Man, What Now?; Miss Fane's Baby Is Stolen; Broadway Bill; There's Always Tomorrow; The Scarlet Letter; Great Expectations.

1935: The Crusades; The Good Fairy; The Last Days of Pompeii; Grand Old Girl; Another Face.

1936: A Message to Garcia; Two in the Dark; The Country Beyond; Our Relations; Parole!; God's Country and the Woman; Yellowstone.

1937: Stella Dallas; The Prince and the Pauper; High, Wide and Handsome; Thin Ice; Music for Madame; When Thief Meets Thief (Jump for Glory).

1938: The Adventures of Robin Hood; Algiers; The Sisters; Four Men and a Prayer; The Adventures of Marco Polo; Valley of the Giants; Listen, Darling.

1939: Dodge City; The Private Lives of Elizabeth and Essex; Dust Be My Destiny; The Man in the Iron Mask; On Your Toes; Pacific Liner.

1940: The Fighting 69th; The Sea Hawk; Santa Fe Trail; Virginia City; They Drive by Night; Three Cheers for the Irish; Green Hell; Tugboat Annie Sails Again.

1941: Strawberry Blonde; Footsteps in the Dark; Manpower; Thieves Fall Out; The Smiling Ghost; The Great Mr. Nobody.

1942: Gentleman Jim; Desperate Journey; Jute Girl; Captains of the Clouds.

1943: Destination Tokyo; Action in the North Atlantic; This Is the Army; Thank Your Lucky Stars.

1944: The Adventures of Mark Twain; Make Your Own Bed; Janie; Hollywood Canteen.

1945: God Is My Co-Pilot; Hotel Berlin; Roughly Speaking; Escape in the Desert.

1946: Night and Day; The Man I Love; The Time, the Place and the Girl; Perilous Holiday.

1947: Pursued; My Wild Irish Rose; Cheyenne; That Way with Women.

1948: The Adventures of Don Juan; My Girl Tisa; Whiplash.

1949: South of St. Louis; The Younger Brothers; The House Across the Street; Always Leave Them Laughing.

1950: Rogues of Sherwood Forest; Colt .45; Stars in My Crown.

That shifty little coward:
PORTER HALL

A shifty, weaseling little coward. That was Porter Hall. He was the type to foreclose your mortgage, or he might just shoot you in the back. He was perpetually a sneak, a meanie, a skinflint, a double-dealer. And you can just bet that it kept him busy for two decades on the screen.

He had a shifty mustache, and beady eyes surrounded by crooked eyebrows and heavy bags. He usually played annoying, grouchy, unhelpful busybodies—snooty little men who are cowards and fools yet exhibit gargantuan self-importance. They never have a good word for anyone, and they try to crush the films' defenseless heroes and heroines (usually by getting them in trouble with the authorities). Also, Hall's characters are suspicious—almost as suspicious as Franklin Pangborn's hotel clerks.

Small, compactly built, with a sour-looking face that could turn either wry or grim, he played prosecutors, crooked businessmen, bigots, blackmailers and murderers with facility and skill. He was one of the men you loved to hate.

Clifford Porter Hall was born September 19, 1888 (some sources say 1883), in Cincinnati, and educated at the University of Cincinnati. He worked in a steel mill and then became an itinerant Shakespearean stage actor, later going to Broadway and playing in comedies during the Twenties.

In 1927 he married Geraldine Brown. They had two children, David and Sarah Jane. (And despite his screen villainy, in private life the actor was a church deacon.)

After acquiring considerable experience on the stage, he turned to the movies in 1934, at age 45. And started right off being nasty, as the lawyer who turns out to be the murderer (of several people) in the classic mystery **The Thin Man.** He was a murder *victim* in **Murder in the Private Car,** but was the killer again in **The Case of the Lucky Legs** (35). He was one of the members of the medical establishment opposing Louis Pasteur (Paul Muni) in **The Story of Louis Pasteur.**

The next three years were Hall's busiest on the screen; he appeared in 27 films in 1936, 1937 and 1938. He was outstanding in **The General Died at Dawn** (36) as Madeleine Carroll's crooked, sniveling father, in league with a Chinese warlord (Akim Tamiroff) but ending up killed by Gary Cooper in self-defense. As if in revenge for this, he in turn killed

Cooper by shooting him in the back in **The Plainsman;** Cooper played Wild Bill Hickok and Hall was Jack McCall. In **The Petrified Forest** he was Bette Davis' sour-faced, super-patriotic father, organizing an impromptu posse to go after escaped convict Humphrey Bogart and later regretting it. He played a slimy blackmailer murdered by Douglass Dumbrille in **The Princess Comes Across,** and was the district attorney in **And Sudden Death.**

Satan Met a Lady was a bizarre version of **The Maltese Falcon** in which, as the partner of private detective Warren William, Hall is murdered by Miss Davis because she thinks he is one of the henchmen of the mysterious Madame Barabbas (Alison Skipworth); in effect, William, Miss Davis and Miss Skipworth played what would later be the Humphrey Bogart, Mary Astor and Sydney Greenstreet roles respectively.

The actor was the cantankerous prosecutor in Carole Lombard's murder trial in **True Confession**

(37) and, in a remarkably similar role, played the prosecutor who tries to convict Gary Cooper of murder in **Souls at Sea.** In the tearjerker **Make Way for Tomorrow** he was the callous son-in-law of elderly Beulah Bondi and Victor Moore, not caring about finding a home for them. He played a crooked oil-stock promoter in **Let's Make a Million,** a sleazy banker in **Wells Fargo,** and a newspaper editor in **King of Gamblers.** As the villain, he menaced hero Ray Milland in both **Bulldog Drummond Escapes** and, in the following year, **Bulldog Drummond's Peril** (in the latter, as the head of a ring of jewel thieves).

Hall was also a jewel thief in **Stolen Heaven** (38), and played the weaseling warden in **Prison Farm,** the head of a shipping company in **King of Alcatraz,** a mayor in **Dangerous to Know,** and a newspaper editor in **Men with Wings.** In **Scandal Street** he and Roscoe Karns are running a crooked mail-order scheme, and he shoots Karns to death. **Mr. Smith Goes to Washington** (39) cast him as one of the senators, and he was again a shady stock promoter in **Grand Jury Secrets.** He was a real meanie in **They Shall Have Music,** as a creditor who threatens to shut down a music school for underprivileged children, at one point sending his men to pry the instruments from the youngsters' hands.

The actor played one of the reporters in **His Girl Friday** (40), and in **Arizona** he and Warren William were the bad guys trying to stop Jean Arthur's railroad freight business until William Holden comes to the rescue. Playing a Civil War-era banker who is a Southern sympathizer in **Dark Command,** he is killed by an angry pro-Northern mob; Claire Trevor and Roy Rogers played his daughter and son. In director Preston Sturges' **Sullivan's Travels** (41) he was one of the studio executives arguing with Joel McCrea, as a film director, over what kind of movies he should make.

He played a small-town crook defeated by Holden in **The Remarkable Andrew** (42), and **The Desperadoes** (43) cast him as a swindling banker. He had a key role in **Double Indemnity** (44) as the man encountered on the train by Fred MacMurray while MacMurray and Barbara Stanwyck are carrying out their murder plot; later he proves to be an unreliable witness. He played the justice of the peace who marries Betty Hutton and Eddie Bracken in Sturges' **The Miracle of Morgan's Creek,** and for the same director portrayed President Franklin Pierce in **The Great Moment,** also supporting Bing Crosby in **Going My Way.**

Hall had a good comedy role in **Murder, He Says** (45), as the mousy but deadly little father of a weird hillbilly family, married to Marjorie Main and ultimately revealed as the killer. **Blood on the Sun** cast him as a treacherous American in league with the Japanese before Pearl Harbor, and in **Kiss and Tell** he was the father of Shirley Temple's boyfriend. He was malicious as the neurotic psychiatrist for Macy's department store in **Miracle on 34th Street** (47), trying to get Kris Kringle (Edmund Gwenn) committed, and he was one of a number of villainous characters in **Unconquered,** once again tangling with Gary Cooper. In **That Wonderful Urge** (48) he played the newspaper attorney bringing a libel suit against Gene Tierney at the behest of Tyrone Power, and he was an escaped embezzler in **You Gotta Stay Happy.**

He had one of his best roles as the leader of the bigoted Southerners in the powerful racial drama **Intruder in the Dust** (49), playing the murdered man's father and leading the lynch mob trying to kill an innocent black man (Juano Hernandez). In **The Beautiful Blonde from Bashful Bend** he was the town judge, succumbing to the wiles of Betty Grable. He was in fine form as newspaper publisher Jacob Q. Boot in director Billy Wilder's grim drama **The Big Carnival** (51) (originally titled **Ace in the Hole**), hiring reporter Kirk Douglas, who ruthlessly capitalizes on the tragedy of a man trapped in a cave. There was a routine part in **Carbine Williams** (52), and his last good role came in **Vice Squad** (53), as the witness to a murder, held in custody by police captain Edward G. Robinson until he helps identify the killer. In his last film, **Return to Treasure Island** (54), he was a crook vying with student Tab Hunter for some buried treasure. By the time it was released, Porter Hall had died at age 65 (late in 1953). He lives on in the memory as one of the great nasties of the screen.

THE FILMS OF PORTER HALL

1931: *Credit uncertain:* Secrets of a Secretary.
1934: The Thin Man; Murder in the Private Car.
1935: The Story of Louis Pasteur; The Case of the Lucky Legs.
1936: The General Died at Dawn; The Petrified Forest; The Plainsman; Satan Met a Lady; The Princess Comes Across; And Sudden Death; Too Many Parents; Snowed Under.

1937: True Confession; Souls at Sea; Wells Fargo; Make Way for Tomorrow; King of Gamblers; Let's Make a Million; Bulldog Drummond Escapes; Hotel Haywire; This Way, Please; Wild Money.
1938: Stolen Heaven; King of Alcatraz; Dangerous to Know; Prison Farm; Scandal Street; Men with Wings; Tom Sawyer—Detective; Bulldog Drummond's Peril; Arkansas Traveler.

1939: Mr. Smith Goes to Washington; They Shall Have Music; Grand Jury Secrets; Henry Goes Arizona.

1940: His Girl Friday; Arizona; Dark Command; Trail of the Vigilantes.

1941: Sullivan's Travels; Mr. and Mrs. North; The Parson of Panamint.

1942: The Remarkable Andrew; Butch Minds the Baby.

1943: The Woman of the Town; A Stranger in Town; The Desperadoes.

1944: Double Indemnity; Going My Way; The Miracle of Morgan's Creek; Standing Room Only; The Great Moment; The Mark of the Whistler.

1945: Weekend at the Waldorf; Murder, He Says; Blood on the Sun; Kiss and Tell; Bring On the Girls.

1947: Miracle on 34th Street; Unconquered; Singapore.

1948: You Gotta Stay Happy; That Wonderful Urge.

1949: Intruder in the Dust; Chicken Every Sunday; The Beautiful Blonde from Bashful Bend.

1951: The Big Carnival (Ace in the Hole).

1952: Carbine Williams; Holiday for Sinners; The Half-Breed.

1953: Vice Squad; Pony Express.

1954: Return to Treasure Island.

Need an affluent protector, young lady?:
JOHN HALLIDAY

In many a Hollywood film of the Thirties there was a part for a suave, dapper, well-to-do middle-aged man who is keeping as his mistress a younger woman (who doesn't love him but needs a wealthy protector, or at least someone to pay the rent). John Halliday and Adolphe Menjou clearly violated the antitrust laws by cornering the market in such roles and dividing them up. When the part was a lecherous theatrical producer, Menjou got it; when it was a sympathetic business tycoon or a gentleman crook, it was Halliday's turn.

Halliday also had a neat line in tolerant husbands, and played the understanding father of several top female stars. With a trim mustache and an incisive manner, he was usually on the nice side, but could develop a mean streak when required. Too self-effacing to be a star, he appreciated it when Paramount obligingly handed him a few top-billed leads in "B" films.

The actor was born September 14, 1880, in Brooklyn, New York (at that time a separate incorporated city), but went to Scotland to train as a mining engineer and then studied at Cambridge University. After service in the British army during the Boer War, he went to the mining camps of the American West and reportedly made a fortune as the owner of the Jumbo Mine at Goldfield, Nevada, only to lose it later through bad investments. While running the mine he had his first taste of show business, presenting Gilbert and Sullivan's **H.M.S. Pinafore** to the miners.

He turned from a mining career to acting, performing in Gilbert and Sullivan and in dramatic presentations in California, then in the Far East and Australia. In 1912 producer William A. Brady (the father of actress Alice Brady) offered him a major part in the smash hit play **The Whip,** in which he made his Broadway debut at age 32.

Although sources do not indicate the dates, the actor was married three times: to Camille Personi, Eva Lang and actress Eleanor Griffith. He was divorced from the first two. Miss Griffith made a few screen appearances, notably as Chester Morris' wife in **Alibi** (29).

Halliday kept busy on the Broadway stage for some 15 years, with two brief side trips to Hollywood to make movies—one in 1916 and two in 1920. On Broadway, he co-starred with Helen Hayes in

Dancing Mothers in 1924 and with Fay Bainter in **Jealousy** in 1928, and had many other starring roles. At the advent of the sound era, along with many other stage-trained actors, he was called back to the film capital and began a 12-year career as a movie character actor.

The first film he then made was an atrocious Poverty Row part-talkie, **East Side Sadie** (29). Things improved in the following year. In **Scarlet Pages** he co-starred with Elsie Ferguson (in her last film); he played a district attorney and she was the mother of Marian Nixon, who was accused of murder. His co-star in **Recaptured Love** was Belle Bennett, and he played for the first time a middle-aged roué, here involved with a young nightclub entertainer, in this case divorcing his wife (Miss Bennett) for the performer (Dorothy Burgess), but eventually seeing his mistake.

The Misses Ferguson and Bennett, however, were over-the-hill silent-screen actresses whose careers were just ending, and better things lay ahead. Halliday, now entering his fifties, starred in **Captain Applejack** (31) as the timid hero who finds the courage to prevent a gang of crooks from robbing his home of a horde of treasure hidden there by a pirate ancestor. He supported Lewis Stone and Irene Rich in **Father's Son,** giving a fine performance as the understanding family doctor who brings their runaway son home. He was Myrna Loy's banker husband in **Transatlantic,** casting his roving eye on Greta Nissen. In **Millie** he played a wealthy man-about-town who dallies with the heroine (Helen Twelvetrees) and years later secretly lures her teen-age daughter (Anita Louise) to his country house for evil purposes, only to be killed by Miss Twelvetrees.

Continuing his run of good roles in that busy year, he was used by Mary Astor to make her straying husband jealous in **Smart Woman;** she nearly marries Halliday but then changes her mind. **Once a Sinner** cast him as the former lover of Dorothy Mackaill, who has thrown him over in favor of Joel McCrea, and he played a newspaper editor, Pat O'Brien's boss, in **Consolation Marriage.**

The actor played a sympathetic college professor in **The Age of Consent** (32), and in **The Impatient Maiden** he paid the rent for Mae Clarke, but she fought off his advances. He was a wealthy rake trying to seduce Joan Bennett in **Week Ends Only.** As a crooked racehorse gambler, he tried unsuccessfully to use Mary Astor to destroy his betting rival, Ricardo Cortez, in **Men of Chance,** and played a philandering husband who accidentally poisons himself in **The Man Called Back.**

He had a key role in **The House on 56th Street** (33) as the wealthy, aging lover whom Kay Francis deserts for Gene Raymond; later he is accidentally killed by her in a struggle for a gun when he threatens suicide, and she spends years in prison. In **The Woman Accused** he spends most of the film trying to pin the murder of his friend Louis Calhern on Nancy Carroll, nearly succeeding; Cary Grant was Miss Carroll's fiancé. **Bed of Roses** cast the actor as a prominent hymn-book publisher keeping riverboat prostitute Constance Bennett in luxury, but he loses her to Joel McCrea. He co-starred with Gloria Swanson and Laurence Olivier in **Perfect Understanding;** Swanson and Olivier are married, and Halliday is a famous explorer who is in love with her anyway. In **Terror Aboard** he was a "civilized" man who kills nearly everyone on an ocean liner, some by rather gruesome methods.

In **Return of the Terror** (34) he played a scientist who fakes insanity to escape prosecution for a series of murders he didn't commit, and then flees to his old sanatorium—where more murders take place. **Registered Nurse** found him as a devoted chief surgeon who ends up winning Bebe Daniels, in the title role, after numerous vicissitudes; film historian Roger Dooley has called it "surely the only time he ever got the girl." In the unusual drama **The Witching Hour,** as a gambling-den owner with the uncanny power to read thoughts and control people's actions, he makes a murderer of his daughter's fiancé. In **Happiness Ahead** he was the father of Josephine Hutchinson, who is in love with Dick Powell, and in **Finishing School** he and Billie Burke were the parents of the nominal star, Frances Dee. He had an important role in **Housewife,** as a cosmetics manufacturer who hires advertising man George Brent but resists the efforts of Brent's wife, Ann Dvorak, to romance him, in order to make Brent jealous, after the ad man gets interested in ex-flame Bette Davis; finally Halliday proposes to Miss Dvorak, but she turns him down and returns to Brent. He was top-billed as a movie director in Monogram Pictures' **A Woman's Man.**

The actor continued to star on the New York stage between film assignments. He was in **Rain from Heaven** in 1934, and in 1936 co-starred in **Tovarich,** in the part later played on screen by Charles Boyer.

As Ann Harding's jealous husband, he was accidentally killed by her lover, Gary Cooper, in **Peter Ibbetson** (35). He played the blinded Fredric March's sympathetic friend in **The Dark Angel.** He was an Italian diplomat in **The Melody Lingers On** and a millionaire art connoisseur in **Mystery Woman.** Probably his finest hour came in **Hollywood Boulevard** (36), in which he starred as a fallen matinee idol whose memoirs are serialized. He was equally superb in **Desire** as Marlene Dietrich's wily, dapper partner in thievery, turning from suave charm to real menace with the subtlest change of expression in his voice. Having played a movie director, he now turned to portraying a film *producer* in **Three Cheers for Love;** this movie was the genesis of that hoary joke that has since appeared in other films, the motto of the low-budget Miracle Pictures studio: "If it's a good picture, it's a Miracle." In **Fatal Lady,** as an opera impresario, he is wrongly suspected of being a murderer.

Halliday was off the screen in 1937, returning the following year to play Deanna Durbin's father in **That Certain Age.** He had a key supporting role in **Blockade,** as a spy who ends up shot by Madeleine Carroll, and was back to jewel thievery in **Arsene Lupin Returns.** In the fine drama **Intermezzo—A Love Story** (39), Ingrid Bergman's first American film, he played violinist Leslie Howard's former accompanist, serving as the *raisonneur* and admonishing Miss Bergman not to destroy Howard's marriage. In **Elsa Maxwell's Hotel for Women** he has Lynn Bari for a mistress, and ends up shot by her when he turns his attentions to the very young Linda Darnell (in her film debut). He played Katharine Hepburn's father in **The Philadelphia Story** (40), divorced and estranged from the family, returning for her wedding and lecturing her on having everything except "an understanding heart."

In the mediocre programmer **Escape to Glory (Submarine Zone)** (41), he played a rotter, a crooked district attorney, who has Constance Bennett for a secretary and mistress, but she spends most of her time with either freewheeling Pat O'Brien or murderous gangster Alan Baxter. His last film, **Lydia**, cast him as Merle Oberon's (and Edna May Oliver's) family butler and the father of Joseph Cotten, who is one of four men in love with Miss Oberon.

The actor then retired to Honolulu, and died there in 1947, aged 66. But any young woman of today who could use an affluent protector would surely welcome the reincarnation of John Halliday.

THE FILMS OF JOHN HALLIDAY

1916: The Devil's Toy.
1920: The Woman Gives; The Love Expert.
1929: East Side Sadie.
1930: Scarlet Pages; Recaptured Love.
1931: Transatlantic; Consolation Marriage; Millie; The Spy; The Ruling Voice; Smart Woman; 50 Million Frenchmen; Once a Sinner; Captain Applejack; Father's Son.
1932: Bird of Paradise; The Age of Consent; The Impatient Maiden; Men of Chance; Week Ends Only; The Man Called Back.
1933: The Woman Accused; The House on 56th Street; Bed of Roses; Terror Aboard; Perfect Understanding.

1934: The Witching Hour; Housewife; Desirable; Happiness Ahead; Registered Nurse; Finishing School; Return of the Terror; A Woman's Man.
1935: Peter Ibbetson; The Dark Angel; The Melody Lingers On; Mystery Woman.
1936: Desire; Hollywood Boulevard; Three Cheers for Love; Fatal Lady.
1938: Blockade; That Certain Age; Arsene Lupin Returns.
1939: Intermezzo—A Love Story; Elsa Maxwell's Hotel for Women.
1940: The Philadelphia Story.
1941: Lydia; Escape to Glory (Submarine Zone).

The hatchet-faced spinster:
MARGARET HAMILTON

Surely there was somebody like her in your town, if you came from a small town. She may have been a gossipy spinster, a snoopy neighbor, a prying house-keeper, or the nightmare schoolteacher who gave you homework every day and warned you about throwing spitballs. Maybe she was the sharp-eyed town busybody with nothing better to do than check up on all the neighbors' peccadilloes. But whoever she was, Margaret Hamilton could have played her on the screen.

Skinny as a rail, with a shrill voice and an instantly recognizable hatchet-faced physiognomy (hawklike nose, beady eyes, firmly clamped mouth), she usually played, as she put it, women "with a heart of gold and a corset of steel." Well, maybe not *all* of them had a heart of gold. Certainly not the Wicked Witch of the West.

Miss Hamilton was born December 9, 1902 (one source says September 12), in Cleveland. Following her schooling she became a kindergarten teacher, but soon joined the Cleveland Playhouse and turned to a stage career. From the start she took character roles, often older women. Among those early roles in Cleveland were such classic spinsters as Miss Prism in Oscar Wilde's **The Importance of Being Earnest** and Prossy in Bernard Shaw's **Candida.** Before long she found herself on the Broadway stage, where she continued to gain experience, although her roles often were unrewarding. In 1932 she played the only likable in-law of new bride Helen Hayes in **Another Language,** and made her film debut in 1933 when both actresses were called upon to repeat the roles on the screen. Thereafter she worked in Hollywood.

Miss Hamilton married landscape architect Paul Meserve in 1931. They had a son, Hamilton, and divorced in 1938; she never remarried.

She was a flashily dressed milliner in **Hat, Coat and Glove** (34), and a maid in **By Your Leave,** also playing small parts in two other films that year. **Way Down East** (35) provided her first "mean" role, as a venomous country gossip whose victims included Henry Fonda. She was also good in another rural drama, **The Farmer Takes a Wife** (which was Fonda's screen debut).

Audiences burst into applause at the conclusion of **These Three** (36) when she, as a servant, administered a well deserved whack to Bonita Granville, the malicious youngster who had stirred up trouble

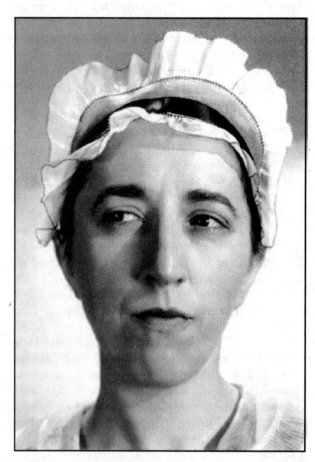

for Merle Oberon, Joel McCrea and Miriam Hopkins. In **The Moon's Our Home** the actress contributed the film's most hilarious moments as a rural boarding-house owner who sneaks in to model Margaret Sullavan's flimsy nightgown before a mirror, only to be discovered by her flabbergasted hayseed husband. She was another boarding-house owner, a sympathetic one, in **Chatterbox,** and a gossipy spinster seamstress in **Laughing at Trouble.**

Miss Hamilton could be memorable even in a one- or two-line cameo, as she was when she played suspicious small-town New Englanders in **Nothing Sacred** and **You Only Live Once** (both 37). She had a nice cameo in the Clark Gable-Jean Harlow starrer **Saratoga** as a plain woman who irately informs Frank Morgan that the beauty product he manufactures hasn't done a thing for her, and in the backwoods drama **Mountain Justice** she played the perennial fiancée of Guy Kibbee. In several other films that year she was cast as a domestic servant.

In **A Slight Case of Murder** (38) she was the disapproving orphanage owner dealing with Edward G. Robinson, and she played Mrs. Harper in **The Adventures of Tom Sawyer.** She was an unpleasant woman plotting to buy the family's home in **Mother Carey's Chickens,** and in **Stablemates** played the five-time widow who owns the farm where Wallace Beery and Mickey Rooney stay while they make plans to enter their horse in a big race.

Then came the role for which Margaret Hamilton will forever be remembered. In a triumph of casting, she appeared in **The Wizard of Oz** (39) as the nasty schoolteacher Miss Gulch, determined to separate Dorothy (Judy Garland) from her dog Toto in the Kansas sequence, then metamorphosing into the unforgettable Wicked Witch of the West, green-faced and red-eyed, with her sinister horde of flying monkeys. She screeches, rants, brews evil potions, menaces Dorothy and threatens her with death, and finally, soaked by Dorothy with a fatal bucket of water, dissolves with the anguished cry, "I'm melting!" This fiendishly cackling performance remains the ultimate in wicked witchcraft. Interestingly, it was not the last time Miss Hamilton would portray a witch; she later played the First Witch in at least two stage productions of **Macbeth.**

Also that year, she was the town busybody in **Babes in Arms,** determined to have Miss Garland and Mickey Rooney removed from a corrupting show-business influence and placed in state work schools. She gave the Dead End Kids a hard time in **Angels Wash Their Faces,** and was a hick in **Main Street Lawyer.** She was perfectly cast in **My Little Chickadee** (40) as the crusading, self-righteous, prudish town gossip who sets out to see the somewhat soiled Mae West redeemed by a man who will marry her; however, W.C. Fields is hardly the man Miss West has in mind. The actress was also good as Anita Louise's mother in the old-fashioned Gay Nineties-style "mellerdrammer" **The Villain Still Pursued Her.**

She played John Barrymore's no-nonsense housekeeper in **The Invisible Woman** (41), and repeated her **Babes in Arms** characterization in **Babes on Broadway.** She played her patented rural woman in **The Shepherd of the Hills.** In the following year she was in such films as **Journey for Margaret** and **Twin Beds.** She was a narrow-minded villager supporting the lynch mob in **The Ox-Bow Incident** (43), and was in support in **Guest in the House** (44) as Ralph Bellamy's maid, suspiciously eyeing newcomer Anne Baxter. Then she didn't get another good

role until **Mad Wednesday (The Sin of Harold Diddlebock)** (47), Harold Lloyd's last movie, playing his spinster sister and wearing horn-rimmed glasses identical to his trademark spectacles.

The actress was in **State of the Union** (48), and in **The Beautiful Blonde from Bashful Bend** (49) she played the battle-ax wife of Porter Hall, who was a judge succumbing to Betty Grable's blandishments. She was a teacher in **The Red Pony.** She was excellent in **Wabash Avenue** (50) as a thinly disguised Carry Nation, a militant temperance advocate who smashes up a saloon. She played an eccentric plane passenger who helps foil the heavies after a robbery and some murders in **The Great Plane Robbery,** and supported Bing Crosby in **Riding High.** Then she got trapped in an Abbott and Costello outing, but followed this by supporting Cary Grant and Jeanne Crain in the interesting and offbeat drama **People Will Talk** (51). At this point Miss Hamilton left the screen for nine years, turning to television and the stage. On TV she appeared in such shows as "Ethel and Albert," "The Patty Duke Show," "The Addams Family" and "Search for Tomorrow." On the boards, she starred in regional productions and sometimes appeared in versions of **The Wizard of Oz.**

She returned to the screen in 1960 in the forgettable **Thirteen Ghosts,** was in a 1962 disaster called **Paradise Alley,** and in 1966 only her voice was heard in **The Daydreamer.** She supported Rosalind Russell in **Rosie!** (67), and had a good role in director Robert Altman's bizarre **Brewster McCloud** (70), also appearing in **The Anderson Tapes** (72). Now in her seventies, making her home in New York City's Gramercy Park section, she became well known to TV watchers as Cora, the New England storekeeper who promotes Maxwell House Coffee, and also made other commercials. Miss Hamilton was the obvious choice to provide the voice for the Wicked Witch again in the animated film **Journey Back to Oz** (74), with Judy Garland's daughter Liza Minnelli as Dorothy. It was her last screen role.

In 1979 she had a featured role in a TV movie, **Letters from Frank.** Then she went back on the stage and was a great success in the national company of the Stephen Sondheim musical **A Little Night Music,** as a sumptuous courtesan at the end of her days.

Margaret Hamilton died at 82 in 1985. But you don't have to worry: Somebody always revives **The Wizard of Oz** on television at least once a year. There she is, up on the screen, cackling evilly and brewing her sinister potions—as wonderfully wicked an old witch as anyone could ever wish for.

THE FILMS OF MARGARET HAMILTON

1933: Another Language.
1934: Broadway Bill; There's Always Tomorrow; Hat, Coat and Glove; By Your Leave.
1935: Way Down East; The Farmer Takes a Wife. *Credit uncertain:* People Will Talk.
1936: These Three; The Moon's Our Home; The Witness Chair; Chatterbox; Laughing at Trouble. *Credit uncertain:* The Trail of the Lonesome Pine.
1937: Nothing Sacred; You Only Live Once; Saratoga; Mountain Justice; I'll Take Romance; Good Old Soak; When's Your Birthday?
1938: The Adventures of Tom Sawyer; A Slight Case of Murder; Four's a Crowd; Stablemates; Mother Carey's Chickens; Breaking the Ice.
1939: The Wizard of Oz; Babes in Arms; Angels Wash Their Faces; Main Street Lawyer.
1940: My Little Chickadee; The Villain Still Pursued Her; I'm Nobody's Sweetheart Now.
1941: The Shepherd of the Hills; The Invisible Woman; Babes on Broadway; Play Girl; The Gay Vagabond.
1942: Journey for Margaret; Twin Beds; Meet the Stewarts; The Affairs of Martha (Once Upon a Thursday).
1943: The Ox-Bow Incident; Johnny Come Lately; City Without Men.
1944: Guest in the House.
1945: George White's Scandals.
1946: Faithful in My Fashion; Janie Gets Married.
1947: Mad Wednesday (The Sin of Harold Diddlebock); Dishonored Lady; Driftwood.
1948: State of the Union; Bungalow 13; Texas, Brooklyn and Heaven.
1949: The Beautiful Blonde from Bashful Bend; The Red Pony; The Sun Comes Up.
1950: Wabash Avenue; Riding High; The Great Plane Robbery.
1951: People Will Talk; Coming Round the Mountain.
1960: Thirteen Ghosts.
1962: Paradise Alley.
1966: The Daydreamer (voice only).
1967: Rosie!
1969: Angel in My Pocket.
1970: Brewster McCloud.
1971: The Anderson Tapes.
1974: Journey Back to Oz (voice only).

The voice of authority:
SIR CEDRIC HARDWICKE

Sir Cedric Hardwicke, one of the most talented character actors ever to appear on the screen, was done in by his personality. Authoritative, remote and aristocratic, he projected absolutely no sympathy, which meant that virtually all his good roles were in villainous parts—but even worse, his great talent was too often squandered in mediocre movies.

You remember him, typically, as a gruff middle-aged man. He usually looked sad, which meant that he seemed understanding when he played kindly men and embittered when he played villains. Basically, his characters were pompous Victorians, and from film to film he switched back and forth between sympathetic gentlemen and black-hearted villains with practiced ease. But best of all the components of his acting was his imposing and plummy voice, which bespoke authority and breeding. You can still hear it in your mind years after seeing a Hardwicke performance.

Cedric Webster Hardwicke was born February 19, 1893, in Stourbridge-on-Lye, Worcestershire, England, the son of a country doctor. His mother reportedly discouraged him from following in his father's footsteps, although one source indicates he was a medical student for a short while. After some amateur dramatics he studied at the Royal Academy of Dramatic Art. He made his stage debut at age 19 in **The Monk and the Woman** in 1912, and in the following year was in a short English film, **Riches and Rogues,** playing six parts because he needed the money. He was offered an American screen contract by Vitagraph, but turned it down.

After serving as an officer in the British army in World War I, the actor joined the Birmingham Repertory Theatre and began to make a name for himself, often appearing as considerably older men. He was frequently cast in Bernard Shaw's plays; Shaw liked him so much as Captain Shotover that he later wrote a part into **Too Good to Be True** for him. However, he really became a favorite with the public in an Eden Phillpotts drama, **The Farmer's Wife,** in 1924. He returned briefly to the screen in 1925 for a supporting part in **Nelson.** Back on the London stage, he was in another Phillpotts play, **Yellow Sands,** in 1928, and also, incredibly, was cast as Captain Andy in **Show Boat.** The next year he originated the part of Magnus in Shaw's **The Apple Cart,** and in 1930 scored a big success as the father in **The Barretts of**

Wimpole Street, which led to his starring the following year in the British film **Dreyfus,** in the title role as the French officer condemned to Devil's Island as a traitor in the famous 1890s case.

Hardwicke made his Broadway debut about 1931 as the optimistic clergyman Dean Harcourt in **Green Light** (which he would later repeat on the screen). In 1933 he was excellent in the film **Rome Express,** as a pompous, falsely philanthropic millionaire, and he played a shady lawyer in the Boris Karloff starrer **The Ghoul.** The following year he was fine as King Charles II in **Nell Gwyn** (with Anna Neagle in the starring role), was the rabbi in **Power (Jew Süss),** and starred in **The King of Paris,** about theatrical life. He was the villain, a swindling financier, in **The Lady Is Willing,** misappropriating the funds of three businessmen, who hire detective Leslie Howard; Howard gets the goods on the swindler and also wins the man's wife (Binnie Barnes).

In that year, 1934, he was knighted by King

George V while appearing on Broadway in **The Late Christopher Bean;** he was to become one of the few knighted actors to use his title professionally. He had to turn down offers by MGM to appear in **David Copperfield** and other films because he was committed to a tour of the play, but in 1935 he went to Hollywood for what would ultimately be a long stay.

The actor played the sympathetic bishop assisting Fredric March in **Les Miserables** (35), and as the Marquis of Steyne he supported Miriam Hopkins in **Becky Sharp,** the first three-color Technicolor feature. He returned to England to film **Peg of Old Drury** (he was good as David Garrick) and **Bella Donna.** Continuing in British films for the moment, he was the evil Theotocopulos in **Things to Come** (36), a sculptor determined to halt further progress for mankind, especially a space gun to shoot people to the moon. He played the crafty villain in **Nine Days a Queen,** and was Edmund Gwenn's pompous, sponging brother-in-law in **Laburnum Grove.**

He then returned to America more or less permanently, appearing next in **Green Light** (37) as the pontificating cathedral dean whose optimism makes Voltaire's Pangloss look like a cynic by comparison. He returned briefly to London that year to film **King Solomon's Mines,** in the lead role as Allan Quartermain, and then was back on Broadway for a while, notably in **Shadow and Substance,** which ran well into 1938.

Three of Hardwicke's best screen roles were played in 1939. In **On Borrowed Time** he was Mr. Brink (i.e., Death), cornered in a magical apple tree by Lionel Barrymore, and in **Stanley and Livingstone** he was the famed missionary Dr. Livingstone ("I presume"), being found in the African jungle by Spencer Tracy as the explorer Stanley. **The Hunchback of Notre Dame** cast him as Frollo, the fanatical lord high justice, Quasimodo's brooding nemesis, an evil and lecherous man lusting after Maureen O'Hara.

The actor had married Helena Pickard in 1928, and they had a son, Edward, who became a stage actor in England; recently he has played Sherlock Holmes' Dr. Watson on TV in an ongoing series. The couple divorced in 1948, and he then married Mary Scott in 1950; they too divorced, in 1961. (One source mentions a third, unspecified, wife.)

In director John Cromwell's version of Joseph Conrad's novel **Victory** (40) he gave what many consider to be his finest screen performance, although the film (starring Fredric March) is scarcely remembered today. He played Mr. Jones, "a soft white homosexual crook in sunglasses" (film historian Charles Higham), who with his two henchmen invades March's hideaway where he has taken Betty Field. Film critic Howard Barnes said at the time, "The Hardwicke characterization of the evil, woman-hating Mr. Jones is the only one that comes through with the impact it had in the book. It is superb. Terror stalks the screen from the moment Mr. Jones appears, and builds into an irresistible crescendo."

In that year he also played the headmaster, Dr. Arnold, in **Tom Brown's School Days;** a crippled reactionary in **The Howards of Virginia,** supporting Cary Grant; and the villain in **The Invisible Man Returns,** in a terribly hammy performance, battling with Vincent Price as the title figure. In 1941 he had a routine part as Joan Fontaine's father in **Suspicion** and was also in **Sundown. In The Ghost of Frankenstein** (42) he was Ludwig Frankenstein, unhappy heir to the family problems, and he played a Nazi officer in the absurd programmer **Invisible Agent** and an English naval officer in **Commandos Strike at Dawn.**

Hardwicke was excellent as the Nazi commandant of a Norwegian town in **The Moon Is Down** (43), but was on the other side as a French priest consoling his countrymen in a Nazi prison camp in **The Cross of Lorraine.** That year he also personally put together the fine film **Forever and a Day,** with an incredible all-star cast in cameo roles, a charity film to help British war relief. It was his energy and passionate concern that made the project work. (He also appeared in a slapstick scene with Buster Keaton, as a pair of plumbers installing a bathtub in the Victorian era.)

In **Wilson** (44), a filmed biography of the World War I-era president, he was the epitome of bitterness and icy contempt in a brief but important part as the senior Senator Henry Cabot Lodge, destroying Wilson's plan to have the United States join the League of Nations; Alexander Knox played the title role. He was again a high-ranking cleric in **The Keys of the Kingdom,** Merle Oberon's father in **The Lodger,** and an admiral in **Wing and a Prayer.** Now in his early fifties, in 1945 he was the plummy-voiced (and uncredited) narrator of **The Picture of Dorian Gray** (but was not seen on the screen), and then he returned to England to appear on the stage again. In 1946 he played a doctor who befriends John Payne in **Sentimental Journey.**

From this point on he shuttled back and forth across the Atlantic, appearing in English and American movies and stage plays. (He co-starred with Katharine Cornell in **Antigone** in 1946.) He had never really deserted the stage, and in fact he rather despised the movies, although he needed the money they provided. Probably one reason he disliked them was that so often he was given mediocre roles in mediocre movies. If anything, this situation was to get worse during the postwar period.

In 1947, however, Hardwicke had both his last good run of dramatic roles and his busiest year on the screen, making eight films. He played a Scotland Yard inspector on the trail of the murderous Joan Fontaine in **Ivy,** and was the red herring nobody suspected in **Lured,** turning out to be the killer menacing Lucille Ball. In **A Woman's Vengeance** he was excellent as the doctor who uses hypnosis to draw from Jessica Tandy the truth—that she murdered Charles Boyer's wife—to save him at the last minute from the gallows. He gave a study of bleak and implacable villainy in **Nicholas Nickleby,** played the industrialist of the title in the John Wayne starrer **Tycoon,** and was in several other films.

The actor had a routine part in 1948 as the father of the murder victim in director Alfred Hitchcock's **Rope,** and his role was small in **I Remember Mama.** The following year he was a comic King Arthur in **A Connecticut Yankee in King Arthur's Court,** singing "Busy Doing Nothing" with Bing Crosby and William Bendix; critics said he was the best thing in the picture. He also starred in Bernard Shaw's **Caesar and Cleopatra** on Broadway. **The Winslow Boy** (50) cast him as the father of the suspected thief defended by Robert Donat, and at this point he was frequently seen in five-minute bit parts, some of them routine, in such films as **The White Tower, The Desert Fox** (51), **Mr. Imperium, The Green Glove** (52), **Caribbean, Botany Bay** (53) and **Salome;** in the latter, at least, he was fine as Tiberius.

The excellent science-fiction thriller **War of the Worlds** used him as the narrator, with just the tone of his voice hinting of impending doom. He continued his cameo parts, playing Priam in **Helen of Troy** (55) and making an appearance in the Lana Turner starrer **Diane.** But during the early Fifties he was much better used on stage, in the touring company of Shaw's **Don Juan in Hell,** as the Statue, with Charles Laughton, Charles Boyer and Agnes Moorehead rounding out the cast. In 1956 Sir Laurence Olivier summoned him to play Edward IV in the superb film version of Shakespeare's **Richard III;** after Hardwicke dies, the evil Richard (Olivier) murders the king's young sons in the tower and claims the throne for himself.

His run of cameo parts continued, including three films in which nearly *everyone* had cameo roles: **The Ten Commandments** and **Around the World in 80 Days** (both 56) and the absurd pastiche **The Story of Mankind** (57), in which he played the high judge of the tribunal. But in 1957 he did have one fine part, demonstrating what he could still do in drama: In **Baby Face Nelson,** starring Mickey Rooney as the gangster, he was the seedy, rundown doctor at the bottom of his profession, consoling himself with alcohol, who runs the sanatorium where Rooney recovers from injuries suffered in a holdup. He is paid to remove the gangster's fingerprints, and also attempts some passes at Rooney's moll, Carolyn Jones, finally being killed by Rooney to prevent his squealing later.

He was now off the screen for four years, sometimes appearing on television and, again, on the stage, notably as the Japanese(!) widower involved in a romance with Jewish matron Gertrude Berg in the hit Broadway play **A Majority of One;** he later appeared on her TV series "Mrs. G. Goes to College." After his second divorce he was financially crippled by alimony payments, reportedly unable to handle money and admitting he would take any role offered him. In 1961 he wrote his autobiography, "A Victorian in Orbit," and supported an over-the-hill Esther Williams in **The Magic Fountain,** appearing the following year in **Five Weeks in a Balloon** as the professor leading the balloon expedition to Africa.

He had a small but effective part in his last film, **The Pumpkin Eater,** which starred James Mason, Anne Bancroft and Peter Finch. It was released in 1964, the year he died in virtual poverty at age 71. (His funeral was paid for by the Actors' Relief Fund.) Sir Cedric Hardwicke had been ill-used by Hollywood over many years, but his dramatic skill still shines through in those films where perceptive filmmakers gave him roles suitable to his splendid talents.

THE FILMS OF SIR CEDRIC HARDWICKE

1926: Nelson.
1931: Dreyfus.
1933: Rome Express; The Ghoul; Orders Is Orders.
1934: Nell Gwyn; Power (Jew Süss); The King of Paris; The Lady Is Willing.
1935: Becky Sharp; Les Miserables; Peg of Old Drury; Bella Donna.
1936: Things to Come; Laburnum Grove; Nine Days a Queen (Tudor Rose); Calling the Tune.
1937: Green Light; King Solomon's Mines.
1939: On Borrowed Time; Stanley and Livingstone; The Hunchback of Notre Dame.
1940: Victory; The Howards of Virginia; Tom Brown's School Days; The Invisible Man Returns.
1941: Suspicion; Sundown.

1942: The Ghost of Frankenstein; Invisible Agent; Commandos Strike at Dawn; Valley of the Sun.

1943: The Moon Is Down; The Cross of Lorraine; Forever and a Day.

1944: Wilson; The Keys of the Kingdom; The Lodger; Wing and a Prayer.

1945: The Picture of Dorian Gray (narrator only).

1946: Sentimental Journey.

1947: Ivy; Lured; A Woman's Vengeance; Beware of Pity; Nicholas Nickleby; The Imperfect Lady; Tycoon; Song of My Heart.

1948: Rope; I Remember Mama.

1949: A Connecticut Yankee in King Arthur's Court; Now Barabbas Was a Robber.

1950: The Winslow Boy; The White Tower.

1951: The Desert Fox; Mr. Imperium.

1952: The Green Glove; Caribbean.

1953: Botany Bay; Salome; War of the Worlds (narrator only).

1954: Bait.

1955: Helen of Troy; Diane.

1956: Richard III; The Ten Commandments; Around the World in 80 Days; The Vagabond King; Gaby; The Power and the Prize.

1957: Baby Face Nelson; The Story of Mankind.

1961: The Magic Fountain.

1962: Five Weeks in a Balloon.

1964: The Pumpkin Eater.

Fidgeting fingertips:

HUGH HERBERT

Probably no comedian in screen history—possibly excepting S.Z. Sakall and Laurel and Hardy—has been so identified in the public mind with a single "piece of business," a trademarked gesture or expression, as was Hugh Herbert.

At some point in just about all his films he would become nervous or agitated. He would then raise fluttering hands, fidget with his fingertips, dart his eyes to and fro, and excitely utter the expression "Woo-woo!" (Evidently this was intended to mean something along the lines of "Boy, have I got problems!")

He was good as a harmless and benevolent eccentric, and frequently played a sheepish philanderer (or *would-be* philanderer). The actor was in nearly 100 comedies and musicals of the Thirties and Forties, usually in small roles, often cameos, but occasionally in leads. During his peak period, at Warner Bros. from 1933 to 1938 (he made 42 films in that short span), he stole many a scene from many a star.

Herbert was born August 10, 1887, in Binghamton, New York, and was educated at Cornell University, although he is said to have been a stage comic as early as age 16. He began his career in vaudeville, writing his own routines. After many years on stage, during which he wrote some of the plays himself, he entered the movies in 1927 as a combination writer and comedy actor, his first part being in **Husbands for Rent** that year, in a small part as a valet. He and Mack Swain were a pair of idiotic detectives in **Caught in the Fog** (28). The actor was the co-author of the first all-talkie, **Lights of New York,** and wrote the dialogue for **The Air Circus** that year and for the Erich von Stroheim starrer **The Great Gabbo** (29). In 1930 he had a cameo as a comic hobo in **Danger Lights** and also was dialogue director, as well as co-directing and co-scripting **He Knew Women.** He played the seedy house detective in the Wheeler and Woolsey comedy **Hook, Line and Sinker,** and co-wrote the script for **The Second Wife**.

Some film reference books confuse the actor with screenwriter F. Hugh Herbert (1897-1958), who is sometimes erroneously given credit for Hugh Herbert's early dialogue work.

The actor was the ambitious first mate in **The Sin Ship** (31), starring Mary Astor; he also wrote the screenplay. He managed to steal the show from Edna

May Oliver in **Laugh and Get Rich,** as her indolent, good-hearted husband, always coming up with a get-rich-quick scheme. He was a traveling salesman in **Traveling Husbands,** and had a featured role in support of Erich von Stroheim, Laurence Olivier and Adolphe Menjou in **Friends and Lovers.** The next year, incredibly, Tallulah Bankhead became his mistress in **Faithless** after he gave her some money (however, she ends up at the finale with Robert Montgomery). He was an aircraft mechanic in **The Lost Squadron,** and the secretary of the Treasury in the weird W.C. Fields farce **Million Dollar Legs.**

He and Frank McHugh were a pair of drunks in **Convention City** (33), and as Genevieve Tobin's husband in **Goodbye Again** he watched her rekindle an old romance with Warren William. He played a detective in **Bureau of Missing Persons,** and had key roles in such films as **Footlight Parade** and **From Headquarters.** He was a stand-out in **Dames** (34), as the hypochondriac moralist Ezra Ounce, an "angel" backing a stage production and also the president of a foundation "for the elevation of American morals." **The Merry Frinks** starred him as a journalistic paterfamilias, a reporter always getting fired for drunkenness; Aline MacMahon played his wife. In **Kansas City Princess** he was a millionaire who threw over his wife in favor of gold-digger Glenda Farrell, and he was an ostrich-feather salesman, with an overstock of the product, in **Fashions of 1934.** He played a newspaper photographer in **Fog over Frisco,** the financial backer of a play in **Sweet Adeline,** and a detective in **Easy to Love.** Miss Farrell was his wife now in **Merry Wives of Reno,** casting her eye on other men.

Herbert had every reason to fidget his fingertips and cry "Woo-woo!" in **Gold Diggers of 1935** (35), because after he dictated a romantic song lyric to a stenographer (who but Miss Farrell?), she converted it into a love letter and sued him for breach of promise. He was fine as the rustic Snout in **A Midsummer Night's Dream,** and he played a lawyer who employed process servers Joan Blondell and—you guessed it—Miss Farrell in **We're in the Money,** and the same two ladies were involved in **Miss Pacific Fleet,** entering the contest of the title, of which Herbert was the creator. You don't even have to guess which two actresses he was involved with in **Traveling Saleslady,** do you? The actor starred in **To Beat the Band** as a man who must marry a widow within three days or forfeit a $59 million inheritance, and weds Helen Broderick.

Perhaps his definitive screen performance was given in **Colleen** (36), as an eccentric millionaire who entrusts gold-digger Blondell with his dress shop, against his family's wishes. He played Donald Meek's old stage role in **Love Begins at Twenty,** a remake of the play **Broken Dishes,** as the henpecked husband who turns the tables, and was a comic kleptomaniac in **Sing Me a Love Song.** He played the economics professor and perpetual alumni secretary in **We Went to College,** and was the priggish president of the Purity League in **One Rainy Afternoon,** shocked when Francis Lederer steals a kiss from Ida Lupino in a movie theater.

Herbert had married Rose Epstein in 1932, and they divorced in 1949, whereupon he married actress Anita Pam.

In 1937 he played a moronic detective investigating strange doings in a lighthouse in **Sh! The Octopus,** also appearing as a hitchhiking poet who gets involved with Miss Blondell and Errol Flynn in **The Perfect Specimen.** He was a promoter who opens a nightclub in **The Singing Marine,** and played a drunk, engineering a romance between a young el-evator operator and a chambermaid, in **That Man's Here Again. In Marry the Girl** he and Mary Boland were a brother and sister running a news syndicate and trying to keep their niece from marrying Mischa Auer. He portrayed a music publisher in **The Great Waltz** (38), and was once more involved with gold-diggers in **Gold Diggers in Paris,** although this time they were not the Misses Farrell and Blondell. In **Men Are Such Fools** he played matchmaker for Wayne Morris and Priscilla Lane.

Herbert starred in the forgettable comedy **Little Accident** (39), as a riotously unhinged newspaper advice columnist who finds an abandoned tot (Baby Sandy) and takes care of her. He was magician David Niven's incompetent valet in **Eternally Yours.** In the weak comedy **The Family Next Door** he starred as a loony plumber whose incompetence forever frustrates his family's ambitions. He was refreshingly subdued in **Private Affairs** (40) as a Scottish cab driver-cum-valet, and starred in **Slightly Tempted** as a fumbling kleptomaniac reforming for his daughter's sake and marrying an elderly spinster. He was a reform-minded philanthropist in the old-fashioned comedy-melodrama **The Villain Still Pursued Her,** and played six parts (a man, his mother, and his four sisters) in **La Conga Nights.** He was Gloria Jean's father in **A Little Bit of Heaven.**

Now in his mid-fifties, the actor appeared as a comic detective in **Hellzapoppin** (41), and he was still "woo-wooing" in **Meet the Chump,** starring as the fumbling executor of a multi-million-dollar estate, reducing the assets to almost nothing. In **Don't Get Personal** (42) he was a pickle manufacturer interfering in the marriage of two radio stars, and played an incompetent advertising man in **You're Telling Me,** also portraying a pudding manufacturer running for mayor in **There's One Born Every Minute.** These last four films were all low-budget Universal comedies in which he was the nominal star. At this point Herbert's screen appearances declined sharply. He made only six films from 1943 through 1947, all in small and forgettable roles. In 1948 he was one of the seven comical professors in the Danny Kaye starrer **A Song Is Born** (a remake of 1941's **Ball of Fire**), and had relatively small parts in such films as **One Touch of Venus.** The following year he was the doctor in the Betty Grable vehicle **The Beautiful Blonde from Bashful Bend,** and in 1951 he was in his last film, a cheap Republic programmer, **Havana Rose.**

Hugh Herbert died in 1952 at age 65, leaving filmgoers with fond memories of fidgeting fingertips and that unforgettable trademark, the "Woo-woo!" by which we will always remember him.

THE FILMS OF HUGH HERBERT

1927: Husbands for Rent.
1928: Caught in the Fog.
1930: Danger Lights; Hook, Line and Sinker; Second Wife.
1931: Friends and Lovers; The Sin Ship; Laugh and Get Rich; Traveling Husbands. *Credit uncertain:* Cracked Nuts.
1932: Faithless; The Lost Squadron; Million Dollar Legs.
1933: Footlight Parade; Bureau of Missing Persons; From Headquarters; College Coach; Convention City; Goodbye Again; Strictly Personal; She Had to Say Yes. *Credit uncertain:* Goldie Gets Along.
1934: Dames; Kansas City Princess; Fog over Frisco; Sweet Adeline; Fashions of 1934; Easy to Love; The Merry Frinks; Wonder Bar; Merry Wives of Reno; Harold Teen.
1935: Gold Diggers of 1935; A Midsummer Night's Dream; We're in the Money; Miss Pacific Fleet; Traveling Saleslady; To Beat the Band.
1936: Colleen; Love Begins at Twenty; Sing Me a Love Song; One Rainy Afternoon; We Went to College. *Credit uncertain:* Mind Your Own Business.
1937: Hollywood Hotel; The Perfect Specimen; The Singing Marine; Top of the Town; Sh! The Octopus; That Man's Here Again; Marry the Girl.
1938: The Great Waltz; Men Are Such Fools; Four's a Crowd; Gold Diggers in Paris.
1939: Little Accident; Eternally Yours; The Family Next Door; The Lady's from Kentucky.
1940: A Little Bit of Heaven; Private Affairs; The Villain Still Pursued Her; Hit Parade of 1941; Slightly Tempted; La Conga Nights.
1941: Hellzapoppin; The Black Cat; Badlands of Dakota; Meet the Chump; Hello, Sucker.
1942: You're Telling Me; Don't Get Personal; There's One Born Every Minute; Mrs. Wiggs of the Cabbage Patch.
1943: Stage Door Canteen.
1944: Kismet; Music for Millions; Ever Since Venus.
1945: One Way to Love.
1947: Blondie in the Dough.
1948: One Touch of Venus; So This Is New York; A Song Is Born; On Our Merry Way (A Miracle Can Happen); The Girl from Manhattan.
1949: The Beautiful Blonde from Bashful Bend.
1951: Havana Rose.

You get older, you get nicer:
JEAN HERSHOLT

Perhaps you've seen both these actors on the screen.

One, in such classics of the silent era as **Greed, Tess of the Storm Country** and **Don Q, Son of Zorro,** played nasty and brutish villains. The other is remembered from the late Thirties as everyone's favorite kindly old country doctor.

Remember these actors? It shouldn't be hard. They were both the same man—Jean Hersholt.

The versatile and phlegmatic Danish character actor appeared on the American movie screen for 40 years, playing many kinds of roles and many nationalities. With his square face and bush of dark hair, he was a familiar figure in some 120 films. And he was also, in private life, one of Hollywood's most notable humanitarians.

Hersholt was born July 12, 1886, in Copenhagen, to parents who were both prominent actors. He trained for the stage at that city's Dagmar Theatre, while also becoming the Danish national champion bicycle racer. Some sources indicate that he appeared in 1906 in what they term the first film ever made in Denmark, **On Walby's Hill,** but at that early date it was almost certainly a short film. He then seems to have turned to the stage for nearly a decade, touring throughout Scandinavia before coming to the United States about 1912 (some sources say 1914) and continuing his stage work there. In 1914 he was touring the country in Henrik Ibsen's plays when he met Lon Chaney, then playing supporting roles in Hollywood, who introduced him to filmmakers. The following year he made his American screen debut with the Ince studio. (But another source says he appeared in European films for six years and made his first American film in 1913.)

In that same year, 1914, the actor married Via Andersen, and they had a son, Allan.

Hersholt is said to have begun his film work by appearing in 80 one-reelers (10-minute films) in 1915. He also supported cowboy star William S. Hart in **The Disciple,** and was in **Don Quixote.** In the following year there were two more Hart outings, **Hell's Hinges** and **The Aryan.** Signing with Universal, he made 10 films for that studio in 1917, supporting such stars as Franklyn Farnum and Ruth Stonehouse. In 1918 he had a key role in **Princess Virtue,** with Mae Murray and Wheeler Oakman, and **Madame Spy,** with Jack Mulhall.

The actor had an important role in the Rudolph Valentino starrer **The Four Horsemen of the Apocalypse** (21), as Professor von Hartrott, and in **A Certain Rich Man** he was unpleasant as an alcoholic newspaper publisher whom the heroine is compelled to marry and who later is killed in a railroad accident. **The Man of the Forest** cast him as a bootlegger. He was the bearded, burly murderer lusting after Mary Pickford in **Tess of the Storm Country** (22), and in **When Romance Rides** he played a half-witted stablehand who abducts the heroine. **The Stranger's Banquet** gave him a small part as "a fiend." During this period he also worked as an assistant director.

He made an excellent villain, usually with a sullen scowl, grease-smeared hair and a loud shirt, such as in **Quicksands** (23), in which he was a drug smuggler. But his greatest and most unforgettable bad-guy role came in 1924 in director Erich von Stroheim's superb classic **Greed.** As Marcus Schouler in this version of Frank Norris' novel **McTeague,** he was the unsuccessful rival to McTeague (Gibson Gowland) for the hand of ZaSu Pitts, and soon afterward tries to kill Gowland. The stunning climax finds the two men in the blazing wastes of Death Valley, where Hersholt tracks down Gowland and is killed by him—but manages to handcuff himself to his rival before he dies, thus ensuring the death of McTeague in the pitiless and trackless desert.

In that same year, in **Torment** he was a Russian nobleman fleeing the revolution with the crown jewels and killed by thugs, played a famous sculptor in **Cheap Kisses,** and supported Colleen Moore in **So Big.** In **Stella Dallas** (25) he was the cheap, tasteless Ed Munn (the part taken by Alan Hale in the 1937 version), temporarily involved with Stella (Belle Bennett), and in **Don Q, Son of Zorro** he played a crafty and calculating blackmailer, Don Fabrique. He was "a crook" in **Fifth Avenue Models,** and tried to take advantage of Laura La Plante in **Dangerous Innocence.** In **If Marriage Fails** he played a doctor.

Hersholt was somewhat miscast as 'Erb 'Uggins, a Cockney costermonger, in **My Old Dutch** (26), and in **The Greater Glory** he played the owner of a gaming den who also deals in war supplies and, oddly, wins the heroine (Anna Q. Nilsson). **Flames** cast him as a construction foreman who disguises himself as an outlaw and abducts heroine Virginia Valli but is himself captured by the real outlaw (Boris Karloff). He was a retired garage owner getting involved with bootleggers in **The Old Soak,** and was Colleen Moore's father, a delicatessen proprietor, in **It Must Be Love.** He played Dr. Juttner, the tutor of the prince (Ramon Novarro), in **The Student Prince in Old Heidelberg** (27); Norma Shearer co-starred. He starred as a corset manufacturer falling for a lady detective in **The Wrong Mr. Right.**

The actor was not yet through with portraying unsavory individuals. In **Alias the Deacon** (28) he was a professional card shark and gambler who, disguised as a deacon, cons himself into solvency whenever the need arises. But **Abie's Irish Rose** cast him as Solomon Levy, father of Abie (Charles [Buddy] Rogers); most critics agreed he stole the film from Rogers and Nancy Carroll. He was up to no good again in **13 Washington Square** as an art thief with whom Alice Joyce gets involved. In director D.W. Griffith's **The Battle of the Sexes** he was a married man seduced by a young gold-digger (Phyllis Haver).

He co-starred with Pola Negri in the first screen version of Sidney Howard's play **They Knew What They Wanted,** here called **The Secret Hour,** as the Italian-American Tony, the aging California grape grower who brings a young mail-order bride to his Napa Valley orchards. (This film would be remade in 1930 as **A Lady to Love** with Edward G. Robinson and Vilma Banky, and in 1940 under the play's original title with Charles Laughton and Carole Lombard.) Hersholt also starred in **Jazz Mad** as a European orchestra conductor unable to sell his musical compositions and suffering a temporary mental breakdown until his daughter (Marian Nixon) and a booking agent (Roscoe Karns) arrange for an orchestra to perform his symphony.

In director Frank Capra's **The Younger Generation** (29) he was an elderly Jewish pushcart peddler named Julius Goldfish who rises to wealth on Park Avenue, and **The Girl on the Barge** cast him as a mean, hard-drinking barge captain trying to keep his daughter (Sally O'Neil) from marrying a tugboat pilot. These were part-talkies. He was back to villainy in **Hell Harbor** (30), as a pearl trader lecherously pursuing Lupe Velez and killing his erstwhile **Greed** rival, Gibson Gowland. As a lawyer, he tried to help escaped prisoner of war Chester Morris in **The Case of Sergeant Grischa,** and he was a teacher of opera singers in **The Climax.** In **Mamba** he was a coarse and unpleasant African planter married to beautiful young Eleanor Boardman and later killed by the natives. **The Third Alarm** found him as a fireman killed in action; Anita Louise played his daughter.

The sound era brought changes to Hersholt's career. Because of his strong foreign accent, his range of roles became more limited, but he continued to be busy in character leads and supporting parts. He was Greta Garbo's unfeeling father in **Susan Lenox: Her Fall and Rise** (31), trying to marry her off to brutish Alan Hale; she flees, and meets Clark Gable. He played a financially ruined watchmaker in **Transatlantic,** supported Norma Shearer in **Private Lives,** portrayed a kindly doctor who is the longtime friend of the hapless Helen Hayes in **The Sin of Madelon Claudet,** and was the villain in **Daybreak,** forcing his attentions on Helen Chandler but losing her to Ramon Novarro. In **The Phantom of Paris** he was a friend of John Gilbert.

The actor had his busiest year on the screen in 1932, with roles in 11 movies. In **Grand Hotel** he was the porter, anxious over his wife's difficulty in bearing their first child, and **The Mask of Fu Manchu** cast him as a professor who undergoes tortures inflicted by Boris Karloff in the title role. He played a gangster in **Beast of the City,** and a kindly old Jewish pawnbroker who adopts an Irish orphan in **Hearts of Humanity.** In **Emma** he was a widower whose children are raised by his housekeeper, Marie Dressler; when they are grown he proposes marriage, but soon after the wedding dies of a heart attack. He was a janitor in **Night Court,** the immigrant proprietor of a beer garden in **Flesh,** a delicatessen owner in **Unashamed,** and played other roles. During this period he was under a contract with MGM (from some point in the Twenties through 1935).

Hersholt had a virtually cameo-sized part in the all-star film **Dinner at Eight** (33) as a Broadway producer insulted by John Barrymore, and in **Song of the Eagle** he was a decent German-American beer baron forced out of business by Prohibition and killed by one of his former truck drivers, now a bootlegger (Charles Bickford). He starred in **Crime of the Century** as a doctor who hypnotizes a banker into giving him $100,000 to satisfy the medic's greedy, philandering wife (Wynne Gibson); then she is murdered, but he turns out to be innocent. In **Christopher Bean** he and George Coulouris were greedy rival art dealers trying to acquire a deceased artist's paintings.

In **Men in White** (34) the actor was the head physician who counsels young doctor Clark Gable in professional integrity and medical ideals; this was the first of his "kindly old doctor" roles, and he would shortly be typecast in such parts. He was Greta Garbo's father again in **The Painted Veil,** and **The Fountain** cast him as the stern Dutch stepfather of Ann Harding. He was a professor, the mentor to composer-pianist Ramon Novarro, in **The Cat and the Fiddle.** In the weak Katharine Hepburn-Charles Boyer starrer **Break of Hearts** (35) he was the only believable character on the screen as Miss Hepburn's kindly old music teacher, but in **Mark of the Vampire** he was back to villainy again, as the murderer (disguised as a vampire) unmasked by Lionel Barrymore via hypnosis. There were still more dastardly deeds in **Murder in the Fleet,** in which he was a crazed naval inspector who murders two men and attempts to blow up a ship, but is thwarted by Robert Taylor. At this point he signed a contract with 20th Century-Fox.

Then came **The Country Doctor** (36). Capitalizing on the immense popularity of the Dionne Quintuplets (born in 1934), it cast Hersholt as the real-life figure Dr. Dafoe, the physician who delivered them; John Qualen was featured as their father, and the Quints of course played themselves. The film was a smash hit. The actor, the Quints and Qualen followed it up the same year in **Reunion,** in which the good doctor dispenses much advice and solves many a problem. He also starred in **Sins of Man** as an old Austrian church-bell ringer; his two sons were both played by Don Ameche in his screen debut. In **One in a Million** he was the Norwegian innkeeper father of Sonja Henie, in her American film debut, and in **His Brother's Wife** he was a professor helping Robert Taylor do research on spotted fever deep in the jungle.

He was the perfect choice to play Shirley Temple's bitter grandfather, whose heart she melts, in **Heidi** (37), and was cast as the priest in the remake of **Seventh Heaven,** with James Stewart and Simone Simon. It was back to the Quints again in **Five of a Kind** (38), and he was once again Miss Henie's dad in **Happy Landing.** Having played professors and music teachers before, he combined the two as Tyrone Power's violin instructor (before he decides to be a band leader) in **Alexander's Ragtime Band,** and he played a circus clown in **I'll Give a Million.**

In 1939 he played his last villain, in **Mr. Moto in Danger Island,** unmasked by Peter Lorre as Oriental detective Mr. Moto. But what was far more important that year, he launched himself as the kindly old Dr. Christian, a persona that would occupy him on screen, radio and television for years to come. In **Meet Dr. Christian** he was the wise country doctor who solves everyone's problems, medical and otherwise. Said the New York Times: "Mr. Hersholt does his customary fine job of healing everything and everybody in sight except the plot."

He also starred as the good doctor in a long-running radio series, getting double mileage out of the character. And on screen, it was strictly Dr. Christian in 1940, in three films. And two more of the same the following year, which concluded the film series—but hardly the character as played by Hersholt, who for years continued as the kindly old physician on the airwaves.

Aside from a cameo in **Stage Door Canteen** (43), his next appearance on the screen wasn't until **Dancing in the Dark** in 1949, in a small part; the actor was now 63. Meanwhile, he had become perhaps better known as a humanitarian than as an actor. During the Thirties he had founded the Motion Picture Relief Fund, a charitable organization which he was to head for 18 years. In 1939 he had received an honorary Academy Award for this work, and in 1949 he got yet another one for services to the film industry as a whole. (And in 1946 he had been knighted by the king of Denmark for humanitarian work.) His service to motion pictures also was signally honored when he served a four-year term (1945-49) as president of the Oscar-awarding Academy of Motion Picture Arts and Sciences; his predecessors had included Douglas Fairbanks, director Frank Capra and Bette Davis, and his successors would include director George Stevens and Gregory Peck.

Hersholt appeared in his last film in 1955—the James Cagney starrer **Run for Cover,** in which he was Viveca Lindfors' father. Upon his death in 1956 the Academy he had headed instituted the Jean Hersholt Humanitarian Award, a special Oscar awarded yearly to film personalities for humanitarian achievements. Winners have included Samuel Goldwyn, Bob Hope, Gregory Peck, Frank Sinatra, Rosalind Russell and Charlton Heston.

Outstanding actor, outstanding human being—Jean Hersholt lives on in the memory of filmgoers everywhere.

THE FILMS OF JEAN HERSHOLT

NOTE: Only feature-length films are listed.

1915: The Disciple; Don Quixote.
1916: The Aryan; Hell's Hinges; The Deserter; Kinkaid—Gambler; Bullets and Brown Eyes.
1917: Fighting for Love; Love Aflame; The Terror; The Soul Herder; The Saintly Sinner; The Show-Down; Southern Justice; The Greater Law; '49-'17; Stormy Knights.
1918: Princess Virtue; Madame Spy.
1919: In the Land of the Setting Sun; Whom the Gods Would Destroy.
1920: The Servant in the House; Merely Mary Ann; The Red Lane.
1921: The Four Horsemen of the Apocalypse; A Certain Rich Man; The Deceiver; The Golden Trail; Man of the Forest.
1922: Tess of the Storm Country; Golden Dreams; The Gray Dawn; When Romance Rides; Heart's Haven; The Stranger's Banquet.
1923: Jazzmania; Quicksands; Red Lights.
1924: Greed; Torment; The Goldfish; The Woman on the Jury; Sinners in Silk; So Big; Her Night of Romance; Cheap Kisses.
1925: Stella Dallas; Don Q, Son of Zorro; Fifth Avenue Models; Dangerous Innocence; A Woman's Faith; If Marriage Fails.
1926: My Old Dutch; The Greater Glory; Flames; The Old Soak; It Must Be Love.
1927: The Student Prince in Old Heidelberg; The Wrong Mr. Wright.
1928: Abie's Irish Rose; Alias the Deacon; The Secret Hour; 13 Washington Square; The Battle of the Sexes; Jazz Mad; Give and Take.
1929: The Younger Generation; The Girl on the Barge; Modern Love.
1930: Hell Harbor; The Case of Sergeant Grischa; East Is West; The Cat Creeps; Viennese Nights; The Climax; Mamba; The Third Alarm.
1931: Susan Lenox: Her Fall and Rise; Private Lives; Transatlantic; The Sin of Madelon Claudet; Daybreak; The Phantom of Paris.
1932: Grand Hotel; The Mask of Fu Manchu; Beast of the City; Emma; Night Court; Flesh; Unashamed; New Morals for Old; Are You Listening?; Hearts of Humanity; Skyscraper Souls.
1933: Dinner at Eight; Christopher Bean; Song of the Eagle; The Crime of the Century.
1934: Men in White; The Painted Veil; The Fountain; The Cat and the Fiddle.
1935: Mark of the Vampire; Break of Hearts; Murder in the Fleet.
1936: The Country Doctor; Reunion; Sins of Man; One in a Million; Tough Guy; His Brother's Wife.
1937: Heidi; Seventh Heaven.
1938: Alexander's Ragtime Band; I'll Give a Million; Happy Landing; Five of a Kind.
1939: Meet Dr. Christian; Mr. Moto in Danger Island.
1940: Courageous Dr. Christian; Dr. Christian Meets the Women; Remedy for Riches.
1941: They Meet Again; Melody for Three.
1943: Stage Door Canteen.
1949: Dancing in the Dark.
1955: Run for Cover.

The flustered fussbudget:
EDWARD EVERETT HORTON

The word "unique"—meaning the only one of its kind—has been misused and over-used in relation to many a movie actor, but it applies precisely in the case of Edward Everett Horton. There was no one remotely like him.

He had an inimitable crooked, uncertain leer that sometimes lapsed into a self-satisfied smirk, and he coupled this with a diffident manner, a startled double-take, and exclamations of "Oh, dear!" to create a tremendously enjoyable comic persona. Flustered, fretting and fuming, often on the verge of an anxiety attack, he was the perennial nervous fussbudget, resembling a worried penguin.

He always tried to help correct a ridiculous situation, usually involving several persons in a romantic entanglement. And he typically rushed about as if his wife had just had sextuplets. He played many a confidant (several times to Fred Astaire), cuckolded husband, hypochondriac, whimsical friend, foppish Milquetoast or unwelcome suitor. One writer adds that he "mastered the art of playing craven, morally dissolute older men." In films for about half a century, he was a favorite of audiences, one of the most popular comic character actors in the history of the screen.

Horton was born March 18, 1886 (some sources say 1887 or 1888), in Brooklyn, the son of a New York Times proofreader. He studied at the Polytechnic Institute in Brooklyn and then at Columbia University, meanwhile making his stage debut in 1908. He launched his professional career in Gilbert and Sullivan operettas with a Staten Island stock company, and continued singing in choruses and appearing in stock with increasing success. For a while he was both an actor and a manager of stage productions, even running his own troupe. He began starring in films, according to one source, at age 32 in 1918, but the first one recorded in reference sources seems to be in 1922, and one source says that was in only an uncredited bit role. In any case, from then on he was primarily a screen actor until after World War II.

He starred in **The Ladder Jinx** (22) as a bank teller involved with robbers, in **Too Much Business** as the proprietor of a day-care center, and in **A Front Page Story** as a newspaperman. He played the title role as the imported butler in **Ruggles of Red Gap** (23), the part taken by Charles Laughton in the 1935

remake. In **To the Ladies** Louise Dresser named him manager of her husband's piano factory. In all these films he was cast in the starring role. He and Bryant Washburn were bill collectors in **Try and Get It** (24), and in **The Man Who Fights Alone** he was wrongly suspected by William Farnum of being involved with the latter's wife (Lois Wilson). **Helen's Babies** cast him as the bachelor uncle of Baby Peggy, left in his charge while her parents toured abroad.

The actor was lauded by critics for his inspired performance in director James Cruze's **Beggar on Horseback** (25), playing an impecunious composer in love with Esther Ralston but proposing to a rich young woman; on the verge of a nervous breakdown, he then goes to sleep and has a surrealistic nightmare in which the vulgarity of the latter's family is greatly magnified, and on awakening he returns to Miss Ralston. He won the love of Florence Vidor in **Marry Me,** and was the henpecked husband of Mae Busch in **The Nut-Cracker.** In **La Boheme** (26), as Colline, he supported Lillian Gish and John Gilbert, and he starred in the comedy **The Whole Town's Talking** as a suitor with an invented lurid past. In **Poker Faces** he played a harassed office worker who unwittingly manages to play a role in the capture of a crook; Laura La Plante was his wife.

In **Taxi! Taxi!** (27) Horton once again was the unwitting agent bringing about the apprehension of a criminal; he played an architectural draftsman and won the love of Marian Nixon. He was widely praised for his first talkie, **The Terror** (28), as a Scotland Yard detective who "is not so stupid as he seems," according to one plot summary. Like those of a few others whose voices had registered well with the microphone, his career suddenly accelerated, and by the end of the year he was in considerable demand.

The actor starred in **The Hottentot** (29) as a man afraid of horses who is mistaken for a champion steeplechase jockey, and he won Patsy Ruth Miller. In **Sonny Boy,** as a lawyer, he loved Betty Bronson. In **The Sap** he, Alan Hale and Franklin Pangborn were involved in speculating on the stock market with misappropriated bank funds. In **The Aviator** he was an author required to pose as having written a book on flying, and winding up accidentally soloing in a plane he doesn't know how to fly, plowing it into a haystack. In the latter two films Miss Miller was once again his love interest. The New York Times commented on **The Aviator:** "Mr. Horton upholds his reputation for being able to get more laughs out of slight facial contortions than most comedians." It was true then, and 40 years later it would still be true.

That was pretty much the end of starring roles in "A" productions for the actor, and, now in his midforties, he settled into supporting parts. He was excellent in the first screen version of **Holiday** (30), in which he and Hedda Hopper were Ann Harding's whimsical older friends; eight years later he would reprise the role (sans Miss Hopper) in the Cary Grant-Katharine Hepburn remake. He played a perfect valet in **Take the Heir** and in **Once a Gentleman,** and a timid bookkeeper, once again winning Patsy Ruth Miller, in **Wide Open.** In the first version of **The Front Page** (31) he was one of the reporters. **Lonely Wives** cast him in a dual role as a lawyer and a vaudeville impersonator, and quite a bevy of his previous leading ladies—Miss Miller, Esther Ralston and Laura La Plante—were involved. He was a sponging pal of Spencer Tracy in **Six Cylinder Love,** and in **Reaching for the Moon** he played Douglas Fairbanks' valet, giving him lessons in love in a hilarious scene of homosexual innuendo.

Horton was a standout in director Ernst Lubitsch's delightful comedy **Trouble in Paradise** (32), as a jealous, middle-aged suitor of Kay Francis, spending the entire film trying to remember where he's seen gentleman thief Herbert Marshall before, with his double-takes and final triumphant recollection providing a superb running gag. (All told, he would play key roles in five Lubitsch films.) He and ZaSu Pitts provided comedy relief in the war drama **Roar of the Dragon.** As Miriam Hopkins' boss (an ad-agency owner), he was married to her and then deserted by her (after Gary Cooper and Fredric March appear on the scene) in Lubitsch's witty **Design for Living** (33), and he was the ideal choice to play the Mad Hatter in **Alice in Wonderland.** He had an unusual occupation in **The Way to Love,** helping the philanderers of Paris deceive their spouses by making fake postcards of them in exotic places and administering suntans to those who are supposed to have been at the beach. He played Maurice Chevalier's valet in **A Bedtime Story.**

For the first of three times, the actor was Fred Astaire's comical confidant, a dithering divorce lawyer, in **The Gay Divorcee** (34), and he was the irate ambassador lecturing the dissolute Chevalier in Lubitsch's **The Merry Widow.** He contended with Cary Grant for the heroine in a pair of films, **Ladies Should Listen** and **Kiss and Make-Up,** and in **Smarty** he married Joan Blondell but divorced her for infidelity after she ran around with Warren William. He was back with Astaire in **Top Hat** (35), and for director Josef von Sternberg played the bearded police chief, Don Paquito, in the Marlene Dietrich starrer **The Devil Is a Woman.** He starred in two weak programmer comedies, and was back as a valet (Ramon Novarro's) in **The Night Is Young.** He played a sidewalk con man, one step ahead of the cops, in **Little Big Shot,** and in **Biography of a Bachelor Girl** he was a senatorial candidate who is engaged to Una Merkel but falls in love with Ann Harding, his childhood flame—to no avail.

In 1936 the actor starred in a few forgotten "B" comedies, such as **Her Master's Voice,** in which he takes mother-in-law Laura Hope Crews' advice and asks for a raise, only to find himself out of a job. But the truth is that while he was a fine comedian in small doses, he tended to be prissy and repetitive as the star of an entire film. In that year he was Al Jolson's valet in **The Singing Kid** and was in several other films.

In director Frank Capra's classic drama **Lost Horizon** (37), Horton played one of the plane passengers, a paleontologist carrying some dinosaur vertebrae around in a little box, and for the third and last time he was Fred Astaire's pal in **Shall We Dance.** In **Let's Make a Million** he was henpecked by two spinster aunts, played by the same ladies who had been the "pixilated" sisters testifying against Gary Cooper in **Mr. Deeds Goes to Town** the previous year. He was a nobleman in **The King and the Chorus Girl** and a penny-pinching newspaper auditor in **Wild Money.** He played Herbert Marshall's valet in the Marlene Dietrich starrer **Angel** (once again directed by Lubitsch), and yet another valet (to Brian Aherne as actor David Garrick) in **The Great Garrick.** He was engaged to Ann Sothern, but lost her to Jack Haley, in **Danger—Love at Work.**

Horton reprised his 1930 role in the remake of **Holiday** (38), as Cary Grant's friend, and played Claudette Colbert's aristocratic father in director Lubitsch's weak comedy **Bluebeard's Eighth Wife.** He married Gracie Allen in **College Swing. Paris Honeymoon** (39) cast him as Bing Crosby's valet, and he was a screenwriter unable to come up with a usable story in the Kay Kyser vehicle **That's Right—You're Wrong.** He took a vacation from the screen in 1940, and by this time he had begun his stage work again. For years he would go on tour in the perennial straw-hat-circuit classic **Springtime for Henry,** playing the philandering bachelor nearly 3,000 times. (In real life, too, the actor was a lifelong bachelor.)

Back on the screen in 1941, Horton, now in his mid-fifties, played one of his most memorable roles, the fussy, petulant Messenger 7013 in the comic fantasy **Here Comes Mr. Jordan,** making a terrible mistake by bringing Robert Montgomery's body to Heaven too soon. He was a theatrical agent in **Ziegfeld Girl,** and in **The Body Disappears** he invented a serum that turned him, Jane Wyman and Jeffrey Lynn invisible. There were also a few tired programmers that year. He supported Jeanette MacDonald and Nelson Eddy in their last film together, the dreary **I Married an Angel** (42), provided a few welcome laughs in the Henry Fonda starrer **The Magnificent Dope,** and was lost in the crowd in a couple of Technicolor musicals for 20th Century-Fox that year and in 1943.

The actor's best performance in a long screen career came in director Douglas Sirk's second American film, **Summer Storm** (44), based on Anton Chekhov's story "The Shooting Party." As the dissolute Count Volsky, competing with a judge (George Sanders) for young temptress Linda Darnell, he broke away from his usual typecasting to give a subtle dramatic portrayal of a decadent nobleman hiding his

despair behind a jaunty front. Clearly, audiences realized that Horton was capable of far more depth than he had ever been allowed in his comedy roles—but filmmakers took no notice of that. Comedy was to be his forte, and he displayed it that year in **Arsenic and Old Lace** as the superintendent of "Happydale," the funny farm awaiting the two sweetly poisonous little old ladies. **San Diego, I Love You** cast him as a professor.

The actor had made more than a hundred films in a quarter of a century; in the ensuing 25 years he would appear in only 15. He supported Deanna Durbin in the mystery **Lady on a Train** (45), in which Ralph Bellamy turns out to be the murderer, and starred in a Poverty Row comedy, **Steppin' in Society,** as an austere judge mistaken for a criminal. The following year brought a few routine parts. In **Down to Earth** (47) he and James Gleason repeated their roles from **Here Comes Mr. Jordan,** although this Rita Hayworth starrer was not a remake of the 1941 film. In **Her Husband's Affairs,** as the head of an advertising agency, he employed married couple Lucille Ball and Franchot Tone.

Horton now took a decade-long sabbatical from Hollywood. He continued to tour on the stage in **Springtime for Henry,** although he was now in his sixties, and also started to make regular appearances on television. In 1957 he made a brief return to the screen to play the cameo role of Sir Walter Raleigh in the bizarre pastiche **The Story of Mankind,** and came back in 1961 to portray the very correct butler in director Frank Capra's last film, **Pocketful of Miracles,** unbending long enough to tell Apple Annie (Bette Davis), "Stay in there and pitch, sister!" Along with many another comedian, he did a cameo in **It's a Mad, Mad, Mad, Mad World** (63), and he was in **Sex and the Single Girl** (64). The following year he played an Indian chief on TV's "F Troop," and he returned to the screen as the 99-year-old second richest man in the world in **The Perils of Pauline** (67); at age 81, he was clearly too young for the role.

He supported Terry-Thomas in **2000 Years Later** (69) and Dick Van Dyke in **Cold Turkey,** his last film, released in 1970, the year he died at age 84. Just before his death Edward Everett Horton had told an interviewer, "I've had a grand time." And moviegoers everywhere might say, so did we, Mr. Horton—so did we.

THE FILMS OF EDWARD EVERETT HORTON

NOTE: Some reference sources say he began starring in films in 1918, but various available checklists do not show any appearances prior to 1922.

1922: The Ladder Jinx; Leave It to Me; Too Much Business; A Front Page Story.
1923: Ruggles of Red Gap; To the Ladies.
1924: Try and Get It; Flapper Wives; The Man Who Fights Alone; Helen's Babies.
1925: Beggar on Horseback; Marry Me; The Business of Love; The Nut-Cracker.
1926: La Boheme; The Whole Town's Talking; Poker Faces.
1927: Taxi! Taxi!
1928: The Terror.
1929: The Hottentot; The Sap; The Aviator; Sonny Boy.
1930: Holiday; Once a Gentleman; Wide Open; Take the Heir.
1931: The Front Page; Smart Woman; Reaching for the Moon; Lonely Wives; The Age for Love; Kiss Me Again; Six Cylinder Love.
1932: Trouble in Paradise; Roar of the Dragon; But the Flesh Is Weak.
1933: Design for Living; The Way to Love; Alice in Wonderland; A Bedtime Story; It's a Boy; The Woman in Command (Soldiers of the King).
1934: The Gay Divorcee; The Merry Widow; Ladies Should Listen; The Poor Rich; Kiss and Make-Up; Easy to Love; Success at Any Price; Uncertain Lady; Sing and Like It; Smarty.
1935: The Devil Is a Woman; The Night Is Young; Top Hat; Little Big Shot; In Caliente; Biography of a Bachelor Girl; $10 Raise; Going Highbrow; All the King's Horses; His Night Out; Your Uncle Dudley.
1936: Hearts Divided; The Man in the Mirror; The Singing Kid; Her Master's Voice; Nobody's Fool.
1937: Lost Horizon; Shall We Dance; Angel; Let's Make a Million; The King and the Chorus Girl; The Great Garrick; Hitting a New High; The Perfect Specimen; Wild Money; Danger—Love at Work; Oh, Doctor!
1938: Holiday; Bluebeard's Eighth Wife; College Swing; Little Tough Guys in Society.
1939: Paris Honeymoon; That's Right—You're Wrong.
1941: Here Comes Mr. Jordan; Ziegfeld Girl; You're the One; Bachelor Daddy; Sunny; Weekend for Three; The Body Disappears.
1942: I Married an Angel; The Magnificent Dope; Springtime in the Rockies.
1943: The Gang's All Here; Thank Your Lucky Stars; Forever and a Day.
1944: Summer Storm; Arsenic and Old Lace; Her Primitive Man; The Town Went Wild; Brazil; San Diego, I Love You.
1945: Lady on a Train; Stepping in Society.
1946: Cinderella Jones; Faithful in My Fashion; Earl Carroll Sketchbook.
1947: Down to Earth; Her Husband's Affairs; The Ghost Goes Wild.
1957: The Story of Mankind.
1961: Pocketful of Miracles.
1963: It's a Mad, Mad, Mad, Mad World.
1964: Sex and the Single Girl.
1967: The Perils of Pauline.
1969: 2000 Years Later.
1970: Cold Turkey.

The greatest of them all:
WALTER HUSTON

Walter Huston just may have been (with the possible exceptions of Spencer Tracy and Laurence Olivier) the finest male screen actor of the first half of the century.

The critics invariably fell over themselves to bestow praise on his performances; "brilliant" and "magnificent" were typical. Oscar-winning actor José Ferrer once said: "Walter is one of the greatest actors who ever lived...Just because every time I saw him do anything he just hit me sort of deeper in the pit of the stomach than most actors ever did." Critic James Agee said after viewing **The Treasure of the Sierra Madre:** "I doubt we shall ever see...better acting than [his] beautiful performance." It was the culmination of a professional lifetime of praise.

Tall, dark, angular, stiff-legged, and authoritative, he was not handsome but was fascinating. His fine presence and the mature intelligence of his acting tended to dominate the films in which he was cast. Middle-aged by the time he came to Hollywood, he was briefly a star and even a romantic lead in his early films, and alternated between heroes and villains with great facility. In the latter part of his career, as a topflight character actor, he vigorously projected roguery and eccentricity, usually appearing vaguely amused by what was happening around him. Remarkably, he made only 46 films in a 22-year career, but his performance stood out in every one. As he once told Gregory Peck, "Son, always give 'em a good show and travel first class!"

Huston was born (as Walter Houghston) April 6, 1884, in Toronto, Ontario, and originally studied engineering, but soon decided that he wanted to be an actor. At 18 he ran away from home and joined a traveling stock company; after a sheriff closed it down, he tried Broadway, getting a three-line part in a play starring matinee idol Richard Mansfield but fumbling his lines due to stage fright and finding himself personally escorted to the stage door by Mansfield with the admonition to try some other line of work. Undaunted, he went from agent to agent and from producer to producer, finally getting the leading role in **In Convict Stripes** about 1904, and touring in that play. When the company played the small hamlet of Rising Sun, Ohio, a little girl aged eight joined the cast; her name was Lillian Gish. In her memoirs Miss Gish recalls being lifted on the shoulders of "the handsome leading man, Walter Huston," for a curtain call.

The actor also appeared in vaudeville in New York City, and in 1905 married newspaperwoman Rhea Gore. She felt that the stage would not provide them a satisfactory living, and prodded him to go back to engineering. The couple moved to the town of Nevada, Missouri, where Huston worked as an engineer at the local water and power company—and where their son, the future film director John Huston, was born in 1906. Family legend has it that one night in 1907 some structures in the town caught fire and Huston was urged by the firemen to supply more water pressure, which overtaxed the system and damaged the machinery, resulting in the family's hasty departure from Nevada. But years later the local newspaper editor reported that while there had indeed been a fire, the water pressure had been normal and no machinery was ruined.

In any case, the Hustons then went to St. Louis, where Walter again worked for the electric utility. But in 1909 the couple split up, and he went back to the stage, and soon became a popular headliner on the vaudeville circuit with his new partner and lover (and future wife), Bayonne Whipple. They did song-and-dance acts together. He divorced Rhea in 1913 and married Bayonne the following year; they would continue to work as a vaudeville act until the early Twenties, by which time they had become headliners on the Keith and Orpheum circuits. But in 1924 serious stage acting came into the picture, with Huston, then 38, cast in the title role of Zona Gale's **Mr. Pitt,** a Broadway play about small-town America, playing a meek little man. He then played a similar role in **The Easy Mark.**

Despite these characterizations, he was chosen by Eugene O'Neill to star as the harsh, tough old farmer in the playwright's new production **Desire Under the Elms** late in 1924. It was a fine opportunity, and he made the most of it. The play was a hit, critics lauded Huston's performance, and he was established as a Broadway star. For several years he appeared in New York productions, including co-starring with ingenue Claudette Colbert in **The Barker** in 1927, but in 1928 there came a flop, **The Commodore Marries,** which impelled him to listen to the siren call of Hollywood, which was summoning a small army of stage-trained players to the movies as the sound era began.

He launched his film career in a starring role as a boozy big-time reporter in **Gentlemen of the Press** (29), which also featured Charlie Ruggles and Kay Francis (billed as "Katherine Francis"). **The Lady Lies** cast him as a widower having a romance with an attractive young salesgirl (Miss Colbert). The actor then went back to Broadway to appear in the hit play **Elmer the Great,** returning to the film capital to make **The Virginian,** with Gary Cooper as the star and Huston as the menacing villain Trampas (played by Brian Donlevy in the 1946 remake).

His big movie break, however, came in 1930 when he starred in the next-to-last film made by pioneer director D.W. Griffith, **Abraham Lincoln.** Although the biographical movie was undistinguished, Huston got enthusiastic notices, with the New Yorker magazine calling it a "towering" performance. Playing Ann Rutledge was Una Merkel in her pre-comedy period. The actor also dominated the mediocre **The Bad Man,** although he really wasn't very convincing as an outlaw named Pancho Lopez, finally killed by a ranger. In the penny-dreadful melodrama **The Virtuous Sin** he was a haughty general who spares the life of an army scientist condemned for disobeying an order; the man's wife (Kay Francis) offers herself to the general but then falls in love with him; the husband, released,

plots to kill the general but ultimately gives his wife up to the man.

Huston starred for director Howard Hawks in **The Criminal Code** (31), a tense and exciting prison drama; he was impressive as the district attorney who becomes the warden of a prison populated by men he has sent up the river. He was also a district attorney in **Star Witness.** In **The Ruling Voice** he played a ruthless racketeer, head of a powerful underworld syndicate, who is rejected by his respectable daughter (the 18-year-old Loretta Young) and betrayed by henchman Dudley Digges; he made the character seem shady and noble at the same time.

In that year, 1931, the actor divorced Bayonne Whipple and married for the last time, to actress Ninetta (Nan) Sunderland, whom he had met when they were both in **Elmer the Great** on Broadway. Miss Sunderland played a few small movie roles in the sound era, receiving screen credit as Lionel Barrymore's wife in **Sweepings** (33) and appearing in **Unconquered** (47).

The year 1932 was to be Huston's busiest on the screen, with nine films, virtually all of them yielding performances that have endured through the years. In director Frank Capra's **American Madness** he was fine as the humanitarian bank president, so busy making loans that he neglects wife Kay Johnson, who ends up spending time with a crooked cashier—who engineers a big bank burglary, resulting in a run on the bank which Huston stops with an impassioned speech to the depositors. He starred in **Beast of the City** as a fighting police captain, exiled to the sticks for being too zealous in arresting a racketeer with connections (Jean Hersholt) but then appointed police chief by the new, honest mayor. In **Rain** he was the fanatical missionary trying to reform prostitute Joan Crawford and then attempting to seduce her, ultimately killing himself; Beulah Bondi played his wife.

He was a crooked, grafting judge in **Night Court,** getting his comeuppance from cab driver Phillips Holmes, whose wife he had framed on a prostitution charge. In director William Wyler's **A House Divided** he was impressive as an embittered, crippled fisherman who recruits a young second wife from a matrimonial agency only to see her fall in love with his son (Kent Douglass, later known as Douglass Montgomery). In this rehash of **Desire Under the Elms,** the fisherman is drowned in a storm. Huston's son John was one of the three screenwriters; he was also co-writer on his father's next film, **Law and Order,** in which Huston gave a fine central performance as the gun-toting marshal trying to make lawless Tombstone, Arizona, law-abiding even if it means decimating the population.

In **The Wet Parade,** an anti-Prohibition tract based on Upton Sinclair's novel, he walked off with the film as a drunken, rundown hotel proprietor who spends his time talking big in saloons. When Prohibition arrives, he must now pay exorbitant prices even for phony whiskey; when his wife breaks one of his bottles, he kills her in a drunken rage and is sentenced to life imprisonment. (The actor was in sympathy with writer Sinclair's views about the evils of Prohibition, for in March 1932, at a rally organized by the author, Huston debated evangelist Aimee Semple McPherson, taking the position that the 18th Amendment was "an appalling and disastrous failure" while Miss McPherson said it hadn't been given enough of a chance. Prohibition was repealed in 1933.)

His last good part in 1932 was in **Kongo,** as the bitter, bestial Deadlegs Flint, a part played by Lon Chaney in the earlier screen version, **West of Zanzibar** (28), but which Huston himself had originated on the stage in 1926. The remarkable plot deserves mentioning: Huston is the wheelchair-bound ruler of a black empire in the Congo, seething with a desire for revenge on the ivory trader who broke his back and stole his wife. He lures the man's virginal daughter (Virginia Bruce) from a convent and turns her into an alcoholic prostitute, only to learn she is really his *own* daughter. Meanwhile, he tortures his mistress (Lupe Velez) by twisting her tongue with a loop of wire, and immerses the daughter's drug-addicted lover up to the neck in a swamp to "let the leeches suck it out of him." Now here is a film that ought to be revived.

His other film that year, **The Woman from Monte Carlo,** was an unsuccessful attempt to introduce German movie star Lil Dagover to the American screen. She played a faithless wife who betrays her aging naval-officer husband (Huston) when she meets Warren William. It was Miss Dagover's first and last American film.

It is likely that Huston's late arrival in Hollywood protected him from the dangers of typecasting—but at the same time prevented him from attaining real stardom, of the kind won by younger actors such as Spencer Tracy and Fredric March. Still, there were a few years of leading roles ahead—not to mention, in the future, his three best performances and an Academy Award.

He gave his usual fine interpretation in **Gabriel over the White House** (33), an unusual and courageous film that was not a big success. He played a party-hack U.S. president who, while recovering from a car crash, has a mysterious vision that converts him into a better man. He fires his corrupt cabinet and, just as he is about to be impeached, dismisses Congress and establishes himself as a benevolent dictator who talks to the people via the radio. (Remember, this was in the first year of Franklin D. Roosevelt's presidency.) When an army of the jobless marches on the capital he meets them in Baltimore, but their leader is killed by a powerful gangster. The president has the gangster executed, solves unemployment and a crime wave, gets the nation's war debts paid by foreign countries, and then dies of a heart attack.

In **Ann Vickers** he was a liberal judge who quietly backs (and falls in love with) social reformer Irene Dunne; when he is unjustly accused of grafting, she repays his confidence, but he is convicted and imprisoned. While he is in jail she gives birth to their child, and after three years he is released and they are married. In **Storm at Daybreak** he was the wealthy peasant husband of Kay Francis; when he realizes that she is love with Nils Asther, he conveniently eliminates himself by driving his carriage over a cliff. He played a brutal submarine commander, clashing with Robert Montgomery, in **Hell Below,** and hammed it up in **The Prizefighter and the Lady,** mugging and yelling as the trainer of prizefighter Max Baer (playing a real-life role; the following year he won the heavyweight title from Primo Carnera).

In the mediocre programmer **Keep 'Em Rolling** (34) Huston played an Army sergeant fighting to keep his horse by his side. After this epic, little wonder that he chose to return to Broadway, where he scored a triumph in the hit play **Dodsworth,** based on Sinclair Lewis' novel. He went to England in 1935 to film **Transatlantic Tunnel (The Tunnel),** playing once again the American president, and **Rhodes of Africa,** starring as British empire builder Cecil Rhodes in this biographical drama.

The actor was then summoned back to Hollywood to do the 1936 film version of **Dodsworth,** starring in the role that made him one of the screen's all-time greats. Under the fine direction of William Wyler, he gave a legendary performance as auto manufacturer Sam Dodsworth, who, retiring rich in his fifties, takes his adored wife (Ruth Chatterton, in her last American film) on an extended European vacation. While he absorbs history and culture, she becomes involved in flirtations (including Paul Lukas and David Niven) and even accepts a marriage proposal. He reluctantly agrees to a divorce, and wanders forlornly around Europe, where he meets Mary Astor, whom he had known before. But his wife tries to come back to him after she is rejected by the mother (Maria Ouspenskaya) of the man who had proposed to her. Now he feels he must stand by his wife. They are on a ship about to sail for home when the realization comes over him that she will never change her vain, shallow ways. In a turn-of-the-worm scene that still brings applause from revival audiences today, he leaves, telling her, "Love has got to stop somewhere short of suicide!"

Huston was magnificent, bringing a driving energy and splendid vitality to the role of the impulsive, bewildered, firm but childlike Sam. It was a beautifully integrated and modulated piece of acting. Critics produced rave reviews. Declared Archer Winsten in the New York Post: "Walter Huston gives a performance that makes you forget acting." The New Yorker said: "It would have been an inexcusable accident had [his] Dodsworth not been fine, but there hasn't been any accident and the [performance] should please people who saw the play and people who didn't." More honors came from the New York film critics, who voted him best actor of the year, and he got an Academy Award nomination as best actor. (He lost to Paul Muni for **The Story of Louis Pasteur,** a good performance but hardly the equal of Huston's.)

Incredibly, after this display of acting brilliance he sharply curtailed his screen activity, making only two films in the next four years and spending some of that time back on Broadway. In 1937 he starred on stage briefly in Shakespeare's **Othello,** returning to Hollywood in 1938 to make **Of Human Hearts,** a fine and now half-forgotten drama in which he was superb as a stern 19th century rural clergyman, the father of James Stewart and, again, the husband of Beulah Bondi. Huston brought to the film a dignity and sense of form it might not otherwise have had. Then it was back to New York to star as Peter Stuyvesant in the Kurt Weill musical drama **Knickerbocker Holiday,** in which he introduced the memorable "September Song." (His famous recording of it was made not during the play's run, but some years later; just before his death it became a hit via the 1950 film **September Affair.**)

His only screen appearance in 1939 was in **The Light That Failed,** in which he was stolid and forceful as Ronald Colman's friend, a war correspondent during the Sudan uprising in the late 19th century. (The picture was stolen by Ida Lupino as a Cockney waif posing for artist Colman; it made her a star.) Huston made no films in 1940, instead starring on Broadway in **Love's Old Sweet Song,** and then returned to the screen in 1941 for the second of his three greatest roles, playing no less than the Devil himself. In **All That Money Can Buy,** Satan was called Mr. Scratch, and materialized as a sly New Hampshire hick with a heavy stubble of beard and a battered hat in this fine version of Stephen Vincent

Benét's short story 'The Devil and Daniel Webster" (which was the name given to the movie when it was reissued later on). Edward Arnold was Webster, fighting Old Nick for control of a man's soul. The critical accolades for Huston this time were even greater than those for **Dodsworth,** if that is possible, and he was once again nominated for a best-actor Oscar. That both he and Orson Welles (for **Citizen Kane**) were beaten by Gary Cooper (for **Sergeant York**) demonstrates all too clearly that the Academy Awards are basically a popularity contest rather than a recognition of the finest screen acting.

Also in 1941, the actor had a role of no great significance in **Swamp Water,** and appeared to advantage in director Josef von Sternberg's bizarre film **The Shanghai Gesture,** a strange study of corruption and decadence, as Gene Tierney's father. He also played an uncredited bit part in his son John's first film as a director, **The Maltese Falcon,** as Captain Jacoby, who staggers into Humphrey Bogart's office and drops dead.

For an utterly routine part as James Cagney's father in **Yankee Doodle Dandy** (42) he was nominated for an Oscar as best supporting actor, and he co-starred again after many years with Kay Francis in the soap opera **Always in My Heart,** in which she was his wife and was unfaithful to him during his 13-year prison term (for a crime he didn't commit, wouldn't you just know it). And, again, he helped out son John by getting together with most of the **Maltese Falcon** cast for a brief bar scene in **In This Our Life;** he was the bartender, and all concerned went uncredited. He also narrated the first two of the nine wartime propaganda documentaries he would do to help the government; Frank Capra, who produced them, had chosen him to do the narration.

Huston was, as always, good in **Edge of Darkness** (43), as Ann Sheridan's father, a bearded Norwegian physician desperately trying to maintain his neutrality in his Nazi-occupied town. Ruth Gordon played his wife, and Errol Flynn was the star. Then came **Mission to Moscow,** a sort of propaganda film in which he starred as real-life diplomat Joseph E. Davies, U.S. ambassador to the Soviet Union. In **The North Star** he was a Russian village leader, matching wits with Nazi officer Erich von Stroheim; in the postwar era this film was considered in retrospect to be such blatant pro-Russian propaganda (the director was the Russian-born, politically leftist Lewis Milestone) that it was heavily re-edited and reissued under a different title. The actor also appeared in Howard Hughes' **The Outlaw,** as Doc Holliday; he was the best thing in this bizarre and not very good movie which spent much of its time concentrating on newcomer Jane Russell's bust.

As Katharine Hepburn's father in **Dragon Seed** (44) he gave one of the few believable performances; hardly anyone looked very Oriental in this drama of the Japanese occupation of China. Aline MacMahon played his wife. He was good as one of the numerous victims (and suspects) in the superb murder mystery **And Then There Were None** (45), and in that year did the last of the war documentaries. He was outstanding in a cameo role as the lecherous preacher called the Sin-Killer in **Duel in the Sun** (46); in the cast was Lillian Gish, that long-ago little girl, now a middle-aged woman, who had appeared in his play **In Convict Stripes** in 1904. He had a routine supporting part in **Dragonwyck,** again playing the father of Gene Tierney, standing by while she marries a man who turns out to be a demented murderer (Vincent Price), but as usual he got the best notices.

In that same year, Huston, now in his early sixties, did his last Broadway play, the short-lived **Apple of His Eye,** and did not return to the screen until 1948, for his last acting triumph and his only Academy Award. Under the direction of his son John, he won the Oscar as best supporting actor for playing the old gold prospector Howard in the classic **The Treasure of the Sierra Madre.** It was a superb performance, notably at the film's ironic ending, when he roars with laughter as he finds the empty gold-dust bags during a sandstorm. To top it off, John also won two Oscars, for direction and screenplay.

The actor also appeared that year in **Summer Holiday,** a remake of 1935's **Ah, Wilderness,** taking Lionel Barrymore's old part and playing the father of Mickey Rooney. He was a roulette-table addict in **The Great Sinner** (49), and in 1950 played his last role, in **The Furies,** as the fond and proud father of Barbara Stanwyck, doing her out of her inheritance of his cattle ranch; Judith Anderson was his second wife. He was then scheduled to play the old counterfeiter in **Mister 880,** but in that year he died at age 66.

Walter Huston's last line in **The Furies** was "There'll never be another like me." And there surely never will. He was the greatest—a towering presence, a brilliant actor.

THE FILMS OF WALTER HUSTON

1929: Gentlemen of the Press; The Lady Lies; The Virginian.
1930: Abraham Lincoln; The Bad Man; The Virtuous Sin.
1931: The Criminal Code; Star Witness; The Ruling Voice.
1932: American Madness; Beast of the City; Rain; Kongo; Night Court; A House Divided; Law and Order; The Wet Parade; The Woman from Monte Carlo.
1933: Gabriel over the White House; Ann Vickers; Storm at Daybreak; Hell Below; The Prizefighter and the Lady.
1934: Keep 'Em Rolling.
1935: Transatlantic Tunnel (The Tunnel).
1936: Dodsworth; Rhodes of Africa (Rhodes).
1938: Of Human Hearts.
1939: The Light That Failed.
1941: All That Money Can Buy; Swamp Water; The Shanghai Gesture; The Maltese Falcon (uncredited bit).
1942: Yankee Doodle Dandy; Always in My Heart; In This Our Life (uncredited bit). *As narrator of documentaries:* Our Russian Front; Prelude to War.
1943: Edge of Darkness; Mission to Moscow; The North Star; The Outlaw. *As narrator of documentaries:* The Nazis Strike; Divide

and Conquer; The Battle of Britain; The Battle of Russia.
1944: Dragon Seed. *As narrator of documentary:* The Battle of China.
1945: And Then There Were None. *As narrator of documentaries:* War Comes to America; Know Your Enemy: Japan.
1946: Duel in the Sun; Dragonwyck.
1948: The Treasure of the Sierra Madre; Summer Holiday.
1949: The Great Sinner.
1950: The Furies.

NOTE: **The North Star** (43) was later (after World War II) heavily re-edited to eliminate what was regarded as pro-Soviet propaganda and was re-released under the title **Armored Attack. All That Money Can Buy** (41) was retitled **The Devil and Daniel Webster** and re-released in 1952; release prints can be found under both titles. **The Outlaw** (43) was actually filmed in 1941. Like several other films made by Howard Hughes, it had a peculiar release history, being released on three or four separate occasions (sources differ as to the years), but probably in 1943, 1946 and 1950; some of them were limited releases. **Summer Holiday** (48) was actually filmed in 1946.

Mugs, lugs and thugs:
ALLEN JENKINS

Ever been in New York City? Then you've met Allen Jenkins—in person.

That cab driver with the Brooklyn accent. The not-too-bright cop on the corner. The mug lounging in front of the drugstore, chewing on a toothpick. They were all Allen Jenkins—or to be more precise, he would have portrayed them in movies.

In any Warner Bros. film of the Thirties, if there was a character named something like Louie, Hunk or Spudsy—usually a sidekick for Humphrey Bogart, Edward G. Robinson or James Cagney—the part might well have been played by Jenkins. He was the one they invariably thought of when the role was a small-time numbskull gangster, a cab driver, a prizefighter's manager, a stool pigeon, or any other urban blue-collar type with a New Yorkish accent. As one writer has put it, "He had the battered but tenacious look of the urban animal who has been around and intends to stay around."

Horse-faced, baggy-eyed and hook-nosed, on screen he was semi-literate, frequently illogical, but usually reasonably friendly even in his roles as a penny-ante crook. He might have come straight from a Damon Runyon story.

Jenkins was born (as Alfred McGonegal) April 9, 1900, in New York City —of course (although one source gives the date as 1890, which seems unlikely). Both parents were musical-comedy performers, and he entered the theater as a stage mechanic following work in the shipyards during World War I. He soon switched to acting, and after studying (via a scholarship) at the American Academy of Dramatic Art he appeared frequently on Broadway, including a stint as a hoofer in the chorus line of **Pitter Patter** in 1922, where one of his fellow hoofers was James Cagney, who became a friend. For several years he was on stage, and shortly after the beginning of the sound era he came to Hollywood and signed a film contract with Warner Brothers, for which he would make the vast majority of his films until World War II.

The actor made his screen debut in **The Girl Habit** (31) for Paramount, playing a notorious killer, and in the following year started getting busy for Warners, with five films. He was one of the convicts in **I Am a Fugitive from a Chain Gang,** a hoodlum in **Rackety Rax** and also in **Three on a Match,** and a hired killer in **Blessed Event.**

He had his most active movie year in 1933, ap-

pearing in 11 films on the fast-paced Warners production line, plus two at RKO. He was James Cagney's sidekick in **The Mayor of Hell,** a radio announcer in **Hard to Handle,** a pickpocket who aids phony clairvoyant Warren William in **The Mind Reader,** a petty thug in both **Blondie Johnson** and **Havana Widows,** a detective in **Bureau of Missing Persons,** a tramp in **The Silk Express,** a detective again in **Tomorrow at Seven,** and a press agent in **Professional Sweetheart.** In **The Keyhole,** as detective George Brent's fortune-hunting partner, he meets gold-digger Glenda Farrell; each erroneously thinking the other wealthy, they hope to marry each other for money.

Jenkins was Cagney's right-hand man again in both **Jimmy the Gent** and **The St. Louis Kid** (both 34), and played a police sergeant in **The Case of the Howling Dog,** a Perry Mason mystery starring Warren William as the detective. **The Merry Frinks** cast him as a foolish radical lawyer, **Bedside** as a press agent, **Happiness Ahead** as a chauffeur, **Whirlpool** as Jack Holt's old carnival buddy, and **Twenty Million Sweethearts** as a radio performer of children's songs.

The actor was married twice. By his first wife, Mary Landes, he had a son. His second marriage, in 1958, was to Lillian Kinsella.

In 1935 he was transformed from a police sergeant to Perry Mason's (Warren William's) assistant Spudsy in **The Case of the Curious Bride** and **The Case of the Lucky Legs.** In the Cagney starrer **The Irish in Us** he played dim-witted prizefighter Carbarn Hammerschlog, and he was a stupid press agent in **Sweet Music** and a sailor hopelessly in love with showgirl Joan Blondell in **Miss Pacific Fleet.** He played a publicist in **I Live for Love.** In films of this period, he was typically billed fourth or fifth in the cast.

Jenkins was one of the three racetrack gamblers trying to exploit Frank McHugh's ability to pick winners in **Three Men on a Horse** (36), and played prizefighter Clark Gable's handler in **Cain and Mabel.** He was ZaSu Pitts' boyfriend, an elevator operator, in **Sing Me a Love Song.** He played a prototypical thug, gangster Humphrey Bogart's sidekick, in **Dead End** (37), and was excellent as an unscrupulous theatrical agent in **Ready, Willing and Able.** He and Hugh Herbert were a pair of dumb detectives in **Sh! The Octopus,** and he was a truck driver in **The Perfect Specimen** and a Marine sergeant in **The Singing Marine.** In **Dance Charlie Dance** he played a theatrical producer, and Glenda Farrell was his wife.

More hoodlums were in the picture in 1938, as the actor played Bogart's stooge again in **The Amazing Dr. Clitterhouse** and Edward G. Robinson's sidekick in **A Slight Case of Murder.** But as an honest truck driver, he was shot down by Bogart's gunmen in **Racket Busters.** He and Rudy Vallee owned a nightclub in **Gold Diggers in Paris,** and he played a Canadian Mountie in **Heart of the North** and a racetrack habitué in **Going Places.** He had a good part in the superior drama **Five Came Back** (39) as a gangster's henchman conveying the man's son to safety, but ending up killed by Indians after a plane crash in the jungle. As Brian Donlevy's chief gun thug in **Destry Rides Again,** he was the murderer of the sheriff, and he played a plagiarizing songwriter in **Naughty But Nice.** As a con man, he fleeced a waitress out of her inheritance in **Sweepstakes Winner.** He succeeded Barton MacLane as girl reporter Torchy Blane's (Glenda Farrell's) love interest in **Torchy Blane...Playing with Dynamite;** like MacLane in the earlier films, he was a not-overly-bright police lieutenant.

Jenkins continued to pay the rent by playing small-time thugs and hoodlums, as in the Edward G. Robinson starrer **Brother Orchid** (40), in the role of Willie the Knife, one of Bogart's menacing sidekicks. He was a Bronx cab driver in **Meet the Wildcat,** and a bank robber called the Weasel in **Oh, Johnny, How You Can Love.** As a former stooge for Perry Mason, he fitted right in as The Falcon's (George Sanders') chauffeur and sidekick in the first two films in that series, **The Gay Falcon** and **A Date with the Falcon** (both 41). In **Ball of Fire** he was hilarious as the Brooklyn-accented garbage man utilized by linguistics professor Gary Cooper to aid him in his study of slang. He assisted amateur sleuth Errol Flynn in **Footsteps in the Dark.**

In **They All Kissed the Bride** (42) the actor played a truck driver who performs a frantic jitterbug with Joan Crawford at a company dance, and in **Tortilla Flat** he was a Mexican fisherman. There was one more Falcon, **The Falcon Takes Over.** He was in only one 1943 film, **Stage Door Canteen,** not returning to the screen for two years. Now his parts began to get smaller, although he was in such films as **Lady on a Train** and **Wonder Man** (both 45). Parts began to get fewer, too, and often they were for Poverty Row studios; of the 14 films he made in the period 1947-52, half were for Monogram, Republic, and Screen Guild. At this point the actor removed himself from the screen scene for seven years.

It seemed like a good idea now to spend some time on the stage again. He also entered a new medium, television, appearing in the series "Hey Jeannie," "The Duke," and as the voice of Officer Dibble in the animated "Top Cat." There was a role in the 1959 Rock Hudson-Doris Day outing **Pillow Talk,** then another long hiatus from movies and more television. He was back on screen in 1964 in **Robin and the Seven Hoods,** as a thug called Vermin, and was far down the cast list in **I'd Rather Be Rich,** as well as doing a cameo in **For Those Who Think Young.** In 1967 he was in the misbegotten comedy **Doctor, You've Got to Be Kidding!,** and in 1974, the year he died, insolvent and in relative obscurity, played his last role, a cameo as a telegraph operator, in the remake of **The Front Page.**

Flashback: It's the Thirties again, it's a Warners crime film, and the chief hoodlum is Bogart, or maybe Edward G. Robinson. Some wise guy needs a good working-over. The gangster silently motions to his sidekick, Muggsy. No problem; Muggsy knows just what to do. And when the lights go up, five will get you ten that the screen credits read: "Muggsy......Allen Jenkins."

THE FILMS OF ALLEN JENKINS

1931: The Girl Habit.

1932: Three on a Match; I Am a Fugitive from a Chain Gang; Blessed Event; Lawyer Man; Rackety Rax.

1933: 42nd Street; Bureau of Missing Persons; The Mayor of Hell; The Keyhole; Hard to Handle; Employee's Entrance; The Silk Express; Tomorrow at Seven; Professional Sweetheart; Blondie Johnson; The Mind Reader; Havana Widows. *Credit uncertain:* Ladies They Talk About.

1934: Jimmy the Gent; The St. Louis Kid; The Big Shakedown; The Case of the Howling Dog; I've Got Your Number; The Merry Frinks; Twenty Million Sweethearts; Happiness Ahead; Bedside; Whirlpool.

1935: The Case of the Curious Bride; The Case of the Lucky Legs; Page Miss Glory; Sweet Music; While the Patient Slept; A Night at the Ritz; I Live for Love; Miss Pacific Fleet; The Irish in Us; Broadway Hostess.

1936: Three Men on a Horse; Cain and Mabel; Sins of Man; The Singing Kid; Sing Me a Love Song.

1937: Dead End; Marked Woman; Ever Since Eve; The Singing Marine; The Perfect Specimen; Sh! The Octopus; Ready, Willing and Able; Dance Charlie Dance; Marry the Girl. *Credit uncertain:* Talent Scout.

1938: A Slight Case of Murder; The Amazing Dr. Clitterhouse; Gold Diggers in Paris; Swing Your Lady; Racket Busters; Fools for Scandal; Hard to Get; Heart of the North; Going Places.

1939: Destry Rides Again; Five Came Back; Naughty but Nice; Sweepstakes Winner; Torchy Blane...Playing with Dynamite.

1940: Brother Orchid; Tin Pan Alley; Margie; Meet the Wildcat; Oh, Johnny, How You Can Love.

1941: Ball of Fire; Dive Bomber; Footsteps in the Dark; Time Out for Rhythm; Go West, Young Lady; The Gay Falcon; A Date with the Falcon.

1942: Tortilla Flat; Eyes in the Night; They All Kissed the Bride; The Falcon Takes Over; Maisie Gets Her Man.

1943: Stage Door Canteen.

1945: Lady on a Train; Wonder Man.

1946: The Dark Horse; Meet Me on Broadway; Singin' in the Corn.

1947: Wild Harvest; The Senator Was Indiscreet; Easy Come, Easy Go; Fun on a Weekend; The Hat Box Mystery; The Case of the Baby-Sitter.

1948: Inside Story.

1949: The Big Wheel.

1950: Bodyhold.

1951: Behave Yourself!; Let's Go, Navy; Crazy over Horses.

1952: Oklahoma Annie; The WAC from Walla Walla.

1959: Pillow Talk.

1964: Robin and the Seven Hoods; I'd Rather Be Rich; For Those Who Think Young.

1967: Doctor, You've Got to Be Kidding!

1974: The Front Page.

Who's your favorite uncle?:
GUY KIBBEE

He was many a filmgoer's favorite uncle or grandfather. Bald, moon-faced, beaming and pink-cheeked, Guy Kibbee was also the ideal small-town editor, doctor or civic leader, which resulted in his getting roles in 84 films in the decade of the Thirties alone—just about a movie every six weeks.

He had a deceptively benign appearance, which meant that although he was often genial he could also be shifty or foxy—and once he was even a murderer. He could be both jovial and venal at the same time. Forever smiling, with a pop-eyed stare and a pot belly, he is one of the most recognizable figures from Thirties comedies, and also made a fair number of appearances in famous dramas. The New York Times has said of him: "One of the cinema's grand personalities...deserving of better things."

Kibbee was born March 6, 1882 (some sources say 1886), in El Paso, Texas, spent his youth in Roswell, New Mexico, where his father was editor of the local newspaper, and began his acting career at about age 13. He was a prop boy with a road show managed by his brother, touring Texas, and also entertained on riverboats on the Mississippi. This led to a long career on the legitimate stage, and eventually to Broadway. After an acclaimed role in the successful play **Torch Song** in 1930, he was called to Hollywood the following year at the age of 49.

The actor married Helen Shea in 1918 and they had two sons, John and Robert, but divorced in 1923. In 1925 he married Esther Reed, with whom he had two children, Guy Jr. and Shirley Ann. In private life he was a gregarious joiner of clubs, and owned a fine horse ranch and a successful printing firm.

In his first film, **Stolen Heaven** (31), he was the police commissioner, and in **Man of the World** he was Carole Lombard's wealthy uncle, being black-mailed by William Powell. He was excellent as the unremorseful, cigar-smoking killer Pop Cooley, the henchman of racketeer Paul Lukas and stepfather of Sylvia Sidney, in **City Streets,** and played a drunken salesman in the Clark Gable-Joan Crawford starrer **Laughing Sinners.** He was a con man outsmarted by an even better con man, James Cagney, in **Blonde Crazy,** a circus owner in **Side Show,** and an inept police sergeant in **The New Adventures of Get Rich Quick Wallingford.**

Kibbee was in an absolute avalanche of movies— 19 of them—in 1932, a rate of one every 19 days and

a mark few major character actors have ever approached, although one or two have topped it. Several involved Cagney: He played the star's father in **The Crowd Roars,** and in the Cagney starrer **Taxi!** he was Loretta Young's dad; in **Winner Take All** he was boxer Jimmy's manager. He was cast as a bookie in **Two Seconds,** a larcenous bum in **Union Depot,** a big-league baseball manager in **Fireman Save My Child,** a bibulous hotel detective in **Big City Blues,** a murdered policeman in **Central Park,** and an alcoholic South Seas trader in **Rain.** Also that year, he was the imbecilic dark-horse candidate for governor in **The Dark Horse,** "so dumb that every time he opens his mouth he subtracts from the sum total of human knowledge." He played Edna May Oliver's doctor husband, a key role, in **The Conquerors,** and was helpful to Barbara Stanwyck in **So Big.**

He appeared in all three of Warner Bros.' blockbuster musicals in 1933. In **42nd Street** he played the show's sugar-daddy financial backer and was cuckolded by Bebe Daniels, and in **Gold Diggers of 1933** money-hungry Aline MacMahon backed him into a corner; he was also in **Footlight Parade** as the show's hayseed "angel." **Convention City** cast him as a wife-avoiding businessman who falls in with gold-digger Joan Blondell. He had a key role in director Frank Capra's **Lady for a Day** as the pool shark hired to pose as "Judge" Blake, the husband of May Robson. **The World Changes** found him playing Paul Muni's partner in a Chicago slaughterhouse, and he was a railroad detective in **The Silk Express.** He tried, and failed, to put the make on young Mary Brian in **Girl Missing,** and Miss Blondell and Glenda Farrell tried to blackmail him in **Havana Widows.** He was a retired detective in **The Life of Jimmy Dolan.**

The actor was perfectly cast in the title role of **Babbitt** (34), with Miss MacMahon as his wife, but the weak film failed to do justice to Sinclair Lewis' satirical novel about a Midwestern real-estate man. Miss Blondell was again trying to blackmail him in **Dames,** and in **Big-Hearted Herbert** he was a crusty old grouch of a bathtub merchant who finally wears down his long-suffering family; once again Miss MacMahon was his wife. But in **The Merry Frinks** she watched as he cooked up his wildly indigestible favorite dish, which killed him; he was the rich, eccentric uncle.

Kibbee was one of Errol Flynn's sidekicks in **Captain Blood** (35), the film that made Flynn a star. In **Don't Bet on Blondes** he was a Kentucky colonel who buys insurance to protect himself against the possibility of his actress daughter's (Claire Dodd's) giving up the stage, the source of his financial support. He was married to ZaSu Pitts, and seeking advice from incompetent business consultant Edward Everett Horton, in **Going Highbrow,** and in **Mary Jane's Pa** it was back to marriage with Aline MacMahon; as a journalist who deserts his job and family to satisfy his wanderlust, he returns years later and manages to win her back. In **While the Patient Slept** he played a policeman who, at the end, proposes to a nurse—who but Miss MacMahon? They were the top-billed co-stars of this murder mystery.

He had one of the top roles in one of Shirley Temple's best films, **Captain January** (36), as the old lighthouse keeper with whom she lives, and in **The Big Noise** he was a retired textile manufacturer who fights protection racketeers when he buys into a dry-cleaning shop. In **M'liss** he played Anne Shirley's father, a drunken saloon dishwasher, and in **Earthworm Tractors** his patience was sorely taxed by tractor salesman Joe E. Brown. He was the kindly grocer who befriends Freddie Bartholomew in **Little Lord Fauntleroy.**

The Big Shot (37) cast the actor as a small-town veterinarian who inherits the money, the estate and the gang of a mysterious relative, and in **The Captain's Kid** he was an old sea captain regaling little Sybil Jason with tales of piracy and murder. In **Don't Tell the Wife** he was a dim-witted innocent foiling stock manipulators through his unintentional blunders; Una Merkel was his wife. But he played an oily stock swindler in the Joe E. Brown vehicle **Riding on Air.** In the backwoods drama **Mountain Justice** he was perennially engaged to hatchet-faced spinster Margaret Hamilton. He and Alice Brady were a married couple visiting France in **Mama Steps Out;** they were the co-stars of this programmer. He was the star, playing a private eye, in the programmer **Jim Hanvey, Detective.**

Kibbee was good as the crabby country storekeeper in **Of Human Hearts** (38), and played one of singer Irene Dunne's parasitical relatives preying on her in **Joy of Living.** He was Janet Gaynor's father in **Three Loves Has Nancy,** and led the supporting cast in the fine drama **Three Comrades.** In director Frank Capra's classic **Mr. Smith Goes to Washington** (39) he was the governor, manipulated by crooked political boss Edward Arnold, and he played the softhearted village judge in the Mickey Rooney-Judy Garland outing **Babes in Arms.** He played a millionaire paint manufacturer in **Bad Little Angel** and a judge in **Let Freedom Ring** and also in **Henry Goes Arizona.**

Now in his late fifties, he played the small-town editor, married to Beulah Bondi and the father of Martha Scott, in the classic **Our Town** (40), and in **Chad Hanna** he was the circus owner employing Henry Fonda and Dorothy Lamour. He was a hobo in **Street of Memories.**

In 1941 the actor launched a three-year, six-film series in the title role of Clarence Budington Kelland's stories about Scattergood Baines, a rural philosopher with a bagful of helpful advice and wise maxims, kicking it off with **Scattergood Baines;** all of them were low-budget programmers. Also that year, he was in **It Started with Eve** and **Design for Scandal.** He played Shirley Temple's grandfather in **Miss Annie Rooney** (42), was a college dean and Judy Garland's grandfather in **Girl Crazy** (43), and wound up the Scattergood series that year with **Cinderella Swings It.** He stayed off the screen for a year, and made just one in 1945, supporting Jack Benny in **The Horn Blows at Midnight.** The next year brought a trio of "B" Westerns and a trip to Monogram on Poverty Row for a Joe Palooka movie.

Kibbee was one of the rustics in **The Romance of Rosy Ridge** (47), and appeared in a boy-and-horse drama, **Red Stallion,** and another "B" Western. But he closed out his film career in a blaze of glory in 1948, supporting John Wayne in two films directed by John Ford; he played the doctor in **Fort Apache** and the judge in **Three Godfathers,** although he was far down the cast list in both.

Guy Kibbee died in 1956 at age 74. There are far fewer parts in today's movies for a benign, beaming uncle, but when they come along, surely many a producer has wished for the reincarnation of this popular and avuncular actor.

THE FILMS OF GUY KIBBEE

1931: City Streets; Laughing Sinners; Stolen Heaven; Man of the World; Blonde Crazy; Side Show; Flying High; New Adventures of Get Rich Quick Wallingford.

1932: Taxi!; The Crowd Roars; Two Seconds; So Big; The Dark Horse; Crooner; Rain; The Mouthpiece; Fireman Save My Child; High Pressure; Union Depot; Play Girl; Man Wanted; The Strange Love of Molly Louvain; Winner Take All; Big City Blues; Scarlet Dawn; Central Park; The Conquerors.

1933: 42nd Street; Gold Diggers of 1933; Footlight Parade; Lady for a Day; They Just Had to Get Married; Girl Missing; Lilly Turner; The Life of Jimmy Dolan; The Silk Express; The World Changes; Havana Widows; Convention City.

1934: Babbitt; Dames; Easy to Love; Big-Hearted Herbert; Harold Teen; Merry Wives of Reno; Wonder Bar; The Merry Frinks.

1935: Captain Blood; Don't Bet on Blondes; While the Patient Slept; Mary Jane's Pa; Going Highbrow; I Live for Love.

1936: Captain January; Little Lord Fauntleroy; Three Men on a Horse; The Big Noise; I Married a Doctor; Earthworm Tractors; M'liss; Stage Struck.

1937: The Captain's Kid; Mama Steps Out; Don't Tell the Wife; Riding on Air; Mountain Justice; The Big Shot; Bad Man of Brimstone; Jim Hanvey, Detective.

1938: Three Comrades; Of Human Hearts; Joy of Living; Three Loves Has Nancy; Rich Man, Poor Girl.

1939: Mr. Smith Goes to Washington; Babes in Arms; It's a Wonderful World; Let Freedom Ring; Bad Little Angel; Henry Goes Arizona.

1940: Our Town; Chad Hanna; Street of Memories.

1941: It Started with Eve; Design for Scandal; Scattergood Baines; Scattergood Meets Broadway; Scattergood Pulls the Strings.

1942: This Time for Keeps; Sunday Punch; Tish; Miss Annie Rooney; Whistling in Dixie; Scattergood Rides High; Scattergood Survives a Murder.

1943: Girl Crazy; Power of the Press; Cinderella Swings It.

1945: The Horn Blows at Midnight.

1946: Singing on the Trail; Cowboy Blues; Lone Star Moonlight; Gentleman Joe Palooka.

1947: The Romance of Rosy Ridge; Red Stallion; Over the Santa Fe Trail.

1948: Fort Apache; Three Godfathers.

NOTE: One source lists an appearance in the 1943 film **White Savage,** but his name does not appear on a published cast list.

Polished and suave:
OTTO KRUGER

Polished, worldly suavity was the stock in trade of Otto Kruger.

With wavy silver hair, a trim mustache, sleek manners and bedroom eyes, he was convincing as a seducer or the "Other Man," and during the Thirties he virtually cornered the market on crooked, immoral lawyers and doctors. He played both good and bad men, but was at his best as a smooth, cynical villain. Always immaculately dressed, his deep metallic voice exuding class, he was one of the most civilized of actors.

Kruger was born September 6, 1885, in Toledo, Ohio; he is said to have been the grandnephew of "Oom Paul" Kruger, president of South Africa in the late 19th century. Trained as a child for a musical career, he switched to acting after studying at Columbia University. After several years in stock, repertory and vaudeville, he made his Broadway debut in 1915 in **The Natural Law,** and that year was also in a film, **When the Call Came.**

In the Twenties he was one of the leading matinee idols of the Broadway stage, in such plays as Eugene O'Neill's **The Straw** in 1921 and in **The Royal Family** in 1927. He played mainly urbane, sophisticated roles. He appeared in another movie, **Under the Red Robe** (23), as a plotter against Louis XIII; the film's other villain, William Powell, was plotting too, but against the prime minister, Cardinal Richelieu. Kruger continued to star on the stage and would not film again for another decade. His Broadway co-stars included Helen Hayes and Alice Brady.

The era of sound films was well under way when the actor was called to Hollywood in 1933. He was in **Turn Back the Clock,** as the rich man exchanging fortunes and wives (only in a dream, as it turned out) with his hard-up friend Lee Tracy. In **The Prizefighter and the Lady** he was the racketeer lover of nightclub queen Myrna Loy, losing her to Max Baer (who was also a boxer in real life). He was a villainous, alcoholic lawyer in **The Women in His Life,** in which he was top-billed. In the soap opera **Gallant Lady** he and his wife adopt Ann Harding's illegitimate child (Dickie Moore); years later, widowed, he marries Miss Harding. In **Beauty for Sale** he breaks up with wife Alice Brady when he falls in love with young Madge Evans.

But these parts, good as they were, couldn't compare with his other role that year, as Barbara Stanwyck's

husband in **Ever in My Heart,** one of Hollywood's finest romantic melodramas. In 1909 a New England girl, Miss Stanwyck, marries a German, Kruger, but during World War I they are caught up in anti-German hysteria and he returns to Germany to fight for his own country, while their friends turn against them. Later, working at a canteen in France, she discovers him operating as a spy, and after one last night together she poisons their wine and they die together as the sound track echoes with "Du, du, liegst mir im Herzen," the song that introduced them. This vastly neglected film is overdue for revival.

Kruger was fine in **Chained** (34) as the older man married to his employee, Joan Crawford, and giving her up to new love Clark Gable. He was one of the senior doctors in the Gable starrer **Men in White,** and played Dr. Livesey in **Treasure Island. The Crime Doctor** starred him as a venomous criminologist who pins the murder he himself committed on the lover (Nils Asther) of his wife (Karen Morley) so skillfully that the charge sticks—but in the end he confesses and kills himself. The critics liked him in **Springtime for Henry** (taking the starring role played so often on stage by Edward Everett Horton); he and Nancy Carroll have romance on their minds, complicated by the fact that she is married to Nigel Bruce. He loved Madge Evans again in **Paris Interlude,** but she finally ends up with Robert Young.

He was good in **Vanessa: Her Love Story** (35) as the crazed husband of Helen Hayes, who finds a new love in Robert Montgomery. **Dracula's Daughter** (36) cast him as a psychoanalyst with whom evil Gloria Holden, in the title role, falls in love—but he calls in the police. In **Lady of Secrets** he fell in love first with young Marian Marsh and later with her older sister, Ruth Chatterton. In the powerful drama **They Won't Forget** (37) he was the defense attorney trying to save an innocent man accused of murder but losing the case to unscrupulous prosecuting attorney Claude Rains. **Counsel for Crime** cast him as a crooked criminal lawyer, going to prison to live up to the ideals of his unacknowledged illegitimate lawyer son (Douglass Montgomery). He played the villain with a guilty secret in **The Barrier.**

The actor married stage actress Sue MacManamy in 1919. They had a daughter, Ottilie.

His parade of crooked lawyers really got under way in 1938. In **Exposed** he was a corrupt district attorney, freed by a jury but ultimately brought to justice by magazine photographer Glenda Farrell. He was good in **I Am the Law** as a corrupt civic leader who has become the crime boss of the city but is no match for Edward G. Robinson, a law professor turned special prosecutor; in the end Kruger kills himself. But in **Housemaster** he was Mr. Nice Guy again, in the title role as a teacher in an English school siding with the boys against the dictatorial new headmaster. He was Bob Hope's employer, a publisher, in **Thanks for the Memory.**

Probably the quintessential crooked lawyer played by Kruger was the one in **Disbarred** (39). Here he was a disbarred mouthpiece who tries to use lawyer Gail Patrick as a stooge to prolong his own unsavory career. The advertising for the film read: "He's America's crooked mouthpiece No. 1." But he was honest again in **A Woman Is the Judge,** as the prosecuting attorney battling Frieda Inescort, a judge who has resigned from the bench to defend her daughter, accused of murder; in the end, Kruger and Miss Inescort fall in love. He was the assistant district attorney in **Another Thin Man.** He and Miss Inescort were in love again in **The Zero Hour,** but he is paralyzed in an auto accident and, to free her to marry another man, kills himself.

After this run of lawyers, the actor probably felt like resigning from the Screen Actors Guild and joining the American Bar Association. But he displayed his versatility in another 1939 film, **Black Eyes,** as a Moscow hotel headwaiter who arranges clandestine romantic assignations for patrons. In **Scandal Sheet** he played a ruthless newspaper publisher without a conscience who murders to protect his illegitimate son. Then he supported Edward G. Robinson in two good biographical films: In **Dr. Ehrlich's Magic Bullet** (40) he was a doctor who aided Robinson in his discovery of a cure for venereal disease, and in **A Dispatch from Reuters** he played the star's father-in-law. In the topical anti-Nazi drama **The Man I Married** he was the father of Francis Lederer, a German who marries Joan Bennett and gradually turns into a Nazi; when Miss Bennett then tries to flee Germany with her son she finds an ally in father-in-law Kruger, who tells Lederer his mother was Jewish, causing him to release his wife. He played Jackie Cooper's father in **Seventeen.**

Now in his mid-fifties, he was a fugitive from justice, living as a hermit, in **Mercy Island** (41), and in the Loretta Young starrer **The Men in Her Life** he played one of them. In **The Big Boss** he was a racketeer trying to take over the state government. He was excellent in director Alfred Hitchcock's **Saboteur** (42) as the suave German agent who temporarily traps Robert Cummings and Priscilla Lane in his New York mansion, and he was a Nazi colonel in the sensationalized drama **Hitler's Children. Secrets of a Co-ed** cast him as a millionaire gangster. He was involved in espionage again in **Night Plane from Chungking** (43), and was a Nazi agent in **Tarzan's Desert Mystery.** He played an unscrupulous press baron in **Power of the Press,** a man who stops at nothing, including murder, to gain his ends, and who tangles with his own managing editor, Lee Tracy. Meanwhile, back on Broadway, he co-starred in **The Moon Is Down.**

Kruger got his teeth into a juicy part in **Murder, My Sweet** (44) as a blackmailing quack psychologist who causes big trouble for Dick Powell. In the Rita Hayworth starrer **Cover Girl** he played a magazine publisher seeking a long-lost beauty. He was a Nazi again in **They Live in Fear,** and a washed-up spy shot to death by Erich von Stroheim in **Storm over Lisbon.** The low-budget chiller **Jungle Captive** (45) featured him as a biochemist restoring life to an ape woman, who kills him, and in the superior horror drama **The Woman Who Came Back** he played a clergyman. He was yet another German spy in **Escape in the Fog,** aided Kay Francis' bigamy racket in **Allotment Wives,** and was the district attorney in **Wonder Man.** He had a small role in the big-budget Western drama **Duel in the Sun** (46). During this period he also returned to the stage; among other work, he starred on Broadway in 1947 in **Laura,** in the role of the decadent murderer Waldo Lydecker (played by Clifton Webb in the 1944 film).

His film roles became fewer now. **Lulu Belle** (48) cast the actor as a millionaire, one of the numerous romantic conquests of Dorothy Lamour; he makes her a stage star. He played the head of a crooked bookmaking syndicate in **711 Ocean Drive** (50), infatuated with Joanne Dru, who unfortunately loves Edmond O'Brien. In **Payment on Demand** (51) he was Bette Davis' lawyer, counseling her on divorce proceedings, and in **Valentino,** as a movie producer, he gave Rudy his first movie break. He played the judge in the classic Western **High Noon** (52), hastily trying to leave town when trouble looms. The actor now also began appearing on television; he was the host on "Lux Video Theatre," and appeared in the series "Climax" and "The Law and Mr. Jones."

In the 1954 remake of **Magnificent Obsession**

he had Ralph Morgan's old role of the family friend counseling Rock Hudson on his plans to study medicine and cure Jane Wyman of blindness. He turned 70 in 1955, and was off the screen for three years. He should have waited longer, because **The Colossus of New York** (58) was an absurd mishmash in which he was a doctor implanting his dead son's brain into a huge robot, which then went on a rampage. In **The Young Philadelphians** (59) it was back to the legal profession; Alexis Smith was his frustrated wife. There were a few more parts, and his last film role, at age 78, came in **Sex and the Single Girl** (64).

A severe stroke Kruger suffered in that year forced his retirement, although he later surmounted the paralysis it brought on. After several years he entered the Motion Picture Country House and Hospital near Hollywood, where in 1974 he died on his 89th birthday.

Today's Hollywood probably hasn't the sense to miss an actor like him. When casting a crooked lawyer, today's producer is likely to choose an uncivilized type to match the less civilized times. Never someone suave, smooth and polished like Otto Kruger.

THE FILMS OF OTTO KRUGER

1915: When the Call Came.
1923: Under the Red Robe.
1933: Ever in My Heart; Turn Back the Clock; Beauty for Sale; The Prizefighter and the Lady; Gallant Lady; The Women in His Life.
1934: Chained; Men in White; Treasure Island; Paris Interlude; The Crime Doctor; Springtime for Henry.
1935: Vanessa: Her Love Story; Two Sinners.
1936: Dracula's Daughter; Lady of Secrets.
1937: They Won't Forget; Counsel for Crime; The Barrier.
1938: I Am the Law; Exposed; Thanks for the Memory; Housemaster; Star of the Circus.
1939: Disbarred; Scandal Sheet; The Zero Hour; A Woman Is the Judge; Another Thin Man; Black Eyes; The Amazing Mr. Forrest.
1940: Dr. Ehrlich's Magic Bullet; A Dispatch from Reuters; The Man I Married; Seventeen.
1941: The Big Boss; The Men in Her Life; Mercy Island.
1942: Saboteur; Hitler's Children; Secrets of a Co-ed; Friendly Enemies.

1943: Power of the Press; Night Plane from Chungking; Tarzan's Desert Mystery; Stage Door Canteen.
1944: Murder, My Sweet; Cover Girl; Storm over Lisbon; They Live in Fear; Knickerbocker Holiday.
1945: Wonder Man; The Great John L.; Jungle Captive; The Woman Who Came Back; On Stage, Everybody!; The Chicago Kid; Escape in the Fog; Allotment Wives; Earl Carroll Vanities.
1946: Duel in the Sun; The Fabulous Suzanne.
1947: Love and Learn.
1948: Lulu Belle; Smart Woman.
1950: 711 Ocean Drive.
1951: Payment on Demand; Valentino.
1952: High Noon.
1954: Magnificent Obsession; Black Widow.
1955: The Last Command.
1958: The Colossus of New York.
1959: The Young Philadelphians; Cash McCall.
1962: The Wonderful World of the Brothers Grimm.
1964: Sex and the Single Girl.

Slimy, shifty, treacherous:
GENE LOCKHART

Gene Lockhart had the versatility to play both good and bad guys, but at the peak of his Hollywood career there was one stereotypical role in which he was cast over and over: the sly, shifty, treacherous nasty who ultimately is undone. He was perfect in parts where his veneer finally crumbles—for example, as an informer who is caught by those he informed on and he winds up cringing in a corner and babbling for mercy.

He could also play doctors, lawyers, fathers, judges, testy businessmen or Nazi spies—not to mention Dickens' Bob Cratchit. In later life he was the picture of crusty benevolence—but you fondly recall him as a slimy informer from films of the Thirties.

Short and chunky, with a chubby, jowly face, he somewhat resembled a pug dog. That face was a familiar one to filmgoers of the late Thirties and the war years, and on into the postwar era as well.

Eugene Lockhart was born July 18, 1891, in London, Ontario. At the age of six he was performing Scottish dances with a band attached to a Canadian regiment, and later was a singer and a newspaper columnist before making his stage debut in the United States, performing Gilbert and Sullivan. He reached Broadway in 1916 in **The Riviera Girl,** and also appeared in such plays as **The Handy Man, Sure Fire** and **Sun Up.**

The actor made one isolated film appearance in the silent era, playing the village clergyman in the first screen version of **Smilin' Through** (22), starring Norma Talmadge. He continued to be active on the stage throughout the Twenties and into the early Thirties. He wrote (and appeared in) a revue, **Bunk of 1926.** He also wrote songs; with Deems Taylor he was the co-composer of "The World Is Waiting for the Sunrise."

In 1924 he married Kathleen Arthur, and they had a daughter, June, the following year. Both Kathleen and June Lockhart were busy film actresses.

In 1933 Lockhart played the bibulous Uncle Sid in the Theatre Guild's Broadway production of Eugene O'Neill's **Ah, Wilderness!,** and this led immediately to Hollywood offers. He left for the film capital and began a long and busy career on the screen. His first sound film is said by some sources to have been the Carole Lombard starrer **The Gay Bride** in 1934, but his name does not appear in the complete

published cast list. However, he was definitely in **By Your Leave,** as a polished drunk who is Frank Morgan's best friend. In director Josef von Sternberg's **Crime and Punishment** (35), based on Tolstoy's novel, he was the pompous, aging Lushin, hoping to marry Peter Lorre's young sister but ending up being mocked and thrown out of the family apartment by Lorre. In **Star of Midnight** he was William Powell's butler, and he played a Cape Cod fisherman in **Captain Hurricane** and a bumbling police lieutenant in **Thunder in the Night.**

The actor's busiest year on the screen was 1936, with 11 releases. He was Joan Crawford's father in the historical drama **The Gorgeous Hussy,** and was good in **Times Square Playboy** as an interfering out-of-towner who comes to New York as the best man for a wedding and makes trouble between the two families. He was the murder victim, killed by H.B. Warner, in **The Garden Murder Case,** and Anita Louise's father, an apple marketer, in **Brides Are Like**

141

That. He played Jackie Cooper's father in **The Devil Is a Sissy,** and was a European archduke in **Wedding Present,** joining newspaper reporters Cary Grant and Joan Bennett in a drunken spree. He played a murdered mayoral candidate in **Mind Your Own Business** and a harassed store owner in **Come Closer, Folks.** At this point in time his real-life wife, Kathleen Lockhart, played his wife in a number of his movies.

Lockhart was heiress Anne Shirley's father in **Too Many Wives** (37), and a scheming producer trying to con James Cagney in **Something to Sing About.** He played a wealthy friend of Guy Kibbee in **Mama Steps Out.** Even better roles came along in 1938. He won an Academy Award nomination as best supporting actor for **Algiers,** as Regis, the informer whose treachery is responsible for the death of Charles Boyer and who ends up killed by members of Boyer's gang of thieves. This may have been the first film in which he portrayed the weaseling informer, trapped and begging for mercy. He was good as the oppressed Bob Cratchit in **A Christmas Carol,** the Dickens classic, and in **Sinners in Paradise,** as a pompous senator with a guilty secret in his past, he was one of a group of people stranded on a tropical island after a plane crash. He played a wealthy hypochondriac in **Meet the Girls,** and in the Judy Garland starrer **Listen, Darling** he was a sour banker who hopes to marry Judy's widowed mother, Mary Astor, but loses her to Walter Pidgeon. In **Blondie,** the first film in that lengthy series, he was the businessman to whom Dagwood Bumstead hopes to make a big sale.

The actor was downright slimy in 1939, with two roles of that type. In **Blackmail** it was he who committed the crime (embezzlement) for which Edward G. Robinson is imprisoned; when Robinson escapes, Lockhart blackmails him and gets him sent back again, but is finally forced to confess on the brink of a flaming oil well. He played this nasty with such zest that he was one of the few performers ever to steal a scene from the redoubtable Robinson, who wasn't bad at scene-stealing himself. Lockhart also was excellent as the treacherous gun-runner selling arms to the Indians in **Geronimo,** once again sweating guiltily when cornered, and meeting a gory end at the dénouement. He was a hotel porter helping some spies in **Hotel Imperial,** and he gave financial backing to telephone inventor Don Ameche in **The Story of Alexander Graham Bell** after Ameche cured Lockhart's son of deafness. He was Robert Young's father, a wealthy industrialist, in **Bridal Suite,** and a tractor magnate in **I'm from Missouri.** In **Tell No Tales** he played a slimy gambling-house owner.

He was good as Stephen A. Douglas, debating Lincoln (Raymond Massey) in **Abe Lincoln in Illinois** (40) and defeating him in the 1858 U.S. Senate election. Continuing to play key roles in important pictures, he was the sheriff in **His Girl Friday,** and one of the financial backers of Edward G. Robinson in his plan to establish a news-wire service in **A Dispatch from Reuters.** In a very similar role, he gave backing to Spencer Tracy as inventor Thomas A. Edison in **Edison, the Man,** but later turned against him. Lew Ayres cured him of meningitis in **Dr. Kildare Goes Home,** and Victor McLaglen murdered him in **South of Pago Pago.** He was a small-minded office manager who fires Lana Turner in **We Who Are Young.**

Lockhart sank his teeth into a juicy dramatic part in **The Sea Wolf** (41), as the drunken ship's doctor who throws himself from the top of the mast into the sea rather than face further humiliation from the crazed captain (Robinson). He was the village squire in **All That Money Can Buy,** Olivia de Havilland's father in **They Died with Their Boots On,** and the mayor who is also the agitated owner of the building from which Gary Cooper threatens to take a suicidal leap in **Meet John Doe.** In **One Foot in Heaven** he and Laura Hope Crews were the stuffy bigwigs battling clergyman Fredric March, and he was slimy once more as a fifth-columnist posing as a loyal American in **International Lady.** He was also villainous as the gang leader with whom Robert Taylor is connected in **Billy the Kid.** Of the latter film, one film historian comments that the role "[reminds] us again that this brilliant character actor was one of the most versatile performers on the screen."

The actor played the villain in **Juke Girl** (42), and supported Barbara Stanwyck in **The Gay Sisters.** He was now in his early fifties, and still more juicy parts lay ahead. Meanwhile, his daughter, June, was beginning to get ingenue roles in films.

Perhaps the quintessence of Gene Lockhart was his part as the collaborationist informer in director Fritz Lang's **Hangmen Also Die** (43), set in Nazi-occupied Czechoslovakia. Patriot Brian Donlevy assassinates Reichsprotektor Reinhard Heydrich, setting off a huge manhunt. Lockhart, the quisling, is exposed as the informer, and the underground decides to frame him for the murder of Heydrich, providing various pieces of incriminating evidence, finally planting the murder weapon and the body of a dead Gestapo inspector in his home. The Nazis arrest him and later find he is innocent, but decide to execute him anyway, to save face. The actor, cringing and babbling in terror, was perfect for this role.

In that same year, he was also cast as Soviet diplomat V.M. Molotov in **Mission to Moscow** and played a greasy, treacherous Nazi agent in the Errol Flynn starrer **Northern Pursuit.** He was a businessman helping priest Bing Crosby in **Going My Way** (44), and played yet another Nazi spy in **The House on 92nd Street** (45), also appearing as the doctor in **Leave Her to Heaven.** He was cast as Hedy Lamarr's aging husband in **Strange Woman** (46), ending up killed by his son by an earlier marriage (Louis Hayward), who then takes up with Miss Lamarr. He was the perplexed judge in **Miracle on 34th Street** (47) and a French nobleman in **The Foxes of Harrow.** He was one of a large troupe of character actors supporting Ingrid Bergman in **Joan of Arc** (48), and in **That Wonderful Urge** he played the judge who helped keep the marriage of Tyrone Power and Gene Tierney from breaking up.

The actor was a college professor in **Apartment for Peggy** (also 48), and played the village mayor (married to Elsa Lanchester) in the Danny Kaye vehicle **The Inspector General** (49), also supporting Jennifer Jones in **Madame Bovary.** He was a grizzled old seafaring man in **Down to the Sea in Ships.** In the forgotten film noir **Red Light** he was the victim of a bizarre murder: Fearfully hiding from villain Raymond Burr in a darkened truck garage, he climbs under a parked trailer, then screams in his death agony as Burr kicks one of the trailer jacks out. In **I'd Climb the Highest Mountain** (51) he played a crusty businessman persuaded by a preacher to allow his (Lockhart's) daughter to marry her lover. And there

were routine parts in a bunch of 1952 and 1953 films, including a Bonzo outing, a Francis the Talking Mule epic and several other tired programmers. In 1953's **Down Among the Sheltering Palms** he was a clergyman serving as a missionary on a tropical island, and he had an exceptionally good part in **World for Ransom** (54) as a black marketeer involved in kidnapping and murder but undone by Dan Duryea.

In this latter part of his career Lockhart also performed in other media, doing plays, television dramas, and dramatic readings on the college lecture circuit. At one point he took Lee J. Cobb's starring role in the play **Death of a Salesman.** He starred in the TV series "His Honor, Homer Bell" as a judge.

The actor was up to no good again in **The Vanishing American** (55), trying to steal land from the Navajo Indians, but he was a conventional businessman in **The Man in the Gray Flannel Suit** (56). He played the benevolent Starkeeper in **Carousel,** and the president of the board of Actors Equity in his last film, **Jeanne Eagels** (57); it had just been completed when he died in 1957 at age 66.

You can still see Gene Lockhart every Christmas when it's time to roll out **A Christmas Carol** once again. He was a fine Bob Cratchit, to be sure—but he's far more fun to watch in a film such as **Algiers** or **Hangmen Also Die,** once again the treacherous informer, once again caught like a rat in a trap, cringing in terror and begging for the mercy he will not get.

THE FILMS OF GENE LOCKHART

1922: Smilin' Through.
1934: By Your Leave. *Credit uncertain:* The Gay Bride.
1935: Crime and Punishment; Star of Midnight; I've Been Around; Captain Hurricane; Thunder in the Night; Storm over the Andes.
1936: The Gorgeous Hussy; Brides Are Like That; Times Square Playboy; Earthworm Tractors; The First Baby; Career Woman; The Garden Murder Case; The Devil Is a Sissy; Wedding Present; Mind Your Own Business; Come Closer, Folks.
1937: Make Way for Tomorrow; Mama Steps Out; Too Many Wives; Something to Sing About; The Sheik Steps Out.
1938: Algiers; Of Human Hearts; A Christmas Carol; Sweethearts; Blondie; Men Are Such Fools; Listen, Darling; Penrod's Double Trouble; Meet the Girls; Sinners in Paradise.
1939: The Story of Alexander Graham Bell; Blackmail; Geronimo; Hotel Imperial; Our Leading Citizen; I'm from Missouri; Tell No Tales; Bridal Suite.
1940: Abe Lincoln in Illinois; His Girl Friday; Edison, the Man; A Dispatch from Reuters; Dr. Kildare Goes Home; We Who Are Young; South of Pago Pago.
1941: The Sea Wolf; Meet John Doe; Billy the Kid; All That Money Can Buy; They Died with Their Boots On; One Foot in Heaven; Keeping Company; Steel Against the Sky; International Lady.
1942: The Gay Sisters; You Can't Escape Forever; Jute Girl.
1943: Hangmen Also Die; Mission to Moscow; Northern Pursuit; Forever and a Day; The Desert Song; Find the Blackmailer. *Credit uncertain:* Madame Curie.

1944: Going My Way; Action in Arabia; The Man from Frisco.
1945: Leave Her to Heaven; The House on 92nd Street; That's the Spirit.
1946: The Strange Woman; A Scandal in Paris (Thieves' Holiday); Meet Me on Broadway.
1947: Miracle on 34th Street; The Foxes of Harrow; The Shocking Miss Pilgrim; Cynthia; Honeymoon; Her Husband's Affairs.
1948: Joan of Arc; That Wonderful Urge; Apartment for Peggy; The Inside Story; I, Jane Doe.
1949: Madame Bovary; Down to the Sea in Ships; The Inspector General; Red Light.
1950: Riding High; The Big Hangover.
1951: I'd Climb the Highest Mountain; The Lady from Texas; Rhubarb; The Sickle and the Cross.
1952: A Girl in Every Port; Face to Face; Androcles and the Lion; Apache War Smoke; Bonzo Goes to College; Hoodlum Empire.
1953: Down Among the Sheltering Palms; Confidentially Connie; Francis Covers the Big Town; The Lady Wants Mink.
1954: World for Ransom.
1955: The Vanishing American.
1956: The Man in the Gray Flannel Suit; Carousel.
1957: Jeanne Eagels.

NOTE: Some sources erroneously credit him with appearances in the 1944 film **The White Cliffs of Dover** and the 1946 film **She-Wolf of London;** it was his daughter, June Lockhart, who was in those films.

Roll those eyeballs:
PETER LORRE

Over many years the American film industry has carelessly squandered many great talents, but surely the most appalling waste of a brilliant actor's skills occurs in the case of Peter Lorre.

The man whom Charlie Chaplin called "the greatest living actor" (this in 1935) hardly ever got the roles he deserved, and after three superb performances (in **M, The Man Who Knew Too Much** and **Mad Love**) that should have made him a great star, was quickly and irretrievably typecast as a mysterious menace, doomed to supporting parts in films that inevitably got worse and worse. At last he figured the hell with it, and walked with his eyes closed through roles that might just as well have gone to Bela Lugosi.

In truth, though, let it be said that Hollywood was not entirely to blame. The actor was to some extent limited by his small stature and his markedly individual screen personality, one utterly unlike any other in films.

The principal components were his sad, rolling eyes, his timid manner and his querulous, whispering voice with its indefinable Mittel-European accent. He came into view with a deceptively friendly smile, but the eyes remained sad. This comic-sinister persona could adapt itself to both sympathetic and villainous roles. Typically he was a mysterious and quietly menacing foreigner, scuttling from the shadier corners of life, speaking in wheedling tones, then snarling, then cringing. Resigned to the follies of others, he made a fetish of his own fastidiousness.

Lorre's criminals are intelligent, often cultured, but too oily to touch. The scariest of them are philosophical "thinking" men who have a touch of melancholy or have suffered greatly. Almost all his characters are eccentric, nervous, excitable, and frustrated in that they never get what they want. They often explode in an infantile rage, literally spitting out words and pulling hair. They are pathetic individuals. But even his wickedest men are hard to hate. One of his screenwriters, Charles Bennett, said, "[He] could kill—calculatedly, malevolently—and still remain amusingly lovable...perhaps because he killed with that alluring smile, or perhaps his personal kindness came through."

He was successful only as a menace. One never warmed up to him as a good man. The only quality he could infuse with dramatic interest was villainy, and for a time he was one of the screen's greatest villains.

The actor was born June 26, 1904, in a town in the Austro-Hungarian Empire whose name is variously given as Rozsahegy, Rosenberg and Ruzmberg; today it is called Ruzomberok and is in eastern Czechoslovakia, near the Polish border. His name at birth was Laszlo (or Ladislav) Loewenstein, and his father (the son of a rabbi) was a comptroller for a textile firm (according to one source) or the owner of a wood lot (according to another). The boy's mother died when he was not quite four, and he was brought up by a stepmother he didn't like. One source says he was as a child "rather peculiar emotionally." The family moved to Romania and then to Vienna, where the child was a brilliant but indifferent student and by his teens was the wayward black sheep who wanted only to become an actor. (He had started early, as a dwarf in **Snow White** in grammar school.)

His father, however, did not approve of that ambition, and so Lorre ran away from home at age 13, in 1918. His first stage appearance was in a comedy role in one of Vienna's small, intimate theaters, and he was caught up as a teen-ager in the Bohemian life. But he agreed to try the business world—for a while, anyway. He studied at a commercial academy and took a job as a bank clerk, submerging himself by night in the café counterculture of Vienna; finally he manipulated the bank manager into firing him and plunged into the world of the stage. He slept on park benches, sold his books and clothes for food, and hunted for acting jobs in postwar Vienna, a hub of cultural activity. After a while he was taken on by an improvisational theater troupe, where his talent emerged in an experimental and spontaneous format. There was no formal instruction, but his instinct and intuition drew from him a strong acting skill. During this period he also entertained in cafés and gave one-man performances and readings.

In 1924 he was hired to work in stock theater in what was then Breslau, Germany (now called Wroclaw, Poland), in small parts, but was shortly fired for putting comedic touches into roles that did not call for them. Then he went to Zurich, Switzerland, where he played an old man in Galsworthy's **Loyalties** and appeared in some children's productions. Work ran out, and he returned to Vienna. From 1925 to 1928 he all but vanished from sight, being swept up in café and theater life, taking small roles in repertory, appearing in plays of every conceivable kind.

But inevitably Lorre was drawn to Berlin, the dazzling and decadent center of Germanic culture in those dying days of the Weimar Republic. He arrived there in 1929 with but a few coins in his pocket, and almost immediately had a fortuitous meeting with playwright Bertolt Brecht, who recommended him for a part in a play to be produced by the Theater am Schiffbauerdamm, Berlin's leading (and most controversial) theater. The play was **Pioniere in Ingolstadt** (Engineers in Ingolstadt), and under Brecht's direction, the actor drew critical raves as a feeble-minded high-school student who aspires to be both lusty and callous toward women, emulating a company of visiting soldiers; when the soldiers ridicule him, he schemes for revenge.

A newspaper critic said: "And a new face was there, a terrifying face; the hysterical bourgeois son, whose bug eyes and corpulent head poured forth in a yellow manner...as this young lad staggers between sluggishness and hysterical breakdown, as he so timorously goes and grabs and sometimes greedily fumbles, such have also older ones that I have hardly seen presented in such an uncanny manner in the theater. This person is Peter Lorre."

His future now seemed assured. He next appeared in **Happy End,** in **Dantons Tod** (Danton's Death) as

a sadistic despot, and then, starring for the first time, in Frank Wedekind's **Frühlings Erwachen** (Spring's Awakening), as a teen-ager who commits suicide when he finds himself unable to deal with his sexual urges. In the audience one night, watching this performance filled with melancholy and hysteria, was the renowned film director Fritz Lang. He asked the young actor to star in his next film—without telling him what role he was to play. Lorre agreed.

While Lang prepared the script, the actor appeared as a corrupt and porcine press lord in the play **Die Unüberwindlichen** (The Unconquerable), and then in a comedic role as a young Communist in **Die Quadratur des Kreises** (Squaring the Circle). Then Lang showed up with the movie script. The film was to be called **M.**

The amiable and mild-mannered Lorre was taken aback to learn that he would be playing a sexual psychopath, a child-murderer. But this remarkable and difficult role posed a challenge for an actor: to portray man's dark instincts in a credible manner. To say that he met the challenge is an understatement. This brilliantly instinctive actor delivered one of the greatest performances in the history of the cinema. He gave the character an almost clinical authenticity with his melancholy expression, at once sinister and pathetic, his round eyes bulging with terror as he is hunted down by both the police and the underworld. He truly *inhabited* the murderer.

The worldwide success of **M** (31) made him, at age 27, an instant star. But, incredibly, although he then proceeded to make eight German films in the next two years, he was merely a supporting actor in all of them—often in very small parts.

He wound up his stage work that same year, appearing in Brecht's **Mann ist Mann** (Man Is Man) as a dock worker who becomes a pugnacious soldier. Then he began work for the leading German film studio, UFA (Universum-Film Aktiengesellschaft), starting with a tiny part as a ship's first engineer in **Bomben auf Monte Carlo** (The Bombardment of Monte Carlo) (31), starring Hans Albers, who was at that point in time to the German film what Burt Reynolds was in America in the Seventies, and Anna Sten. Next came **Die Koffer des Herrn O.F.** (The Trunks of Mr. O.F.), in a good role as a comic journalist, followed by **Fünf von der Jazzband** (The Jazzband Five) (32), again in a small part, as a car thief, and **Schuss im Morgengrauen** (A Shot at Dawn), as one of a ring of thieves.

In **F.P. 1 antwortet nicht** (F.P. 1 Doesn't Answer), again starring Albers, Lorre was once more a journalist, and he also appeared in the French version, **F.P. 1 ne répond plus,** with Charles Boyer as the star. (For the record, F.P. means floating platform.) In Albers' next film, **Der weisse Dämon** (The White Demon), the actor finally got a major part, being billed third as the hunchbacked leader of a drug-smuggling ring. He was a detective in **Was Frauen träumen** (What Women Dream) (33), a film for which future director Billy Wilder co-authored the screenplay. His last German film, **Unsichtbare Gegner** (Invisible Opponent), featured him and Oscar Homolka as international swindlers; he also made the French version, **Les réquins du petrole** (The Oil Sharks).

During the filming of **Unsichtbare Gegner** the Nazis came to power. Producer Sam Spiegel (later a prominent American producer) and the largely Jewish cast and crew hastily fled from Berlin to Vienna without so much as their baggage; Spiegel had only the script. Then it was on to Paris for one last European film, director G.W. Pabst's **Du haut en bas** (From Top to Bottom), starring Jean Gabin, in which Lorre had a tiny role as a beggar.

He now urgently needed work, but is said to have turned down more than 300 offers to play psychopathic murderers since the release of **M**. Still, he agreed to appear in director Alfred Hitchcock's next film—as a murderous psychopath. This was **The Man Who Knew Too Much** (34). Playing an inhuman professional assassin and kidnapper, he filled his performance with dark and terrifying emotions without seeming to disturb his placid moon face. American critics were lavish in their praise, and, clearly, Hollywood would be the next step in his career.

For MGM, he gave the last of his three truly great performances, in the film that brought about the typecasting that would irreparably harm his career. This was **Mad Love** (35), a remarkable foray into the world of Grand Guignol. Based on the novel "The Hands of Orlac," it starred Lorre as Dr. Stephen Gogol, a maniacal and love-crazed surgeon obsessed with an actress; he grafts the hands of a guillotined murderer onto the mangled arms of her husband, a concert pianist, and later tries to strangle the actress, but is knifed by the husband. The actor exuded a vicious sadism as the lecherous, giggling maniac, popeyed, baby-faced and bald. Truly, this was a villain for connoisseurs, and it is understandable that this performance was to influence Orson Welles in some of the key scenes in **Citizen Kane.** (Especially the one when Kane, just after his second wife has left him, walks slowly and heavily down the mirrored corridor.)

Lorre then starred for director Josef von Sternberg in Columbia's version of Dostoyevsky's **Crime and Punishment,** making a convincing murderer Raskolnikov, pursued by Edward Arnold as Inspec-

tor Porfiry, in a weak film. He was really too old at 31 to portray the student, but delivered an insightful and expertly shaded performance. He then refused Columbia's offer of a contract, and worked for Hitchcock again in **Secret Agent** (36), in a supporting role as the murderous little spy known as "the general"; he had no trouble stealing the film from stars John Gielgud, Madeleine Carroll and Robert Young. Critic Otis Ferguson commented, "He is one of the true characters of the theater, having mastered loose oddities and disfigurements until the total is a style, childlike, beautiful, unfathomably wicked, always hinting at things it would not be good to know."

The actor's career now reached a fatal turning point. He had established himself as a dramatic star, albeit with an image as a demented killer. But he signed a contract with 20th Century-Fox to guarantee himself steady work—and that studio (like most studios) simply did not have a steady supply of parts of the right type for such a performer. Instead, he would have to fit into the Hollywood mold. He next appeared in **Crack-up** (37), the nominal star, as the head of a foreign spy ring out to get documents on new planes; co-starred was Brian Donlevy as a double-crossing pilot. Lorre was third in the cast list in **Nancy Steele Is Missing,** playing kidnapper Victor McLaglen's prison cellmate, a treacherous little professor with homicidal tendencies. This hardly looked as though it was leading Lorre to stardom—in fact, it seemed to be leading him in an entirely different direction.

The actor married stage and screen actress Celia Lovsky in 1934 (according to one source, but another says they were already married and fled Germany together in 1933); she was active on the screen after 1944, the year they were divorced. He then married another screen actress, Kaaren Verne, whose best role was as Robert Cummings' sweetheart in the concluding portion of the 1941 **Kings Row.** They were divorced in 1954, and that same year he married Annemarie Brenning; this marriage gave him his only child, Kathryn.

The only thing 20th Century-Fox could come up with next was a starring part as a Japanese detective in a low-budget "B" film, **Think Fast, Mr. Moto,** based on John P. Marquand's stories in the Saturday Evening Post. Possibly the character could be developed into a series—after all, the studio already had the profitable and long-running Charlie Chan series with Warner Oland, also featuring an Oriental detective as the star. To promote the film, publicity men called Lorre "Europe's One-Man Chamber of Horrors." But in fact the screenplay did not reveal the actor to be any kind of ghoul; as film historian Jon

Tuska has said, "He was soft-spoken, wily, very much the enchanting little character of the novels. Possibly Lorre was apt for the role precisely because he left the personality of Moto unaffected." And the screen Moto is a gentle, scholarly little man, a master of disguise and deduction—although he is someone who kills without compunction when necessary.

Peter Lorre as Mr. Moto does not come across to the viewer as a European playing a Japanese; there is the feeling of a real Oriental actor (this was never the case with Oland as Charlie Chan). And this first film did well, launching a series of eight—all featuring the actor's subtle underplaying—that began in 1937 and ended in 1939. (All had "Mr. Moto" as part of the title.)

During the Moto period, though, he worked on other films as well. He was in **Lancer Spy** (also 37), billed third, in which he and Sig Rumann were German counterintelligence officers trailing British counterspy George Sanders. The year 1938 brought three more Motos to add to the two from the previous year, plus **I'll Give a Million,** in which he and John Carradine were comic standouts as hoboes. The following year offered nothing but three Motos—and they were the last of the hackneyed series. The final one was **Mr. Moto Takes a Vacation,** and at this point Mr. Lorre also took a vacation. He rebelled at being kept in a "B" series, and asked for, and was given, a release from his 20th Century-Fox contract. Actually, the studio had wanted to keep the series going, but if the truth be told, growing tension between the United States and Japan would shortly have made it seem like a bad idea in any case.

Oriental detectives were no longer in vogue, and there were alarmingly few parts for psychopathic killers in late 1939 and early 1940. What next? MGM saw Lorre as an ideal slimy little stool pigeon, and cast him as just that—lusting after Joan Crawford, who manages to escape his clutches and get back to Clark Gable—in director Frank Borzage's **Strange Cargo** (40). The actor would play many another such role in the next decade. He was now irretrievably typecast—and in supporting roles.

He and Erich von Stroheim were confidence artists in **I Was an Adventuress,** which allowed him to unleash his comedic talents again. But in reviewing the film, Time magazine remarked that his "best characterizations are as creepy as a psychopathic giggle." What next, then? If not slimy informers, what about vicious sadistic killers again? In the cheap programmer **Island of Doomed Men** he played the owner of an obscure Pacific island where convicts, paroled into his custody, are forced to slave in the diamond mines; he listens to Chopin nocturnes when not flogging his slaves. Then he was top-billed in **Stranger on the Third Floor,** a remarkable and fascinating little "B" film, as an escaped lunatic who murders anyone who threatens to reveal his whereabouts. In one scene the heroine describes the madman to a postman, who comments, "I never thought of anybody that would look like *that!*" In truth, nobody else ever looked "like that"—either like the character or like Peter Lorre.

Parts got worse and worse. In **You'll Find Out** he, Boris Karloff and Bela Lugosi were a trio of menaces out to kill off a young heiress; lobby-card billing for the film (which starred comic bandleader Kay Kyser) called them "The Three Horror Men." The real horror, however, was not on the screen—it was in this absurd and fatal typecasting. He then starred in **The Face Behind the Mask** (41) as an immigrant Hungarian watchmaker whose face is horribly burned in a fire, so he joins a criminal gang and becomes its leader. Critics still had good things to say about his work even in such quickie programmers as this. The actor then did a Poverty Row picture, **Mr. District Attorney,** as a murderous embezzler. After that it was back to informers, playing the skipper of a Chinese tramp steamer who turns in escaping jewel thieves Clark Gable and Rosalind Russell for the reward money in **They Met in Bombay.**

Now came an upward turn in Lorre's fortunes. He got a juicy supporting part in the classic **The Maltese Falcon**—his first film for Warner Bros. and also his first with fellow character actor Sydney Greenstreet; in addition, it marked the directorial debut of John Huston. He played Greenstreet's criminal confederate Joel Cairo, an effeminate little man with frizzy hair, perfume, spats, and saucer eyes—cowardly, querulous, getting slapped around by Humphrey Bogart, and bursting into tears or screaming abuse at his colleagues. This distinctive characterization was to assure him of mostly better parts—for five years, anyway.

In **All Through the Night** (42) he was a murderous little Nazi spy posing as a nightclub pianist, ultimately shot by his colleague Conrad Veidt. The nightclub singer was played by a pretty but bovine young actress named Kaaren Verne; in the film, she ended up with Bogart, but in real life as the second wife of Peter Lorre. Next, he was a Japanese agent, ultimately committing hara-kiri, in the cheesy programmer **Invisible Agent,** and he and Boris Karloff co-starred in the cheap horror-comedy **The Boogie Man Will Get You,** which was neither scary nor funny.

Another good part came along in an even better classic, **Casablanca** (43), as the sinister little weasel Ugarte, who makes his living providing exit visas for refugees. It is only a small part, but it is very well handled. Ugarte's activities are halted when the gendarmes arrest him, and he cries out to Bogart for help. Bogie replies, "I stick my neck out for nobody." Claude Rains, Veidt and Greenstreet headed a superb troupe of character actors who also appeared. In **Background to Danger,** as a friendly Russian agent, he saves George Raft from Greenstreet. The New York Times called Lorre and Greenstreet "two fascinating rascals in the art of duplicity"—and their best films together still lay ahead.

The actor had an offbeat role in **The Constant Nymph,** billed seventh, as a wealthy man who marries one of four sisters, Brenda Marshall (the real-life wife of William Holden); Charles Boyer and Joan Fontaine starred. Then he was a viciously sadistic Nazi sergeant at a camp for French prisoners in **The Cross of Lorraine;** he shoots a priest (Sir Cedric Hardwicke) but is later killed by Jean-Pierre Aumont. He and Greenstreet again supported Bogart in **Passage to Marseille** (44); Lorre was one of a group of convicts escaped from Devil's Island and intent on fighting for France.

The Mask of Dimitrios was the first film in which he and Greenstreet actually *co-starred.* Lorre was a mystery writer and Greenstreet a blackmailer. The two actors were now the ace character performers of Warners' stock company, and Lorre also formed a friendship with "the old man," who at this point was 64 to his friend's 40. They made a splendid team, Lorre's small frame providing a contrast to the bulk of Greenstreet, who was forever seizing him by the lapels. One writer has called them "a sort of unholy Laurel and Hardy."

The actor now had a good comedy role in **Arsenic and Old Lace,** as the plastic surgeon who is the sidekick of the murderous Raymond Massey; Cary Grant was the star. **The Conspirators** cast him and Greenstreet in the title roles as anti-Nazi plotters, but they weren't the stars. In **Hotel Berlin** (45) he was excellent as a clandestinely anti-Nazi professor, providing the best scene in the film as he bitterly ransacks his hotel room, peering under the sofa and into closets, looking for a hypothetical "good German." He played a spy traitorously planning to sell out to Franco Spain in **Confidential Agent,** dying of shock while threatened with a gun by Charles Boyer.

In **Three Strangers** (46) he was reunited with Greenstreet. They and Geraldine Fitzgerald are the trio of the title, sharing a sweepstakes ticket; Lorre is falsely implicated in a killing and sentenced to hang, but is freed by the dying confession of the real murderer; meanwhile Greenstreet kills Miss Fitzgerald and then goes mad. In this film Lorre also finds romance with young Joan Lorring. In **Black Angel,** an imaginative film noir, he was a too-obvious red herring as a nightclub owner who is a murder suspect; the real killer was Dan Duryea. Then he played racketeer Steve Cochran's bodyguard in **The Chase.**

He and Greenstreet were together for the last time in **The Verdict,** which marked the directorial debut of Don Siegel. They were the indubitable co-stars of this fine mystery thriller, with Greenstreet as a Scotland Yard superintendent forced to resign after a convicted murderer is found to have been innocent, and Lorre as his friend. Shortly, a new and mysterious murder occurs, and Lorre becomes another blatant red herring, skulking about so obviously that you know he couldn't have done it. Greenstreet, however, could, and did—to embarrass the new police administration with an unsolvable crime. His last line to Lorre, viewed in retrospect after the demise of their screen teaming, is ironic: "Things over which we have no control have come between us."

The actor closed out 1946 with **The Beast with Five Fingers,** which ended his Warners contract. He was at his most unrestrained as a deranged secretary, fleeing in terror from a disembodied hand that pursues and finally strangles him. At this point roles became much fewer and farther between. His only 1947 appearance was in the Bob Hope outing **My Favorite Brunette,** as one of the villains, a murderous, knife-throwing thug called Kismet, but not without comic overtones. In 1948, again in just one film, he took Joseph Calleia's old part as Inspector Slimane in **Casbah,** underplaying smoothly in this remake of **Algiers;** alas, Tony Martin was no Charles Boyer. Most critics said Lorre was the only good thing in the film. The following year, once again there was only one movie, **Rope of Sand,** in which he was back in his slimy-little-informer persona as a character called Toady, a philosophical inebriate, a conniving desert wastrel. At one point he tells Burt Lancaster, "I am here, free as the wind, a fountain of extraordinary knowledge, splendidly corrupt and eager to be of profitable service."

He also did vaudeville appearances in New York in 1949. In 1950 he played a penny-arcade operator who blackmails Mickey Rooney in **Quicksand.** Then he did a British film, **Double Confession,** giving a particularly unsubtle performance as a red herring in this murder mystery. At this point his screen career was becoming deeply mired in mediocrity, and he wondered what could resuscitate it. One project that might have done it—a collaboration with Bertolt Brecht to provide him with truly outstanding dramatic parts—had failed a few years earlier when no suitable vehicles could be found. The actor decided to return to Germany after 17 years, there to write, direct and star in a film of his own devising.

The remarkable **Der Verlorene** (The Lost One) (51) was made in an expressionist style reminiscent of German films of the Twenties. Lorre played Dr. Rothe, a scientist consumed with guilt for a wartime murder (of his fiancée, who had tried to betray him to the Nazis); later, in the present, he kills once again, and decides to take his own life, which he does by walking in front of a moving train. The waxen features, wary glance and look of chained desperation that characterize Rothe made the Germans see the film—correctly—as a portrayal of national guilt, as well as a study of Nazi mentality, and they reacted with either apathy or hostility. It was a commercial failure, the wrong film at the wrong time; five years earlier it might have been accepted, but the Germans now wanted to put their past guilt behind them. The film was not even exported, and has never been dubbed or subtitled in English.

It was three years before Lorre returned to Hollywood. His physical appearance had by now changed; a glandular problem had caused him to put on considerable weight, and there was a strange sidewise twist to the mouth. This odd-looking individual surely could no longer be a menace; in fact, he was now castable mainly in cheap programmers, horror-comedies and Jerry Lewis vehicles, which is how he closed out his Hollywood career.

In John Huston's peculiar but enjoyable shaggy-dog-story film, **Beat the Devil** (54), he was one of a motley group of petty crooks (including Humphrey Bogart and Robert Morley) trying to get illegal control of some uranium-rich African acreage. He was professor Paul Lukas' assistant in **20,000 Leagues Under the Sea,** and hammed it up in **Congo Crossing** (56) as an African police chief. In **Around the World in 80 Days** he played a Japanese steward. He gave probably the worst performance of his career as a von Stroheim-like film director in **The Buster Keaton Story** (57), was a comic Russian in **Silk Stockings,** and in the absurd farrago **The Story of Mankind** portrayed Nero. He was a dissolute French judge in the cheesy programmer **Hell Ship Mutiny,** and appeared in the Jerry Lewis outing **The Sad Sack** as a comic villain named Abdul.

The actor was good as a circus clown in **The Big Circus** (59), and had a key role as a cab driver in **Scent of Mystery** (60). In **Voyage to the Bottom of the Sea** (61) he was a famous physicist. **Tales of Terror** (62), based on three Edgar Allan Poe stories, found him walling up Vincent Price behind bricks à la "The Cask of Amontillado." (This was old home week, because for years Lorre performed the works of Poe on radio, in vaudeville, wherever and whenever he could.) He played a slave trader named Ahmed in **Five Weeks in a Balloon.** There was another Poe-like outing, **The Raven** (63), in which he, Price and Boris Karloff did a horror-comedy send-up to end all horror-comedy send-ups; a young Jack Nicholson played his son. Lorre, Price and Karloff were back at it again in **The Comedy of Terrors** (64), with Price an undertaker and Lorre his assistant. It goes without saying that the performers hammed it up unmercifully. The New York Times said Lorre "waddles through the picture like a stuffed owl." He had an unbilled cameo in **Muscle Beach Party,** and his final role was as a film director in the Jerry Lewis vehicle **The Patsy.** Four days after it wound up, he was dead at age 59.

Vincent Price (who delivered the eulogy at his funeral) later said of him: "He was set into a mold [by Hollywood] and it fit him. The mold was many-sided, pathetic, wistful, sinister, cute, vague, lethargic, and also quick-witted-in-a-wicked-way. It all went to make him irresistible, unforgettable."

Forget—if you can—the hammy absurdities of the postwar years. Remember him as the acting genius who gave us the definitive psychopathic murderer in **M, The Man Who Knew Too Much** and **Mad Love.** Remember the greatness that once belonged to Peter Lorre.

THE FILMS OF PETER LORRE

1931: M; Bomben auf Monte Carlo (The Bombardment of Monte Carlo); Die Koffer des Herrn O.F. (The Trunks of Mr. O.F.).

1932: Fünf von der Jazzband (The Jazzband Five); Schuss im Morgengrauen (A Shot at Dawn); F.P. 1 antwortet nicht (F.P. 1 Doesn't Answer) (also French version, F.P. 1 ne répond plus); Der weisse Dämon (The White Demon).

1933: Was Frauen träumen (What Women Dream); Unsichtbare Gegner (Invisible Opponent) (also French version, Les réquins du petrole [The Oil Sharks]); Du haut en bas (From Top to Bottom).

1934: The Man Who Knew Too Much.

1935: Mad Love; Crime and Punishment.

1936: Secret Agent.

1937: Crack-up; Nancy Steele Is Missing; Lancer Spy; Think Fast, Mr. Moto; Thank You, Mr. Moto.

1938: I'll Give a Million; Mr. Moto's Gamble; Mr. Moto Takes a Chance; Mysterious Mr. Moto.

1939: Mr. Moto's Last Warning; Mr. Moto in Danger Island; Mr. Moto Takes a Vacation.

1940: Strange Cargo; Stranger on the Third Floor; I Was an Adventuress; Island of Doomed Men; You'll Find Out.

1941: The Maltese Falcon; They Met in Bombay; The Face Behind the Mask; Mr. District Attorney.
1942: All Through the Night; Invisible Agent; The Boogie Man Will Get You.
1943: Casablanca; Background to Danger; The Constant Nymph; Cross of Lorraine.
1944: Passage to Marseille; The Mask of Dimitrios; Arsenic and Old Lace; The Conspirators; Hollywood Canteen.
1945: Hotel Berlin; Confidential Agent.
1946: Three Strangers; Black Angel; The Chase; The Verdict; The Beast with Five Fingers.
1947: My Favorite Brunette.
1948: Casbah.
1949: Rope of Sand.

1950: Quicksand; Double Confession.
1951: Der Verlorene (The Lost One).
1954: Beat the Devil; 20,000 Leagues Under the Sea.
1956: Congo Crossing; Around the World in 80 Days; Meet Me in Las Vegas (unbilled cameo appearance).
1957: Silk Stockings; The Buster Keaton Story; The Story of Mankind; Hell Ship Mutiny; The Sad Sack.
1959: The Big Circus.
1960: Scent of Mystery.
1961: Voyage to the Bottom of the Sea.
1962: Tales of Terror; Five Weeks in a Balloon.
1963: The Raven.
1964: The Comedy of Terrors; The Patsy; Muscle Beach Party (unbilled cameo appearance).

From sinister to sympathetic:
PAUL LUKAS

Paul Lukas started out in Hollywood as a suave Mittel-European seducer, went on to portray slick villains and "The Other Man" in romantic triangles, and in later years played kindly elderly men. A stolid performer with very little warmth or sympathy, he won the best-actor Oscar in a fluke. Elegant, sinister and erect, with mustache and sleek hair, he was type-cast irretrievably, and rarely had a chance to display his versatility in a role that fell outside the niche that had been selected for him.

Pál Lukács (or Lugács) was born May 26, 1894 (some sources say 1895 or 1897), in Budapest, Hungary, just as his mother's train was pulling into the station. His father was an advertising executive. At 18 the young man was a member of Hungary's Olympic wrestling team in 1912, and during this period he also received stage training at the Royal Academy of Acting. He went into war service in 1914 with the Austro-Hungarian army, but was shell-shocked and injured by shrapnel while serving with the 5th Dragoons, Hungarian Cavalry. This took him out of the war for a time, and he studied at the Actors' Academy of Hungary, making his Budapest stage debut in 1916 in the title role of Ferenc Mólnar's **Liliom.** But he soon went back into service, piloting a plane.

After the war he appeared in repertory, then joined Budapest's Comedy Theatre, where for nine years he played every conceivable character in plays by such masters as Shakespeare, Chekhov, Wilde, Shaw and Galsworthy. Meanwhile, in 1915 he had begun making films as well, and by 1924 had appeared in about 25 of them, mostly in Hungary but a few in Germany. (One of the German ones, **Samson und Dalila,** was directed by Michael Curtiz.) He continued to be busy on the stage in Budapest, Berlin and Vienna, achieving matinee-idol status and gaining a reputation throughout central Europe, and frequently starred in the productions of Max Reinhardt. While appearing in a play in Budapest in 1926, he was seen by American movie tycoon Adolph Zukor, the Hungarian-born head of the Paramount studio, who brought Lukas to America to work for him.

The actor made his Hollywood debut in **Two Lovers** (28) as Vilma Banky's rejected lover, a Spanish officer, killed by Ronald Colman. (Interestingly, Miss Banky was also a fellow Hungarian.) Then he was in three Pola Negri films: **Three Sinners,** as her husband, being unfaithful with Olga Baclanova;

Loves of an Actress, as a newspaper publisher, one of three men in love with her; and **The Woman from Moscow,** as her fiancé, killed off early in the film (he had seduced the killer's sister). He was a jewel thief in **Hot News,** a French naval commander in **The Night Watch,** and a lecherous theatrical producer in the Nancy Carroll starrer **Manhattan Cocktail.**

When sound films came in, Lukas knew little English and of course had a heavy accent. Hastily he took eight months of intensive English lessons. In his early sound films his voice was dubbed (by Lawford Davidson), but he later got to use his own voice as Hollywood's Continental-in-residence. He became a success with his Hungarian accent even as Vilma Banky fell by the wayside because of hers.

Lukas married Gizella Benes in 1927, a marriage that endured until her death in 1962. (There had been an earlier and very brief marriage during the war, to someone whose name the actor never disclosed.)

After Gizella died he married Annette (or Anna) Driesens in 1963.

In **The Wolf of Wall Street** (29) he played a copper trader who seeks revenge on ex-partner George Bancroft but instead is deceived by him and ends up penniless. He was the wealthy playboy paying the rent for Nancy Carroll in **The Shopworn Angel**—but she ends up marrying Gary Cooper. He was far down the cast list in the Carroll vehicle **Illusion.** In **Half-way to Heaven,** as a circus trapeze artist, he loves his partner, Jean Arthur, and kills a rival to try to win her. He played a master crook holding power over Evelyn Brent in **Slightly Scarlet** (30), and in **Young Eagles** was a German pilot involved in two exciting air duels with Charles (Buddy) Rogers, who loves Miss Arthur, a counterspy. He was a check forger, one of the suspects in a killing, in **The Benson Murder Case,** and supported Miss Carroll again in **The Devil's Holiday.** Now he co-starred three times with Ruth Chatterton: in **Anybody's Woman,** as her lover before she returns to husband Clive Brook; **The Right to Love,** in which she falls in love with Lukas; and **Unfaithful** (31), in which she is just that while married to him.

In director Rouben Mamoulian's **City Streets** he was a top gangster, tossing aside mistress Wynne Gibson when he meets Sylvia Sidney, only to be shot by the vengeful Miss Gibson. He was an embassy aide turned informer (and loved by Kay Francis) in **Vice Squad,** and a suave Italian singer with seduction on his mind in **Strictly Dishonorable.** He played a Daddy Long Legs-like role in **The Beloved Bachelor,** adopting young Dorothy Jordan as a child and falling in love with her when she grows up. In **Working Girls** he was a slick Lothario.

No One Man (32) cast Lukas as a gynecologist loved by Carole Lombard, and in **Tomorrow and Tomorrow** he was a Viennese doctor who seduces, and fathers a child by, his patient, the married Ruth Chatterton. In **Thunder Below** he, Tallulah Bankhead and Charles Bickford were all steamed up in the old eternal triangle in some tropical outpost, with faithless Tallulah loving him while married to Bickford, and **Passport to Hell** involved another outpost and another triangle, with Elissa Landi. He played a theatrical agent who, as her manager, molds Constance Bennett into a Broadway sensation and then waits hopelessly for her love while she dallies with Joel McCrea and Walter Pidgeon in director George Cukor's **Rockabye.** In the unusual drama **Downstairs** he was a virtuous butler in conflict with John Gilbert as an unscrupulous chauffeur.

In Cukor's classic **Little Women** (33) the actor was ingratiating as the gentle Professor Bhaer, win-

ning the love of Katharine Hepburn, and he was good in **Grand Slam,** as a Russian waiter who becomes a bridge champion, married to his partner, Loretta Young. He gave a strong performance in **The Kiss Before the Mirror** as a distinguished Viennese doctor (what, again?), killing faithless wife Gloria Stuart in the arms of her lover (Pidgeon), and was a humane German prisoner-of-war camp commander in **Captured!** He was one of three suitors of Miss Stuart in **Secret of the Blue Room.**

He had a chance to display his comedic talents in **By Candlelight** (34), as the butler to prince Nils Asther, finding himself mistaken for his employer, and in director William Wyler's **Glamour** he was the composer husband of showgirl Constance Cummings. In **The Fountain** he played a crippled German officer, married to Ann Harding and conveniently dying so she can marry Brian Aherne, and in **The Countess of Monte Cristo** he was a crook unmasked by Fay Wray. He was a Casanova killed off at the outset in **Affairs of a Gentleman,** and in **I Give My Love** he was (once again) murdered by Wynne Gibson, as his wife.

Lukas was miscast as the killer tracked down by Walter Connolly in **Father Brown—Detective** (35), but was acceptable as detective Philo Vance in **The Casino Murder Case.** (William Powell had earlier made a better Vance.) In **Age of Indiscretion** Helen Vinson was his unfaithful wife, and **The Three Musketeers** found him playing Athos. He had a small but telling part as a Continental charmer with whom Ruth Chatterton dallies in Wyler's **Dodsworth** (36), and was Constance Bennett's "protector" in **Ladies in Love.** He played a munitions magnate in **Espionage** (37), and was sinister in **Brief Ecstasy** and in **Dinner at the Ritz** (in the latter, losing Annabella to David Niven; later it turns out that Lukas murdered her father). At the end of that year he returned to the Broadway stage temporarily, appearing with Ruth Gordon in Ibsen's **A Doll's House,** as Dr. Rank. He returned to the screen as the menacing spy in director Alfred Hitchcock's classic thriller **The Lady Vanishes** (38), and his villainy continued in **Dangerous Secrets** and **The Mutiny on the Elsinore.**

In the topical drama **Confessions of a Nazi Spy** (39) the actor was the Nazi propaganda chief in the U.S., one of a number of those caught in FBI agent Edward G. Robinson's net. He, Victor McLaglen and John Carradine were all nasties in **Captain Fury.** In **Strange Cargo** (40) he played a fascistic, cynical, philosophical wife murderer, one of a group of convicts, led by Clark Gable, escaping from Devil's Island. He menaced Bob Hope in **The Ghost Breakers.** In **The Monster and the Girl** (41) he was a gangster involved in white slavery, and in **They Dare Not Love** a Gestapo chief, in an entertainingly ripe performance. He was again the heavy in **The Chinese Bungalow (The Chinese Den).**

After this long siege of villainy, including a couple of Nazis, surely no one was prepared for the next turn in Lukas' career. In the spring of 1941, without his ever-present mustache, he opened on Broadway in the starring role of a dedicated anti-Nazi, a fighter against fascism, in Lillian Hellman's fine play **Watch on the Rhine.** The drama was a smash hit, and the actor was acclaimed. After a long run, he was asked to repeat the role in the film version (43), with Bette Davis brought in to play his wife (with top billing) to add star value. Without his mustache (thus changing his whole persona), he was fine in the lead role of one of Hollywood's biggest films of the year. His Academy Award as *best actor* stemmed from a combination of two things: the popularity of the film and the message it carried, and the fact that the Oscar competition in his category that year was relatively weak. But in truth, film critics hailed his performance with a barrage of superlatives. The inevitable question arose: If this actor was this good, why had he not been a major star all along?

It was in fact a fluke so far as Hollywood producers were concerned, for he continued to work out his career in supporting roles. His only other film in 1943, **Hostages,** cast him as—you guessed it, a Nazi again, this time a Gestapo chief. **Uncertain Glory** (44) gave him a role as a French detective hunting down Errol Flynn, and in **Address Unknown** he played yet another devoted Nazi. There was a **Gaslight**-type role in **Experiment Perilous,** in which he menaced wife Hedy Lamarr.

There were only 15 films remaining for Lukas in the next quarter-century. In **Deadline at Dawn** (46) he was a philosophical cab driver helping Susan Hayward track down suspects in the murder of a young woman (Lola Lane); it turns out at the end that he killed her himself to keep the vicious tramp from hurting more people. He was Merle Oberon's husband in **Temptation;** she nearly succeeds in poisoning him at the behest of her lover (Charles Korvin). Now in his early fifties, he played a prominent lawyer with a sordid past in **Whispering City** (47), and had a key role as an anti-Nazi statesman in **Berlin Express** (48), which also starred Miss Oberon. In 1950 he was the elderly lama, or holy man, in the Errol Flynn starrer **Kim,** based on a Kipling story. Later that year he also appeared as the love interest opposite Ethel Merman in the hit Broadway musical **Call Me Madam** (the part later taken in the movie version by George Sanders), and even sang a couple of songs.

Back in Hollywood after a few years, the actor played the professor in **20,000 Leagues Under the Sea** (54), and then, at age 60, drifted into semi-retirement, with occasional stage appearances and television roles—and occasional films. He returned to the screen in **The Roots of Heaven** (58), sixth in the cast. He had a small part as a psychiatrist in **Tender Is the Night** (60), and an equally small one in **Scent of Mystery. The Four Horsemen of the Apocalypse** (62) found him playing a German patriarch. He was a doctor in **55 Days at Peking** (63), and appeared in an Elvis Presley vehicle, **Fun in Acapulco.** In 1965 he was in support in **Lord Jim,** and the following year had a part in **Holiday in Spain.** He had his last role in **Sol Madrid** (68), billed seventh.

In 1970 he retired to Majorca, but then decided to make his home in Tangier, Morocco. While looking for a house he died in that city in 1971 at age 77. He had given half a century to films and 40 years to the American screen, and in truth Paul Lukas was a much better actor than his long run of middling (and typecast) roles would indicate. His Oscar was the ultimate proof of that.

THE FILMS OF PAUL LUKAS

NOTE: In the case of his early (Hungarian and German) films, 1915 to 1924, some of the titles are translated into English and some are not. In the latter case, sources do not supply the translations.

1915: Man of the Earth.
1917: Sphinx; Song of the Heart.
1918: Udvari Lovego; Vorrei Morir.
1920: The Yellow Shadow; Little Fox; The Castle Without a Name; The Milliner; The Actress; Sarga Arnyek; Szinesno; Olavi; Nevtelen Var; Masamod; A Szurkeruhas Holgy.
1921: Telegram from New York; Love of the 18th Century; Hetszazeves Szerelem.
1922: The Lady in Grey; Samson und Dalila; Lady Violette; Eine versunkene Welt.

1923: The Glorious Life; A Girl's Way; Der unbekannte Morgen.
1924: Egy Fiunak a Fele.
1928: Two Lovers; Three Sinners; Loves of an Actress; The Woman from Moscow; Manhattan Cocktail; The Night Watch.
1929: The Wolf of Wall Street; The Shopworn Angel; Illusion; Half-way to Heaven.
1930: Slightly Scarlet; Behind the Make-up; Young Eagles; Grumpy; The Benson Murder Case; The Devil's Holiday; Anybody's Woman; The Right to Love.
1931: City Streets; Unfaithful; Vice Squad; Women Love Once; Strictly Dishonorable; The Beloved Bachelor; Working Girls.
1932: No One Man; Tomorrow and Tomorrow; Thunder Below; Passport to Hell; Rockabye; Downstairs.
1933: Little Women; The Kiss Before the Mirror; Captured!; Grand

Slam; Secret of the Blue Room; Sing Sinner Sing.
1934: By Candlelight; Glamour; The Fountain; The Countess of Monte Cristo; Affairs of a Gentleman; I Give My Love; Gift of Gab.
1935: Father Brown—Detective; The Casino Murder Case; Age of Indiscretion; The Three Musketeers; I Found Stella Parish.
1936: Dodsworth; Ladies in Love.
1937: Espionage; Brief Ecstasy; Dinner at the Ritz.
1938: The Lady Vanishes; Dangerous Secrets; The Mutiny on the Elsinore.
1939: Confessions of a Nazi Spy; Lady in Distress; Captain Fury.
1940: Strange Cargo; The Ghost Breakers.
1941: The Monster and the Girl; They Dare Not Love; The Chinese Bungalow (Chinese Den).

1943: Watch on the Rhine; Hostages.
1944: Uncertain Glory; Address Unknown; Experiment Perilous.
1946: Deadline at Dawn; Temptation.
1947: Whispering City.
1948: Berlin Express.
1950: Kim.
1954: 20,000 Leagues Under the Sea.
1958: The Roots of Heaven.
1960: Tender Is the Night; Scent of Mystery.
1962: The Four Horsemen of the Apocalypse.
1963: 55 Days at Peking; Fun in Acapulco.
1965: Lord Jim.
1966: Holiday in Spain.
1968: Sol Madrid.

Toughest of the tough, meanest of the mean:
BARTON MacLANE

Many a movie villain was suave, cultured and polished—but in that respect Hollywood did not hold a mirror up to real life. We all know that bad guys are really, for the most part, rough and brutish thugs. And when producers wanted to cast an actor who filled *that* bill, they often turned to Barton MacLane.

Big, burly, raspy-voiced and squinty-eyed, he played many a trigger-happy gangster, crooked cop, snarling convict, or mean Western outlaw. These were villains without any culture whatever. Nor did they have well modulated voices; on the screen, MacLane never seemed to speak when shouting would do. In truth, he was a highly satisfactory louse.

He was born on Christmas Day, 1902, in Columbia, South Carolina, and attended Wesleyan University in Connecticut, where he starred in football. After graduation he studied for a while at the American Academy of Dramatic Art, and then went on the stage. He made his film debut in a small, uncredited part in **The Quarterback** (26), as a football player, and is said to have appeared in 1929 in the Marx Brothers' first film, **The Cocoanuts,** but if so, this must have been a really minuscule bit part. He continued his stage work until being called to Hollywood in 1933, when he began an active career that would ultimately total some 150 films.

If the actor had been hoping to portray heroes or nice guys, he was disappointed. He once said, "I thought an actor should be a man of fine physical build, so I developed my muscles to be able to tear a villain limb from limb." Ironically, he almost always played the villain himself.

During 1933 and 1934 he worked for Paramount, playing meanies of all sorts. He may have appeared in the Claudette Colbert starrer **Torch Singer** (33), but this is uncertain. He was a public official in the W.C. Fields vehicle **Tillie and Gus,** and a dance-hall manager in **Hell and High Water.** Five of his nine films in this period were Westerns, and four of those were part of the long series based on Zane Grey's novels, all directed by Henry Hathaway (his first work as a director in his own right) and all but one starring Randolph Scott. MacLane probably was a villain in a few of these, but he was a good guy in **To the Last Man** (33), in which he marries Gail Patrick. He had a small role as a policeman in **All of Me** (34).

In 1935 MacLane moved to Warner Bros., and immediately got better parts. In **Black Fury** (35), star-

ring Paul Muni, he played the leader of a gang of strike-breaking thugs, shooting down hapless coal miner John Qualen, and in the James Cagney starrer **G-Men** he was a vicious gangster who shoots his wife (Ann Dvorak) in a phone booth. He menaced Cagney in **The Frisco Kid,** trying to shanghai him aboard a ship, and he was pilot Cagney's boss in **Ceiling Zero.** In **Dr. Socrates** he was a gang leader undone by small-town physician Muni (and losing his girlfriend, Miss Dvorak, to the doctor). In the "B" picture **Man of Iron** he was actually the star, as a factory foreman who crashes high society. He was a racketeer in **Stranded,** a detective in **The Case of the Curious Bride,** Kay Francis' blackmailing husband in **I Found Stella Parish,** and yet another gangster in **Go into Your Dance,** in which his wife (Helen Morgan) was dallying behind his back with Al Jolson.

The actor was now established as one of the screen's top supporting players, and Warners kept him busy. In **Bullets or Ballots** (36) he was a big-time

155

racketeer who employs Edward G. Robinson, not knowing that he is a police undercover man. Racketeering was still his game in **The Walking Dead,** as he tries to frame Boris Karloff for murder but instead ends up electrocuted by a power pole. In **Jailbreak** he got a change of pace as a captain of police detectives who solves a murder, and he starred in **Bengal Tiger** as a drunken lion tamer, also appearing as the chief villain in **God's Country and the Woman.** And he launched, as Glenda Farrell's co-star, the Torchy Blane series, in which she was Torchy, a wisecracking newspaper reporter, and he was her boyfriend, police lieutenant Steve McBride of the homicide division, helping her track down evildoers; the five-year series kicked off with **Smart Blonde.**

MacLane was on the side of the law as the public defender helping Henry Fonda in **You Only Live Once** (37), but was back in form as a brutish thug routed by Errol Flynn in **The Prince and the Pauper.** There were two more Torchy Blanes with Miss Farrell, and there was **Draegerman Courage,** a "B" in which he starred as an expert who rescues three people trapped in a mine disaster. **Born Reckless** cast him as a racketeer trying to control a city's taxicab business but brought to justice by Brian Donlevy, and in **San Quentin** he was a stand-out as a tough prison guard harassing convict Humphrey Bogart. He starred in **Wine, Women and Horses** (a remake of the Edward G. Robinson film **Dark Hazard**) as a (momentarily) reformed gambler whose wife (Ann Sheridan) leaves him when he can't resist returning to the gaming tables.

The actor was married at an unspecified date to Martha Stewart, by whom he had two children. After they were divorced, he married Charlotte Wynters in 1939.

He starred in **The Kid Comes Back** (38) as a veteran boxer hoping for a shot at the title, and did two more Torchy Blanes. He was a ship's captain in **The Storm,** an unpleasant thug again in **Gold Is Where You Find It,** and a criminal in **You and Me.** In **Prison Break** he played an honest tuna fisherman in prison for a murder he didn't commit, with the parole system preventing him from marrying his girlfriend, who was—would you believe Glenda Farrell? He was in one more Torchy Blane in 1939. He was now well identified with prison films, and did **I Was a Convict** as a manufacturer sent up for tax evasion, also playing a tough inmate in **Mutiny in the Big House.** Both those films were for Poverty Row studios; he had left Warners and was now freelancing. But mainly he worked for major studios. He was one of the heavies bested by Robert Taylor in **Stand Up and Fight,** and in the title role

of **Big Town Czar** he was a gangster who goes to the electric chair.

In **Men Without Souls** (40) he was an ultra-tough prison inmate, snarling at the chaplain, "We don't want any psalm-singing rats hanging around. Go peddle your prayers!" He finally wound up the Torchy Blane series with **Torchy Runs for Mayor.** He was yet another vicious, murdering gangster in **The Secret Seven,** and still another in **Gangs of Chicago,** and played a villainous saloon-keeper threatening Gene Autry in **Melody Ranch.**

MacLane had one of his best years in 1941, appearing in nine films that included two enduring Hollywood classics and several other superior pictures. He played a policeman, Lt. Dundy, in **The Maltese Falcon** and was a tough mobster in **High Sierra,** both starring Humphrey Bogart. In **Western Union** he was the chief villain, trying to block the telegraph wires from going up and finally shot down by his brother (Randolph Scott), and in **Manpower** he played the proprietor of a clip joint, with Marlene Dietrich as one of the "hostesses." He was the murderer unmasked by the Dead End Kids in **Hit the Road,** and in **Wild Geese Calling** he lost his Klondike hotel to Warren William in a card game; later he shoots and wounds Henry Fonda, but is killed by William.

Insufficient variety in his parts now sent him farther down cast lists, although he was to continue busy for a quarter-century to come. He was a nightclub owner in **All Through the Night** (42), and now managed to become as thoroughly typecast as the proprietor of a nightclub as he had been earlier as an imprisoned convict, for in **The Big Street** he was the crooked owner of a bistro, slapping his paramour, Lucille Ball, and causing her to fall downstairs and become permanently crippled, whereupon adoring busboy Henry Fonda takes over and cares for her. But he was back at his old stand as a racketeer in **Highways by Night.** With the war on, he donned military uniform for **Bombardier** (43), and also starred in a couple of cheapies for PRC, the bottom of the barrel among Poverty Row studios. He played a police inspector in **The Mummy's Ghost** (44) and a Marine sergeant in **Marine Raiders,** and was in more cheapies. **The Spanish Main** (45) cast him as a pirate captain. He starred in a low-budget outing called **Jungle Flight** (47), and was a nasty in **Tarzan and the Huntress.**

The actor had a good cameo in the classic **The Treasure of the Sierra Madre** (48), as a tough guy brawling with Humphrey Bogart over gambling stakes, and was the villain in the Errol Flynn Western **Silver River.** In the interesting film noir **Red**

Light (49) he was one of the villains, but was upstaged by Raymond Burr as an even nastier one. He and Ward Bond were a pair of crooked cops shaking down James Cagney in **Kiss Tomorrow Goodbye** (50). And from there on out it was routine roles in films that were mostly dull programmers.

Virtually all of MacLane's remaining movies were forgettable Westerns and action films. In the Fifties, for example, titles included **Cow Country, Sea of Lost Ships, Rails into Laramie, Jail Busters, Hell's Outpost, Backlash** and **Gunfighters of Abilene.** In them he might be a meanie (usually) or a lawman (occasionally). He played an Army general in **The Glenn Miller Story** (54), and was the police commissioner in **Pocketful of Miracles** (61). Now he took roles with sharply decreasing frequency as he entered his sixties. He was far down the cast list in **The Rounders** (65), and made his last two films in 1968, as the sheriff in **Arizona Bushwhackers** and a doctor in **Buckskin.** During the Sixties he also appeared on television, as a lawman in the series "The Outlaws" and also getting a role in "I Dream of Jeannie."

The actor died in 1969 at age 66. It had been a long time since his heyday in the Thirties—since the time when, if a producer wanted a *cultured* villain, he called on someone like Basil Rathbone, but if he wanted a mean, brutish, snarling thug, the best choice was Barton MacLane.

THE FILMS OF BARTON MacLANE

1926: The Quarterback.
1929: *Credit uncertain:* The Cocoanuts.
1933: Tillie and Gus; Big Executive; Man of the Forest; To the Last Man (Law of Vengeance); The Thundering Herd; Hell and High Water. *Credit uncertain:* Torch Singer.
1934: Lone Cowboy; The Last Round-Up; All of Me.
1935: G-Men; Black Fury; Ceiling Zero; The Frisco Kid; The Case of the Curious Bride; The Case of the Lucky Legs; Stranded; Dr. Socrates; Page Miss Glory; I Found Stella Parish; Man of Iron; Go into Your Dance.
1936: Bullets or Ballots; The Walking Dead; Smart Blonde; Times Square Playboy; Jailbreak; Bengal Tiger; God's Country and the Woman.
1937: You Only Live Once; The Prince and the Pauper; Ever Since Eve; San Quentin; Draegerman Courage; Born Reckless; Wine, Women and Horses; Torchy Blane, the Adventurous Blonde; Flyaway Baby.
1938: The Kid Comes Back; Blondes at Work; The Storm; Gold Is Where You Find It; You and Me; Prison Break; Torchy Gets Her Man.
1939: Stand Up and Fight; Big Town Czar; I Was a Convict; Mutiny in the Big House; Torchy Blane in Chinatown.
1940: Men Without Souls; The Secret Seven; Gangs of Chicago; Melody Ranch; Torchy Runs for Mayor.
1941: The Maltese Falcon; High Sierra; Western Union; Manpower; Dr. Jekyll and Mr. Hyde; Come Live with Me; Barnacle Bill; Wild Geese Calling; Hit the Road.
1942: All Through the Night; The Big Street; Highways by Night.
1943: Bombardier; Man of Courage; Song of Texas; The Underdog; Crime Doctor's Strangest Case.

1944: Marine Raiders; Secret Command; Gentle Annie; The Mummy's Ghost; Cry of the Werewolf; Nabonga.
1945: The Spanish Main; Scared Stiff (Treasure of Fear); Tarzan and the Amazons.
1946: The Mysterious Intruder; Santa Fe Uprising.
1947: Cheyenne; Jungle Flight; Tarzan and the Huntress.
1948: The Treasure of the Sierra Madre; The Walls of Jericho; Silver River; Relentless; Unknown Island; The Dude Goes West; Angel in Exile.
1949: Red Light.
1950: Kiss Tomorrow Goodbye; Rookie Fireman; Let's Dance; The Bandit Queen.
1951: Drums in the Deep South; Best of the Badmen.
1952: Bugles in the Afternoon; The Half-Breed; Thunderbirds.
1953: Jack Slade; Kansas Pacific; Cow Country; Sea of Lost Ships; Captain Scarface.
1954: The Glenn Miller Story; Rails into Laramie; Jubilee Trail.
1955: Foxfire; Jail Busters; The Treasure of Ruby Hills; Hell's Outpost; The Silver Star; Last of the Desperadoes.
1956: Three Violent People; Backlash; Wetbacks; Jaguar; This Man Is Armed; The Naked Gun.
1957: The Storm Rider; Sierra Stranger; Hell's Crossroads; Naked in the Sun.
1958: The Geisha Boy; Frontier Gun; The Girl in the Woods.
1960: Gunfighters of Abilene; Noose for a Gunman.
1961: Pocketful of Miracles.
1964: Law of the Lawless.
1965: The Rounders; Town Tamer.
1968: Arizona Bushwhackers; Buckskin.

The anatomy of melancholy:
ALINE MacMAHON

Hollywood has never known how to deal properly with the great performers of the stage, especially actresses. Such ladies as Ethel Barrymore, Helen Hayes, Lynn Fontanne and Alla Nazimova gave it a try in movies, but found far greater rewards on Broadway. Such was also the case with Aline MacMahon, who in the early Thirties was on the verge of becoming a film star but decided there was far less to be derived from playing Guy Kibbee's wife than from appearing in plays by Eugene O'Neill, Shakespeare and T.S. Eliot, and subsequently returned to the screen only rarely.

Critics have raved over her, though. Film historian David Shipman has called her "one of the screen's few perfect actresses." She was in fact unique, a sad-faced, soulful, gentle-mannered lady who portrayed touching and sympathetic women with a real warmth. Tall, dark-haired and distinguished-looking, with large, heavy-lidded eyes, she had a face like a tragic mask and bore an interesting resemblance to another famed stage actress, Katharine Cornell. She could provide a blunt, earthy and practical note to a film, and there was a touch of melancholy in most of her roles. She could, however, handle comedy equally well, and dished up the wisecracks with facility.

What Hollywood ultimately lost can be seen in her filmography. She made 42 films, and exactly half of them came in the years 1932-35, when Warner Bros. thought it had a new star but was unwilling or unable to give her decent parts. She made fewer films in the next 28 years than she had in that four-year burst of activity.

Miss MacMahon was born May 3, 1899, in McKeesport, Pennsylvania, the daughter of a telegraph operator who, sources say, became editor-in-chief of Munsey's Magazine; she was raised in New York City. After graduation from Barnard College there, she made her stage debut at the Neighborhood Playhouse in Manhattan, playing (at age 22) a 39-year-old spinster in **The Madras House.** She got a small Broadway role in **The Mirage,** and then made a hit in the Neighborhood Playhouse's **Grand Street Follies** with a wickedly clever impersonation of Gertrude Lawrence. The Shuberts signed her up and she did more impersonations in their **Artists and Models** in 1925. She scored a hit in the 1926 revival of Eugene O'Neill's **Beyond the Horizon,** in a performance that Noel Coward described as "astonish-

ing, moving and beautiful," and in the next few years appeared in **Spread Eagle, Her First Affair, Winter Bound** and **Maya.** (The latter play, a symbolic biography of a Paris prostitute, was closed by the police, but it still brought her critical acclaim.)

In 1929 she was signed by Moss Hart for a key role in **Once in a Lifetime,** as the over-the-hill vaudeville star who teaches silent-film actors how to speak for the talkies. Instead of the Broadway cast, she ended up in the West Coast company. A Warners casting director saw her play the part in Los Angeles and promptly offered her a contract.

The actress made her screen debut as newspaper editor Edward G. Robinson's secretary in **Five Star Final** (31), in love with him (without his knowing it) and masking her feelings by acerbic comments on his behavior, meanwhile quietly making her own moral judgments. She got rave notices, and was asked to repeat her stage role in **Once in a Lifetime** (32). She was superb as the acid-tongued voice expert determined to make good in Hollywood; critic Richard Watts Jr. said she "provides the best acting in the picture." She played a tenement cleaning woman in **The Heart of New York,** and was fine as another wise secretary, lawyer Warren William's, in **The Mouthpiece,** stealing the film in support. She was Loretta Young's sister in **Weekend Marriage,** and played the fake countess, otherwise known as "Barrelhouse Betty," in the fine drama **One Way Passage.** As the head nurse in **Life Begins,** she held the threads together in this drama about a maternity ward, and she was a stand-out in **Silver Dollar** as Robinson's discarded wife (the movie was a thinly disguised version of the lives of Silver Dollar Tabor and Baby Doe).

Miss MacMahon was married in 1928 to a prominent New York architect, Clarence S. Stein, whose works included that city's most famous synagogue, Temple Emanu-El. She had known him for 10 years. Her Warners contract stipulated that her filming be restricted to certain times of the year so she could live in New York with him. They had a son. Stein died in 1974 (some sources say 1975).

The key figure in the actress' early screen career was Warners director Mervyn LeRoy. He had already worked with her on **Five Star Final** and **The Heart of New York,** and now he gave her one of her best roles in **Gold Diggers of 1933** (33)—the delightfully opportunistic, ruthless Trixie, an aging showgirl determined to bleed Warren William and millionaire Guy Kibbee of everything they have, and ending up at the fade-out with Kibbee. In that year she was also active on screen in social work, being the proprietor of a soup kitchen in **Heroes for Sale** (she comforts Richard Barthelmess when his wife, Loretta Young, is killed) and devoting her life to caring for orphans in **The Life of Jimmy Dolan,** which also featured Miss Young. She worked for LeRoy again in **The World Changes,** playing the mother of Paul Muni (who was older in real life than she was), aging through the picture and finally, in her nineties, telling off her useless descendants.

What was possibly her finest film role came in the last of her films to be directed by LeRoy, **Heat Lightning** (34), in which she and her younger sister (Ann Dvorak) run a desert gas station. Suddenly into the picture comes evil Preston Foster, an old flame of the elder sister's, but this time making a play for Miss Dvorak; Miss MacMahon kills him to protect her sister. It was a dramatic performance of quiet strength and tender poignancy. In **Side Streets** she was a love-starved businesswoman who marries a destitute sailor (Paul Kelly); the marriage is later threatened by Miss Dvorak. She was the downtrodden wife of Hugh Herbert in the comedy **The Merry Frinks,** in which, unappreciated by her family, she futilely tries society life. And then along came Guy Kibbee again; she co-starred with him in four straight films, starting with **Big-Hearted Herbert,** in which he was the grouchy husband she decides to reform. She was again his wife in **Babbitt,** from Sinclair Lewis' novel, delivering a stand-out performance, and also in **Mary Jane's Pa** (35), in which they parted but were reunited. They were both in **While the Patient Slept,** but not married; she was a nurse again, this time playing detective and solving the mystery.

Her last good part for some years to come was in **Kind Lady,** an excellent melodrama in which, as a kindly spinster, she befriends impoverished painter Basil Rathbone, who then proceeds to drug her, murder her maid, and imprison her in an attic room where he plans to kill her (she is saved at the end). She played the spinster aunt wooed by Wallace Beery in **Ah, Wilderness,** from an O'Neill play, and was archaeologist Brian Aherne's assistant in **I Live My Life,** giving him guidance as he woos Joan Crawford. And at this point she bowed out of films for a while. She had grown restless, she wanted better parts, she wanted to act on the stage again. But she would be back.

At one time she apparently was scheduled to co-star with Paul Muni in **The Good Earth,** but lost the part to Luise Rainer—who won the first of two back-to-back best-actress Oscars for it. Instead, Miss MacMahon's only 1937 screen role was as Grace Moore's secretary in **When You're in Love.** She was back in stage roles now, including starring in **Candida** in summer stock. She played a schoolteacher in the film **Back Door to Heaven** (39), receiving top billing, and was Ida Lupino's shrewish mother (Thomas Mitchell played the father) in **Out of the Fog** (41). Now in her early forties, she portrayed another secretary—Marlene Dietrich's—in **The Lady Is Willing** (42). In **Tish** she, ZaSu Pitts and Marjorie Main were three middle-aged women constantly getting into some kind of trouble. (Meanwhile, she co-starred on Broadway in **The Moon Is Down.**)

In Oriental makeup, the actress was Walter Huston's wife in the film **Dragon Seed** (44), a drama of war-torn China starring Katharine Hepburn as her daughter-in-law, and for this role Miss MacMahon won an Oscar nomination as best supporting actress. She also supported Ralph Bellamy and Anne Baxter in **Guest in the House;** she was the aunt, the only one in Bellamy's family who sees through the scheming Miss Baxter, and ends up driving her to suicide before she can destroy the family. There was a strictly routine part as Wallace Beery's pawnbroker girlfriend in **The Mighty McGurk** (46), and she had one last good role in **The Search** (48), crisply professional yet compassionate as the director of a camp for displaced persons; it was Montgomery Clift's debut film. Once again she won critical raves. Then she played a rural matriarch in **Roseanna McCoy** (49), and an old crone in **The Flame and the Arrow** (50). And from here on her screen appearances became scarce indeed.

In **The Eddie Cantor Story** (53) she was his grandmother, and she played a lonely rancher in **The Man from Laramie** (55). Meanwhile there were many stage roles, including parts in **The Eve of St. Mark,** T.S. Eliot's **The Confidential Clerk, A Day by the Sea, The Madwoman of Chaillot,** and lots of Shakespeare: the Nurse in **Romeo and Juliet,** the Countess in **All's Well that Ends Well** and Volumnia in **Coriolanus.** Now in her sixties, she was back in Hollywood to play the newspaper editor in the re-

make of **Cimarron** (60), well down the cast list, and she was a kindly doctor in **The Young Doctors** (61) and a Hawaiian woman in **Diamond Head** (63). There were good parts in her last two films, both 1963 releases. She was skeptical and affectionate—and unforgettable—as Judy Garland's dresser and companion in that doomed star's last movie, **I Could Go On Singing,** and gave a fine farewell to the screen as the aunt in **All the Way Home.**

Widowed in 1974, she lived in Manhattan. As late as 1975 (when she was 76) she co-starred at Lincoln Center in a revival of Sir Arthur Wing Pinero's **Trelawny of the Wells.** In 1991 she died at age 92, one of the last survivors of Hollywood's Golden Era. Had circumstances worked out differently, Aline MacMahon might have become one of the great stars of the screen more than half a century earlier. But in any case, she was unique, and a magnificent actress.

THE FILMS OF ALINE MacMAHON

1931: Five Star Final.
1932: Once in a Lifetime; Silver Dollar; Life Begins; The Mouthpiece; One Way Passage; The Heart of New York; Weekend Marriage.
1933: Gold Diggers of 1933; The World Changes; Heroes for Sale; The Life of Jimmy Dolan.
1934: Heat Lightning; Babbitt; Side Streets; The Merry Frinks; Big Hearted Herbert.
1935: Kind Lady; Ah, Wilderness; I Live My Life; While the Patient Slept; Mary Jane's Pa.
1937: When You're in Love.
1938: *Credit uncertain:* The Patient in Room 18.
1939: Back Door to Heaven.
1941: Out of the Fog.

1942: The Lady Is Willing; Tish.
1943: Stage Door Canteen; Seeds of Freedom (narrator only).
1944: Dragon Seed; Guest in the House.
1946: The Mighty McGurk.
1948: The Search.
1949: Roseanna McCoy.
1950: The Flame and the Arrow.
1953: The Eddie Cantor Story.
1955: The Man from Laramie.
1960: Cimarron.
1961: The Young Doctors.
1963: I Could Go On Singing; All the Way Home; Diamond Head.

She knew what was fittin':
HATTIE McDANIEL

It was nothing so minor as the Hollywood studio system that worked against any possible variety in the screen roles of Hattie McDaniel. Rather, American history itself conspired against her breaking free from her stereotype.

Miss McDaniel—the best-known female Afro-American performer in the movies of the Golden Era—played the same role in 80 films: a domestic servant, almost invariably somebody's maid. That she was able to win an Academy Award in such circumstances is a tribute to her acting skill—not to mention a minor miracle.

In just about any major production of the Thirties and early Forties where there was a black maid with a substantial speaking part, the role was played either by her or by Louise Beavers. She was the archetypal lady's maid, in an apron and white bandana or lace cap. Immense, heavy-set, beaming and cheerful, and much loved by her fellow actors, she at least had some variations on that role during her career, starting out as a bossy, sassy or cantankerous domestic, later becoming a loyal, perceptive, protective and outspoken (and hilarious) mother-surrogate, guarding her mistress' home like a fierce bulldog.

To say that she was required to play domestic servants is to reiterate what is well known historically—in real life, as well as on the screen, there was virtually no other role a black woman could or did play in the Thirties and Forties. Hollywood in this instance was simply reflecting the reality of the times. Not that the actress was happy with this typecasting, but she knew full well that if she did not play maids on the screen for $700 a week she would end up *working* as a maid for $7 a week. The choice was obvious.

Miss McDaniel was born June 10, 1895, in Wichita, Kansas, the daughter of a Baptist preacher and his spiritual-singing wife, and the granddaughter of a slave. The 13 children included two other future film actors, Sam and Etta. Hattie, the youngest, won a Women's Christian Temperance Union medal for dramatics at age 15 while attending high school in Denver, and after graduation became a singer with Professor George Morrison's Colored Orchestra in Denver, touring the West. She moved over to vaudeville, touring the South with the Shrine and Elks circuits and later the more prestigious Pantages and Orpheum circuits, still as a vocalist; she was billed as "the colored Sophie Tucker." She

also appeared on radio, reputedly becoming the first black woman to sing on that medium, and began work on the stage as well, touring in road companies of the musical **Show Boat** (which she would later film). Oddly enough, she rarely got to sing when she was in the movies.

She was called to Hollywood after talent scouts had seen her in the musical. Her screen debut was in a George O'Brien "B" Western, **The Golden West** (32), playing a servant called "Mammy Lou." She was also in a major production, the Lionel Barrymore starrer **Washington Masquerade**, here being billed, as she would be so often, simply as "Maid." In the Marlene Dietrich vehicle **Blonde Venus** she was nearly at the bottom of the cast list, billed as "Negro Girl" (she was then 37 years old). She was lost in the crowd as one of *three* maids employed by Mae West in **I'm No Angel** (33).

The actress' first *prominent* role as a maid was in the Will Rogers film **Judge Priest** (34). This movie featured a fascinating scene in which she is singing a conversational blues song and Rogers joins in, singing antiphonally. She played a cook in the Civil War drama **Operator 13,** with Gary Cooper and Marion Davies, which also gave a role to her brother Sam. She had a small bit as a mourner at the funeral of black Louise Beavers in **Imitation of Life,** and appeared in **Babbitt** and other films, invariably as a servant. Then she had one of her best comic parts, as the maid hired to serve a dinner in **Alice Adams** (35); Katharine Hepburn and her family are eager to impress boyfriend Fred MacMurray, but the dinner is turned into a disaster as the tipsy Miss McDaniel, chewing her gum and with cap askew, lurches about spilling and dropping things.

She was prominently cast in the Shirley Temple starrer **The Little Colonel,** as the family cook; the film was set in a never-never land of magnolias and mint juleps. She played Jean Harlow's maid in **China Seas.** In the Alice Faye starrer **Music Is Magic** her character's name was Hattie; this was not the last time this would occur. She appeared in the cast list as "Black Woman" in the Joan Blondell-Glenda Farrell vehicle **Traveling Saleslady,** and was in other films that year.

Miss McDaniel was in the impressive total of 27 movies in 1936 and 1937. The best of these roles was as the cook in **Show Boat** (36), starring Irene Dunne; she is married to shiftless Paul Robeson, and shouts at him, "You don't work like me...!", whereupon he breaks into song with "Ah Still Suits Me." Later, she sings an up-tempo reprise of "Can't Help Lovin' Dat Man" after Helen Morgan has sung it. And she was in such major productions as **Libeled Lady, The Bride Walks Out** and **Hearts Divided,** in the latter film playing a character called "Mammy," which was a harbinger of things to come; a similar foretaste of the future was provided in the Jane Withers vehicle **Can This Be Dixie?,** involving doings on "an old Southern plantation."

The actress was in two fine 1937 screwball comedies, both starring Carole Lombard: **Nothing Sacred** (in which she broke away from her maid stereotype to play a very small mother role, basically just a bit part) and **True Confession.** She was Jean Harlow's maid again in the young star's last film, **Saratoga,** and Una Merkel's maid in **Don't Tell the Wife,** and had a small part in **Stella Dallas.** As Ginger Rogers' maid in **Carefree** (38), her character name once again was Hattie. She played Barbara Stanwyck's servant in **The Mad Miss Manton,** was Margaret Sullavan's maid in **The Shopworn Angel,** and was the domestic in the star-studded drama **The Shining Hour.**

It all became worthwhile in 1939, when she was cast as Mammy in **Gone With the Wind.** Mammy was the head of a small army of domestics (actually they were slaves, of course) serving the O'Hara family (notably Vivien Leigh as Scarlett) in the antebellum South. As the ever-scolding but ever-loving servitor, the most faithful of faithful souls, she stays with Scarlett through good times and bad, even after the war has freed the slaves. It has to be said that the character of Mammy is *not* a stereotype; rather, she is one of the strongest and most dignified people in the film, assertive, haughty, protective and maternal, and repeatedly serves as Scarlett's conscience as well as the ultimate authority on what's "fittin'." And the relationship of mutual respect that grows between her and Clark Gable is well depicted.

Miss McDaniel was nominated for an Academy Award as best supporting actress for this role, and the competition was potent; besides Olivia de Havilland in **GWTW** itself, there were Edna May Oliver in one of her finest roles, in **Drums Along the Mohawk;** Maria Ouspenskaya in **Love Affair,** and Geraldine Fitzgerald in **Wuthering Heights.** But there was little question as to who was the popular favorite for the honors. A tremendous cheer went up as Hattie McDaniel was announced as the winner. Director Frank Capra later wrote, "When that beloved performer received her Oscar, there was a wet-eyed demonstration that lasted for minutes. Hattie sobbed her gratitude, clutched the statuette to her breast, and sobbed her way back to her seat through a standing ovation—one of the Academy's great moments."

That this great honor should have changed the career of the actress, however, was simply not in the cards. Things went on just about as before. She was Bette Davis' housekeeper in **The Great Lie** (41), and Miss de Havilland's maid in **They Died with Their Boots On,** still doing her "sassy mammy" routine. She had a better-than-usual part in **In This Our Life** (42), in which, as the family cook, she stood by helplessly as Miss Davis tried to frame up Miss McDaniel's son on a charge of vehicular homicide. Then she displayed a dormant talent in the all-star revue **Thank Your Lucky Stars,** singing and dancing "Ice Cold Katie" with Willie Best.

The actress was married twice, but sources are hazy on some of the details. The first marriage was to James Crawford, with a divorce, and the second to Larry Williams, with a divorce in 1950. Some sources indicate that there was a third marriage and that she was widowed once.

In one of 1944's best productions, **Since You Went Away,** she had a good role as the family cook for Claudette Colbert and daughters Jennifer Jones and Shirley Temple, taking a factory job when the family can no longer afford her but hurrying back to them after hours to provide malapropisms, comic relief, mother wit—and free labor. Meanwhile, how did she feel about this endless string of domestic servants? At a 1943 conference on blacks in the movies she commented, "I know there is much room for improvement, but being part and parcel of this industry, I have seen great strides made."

She supported Jeanne Crain in **Margie** (46) and Errol Flynn in **Never Say Goodbye,** and was in Walt Disney's **Song of the South.** She was Miss Colbert's maid again in **Family Honeymoon** (48), and appeared in her last film, **The Big Wheel,** in 1949, at age 54.

The actress now retired from the screen, partly because of ill health, but turned to the medium of radio. She had earlier appeared many times on such shows as "Amos 'n' Andy" and "The Eddie Cantor Show." Now she was given the starring role in the "Beulah" series—but the stereotype was unchanged. She was still a domestic servant, albeit a comedy star. "Beulah" started off on radio and later moved to television. While still starring in this role she died in 1952 at age 57.

We can regret the historical mischance that robbed Hattie McDaniel of the opportunity to play anything but servants throughout her film career. But let us also fondly remember her hour of glory as **Gone With the Wind's** indomitable Mammy.

THE FILMS OF HATTIE McDANIEL

1932: Blonde Venus; Washington Masquerade; The Golden West; Hypnotized; Crooner; Are You Listening?
1933: I'm No Angel. *Credit uncertain:* The Story of Temple Drake.
1934: Judge Priest; Operator 13, Babbitt; Imitation of Life; Lost in the Stratosphere; Little Men; Merry Wives of Reno.
1935: Alice Adams; The Little Colonel; China Seas; Music Is Magic; We're Only Human; Traveling Saleslady; Another Face; Harmony Lane; Murder by Television.
1936: Show Boat; Libeled Lady; The Bride Walks Out; Hearts Divided; Gentle Julia; Next Time We Love; The Singing Kid; High Tension; Reunion; Postal Inspector; Can This Be Dixie?; The First Baby; Star for a Night; Valiant Is the Word for Carrie.
1937: Nothing Sacred; True Confession; Saratoga; Stella Dallas; Racing Lady; The Crime Nobody Saw; 45 Fathers; The Wildcatter; Over the Goal; Don't Tell the Wife; Merry-Go-Round of 1938; Quick Money; Sky Racket.
1938: Carefree; The Mad Miss Manton; Vivacious Lady; The Shopworn Angel; The Shining Hour; Battle of Broadway.

1939: Gone With the Wind; Everybody's Baby; Zenobia.
1940: Maryland.
1941: The Great Lie; They Died with Their Boots On; Affectionately Yours.
1942: In This Our Life; The Mare Animal; George Washington Slept Here.
1943: Johnny Come Lately; Thank Your Lucky Stars.
1944: Since You Went Away; Janie; Three Is a Family.
1945: Hi, Beautiful.
1946: Margie; Never Say Goodbye; Janie gets Married; Song of the South.
1947: The Flame.
1948: Family Honeymoon; Mickey.
1949: The Big Wheel.

NOTE: Contrary to some sources, she did not appear in the 1942 film **Reap the Wild Wind** or the 1948 film **Mr. Blandings Builds His Dream House.** The actress involved in both cases was Louise Beavers.

A beaming face, a nervous laugh:
FRANK McHUGH

Frank McHugh had little to offer the movies other than a permanent look of amiable bafflement and an unusual laugh, but he parlayed the combination into a long career in which he made some 120 films.

Fast-talking and perpetually beaming, with a surprised look, he was frequently cast as the loyal but not-overly-bright friend or assistant of the hero, who was often James Cagney. His trademark was a high-pitched, nervous, braying, and triumphantly insulting laugh: "Haaa-haaa-haaaaa!"

As a regular member of the Warner Bros. stock company, he probably appeared in more films for that studio than any other performer in its history—74 of them in the period 1930-42 alone. Thus anyone who saw a lot of Warners films in the Golden Era soon had more than a sufficiency of McHugh—especially since the chunky, wavy-haired actor's performances hardly ever varied from one film to the next.

Francis Curray McHugh was born May 23, 1898 (some sources say 1899), in Homestead, Pennsylvania, a suburb of Pittsburgh. The son of an actor, he was practically "born in a trunk," and made his stage debut at age 11 with his parents' traveling stock company, and at 17 graduated to juvenile roles with the Marguerite Bryant Players, later joining the Sherman Kelly Stock Company. Going into vaudeville, he played the Orpheum and Keith circuits, did resident stock, and in 1925 made it to Broadway, his first role there being in the hit comedy **The Fall Guy.** He reportedly was in one silent film, **Mademoiselle Modiste** (26), apparently in a very small part, and in 1927, back on the boards, co-starred with Miriam Hopkins in the play **Excess Baggage.** He made one short film in 1928, but finally landed in Hollywood for good in 1930.

He debuted for Warners in support of Joe E. Brown in **Top Speed** (30), and was irritating as a drunken reporter in **Bright Lights.** (He frequently played alcoholics.) He supported Edward G. Robinson in **The Widow from Chicago,** and was also in a small role in **The Dawn Patrol.** He played one of the reporters in the 1931 version of **The Front Page,** and made heavy weather of his comedy bits in **Kiss Me Again.** In **Up for Murder** he was again an intoxicated newsman, and he played Chester Morris' wealthy college classmate in **Corsair** and a traveling salesman in **Traveling Husbands.**

The actor played William Powell's con-artist as-

sociate in **One Way Passage** (32), a role he would repeat in the 1940 remake, and was James Cagney's loyal buddy for the first time in **The Crowd Roars.** (Off-screen, both Cagney and Spencer Tracy were his close friends.) He was a genial drunk in **Union Depot** and a perplexed father-to-be in **Life Begins,** and for the second time that year was a con man working with William Powell in **High Pressure.**

Whatever the salary paid to McHugh in 1933, he earned it, making 16 movies—one rolled off the assembly line nearly every three weeks. In **Footlight Parade** he was the harassed dance director, clumsily leading the evolutions of the chorus line, and in the classic horror film **The Mystery of the Wax Museum** he brought comic relief as reporter Glenda Farrell's editor. He played the drink-sodden carnival barker who offers to make a respectable woman of Ruth Chatterton in **Lilly Turner** (sorry, she prefers George Brent), and was also an alcoholic in **Convention City** (as was Hugh Herbert) and **Havana**

Widows. He and Allen Jenkins were a pair of bumbling detectives in **Tomorrow at Seven,** and in **Grand Slam** he ghost-writes a book for bridge expert Paul Lukas because he is hopelessly in love with Lukas' wife, Loretta Young. He played Douglas Fairbanks Jr.'s buddy in **Parachute Jumper,** a salesman in **Convention City,** a lawyer in **Havana Widows,** and a press agent in **Professional Sweetheart.**

McHugh married actress Dorothy Spencer in 1933 (but one source says 1928). They had three children, Susan, Peter, and another son whom sources don't name (one son was killed in a car crash). Frank also had an elder brother and sister, Matt and Kitty McHugh, who were kept busy in small parts in films, and even their mother, Catherine McHugh, had some film roles.

The actor played Glenda Farrell's chauffeur in **Heat Lightning** (34), and for the third time was con man William Powell's assistant in **Fashions of 1934,** hiding a tiny camera in the top of his cane to surreptitiously photograph new Paris fashions for Powell's other assistant, Bette Davis, to copy. He played a reporter again in **Return of the Terror** and a sailor pal of James Cagney's in **Here Comes the Navy,** among the 10 movies he made that year.

He did a beautifully judged cameo as Quince in a Shakespearean film, **A Midsummer Night's Dream** (35), and was Alice Brady's idiotic, girl-chasing son in **Gold Diggers of 1935.** He and Cagney were Marine pilots in **Devil Dogs of the Air,** and he was the brother of Cagney and Pat O'Brien in **The Irish in Us;** McHugh was a city fireman and not too bright. He and O'Brien were a couple of con men in **Page Miss Glory.** He starred in the comedy **Three Men on a Horse** (36), repeating his stage role as a timid writer of greeting-card verse whose surefire system for picking horse-race winners draws the attention of gamblers, and he was also top-cast in **Freshman Love,** as a college coach frustrated in his efforts to turn the varsity crew into a winner. And he supported Edward G. Robinson and Humphrey Bogart in **Bullets or Ballots.**

McHugh played a sailor in **Submarine D-1** (37), and he wooed and won Alice Brady in **Mr. Dodd Takes the Air,** also co-starring and winning the ingenue, Carol Hughes, in **Marry the Girl.** In the fine drama **Four Daughters** (38) he provided comedy relief as the prattling, piggish real-estate agent whom Lola Lane settles for; in the next three years he would repeat the role in three sequels, **Daughters Courageous, Four Wives** and **Four Mothers** (fortunately, audiences were spared seeing the ladies as grandmothers). He starred as a timid advertising clerk who wins the girl of his dreams (Jane Wyman) in **He Couldn't Say No,** and supported Cagney and O'Brien

again in **Boy Meets Girl.** He played a gambler in **Valley of the Giants** and also in **Little Miss Thoroughbred,** and he and Allen Jenkins were the trainers of wrestler Nat Pendleton in **Swing Your Lady.**

He was Cagney's pal once again in **The Roaring Twenties** (39), helping him make bathtub gin during Prohibition, and was back piloting an airplane in **Wings of the Navy.** In the Errol Flynn starrer **Dodge City** he played a newsman who is killed after he unearths the evidence that would send Bruce Cabot, the town boss, to prison. He repeated his 1932 **One Way Passage** role (a con man) in the 1940 remake, **'Til We Meet Again,** and was Cagney's friend again in **City for Conquest** and one of his Army buddies in **The Fighting 69th.** Once again he and William Powell were con artists in **I Love You Again,** and he supported Flynn in **Virginia City.** He was Edward G. Robinson's fellow power lineman in **Manpower** (41), and played a traveling salesman who gives Margaret Sullavan a hard time in **Back Street.**

McHugh was Robert Taylor's song-writing partner in **Her Cardboard Lover** (42), which was Norma Shearer's last film, and was Humphrey Bogart's henchman in **All Through the Night.** His long Warners contract was now over, and he freelanced. He was one of Bing Crosby's fellow priests in **Going My Way** (44), and a Marine again in **Marine Raiders.** Now in his mid-forties, he was appearing in considerably fewer films. He played an impoverished barber whose family takes in and assists an elderly woman in **Little Miss Big** (46), and supported Powell again in **The Hoodlum Saint.** In **Easy Come, Easy Go** (47) he was hanging around racetracks again, and he supported Rosalind Russell in **The Velvet Touch** (48). He was in the anti-Communist tract **My Son John** (52) and worked with Cagney for the last time in **A Lion Is in the Streets** (53). He was off the screen for three years in the Fifties, returning to play a small role in **The Last Hurrah** (58), with Spencer Tracy. He was a waiter in **Career** (59).

He now took up with television at age 60, appearing on the series "The Bing Crosby Show," and after a five-year screen hiatus returned for a part in **The Tiger Walks** (64). His last film, in 1967, starred Elvis Presley, and it was the second time he had been in a movie called **Easy Come, Easy Go.**

The actor retired to Cos Cob, Connecticut, where he died in 1981 at the age of 83. But his beaming countenance can still be seen, and his high-pitched laugh still heard, late at night when some old Warners epic turns up on the tube. Just watch for something with Cagney in it. Who's his smiling buddy? Why, Frank McHugh, of course.

THE FILMS OF FRANK McHUGH

1926: *Credit uncertain:* Mademoiselle Modiste.
1930: The Dawn Patrol; Bright Lights; Top Speed; College Lovers; The Widow from Chicago. *Credit uncertain:* Little Caesar.
1931: The Front Page; Corsair; Millie; Traveling Husbands; Men of the Sky; Bad Company; Up for Murder; Kiss Me Again.
1932: One Way Passage; The Crowd Roars; Union Depot; The Strange Love of Molly Louvain; Life Begins; The Dark Horse; Blessed Event; High Pressure.
1933: Footlight Parade; The Mystery of the Wax Museum; Ex-Lady; Grand Slam; Parachute Jumper; Elmer the Great; Convention City; Son of a Sailor; Lilly Turner; Havana Widows; Private Jones; Professional Sweetheart; Tomorrow at Seven; Hold Me Tight; The House on 56th Street; The Telegraph Trail.
1934: Heat Lightning; Happiness Ahead; Fashions of 1934; Maybe It's Love; Merry Wives of Reno; Smarty; Here Comes the Navy; Let's Be Ritzy; Return of the Terror; 6 Day Bike Rider.
1935: A Midsummer Night's Dream; Gold Diggers of 1935; Page Miss Glory; The Irish in Us; Devil Dogs of the Air; Stars over Broadway.
1936: Bullets or Ballots; Three Men on a Horse; Freshman Love; Snowed Under; Stage Struck; Moonlight Murder.
1937: Ever Since Eve; Mr. Dodd Takes the Air; Marry the Girl; Submarine D-1.
1938: Four Daughters; Boy Meets Girl; Valley of the Giants; Swing Your Lady; He Couldn't Say No; Little Miss Thoroughbred.
1939: Daughters Courageous; Four Wives; The Roaring Twenties; Dust Be My Destiny; Dodge City; Wings of the Navy; On Your Toes; Indianapolis Speedway.
1940: 'Til We Meet Again; The Fighting 69th; City for Conquest; Virginia City; I Love You Again.
1941: Four Mothers; Back Street; Manpower.
1942: All Through the Night; Her Cardboard Lover.
1944: Going My Way; Marine Raiders; Bowery to Broadway.
1945: State Fair; A Medal for Benny.
1946: The Hoodlum Saint; Little Miss Big; The Runaround.
1947: Easy Come, Easy Go; Carnegie Hall.
1948: The Velvet Touch.
1949: Mighty Joe Young; Miss Grant Takes Richmond.
1950: Paid in Full; The Tougher They Come.
1952: My Son John; The Pace that Thrills.
1953: A Lion Is in the Streets; It Happens Every Thursday.
1954: There's No Business Like Show Business.
1958: The Last Hurrah.
1959: Say One for Me; Career.
1964: A Tiger Walks.
1967: Easy Come, Easy Go.

NOTE: Some sources erroneously credit him with appearances in **The Mad Game** (33) and **Deadline for Murder** (46); those roles were played by his brother, Matt McHugh. Credits to Frank McHugh for appearances in **42nd Street** (33) and **Saturday's Children** (40) also appear to be erroneous.

Oh, so ya wanna fight?:
VICTOR McLAGLEN

The title of Victor McLaglen's first American film was **The Beloved Brute,** and it was a sobriquet that suited him. Burly, barrel-chested, craggy-faced, with an impudent grin and flashing teeth, he was blustery, brawling and garrulous, grinning and fighting his way through scores of action-filled adventure films.

Gruff but soft-hearted, he had a persona that was ideal for roles as a tough top sergeant, and he played many variations of that part over a long screen career. But he also found time to be the romantic interest for such stars as Jeanette MacDonald, Marlene Dietrich, Mae West, Louise Brooks and Dolores Del Rio. And when the right role came along, he won an Academy Award as *best actor*—one of the few character actors ever to do so. But overall he was not a performer of great subtlety, and despite the Oscar, during much of his career he was used largely as Irish comedy relief.

McLaglen was born December 10, 1886 (some sources say 1883, and there is also a December 11 date given), in Tunbridge Wells, Kent, England, the son of a clergyman (who was later a South African bishop) and the eldest of eight brothers. (Five of the others—Arthur, Clifford, Cyril, Kenneth and Leopold—also became film actors.)

The conflicting source information on his year of birth creates a further problem regarding his army service during the Boer War in 1900. The sources that list 1886 as the year say he ran away from home at 14 to join the Life Guards regiment but that his father managed to buy him out so that he did not see action. But those that opt for the 1883 date (which would have made him 17 in 1900) say he was in the fighting. In any case, after the war he began a life that was considerably more interesting than the plots of many of his future movies.

He went to Canada, where he worked on farms, did casual labor, prospected for gold and silver, worked on a railroad, and became a prizefighter and a professional strong man. He is also said to have posed for statues of Hercules and Adonis, and to have been the physical-culture adviser to an Indian rajah. He did exhibition boxing with Wild West shows and circuses, then went into vaudeville, touring in the United States and Australia (where he took part in the Kalgoorlie gold rush). At some point during the reign of heavyweight boxing champion Jack Johnson (1908-15), McLaglen was matched against him, but lost the much-promoted bout in six rounds. In World

War I he served as a captain in the Irish Fusiliers, and for a while was provost marshal of Baghdad, Iraq. After the armistice he took up boxing again and was with London's National Sporting Club when a movie producer saw him and offered him the lead in the British film **The Call of the Road** (20). The costume romance was judged Britain's best picture of the year, and the actor, now in his mid-thirties, was on his way in movies.

For the next several years McLaglen ran roughshod through nearly a score of swashbuckling action films, including the first British color film, **The Glorious Adventure** (22), in which he was the ruffian who abducts the heroine. English productions were not particularly good in those days, and most of these movies are forgotten today. Soon he was summoned to Hollywood, and in 1924 made his first American film, **The Beloved Brute,** as a tough wrestler; he co-starred with Marguerite De La Motte.

In director John Ford's **The Fighting Heart** (25)

he was a brutish bootlegger who becomes the heavyweight boxing champion, in a supporting role, and he played a dance-hall proprietor in **The Hunted Woman** and a political boss in **Percy.** He was a standout in director Tod Browning's **The Unholy Three,** starring Lon Chaney; a member of a robbery trio, he kills one of his confederates (midget Harry Earles) and then is himself killed by a gorilla. He and Edmund Lowe co-starred (for the first of many times) as the brawling Captain Flagg and Sergeant Quirt, respectively, in the war drama **What Price Glory** (26), directed by Raoul Walsh and featuring Dolores Del Rio as Charmaine; it was a smash hit and made McLaglen a star. Just previously he had had a minor role as one of the Legionnaires in the first screen version of **Beau Geste** and was the villain in both **Men of Steel** and **The Isle of Retribution.**

In Walsh's **The Loves of Carmen** (27) he was the bullfighter Escamillo to Miss Del Rio's Carmen, and he worked for John Ford twice again: in **Hangman's House** (28), as a soldier of fortune in this Irish drama, and **Mother Machree,** as the owner of a sideshow. He starred in director Howard Hawks' **A Girl in Every Port** as a sailor with just that, his chief love being Louise Brooks in France, and in **The River Pirate,** as an ex-convict unable to go straight. In his first talkie, Ford's **The Black Watch** (29), he was an officer thought to be a coward but in fact on a secret mission, meanwhile vamped by Myrna Loy in her early "bad girl" persona. Walsh's **The Cock-Eyed World** reunited him with Edmund Lowe, as Flagg and Quirt again, and this too was a big hit. In **Captain Lash** he headed the gang of stokers on an ocean liner and romanced a society lady, and in Ford's **Strong Boy** he was a baggage porter who outwits a gang of train robbers; Leatrice Joy was his sweetheart. He played a rough, uncouth sailor who wins a lottery (and the girl) in Walsh's **Hot for Paris.**

McLaglen was now one of the top draws for the Fox studio, with which he had had a contract since 1926, and to an increasing extent formula pictures were being built around him. In **A Devil with Women** (30) he played a soldier of fortune who loses the girl of his dreams to a rich young man who has been following him around; the young actor, making his film debut, was Humphrey Bogart. McLaglen was a romantically inclined iron riveter in **On the Level,** and played the Russian officer who falls in love with, and then is betrayed by, spy Marlene Dietrich in director Josef von Sternberg's **Dishonored** (31). In Walsh's **Women of All Nations** he and Lowe were Flagg and Quirt again, only he had been demoted to *Sergeant* Flagg. He was a strong and silent Westerner married to Jeanette MacDonald in **Annabelle's Affairs,** and

was involved with Fay Wray in **Not Exactly Gentlemen.**

The actor married Enid Lamont (or Enid Leonard, according to one source) in 1918; they had a son, Andrew (the future film director), and a daughter, Sheila. After his wife died in 1942, he married his secretary, Suzanne Brueggsman (or Brueggemann), in 1943, and they divorced in 1948; that same year he married Margaret Humphrey.

He played a big-shot mobster who muscles in on football betting in **Rackety Rax** (32), and was back with Lowe in **Guilty as Hell,** a murder mystery (they were no longer Flagg and Quirt). In **Devil's Lottery** he won the Calcutta Sweepstakes, and in **While Paris Sleeps** he played a murderer escaped from Devil's Island. He and Lowe were teamed again (with Lupe Velez) in a weak picture, **Hot Pepper** (33), and he returned to England to make **Dick Turpin.** His career had started to go downhill at this point, and who should ride to the rescue but John Ford. He starred him as the (ultimately) last survivor of **The Lost Patrol** (34), a fine film that erased the Captain Flagg image. McLaglen was a detective in **Murder at the Vanities** and also in **The Captain Hates the Sea,** the last film of the doomed star John Gilbert. He and Preston Foster were romantic rivals for Dorothy Dell in **Wharf Angel,** and he appeared with Lowe again in **No More Women.**

Director John Ford was the best thing that had happened to the actor's career, and now he starred him in **The Informer** (35), based on Liam O'Flaherty's novel about an Irishman who sells out his pal to the British for the price of a steamship ticket to America. In retrospect, the film is good but not exceptional, and McLaglen's performance in the title role somewhat hammy and obvious. But the critics of the time felt otherwise. The London Daily Telegraph said, "[His] Gypo Nolan could not be bettered by any actor living." The New York Times commented, "There is something just a bit sinister about the way [he] becomes brilliant under Mr. Ford's guidance...[He] makes something stark and memorable out of the stupid giant...The animal cunning of the man, his transparent deceits and his naive belief in the powers of deception are woven into the fabric of a character that is worthy...of a Dostoevsky...He becomes some dreadful and pathetic creature of darkness...There is a tragic quality in this man's bewildered terror."

Reviews like these catapulted the film into a box-office success (although it was really appreciated only by highbrow audiences), and at Oscar time it won five Academy Awards—including one for McLaglen as *best actor.* His future as a screen actor was fairly well assured—but he was turning 50, and stardom was not in the cards.

In the same year as **The Informer**—besides writing his autobiography, "Express to Hollywood"—he was in **Professional Soldier** as a man hired to kidnap young Freddie Bartholomew but who befriends him instead, and was in two more programmers with Edmund Lowe: **The Great Hotel Murder,** as the dumb house detective, and Raoul Walsh's **Under Pressure,** as the boss of a crew of tunnel-building sandhogs, tangling with rival crew boss Charles Bickford. He was the bruiser who falls for (but is not fooled by) Mae West in **Klondike Annie** (36), and was good as the Foreign Legion commandant who is jealous of Ronald Colman, loved by Claudette Colbert, in **Under Two Flags.** He starred as a roughneck steel blast-furnace boss in **The Magnificent Brute.** In Ford's **Wee Willie Winkie** (37) he came near stealing the picture from Shirley Temple; he was the tough sergeant who befriends her but is killed. He played a reformed kidnapper in **Nancy Steele Is Missing,** falling afoul of Peter Lorre; was a Coast Guardsman in **Sea Devils,** with Ida Lupino as his daughter; and headed a gang of bank robbers infiltrated by undercover agent Robert Taylor in **This Is My Affair.**

In **Battle of Broadway** (38) he and Brian Donlevy were a pair of bickering buddies who both fall for Gypsy Rose Lee (under her sometime screen name of Louise Hovick). He co-starred with English comedienne Gracie Fields in **We're Going to Be Rich,** and was a good/bad guy as an underworld nightclub owner in **The Devil's Party.** He, Cary Grant and Douglas Fairbanks Jr. were Kipling's three British sergeants in the classic adventure tale **Gunga Din** (39), and he was a prison warden in **The Big Guy. Full Confession** cast him as a murderer who confesses (to priest Joseph Calleia) when he thinks he's dying, but later recants, only to confess again to the police and save innocent Barry Fitzgerald from execution. He was an ex-convict in **Captain Fury,** the villain bested in a fistfight by Nelson Eddy(!) in **Let Freedom Ring,** a ship's chief engineer in **Pacific Liner,** a former boxing champion working as a doorman in **Ex-Champ,** and an aide to crooked financier Basil Rathbone in **Rio,** undergoing a change of heart at the end and killing his mentor.

McLaglen had now reached the point where he was either starring in fairly tedious programmers or else supporting bigger names in major pictures. He was involved in the South African diamond rush in **Diamond Frontier** (40), and he and Gene Lockhart were pirates trying to steal the natives' supply of pearls in **South of Pago Pago.** His only 1941 film was a weak comedy. Incredibly, he was reunited with Edmund Lowe—16 years after their first teaming—in **Call Out the Marines** (42), and they were once again brawling and cussing at each other. He played a munitions-plant foreman in **Powder Town** and a spy in the pay of Japan in **China Girl.** Continuing to be villainous, he was tanker captain Edward G. Robinson's first mate, secretly working for the Nazis, in **Tampico** (44), and a pirate menacing Bob Hope in **The Princess and the Pirate. Roger Touhy, Gangster** found him playing a criminal associate of Preston Foster, who had the title role. On Poverty Row (for Republic), he brawled with Chester Morris in **Rough, Tough and Ready** (45), and also worked for that studio in **Love, Honor and Goodbye,** billed below the (even then) long-forgotten Nils Asther.

He was an uncouth nightclub owner involved with screen newcomer Ava Gardner in **Whistle Stop** (46), and supported Rex Harrison and Maureen O'Hara in **The Foxes of Harrow** (47), also appearing in a mediocre programmer and a "B" Western. What next? Once again director John Ford rode to the rescue, this time bringing the U.S. Cavalry with him. He featured the actor in his classic "Cavalry trilogy"—**Fort Apache** (48), **She Wore a Yellow Ribbon** (49) and **Rio Grande** (50); McLaglen played Sergeant Mulcahy in the first outing and then was Sergeant Quincannon in the other two, and the parts were routine and relatively small. But Ford's superb **The Quiet Man** (52) was something else again. Here McLaglen had an important role as Maureen O'Hara's brother, and was involved in a marathon knock-down-drag-out fistfight with John Wayne—reputedly the longest ever filmed. His still-massive physique allowed viewers to believe that the 66-year-old actor was every bit a match for the 45-year-old Wayne. And to top it off, he was nominated for another Oscar, as best supporting actor.

There wasn't much left. He had secondary roles in some unimportant films in the Fifties to close out his career. He played the owner of an underworld cafe in **Bengazi** (55), and was the father of Eleanor Parker, presiding over her shotgun wedding to Robert Taylor, in **Many Rivers to Cross.** He supported Miss O'Hara again in **Lady Godiva,** putting out the eyes of Tom the Tailor, who dared to sneak a peek as the lady rode through the town clad in nothing more than a lot of long red hair. He did a cameo as a ship's helmsman in **Around the World in 80 Days** (56), and starred under his son Andrew's direction in **The Abductors** (57), as an ex-convict who plots in 1876 to steal Abraham Lincoln's body from the grave.

In what was apparently his last film, **Sea Fury** (58), he played at age 72 a belligerent, hard-drinking tugboat captain who is set to marry luscious young Luciana Paluzzi, but she falls for first mate Stanley Baker. At least one source indicates that he also made a film called **The Italians Are Crazy** that year, but a search through standard checklists fails to turn up any movie with that name.

Victor McLaglen died in 1959, leaving memories of his glory days as the screen's rough, tough, grinning, rip-roaring brawler. In truth, he was a lot of fun to watch.

THE FILMS OF VICTOR McLAGLEN

1920: The Call of the Road.
1921: Carnival; The Prey of the Dragon; The Sport of Kings; Corinthian Jack.
1922: The Glorious Adventure; A Romance of Old Bagdad; A Sailor Tramp; Little Brother of God; The Crimson Circle.
1923: The Romany; M'Lord of the White Road; Heartstrings; In the Blood.
1924: The Beloved Brute; Women and Diamonds; The Gay Corinthian; The Passionate Adventure.
1925: The Unholy Three; The Fighting Heart; The Hunted Woman; Percy; Winds of Chance.
1926: Beau Geste; What Price Glory; The Isle of Retribution; Men of Steel.
1927: The Loves of Carmen.
1928: A Girl in Every Port; Hangman's House; Mother Machree; The River Pirate.
1929: The Black Watch; The Cock-Eyed World; Captain Lash; Strong Boy; Hot for Paris; Happy Days.
1930: A Devil with Women; On the Level.
1931: Dishonored; Women of All Nations; Annabelle's Affairs; Not Exactly Gentlemen; Wicked.
1932: Rackety Rax; The Gay Caballero; The Devil's Lottery; While Paris Sleeps; Guilty as Hell.
1933: Hot Pepper; Laughing at Life; Dick Turpin.
1934: The Lost Patrol; Murder at the Vanities; The Captain Hates the Sea; Wharf Angel; No More Women.
1935: The Informer; Under Pressure; Professional Soldier; The Great Hotel Murder.
1936: Under Two Flags; Klondike Annie; The Magnificent Brute.
1937: Wee Willie Winkie; This Is My Affair; Sea Devils; Nancy Steele

Is Missing; Ali Baba Goes to Town.
1938: Battle of Broadway; The Devil's Party; We're Going to Be Rich.
1939: Gunga Din; Full Confession; Captain Fury; The Big Guy; Rio; Let Freedom Ring; Pacific Liner; Ex-Champ.
1940: Diamond Frontier; South of Pago Pago.
1941: Broadway Limited.
1942: China Girl; Call Out the Marines; Powder Town.
1943: Forever and a Day.
1944: Tampico; The Princess and the Pirate; Roger Touhy, Gangster.
1945: Rough, Tough and Ready; Love, Honor and Goodbye.
1946: Whistle Stop.
1947: The Foxes of Harrow; Calendar Girl; The Michigan Kid.
1948: Fort Apache.
1949: She Wore a Yellow Ribbon.
1950: Rio Grande.
1952: The Quiet Man.
1953: Fair Wind to Java.
1954: Prince Valiant; Trouble in the Glen.
1955: Bengazi; Many Rivers to Cross; Lady Godiva; City of Shadows.
1956: Around the World in 80 Days.
1957: The Abductors.
1958: Sea Fury.

NOTE: Some sources indicate appearances in films called **Sez You— Sez Me** (29), **Wings of Adventure** (30), **Dust and Sun** (30) and **The Italians Are Crazy** (58), but a search through standard title checklists does not turn up any films with those titles. **Sez You—Sez Me** may have been an alternate title for **The Cock-Eyed World** (29).

The timid soul:
DONALD MEEK

No other actor has ever had so apt a name. For in his screen persona, meek is precisely what he was. Donald Meek portrayed timidly respectable little men who were worried, confused and ineffectual, the personification of Caspar Milquetoast.

With a quavery and bleating voice emerging from his thin mouth, and with chubby cheeks, a small nose and blinky eyes, he held a monopoly on the role of the nervous little man who is the victim of fate or adversity. The fact that he stood five feet, four inches tall and weighed 130 pounds didn't detract from that image.

Ironically, off-screen the bald comic was forceful and erudite, a strong, determined man who served in two wars and had been a professional acrobat.

Meek was born July 14, 1880, in Glasgow, Scotland, the son of an artist. He acted professionally even as a child, touring Australia as the lead in **Little Lord Fauntleroy.** At 14 he came to the United States as the "top man" in an acrobatic troupe, but a fall from the high wire in which he broke both legs turned him back to the stage. He served with the U.S. Army in Cuba during the Spanish-American War, and contracted tropical fever, which caused him to lose most of his hair.

Becoming a character actor at age 18, he joined the Castle Square Stock Company in Boston, appearing with that group for many years, during which time he married Belle Walken in 1909. He also worked with the Denver-based Countess Stock Company. In 1913 he made his Broadway debut in the musical **Going Up.**

The actor tried to enlist in the Army again when World War I broke out, but was turned down, so he served in the Canadian army instead. After the Armistice he toured South Africa, India and Australia in road shows, eventually returning to Broadway to begin a long career there. A part in **Six Cylinder Love** led to an early film appearance in the 1923 screen version of that play, which also, by coincidence, featured the screen debuts of character actors Thomas Mitchell and Berton Churchill. (All three actors were together again 16 years later in **Stagecoach.**) He continued to be busy on the New York stage all through the Twenties, starring in **The Potters** (1923) and appearing in **Love 'Em and Leave 'Em, After Tomorrow** and **Little Old New York.** All told, he played hundreds of roles.

In 1929 he starred in the domestic drama **Broken Dishes,** as a Milquetoast drudge who rebels against his tyrannical wife and is aided and abetted by his daughter. In the final scene the daughter denounces her mother in a powerful speech. The young actress who had this part was an unknown just starting her career, and the play's success propelled her toward future stardom. Her name was Bette Davis.

During the play's run Meek lost his life's savings in the Wall Street crash. The night the market plunged, he came on stage and gave a brilliant performance, Miss Davis later recalled.

As talkies took over the screen, he was called to Hollywood. As a character called Goofy, he supported Claudette Colbert and Edward G. Robinson in **The Hole in the Wall** (29), and then was in a Poverty Row outing, **The Love Kiss** (30). He was Nancy Carroll's poor Irish father in **Personal Maid** (31), and supported Charlie Ruggles in **The Girl Habit.** These films were all made for Paramount, but now

171

he began to freelance, which he would do throughout his film career. At this point he also starred in many Vitaphone two-reel (20-minute) mystery shorts scripted by S.S. Van Dine.

In 1933 he repeated an earlier stage role by playing a friend of ZaSu Pitts in **Love, Honor and Oh, Baby!** and had a small part in the Dick Powell vehicle **College Coach.** And then (he was now in his mid-fifties) he really came into his own in 1934, with 11 film appearances. He was a valet in **The Merry Widow,** a doctor in **Murder at the Vanities,** and a clergyman in **Romance in Manhattan. The Last Gentleman** cast him as George Arliss' scheming son, who tries to inherit his wealth, and in **Mrs. Wiggs of the Cabbage Patch** he was the absent Mr. Wiggs, finally returning home to renew his henpecked existence. In **Bedside,** as a physician again, he was the assistant to medical charlatan Warren William, doing all the latter's work, and he had fairly small parts in such films as **What Every Woman Knows, The Captain Hates the Sea** and **Hi, Nellie!**

In 1935 the actor was in the astonishing total of 20 movies, a mark few have equaled. In director John Ford's **The Whole Town's Talking** he was the excitable little man who mistakes mild-mannered office worker Edward G. Robinson for a killer (understandably, since Robinson also played the murderer, in a dual role). He had a good cameo in Ford's **The Informer** as the timid tailor falsely accused by Victor McLaglen of being the informer; in the drama's only humorous scene, he readily clears himself of the charge. He was a doctor again in **Mark of the Vampire,** and in **Barbary Coast** played the gutsy little Scottish prospector who stands up to the bad guys and ends up murdered by Brian Donlevy. He was once more a doctor in **Captain Blood,** portrayed a chess player in **China Seas** and a clergyman in **Top Hat,** and played Gary Cooper's blind employer in **Peter Ibbetson.** He was the judge in **The Bride Comes Home** and played Randolph Scott's timid hired hand, murdered by Robert Barrat, in **Village Tale.** And he was in other important pictures that year, such as **Kind Lady, The Gilded Lily, Biography of a Bachelor Girl, Accent on Youth** and **Society Doctor.**

Meek had a delightful comic cameo in **Love on the Run** (36), as the batty caretaker at the Palace of Fontainebleau, visited by Clark Gable and Joan Crawford. He was the feeble grandfather of the down-on-their-luck family helped out by Bing Crosby in **Pennies from Heaven,** and the judge in **One Rainy Afternoon,** also playing a hotel manager in **And So They Were Married.** In **The Toast of New York** (37) he was perfect as the penny-pinching, God-fearing, hypocritical 19th century financier Daniel Drew,

and in **Maid of Salem** he was a village elder caught up in the 1692 Salem witchcraft hysteria. He played another doctor in **Artists and Models,** and was a clergyman in both **Double Wedding** and **Breakfast for Two,** also portraying Basil Rathbone's valet in **Make a Wish.** In **Behind the Headlines** he had a rare villainous role as a rogue government agent planning to hijack a gold shipment en route to Fort Knox.

In director Frank Capra's 1938 screwball comedy **You Can't Take It with You** he played the timid Mr. Poppins, an inventor of toys and party masks who is Lionel Barrymore's best friend. He was the Sunday school superintendent in **The Adventures of Tom Sawyer,** George Murphy's father in **Little Miss Broadway,** and an eccentric jeweler helping to track down some thieves in **Double Danger.** In **Hold That Co-ed** he played a college dean.

His most famous role came in John Ford's Western classic **Stagecoach** (39), as Mr. Peacock, the whiskey salesman in the deerstalker hat, losing his samples to alcoholic doctor Thomas Mitchell. In **Jesse James** he was the weasely, vengeful railroad president who talks Jesse (Tyrone Power) into surrendering and then tries to have him hanged, and in Ford's **Young Mr. Lincoln** he played the spellbinding prosecutor at the climactic trial, losing the case to Henry Fonda as Lincoln. He had an offbeat part in **Nick Carter, Master Detective,** as "Bartholomew, the Bee Man," a mild little man wrapped up in his world of beekeeping and functioning as a sort of Dr. Watson to Walter Pidgeon as Carter (he repeated the role the following year in **Phantom Raiders and Sky Murder**). He played the head of a movie studio in **Hollywood Cavalcade,** and was an apoplectic newspaper editor in **The Housekeeper's Daughter.**

The actor was card sharp Amos W. Budget in the W.C. Fields-Mae West outing **My Little Chickadee** (40), repeated his **Jesse James** role in **The Return of Frank James,** and supported Edward G. Robinson in **Dr. Ehrlich's Magic Bullet.** He was the confused butler in **Turnabout,** a crooked banker in **The Ghost Comes Home,** a movie casting director in **Star Dust,** and an eccentric inventor in **Oh, Johnny, How You Can Love.** He played one of Joan Crawford's crooked accomplices in **A Woman's Face** (41) and a philosophical bum encountered by James Stewart in **Come Live with Me,** as well as a screwloose college professor in **Rise and Shine.** He was hilarious as a Western novelist in **Blonde Inspiration,** and was in key roles in **The Feminine Touch** and **Babes on Broadway.** In 1942 he was in two Spencer Tracy starrers, **Tortilla Flat** and **Keeper of the Flame.**

Meek was a little old man who turns out to be a

murderous maniac in the Bob Hope outing **They Got Me Covered** (43). He played a customer of grocer Wallace Beery in **Rationing** (44) and the proprietor of a small art gallery in **The Thin Man Goes Home.** In **State Fair** (45) he was a standout as a judge for the food awards at the fair, getting progressively drunker as he keeps tasting the liquor-spiked mincemeat, and **Colonel Effingham's Raid** cast him as a doctor again. The following year he supported Deanna Durbin and Jane Withers in a couple of forgettable films.

The actor's last screen appearance was in support of James Stewart in **Magic Town** (47). By the time it was released Donald Meek had died at age 66, in the fall of 1946. He was unique, he was inimitable, and his is one of the most instantly recognizable faces to appear on the screen in Hollywood's Golden Era.

THE FILMS OF DONALD MEEK

1923: Six Cylinder Love.
1929: The Hole in the Wall.
1930: The Love Kiss.
1931: The Girl Habit; Personal Maid.
1932: *Credit uncertain:* Wayward.
1933: College Coach; Love, Honor and Oh, Baby!
1934: The Merry Widow; What Every Woman Knows; Hi, Nellie!; Murder at the Vanities; Romance in Manhattan; The Last Gentleman; The Mighty Barnum; The Captain Hates the Sea; Mrs. Wiggs of the Cabbage Patch; Bedside; The Defense Rests.
1935: The Whole Town's Talking; The Informer; Mark of the Vampire; Kind Lady; Barbary Coast; Captain Blood; China Seas; Peter Ibbetson; Top Hat; Biography of a Bachelor Girl; Village Tale; The Return of Peter Grimm; Old Man Rhythm; The Gilded Lily; Accent on Youth; The Bride Comes Home; Society Doctor; Baby Face Harrington; She Couldn't Take It; Happiness C.O.D.
1936: Love on the Run; Pennies from Heaven; Everybody's Old Man; And So They Were Married; One Rainy Afternoon; Three Wise Guys; Old Hutch; Three Married Men; Two in a Crowd.
1937: Maid of Salem; Parnell; The Toast of New York; Artists and Models; Double Wedding; Behind the Headlines; Make a Wish; Breakfast for Two; You're a Sweetheart; Three Legionnaires. *Credit uncertain:* The Perfect Specimen.

1938: You Can't Take It with You; The Adventures of Tom Sawyer; Little Miss Broadway; Having Wonderful Time; Hold That Coed; Goodbye Broadway; Double Danger.
1939: Stagecoach; Jesse James; Young Mr. Lincoln; Hollywood Cavalcade; The Housekeeper's Daughter; Nick Carter, Master Detective; Blondie Takes a Vacation.
1940: My Little Chickadee; Dr. Ehrlich's Magic Bullet; The Return of Frank James; Turnabout; The Man from Dakota; The Ghost Comes Home; Oh, Johnny, How You Can Love; Phantom Raiders; Sky Murder; Third Finger, Left Hand; Hullabaloo; Star Dust.
1941: A Woman's Face; Come Live with Me; The Feminine Touch; Barnacle Bill; Wild Man of Borneo; Blonde Inspiration; Rise and Shine; Babes on Broadway.
1942: Keeper of the Flame; Tortilla Flat; Seven Sweethearts; The Omaha Trail; Maisie Gets Her Man.
1943: They Got Me Covered; Lost Angel; Du Barry Was a Lady; Air Raid Wardens.
1944: Two Girls and a Sailor; Rationing; Bathing Beauty; Barbary Coast Gent; The Thin Man Goes Home; Maisie Goes to Reno.
1945: State Fair; Colonel Effingham's Raid.
1946: Because of Him; Janie Gets Married; Affairs of Geraldine.
1947: Magic Town; The Fabulous Joe (segment of The Hal Roach Comedy Carnival).

Dapper Dan, the best-dressed man:
ADOLPHE MENJOU

Suave and debonair, impeccably dressed and with an elegantly waxed mustache, Adolphe Menjou was typecast as the insouciant and cynical man of the world for several decades.

Starting as a caddish matinee idol in sophisticated drawing-room comedies of the silent era, during the Thirties he was frequently the middle-aged Lothario with whom the ingenue was temporarily infatuated, and he also was often cast as a lecherous, avuncular theatrical producer who is paying the rent for one or more young actress protégées.

Polished, sharp-spoken and supercilious, he was for years known as Hollywood's best-dressed man, a reputation he cultivated as part of his image. His screen tenure was a long one, extending nearly half a century and including films made for directors ranging from D.W. Griffith to Stanley Kubrick.

Adolph Jean Menjou (the "e" on "Adolphe" was added later) was born February 18, 1890, in Pittsburgh, the son of a French restaurateur; his mother was Irish, and reportedly closely related to author James Joyce. He attended Culver Military Academy and then trained as an engineer at Cornell University, leaving to join his father in the restaurant business. He decided that he wanted to be an actor, however, and in 1913, at age 23, began to get work as an extra in Vitagraph films made in New York City, appearing in three- and four-reelers (movies 30 to 40 minutes long). By 1916 he was working in feature-length films, and then started to get bigger parts; in **The Moth** (17) he was the villain, opposite Norma Talmadge. But his acting career was briefly interrupted by a stint of Army service in World War I, from which he emerged a captain.

Not long after the war ended he decided to try his luck in Hollywood, and immediately began getting important roles in major productions. In **The Sheik** (21) he was Rudolph Valentino's friend and confidant, a French doctor, and he played Louis XIII (according to one source) or Cardinal Richelieu (another source) in the Douglas Fairbanks starrer **The Three Musketeers. The Faith Healer** cast him as a cynical doctor who sneers at hero Milton Sills, and he was a suave, unsavory blackmailer in **Through the Back Door.** He killed his father in a robbery attempt in **Courage,** and played a nobleman in **Queenie.** In the action-packed **The Fast Mail** (22) he was the villain, losing a fistfight to hero Buck

Jones, and in **Clarence,** as a scheming private secretary, he was prevented from eloping with May McAvoy. **The Eternal Flame** found him co-starring with Norma Talmadge as her nobleman husband, and in **Head over Heels,** as a theatrical agent, he hired Mabel Normand. He was a law student in **Is Matrimony a Failure?** and made a losing play for Bebe Daniels in **Singed Wings.**

Menjou's big breakthrough, at age 33, came in director/producer Charlie Chaplin's **A Woman of Paris** (23), as the wealthy, sympathetic seducer of the heroine (Edna Purviance). The film was a box-office failure but a critical success, and it made him a star—for the rest of the silent era, at least. He was Pola Negri's husband in **Bella Donna,** getting himself convicted of murder and conveniently out of her way. In **The World's Applause,** while married to Kathlyn Williams, he again unsuccessfully made advances to Miss Daniels, who preferred Lewis Stone.

The actor was now a big name on the screen, and

174

he starred or co-starred in 10 films in 1924. He won critical plaudits in director Ernst Lubitsch's smash-hit social comedy **The Marriage Circle,** about the tangled flirtations of two married couples (he was married to Marie Prevost, and the other pair were Florence Vidor and Monte Blue). In Lubitsch's **Forbidden Paradise,** starring Miss Negri, he was the chancellor quelling a Ruritanian revolution, and in **Broadway After Dark** he played a wealthy man about town rejecting flirtatious Anna Q. Nilsson for working girl Norma Shearer, a young ingenue whose first major role this was. He was a roué adept at sympathizing with neglected wives in **The Fast Set,** and in **For Sale** he played a jaded millionaire willing to save the heroine's father from financial ruin if she will marry him. He was the philandering husband of Leatrice Joy in **The Marriage Cheat,** and also had roving eyes in **Open All Night.** He threatened to expose Miss Negri's unsavory past unless she yielded to him in **Shadows of Paris,** and in **Sinners in Silk** he was outstanding as an aging ladies' man who gets rejuvenation surgery (from Jean Hersholt) and goes in for some lechery.

Menjou played an eastern European prince with an eye for the women in **The Swan** (25), and was "Serge IV, King of Molvania," in **The King on Main Street,** falling for Bessie Love while visiting the United States but forced to give her up. He still had a weakness for the ladies in **A Kiss in the Dark,** and played a compulsive gambler marrying Greta Nissen to win a bet in **Lost—a Wife.** The mustachioed actor had always looked older than his real age, and in **Are Parents People?** was distressed to find himself, at 35, playing the father of Betty Bronson, who was then 18. (Florence Vidor was his wife.)

He scored a notable success in **The Grand Duchess and the Waiter** (26), as a millionaire turfman winning an impoverished duchess (Miss Vidor) only after posing as a waiter; he stirred up peals of laughter by simply raising his eyebrows. His leading lady in **A Social Celebrity** was Louise Brooks; he was a small-town barber and she was the manicurist who leaves to become a showgirl, but eventually returns to him. In D.W. Griffith's **The Sorrows of Satan,** a contemporary version of the Faust legend, he played the Devil disguised as a suave and worldly nobleman, corrupting a young writer (Ricardo Cortez) by leading him into the fleshpots of society with the help of a vamp. Oddly enough, he was not in the title role of **The Ace of Cads,** but played a victim of same.

The actor was in top form in **Service for Ladies** (27) as a Parisian headwaiter courting an American heiress, and in **Serenade** he was a Viennese composer temporarily being unfaithful to his wife. Once

again he had "a weakness for women" in **A Gentleman of Paris** and, apparently unable to remain far from that city for long, cut capers there with Louise Brooks after wife Virginia Valli left him (temporarily) in **Evening Clothes,** an ideal title for a Menjou film. In **Blonde or Brunette** he was—surprise!—a Parisian, involved with two women. He was a suave *boulevardier* romancing an American woman in **His Private Life** (28), and there are no prizes for guessing the city where the action took place. Likewise with **His Tiger Lady,** in which he was a Folies Bergere stagehand in love with a duchess. In **A Night of Mystery** he played a French army officer who tries to confess to a murder done by someone else.

It was now 1929, and talkies took over the screen. Menjou was making an impressive $8,500 a week, but many stars were falling by the wayside; would he come through? Some movie moguls doubted it. In **Fashions in Love** (29) he was a temperamental musician who nearly gets involved in wife-swapping; to cover his screen options, he sang and played the piano. The reaction? Said one critic, "His wonderful command of gesture and emotion are more than ever admirable, as is his ability to express a wealth of meaning in the smallest movement." He also starred in **Marquis Preferred** as a nobleman whose creditors organize him into a corporation and marry him off to a wealthy woman.

But he promptly found himself in a supporting role in director Josef von Sternberg's **Morocco** (30), playing (at age 40) "the older man" who loses Marlene Dietrich to Gary Cooper. And for a brief time he did foreign-language versions of movies first filmed in English.

Menjou married writer Katherine Tinsley in 1919, and they were divorced in 1927, the same year he married actress Kathryn Carver, his co-star in several of his late silent films. In 1933 they were divorced, and the following year he married actress Verree Teasdale, by whom he had a child, Peter. Miss Teasdale played glamorous and sometimes bitchy blondes in a number of Thirties films.

The actor won his only Oscar nomination—as best actor—when he starred in **The Front Page** (31), giving a masterly performance as the editor in the part that Cary Grant would play in the remake. In **The Easiest Way** he was a rich man paying the rent for Constance Bennett, but she loves Robert Montgomery. He was brilliant as a temperamental, philandering opera star in **The Great Lover;** protégée Irene Dunne (a newcomer in her fourth film) finally realizes she doesn't love him. In **Friends and Lovers** he and young Laurence Olivier were British military men contending for the affections of Lili Damita after her husband (Erich von Stroheim) has been shot to death. He was still the suave seducer in **Men Call It Love,** and he lost Grace Moore to Lawrence Tibbett in **New Moon.**

He was a standout in **A Farewell to Arms** (32) as Gary Cooper's friend, Major Rinaldi, and equally good in director Frank Capra's **Forbidden** as Barbara Stanwyck's lover. In **Prestige,** when Ann Harding discovers that husband Melvyn Douglas is an alcoholic, she becomes susceptible to the wooing of his commanding officer, Menjou. He was excellent in comedy as the troubled fiancé of a young woman who runs around on him in **Bachelor's Affairs;** he finally discovers that his loyal secretary has long been secretly in love with him. In a different kind of role, he played New York Police Commissioner Thatcher Colt, who likes operating as a detective, in **Night Club Lady** (and would play him again the following year in **The Circus Queen Murder**). He was the obvious choice for the stage producer who has a brief affair with young Katharine Hepburn in **Morning Glory** (33), and was the best thing about **Convention City,** as a worldly-wise salesman just as good at selling himself as his product. (The New York Times said he "stands out like a diamond in a 10-cent-store jewelry counter.") In **The Worst Woman in Paris?** he was a wealthy, jaded sophisticate who loses his fortune but manages to retain the woman he loves.

Menjou was the racetrack bookie reformed by Shirley Temple in **Little Miss Marker** (34). In **The Mighty Barnum,** which had Wallace Beery in the title role, he was his partner. In **Journal of a Crime** he was unfaithful to wife Ruth Chatterton with that quintessential "Other Woman" Claire Dodd, and he was at it again in **Easy to Love,** running around with Mary Astor behind wife Genevieve Tobin's back. In a bizarre concoction called **The Trumpet Blows** he and George Raft were brothers, with Menjou playing a Mexican Robin Hood in tight pants and Raft portraying a bullfighter. He was a fading matinee idol (and not for the last time) in **The Great Flirtation,** and in **The Human Side** played a bankrupt producer trying to get his ex-wife to marry money but eventually reconciling with her.

Gold Diggers of 1935 (35) cast him as a maniacal Russian impresario constantly exclaiming, "Leave everything to Nikoleff!", and he was Dick Powell's singing teacher in **Broadway Gondolier.** In **Sing, Baby, Sing** (36) his new persona was appropriate for his casting as a broken-down, alcoholic matinee idol (clearly a takeoff on the real life of John Barrymore), involved for a time with Alice Faye; here he was in brilliant comic form. He played the manager of comic

prizefighter Harold Lloyd in **The Milky Way,** and also of skater Sonja Henie in **One in a Million** (her screen debut).

The term "casting couch" might well have been invented for some of the theatrical producers the actor played in the Thirties. In **Stage Door** (37) his protégées included Katharine Hepburn, Ginger Rogers and Gail Patrick. He was a film producer in the classic first version of **A Star Is Born,** but this time no protégées were visible. He played Deanna Durbin's widowed father in her second film, **One Hundred Men and a Girl,** and was a nightclub owner in **Cafe Metropole.** He was a producer (again) in **The Goldwyn Follies** (38), and a fading matinee idol (again) in **Letter of Introduction,** doing another John Barrymore takeoff. He and Jack Oakie were hot-shot advertising men in **Thanks for Everything.**

Menjou played the manager of prizefighter/violinist William Holden (a screen newcomer) in **Golden Boy** (39), with Barbara Stanwyck also starring, and in **King of the Turf** he was a drunken derelict befriended by a stable-boy who turns out to be, you guessed it, his son; the derelict then rises to become a racing magnate. He was (ho hum) a producer in **That's Right—You're Wrong,** and in **The Housekeeper's Daughter** played an ace newspaper reporter. In the forgotten 1940 remake of **A Bill of Divorcement** he was fine in John Barrymore's old role as the demented father, with Fay Bainter and Maureen O'Hara in the parts originally played by Billie Burke and Katharine Hepburn. Film fans must have been surprised that year to read that the actor had turned 50; he had seemed to be at least that age on screen for quite some time.

He gave a mediocre performance (unusual for him) in **Father Takes a Wife** (41), as a widower falling in love with a famous actress (Gloria Swanson, in her last film before **Sunset Boulevard** nine years later). He got back into form with one of his greatest performances, in the comedy **Roxie Hart** (42), as the frenetic shyster lawyer defending accused murderer Ginger Rogers and coaching her every courtroom move. As an Argentine hotel tycoon, he schemed to marry off daughter Rita Hayworth in **You Were Never Lovelier;** she ends up with Fred Astaire, who was not his choice. And he was top-billed as Bonita Granville's architect father in **Syncopation.** He played the harassed editor of the raffish Police Gazette in **Sweet Rosie O'Grady** (43), and starred in the screwball comedy **Hi Diddle Diddle,** as the husband of Pola Negri, his co-star of a generation earlier.

Menjou supported Frank Sinatra in **Step Lively** (44), and had an absurd role as a weird magician called Kismet in **Man Alive** (45). But during much of this period he also made broadcasts in five languages for the Office of War Information. In **Heartbeat** (46), as an ambassador, he hires pickpocket Ginger Rogers to steal someone's watch, and in **The Bachelor's Daughters** he was an unmarried department-store floorwalker who pretends to be the father of four of his salesgirls (Ann Dvorak, Jane Wyatt, Claire Trevor, Gail Russell) in an effort to find them rich husbands. He supported Clark Gable in **The Hucksters** (47), had the title role in **Mr. District Attorney,** and played a meat packer in a Deanna Durbin outing, **I'll Be Yours.**

In 1948 the actor published his autobiography, "It Took Nine Tailors." (Director Robert Florey at one time penned a biography of him, in French.) He appeared in the powerful political drama **State of the Union** (48), directed by Frank Capra, in which, as an experienced political wheeler-dealer, he worked to get Spencer Tracy (and wife Katharine Hepburn) into the White House. The *real* political drama, however, was unfolding off-screen during the making of the film, with Menjou leading the parade of right-wingers testifying before the witch-hunting House Committee on Un-American Activities (HUAC) in Washington.

A deep-dyed reactionary who loathed Franklin D. Roosevelt (among others), he was Hollywood's most prominent supporter of HUAC during these investigations into alleged Communist subversion in the film industry (Tracy and Miss Hepburn were among its most prominent foes). Menjou pointed a finger; he named names; he was an informer. Director Capra has called him "a super-patriot who invested his American dollars in Canadian bonds," adding that he "had a manic thing about Communists. 'Scratch do-gooders like Hepburn,' he used to mutter, 'and they'll yell Pravda!' " Much of the film colony turned against the veteran actor; he was shunned by old colleagues. (After his death director George Cukor called him "the late, unlamented Adolphe Menjou," and Edward G. Robinson was to say of him, "I had no

wish to live near Menjou. He never forgave King John for signing the Magna Carta.")

He continued to make films, though. He supported Doris Day in **My Dream Is Yours** (49), and played a movie producer again in **Dancing in the Dark.** As he turned 60, he supported Clark Gable and Barbara Stanwyck in **To Please a Lady** (50), and was excellent as a demented old fur trapper in **Across the Wide Missouri** (51), with Gable again. He was a detective trying to track down **The Sniper** (52). He must have appreciated the incredible irony of being cast as a Czech Communist official in **Man on a Tightrope** (53), for he gave a fine performance as he investigated circus owner Fredric March, who was secretly trying to move his show out of the country and defect to the West.

The actor also went into television during these latter years, appearing as the host of "My Favorite Story," and became heavily involved in Republican politics. But screen appearances continued. He was in a cheap Republic programmer, **Timberjack** (55), and played a senator married to Myrna Loy in **The Ambassador's Daughter** (56); Miss Loy, one of Hollywood's most dedicated liberals, must have had mixed feelings about the casting. He also had Charles Coburn's old part as a department-store owner in **Bundle of Joy,** a remake of **Bachelor Mother.**

Menjou had one last good role as a corrupt French army general in director Stanley Kubrick's fine anti-war drama **Paths of Glory** (57), starring Kirk Douglas. He was advertising man George Gobel's boss in the appallingly bad I **Married a Woman** (58), and closed out his film career supporting Hayley Mills in **Pollyanna** (60).

He died in 1963 at age 73, after 47 years as a movie actor and some 138 feature-length films. Let's charitably pull the curtain on his political views and remember Adolphe Menjou as the best of all caddish and cynical Lotharios, as that debonair man of the world, and above all as that actor for whom evening clothes seemed to have been created—the best-dressed man ever to grace the silver screen.

THE FILMS OF ADOLPHE MENJOU

NOTE: Only feature-length films are listed, so his films of less than feature length during the period 1913-16 are omitted.
Additionally, despite a credit by some sources for the 1932 film **The Man from Yesterday,** he apparently was not in it.

1916: The Habit of Happiness; Manhattan Madness; The Blue Envelope; The Kiss; A Parisian Romance; Romeo and Juliet; The Price of Happiness; The Crucial Test; The Reward of Patience.
1917: The Amazons; The Valentine Girl; The Moth.

1921: The Sheik; The Three Musketeers; Courage; The Faith Healer; Queenie; Through the Back Door.
1922: Clarence; The Eternal Flame; The Fast Mail; Head over Heels; Pink Gods; Is Matrimony a Failure?; Singed Wings; Arabian Love.
1923: A Woman of Paris; Bella Donna; Rupert of Hentzau; The Spanish Dancer; The World's Applause.
1924: The Marriage Circle; Forbidden Paradise; Broadway After Dark; Broken Barriers; The Fast Set; For Sale; The Marriage Cheat; Open All Night; Shadows of Paris; Sinners in Silk.

1925: Are Parents People?; The King on Main Street; A Kiss in the Dark; The Swan; Lost—a Wife.

1926: The Grand Duchess and the Waiter; The Sorrows of Satan; A Social Celebrity; The Ace of Cads; Fascinating Youth.

1927: Service for Ladies; Serenade; A Gentleman of Paris; Evening Clothes; Blonde or Brunette.

1928: His Private Life; His Tiger Lady; A Night of Mystery.

1929: Fashions in Love; Marquis Preferred. *Credit uncertain:* The Bachelor Girl.

1930: Morocco; Mon Gosse de Père (also filmed English-language version, title uncertain); L'Enigmatique Monsieur Parkes (French version of Slightly Scarlet, which he did not film in English); Amor Audaz (Spanish version of Slightly Scarlet).

1931: The Front Page; The Easiest Way; The Great Lover; Friends and Lovers; Men Call It Love; New Moon; Soyons Gais (French version of Let Us Be Gay, which he did not film in English).

1932: A Farewell to Arms; Forbidden; Prestige; Bachelor's Affairs; Night Club Lady; Diamond Cut Diamond (Blame the Woman).

1933: Morning Glory; Convention City; The Circus Queen Murder; The Worst Woman in Paris?

1934: Little Miss Marker; The Mighty Barnum; Journal of a Crime; Easy to Love; The Trumpet Blows; The Great Flirtation; The Human Side.

1935: Gold Diggers of 1935; Broadway Gondolier.

1936: Sing, Baby, Sing; The Milky Way; One in a Million; Wives Never Know.

1937: Stage Door; A Star Is Born; One Hundred Men and a Girl; Cafe Metropole.

1938: The Goldwyn Follies; Letter of Introduction; Thanks for Everything.

1939: Golden Boy; King of the Turf; The Housekeeper's Daughter; That's Right—You're Wrong.

1940: A Bill of Divorcement; Turnabout.

1941: Father Takes a Wife; Road Show.

1942: Roxie Hart; You Were Never Lovelier; Syncopation.

1943: Sweet Rosie O'Grady; Hi Diddle Diddle.

1944: Step Lively.

1945: Man Alive.

1946: Heartbeat; The Bachelor's Daughters.

1947: The Hucksters; Mr. District Attorney; I'll Be Yours.

1948: State of the Union.

1949: My Dream Is Yours; Dancing in the Dark.

1950: To Please a Lady.

1951: Across the Wide Missouri; The Tall Target.

1952: The Sniper.

1953: Man on a Tightrope.

1955: Timberjack.

1956: The Ambassador's Daughter; Bundle of Joy.

1957: Paths of Glory; The Fuzzy Pink Nightgown.

1958: I Married a Woman.

1960: Pollyanna.

Every heroine needs a wisecracking friend:
UNA MERKEL

In many a film of the Thirties the female star played what amounted to straight woman to a character actress cast as her best friend or sidekick, who provided comedy relief. And perhaps the best of these comic sidekicks was Una Merkel.

As the friend of Jean Harlow, Carole Lombard, Ruby Keeler, Janet Gaynor, Myrna Loy or Eleanor Powell, among others, she was always ready with a nifty retort, delivered deadpan in a slight Southern drawl. To her female friends she dispensed caustic or sensible advice; to a variety of suitors she conveyed sharp, no-nonsense opinions.

Pretty and pixyish, with reddish-gold hair and dimpled cheeks, in films of the Thirties she typically played a character who might have been called Tootsie or Trixie. After the war she turned up as a sassy spinster, maiden aunt or mother, and with even more polished acting skills that ultimately brought her an Oscar nomination in a strong dramatic role. But you remember her best dishing up the wisecracks.

Miss Merkel was born December 10, 1903, in Covington, Kentucky, the daughter of a traveling salesman. She worked as a magazine model, posing for photos that illustrated true-confession-type stories in such magazines as True Story, and also attended dramatic school. She began to get small stage roles, such as the cigarette girl in the Broadway production **Montmartre.** While it is true that at some point she was hired by pioneer director D.W. Griffith as Lillian Gish's stand-in (because a film executive noticed a resemblance), she said it was not true that that occurred as early as 1920 (when she was 16) or that she had a part in Griffith's **Way Down East** that year. Rather, the stand-in work seems to have begun about 1923, and she did work as an extra in Griffith's **The White Rose** (starring Mae Marsh) that year.

She then played the ingenue lead in an obscure small-budget film, **The Fifth Horseman** (24). Following this, a twist of fate prevented her from making screen history; it was nearly Una Merkel's voice, rather than Al Jolson's, that was the first one to be heard on the screen. She was hired in 1924 by Dr. Lee De Forest, the inventor, to star in what was planned to be the first talkie, a two-reel (20-minute) short entitled **Love's Old Sweet Song.** De Forest's soundtrack was directly on the film, eliminating any need for separate sound equipment. According to the actress, the film was completed but the inventor "lost

the rights" to it, and it apparently has never been released. Audiences had to wait until 1927's **The Jazz Singer** to hear a voice on the screen.

She returned to Broadway and spent a busy six years there, including a two-year run with Helen Hayes in **Coquette.** As the sound era began, she came to Hollywood at age 26, where her first job was once again with D.W. Griffith, whose career was just about over. She co-starred with Walter Huston in the veteran director's **Abraham Lincoln** (30), playing the ill-fated Ann Rutledge, the future president's sweetheart who died young. She received good reviews, but the romantic scenes were panned as being cloyingly reminiscent of the most saccharine silent films. She then co-starred as a simple mountain girl in **The Eyes of the World,** from Harold Bell Wright's novel, and played the nervous heroine of **The Bat Whispers,** from a Mary Roberts Rinehart play; Chester Morris co-starred.

Miss Merkel proved herself adept at scatterbrained comedy in **Private Lives** (31), as Robert Montgomery's whiny, boring and very temporary second wife before he returns to Norma Shearer in this version of Noel Coward's play. She was perfect as the secretary in the original version of **The Maltese Falcon** (Ricardo Cortez was Sam Spade), and played Janet Gaynor's best friend (her first "friend" role) in **Daddy Long Legs.** She flirted with Spencer Tracy in his third film, **Six Cylinder Love,** and was good in a supporting role as a servant turned artist's model in **The Bargain.** She provided comic relief again in the Jeanette MacDonald starrer **Don't Bet on Women,** and co-starred in **Command Performance** as a princess in this Graustarkian romance, also starring as the heroine in **The Secret Witness,** a murder mystery.

The actress played the best friend of girl-on-the-make Jean Harlow in **Red Headed Woman** (32), and as a husband-hunting working girl in **They Call It Sin** her comedic talent got her better notices than the ingenue star, Loretta Young. She was the hat-check girl in whom Leo Carrillo is interested in **Men Are Such Fools,** and was courted by Andy Devine in **The Impatient Maiden.** She played Joan Bennett's friend, a newspaper reporter, in **She Wanted a Millionaire,** and in **Man Wanted** she was engaged to David Manners, but he fell in love with Kay Francis instead. At this point in time she was almost invariably billed third on cast lists.

She was one of the more caustic chorus girls in **42nd Street** (33), and was good as Miss Harlow's uppity secretary in **Bombshell.** She and Miss Young were on the wrong side of the law as members of a robbery gang in **Midnight Mary,** and she was one of three beauty-salon employees in **Beauty for Sale.** She was the heroine of **Whistling in the Dark,** menaced by Edward Arnold as the heavy, and played Lee Tracy's girlfriend in **Clear All Wires** and Richard Dix' maid in **Day of Reckoning.** She was lawyer Otto Kruger's secretary in **The Women in His Life,** and her films that year also included **Reunion in Vienna.**

Supporting Jeanette MacDonald again, she was the Queen in **The Merry Widow** (34), vouching for the virility of Maurice Chevalier, and was Myrna Loy's best friend in **Evelyn Prentice** (which also marked Rosalind Russell's screen debut). She played an American expatriate commercial artist wooed by newspaperman Kruger in **Paris Interlude,** and was teamed with comedian Charles Butterworth in support of Ronald Colman and Miss Young in **Bulldog Drummond Strikes Back.** She was Harold Lloyd's girlfriend in **The Cat's Paw,** and played politician Edward Everett Horton's fiancée in **Biography of a**

Bachelor Girl, irked when he falls in love with Ann Harding (who isn't interested). She was romanced by Charlie Ruggles in **Murder in the Private Car,** and was a beautician wooed by Stuart Erwin in **Have a Heart.**

Miss Merkel was Eleanor Powell's comedic sidekick in **Broadway Melody of 1936** (35), and played Jean Harlow's sister in **Riffraff.** Of the latter film a reviewer said, "[Miss Merkel] is making herself more valuable to the screen. She is intelligent, adaptable, and has a lively sense of humor." She co-starred with Butterworth in **Baby Face Harrington,** and was Jack Benny's wife in **It's in the Air.** She was a ballerina loved by Butterworth in **The Night Is Young,** but she turns from him to make an unsuccessful play for Ramon Novarro. In **One New York Night** she was more successful, as a hotel telephone operator who wins wealthy Franchot Tone. She was once again Miss Powell's friend in the musical **Born to Dance** (36)—this time joining her, James Stewart and three others in a song-and-dance number—and also supported Stewart in **Speed,** in which he was an auto test driver and she was an executive who loves him but loses him to Wendy Barrie. In **We Went to College** she was Hugh Herbert's philandering wife.

She sparkled as Carole Lombard's best friend in **True Confession** (37), and was Frank Morgan's mistress ("I've been around the block") in **Saratoga,** the last film of Jean Harlow. She played a sympathetic ranch owner helping Jane Withers in **Checkers,** was Guy Kibbee's wife in **Don't Tell the Wife,** and was Wallace Beery's maid in **The Good Old Soak.** Then she was off the screen for a year.

Miss Merkel married aircraft designer Ronald Burla in 1932. They divorced in 1946, and she never remarried.

The actress, playing Mischa Auer's wife, had her famous knock-down-drag-out saloon brawl with Marlene Dietrich in **Destry Rides Again** (39), and at age 35 still looked youthful enough to play a student nurse, one of the **Four Girls in White;** she ends up with Buddy Ebsen. She was Lionel Barrymore's loyal housekeeper in **On Borrowed Time.** She played W.C. Fields' daughter in **The Bank Dick** (40), and in **Sandy Gets Her Man** she was Baby Sandy's mother, with Jack Carson and Stuart Erwin vying for her affections. She played a hillbilly in **Comin' 'Round the Mountain.** There was another best-friend role as she and Dorothy Lamour went on **The Road to Zanzibar** (41) with Bob Hope and Bing Crosby, and she co-starred in two weak programmers, one with Erwin and one with Edmund Lowe.

She supported Joan Bennett (and was Mischa Auer's wife again) in **Twin Beds** (42), and was one of the people trapped on a desert island with **The Mad Doctor of Market Street** (Lionel Atwill). Her only 1943 film was the all-star musical **This Is the Army,** and she was in a Monogram cheapie in 1944. Then she vanished from the screen for three years, returning in **It's a Joke, Son** (47). She played publisher Hume Cronyn's flip-tongued secretary in the Van Johnson-June Allyson starrer **The Bride Goes Wild** (48). Now in her mid-forties, she was William Bendix' wife in **Kill the Umpire** (50), and she started moving farther down cast lists in forgettable pictures. She reprised her old **Merry Widow** role in the 1952 remake, and had a cameo as a nun in **With a Song in My Heart.**

Another two-year absence from filming ended when she appeared in **The Kentuckian** (55), and she worked for a while on the Broadway stage again, winning a Tony award for her role in the Eudora Welty play **The Ponder Heart** in 1956 and co-starring in the musical **Take Me Along.** That year she was back on screen in **Bundle of Joy,** and was involved in a 20-year fence-sitting romance with Arthur Hunnicutt in **The Kettles in the Ozarks.** She was in the last film ever made by RKO, **The Girl Most Likely** (58), and was Paul Douglas' wife and Debbie Reynolds' mother in **The Mating Game** (59).

Miss Merkel's fine work on stage in **The Ponder Heart** led to her casting as the embittered, emotionally disturbed mother of Geraldine Page in Tennessee Williams' play **Summer and Smoke** on Broadway, and both she and Miss Page were asked to repeat their roles in the 1961 film. This outstanding performance gained her an Oscar nomination as best supporting actress, but it did not lead to better roles. She was also in **The Parent Trap** that year, and in **Summer Magic** in 1963; both films starred Hayley Mills. Now in her sixties, she had a role in **the Tiger Walks** (64), and made her last screen appearance supporting Elvis Presley in **Spinout** (67).

The actress later did some more stage work, and for some time expressed a desire to film again, but that never occurred. In 1974 she was reported to be living with her father near the beach in Los Angeles; since she was 70 at the time, he was probably in his nineties. In 1976 she told an interviewer that she would like more acting jobs, but presumably she did not get them. Una Merkel died in 1986 at age 82, but film fans can still enjoy watching her on the screen, for TV showings and revival houses continue to offer films featuring her pert and sassy personality and her knowing way with a neat retort. She was a lot of fun.

THE FILMS OF UNA MERKEL

1923: The White Rose (as an extra).
1924: The Fifth Horseman.
1930: Abraham Lincoln; The Eyes of the World; The Bat Whispers.
1931: Private Lives; The Maltese Falcon; Daddy Long Legs; Six Cylinder Love; The Bargain; Don't Bet on Women; Wicked; The Secret Witness; Command Performance.
1932: Red Headed Woman; Men Are Such Fools; The Impatient Maiden; She Wanted a Millionaire; They Call It Sin; Man Wanted; Huddle.
1933: 42nd Street; Bombshell; Reunion in Vienna; Clear All Wires; Midnight Mary; Broadway to Hollywood; Beauty for Sale; Whistling in the Dark; Day of Reckoning; Her First Mate; The Secret of Madame Blanche; The Women in His Life.
1934: The Merry Widow; Evelyn Prentice; Murder in the Private Car; Biography of a Bachelor Girl; Paris Interlude; Bulldog Drummond Strikes Back; Have a Heart; This Side of Heaven; The Cat's Paw.
1935: Broadway Melody of 1936; Riffraff; Murder in the Fleet; The Night Is Young; One New York Night; Baby Face Harrington; It's in the Air.
1936: Born to Dance; Speed; We Went to College.
1937: True Confession; Saratoga; Checkers; Don't Tell the Wife; The Good Old Soak.
1939: Destry Rides Again; On Borrowed Time; Four Girls in White; Some Like It Hot.
1940: The Bank Dick; Comin' 'Round the Mountain; Sandy Gets Her Man.
1941: The Road to Zanzibar; Double Date; Cracked Nuts.
1942: Twin Beds; The Mad Doctor of Market Street.
1943: This Is the Army.
1944: Sweethearts of the U.S.A.
1947: It's a Joke, Son.
1948: The Bride Goes Wild; The Man from Texas.
1950: My Blue Heaven; Emergency Wedding; Kill the Umpire.
1951: Rich, Young and Pretty; Golden Girl; A Millionaire for Christy.
1952: The Merry Widow; With a Song in My Heart.
1953: I Love Melvin.
1955: The Kentuckian.
1956: Bundle of Joy; The Kettles in the Ozarks.
1957: The Girl Most Likely; The Fuzzy Pink Nightgown.
1959: The Mating Game.
1961: Summer and Smoke; The Parent Trap.
1963: Summer Magic.
1964: A Tiger Walks.
1967: Spinout.

You name it, he could play it:
THOMAS MITCHELL

No character actor in Hollywood's history was more versatile than Thomas Mitchell, a performer whose range was virtually unlimited. It is difficult to think of a character role he could not have played. He could be humane or evil, tragic or comic. His great talent allowed him to give substance, credibility and power to any portrayal.

He was in fact a character star, and one of the screen's best actors. His performances were deeply thought and always highly enjoyable. And although he did not turn to screen acting until middle age and made only 58 films, his is one of the most instantly recognizable faces in movie history.

Stubby, curly-haired and fleshy-faced, with small, staring eyes, he frequently drew on his own heritage to play Irishmen, and he also often portrayed alcoholics (one such role won him an Oscar). He played several memorable death scenes, too. And in his heyday his appearances were usually in major productions; a list of his films in the period 1936-46 reads like a catalogue of Hollywood's top films of the era. Truly, he was one of the greatest of character actors.

Mitchell was born July 11, 1892 (one source says 1895), in Elizabeth, New Jersey, and originally set out to be a journalist, starting as a reporter with the Elizabeth Daily Journal. He later wrote a number of plays, some of which were successfully produced on stage; several were adapted to the screen. **Little Accident,** which he wrote with Floyd Dell, was filmed in 1930 and 1939, and again in 1943 as **Casanova Brown;** he also collaborated on the screenplay of the 1934 film **All of Me.**

But he soon turned to acting, and seems to have worked on the stage beginning about 1918, the year he appeared with John Barrymore on Broadway in **Redemption.** He starred in J.M. Synge's Irish classic **The Playboy of the Western World** in 1921. There was a one-shot screen appearance in **Six Cylinder Love** (23), which also marked the movie debuts of Donald Meek and Berton Churchill, but otherwise he kept busy on stage for many years. In 1930, at age 38, he replaced Spencer Tracy in the starring role of Killer Mears in **The Last Mile** on Broadway. Given his acting skill, it is unlikely that he had no offers from Hollywood; more likely is that he had them and turned them down. Not until 1936, when he was 44 years old, did he finally turn to screen acting for good.

The actor's first appearance in talkies (other than a 1934 short, **Cloudy with Showers**) was in the Rosalind Russell starrer **Craig's Wife** (36), as an acquaintance of her husband's who murders his philandering young wife and then commits suicide (all this happens off-screen). In **Theodora Goes Wild** he was good as the small-town newspaper editor who is the only defender of Irene Dunne's racy novel, and he was also a newspaper editor (whose ace crime reporter is Joel McCrea) in **Adventure in Manhattan.**

His roles kept getting better. He was a fugitive from justice in director Frank Capra's classic **Lost Horizon** (37), and won his first Oscar nomination as best supporting actor in director John Ford's **The Hurricane** as the alcoholic physician Dr. Kersaint, who narrates the film in flashback. (He lost the Oscar to Joseph Schildkraut in **The Life of Emile Zola.**) **In Make Way for Tomorrow** he played the eldest son of senior citizens Beulah Bondi and Victor Moore, and he co-starred as a villainous politician in **Man of** the People. He then appeared in **I Promise to Pay,** helping Chester Morris testify against loan sharks, and played singer Grace Moore's publicist in **When You're in Love.** He was the chief of detectives sending Fredric March to track down murder suspect Joan Bennett in **Trade Winds** (38), and played Wayne Morris' father, losing his wife after he philanders, in **Love, Honor and Behave.**

Several character actors have experienced an *annus mirabilis*, but surely none to the extent that Mitchell did in 1939. The highlight of these highlights was his Academy Award as best supporting actor (it would be his final nomination) for the whiskey-soaked physician Doc Boone in John Ford's Western classic **Stagecoach,** swiping liquor salesman Donald Meek's samples, delivering a baby, and advising John Wayne and Claire Trevor to find happiness together. He was also excellent as Scarlett O'Hara's (Vivien Leigh's) father in **Gone With the Wind,** sinking into drunken fantasies after the war has left the family impoverished. And he was a standout in director Howard Hawks' **Only Angels Have Wings,** delivering a death scene that has become something of a classic. He was the alcoholic reporter who loves Jean Arthur (but she loves James Stewart) in director Capra's memorable **Mr. Smith Goes to Washington,** and topped off the year by playing Clopin, "king of the beggars," in **The Hunchback of Notre Dame.**

The actor was now in the top rank of Hollywood character players, and his future was set. He was William Holden's father (and Fay Bainter's husband) in **Our Town** (40), and was a standout as one of the merchant seamen in John Ford's **The Long Voyage Home.** He played the paterfamilias of the castaway family in **The Swiss Family Robinson,** and was a retired Irish cop, the father of Priscilla Lane, disliking son-in-law Dennis Morgan, in **Three Cheers for the Irish.** In **Angels over Broadway** he was fine as an alcoholic playwright, delivering some of the most flamboyant lines of writer/co-director Ben Hecht.

Out of the Fog (41) cast him and John Qualen as fishermen whose money is taken by protection racketeer John Garfield, who incidentally is trying to seduce Mitchell's daughter, Ida Lupino; the fishermen plan to murder Garfield, but he conveniently falls overboard from their boat, saving them the trouble. Mitchell also starred (and was excellent) in **Flight from Destiny** as an elderly college professor who learns he has just six months to live; wishing to do one worthwhile deed, he reunites two former pupils (Geraldine Fitzgerald and Jeffrey Lynn) and makes a conscious decision to murder ruthless Mona Maris, who has been having an affair with Lynn.

He played a derelict acquaintance of Jean Gabin in **Moontide** (42), a treacherous parasite who turns into a rapacious blackmailer and threatens the seaman's happiness with Miss Lupino but is killed accidentally by Gabin. In the opening episode of the multi-story **Tales of Manhattan** he was Rita Hayworth's jealous husband, shooting her lover, Charles Boyer (but not fatally). He was a piratical pal of Tyrone Power in **The Black Swan,** and also played Power's friend in **This Above All.** He was an Irish planter in Hawaii (and Betty Grable's father) in **Song of the Islands,** and a French priest in **Joan of Paris.**

As the tough old noncom in the title role of **The Immortal Sergeant** (43) he delivered another potent death scene, inspiring soldier Henry Fonda to fight on in the African desert. He was Sheriff Pat Garrett in Howard Hughes' bizarre **The Outlaw,** falling afoul of Billy the Kid (Jack Buetel), Doc Holliday (Walter Huston), and of course Jane Russell. In another multi-episode film, **Flesh and Fantasy,** he was a palm reader who predicts Edward G. Robinson will commit murder; Robinson strangles Mitchell to make the prediction come true. In **Bataan** he played a Jewish corporal.

The actor was Gregory Peck's doctor friend in **The Keys of the Kingdom** (44), and played Woodrow Wilson's secretary, Joseph Tumulty, in **Wilson** (Alexander Knox had the title role). He turned villainous again in **Dark Waters,** joining with Fay Bainter, John Qualen and Elisha Cook Jr. in an attempt to drive heiress Merle Oberon insane. He was circus promoter Ned Buntline in **Buffalo Bill,** and played the father of **The Sullivans,** five young sailors who gave their lives in World War II.

Mitchell was Clark Gable's lovable, eccentric sailor pal in **Adventure** (45), once again having a memorable death scene. He supported Fred MacMurray in **Captain Eddie,** and played a prison warden whose son is one of the inmates in **Within These Walls.** He had a key role in Frank Capra's classic drama **It's a Wonderful Life** (46), as James Stewart's Uncle Billy, mislaying a crucial money deposit, which malevolent banker Lionel Barrymore scoops up. In **The Dark Mirror,** as the baffled police lieutenant, he gave a performance judged by some to be better than that of the star, Olivia de Havilland, and in the tearjerker **Three Wise Fools** he and Margaret O'Brien caused the dampening of many a handkerchief. He was Van Johnson's uncle in **High Barbaree** (47), but in **The Romance of Rosy Ridge,** as the father of Janet Leigh (in her screen debut), he kept a wary eye on suitor Johnson. In that year he also starred on Broadway in **An Inspector Calls.**

He was excellent as Errol Flynn's alcoholic, Shakespeare-quoting lawyer in **Silver River** (48), and played an honest politician corrupted by the Devil (Ray Milland) in **Alias Nick Beal** (49). In **The Big Wheel,** as a race-car driver, he is killed in an accident on the track, leaving son Mickey Rooney to follow in his footsteps. His film appearances now declined sharply, and in 1950 he made none at all. He was in **Journey into Light** (51), and was second-billed as the judge in the classic Western **High Noon** (52), starring Gary Cooper.

Although sources do not give the dates, the actor was married twice, to Anne Brewer (with a child, Anne) and Rachel Hartzell. Both marriages ended in divorce.

Now in his sixties, Mitchell supported Audie Murphy in **Destry** (54) and Charlton Heston in **Secret of the Incas.** He was the tough managing editor in **While the City Sleeps** (56), and was in a programmer, **Handle With Care** (58). He also worked in television, appearing in the series "Mayor of the Town," "O. Henry Playhouse" and "Glencannon." In 1961 he made his last two films; Frank Capra's **Pocketful of Miracles** cast him as the alcoholic judge who poses as derelict Bette Davis' husband, and, playing an embezzler, he supported Lana Turner in the soap opera **By Love Possessed.**

Thomas Mitchell died at 70 in 1962. He left a legacy of brilliant and versatile screen acting, a gallery of unforgettable portrayals that few performers have ever matched. He was one of the giants of his profession.

THE FILMS OF THOMAS MITCHELL

1923: Six Cylinder Love.
1936: Craig's Wife; Theodora Goes Wild; Adventure in Manhattan.
1937: Lost Horizon; The Hurricane; Make Way for Tomorrow; When You're in Love; Man of the People; I Promise to Pay.
1938: Trade Winds; Love, Honor and Behave.
1939: Stagecoach; Gone With the Wind; Only Angels Have Wings; Mr. Smith Goes to Washington; The Hunchback of Notre Dame.
1940: Our Town; The Long Voyage Home; The Swiss Family Robinson; Angels over Broadway; Three Cheers for the Irish.
1941: Out of the Fog; Flight from Destiny.
1942: Tales of Manhattan; The Black Swan; Moontide; This Above All; Joan of Paris; Song of the Islands.
1943: The Immortal Sergeant; The Outlaw; Flesh and Fantasy; Bataan.

1944: The Keys of the Kingdom; Wilson; Dark Waters; Buffalo Bill; The Sullivans.
1945: Adventure; Captain Eddie; Within These Walls.
1946: It's a Wonderful Life; The Dark Mirror; Three Wise Fools.
1947: High Barbaree; The Romance of Rosy Ridge.
1948: Silver River.
1949: Alias Nick Beal; The Big Wheel.
1951: Journey into Light.
1952: High Noon.
1954: Destry; Secret of the Incas.
1956: While the City Sleeps.
1958: Handle with Care.
1961: Pocketful of Miracles; By Love Possessed.

The beloved rogue:
FRANK MORGAN

Few character actors in screen history were better loved by audiences than Frank Morgan. He perfected a characterization of an endearingly befuddled, absent-minded, roguish and sometimes eccentric middle-aged man, and at the peak of his career these performances were more or less unvarying. He got so good at it that for years he shamelessly stole scenes—and sometimes entire films—from under the nose of many a major star.

A longtime (1933-49) member of the MGM stock company, and Lionel Barrymore's rival as that studio's top character player (although its *busiest* one was Reginald Owen), he had a robust laugh, an air of perpetual surprise and a unique cracked voice. Film historian David Shipman has noted, "His neigh of astonishment ['We-e-e-ell!'] is one of the soundtrack's enduring memories."

Often cast as the dithering family fool, he occasionally played strong dramatic roles (especially in the early Thirties, and also a few times in the early Forties), and was twice nominated for Oscars, once as best actor. Square-faced, stocky, mustachioed and crusty-looking, he was one of the most instantly recognizable performers ever to appear on the screen.

Morgan was born as Francis Wuppermann on June 1, 1890 (some sources say July 1), in New York City, one of 11 children of the prosperous manufacturer of Angostura Bitters, a cocktail ingredient that is still on the market today. He started out as a professionally successful boy soprano, studied for a while at Cornell University (where Adolphe Menjou was a classmate), sold real estate, sold toothbrushes door to door, sold advertising for a Boston newspaper, and worked as a cowboy and as a stoker on a tramp steamer. His MGM studio biography says he then worked up a stage sketch and was performing it in vaudeville when he was offered the juvenile lead in **Mr. Wu** on Broadway in 1914 (following in the footsteps of his elder brother Ralph [see next chapter]). But a biographical note in Who's Who in the Theatre in 1933 said he studied at the American Academy of Dramatic Art and made his Broadway debut in **A Woman Killed with Kindness** and later was in stock, playing leads, based in Northampton, Massachusetts.

In any case, the Vitagraph film studio signed him to a contract in 1916, when he was 26, and he began playing leads in its productions filmed in New York. When the star Anita Stewart lost her usual leading

man, Earle Williams, Morgan stepped into his shoes and partnered Miss Stewart in his first film, **The Suspect** (16), and others. He made eight films in 1917 and four more in the period 1918-19, but then returned to the stage. His Broadway appearances included top roles in **Rock-a-Bye Baby** with Louise Dresser in 1918, **Seventh Heaven** in 1922, **The Lullaby** in 1923, **The Firebrand** with Joseph Schildkraut in 1924, **Gentlemen Prefer Blondes** in 1926, and **Rosalie** with Marilyn Miller in 1928.

Meanwhile, he worked intermittently in films. He was the financial adviser cheating Bert Lytell in **Born Rich** (24), and played the proprietor of a fashion salon, giving a job to Gloria Swanson, in **Manhandled. In The Man Who Found Himself** (25) he was a crooked banker, trying to hang a bum rap on Thomas Meighan and ending up killed by a bank watchman; his brother Ralph was also in it. **Scarlet Saint** cast him as a baron in love with Mary Astor but giving her up, and he supported Bebe Daniels in

The Crowded Hour. In **Love's Greatest Mistake** (27) he was a financier whom William Powell tries unsuccessfully to blackmail over some love letters.

Morgan married Alma Muller in 1914. They had two children, one of whom was a son, Tom, but sources do not give further details, except to say the marriage was a long and happy one.

On Broadway he starred in **Topaze** in 1930, in the role later played on screen by John Barrymore, and that same year Paramount starred him in a short film and then signed him to a contract. In **Laughter** (30) he was an affable, aging millionaire who marries young Follies beauty Nancy Carroll, but she leaves him to resume an old affair with Fredric March. In **Fast and Loose** Miriam Hopkins (in her screen debut) was his daughter and Carole Lombard was in love with his son. He and Charlie Ruggles were partners in a garter business in **Queen High,** also featuring flapper Ginger Rogers in her second film, and he played a comic bank robber in **Dangerous Nan** [sic] **McGrew.** Then he was off the screen for more than a year to appear with Fred and Adele Astaire on Broadway in **The Band Wagon.** He returned to settle permanently in Hollywood.

In **The Half-Naked Truth** (32) he was a theatrical impresario blackmailed by shady advertising man Lee Tracy over a compromising photo of Morgan and Lupe Velez, and, as a police inspector, he was one of many caught up in a web of intrigue in **Secrets of the French Police.** Then, in 1933, he had the busiest year of his screen career, making 10 movies that included some of his best roles. The most important was director James Whale's **The Kiss Before the Mirror,** in which he played a lawyer defending Paul Lukas, who has killed his wife, Gloria Stuart, in a jealous rage. Meanwhile, Morgan has good reason to suspect his own wife, Nancy Carroll, of infidelity, and tests her with the kiss of the title, which she appears to shrug off; now it seems that a parallel murder may take place. But Morgan insists that his wife be present in court for his summation to the jury in Lukas' trial. So powerfully does he re-enact the crime that Miss Carroll screams and faints, later coming to her senses in more ways than one. Morgan, not yet typed in comic roles, gave an extraordinarily strong dramatic performance, and walked off with the film with his powerful courtroom speech.

Also that year, the actor played Jean Harlow's disreputable father in **Bombshell,** and gave a fine performance co-starring with Alice Brady as a married vaudeville team in **Broadway to Hollywood.** In **When Ladies Meet** he was a publisher loved by one of his young authors, Myrna Loy, but married to Ann Harding; Miss Loy becomes his mistress and spurns Robert Montgomery because of her relationship with Morgan, but in the end the publisher stays with his wife. He was a standout in **Reunion in Vienna** as the enlightened Freudian psychiatrist who urges his wife (Diana Wynyard) to confront and dispel a ghost from her past in the form of her ex-lover (John Barrymore). In the Al Jolson starrer **Hallelujah, I'm a Bum** he gave an intensely moving performance as the mayor, gradually realizing how desperately in love he is. He played a wealthy shipping magnate who ends up murdered by Verree Teasdale in **Luxury Liner,** and in **The Nuisance** he was an alcoholic quack doctor who helps ambulance-chasing lawyer Lee Tracy defraud insurance companies; later, ashamed of his actions, he kills himself. In **Billion Dollar Scandal** he was a rich promoter and speculator trying to put over a shady Teapot Dome-style oil-lands deal, and he played Buddy Rogers' father in **Best of Enemies.** Thus in 1933 he was Morgan the dramatic actor, not yet typecast as a comic buffoon.

Morgan's skill was recognized not only by MGM but also elsewhere; virtually every other studio clamored for him, and he was on numerous loan-outs in 1934. He won an Academy Award nomination as *best actor* for his picture-stealing performance as the perpetually bumbling Duke of Florence in **The Affairs of Cellini;** his hot pursuit of Cellini's (Fredric March's) lovely, stupid model (Fay Wray) enables his designing duchess (Constance Bennett) to have an affair with March. But he actually gave a better performance in **There's Always Tomorrow,** as a gentle, patient family man whose wife (Lois Wilson) and children have gradually tuned him out of their lives. Then into the picture steps Binnie Barnes, who has loved him from afar for years. Robert Taylor, in his second film, played the eldest son.

Also that year, he was Barbara Stanwyck's aging husband in **A Lost Lady.** He has restored her will to live, so she plans to leave him, but now *he* loses the will to live, so she decides to stay with him. This artificial ending (not in Willa Cather's novel) was tacked on by the studio. As a comic villain, he lost Jeanette MacDonald to Ramon Novarro in **The Cat and the Fiddle,** and in **By Your Leave** played a man having a mid-life crisis and almost losing his wife (Genevieve Tobin). In **Sisters Under the Skin** he was an older married man who loses his young mistress (Elissa Landi) to bohemian composer Joseph Schildkraut, and in **Success at Any Price** he was the head of an advertising agency employing Douglas Fairbanks Jr. and Colleen Moore (in her next-to-last film); ultimately Fairbanks buys him out.

Now in his mid-forties, again supporting Miss MacDonald, he was amusing as the governor of colonial New Orleans in **Naughty Marietta** (35), with Elsa Lanchester as his suspicious wife. He stole the show from stars Margaret Sullavan and Herbert Marshall in **The Good Fairy,** as the bewildered, imperious, resentful millionaire meat packer who promises to turn whomever Miss Sullavan marries into a wealthy man. He was superbly comic as Joan Crawford's father in **I Live My Life,** and was Ann Harding's estranged husband in **Enchanted April.** He and Reginald Owen were brothers involved with Luise Rainer in her first American film, **Escapade,** and in **The Perfect Gentleman** he starred in the title role, as a British aristocrat who falls in love with a music-hall singer (England's Cicely Courtneidge).

He was a standout as William Powell's showman rival in **The Great Ziegfeld** (36), and played Robert Montgomery's friend in **Trouble for Two.** Then he virtually made screen history as the only performer ever to steal a film from Shirley Temple in her prime; it happened in **Dimples,** in which he was her grandfather, a street thief spouting flowery language. He played Montgomery's father in **Piccadilly Jim,** and was the befuddled mayor of a village invaded by pirates in **The Dancing Pirate.** He played Una Merkel's fond and foolish sugar daddy in the Clark Gable-Jean Harlow starrer **Saratoga** (37), Miss Harlow's last film, and repeated his 1928 stage role as the dithering king in **Rosalie,** married to battle-ax Edna May Oliver. He played a rather asinine suitor for Joan Crawford's hand in **The Last of Mrs. Cheyney,** but Powell and Montgomery found more favor from the lady. He was the star of **Beg, Borrow or Steal,** as an expatriate con man selling fake art objects on the French Riviera.

Morgan was an impresario again in the Jeanette MacDonald-Nelson Eddy outing **Sweethearts** (38), and was excellent as prizefighter Robert Taylor's shrewd, driving, alcoholic father in **The Crowd Roars.** In **Port of Seven Seas,** MGM's version of Marcel Pagnol's **Fanny** trilogy, he was the elderly husband of Maureen O'Sullivan (the part originally played by Raimu in the French films), and was a standout. He was top-billed in **Paradise for Three,** as a millionaire soap manufacturer contending with a breach-of-promise suit by Mary Astor and also with a bossy housekeeper, Edna May Oliver.

The capstone of the actor's career, the role for which he will eternally be remembered (but hardly his best one), came in the classic fantasy **The Wizard of Oz** (39). Not only did he play the Wizard, but he was also a cranky doorman, a Cockney cab driver and a softhearted palace guard—four Morgans for the price of one. Scraps of Morgan's dialogue still linger in the memory more than half a century later:

"I am the great and powerful Oz! Who are you?" and "Pay no attention to that man behind the curtain!" are a couple of the better ones. Also that year, he was a Broadway producer who hires singer Jeanette MacDonald in **Broadway Serenade,** and a Russian aristocrat in **Balalaika.**

He delivered several fine dramatic performances in 1940. Combining comedy and pathos, he was the cuckolded (by Joseph Schildkraut) luggage-shop owner in the James Stewart-Margaret Sullavan starrer **The Shop Around the Corner,** directed by Ernst Lubitsch. And he was excellent as the Jewish professor sent to a Nazi concentration camp in **The Mortal Storm;** Miss Sullavan was his daughter and Stewart again her co-star. He played a rascally oilfield promoter in the Clark Gable-Spencer Tracy outing **Boom Town,** and co-starred with Billie Burke in **Hullabaloo,** adding song, dance and imitations of other stars to his repertoire. He was with Miss Burke again in **The Ghost Comes Home,** and supported Fred Astaire in **Broadway Melody of 1940.**

Morgan was Lana Turner's alcoholic father, killed off early in the picture, in the Clark Gable starrer **Honky Tonk** (41), and played a kindly do-gooder in **Washington Melodrama.** In **The Vanishing Virginian** he was Spring Byington's husband and Kathryn Grayson's father, and in **Wild Man of Borneo** a super-salesman, once again with Miss Burke. Then he won another Oscar nomination, as best supporting actor, for his role as a religious, dog-loving, filthy derelict in **Tortilla Flat** (42), stealing the picture from Spencer Tracy and John Garfield. He played the small-town telegraph operator in **The Human Comedy** (43), dying at his post while messenger boy Mickey Rooney is out delivering telegrams, and had a major role as Irene Dunne's father in **the White Cliffs of Dover.** He had a fine comic cameo in **Thousands Cheer** as a lecherous doctor giving physical exams to a procession of gorgeous young ladies, and he was a Supreme Court justice on vacation who cleans up a small town's judicial corruption in **Stranger in Town.**

In his only 1944 screen appearance, the actor, now in his mid-fifties, played Anita Louise's father in the Gary Cooper starrer **Casanova Brown.** He was good as a con man in the Fred Astaire vehicle **Yolanda and the Thief** (45), and was a bearded old codger friendly to little Elizabeth Taylor in **Courage of Lassie.** He played the grandfather of Robert Young's wife, Barbara Hale, in **Lady Luck** (46), and Keenan Wynn's father (they were both ghosts) in **The Cockeyed Miracle.** Then he portrayed *himself* in an oddity called **The Great Morgan;** he was an actor producing a movie and getting things all mixed up in the cutting room. His only 1947 film was **Green Dolphin Street,** supporting Lana Turner. In **Summer Holiday** (48) he was the bachelor uncle wooing spinster Agnes Moorehead in this remake of 1935's **Ah, Wilderness** (the parts originally played by Wallace Beery and Aline MacMahon). And he was Louis XIII in the Gene Kelly version of **The Three Musketeers.**

He portrayed a habitué of the gaming tables in two 1949 films—**Any Number Can Play,** with Clark Gable, and **The Great Sinner,** with Gregory Peck. For a change of pace, he was a has-been ex-baseball player who develops James Stewart into a star pitcher in **The Stratton Story.** Then he played the right-hand man of mayor Clark Gable in **Key to the City,** and started working on **Annie Get Your Gun,** in the role of Buffalo Bill, a role he was born to play. During the filming he died at the relatively early age of 59 in the summer of 1949. Louis Calhern took over his part as Buffalo Bill, and **Key to the City,** his last film, was released in 1950 after his death. His untimely passing robbed filmgoers of what could have been many more years of enjoyable performances. But Frank Morgan's great comic and dramatic roles in 96 movies are preserved on film for posterity, so we can still see him on the screen, dithering and befuddled or in a dramatic role of pathos and power. He ranks among the immortals.

THE FILMS OF FRANK MORGAN

1916: The Suspect.
1917: The Daring of Diana; Light in the Darkness; A Modern Cinderella; The Girl Philippa; Who's Your Neighbor?; Raffles—The Amateur Cracksman; A Child of the Wild; Baby Mine.
1918: The Knife; At the Mercy of Men.
1919: Gray Towers of Mystery; The Golden Shower.
1924: Manhandled; Born Rich.
1925: The Man Who Found Himself; Scarlet Saint; The Crowded Hour.
1927: Love's Greatest Mistake.
1930: Laughter; Fast and Loose; Queen High; Dangerous Nan McGrew.
1932: The Half-Naked Truth; Secrets of the French Police.
1933: The Kiss Before the Mirror; Bombshell; When Ladies Meet; Broadway to Hollywood; Reunion in Vienna; Hallelujah, I'm a Bum; Luxury Liner; The Nuisance; Best of Enemies; The Billion Dollar Scandal.
1934: The Affairs of Cellini; There's Always Tomorrow; A Lost Lady; The Cat and the Fiddle; By Your Leave; Success at Any Price; Sisters Under the Skin.
1935: Naughty Marietta; The Good Fairy; Escapade; I Live My Life; Enchanted April; The Perfect Gentleman.

1936: The Great Ziegfeld; Trouble for Two; Dimples; Piccadilly Jim; The Dancing Pirate.
1937: Saratoga; Rosalie; The Last of Mrs. Cheyney; The Emperor's Candlesticks; Beg, Borrow or Steal.
1938: Sweethearts; The Crowd Roars; Port of Seven Seas; Paradise for Three.
1939: The Wizard of Oz; Broadway Serenade; Balalaika; Henry Goes Arizona.
1940: The Shop Around the Corner; The Mortal Storm; Boom Town; Broadway Melody of 1940; Hullabaloo; The Ghost Comes Home.
1941: Honky Tonk; Washington Melodrama; The Vanishing Virginian; Keeping Company; Wild Man of Borneo.
1942: Tortilla Flat; White Cargo.
1943: The Human Comedy; The White Cliffs of Dover; Thousands Cheer; Stranger in Town.
1944: Casanova Brown.
1945: Yolanda and the Thief; Courage of Lassie.
1946: Lady Luck; The Cockeyed Miracle; The Great Morgan.
1947: Green Dolphin Street.
1948: Summer Holiday; The Three Musketeers.
1949: Any Number Can Play; The Great Sinner; The Stratton Story.
1950: Key to the City.

Watch out for the red herring:
RALPH MORGAN

In many a low-budget mystery film of the Thirties and early Forties, the presence of Ralph Morgan's name in the cast list meant only one thing. Let film historian William K. Everson explain:

"Stalking through detective films was the urbane and smiling Ralph Morgan, the self-effacing Uriah Heep of whodunits. Detective buffs who were interested only in whodunit, and not in why or how, could safely go home early when his name appeared in the cast list, confident that he and the Hollywood typecasting system would not let them down. He would be the killer."

In other words, his seeming innocence was the red herring that was dragged across the plot early on. Him? He couldn't possibly have done it, said members of the audience. Such a nice, upstanding fellow... But then—surprise, surprise!

Frank Morgan's elder brother—whom he strongly resembled—appeared in 98 films, occasionally in character leads but usually in supporting roles—frequently small ones—that ranged from kindly gentlemen to unpleasant villains, from gentle personages to dominating types. He was what is known in the baseball world as a good utility infielder.

Morgan was born July 6, 1882 (one source says 1883), in New York City, with the name Raphael Wuppermann; he and Frank (born eight years later) were among 11 children of the manufacturer of Angostura Bitters for cocktails. A law graduate of Columbia University, he soon abandoned a legal career for the stage, although sources don't indicate when that happened or name most of the plays he appeared in. One was **The National Anthem** in 1922, in which he co-starred with Laurette Taylor; in that same year he was the male star in George Cukor's fledgling Rochester, New York, stock company, the Lyceum Players (but curiously, he never appeared in any of director Cukor's movies later on). Now in his forties, he also made two silent films. He starred for a small independent company in **Penny Philanthropist** (23), and then, in **The Man Who Found Himself** (25), he was Thomas Meighan's brother, speculating with a bank's funds; brother Frank played the villain (it was their only film together).

A key Broadway role in the Eugene O'Neill drama **Strange Interlude** in 1931 led to an offer from Hollywood, and Morgan, now 49, moved to the film capital permanently. He was far down the cast list in

Honor Among Lovers (31), and appeared in **Charlie Chan's Chance.**

Then his parts started getting much bigger. He repeated his stage role in the film version of **Strange Interlude** (32), supporting Clark Gable and Norma Shearer. He was the prissy bachelor novelist with a mother complex, loving Miss Shearer in a wistful, sexless way. After she marries Alexander Kirkland she secretly has a son by Gable, but years later she finally turns to Morgan and what will clearly be a platonic marriage. Unfortunately, the script eliminated the dramatic aspects of his role and left him playing mainly comedy relief. But he was excellent as the gentle, naive czar of Russia in **Rasputin and the Empress,** the only film to star all three Barrymores. Ethel played his wife, John was the hero, and Lionel—as usual—walked off with the film as the mad monk Rasputin.

In **Disorderly Conduct** Morgan was a powerful politician and bootlegger who causes problems for motorcycle cop Spencer Tracy, and he portrayed a Chinese in the Helen Hayes starrer **The Son-Daughter.** There were also several programmers for Fox, the studio for which he made most his films during the period 1932-34; he was a thief in **Cheaters at Play,** a millionaire who runs nightclubs for fun in **Dance Team,** and a paralyzed British officer in **The Devil's Lottery.**

Morgan was married to actress Grace Arnold; some sources give her name as Georgiana Iversen. Their only child, Claudia, became an actress under the name Claudia Morgan and appeared in many films, as well as performing on the stage and on radio.

In **The Power and the Glory** (33) (a film that was to influence Orson Welles when he made **Citizen Kane**) the actor was the narrator, Spencer Tracy's secretary and lifelong friend. He was also in two other Tracy films that year: **Shanghai Madness,** again as a Chinese, and **The Mad Game,** as a judge who won't be bribed and who sends bootlegger Tracy to prison. He had a small part as a doctor in the Will Rogers vehicle **Doctor Bull,** and played one of his earliest red herrings in **The Kennel Murder Case,** as the helpful secretary to the murdered man—one of the suspects, and of course the killer.

That same year, he was the star of **Humanity,** as a kindly old Lower East Side doctor sacrificing to put his motherless son through medical school in Europe; the son returns with a society girl who wants him to practice on Park Avenue, so the young man tends a fleeing rumrunner, Morgan takes the blame, loses his medical license and dies. In **Walls of Gold** he was involved in a loveless marriage with young Sally Eilers, and he starred as a magician in a programmer, **Trick for Trick.**

The actor played the father of the boy hero (George Breakston) in **No Greater Glory** (34), and was once again a secretary, this time to the president of the United States, in the Shirley Temple outing **Stand Up and Cheer.** He turned out to be the murderer in **Transatlantic Merry-Go-Round,** played George Arliss' faithful secretary in **The Last Gentleman,** and took Paul Lukas' **Little Women** role as Professor Bhaer in **Little Men,** made by Mascot, a small Poverty Row studio (Erin O'Brien-Moore was Jo). In **Orient Express** he played an anarchist posing as a family doctor, and he was in several other programmers that year.

In the first screen version of **Magnificent Obsession** (35) he was the mystical old stonecutter (the part played by Otto Kruger in the 1954 version) who inspires Robert Taylor by expounding the philosophy indicated in the title. He turned out to be the

murderer in the William Powell-Ginger Rogers outing **Star of Midnight,** and in a Poverty Row horror film, **Condemned to Live,** he played a gentle professor by day who at night turns into a batlike monster (actually, a vampire) terrorizing an English village. In **The Unwelcome Stranger** he was a stablehand.

Morgan was an opera impresario in **Anthony Adverse** (36), played the district attorney in **Human Cargo,** and as one of the three murder suspects in **The Ex-Mrs. Bradford** he fooled everyone by *not* being the killer. In **Muss 'Em Up** he was millionaire Alan Mowbray's eccentric brother-in-law, and in **Little Miss Nobody** the prosecuting attorney who turns out to be Jane Withers' real father. He played James Stewart's boss in **Speed,** a Civil War general on the Union side in **General Spanky,** and a gangster in **Yellowstone.** He was one of the bad guys, the Commandant of Paris, in **The Life of Emile Zola** (37), played an airplane manufacturer involved with spies in **Crack-Up,** and in **Exclusive** was a mayoral candidate who kills himself when he is revealed as an ex-convict. He was also an ex-convict in **The Man in Blue,** a crook shot by Edward Ellis in self-defense, and a city editor in **That's My Story,** a film in which his daughter Claudia played the ingenue.

Mannequin (38) cast him once again as Spencer Tracy's assistant; this time Tracy was a shipping magnate in love with Joan Crawford. In **Wives Under Suspicion** Morgan was a professor suspected of killing his actress wife (who is never seen) and is harassed by ruthless district attorney Warren William. He was an officer killed in the Spanish-American War in **Mother Carey's Chickens,** leaving widow Fay Bainter and four children who include Ruby Keeler and Anne Shirley. In **Love Is a Headache** he played a millionaire who loses Gladys George to Franchot Tone, and he was a spy in **Shadows over Shanghai** and a nasty dog-kennel owner in **Orphans of the Street.**

The actor was a villainous spymaster, with young Rita Hayworth as his Mata Hari-style agent (and mistress) in **The Lone Wolf Spy Hunt** (39), and played historical figure Stephen F. Austin in **Man of Conquest,** about the early days of Texas. He joined Bobby Breen, the boy soprano, in a song in **Way Down South,** and was an Army general in **Geronimo.** He played a millionaire murdered by Reginald Owen in **Fast and Loose.** In the Eddie Cantor vehicle **Forty Little Mothers** (40) he was a sympathetic judge, and he was a movie producer in **I'm Still Alive.** In **The Mad Doctor** (41) he played a physician, but not the mad one—that was Basil Rathbone. He was a U.S. senator in **Adventure in Washington,** and portrayed the villain in the serial **Dick Tracy vs. Crime, Inc.** There was another good red-herring plot in **Night Monster** (42), in which he was a wealthy wheelchair-bound cripple who turns out to be the murderer, and in the serial **Gang Busters** he was the villain, Prof. Mortis (hmmm...wonder what his first name was?). In that year he also co-starred on Broadway in **The Moon Is Down.**

As he turned 60, Morgan played the mayor of the ill-fated town of Lidice, Czechoslovakia, in **Hitler's Madman** (43). He had the title role in the Poverty Row horror film **The Monster Maker** (44), as a doctor creating monsters with his "secretly invented glandular injections." But in the serial **The Great Alaskan Mystery** he was the heroine's upstanding father. At this point many of the actor's film appearances were in cheap Poverty Row programmers. He had the lead role in **Black Market Babies** (45) as an alcoholic, unwilling obstetrician. This was meager fare indeed for the man who had been one of the founders of the Screen Actors Guild and served for a time as its president.

Off the screen for a year, he returned in **Song of the Thin Man** (47) as a murder suspect who was not in fact the killer. He played the villain in the Gene Autry outing **The Last Roundup.** He had a small part as a doctor in the Claudette Colbert starrer **Sleep, My Love** (48), and in **The Creeper** he was a scientist trying to stop a mad colleague from continuing his serum experiments (involving changing humans into cats), and getting killed for his efforts. Now all his remaining films were made on Poverty Row. In **Heart of the Rockies** (51), a Roy Rogers outing, he tried to sabotage the building of a road across his land because he was afraid people would find out how he acquired it. In his last film, **Gold Fever** (52), he was an aging gold prospector grubstaked by a young man to work a secret mine—but then crooks take it over.

Ralph Morgan died in 1956 at age 74. He had had one brief moment, in 1932, when he not only had important dramatic parts but was also married on screen to Ethel Barrymore and loved by Norma Shearer. But he quickly found his niche as Hollywood's finest red herring. As he glided in a smooth and self-effacing manner through the plot of many a murder mystery, audiences quickly got the message: *Don't trust this man.*

THE FILMS OF RALPH MORGAN

1923: Penny Philanthropist.
1925: The Man Who Found Himself.
1931: Honor Among Lovers; Charlie Chan's Chance.
1932: Strange Interlude; Rasputin and the Empress; Disorderly Conduct; The Son-Daughter; The Devil's Lottery; Dance Team; Cheaters at Play.
1933: The Power and the Glory; Shanghai Madness; Doctor Bull; The Kennel Murder Case; Humanity; The Mad Game; Walls of Gold; Trick for Trick.
1934: No Greater Glory; Stand Up and Cheer; Transatlantic Merry-Go-Round; Their Big Moment; The Last Gentleman; Hell in the Heavens; Orient Express; She Was a Lady; Little Men; Girl of the Limberlost.
1935: Magnificent Obsession; Star of Midnight; Calm Yourself; I've Been Around; The Unwelcome Stranger; Condemned to Live.
1936: Anthony Adverse; The Ex-Mrs. Bradford; Human Cargo; Muss 'Em Up; Little Miss Nobody; Speed; General Spanky; Yellowstone.
1937: The Life of Emile Zola; Wells Fargo; Crack-Up; Exclusive; The Man in Blue; The Outer Gate; That's My Story.
1938: Mannequin; Wives Under Suspicion; Out West with the Hardys; Mother Carey's Chickens; Love Is a Headache; Army Girl; Orphans of the Street; Barefoot Boy; Shadows over Shanghai.
1939: Fast and Loose; Way Down South; Geronimo; The Lone Wolf Spy Hunt; Man of Conquest; Trapped in the Sky; Smuggled Cargo.
1940: Forty Little Mothers; I'm Still Alive.
1941: The Mad Doctor; Adventure in Washington; Dick Tracy vs. Crime, Inc. (serial).
1942: Night Monster; A Close Call for Ellery Queen; The Traitor Within; Klondike Fury; Gang Busters (serial).
1943: Hitler's Madman; Jack London; Stage Door Canteen.
1944: Weird Woman; The Impostor; The Monster Maker; Enemy of Women; Trocadero; The Great Alaskan Mystery (serial).
1945: This Love of Ours; Black Market Babies; The Monster and the Ape; Hollywood and Vine.
1947: Song of the Thin Man; Mr. District Attorney; The Last Roundup.
1948: Sleep, My Love; The Creeper; Sword of the Avenger.
1950: Blue Grass of Kentucky.
1951: Heart of the Rockies.
1952: Gold Fever.

Pompous and stuffy:
ALAN MOWBRAY

He was imperious, pompous and elegant. And since such a personage could not be taken seriously, Alan Mowbray spent most of his considerable film career in comedy roles, such as a butler, a stuffy ambassador, an ultra-snob, an aloof headwaiter or an eccentric English nobleman.

Tall, suave and robust, he started his Hollywood career in a more serious vein, portraying famous historical characters or dignified and austere professional men such as doctors and lawyers. But before long he found his true forte in parts that drew laughter from the audience.

Mowbray was born August 18, 1893 (some sources say 1896), in London. Little seems to be known about his younger days, but he acted on the English stage after World War I, and in 1923 arrived in the United States after working his way across on a ship. He spent his first few months in New York sleeping in Central Park, using the Harvard Club to wash and shave and the Automat for free meals of tomato soup—made from ketchup and hot water. But before long he got acting work touring with the Theater Guild. He appeared in many stage plays in the Twenties, and shortly after the advent of the sound era was called to Hollywood.

He was ideally cast as George Washington in the George Arliss starrer **Alexander Hamilton** (31), a role for which he won critical praise. In **Guilty Hands** he was the notorious roué murdered by Lionel Barrymore to save the latter's daughter (Madge Evans) from marrying him, and he played the swordsman lover of temptress Bebe Daniels in **Honor of the Family.**

The following year, 1932, saw the actor cast in 13 films—his busiest year on the screen. He had a comic cameo as Washington in **The Phantom President,** played a physician in **The Man from Yesterday,** and was excellent as a Russian duke, with Miriam Hopkins as his mistress, in **The World and the Flesh.** In **Nice Women** he was a millionaire whom the ingenue is persuaded to marry by her avaricious mother, and he was a detective in **Jewel Robbery.** He played a police official in **Sherlock Holmes,** a notorious spy killed by Karen Morley in **Man About Town,** and had parts in half a dozen other films.

He played the villain in another George Arliss outing, **Voltaire (33),** and was the comic Major-Domo in the Eddie Cantor vehicle **Roman Scandals. In Our**

Betters he had a key role as the nobleman who marries hardware heiress Constance Bennett, but is only interested in her money and has no intention of giving up his mistress. He played Inspector Lestrade in the Sherlock Holmes film **A Study in Scarlet,** was a jewel thief in **Midnight Club,** and had four other roles that year. Typically, at this point in time, he would be billed sixth or seventh on a cast list.

Mowbray was Prince Metternich in yet another Arliss starrer, **The House of Rothschild** (34), and in **One More River** played barrister "Very Young" Roger Forsyte, hired by Diana Wynyard to defend the divorce suit brought by Colin Clive. He was cast as a German matinee idol in **Little Man, What Now?,** and was a nightclub owner in **Long Lost Father,** employing John Barrymore and his daughter, Helen Chandler. In **Where Sinners Meet** he and Billie Burke started to elope, but he was talked out of it by Clive Brook and fled. He was revealed as a spy in **Charlie Chan in London,** and played a reclusive millionaire whose jewels are stolen in **Cheaters.**

Now in his early forties, he was the snobbish Rawdon Crawley, loved by Miriam Hopkins, in **Becky Sharp** (35), and was another British nobleman in **The Gay Deception.** He was an egotistical movie star, the regular co-star of Ginger Rogers, in **In Person,** and he starred in **Night Life of the Gods** as a scientist who dreams he can turn statues into humans and vice versa. He ended up marrying Alice Brady in **Lady Tubbs,** and in **She Couldn't Take It** he was a pompous actor whose engagement to Joan Bennett was canceled by George Raft.

The actor was married to Lorraine Carpenter. They had two children—one of whom, Patricia, at age 28 would marry the 69-year-old character actor Douglass Dumbrille, a friend of her father's.

Mowbray played a society man about town in the classic screwball comedy **My Man Godfrey** (36) (some sources erroneously state that his role was that of a butler). He was one of the Scottish lords in **Mary of Scotland,** and in **Desire** he played a French psychiatrist duped by jewel thief Marlene Dietrich. He had a cameo as the prime minister of Quebec in the operetta **Rose Marie,** was comical as a conceited magician employing Janet Gaynor as a stooge in **Ladies in Love,** and was snobbish to boy soprano Bobby Breen in **Rainbow on the River.** He played a millionaire who is revealed as a murderer in **Muss 'Em Up,** an Italian tenor who is hooted off the stage in **Give Us This Night,** and a murder victim in **Fatal Lady.** In **The Case Against Mrs. Ames** he played Madeleine Carroll's lawyer, defending her on a charge of murdering her husband; then it comes out that the lawyer is actually the killer.

He was excellent as the sardonic butler in **Topper** (37), employed by Roland Young and Billie Burke and ending the film with his acid delivery of the line "Bless our happy home." In **Hollywood Hotel** he was an actor who can't sing and hires Dick Powell as his musical voice-double; if you've seen **Singin' in the Rain** you know the rest of the plot. **Stand-In** cast him as an unscrupulous, temperamental film director, and **Music for Madame** as a distinguished but eccentric orchestra conductor. In **Vogues of 1938** Joan Bennett (once again) backed out of marriage with him, and so he founded a fashion-design house to compete with her new employer, Warner Baxter. He lost Madeleine Carroll to Dick Powell in **On the Avenue,** and played a flamboyant magician in **On Such a Night.**

He was Billie Burke's butler again in the screwball comedy **Merrily We Live** (38), and also in **Topper Takes a Trip.** He played Patsy Kelly's boyfriend,

a correspondence-school chiropractor, in **There Goes My Heart.** Now his film roles started on a slow nosedive in importance and quality. He was a New Orleans innkeeper in another Bobby Breen vehicle, **Way Down South** (39), lost Martha Raye to Bob Hope in **Never Say Die,** and joined forces with Gale Sondergaard (playing his wife) in an attempt to defraud the ingenue in a "B" Western, **The Llano Kid.** He was a lecherous newspaper publisher chasing Rita Hayworth in **Music in My Heart** (40), and an unethical Broadway producer out to exploit playwright Rosalind Russell in **Curtain Call.** He and Eric Blore were tailors running a shop together in **The Boys from Syracuse,** and he played a film producer in **Scatterbrain,** a villainous lawyer in **The Villain Still Pursued Her,** and a college professor in **The Quarterback.**

Possibly the best role of Mowbray's career came in **That Hamilton Woman (Lady Hamilton)** (41), with Vivien Leigh (as his wife) cuckolding him with Laurence Olivier; his performance was masterly. He was Merle Oberon's idiotic psychiatrist in **That Uncertain Feeling,** overacted hammily as a theatrical producer in **Footlight Fever,** and was one of the potential murder suspects in **I Wake Up Screaming.** He was a foppish grand duke in the Norma Shearer starrer **We Were Dancing** (42), and played Jane Withers' father in **The Mad Martindales.** In **The Powers Girl** he was John Robert Powers, head of the famous modeling agency, and he portrayed the Devil in **The Devil With Hitler.** In **His Butler's Sister** (43) he, Akim Tamiroff, Hans Conried, Sig Arno and Frank Jenks were a quintet of comic butlers all romancing Deanna Durbin; however, the butler of the title was Pat O'Brien, and his employer was Franchot Tone, who ends up with Deanna. He played a vitamin manufacturer in **My Gal Loves Music** (44).

He again did a cameo as George Washington in **Where Do We Go From Here?** (45); four of his seven pictures that year were made on Poverty Row. But then he got his last really good role, that of the alcoholic Shakespearean ham actor in director John Ford's **My Darling Clementine** (46). He played the villainous Col. Sebastian Moran in a Sherlock Holmes entry, **Terror by Night.** The actor was a professor in **Captain from Castile** (47), and played a silent-movie director in **You're My Everything** (49). Once again he portrayed a hammy nomadic actor for John Ford, in **Wagonmaster** (50), as well as a bizarre interior decorator in **The Jackpot.**

A succession of boring programmers ensued, in which his parts grew increasingly more trivial. After a Ma and Pa Kettle vehicle in 1954 he turned to a considerable extent to television work as he entered his sixties, appearing in the series "Colonel Flack" (in the starring role), "Hey, Mulligan," "Dante" and "The Best in Mystery." Meanwhile, however, in 1956 he had one last run of good films (if not outstanding parts). He was the British ambassador to Siam in **The King and I,** supported James Stewart in **The Man Who Knew Too Much,** and played a consul in **Around the World in 80 Days.** That was his last screen work for five years. He came back in 1961 for one last film, **A Majority of One,** far down the cast list in this bizarre outing starring Rosalind Russell and Alec Guinness.

Alan Mowbray died in 1969 at age 75. But in the impressive total of 135 movies we can still see him up there on the screen—stuffy, pompous and imperious.

THE FILMS OF ALAN MOWBRAY

1931: Alexander Hamilton; The Man in Possession; God's Gift to Women; Guilty Hands; Honor of the Family; Leftover Ladies.

1932: Sherlock Holmes; The Phantom President; Lovers Courageous; Jewel Robbery; The Man from Yesterday; The World and the Flesh; The Silent Witness; Nice Women; Man About Town; Winner Take All; Two Against the World; The Man Called Back; Hotel Continental.

1933: The World Changes; Berkeley Square; Voltaire; Roman Scandals; Our Betters; A Study in Scarlet; Peg o' My Heart; Midnight Club; Her Secret.

1934: The House of Rothschild; One More River; Little Man, What Now?; Long Lost Father; The Girl from Missouri; Where Sinners Meet; Charlie Chan in London; Embarrassing Moments; Cheaters.

1935: Becky Sharp; The Gay Deception; In Person; Night Life of the Gods; Lady Tubbs; She Couldn't Take It.

1936: My Man Godfrey; Mary of Scotland; Desire; Rose Marie; Ladies in Love; Give Us This Night; The Case Against Mrs. Ames; Rainbow on the River; Muss 'Em Up; Fatal Lady.

1937: Topper; On the Avenue; Hollywood Hotel; Stand-In; Music for Madame; Vogues of 1938 (Walter Wanger's Vogues of 1938); Four Days' Wonder; As Good as Married; On Such a Night; The King and the Chorus Girl; Marry the Girl.

1938: Merrily We Live; Topper Takes a Trip; There Goes My Heart.

1939: Never Say Die; Way Down South; The Llano Kid.

1940: Music in My Heart; Curtain Call; The Boys from Syracuse; Scatterbrain; The Quarterback; The Villain Still Pursued Her.

1941: That Hamilton Woman (Lady Hamilton); I Wake Up Screaming; That Uncertain Feeling; Moon over Her Shoulder; The Cowboy and the Blonde; Footlight Fever; Ice-Capades Revue; The Perfect Snob.

1942: We Were Dancing; A Yank at Eton; Panama Hattie; So This Is Washington; The Mad Martindales; The Devil with Hitler; The Powers Girl; Yokel Boy; Isle of Missing Men.

1943: His Butler's Sister; Holy Matrimony; Slightly Dangerous; Stage Door Canteen.

1944: The Doughgirls; Ever Since Venus; My Gal Loves Music.

1945: Bring On the Girls; Where Do We Go from Here?; Men in Her Diary; Tell It to a Star; Earl Carroll's Vanities; Sunbonnet Sue; The Phantom of 42nd Street.

1946: My Darling Clementine; Terror by Night; Idea Girl.

1947: Captain from Castile; Lured; Merton of the Movies; Man About Town; The Pilgrim Lady.

1948: Every Girl Should Be Married; Don't Trust Your Husband (An Innocent Affair); The Prince of Thieves; My Dear Secretary; The Main Street Kid.

1949: You're My Everything; The Lone Wolf and His Lady; The Lovable Cheat; Abbott and Costello Meet the Killer—Boris Karloff.

1950: Wagonmaster; The Jackpot.

1951: The Lady and the Bandit; Crosswinds.

1952: Blackbeard the Pirate; Androcles and the Lion; Just Across the Street.

1954: The Steel Cage; Ma and Pa Kettle at Home.

1955: The King's Thief.

1956: The King and I; The Man Who Knew Too Much; Around the World in 80 Days.

1961: A Majority of One.

But never an Irishman:
J. CARROL NAISH

He was Hollywood's one-man United Nations.

J. Carrol Naish played Italians, Spaniards, Chinese, Japanese, Arabs, Jews, American Indians, *Indian* Indians, Russians, Greeks and Mexicans, among others. He could be amiable or villainous, comic or tragic, and his range of portrayals in some 170 films was astounding. He was seen on screen as a mobster, a shyster lawyer, a radical agitator, a snake charmer, a detective, a cowboy, an ape-man, a hunchbacked killer, a painter, a doctor, and countless other roles, plus assorted fiends in horror outings, not to mention Arsene Lupin, Sitting Bull and Leon Trotsky. And he won two Oscar nominations in the process.

But one kind of role the swarthy, black-haired actor never played: an Irishman. Which is interesting, because Joseph Patrick Carrol Naish (pronounced "Nash") was the descendant of a long line of Irish peers and the great-great-grandson of a lord chancellor of Ireland.

A master of dialect, he was frequently seen in some kind of disguise; you might not have recognized him offscreen. But, of course, with a busy shooting schedule he didn't spend much time off a movie set. In any case, he was one of the movies' greatest utility infielders.

Naish was born January 21, 1900 (some sources say 1897 or 1901), in New York City and grew up in the tough Yorkville-East Harlem section of that city. One source says he dropped out of school at age 14 to work as a song plugger, but another declares he left at 16 to join the Navy. During World War I he is said to have seen action, but in the aviation section of the Army Signal Corps. After the war he roamed about Europe, doing odd jobs and learning several languages. Returning to the United States on a tramp steamer that dropped him off on the West Coast, he appeared in a few silent films as an extra and stuntman (one of them is said to have been **What Price Glory?** in 1926, as one of the soldiers). He then headed for Broadway and signed on as an understudy with the road company of **The Shanghai Gesture,** later appearing in other stage plays.

In 1930, as the talkie era got under way, the actor was called back to Hollywood to begin an extremely busy career as a character actor, one that would continue for more than four decades. He was a plastic surgeon in **Scotland Yard** (30), a crook in **Good Intentions,** and had small parts in two other films that

year. As a small-time thug, he didn't even get a screen credit for **Ladies of the Big House** (31), or for **Tonight or Never,** but he did for **The Royal Bed.** He was a racketeer in **Homicide Squad,** and a cowpoke in **Gun Smoke.**

Then, suddenly, the face of J. Carrol Naish was seen everywhere for the next five years, during which time he appeared in the astonishing total of at least 71 movies (and possibly two more), many of them important ones—although in virtually all of them he had small, insignificant roles.

He played a hoodlum again in **Beast of the City** (32), and in **Two Seconds** he was the slimy dance-hall proprietor running around with Edward G. Robinson's two-timing wife; Robinson thereupon kills her. As if that weren't enough, he tried to make a pass at one-handed tuna fisherman Robinson's girlfriend in **Tiger Shark,** and got slashed with the hook on the other arm. His first really good role came in **The Hatchet Man,** in which everybody was Chinese;

he was "Sun Yat Sen"(!), Loretta Young's father, executed on orders from the tong by his close friend, none other than Robinson (with a hatchet, of course). In **The Conquerors** he played a radical agitator, and in **The Kid from Spain** he was a matador's sinister sidekick, pursuing Eddie Cantor's girlfriend. He was a mobster again in **The Mouthpiece,** a bootlegger in **Big City Blues,** a naval officer in **It's Tough to Be Famous,** the prosecutor in **The Famous Ferguson Case,** and a murderous gangster in **Afraid to Talk.**

He had his busiest year on the screen in 1933, appearing in 19 movies, which were churned out at a rate faster than one every three weeks; he worked for nine different studios, including four Poverty Row cheapie outfits. He played a nervous plane passenger in **Central Airport** and a prisoner of war in **Captured!** In **The Mad Game** he was a bootlegger turned kidnapper, and in **No Other Woman** he was especially good as Charles Bickford's slippery shyster lawyer, arranging to bribe witnesses to get Bickford a divorce from Irene Dunne. He played a crook in **Elmer the Great,** and was shot to death by Louis Calhern in **Frisco Jenny** for cheating in a crap game. He was a French Foreign Legionnaire who poisons his commanding officer in **The Devil's in Love,** and also appeared in several "B" Westerns, an abysmal serial, and a raft of cheap programmers.

Naish had a cameo as a Communist agitator in **The President Vanishes** (34), and portrayed a more famous Communist, Leon Trotsky, in **British Agent.** As her blackmailing ex-lover, he killed showgirl Ginger Rogers in **Upper World** and was in turn killed by Warren William (it's the only film in which Miss Rogers was ever murdered). In **Hell in the Heavens** he was a World War I pilot, in **Murder in Trinidad** a murdered diamond smuggler, and in **One Is Guilty** a murdered boxing manager. Apparently he was seen by casting directors as an ideal murder victim, for in **Return of the Terror** he was done in by Lyle Talbot. He played an underworld boss in **Girl in Danger,** and was once again an agitator in **Bachelor of Arts.** He was a gambling-ship owner who was—you guessed it—murdered in **The Defense Rests.**

The actor married actress Gladys Heaney in 1928. They had a daughter, Elaine.

He was cast as the Grand Vizier in **The Lives of a Bengal Lancer** (35), and was an Arab slave dealer in **The Crusades.** Once again he played a radical agitator in **Black Fury,** only this time a fake one, planted by a strike-breaking detective agency to stir up trouble among the coal miners led by Paul Muni. He was a French pirate in **Captain Blood,** played a racketeer again in **Little Big Shot,** and looked authentic as a gaucho in **Under the Pampas Moon** (Rita

Hayworth's first film). And in two Bette Davis crime films, **Front Page Woman** and **Special Agent,** he was a hoodlum.

In **The Charge of the Light Brigade** (36) he bore the imposing name of Subahdar Major Puran Singh, and in **Anthony Adverse** he was a French army officer. He was an American Indian in **Ramona,** a spy working for Peter Lorre in **Crack-Up,** and in **Charlie Chan at the Circus** he played the murderer, a snake charmer who kills while dressed in an ape suit. He had a key role in **Robin Hood of El Dorado,** as the murderous bandit Three-Fingered Jack, whose gang Warner Baxter joins; most of the cast is wiped out at the end in a savage massacre that anticipates **The Wild Bunch** many years later. In **Special Investigator** he was good as the brutal gang leader brought to justice by G-Man Richard Dix, and he played a convict in **We Who Are About to Die** and a member of Joseph Calleia's gang in **Exclusive Story.** Another gangster role came along in **The Return of Jimmy Valentine,** and he was a murder victim again in **The Leathernecks Have Landed,** also playing an insane opera composer shot to death by the police in **Moonlight Murder.**

As a member of a smuggling ring (a part he played several times), he tried to kill Peter Lorre in **Think Fast, Mr. Moto** (37), but was foiled by a bulletproof vest. He was a gang leader in **Border Cafe,** and also in **Hideaway**—but this time a *sympathetic* gang leader. And, for an encore, a gangster in **Night Club Scandal**—but for a change of pace, he was a fisherman in love with Margaret Lindsay but losing her to Dean Jagger in **Song of the City.** Then it was back to being an unpleasant criminal in **Bulldog Drummond Comes Back.** He was a Mexican prospector who helps orphan Gilbert Roland in **Thunder Trail,** and a fur smuggler in **Sea Racketeers.**

At this point the Paramount studio came up with a plan to build a large number of classy "B" pictures—superior programmers, but not quite top-of-the-line productions—around Naish and Akim Tamiroff (mostly in separate films), making them character stars. And for the next three years the actor primarily played the leading roles—although not always top-billed—in a string of interesting and well handled crime melodramas for that studio.

He smuggled illegal aliens in **Daughter of Shanghai** (38), and was the real star (although third-billed behind Gail Patrick and Lloyd Nolan) of **King of Alcatraz,** with the ads reading, "Meet Steve Murkil...he crashed his way out of Alcatraz!" He led a gang of hijackers in **Tip-Off Girls,** and ran an escape route for wanted criminals in **Illegal Traffic** (the ads called him "more dangerous, more menacing than ever"); in this film he was top-billed over Robert Preston. He was a racketeer again in **Hunted Men,** and a brutal guard in **Prison Farm.** In the Dorothy Lamour starrer **Her Jungle Love** he played the villainous native who hopes to feed the white men to the crocodiles. In **Bulldog Drummond in Africa** he was a murderous international spy.

In a change of pace now, Naish played the treacherous and cowardly Private Rasinoff in **Beau Geste** (39), trying to steal Gary Cooper's money belt, informing on Cooper to the cruel Sergeant Markoff (Brian Donlevy), and ultimately falling to his death from a watchtower. He and Akim Tamiroff joined forces as mobsters trying to gain control of the Chinatown rackets in **King of Chinatown.** In **Persons in Hiding** he was a brutal, stupid small-time hood who teams up with (and marries) cold-blooded, greedy beauty Patricia Morison to become the nation's most wanted criminal pair. **Undercover Doctor** cast him as the private physician for a mob of gangsters; the ads said, "A king of crime! The murder mob's most dangerous ally, and the law's most vicious enemy!" In **Island of Lost Men** he played an Oriental general who disappears, becomes a wicked exploiter of men in the jungle, and is later found by his daughter (Anna May Wong). In **Hotel Imperial** he was a World War I spy (for the Russians against the Austrians).

Queen of the Mob (40) cast him as the chief henchman for a lady gangster (Blanche Yurka), and in the Dorothy Lamour outing **Typhoon** he did a virtual replay of his part in **Her Jungle Love,** as a native plotting to destroy the visiting white men. He had a comic role in **Down Argentine Way,** was a gangster again in **A Night at Earl Carroll's,** and played an unscrupulous boxing promoter in **Golden Gloves.**

Now in his forties, he was good as the former matador, Tyrone Power's boyhood idol, now reduced to begging, in **Blood and Sand** (41); Power, the current star matador, gives him a job as his dresser. In the Bing Crosby starrer **The Birth of the Blues** he was a racketeer who uses his nightclub as a front for his criminal interests, and he had a key role in **The Corsican Brothers.** The actor played a robber in the multi-episode drama **Tales of Manhattan** (42), stuffing his $40,000 loot into a coat and making his getaway by plane, but the coat catches fire and he absent-mindedly throws it out the plane window. He was a Frenchman (and Anne Baxter's father) in **The Pied Piper,** and was good in the horror outing **Dr. Renault's Secret,** turned by George Zucco from a jungle ape into a semi-human and then killing Zucco and several other people. He was the murderer in **The**

Man in the Trunk, a gangster in **Dr. Broadway,** and an unethical painter who copies classics and sells them as originals in **Gentleman at Heart.**

Naish got his first Academy Award nomination as best supporting actor for his portrayal of the bewildered and pathetic Italian soldier taken prisoner by Humphrey Bogart and his tank crew in **Sahara** (43). In **Behind the Rising Sun** he was a Japanese publisher and diplomat, vacillating between liberal and imperialist, who forces his American-educated son (Tom Neal) to join the Japanese army, with tragic results: The son is killed in battle, and Naish commits hara-kiri. He was a remarkably shrewd detective solving the murder of Lon Chaney Jr.'s wife in **Calling Dr. Death,** and played the villain, the dastardly Dr. Daka, in the serial **Batman,** as well as appearing as a Marine officer in **Gung Ho!**

In the war drama **Dragon Seed** (44) he was the Japanese kitchen overseer, distracted by Katharine Hepburn so she can poison an entire banquet hall full of Japanese troops. **House of Frankenstein** cast him as the psychopathic hunchbacked killer, mad doctor Boris Karloff's assistant, murdered by the monster. In **Enter Arsene Lupin** he played the famed detective, and in **Waterfront** he and John Carradine were murderous Nazi agents. He was a hired killer in **The Whistler,** a man who thinks of his calling as "an art" and continually schemes up new ways to kill his "clients."

He won critical raves for his second and last Oscar-nominated performance in **A Medal for Benny** (45), as a Mexican-American *paisano* receiving a posthumous Medal of Honor for his son, who had been driven out of town as an incorrigible delinquent. But he didn't ring true as a poor Southern farmer in **The Southerner,** acting in a stingy and unfriendly manner toward neighbor Zachary Scott; it just wasn't his kind of role. In **Strange Confession** he was a drug dealer murdered by his chemist employee, Lon Chaney Jr. He played John Garfield's father in **Humoresque** (46), trying to discourage him from playing the violin, and had a key role in support of Peter Lorre in **The Beast with Five Fingers.** He was a Mexican peasant working as a police informer in **The Fugitive** (47), and played Cesar Romero's father in **Carnival in Costa Rica.**

The Ingrid Bergman starrer **Joan of Arc** (48) cast him as a nobleman from Luxembourg, and in **The Kissing Bandit** he was a former womanizing desperado whose son (Frank Sinatra) takes over his role; it was the biggest flop of Sinatra's career. The actor supported Mario Lanza in the latter's debut film, **That Midnight Kiss** (49), and was a French-Canadian trapper opposed to the building of a railroad in **Canadian Pacific.** He played Chief Sitting Bull in **Annie Get Your Gun** (50), and was Lanza's doting fisherman uncle in **The Toast of New Orleans.** In **The Black Hand** he was a turn-of-the-century Mafioso hunted down by Gene Kelly, and he portrayed General Philip Sheridan in the John Wayne Western **Rio Grande.** In **Across the Wide Missouri** (51) he gave an offbeat conception of an Indian chief.

Early in the postwar period Naish interspersed his film work with a starring role in the radio comedy series "Life with Luigi," about a harassed Italian-American, and later played the role on television. Now his screen appearances started to become fewer as his work in the broadcast media increased. He was a fisherman in the Barbara Stanwyck outing **Clash by Night** (52), but it was a very small part, and his roles in two Westerns that year were minor, as was his part as a Florida sponge fisherman in Beneath the **Twelve-Mile Reef** (53). He was the obvious choice for the title role in **Sitting Bull** (54), having played the role before, and in **Saskatchewan** he was an Indian scout aiding Alan Ladd. In **Violent Saturday** (55) he, Lee Marvin and Stephen McNally pulled off a bank robbery, and he was a gangster again in **New York Confidential.** He was the murderer in **Desert Sands,** one of a trio of Western outlaws lynched by an angry mob in **Rage at Dawn,** and played the Mexican general Santa Anna in **The Last Command,** about the battle of the Alamo.

Now in his mid-fifties, he was a Confederate patriarch, one of whose sons accidentally kills a child, in **Rebel in Town** (56), and he played a criminal saloon owner in the old West in **Yaqui Drums.** After parts in two 1957 films, his screen career virtually ended as he took on the starring role in the television series "The New Adventures of Charlie Chan." A few years later he appeared as Chief Hawkeye in the series "Guestward Ho!" In 1961 he was in another film, and did another in 1964. Seven years later occurred one of those things that fall into the category of "It seemed like a good idea at the time": Somebody decided to bring back Naish (at age 71) and an old colleague, Lon Chaney Jr., in something called **Dracula vs. Frankenstein** (alternate title: **Blood of Frankenstein**) (71). This atrocious production was the last film for both actors.

J. Carrol Naish died in 1973. He is still remembered as one of the screen's most prolific character actors, and unquestionably one of the best.

THE FILMS OF J. CARROL NAISH

NOTE: No listing is given for the silent films in which he appeared as an extra or stuntman (except for **What Price Glory?**), because reference sources do not identify them.

1926: *Credit uncertain:* What Price Glory? (as extra).
1930: Scotland Yard; Good Intentions; Cheer Up and Smile; Double Cross Roads.
1931: The Royal Bed; The Homicide Squad; Gun Smoke. *Credit uncertain:* Ladies of the Big House; Tonight or Never; Kick In.
1932: Beast of the City; Two Seconds; Tiger Shark; The Hatchet Man; The Kid from Spain; The Conquerors; The Mouthpiece; Weekend Marriage; Big City Blues; It's Tough to Be Famous; Crooner; The Famous Ferguson Case; No Living Witness; Afraid to Talk; *Credit uncertain:* Cabin in the Cotton; Washington Merry-Go-Round.
1933: Central Airport; Captured!; Frisco Jenny; The Mad Game; The Devil's in Love; Ann Vickers; The Past of Mary Holmes; No Other Woman; Elmer the Great; Infernal Machine; Arizona to Broadway; The Whirlwind; Silent Men; The Last Trail; The World Gone Mad; The Avenger; Notorious But Nice; The Big Chance; Mystery Squadron (serial).
1934: The President Vanishes; British Agent; Marie Galante; Upper World; Murder in Trinidad; One Is Guilty; The Hell Cat; Sleepers East; Return of the Terror; Bachelor of Arts; Girl in Danger; The Defense Rests; Hell in the Heavens; What's Your Racket?
1935: The Lives of a Bengal Lancer; The Crusades; Black Fury; Captain Blood; Front Page Woman; Special Agent; Under the Pampas Moon; Little Big Shot; Behind Green Lights; Confidential.
1936: The Charge of the Light Brigade; Anthony Adverse; Ramona; Crack-Up; Two in the Dark; Robin Hood of El Dorado; Special Investigator; We Who Are About to Die; Exclusive Story; The Return of Jimmy Valentine; Charlie Chan at the Circus; Moonlight Murder; Absolute Quiet; The Leathernecks Have Landed.
1937: Night Club Scandal; Think Fast, Mr. Moto; Song of the City; Border Cafe; Hideaway; Bulldog Drummond Comes Back; Thunder Trail; Sea Racketeers.
1938: Daughter of Shanghai; Her Jungle Love; King of Alcatraz; Tip-Off Girls; Illegal Traffic; Bulldog Drummond in Africa; Hunted Men; Prison Farm.
1939: Beau Geste; King of Chinatown; Persons in Hiding; Hotel Imperial; Island of Lost Men; Undercover Doctor.
1940: Typhoon; Queen of the Mob; Down Argentine Way; Golden Gloves; A Night at Earl Carroll's.
1941: Blood and Sand; The Corsican Brothers; Birth of the Blues; That Night in Rio; Accent on Love; Forced Landing; Mr. Dynamite.
1942: Tales of Manhattan; The Pied Piper; Dr. Renault's Secret; The Man in the Trunk; Dr. Broadway; Gentleman at Heart; Sunday Punch; Jackass Mail.
1943: Sahara; Behind the Rising Sun; Gung Ho!; Good Morning, Judge; Harrigan's Kid; Calling Dr. Death; Batman (serial).
1944: Dragon Seed; House of Frankenstein; Voice in the Wind; The Whistler; Mark of the Whistler; Enter Arsene Lupin; Two-Man Submarine; Jungle Woman; The Monster Maker; Waterfront.
1945: A Medal for Benny; The Southerner; Strange Confession; Getting Gertie's Garter.
1946: Humoresque; The Beast with Five Fingers; Bad Bascomb.
1947: The Fugitive; Carnival in Costa Rica.
1948: Joan of Arc; The Kissing Bandit.
1949: That Midnight Kiss; Canadian Pacific.
1950: Annie Get Your Gun; The Toast of New Orleans; Please Believe Me; The Black Hand; Rio Grande.

1951: Across the Wide Missouri; Bannerline; Mark of the Renegade.
1952: Clash by Night; The Denver and Rio Grande; Ride the Man Down; Woman of the North Country.
1953: Beneath the Twelve-Mile Reef; Fighter Attack.
1954: Sitting Bull; Saskatchewan.
1955: Violent Saturday; Hit the Deck; New York Confidential; Rage at Dawn; The Last Command; Desert Sands.
1956: Rebel in Town; Yaqui Drums.
1957: This Could Be the Night; The Young Don't Cry.
1961: Force of Impulse.
1964: The Hanged Man.
1971: Dracula vs. Frankenstein (Blood of Frankenstein).

King of the triple-take:
JACK OAKIE

In the Thirties, whenever a film had a major part for a not-overly-bright comic actor, the casting director frequently called up Jack Oakie's agent right away to see whether he was available.

The chubby, dark-haired, grimacing, fast-talking Oakie invariably played slow-witted, happy-go-lucky buffoons, often the hero's friend or someone's beaming brother. Short of stature but full of energy, he also not only mastered the startled double-take but virtually patented the *triple*-take, or, as he called it, the triple fade—and invariably found a way to fit it into each role he played.

He was born (as Lewis Delaney Offield) November 12, 1903, in Sedalia, Missouri; his mother was actress Evelyn Offield. Raised from age five in Oklahoma (he arrived there when it was still called Indian Territory), he later adopted the appellation "Okie" as his stage name, Oakie. After high school he went to New York, where he attended business school and worked as a telephone clerk for a Wall Street brokerage firm. Displaying comic talent in the company's annual benefit show, he was persuaded to turn to acting professionally, and in 1922 made his stage debut in the chorus of George M. Cohan's **Little Nellie Kelly.** Then he opened in Atlantic City in the musical **Innocent Eyes,** starring Mistinguett. For a number of years he was the partner of vaudeville star Lulu McConnell in two-a-day shows and on Broadway. There was a part as a chorus boy in the Shuberts' **Artists and Models** (with Miss McConnell) in 1925, and then he was a hoofer in Rodgers and Hart's **Peggy-Ann** in 1926.

Deciding to try his luck in Hollywood, he met director Wesley Ruggles, who got him a job at Paramount, the studio for which he made most of his films for the next nine years. His debut was in a small (in fact, uncredited) part in Ruggles' **Finders Keepers** (28), at age 25. But in **The Fleet's In** he had an important role as sailor Searchlight Doyle, momentarily distracting Clara Bow from her true love. In **Sin Town** he played a lazy ranch hand. In his first talkie, the Clara Bow-Fredric March starrer **The Wild Party** (29), he was well down the cast list, but in **Close Harmony** he and Skeets Gallagher were a harmony singing act broken up by jealousy when Nancy Carroll flirts with both of them. He starred in **Fast Company** as a small-town baseball hero who rises to the big leagues and stars in the World Series, and in

Sweetie (again with Miss Carroll) he scored a hit as a Broadway hoofer named Tap-Tap Thompson, singing a college song, "Alma Mammy." He was a jazz clarinetist in **Street Girl,** the first film ever made by the RKO studio, and played a reporter in **Chinatown Nights** (the last film of star Florence Vidor), also taking parts in **The Dummy** and **The Man I Love.**

Playing a cab driver named Voltaire McGinnis, Oakie co-starred with Jeanette MacDonald in **Let's Go Native** (30), and he starred in **The Sap from Syracuse** as a crane operator who wins a young flapper who is a wealthy heiress (screen newcomer Ginger Rogers in her third film). In the musical **Hit the Deck** he was again the star, a sailor called Bilge, but some critics said he wasn't versatile enough to meet the demands of the role. For the *second* time he was a sailor named Searchlight Doyle in **Sea Legs,** this time the lightweight boxing champion of the Navy, and winning the love of Lillian Roth. In **The Social Lion** he was a combination never heard of before or since: a prizefighter who is also a crack polo player. He played a dumb insurance salesman in **The Gang Buster** (31), getting involved with gangsters and winning Jean Arthur, and was a not-so-bright songwriter in **June Moon** and an actor posing as a Western gunman in **Dude Ranch. In Touchdown!** he was a college football hero.

Oakie's first marriage was to Ziegfeld Follies beauty Venita Varden; it ended in divorce in 1945. In the early 1950s he married comedienne Victoria Horne, who had small roles in some Forties films.

One of the actor's finest comedic turns on screen came in **Once in a Lifetime** (32). As a dim-witted newcomer trying to crash Hollywood, he tells off a studio head, who is so impressed with his honesty that he makes him a supervisor. Oakie then stars his untalented girlfriend in a film he produces by mistake from a 1910 script, shoots scenes in virtual darkness while cracking nuts (which the microphone picks up), and is fired when the producer sees the result. However, the critics see subtle artistry in this mishmash, and so he's back on top again. The comedian's on-screen stupidity generated most of the laughs in this half-forgotten classic. He was one of Gary Cooper's Marine buddies in **If I Had a Million,** and in **Million Dollar Legs** he was top-billed (over W.C. Fields) as a brush salesman who gets involved with a mythical country. He had an unexpectedly strong serious role in **Dancers in the Dark,** cast against type as a grasping bandleader who for a while has a love affair with taxi-dancer Miriam Hopkins. He was a barker for a flying circus in **Sky Bride,** a prizefighter in **Madison Square Garden,** and a gumball-machine salesman in **Uptown New York.**

He, Fredric March and Cary Grant were wartime fighter pilots in **The Eagle and the Hawk** (33), and in **Sitting Pretty** he and Jack Haley were a songwriting team hitchhiking across the country to Hollywood (he sang a current hit, "Did You Ever See a Dream Walking?"). He played a sports announcer who wants to become a crooner in **From Hell to Heaven,** a college football star in the Bing Crosby outing **College Humor,** and Tweedledum (to Roscoe Karns' Tweedledee) in **Alice in Wonderland. In Sailor Be Good** he starred once again as a Navy boxing champion, and in **Too Much Harmony** he provided what laughs there were while Crosby provided the songs. He played the stage manager in **Murder at the Vanities** (34), and he and Spencer Tracy were a pair of telephone-company troubleshooters in **Looking for Trouble.** He was a former college football hero running a department store in **College Rhythm,** and **Shoot the Works** cast him as a sideshow barker deserted by

his friends when he gambles away the rights to a song he has written.

Oakie had a good part in **Call of the Wild** (35) as Clark Gable's sidekick in the Alaska gold fields, and he made the most of it; many critics liked his cutting-up better than Gable's emoting with Loretta Young. He served up the comedy, and Alice Faye the tunes, in **King of Burlesque,** and he was a Broadway playboy who becomes dean of a girls' school in **Collegiate,** deciding that the curriculum should emphasize rhythm, not mathematics. In **The Big Broadcast of 1936** he owned the radio station. He didn't quite jell as the bandit who becomes a ranger in **The Texas Rangers** (36). He was a band guitarist in **That Girl from Paris,** danced with Joan Blondell in the last of the Dick Powell-Ruby Keeler vehicles, **Colleen,** and starred as a newspaper reporter in **Florida Special.**

In **The Toast of New York** (37) he was the partner of Cary Grant and Edward Arnold in some shady business deals circa 1870, and in **Hitting a New High** he played the ace publicity man trying to pass off opera singer Lily Pons as something unearthed in the African jungle. His comedy relief was welcome in **Champagne Waltz,** featuring yet another opera star (Gladys Swarthout); he was the owner of the jazz club where Fred MacMurray played the trumpet. In **Super-Sleuth** he was a simple-minded detective trained in Hollywood-style criminology techniques who ends up capturing arch-villain Eduardo Ciannelli, and he walked off with **Fight for Your Lady,** playing a wrestling manager. He was in top form as movie star Lucille Ball's gimmick-a-second press agent in **The Affairs of Annabel** (38), but the sequel, **Annabel Takes a Tour,** seemed to overstay its welcome. He and Adolphe Menjou were a couple of hotshot promoters for an advertising agency in **Thanks for Everything,** and he teamed with young Milton Berle as a pair of no-talent, tune-stealing songwriters in **Radio City Revels.**

Now came a crisis in the actor's career. Once a comedy star, he had been reduced to supporting roles. His career seemed to be declining, he was putting on a lot of weight, and RKO, the studio he had been working for since 1936, now felt his salary demands were excessive. He took a long trip to Europe, and on his return found he had been dropped from the studio's contract list. His telephone wasn't ringing, and he appeared in no films at all in 1939. But a somewhat improbable personage rode to the rescue: Charlie Chaplin. He cast Oakie in **The Great Dictator** (40) as dictator Benzino Napaloni of Bacteria (i.e., Benito Mussolini), as the counterpart to Chaplin's Hynkel (Hitler). Mugging and grimacing for all he was worth, Oakie picked up an Academy Award nomination as best supporting actor for this comedy performance. In **Tin Pan Alley** he and John Payne were struggling songwriters involved with Betty Grable and Alice Faye, and in **Young People** he played Shirley Temple's father. In **Little Men** he was an ingratiating thief called Willie the Fox, and once again he walked off with the picture.

He starred in **Rise and Shine** (41) as a dumb football player kidnapped by racketeers to prevent him from playing, and he played a sailor in **Navy Blues.** He teamed up again with Payne (they owned a radio station) and Miss Faye in **The Great American Broadcast,** during the course of which he recited the poem "The Shooting of Dan McGrew." There was only one film in 1942, **Song of the Islands,** with Miss Grable. In **Hello, Frisco, Hello** (43) he was the comedy relief for—would you believe Payne and Miss Faye? Then it was Sonja Henie in **Wintertime;** he was a hotel owner persuading her to invest in it. As he entered his forties, he played the owner of a Bowery night spot in **Bowery to Broadway** (44), a vaudevillian in **The Merry Monahans,** and was in two other films. **That's the Spirit** (45) cast him as a long-dead hoofer returning to Earth to help his daughter (Peggy Ryan) win a stage career, and in **On Stage, Everybody** he was her father again and they were vaudeville partners.

Oakie's career now wound down sharply, but it hardly mattered. During the Thirties he had invested heavily in land in a sparsely settled valley not far from the film capital; now, with the war over, house-hungry hordes poured into the Los Angeles area, and land values in the San Fernando Valley suddenly went through the roof; the actor soon became a mul-

timillionaire. (He had also made wise stock investments.) In 1941 he bought Barbara Stanwyck's ranch for his own home. But he made a few films. He co-starred with comedienne Joan Davis in **She Wrote the Book** (46), in which he was a book publisher's hotshot publicity man. Then he took a long vacation, returning in another Betty Grable outing, **When My Baby Smiles at Me** (48), as Dan Dailey's buddy, also appearing in a "B" Western. He had a role in the melodrama **Thieves' Highway** (49), and was in **Last of the Buccaneers** (50). He was a cowpoke in **Tomahawk** (51), and then was off the screen for five years, doing some TV guest spots and counting his money.

The actor had one of the cameo roles in **Around the World in 80 Days** (56), playing a ship's captain, and was back in Western garb for **The Wonderful Country** (59). He had a comic cameo as a bartender in **The Rat Race** (60), and concluded his screen career with the Rock Hudson-Doris Day outing **Lover Come Back** (61), as a floor-wax manufacturer who gives his account to the advertising agency most willing to supply him with women and liquor, and delivering one last hilarious comedy routine in a scene where he tears into a box of alcohol-laced candy.

He was through with filming at age 58. Now, although he was growing deaf, he enjoyed life as only a millionaire can, meanwhile doing occasional TV stints. The years rolled by without any no-longer-needed summonses from casting directors.

Jack Oakie died in 1978 at age 74. His contribution to the cinema was a long parade of laughs, much appreciated by audiences—especially in those dark days of the Depression in the early Thirties, when he was at his peak, an authentic comedy star.

THE FILMS OF JACK OAKIE

1928: Road House; The Fleet's In; Finders Keepers; Someone to Love; Sin Town.

1929: The Wild Party; Close Harmony; The Dummy; The Man I Love; Fast Company; Sweetie; Hard to Get; Street Girl; Chinatown Nights.

1930: Let's Go Native; The Sap from Syracuse; Paramount on Parade; Hit the Deck; Sea Legs; The Social Lion.

1931: June Moon; Dude Ranch; The Gang Buster; Touchdown!

1932: Once in a Lifetime; If I Had a Million; Make Me a Star; Million Dollar Legs; Dancers in the Dark; Madison Square Garden; Sky Bride; Uptown New York.

1933: The Eagle and the Hawk; Sitting Pretty; From Hell to Heaven; College Humor; Alice in Wonderland; Sailor Be Good; Too Much Harmony.

1934: Murder at the Vanities; Looking for Trouble; College Rhythm; Shoot the Works.

1935: Call of the Wild; King of Burlesque; Collegiate; The Big Broadcast of 1936.

1936: The Texas Rangers; That Girl from Paris; Colleen; Florida Special.

1937: The Toast of New York; Champagne Waltz; Fight for Your Lady; Hitting a New High; Super-Sleuth.

1938: The Affairs of Annabel; Annabel Takes a Tour; Thanks for Everything; Radio City Revels.

1940: The Great Dictator; Tin Pan Alley; Young People; Little Men.

1941: Rise and Shine; Navy Blues; The Great American Broadcast.

1942: Song of the Islands.

1943: Hello, Frisco, Hello; Wintertime; Something to Shout About.

1944: It Happened Tomorrow; Bowery to Broadway; Sweet and Low Down; The Merry Monahans.

1945: That's the Spirit; On Stage, Everybody.

1946: She Wrote the Book.

1948: When My Baby Smiles at Me; Northwest Stampede.

1949: Thieves' Highway.

1950: The Last of the Buccaneers.

1951: Tomahawk.

1956: Around the World in 80 Days.

1959: The Wonderful Country.

1960: The Rat Race.

1961: Lover Come Back.

With an ear-piercing shriek:
UNA O'CONNOR

She was a great screamer.

Confronted by Frankenstein's monster or the half-unwrapped Invisible Man, Una O'Connor would let loose with a terrified shriek that could shatter glass tumblers at 30 paces. It differed only in volume from her cries of anguish in many another famous film, and as often as not it was accompanied by loud wailing and keening. One writer has dubbed her "the queen of hysteria."

The pinch-faced, purse-lipped, frail, birdlike actress made a career of playing jittery, fussy, worrisome Irish or Cockney maidservants, ladies-in-waiting, spinsters or gossips—and sometimes a combination of these. Her huge eyes could make her look like a hunted animal—or, when she was playing a servant, could send forth icy and contemptuous glances. She made fewer films than many character performers, but she lingers in the memory.

Miss O'Connor was born (as Agnes Teresa McGlade) October 23, 1880, in Belfast, Northern Ireland (some sources say 1881 or, surprisingly, even 1893). She made her stage debut in 1911 with Dublin's famed Abbey Theatre in Bernard Shaw's **The Shewing-Up of Blanco Posnet,** a play that took her to Broadway, and also appeared in plays by J.M. Synge. Once in New York, she never acted in Ireland again, working on stage in London and on Broadway for many years. At the beginning of the movies' sound era she was in a few British films, starting at age 49: **Dark Red Roses** (29); a possible appearance in director Alfred Hitchcock's **Murder** (30), although her name doesn't appear in a published cast list; and a few others. She then returned to the stage, ultimately appearing as the Cockney maid in Noel Coward's **Cavalcade.** She was brought to Hollywood to repeat that role.

She drew many a chuckle with her mournful countenance in the film version of **Cavalcade** (33), teaming with comedian Herbert Mundin as the former servants of Clive Brook and Diana Wynyard. She had one of her best moments as the innkeeper's hysterical wife in **The Invisible Man,** confronting Claude Rains (in his screen debut) with his head half unwrapped as she shrieks, " 'E's all eaten away!", followed by a barrage of terrified screams. She also drew good notices in **Pleasure Cruise** (as a woman with a crush on Roland Young) and **Mary Stevens, M.D.,** and played an English noblewoman in **Horseplay.**

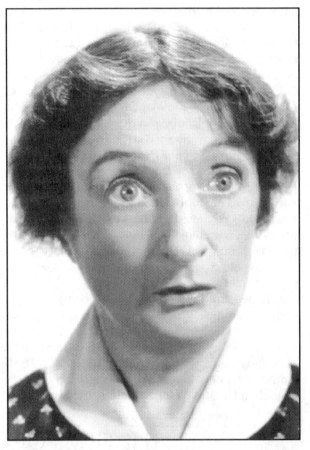

She portrayed Norma Shearer's maid in **The Barretts of Wimpole Street** (34), provoking smiles whenever she glided across the floor as if on wheels, and was a maid in the Clark Gable-Joan Crawford starrer **Chained,** also playing a servant in **Stingaree.** In **The Poor Rich** she was Thelma Todd's mother, an English aristocrat, and she was teamed with Mundin again in two more films: as a vulgar Cockney couple in **Orient Express,** and also in **All Men Are Enemies.**

The actress' best year on screen was 1935. She had a small but good dramatic role as the mother of the betrayed and murdered Wallace Ford in director John Ford's classic **The Informer,** forgiving Victor McLaglen for the crime as she kneels to pray in church. And she was unforgettable in **Bride of Frankenstein,** as the old crone, a family retainer, muttering and scuttling about. When Dr. Pretorius (Ernest Thesiger) knocks on the castle door, she cries out, "All right, don't knock the castle over; we're not all dead yet!" Later, confronted by the monster (Boris Karloff), she gives out with several of her patented shrieks. She had a nice cameo in **David Copperfield** as the pathetic old Mrs. Gummidge, teamed again with Mundin in **The Perfect Gentleman** (she played Frank Morgan's sister), and was a maid again in **Thunder in the Night.**

As the old sot in John Ford's **The Plough and the Stars** (36), Miss O'Connor was reunited with other graduates of Dublin's Abbey Theatre in support of Barbara Stanwyck in this version of Sean O'Casey's play. She played a widow in **Lloyd's of London,** was Jeanette MacDonald's maid in **Rose Marie,** played a landlady in Suzy, and was in **Little Lord Fauntleroy.** She portrayed Jean Harlow's agitated maid in **Personal Property** (37), and a charwoman in **Call It a Day.** Then it was back with Herbert Mundin for the last time in the classic **The Adventures of Robin Hood** (38); she was Olivia de Havilland's coy maid and he was Much, the Miller. She also appeared in the British film **The Return of the Frog.** In **We Are Not Alone** (39) she was the gossiping old crone who causes Paul Muni's destruction.

In the Errol Flynn epic **The Sea Hawk** (40) she was the heroine's watchful duenna, and she played Alice Faye's maid in **Lillian Russell.** Her comic timing and delivery were impeccable in portraying Ann Sheridan's mother, a boardinghouse keeper, in **It All Came True,** unwittingly aiding gangster Humphrey Bogart. In **He Stayed for Breakfast** she was Loretta Young's confused maid, swigging on a bottle of brandy. She supported Miss de Havilland and James Cagney in **The Strawberry Blonde** (41), and in **Random Harvest** (42) she had a nice cameo as a tobacco-shop proprietor, suspiciously eyeing escaped mental patient Ronald Colman. One of her best dramatic parts came in director Jean Renoir's **This Land Is Mine** (43), as the domineering (in fact, castrating) mother of Charles Laughton.

Now in her sixties, the actress (who never married) supported Laughton and Margaret O'Brien in **The Canterville Ghost** (44). Her roles were getting smaller now. She was a servant in priest Bing Crosby's rectory in **The Bells of St. Mary's** (45), and also played a domestic in **Christmas in Connecticut.** She provided a few laughs in **Cluny Brown** (46), as Richard Haydn's elderly mother, never speaking but constantly clearing her throat loudly. In **Ivy** (47) she was the fortune-teller who opens the film by predicting to wicked Joan Fontaine some of the events to follow. She virtually replayed her **Sea Hawk** role as a duenna in another Flynn film, **The Adventures of Don Juan** (48). There was a nine-year hiatus from the screen, and she came back at age 77 in 1957 for her last movie role in **Witness for the Prosecution,** as the maid of the murdered Norma Varden, whom Tyrone Power is accused of killing.

Una O'Connor died in 1959, but her shrieks of terror on the screen still ring down the corridors of time. Hers was a face—and a scream—you won't soon forget.

THE FILMS OF UNA O'CONNOR

1929: Dark Red Roses.
1930: Timbuctoo; To Oblige a Lady. *Credit uncertain:* Murder.
1933: Cavalcade; The Invisible Man; Pleasure Cruise; Mary Stevens, M.D.; Horseplay.
1934: The Barretts of Wimpole Street; Chained; Stingaree; The Poor Rich; Orient Express; All Men Are Enemies.
1935: The Informer; Bride of Frankenstein; David Copperfield; Father Brown, Detective; The Perfect Gentleman; Thunder in the Night.
1936: The Plough and the Stars; Lloyd's of London; Rose Marie; Suzy; Little Lord Fauntleroy.
1937: Personal Property; Call It a Day.
1938: The Adventures of Robin Hood; The Return of the Frog.
1939: We Are Not Alone.

1940: The Sea Hawk; Lillian Russell; It All Came True; He Stayed for Breakfast; All Women Have Secrets.
1941: The Strawberry Blonde; Kisses for Breakfast; Three Girls About Town; Her First Beau.
1942: Random Harvest; My Favorite Spy; Always in My Heart.
1943: This Land Is Mine; Forever and a Day; Holy Matrimony; Government Girl.
1944: The Canterville Ghost; My Pal Wolf.
1945: The Bells of St. Mary's; Christmas in Connecticut.
1946: Cluny Brown; Of Human Bondage; The Return of Monte Cristo; Child of Divorce; Banjo; Unexpected Guest.
1947: Ivy; The Corpse Came C.O.D.; Lost Honeymoon.
1948: The Adventures of Don Juan; Fighting Father Dunne.
1957: Witness for the Prosecution.

Darned clever, these Chinese:
WARNER OLAND

It is highly doubtful that any performer in movie history was more thoroughly identified with one character he repeatedly played than was Warner Oland with Charlie Chan.

He was only one of seven actors to portray the sagacious Chinese detective on the screen, but it's hard to remember anyone else in the part. Yet Chan was not the only Oriental he played in films; he did quite a variety of slant-eyed villains, among them Dr. Fu Manchu. His features seemed perfect for Oriental parts. And his ancestry? Why, Swedish, of course.

Oland was (although most film fans are unaware of it) a film pioneer as well, first appearing on screen at the very early date of 1909. Stocky, barrel-chested, bluff, dark and mustachioed, with menacing eyes, he was first into Oriental skulduggery in 1916 and occasionally continued to practice it even after he became Chan. But more than half of his Thirties films cast him as the aphorism-spouting Chinese sleuth (all told, he played the role sixteen times in seven years), and if you remember him, it's almost certainly as Charlie Chan.

He was born (as Johan Werner Ohlund, or Ölund) October 3, 1880, in Umea, Sweden, a coastal town in the northern part of the country. In the United States from about the age of 10, he was educated in Boston and spoke with no foreign accent whatever. As a young man he acted in plays by Ibsen and Strindberg; one source says he made his debut with Sarah Bernhardt's company. He also worked as a set designer and Strindberg translator. In 1909—still the infancy of the American film—he appeared in one movie, **The Jewels of the Madonna** (a short film, as were all U.S. films until the feature-length film arrived in 1914). In 1912 he was in **The Life of John Bunyan: Pilgrim's Progress,** in a dual role as Bunyan and Christian. (Some sources say this film was two separate movies.) At this point he had good reason to abandon the stage for the cinema: Following a season working with Alla Nazimova, he lost his savings producing his own plays at a New York theater. So in 1914 he came to Hollywood to begin a film career.

He appeared in **Sin** in 1915, supporting Theda Bara, and then was quite busy in 1916, making seven films. In the serial **Patria,** starring dancer Irene Castle, he was a villainous Japanese baron, the head of the enemy spy apparatus. He played the villain in

The Eternal Question, sporting a monocle and menacing the heroine, and worked with Miss Bara again in **Destruction.** He was the villain again in the Pearl White serial **The Fatal Ring** (17) and made several other films that year, invariably as a menace and usually as an Oriental one. He played an Eastern potentate in **The Naulahka** (18), and was in **The Yellow Ticket** and the serial **The Yellow Raider** (presumably wearing yellow makeup). He supported the popular Elsie Ferguson in **The Avalanche** (19), and was in seven movies altogether that year, including another Pearl White serial. He worked exclusively in serials in 1920 and 1921, with a total of four (one was **The Yellow Arm;** guess who it belonged to). In fact, he was the chief villain of silent serials.

In **East Is West** (22) Oland, now in his early forties, was a powerful Chinatown figure who covets Constance Talmadge (the roles played by Edward G. Robinson and Lupe Velez in the 1930 remake), and in **The Pride of Palomar** he played "a Japanese potato baron" seeking to appropriate a ranch from its rightful owner for a colonization scheme. He supported Bebe Daniels in **His Children's Children** (23), was a Chinese again in **The Fighting American** (24), and played "a sinister, half-caste Chinese mesmerist" in **Curlytop;** in the latter film he owns a floating barge-*cum*-restaurant and hires Shirley Mason to work on it as a waitress, but just as he is hypnotizing her in a locked cabin the barge collides with a schooner, and the villain (but not the heroine) sinks into the Thames. **One Night in Rome** cast him as an Italian singer, and **So This Is Marriage** as King David in the biblical sequence.

The actor played an assassinated Austrian archduke in the Douglas Fairbanks starrer **Don Q, Son of Zorro** (25) (directed by Donald Crisp), although the plot had nothing to do with the 1914 murder in Sarajevo. In **Flower of Night** he was the sinister head of a band of vigilantes in the California of Gold Rush days, infatuated with Pola Negri but killed by her lover. As a crooked lawyer run out of town in the Tom Mix vehicle **Riders of the Purple Sage,** he abducts the heroine and later manages to become a judge, but is killed by Mix in a courtroom. He played an Egyptian pasha in **Infatuation.** In **Don Juan** (26), the John Barrymore starrer that made movie history as the first film with sound effects and a musical score, he was the villainous Cesare Borgia, and he played a Chinese bandit leader in the Lon Chaney outing **Tell It to the Marines.** He was downright nasty in **Man of the Forest,** scheming to kidnap the heroine (Georgia Hale) and force his attentions on her, but ending up killed by the hero (Jack Holt), and as a theatrical producer he out-acted the stars, Francis X. Bushman and Billie Dove, in **The Marriage Clause.** As music-hall dancer Colleen Moore's manager in **Twinkletoes** he tried unsuccessfully to seduce her.

After this barrage of villainy, filmgoers must have been startled to see him as Al Jolson's father in the first part-talkie, **The Jazz Singer** (27)—an elderly Jewish cantor, rolling his eyes, beating his breast and pulling his hair in an acting style that should have gone out with buggy whips. (At the time, he was 46 to Jolson's 41.) But nastiness as practiced in the back alleys of Chinatown was once again in full sway in **Old San Francisco,** in which he played the vice lord of that city in 1906, persecuting the Chinese although he is in fact secretly Chinese himself. He abducts Dolores Costello, but is killed in the great earthquake. In **A Million Bid** Miss Costello is induced to marry him; later he is believed drowned, but turns up as an amnesia victim; ultimately he leaves the heroine to her true lover.

Also that year, he was a put-upon actor cruelly

beset by misfortune in **Good Time Charley,** but it was back to malevolence in **When a Man Loves,** in which, as Miss Costello's brother, he attempts to force her into an alliance with a lustful nobleman, but her true love, John Barrymore, ultimately wins out (as in real life; he married Miss Costello the following year). Oland was the star of **What Happened to Father,** as an absent-minded Egyptologist who, unknown to his family, writes musical comedies on the side; he changes from a henpecked husband to a dominating one. And in **Sailor Izzy Murphy** he was a millionaire French perfume merchant, saved by George Jessel from a murderous maniac.

In **Stand and Deliver** (28) the actor gave a bravura performance as a greed-crazed mountain bandit who captures Lupe Velez and Rod La Rocque, and in the now long-forgotten Joan Crawford vehicle **Dream of Love** he was a duke who usurps a kingdom and rules as a dictator, while his duchess (Aileen Pringle) plans to depose him and marry Nils Asther. He played a hated Russian Communist leader of revolutionary days in **The Scarlet Lady,** killed by his former mistress (Lya de Putti), and in **Wheel of Chance** he was the Russian immigrant father of Richard Barthelmess (who played a dual role).

Oland married actress and painter Edith Shearn, who was 10 years his senior, in 1908. She isn't listed in reference sources as having played any credited film roles. The marriage lasted until she sued for separate maintenance in 1937, the year before he died; she would outlive him by 30 years and die at age 98. Offscreen, the actor had mansions in Santa Barbara, Beverly Hills and Boston, plus a 7,000-acre Mexican island where he raised cattle and cocoanuts. Widely read, especially in philosophy, he was a devotee of classical music, a painter like his wife, and an art connoisseur.

As talkies came in, Hollywood's best-known player of Oriental roles was the natural choice for the starring role as Sax Rohmer's satanic master criminal in **The Mysterious Dr. Fu Manchu** (29). The heroine, under his hypnotic spell, was young Jean Arthur, but ultimately the doctor's nefarious plans are foiled and he apparently commits suicide. The film was a big success, and the actor was now virtually a star. In **Chinatown Nights** he was Wallace Beery's rival in a tong war, named Boston Charley. Playing a film director, he was revealed as the killer of one of his actors, Fredric March, in **The Studio Murder Mystery.** In **The Mighty** he was a mobster who employs George Bancroft as a gunman, and he had the title role in **The Faker** as a phony spiritualist.

He starred in **The Return of Dr. Fu Manchu**

(30), in which Miss Arthur and most of the other featured players from the previous film repeated their roles. No, he hadn't really killed himself, just went into a cataleptic trance, and now he swears revenge on the English families responsible for the earlier death of his wife and son, but he is killed (it says here) in a gunfight. In **Dangerous Paradise,** the first screen version of Conrad's novel "Victory," he played the lecherous hotel owner Schomberg, pursuing Nancy Carroll but killed off by the three desperadoes (his role was taken by Sig Rumann in the 1940 remake). He played the grand marshal of France in the Jeanette MacDonald operetta **The Vagabond King,** secretly in league with the Burgundians against the king and plotting his murder and that of the heroine as well. In the all-star revue **Paramount on Parade** he had a comic cameo as Fu Manchu.

His last outing as the Oriental arch-criminal came in **Daughter of the Dragon** (31), with Anna May Wong in the title role; it was full of secret panels and passages and had a thrilling last-minute rescue by Scotland Yard. But now came the most significant piece of casting in the screen career of Warner Oland. Instead of an Oriental villain, his next role was an Oriental *nice* guy—a detective named Charlie Chan.

Chan, the creation of writer Earl Derr Biggers, had already been played on the screen by three other actors, to no great effect. Oland changed all that. Thanks to his acting skill, the series of what were basically formula "B" detective films became extremely popular with fans (so much so, in fact, that they're still shown on late-night television some 60 years later). Chan was a Honolulu detective of Chinese ancestry who had a large family and a penchant for continually spouting wise and witty aphorisms that sounded like they might have originated with Confucius. (Example: "Alibi, like dead fish, cannot stand test of time!") Just before the end of each film Chan would assemble all the suspects in one room, review each one's recent activities, and finally turn to the guilty individual with an exclamation of "You are murderer!" (The latter's usual response was "Very clever, Mr. Chan.") Also memorable were his eldest offspring, invariably called Number One Son (played by Keye Luke) and Number Two Son. Interestingly, Oland did not wear makeup to play Chan.

In the same year that he stopped being Fu Manchu, he started being Charlie Chan. His first film in the role was **Charlie Chan Carries On** (31), made, like all his Chan films, by Fox (later to become 20th Century-Fox). Commented the New York Times: "Mr. Oland's conception of Chan's manner of speaking is quite acceptable, and he relies on very little change in his appearance to play the part." Unfortunately for

film historians, this movie is now a lost film. He then made **The Black Camel,** the only one of his 16 Chan films not to carry the detective's name in the title. He also supported Marlene Dietrich in the spy drama **Dishonored,** as a traitorous Austrian general passing secrets to the Russians (unmasked by Miss Dietrich, he shoots himself). He was the villain, a gangster, in **The Big Gamble,** and a mad scientist in **Drums of Jeopardy.**

It was back to sleuthing in **Charlie Chan's Chance** (32), and he again supported Miss Dietrich in the classic **Shanghai Express,** as a revolutionary Chinese general who is also the sadistic villain. In **The Son-Daughter** Helen Hayes, to aid the cause of overthrowing the Manchu dynasty, sells herself to Oland, the highest bidder and a secret royalist, who is plotting to assemble the rebels at his wedding feast and kill them all. After seeing her father (Lewis Stone) and her lover (Ramon Novarro) die, she strangles Oland with his own pigtail. Then he played a German police commandant being nasty to Elissa Landi in **Passport to Hell.**

Oland was busy sleuthing again in Charlie Chan's **Greatest Case** (33), and was the murderous villain, a crazed Austrian doctor, in **Before Dawn.** Now the Chan series started getting more popular with fans. He did **Charlie Chan in London** (34) and **Charlie Chan's Courage.** He played a Chinese warlord again in the Greta Garbo starrer **The Painted Veil,** and a smuggler and kidnapper named Prince Achmed trying to unload a fortune in furs from a cholera-plagued ship in **Bulldog Drummond Strikes Back.** In **Mandalay,** Kay Francis is turned over by her smuggler lover (Ricardo Cortez) as a virtual white slave to Oland, his evil boss.

Now, as Fox became 20th Century-Fox, new studio boss Darryl F. Zanuck increased the Chan films to three in 1935. One of the best in the entire series was **Charlie Chan in Egypt,** involving exciting doings amid some ancient tombs and featuring 16-year-old Rita Cansino (later Rita Hayworth), in her second film appearance, as one of the suspects. **Charlie Chan in Shanghai** dealt with the breaking up of an opium ring; there was also **Charlie Chan in Paris.** And he made his last two non-Chan movies. In the interesting horror film **Werewolf of London** the actor played a werewolf named Dr. Yogami (of "the University of Carpathia"), who bites medical researcher Henry Hull while in Tibet, converting *him* into a werewolf, and is later killed by him. He was a friend of Charles Boyer in **Shanghai,** once again as an Oriental.

By this point in time Oland had so identified himself with the role of Chan that off the screen he frequently spoke to friends, associates and visitors in Oriental aphorisms. And in a conversation he tended to refer to himself in the third person. He was also battling a longtime problem with alcoholism. Directors and producers were now saying it was affecting the work of the actor, who at this point was in his mid-fifties.

All seven of his remaining films would be Chans. **Charlie Chan's Secret** (36) was a weak entry with a mediocre cast. In **Charlie Chan at the Circus,** the killer was J. Carrol Naish as a snake charmer, and in **Charlie Chan at the Opera** Boris Karloff was a sinister-looking red herring who turns out to be innocent. There was skulduggery afoot involving horse racing in **Charlie Chan at the Race Track.** Footage from the 1936 Olympic Games in Berlin was used in **Charlie Chan at the Olympics** (37), which dealt with spies and plans for a remote-control aircraft. **Charlie Chan on Broadway** had a background of New York night life, and **Charlie Chan at Monte Carlo** of course took place at the famous casino.

Oland now began work on the never-to-be-completed **Charlie Chan at Ringside,** but his health was failing. He journeyed to his native Sweden, and in the summer of 1938 died in Stockholm of bronchial pneumonia at age 57. But you can still see him by twirling your television dial in the wee small hours. And if it is true that Charlie Chan made Warner Oland immortal, the reverse is equally true.

THE FILMS OF WARNER OLAND

NOTE: Only feature-length films are listed, so the films he made in 1909 and 1912 are not included. Additionally, some sources erroneously list a 1928 film called **Tong War;** that was just the working title for the 1929 film **Chinatown Nights.**

1915: Sin.
1916: The Rise of Susan; The Eternal Question; The Serpent; Destruction; The Fool's Revenge; The Reapers; Patria (serial).
1917: The Cigarette Girl; The Mysterious Client; Convict 993; The Fatal Ring (serial).
1918: The Yellow Ticket; The Naulahka; The Yellow Raider (serial).
1919: The Avalanche; Witness for the Defense; Mandarin's Gold; Twin Pawns; The Mad Talon; Roaring Oaks; The Lightning Raider (serial).
1920: The Third Eye (serial); The Phantom Foe (serial).
1921: Hurricane Hutch (serial); The Yellow Arm (serial).
1922: East Is West; The Pride of Palomar.
1923: His Children's Children.
1924: The Fighting American; Curlytop; One Night in Rome; So This Is Marriage; The Throwback.
1925: Don Q, Son of Zorro; Flower of Night; Infatuation; The Winding Stair; Riders of the Purple Sage.
1926: Don Juan; Tell It to the Marines; Man of the Forest; The Marriage Clause; The Mystery Club; Twinkletoes.

1927: The Jazz Singer; Old San Francisco; A Million Bid; Good Time Charley; When a Man Loves; What Happened to Father; Sailor Izzy Murphy.
1928: Dream of Love; The Scarlet Lady; Stand and Deliver; Wheel of Chance.
1929: The Mysterious Dr. Fu Manchu; Chinatown Nights; The Studio Murder Mystery; The Mighty; The Faker.
1930: The Return of Dr. Fu Manchu; Dangerous Paradise; The Vagabond King; Paramount on Parade.
1931: Charlie Chan Carries On; The Black Camel; Daughter of the Dragon; The Big Gamble; Dishonored; Drums of Jeopardy.
1932: Shanghai Express; Charlie Chan's Chance; The Son-Daughter; A Passport to Hell.
1933: Charlie Chan's Greatest Case; Before Dawn; As Husbands Go.
1934: Charlie Chan in London; Charlie Chan's Courage; The Painted Veil; Mandalay; Bulldog Drummond Strikes Back.
1935: Charlie Chan in Paris; Charlie Chan in Egypt; Charlie Chan in Shanghai; Werewolf of London; Shanghai.
1936: Charlie Chan's Secret; Charlie Chan at the Circus; Charlie Chan at the Opera; Charlie Chan at the Race Track.
1937: Charlie Chan at the Olympics; Charlie Chan on Broadway; Charlie Chan at Monte Carlo.

A horse face, a disapproving sniff:
EDNA MAY OLIVER

If a poll were taken to determine present-day film fans' favorite character actress of the Thirties, there's a good chance that Edna May Oliver would come out on top. And she was just as popular in her own time, with both moviegoers and critics.

Film historian John Springer has described her with pinpoint accuracy: "[She] was triumphantly herself among character actresses—inimitable, if occasionally imitated. Her appearance was unique: the spare, ramrod-straight frame, the great horse-face with its incomparable sniff, the owlish, watchful eyes. And above all, that voice—the ultimate aristocratic rasp."

Her almost invariable role was that of a spinster, sometimes acidulous, sometimes warm-hearted, sometimes droll, sometimes sarcastic, but usually formidable. She once said, "They always hand me an old hyena role, and I keep right on barking." Certainly no beauty, she capitalized superbly on her unprepossessing countenance, arching her eyebrows, staring purposefully, and always giving her famous disapproving sniff. She usually spoke truths that others avoided, and she stood no nonsense from anyone.

Miss Oliver was born November 9, 1883, in Malden, Massachusetts. (Her real name is variously given by sources as Edna May Cox Nutter, Edna May Nutter, and Edna May Cox-Oliver.) After studying music, she was a light-opera singer for a while, but turned to the legit stage, making her debut in Boston in 1911 and proceeding to Broadway in 1916, where she opened in **The Master.** She appeared in other plays, including **Oh, Boy, Icebound** (she was the star) and **The Cradle Snatchers** (the latter play also featuring Mary Boland and a young Humphrey Bogart), before making her film debut at age 39 in 1923 (she would also later appear on stage as the original Parthy Ann Hawks, the riverboat captain's wife, in **Show Boat**).

Her first movie was **Three O'Clock in the Morning** (23), made by a small independent studio, C.C. Burr Pictures; it was a relatively small part. Also for Burr, she played James Rennie's secretary in **Restless Wives,** the second picture directed by Gregory La Cava. She had a mother role in **Wife in Name Only;** playing her husband was Tyrone Power (Sr.), father of the future superstar. She was one of the small-town spinsters gossiping about Richard Dix in

the screen version of **Icebound** (24), and also supported him in **Manhattan.** Dix was again the star in **Lucky Devil** (25), in which she was the aunt of the heroine (Esther Ralston), and she played the spinster chaperone of Bebe Daniels and Eden Gray in **Lovers in Quarantine.** Her role in **The Lady Who Lied** was little more than a bit.

The actress played the wife of comedian Ford Sterling and the mother of Miss Ralston's sappy fiancé (Kenneth MacKenna) in **The American Venus** (26), and it was back to supporting Dix again in **Let's Get Married**—but this time she had an offbeat role as an inebriated woman who sells hymnals. She was then off the screen and working on the stage for three years, returning in a key supporting role in her first talkie, **The Saturday Night Kid** (29), starring Clara Bow and Jean Arthur as a pair of feuding sisters and also featuring Jean Harlow in her first credited film role. Now RKO decided to let her play comic support to funnymen Bert Wheeler and Robert

Woolsey; as an Army colonel's wife in **Half Shot at Sunrise** (30) she sniffed in disgust at their antics, a reaction that was not in the script but which became her screen trademark.

Miss Oliver drew good notices as the frontier-town busybody in the smash hit drama **Cimarron** (31), starring Irene Dunne and, once again, Richard Dix. In the homespun comedy **Laugh and Get Rich** she ran a boardinghouse and henpecked indolent husband Hugh Herbert. RKO now had hopes of building her into a comedic character star à la Marie Dressler, and cast her in **Fanny Foley Herself** as a vaudeville performer with two daughters (Rochelle Hudson and Helen Chandler), but the film was an unsuccessful mishmash. It was back to Wheeler and Woolsey in **Cracked Nuts,** in which she played the secretary of war of a mythical kingdom, and in **Newly Rich** (alternate title: **Forbidden Adventure**) she was the mother of child star Mitzi Green.

As the wife of town doctor Guy Kibbee, she supported Ann Harding—and, inevitably, Richard Dix—in **The Conquerors** (32), and she was in another Wheeler and Woolsey outing, **Hold 'Em Jail,** as a prison warden's sister romanced by the redoubtable Woolsey. In **Ladies of the Jury** she finally got the hit she had been waiting for, starring as a determined society woman sitting on a jury, certain that a young actress did not kill her husband and bringing the 11 others around to her view (à la **Twelve Angry Men** years later) by interrogating witnesses and breaking up the courtroom in her own unique style.

But her best casting that year came in **The Penguin Pool Murder,** as Hildegarde Withers, a spinster schoolteacher playing detective. Dressed like England's Queen Mary and carrying a silver-handled umbrella no matter what the weather, she teamed up with James Gleason as know-it-all Inspector Oscar Piper of the police to solve a pair of murders and sundry other matters. At film's end, she accepts Gleason's marriage proposal. Audiences loved it, and RKO made plans to convert the outing into a detective series, starring the woman who was surely Hollywood's most unusual sleuth.

She was a standout in director George Cukor's classic **Little Women** (33) as the testy Aunt March, whose nieces included Katharine Hèpburn and Joan Bennett. **Alice in Wonderland** cast her as the imperious Red Queen, and she was billed third in support of Margaret Sullavan in the latter's film debut in **Only Yesterday.** In the fine drama **Ann Vickers** she was Irene Dunne's best friend, and in **The Great Jasper** she was a fortune teller who was a friend of—would you believe Richard Dìx? In the strange fantasy **It's Great to Be Alive** she was a doctor working on a disease that kills only men; later, the last man on Earth has died and she tries to create a synthetic man. She was the dean of a women's college in **Meet the Baron.**

The Hildegarde Withers detective series resumed with **Murder on the Blackboard** (34), in which she nabbed the killer (Bruce Cabot) of her school's music teacher despite the sneers of policeman Gleason (who apparently had forgotten about their marriage in the previous film). She played George Arliss' spinster sister in **The Last Gentleman,** and in **The Poor Rich** she was the wife of Edward Everett Horton, pretending to be wealthy to impress their friends. In **We're Rich Again** she was a polo-playing grandmother.

Although she frequently portrayed spinsters on the screen, Miss Oliver was once married—very briefly. She wed New York stockbroker David M. Pratt in 1928, and they separated three months later (and were divorced in 1931).

The actress, now in her early fifties, had two of her best and most famous roles—interestingly, both of them Dickens characters—in 1935. In George Cukor's **David Copperfield** she was excellent as the outspoken Aunt Betsey Trotwood, taking the orphaned David under her wing. And she was absolutely superb in the Ronald Colman starrer **A Tale of Two Cities** as the faithful family retainer Miss Pross, fighting to the death with the vicious Madame Defarge (Blanche Yurka) to save the master and mistress she loves. She played Joan Crawford's mother in **No More Ladies,** and was sleuth Hildegarde Withers for the third and last time in **Murder on a Honeymoon,** still sparring with Gleason. (The series continued with Helen Broderick and then ZaSu Pitts, but soon died.) Her only 1936 film (again for director Cukor) was **Romeo and Juliet,** as Norma Shearer's droll, wise and impish nurse. She did her patented spinster thing as Myrna Loy's aunt in the Clark Gable starrer **Parnell** (37), played the battle-ax queen to Frank Morgan's king in the musical **Rosalie,** and was an eccentric matron in **My Dear Miss Aldrich.**

In the Shirley Temple outing **Little Miss Broadway** (38) she was the grumpy owner of a hotel catering to entertainers, objecting to the noise they make and having the manager (Edward Ellis) send Shirley back to an orphanage—but her nephew (George Murphy) persuades her to change her mind. She played Frank Morgan's bossy housekeeper in **Paradise for Three.**

She garnered a well deserved Academy Award nomination as best supporting actress for her fine portrayal of the widow Sarah McKlennar in director John Ford's superb drama of Revolutionary times,

Drums Along the Mohawk (39). At the top of a large supporting cast of character actors, she was a doughty pioneer woman who helps the colonists battle marauding Indians and takes into her home newlyweds Henry Fonda and Claudette Colbert. Nor was she above challenging military authority; using a line that might have been borrowed from comedian Oliver Hardy, she declares, "Well, General Herkimer, a fine mess you've gotten yourself into this time!"

Also in 1939, Miss Oliver played the close friend of Fred Astaire and Ginger Rogers in **The Story of Vernon and Irene Castle,** and was Sonja Henie's aunt in **Second Fiddle** (at one point dancing with young Tyrone Power), also appearing as a countess in **Nurse Edith Cavell,** helping to smuggle escaped Allied prisoners into Holland in World War I. She was a standout as the aristocratic Lady Catherine de Bourgh in **Pride and Prejudice** (40), in support of Greer Garson and Laurence Olivier (she was Olivier's aunt). In her last film, **Lydia** (41), she played Merle Oberon's shrewd and salty New England grandmother, urging her to be an individualist.

She died on her 59th birthday in 1942, of an intestinal ailment, her early passing robbing filmgoers of many more years of wonderful performances by one of the greatest of all character actresses. Close your eyes for a moment and you can still see Edna May Oliver up there on the screen—arching her eyebrows, staring intently and, inevitably, giving an aristocratic sniff of disapproval to some hapless miscreant.

THE FILMS OF EDNA MAY OLIVER

1923: Wife in Name Only; Restless Wives; Three O'Clock in the Morning.
1924: Icebound; Manhattan.
1925: Lucky Devil; Ladies in Quarantine; The Lady Who Lied.
1926: The American Venus; Let's Get Married.
1929: The Saturday Night Kid.
1930: Half Shot at Sunrise.
1931: Cimarron; Laugh and Get Rich; Fanny Foley Herself; Forbidden Adventure (Newly Rich); Cracked Nuts.
1932: The Penguin Pool Murder; Ladies of the Jury; The Conquerors; Hold 'Em Jail.
1933: Little Women; Alice in Wonderland; Ann Vickers; Only Yesterday; It's Great to Be Alive; Meet the Baron; The Great Jasper.
1934: Murder on the Blackboard; The Last Gentleman; The Poor Rich; We're Rich Again.
1935: David Copperfield; A Tale of Two Cities; Murder on a Honeymoon; No More Ladies.
1936: Romeo and Juliet.
1937: Parnell; Rosalie; My Dear Miss Aldrich.
1938: Little Miss Broadway; Paradise for Three.
1939: Drums Along the Mohawk; The Story of Vernon and Irene Castle; Second Fiddle; Nurse Edith Cavell.
1940: Pride and Prejudice.
1941: Lydia.

MARIA OUSPENSKAYA

For an actress who had such a brief moment in the Hollywood spotlight, Maria Ouspenskaya carved out quite a niche for herself.

She won Academy Award nominations in her first and third American films. And although she appeared in only 20 U.S. movies altogether, she is one of the best-remembered figures among the screen's character performers. Of those 20 films, 10 were enduring classics, with performances by the elderly actress that linger in the memory, even if many of them amounted to cameo roles with relatively little screen time. What it all adds up to is that she was a great scene-stealer.

With a tiny, gnarled body, a little face wrinkled like a monkey's, beady eyes and a quavery voice with a thick Slavic accent—all unchanged from film to film—she was still forceful and distinguished. She sometimes played quiet women with great warmth and a philosophical bent, and sometimes cruel, autocratic figures, but despite the fact that she was in real life a renowned teacher of acting technique, her own performances varied hardly at all. For if you saw one of them, you had for all practical purposes seen them all. What she did, then, was portray herself.

Miss Ouspenskaya was born July 29, 1876, in Tula, Russia, the daughter of a lawyer. (One source gives a date of 1867, possibly a typographical error.) She studied singing at the Warsaw Conservatory and then was a student at Adasheff's School of the Drama in Moscow. Beginning as an actress in the provinces in 1911, at age 35, she joined the famed Moscow Art Theatre headed by Konstantin Stanislavsky. Interspersed with her stage performances were appearances in six Russian silent films between 1915 and 1929 (they are listed in the filmography at the end of the chapter).

The Moscow Art Theatre troupe visited the United States in 1923, and when it returned home she stayed behind, her primary goal being the establishment of an acting school, although she also acted in Broadway plays. A dominant figure on the New York stage for more than a decade, she appeared in **The Saint, The Jest, Three Sisters,** and many more.

With Richard Boleslavsky (also known as Boleslawski), a fellow Moscow Art Theatre alumnus who had directed Soviet films and would direct some important Hollywood movies in the Thirties, she founded the American Laboratory Theatre to teach the Stanislavsky method, and in 1929 she

founded the Maria Ouspenskaya School of Dramatic Art, with branches in New York and Hollywood. Both efforts were successful, and the Ouspenskaya school profoundly influenced acting on the American stage and screen for a generation. Many notable film stars learned technique from her.

It wasn't until 1936, at the age of 60, that she agreed to appear in films in Hollywood. And, in truth, the main reason the actress (who never married) did so was to support the acting school. But whatever the reason, she scored a hit and won an Oscar nomination as best supporting actress in her first American film, director William Wyler's **Dodsworth** (36), in a part she had played on Broadway two years earlier—the Baroness von Obersdorf, an icy Viennese aristocrat who sternly forbids Fran Dodsworth (Ruth Chatterton, who is divorcing Walter Huston) to marry the baroness' son (Gregory Gaye). This superb five-minute cameo made her screen career. In fact, it deserved to win the Oscar in this first year of the supporting categories, but the award went to Gale Sondergaard for her much weaker performance (in what was also *her* screen debut) in **Anthony Adverse.** Meanwhile, Miss Ouspenskaya returned briefly to Broadway to co-star in the play **Daughters of Atreus.**

Back in Hollywood, the actress was again an aristocrat, this time a countess, in the Greta Garbo starrer **Conquest** (37), playing cards with Napoleon (Charles Boyer) in a relatively brief scene, and then was off the screen for two years. She won a second Oscar nomination for her fine cameo as Boyer's wise grandmother in **Love Affair** (39), and was good as the Maharanee (married to H.B. Warner) in **The Rains Came,** disapproving of Myrna Loy as not being right for Tyrone Power.

She was very busy in 1940, making seven films. She played a ruthless, demanding ballet teacher in **Waterloo Bridge,** her troupe including Vivien Leigh. **Dr. Ehrlich's Magic Bullet** cast her as a wealthy dowager whose dinner party is shocked by the discussion of syphilis by medical researcher Edward G. Robinson; she is the only one not shocked, and gives him money for his experiments. She was James Stewart's mother in the powerful anti-Nazi drama **The Mortal Storm,** and in **Dance, Girl, Dance** she played a former ballet teacher now running a professional dancing troupe that includes Maureen O'Hara and Lucille Ball. In another anti-Nazi tract, the Joan Bennett starrer **The Man I Married,** she was the widow of a German philosopher killed in a concentration camp, and in **Beyond Tomorrow** she was the housekeeper for Sir C. Aubrey Smith, Harry Carey and Charles Winninger. In the Hardy Family vehicle **Judge Hardy and Son** she and Egon Brecher were a destitute elderly couple helped by the judge (Lewis Stone).

In the classic drama **Kings Row** (41), in one of her best-remembered roles, she played Robert Cummings' grandmother, a pillar of wisdom and strength, dying at last behind the shutters of the white house on the hill. In the superior horror film **The Wolf Man** she was Maleva, the wise but superstitious old gypsy (Bela Lugosi was her son) who foretells the

doom of Lon Chaney Jr. ("Whoever is bitten by a werewolf and *lives* becomes a werewolf himself"); Claude Rains and Ralph Bellamy were also in the cast. And in director Josef von Sternberg's bizarre, baroque **The Shanghai Gesture** she played the mute old Amah; others on hand included Walter Huston, Gene Tierney, Victor Mature and Eric Blore. (The actress, who did not suffer fools lightly, said of Sternberg, "The man is an idiot.")

That was pretty much the end of anything significant in her screen career, but there were more films to come. Meanwhile, though, she had become something of a minor Hollywood legend, sporting a cane and monocle offscreen and gaining a reputation as a painter in her spare time. She walked off with **The Mystery of Marie Roget** (42) as the murdered Maria Montez' peppery grandmother, garnering most of the critical notices, and repeated her role as the gypsy in **Frankenstein Meets the Wolf Man** (43). She was the venerable Amazon queen in the silly **Tarzan and the Amazons** (45), and again stole the show in **I've Always Loved You** (46), as Philip Dorn's mother. In **Wyoming** (47) she played Vera Ralston's chaperone in the wild West. And there had, meanwhile, been more stage appearances, too; the last was in **Outrageous Fortune** on Broadway in 1943.

The actress made her last film in 1949. The David Niven-Jane Wyman starrer **A Kiss in the Dark** featured, as one reviewer put it, "Maria Ouspenskaya as Maria Ouspenskaya." He was merely reiterating what had always been the case. But considering the years of critical plaudits, the two Oscar nominations and the successful acting school, what did the 73-year-old actress care?

A tragedy ended her life. Toward the end of 1949 she was smoking in bed in her Hollywood apartment. The bedclothes caught fire and blazed up; Miss Ouspenskaya died of burns. Her place in screen history is secure; she overcame the seeming handicap of only a handful of film roles by delivering a small but memorable gallery of vivid performances that you still recall today.

THE FILMS OF MARIA OUSPENSKAYA

1915: Sverchok Na Pechi (The Cricket on the Hearth).
1916: Nichtozhniye (Worthless).
1917: Tsveti Zapozdaliye (Belated Flowers) (or Dr. Toporkov).
1919: Zazhivo Pogrebennii (Buried Alive).
1923: Khveska (Hospital Guard Khveska).
1929: Tanka-Traktirschitsa Protiv Otsa (Tanka the Innkeeper Against Her Father).
1936: Dodsworth.
1937: Conquest.
1939: Love Affair; The Rains Came.

1940: Waterloo Bridge; Dr. Ehrlich's Magic Bullet; The Mortal Storm; Dance, Girl, Dance; Beyond Tomorrow; The Man I Married; Judge Hardy and Son.
1941: Kings Row; The Wolf Man; The Shanghai Gesture.
1942: The Mystery of Marie Roget.
1943: Frankenstein Meets the Wolf Man.
1945: Tarzan and the Amazons.
1946: I've Always Loved You.
1947: Wyoming.
1949: A Kiss in the Dark.

The one-man stock company:
REGINALD OWEN

Reginald Owen was a one-man stock company. He played kings, beggars, diplomats, butlers, cripples, giants, professional men, thieves, policemen, couturiers and spies—not to mention Scrooge, Sherlock Holmes *and* Dr. Watson. Almost never cast in low-budget programmers, he was usually seen in first-rank productions supporting the top stars of his day; the list of his MGM films in the period 1935-45, especially, reads like a catalogue of Hollywood classics.

He was an actor who belongs in the record books. Item: A screen career that extended over an incredible 60 years, from age 24 to age 84 (surpassed only by Lillian Gish, Ruth Gordon and possibly a tiny handful of others). Item: Of his 126 films, an amazing 73 of them were made for MGM (in only a 23-year span), almost certainly more movies than any other credited performer except Lionel Barrymore ever made for that studio.

Tall (six feet, three inches), genial and fair-haired, with owlish good looks, he was at his best portraying self-controlled and somewhat stuffy Englishmen, although he could become quite irritated on occasion. An effortless scene-stealer, he often outshone the top stars he worked with, in acting skill (of which he had a great deal) if not in charisma (of which he had very little). He was the consummate character actor.

John Reginald Owen was born August 5, 1887, in Wheathampstead, Hertfordshire, England. A graduate of Sir Herbert Beerbohm Tree's Academy of Dramatic Art, he made his professional acting debut at age 18 on the London stage in 1905. In 1911 he was in the first British two-reel (20-minute) film, **Henry VIII,** starring Tree as Henry and featuring Owen as his chief minister, Thomas Cromwell. He made occasional films during the next 20 years, interspersed with a busy stage schedule. There was apparently one called **The Flight of Death** (14), which is unrecorded by all but one source, and then he was in an American movie, **Sally in Our Alley** (16), and the British **A Place in the Sun** (19). He had a role in **The Grass Orphan** (23), probably English, and that same year was in a French production, **Phroso.** He made his first Broadway appearance in 1924 and was seen in many plays, including Mólnar's **The Play's the Thing** in 1926 and **Candle Light** (with Gertrude Lawrence and Leslie Howard) in 1929. But his film career as most

of us know it didn't really begin until the start of the sound era in 1929, when he was 42.

His first talkie was the earliest screen version of **The Letter** (29), starring Jeanne Eagels, the drug-addicted, doomed actress whose next-to-last film this was and who died that same year of a heroin overdose. He played her tormented husband; the murdered lover was portrayed by Herbert Marshall, who would take over the husband role in the 1940 remake starring Bette Davis. Owen returned to the stage for two more years and then came back to Hollywood to make a permanent career in films.

As an arrogant and unpleasant lawyer, he supported Jean Harlow and Loretta Young in **Platinum Blonde** (31), and then made his first MGM movie, **The Man in Possession,** as Robert Montgomery's stuffy brother (a role he would play again in the 1937 remake). In **Sherlock Holmes** he was Watson, assisting Clive Brook's Holmes, and in **Lovers Courageous** he was a millionaire to whom Madge Evans is engaged until Montgomery comes along. He was a Ruritanian prime minister in **A Woman Commands,** with Pola Negri, Basil Rathbone and Roland Young, and in **Downstairs** he was the Austrian baron who employs scheming chauffeur John Gilbert and upright butler Paul Lukas.

From Watson, he moved up to starring (not very successfully) as Sherlock Holmes (and also wrote the screenplay) in **A Study in Scarlet** (33), with Alan Mowbray as Watson. In the Greta Garbo starrer **Queen Christina** he was Prince Charles of Sweden, scheduled to marry her but then rejected, and in **Voltaire** he played the amiably stupid Louis XV, the first of three times he would portray that French monarch; George Arliss was Voltaire. Owen was droll as a butler in **Double Harness,** and played Maureen O'Sullivan's father, the English owner of a ranch in the West, in **Robbers' Roost.** He played a swindling card sharp in **The Big Brain.**

His most active year on screen was 1934, with a dozen films. He was the shadow-like aide to theatrical impresario Richard Bennett in **Nana,** Samuel Goldwyn's ill-fated introduction of Anna Sten to the American screen, and in the Bette Davis starrer **Of Human Bondage** he played the father of Frances Dee. He supported Arliss again in **The House of Rothschild,** and was outstanding as (once again) the jaded and profligate Louis XV (a few years older and more fatuous) in **Madame Du Barry.** In **Fashions of 1934** he played a crusty, snobbish Parisian couturier, the emperor of the fashion industry, whose dress designs William Powell and Miss Davis try to steal, and in **Mandalay** he was the police captain. **Stingaree** cast him as the governor general, and he was a Russian prince in **Here Is My Heart.** In **Where Sinners Meet** Clive Brook talked him out of eloping with Diana Wynyard, and he was a music publisher helping singer Gloria Swanson in **Music in the Air.** He played a confidence man trying (unsuccessfully) to get Fay Wray involved in his schemes in **The Countess of Monte Cristo,** and in **The Human Side** Doris Kenyon plans to marry him but eventually reconciles with her ex-husband (Adolphe Menjou). (On numerous occasions Owen emulated Ralph Bellamy in that he "didn't get the girl.")

The actor was married to Lydia Bilbrooke in 1908, and they were divorced in 1923. He wed stage actress Mrs. Harold Austin in an unspecified year, and they had two children. Widowed in 1956, he married Barbara Haveman that year.

Owen played the villainous gold prospector Smith, Clark Gable's rival, in **Call of the Wild** (35), and was Ronald Colman's clever lawyer, Stryver, in **A Tale of Two Cities.** In the Margaret Sullavan starrer

The Good Fairy he was in top form as an eccentric waiter who helps her, and in **Anna Karenina** he played Greta Garbo's philandering brother. As a grandiloquent eccentric, he stole **Enchanted April** from Ann Harding and Frank Morgan, and he played Morgan's brother, an orchestra conductor, in **Escapade.** In **The Bishop Misbehaves** he cheated Maureen O'Sullivan's father out of a valuable patent on an invention.

He played a shrewd and ruthless international spy who captures Clark Gable and Joan Crawford in **Love on the Run** (36), and was opera star Jeanette MacDonald's nervous manager in **Rose Marie.** He played the stuffy English nobleman who loses his fiancée, Myrna Loy, to Robert Montgomery in **Petticoat Fever,** and he was the president of the bizarre Suicide Club in **Trouble for Two,** starring Montgomery and Rosalind Russell; ultimately he is killed by Montgomery in a duel. In **Yours for the Asking** he played a con artist who, with gold digger Ida Lupino, is hired to break up a romance between George Raft and Dolores Costello (who was then being billed as Dolores Costello Barrymore); he and Miss Lupino easily stole the film. He was a master criminal whose planned bank robbery is foiled by Joel McCrea and Jean Arthur in **Adventure in Manhattan,** and was good as Gloria Stuart's thieving, blackmailing butler in **The Girl on the Front Page.** He also had a prominent role in **The Great Ziegfeld.**

In the Greta Garbo starrer **Conquest** (37), also featuring Charles Boyer as Napoleon, Owen was cast as Talleyrand, and he was an Italian admiral visiting a Tyrolean resort in **The Bride Wore Red.** He re-did his 1931 **Man in Possession** role in the remake, called **Personal Property;** he was Robert Taylor's insufferable brother, whom Jean Harlow wants to marry (and vice versa) until each finds out the other has no money. He played the chancellor in **Rosalie,** and was a friend of Gladys George in **Madame X.**

Then came the role for which filmgoers surely remember him best: starring as Scrooge in the Dickens classic **A Christmas Carol** (38), a part in which he was superb; the film is still shown regularly on television every Christmas. He was Freddie Bartholomew's evil uncle in **Kidnapped,** and he and Billie Burke were the nutty heads of a theatrical family in **Everybody Sing,** which featured 15-year-old Judy Garland as their younger daughter. He played Franchot Tone's friend in **The Girl Downstairs.** He was Gary Cooper's commanding officer in **The Real Glory** (39), and he and Miss Burke were reunited in **Remember?,** as the parents of Greer Garson. He played a Russian general in **Hotel Imperial,** and in **Fast and Loose** Robert Montgomery exposed him as the murderer of Ralph Morgan. He was Guy Kibbee's valet in **Bad Little Angel.**

The actor's roles were beginning to diminish in 1940. He was a lawyer in **The Earl of Chicago** (Montgomery was again the star), played the Emperor Franz Joseph of Austria-Hungary in **Florian,** and was in a couple of minor programmers. He and Donald Meek were among the members of a blackmailing gang led by Joan Crawford in **A Woman's Face** (41), and he was a British commanding general in the Clark Gable starrer **They Met in Bombay.** The Jack Benny vehicle **Charley's Aunt** cast him as a bumbling, doddering Oxford don, and he was an unscrupulous gold-hunter in **Tarzan's Secret Treasure.**

Owen was Mr. Foley, the grocer and air-raid warden, in the popular Greer Garson-Walter Pidgeon hit **Mrs. Miniver** (42), and a British pub-keeper in **Random Harvest,** also starring Miss Garson (with Ronald Colman). He played a friendly lawyer in the first Spencer Tracy-Katharine Hepburn starrer, **Woman of the Year,** and an aristocratic Southerner in **We Were Dancing.** He was a Nazi official giving Joan Crawford and John Wayne a hard time in **Reunion in France.** He played a doctor in another Garson-Pidgeon hit, **Madame Curie** (43), and he was once again a Nazi harassing Miss Crawford in **Above Suspicion.** He played a Nazi colonel in **Assignment in Brittany.**

The actor portrayed a neighboring farmer to Elizabeth Taylor's family (with Donald Crisp as the father) in **National Velvet** (44), and did his patented high-born Englishman in **The Canterville Ghost.** Then he had one of his best screen roles in **Kitty** (45), as the elderly Duke of Malmunster, eager to wed Paulette Goddard; she is pregnant by her late first husband, but allows the duke to think the child, born after their marriage, is his, and his joy is so great that he becomes exhausted and dies of a heart attack. He played martinet Judith Anderson's repressed and doddering husband in director Jean Renoir's **The Diary of a Chambermaid** (46), with Miss Goddard again, and played Louis XV for the third and last

time in the Bob Hope romp **Monsieur Beaucaire.** He was yet another British nobleman in **Cluny Brown,** the last film completed by director Ernst Lubitsch.

He played a sea captain in **Green Dolphin Street** (47) and a rural Scotsman in **Thunder in the Valley.** Now in his early sixties, he played roles that were farther and farther down the cast list in such films as **The Three Musketeers** and **The Pirate** (both 48). He repeated his earlier role in **The Miniver Story** (50), and played a priest in the Errol Flynn vehicle **Kim.** Then he sharply cut back his filming schedule, although he would continue on the screen for a generation to come. After a three-year hiatus, he was in small parts in two 1953 and 1954 films, and then stayed away from the cameras for four years. He was far down the cast list in **Darby's Rangers** (58), playing yet another titled Briton.

After four more years the actor, now 75, appeared in a small role as a consul in **Five Weeks in a Balloon** (62). He also did some television work, including a regular part in the series "The Queen and I." Back on screen, he supported Doris Day in **The Thrill of It All** (63), and was comical as Admiral Boom in **Mary Poppins** (64). He came back again with a small role in the Rosalind Russell outing **Rosie!** (67), and after another four years had his final screen role in **Bedknobs and Broomsticks** (71)—a tiny part as a British officer, at age 84.

Owen had begun his screen career just after the Edwardian era ended, and well before the beginning of World War I; now it was almost the year of Watergate, and 60 long years had elapsed. Film stars he had supported in Hollywood's Golden Era, some of them mere toddlers and others not yet even born when he first appeared on the screen, were now, many of them, retired or dead. He was a survivor.

In 1972, at 85, he returned to Broadway in the musical farce **A Funny Thing Happened on the Way to the Forum.** But that fall the veteran actor died. It is impossible to believe that Hollywood will ever again spawn another one-man stock company like Reginald Owen.

THE FILMS OF REGINALD OWEN

NOTE: This filmography omits his 1911 appearance in **Henry VIII,** which was only two reels long. Additionally, it should be noted that while some sources list him as having appeared in the 1938 film **Sweethearts,** the 1939 film **Balalaika** and the 1940 film **Pride and Prejudice,** those sources are apparently in error, at least according to the dependable American Film Institute Catalog.

1914: The Flight of Death.

1916: Sally in Our Alley.
1919: A Place in the Sun.
1923: The Grass Orphan; Phroso.
1929: The Letter.
1931: Platinum Blonde; The Man in Possession.
1932: Sherlock Holmes; Lovers Courageous; Downstairs; A Woman Commands; The Man Called Back.
1933: A Study in Scarlet; Queen Christina; Voltaire; Double Harness; the Narrow Corner; The Big Brain; Robbers' Roost.

1934: Nana; Of Human Bondage; The House of Rothschild; Madame Du Barry; Fashions of 1934; Mandalay; Stingaree; Here Is My Heart; Music in the Air; The Countess of Monte Cristo; where Sinners Meet; The Human Side. *Credit uncertain:* Outcast Lady.

1935: Call of the Wild; A Tale of Two Cities; The Good Fairy; Anna Karenina; Escapade; Enchanted April; The Bishop Misbehaves.

1936: Love on the Run; Rose Marie; The Great Ziegfeld; Petticoat Fever; Trouble for Two; Yours for the Asking; Adventure in Manhattan; The Girl on the Front Page.

1937: Conquest; The Bride Wore Red; Rosalie; Personal Property; Madame X; Dangerous Number.

1938: A Christmas Carol; Kidnapped; Stablemates; Everybody Sing; Paradise for Three; The Girl Downstairs; Three Loves Has Nancy; Vacation from Love.

1939: The Real Glory; Hotel Imperial; Remember?; Fast and Loose; Bridal Suite; Bad Little Angel.

1940: The Earl of Chicago; The Ghost Comes Home; Florian; Hullabaloo.

1941: A Woman's Face; They Met in Bombay; Charley's Aunt; Lady Be Good; Free and Easy; Blonde Inspiration; Tarzan's Secret Treasure.

1942: Mrs. Miniver; Random Harvest; Woman of the Year; White Cargo; We Were Dancing; Somewhere I'll Find You; Reunion in France; I Married an Angel; Cairo; Pierre of the Plains.

1943: Madame Curie; Above Suspicion; Forever and a Day; Assignment in Brittany; Salute to the Marines; Three Hearts for Julia.

1944: National Velvet; The Canterville Ghost.

1945: Kitty; The Valley of Decision; Captain Kidd; The Sailor Takes a Wife; She Went to the Races.

1946: The Diary of a Chambermaid; Cluny Brown; Monsieur Beaucaire; Piccadilly Incident.

1947: Green Dolphin Street; If Winter Comes; The Imperfect Lady; Thunder in the Valley.

1948: The Three Musketeers; The Pirate; Julia Misbehaves; The Hills of Home.

1949: The Secret Garden; Challenge to Lassie.

1950: The Miniver Story; Kim; Grounds for Marriage.

1953: The Great Diamond Robbery.

1954: Red Garters.

1958: Darby's Rangers.

1962: Five Weeks in a Balloon.

1963: The Thrill of It All; Tammy and the Doctor.

1964: Mary Poppins; Voice of the Hurricane.

1967: Rosie!

1971: Bedknobs and Broomsticks

The 300-pound bullfrog:
EUGENE PALLETTE

Nobody looked or sounded remotely like Eugene Pallette. Extremely overweight, moon-faced and jowly, with bushy eyebrows and dark hair, he looked like some huge black beetle, albeit one dressed in immaculately cut suits. The voice was even more unusual: It was an incredibly deep, gravel-grating bullfrog rasp that didn't sound like it could be issuing from anything human; actually, it was more like a foghorn. To put it mildly, when he appeared on the screen there was no mistaking him for some other actor.

During the Thirties he became stereotyped in the role of a grouchy, exasperated, loudly grumbling, vulgar slob of a millionaire, usually in classic screwball comedies, although sometimes he was good-natured. Much of the time he was cast as the father of some major star, usually female. A skillful scene-stealer, he was a character comedian, and rarely had a dramatic role. But his figures of authority usually proved to be neither as dumb nor as grouchy as they first appeared.

In a typical film, Pallette can never get a straight answer from anyone, and his opinions are usually wrong and/or ignored. He sees himself as the master of the household, but his wife or flighty daughter pretends to listen to him only when she feels sorry for him.

Surprisingly, the actor started out in the movies way back in the D.W. Griffith days as a slim(!) and handsome young hero. (Ultimately his screen appearances would total 192 feature-length films.) Putting on an enormous amount of weight during the Twenties, although it was not done deliberately, is probably what made his career as a top character actor in the sound era; his girth and that basso profundo were basically his screen persona.

He was born July 8, 1889, in Winfield, Kansas, to a theatrical couple who were touring in that melodramatic standby, **East Lynne.** He left Culver Military Academy in Indiana and, while still a teen-ager, served his acting apprenticeship in touring companies, although some sources say he also worked for a while as a streetcar conductor and as a jockey. He entered films in 1910, when he was 21, as an extra. American movies were still basically in their infancy at that time, most of them being one-reelers (10 minutes long) until Griffith introduced the two-reeler late in the year. The newcomer soon became a leading

player in these short films. The feature-length film arrived in 1914, and for several years thereafter he appeared in at least 10 movies a year. He had a small part as a Union soldier in Griffith's landmark film **The Birth of a Nation** (15), but in the same director's classic **Intolerance** (16) he had moved up the cast list considerably, co-starring as handsome hero Prosper Latour in the sequence about the 1572 massacre of the Huguenots.

He now appeared in two films with the young star Norma Talmadge, in one of which, **Going Straight,** he was a gang member attempting to blackmail her and ending up strangled by her husband. There was brief military service during World War I, involving an enlistment in the Army Air Corps, but he still managed to make 18 films in 1917 and 1918; among those in the latter year were **Tarzan of the Apes,** starring Elmo Lincoln, and **His Robe of Honor,** with Henry B. Walthall. He supported Bert Lytell in **Alias Jimmy Valentine** (20), Harry Houdini in **Ter-**

ror Island (as the principal villain), and had a chance to co-star opposite Ruth Stonehouse in **Parlor, Bedroom and Bath.**

A lover of food who refused to diet, he was now seen as a stocky Aramis in **The Three Musketeers** (21), starring Douglas Fairbanks as D'Artagnan, and he starred in **Fine Feathers** as a construction engineer who kills a man who has ruined him and then commits suicide. He played a ranch hand in **Two Kinds of Women** (22), and had a very small part in director Cecil B. DeMille's biblical epic **The Ten Commandments** (23). In director Jack (John) Ford's **North of Hudson Bay** he was Tom Mix' murdered brother, and he supported Richard Dix in **To the Last Man.** He was the train robber (but only in Buck Jones' lengthy dream) in **Hell's Hole,** and a South American military officer in the remake of **A Man's Man,** which he had also filmed in 1917.

Pallette played John Gilbert's villainous brother in **The Wolf Man** (24), engaging him in a savage knife fight; the ingenue was Norma Shearer, at that time not yet a star. He was a cowpoke in **The Light of Western Stars** (25) and in **Mantrap** (26) he disgustedly parted company with the pampered Percy Marmont during their North Woods camping trip; the star was Clara Bow. He was one of a gang of smugglers in **The Fighting Edge,** and in **Whispering Smith** he was on the other side of the law, helping lawman H.B. Warner track down the villain. He played a deputy sheriff in **Desert Valley,** a cocky Englishman out West in **Whispering Canyon,** and one of a band of Alaskan fur poachers in **Rocking Moon.**

In **Chicago** (27) the actor was Phyllis Haver's clandestine lover, a car salesman, whom she is accused of murdering. He appeared in the first all-talkie, **Lights of New York** (28), and played an insanely jealous Parisian hotel owner in the Adolphe Menjou starrer **His Private Life.** Reviewers were already describing him as "corpulent," since he now weighed in at 275 pounds (and would go well over the 300 mark in the Thirties). He was a World War I Army captain in **The Good-Bye Kiss,** a French soldier in the same war (with Richard Barthelmess) in **Out of the Ruins,** and a convict in **The Red Mark.**

With his distinctive appearance and voice (as revealed by talkies), he was right in line to find better parts as a character actor. And now he was cast for the first of five times as the dense police detective, Sergeant Heath, always arresting the wrong suspects, in **The Canary Murder Case** (29), one of the series based on books by S.S. Van Dine featuring detective Philo Vance and all of whose titles had a six-letter name or word preceding "Murder Case." This first one starred William Powell as the smooth and urbane detective Vance, investigating the murder of blackmailing musical-comedy star Louise Brooks; also featured was ingenue Jean Arthur, not yet a star. Powell starred again in **The Greene Murder Case,** and this time the squeaky-voiced Miss Arthur turned out to be the surprise murderer (of three people, no less). **The Studio Murder Mystery** had no connection with Philo Vance or with Van Dine, but he was still the investigating police officer, pinning the murder of film actor Fredric March (in his third movie) on his director, Warner Oland.

Pallette played the minister of war in the very early musical **The Love Parade,** and was a cowpoke in **The Virginian,** also appearing as theatrical producer Powell's dance director in **Pointed Heels.** Then it was back to Sergeant Heath (and, once again, Powell as Vance) in **The Benson Murder Case** (30). In **Slightly Scarlet** he was a *nouveau riche* who becomes the target of jewel thief Evelyn Brent, working for master criminal Paul Lukas, and as a French seaman he supported Jack Oakie in **Sea Legs.** He was a "creditor's man" in **Let's Go Native** and the first mate of a treasure-hunting ship in **The Sea God.** As a reformed outlaw, he was shot down by gang members in **The Border Legion,** and he played a traffic cop in **Men Are Like That** and a sheep rancher in **The Santa Fe Trail.** Now in his early forties, the actor was a frontiersman in the Gary Cooper starrer **Fighting Caravans** (31), and a soap manufacturer in **It Pays to Advertise.** He played the disreputable "King" in **The Adventures of Huckleberry Finn,** was a cowpoke in **Gun Smoke** and **Dude Ranch,** and appeared as a philandering married man in **Girls About Town.**

The Marlene Dietrich starrer **Shanghai Express** (32) cast him as one of the train passengers, an engineer who loves to gamble, and in **The Half Naked Truth** he was hired by publicist Lee Tracy to pose as the Turkish retainer of "Madame Exotica"—Lupe Velez as an actress pretending to be an escaped harem beauty. He played a quirky, folksy stagecoach driver called Yuba Bill in **Wild Girl,** and an oilfield worker in **Thunder Below.** He was the political mentor of **The Night Mayor** (Lee Tracy), and played another police detective in **Strangers of the Evening.** After a three-year hiatus from the role, he was back as Sergeant Heath in **The Kennel Murder Case** (33). He played sailor Spencer Tracy's buddy in **Shanghai Madness** and was one of a submarine's crew, a pugnacious warrant officer, in **Hell Below.** Now becoming typecast as a police detective, he played another one in **From Headquarters,** and he was a drinking buddy of Will Rogers in **Mr. Skitch.**

He played Sergeant Heath for the last time in **The Dragon Murder Case** (34), and was the rather improbable chief of a Hungarian gypsy band in **Caravan**, also portraying the old college chum of Charlie Ruggles in **Friends of Mr. Sweeney,** forcing him to face some truths about his life. He was yet another police detective in **I've Got Your Number,** and was also a gumshoe in **One Exciting Adventure.** He played a noisy bus passenger in **Cross Country Cruise.** There was a good part in **Bordertown** (35), as a café owner who hires Paul Muni as a manager; soon Pallette's young and flirtatious wife, Bette Davis, is making eyes at Muni, and not long after that she kills her husband by letting his car engine run in a closed garage while he is sleeping off a drunk. He was the sheriff in the Will Rogers outing **Steamboat 'Round the Bend,** and a wealthy, poker-playing oilman in **Black Sheep.**

Pallette married Marjorie Cagnacci in 1932, when he was 43. Sources do not list any children.

The actor had one of his best-remembered roles in the classic screwball comedy **My Man Godfrey** (36), as the husband of Alice Brady, the father of Carole Lombard and Gail Patrick, and the temporary employer of down-and-out William Powell as the family butler. He was in fine fettle in **The Ghost Goes West** as the boorish American millionaire who buys a castle haunted by Robert Donat and wants it transported to the United States, and he played a *nouveau riche* oil tycoon in the Bette Davis starrer **The Golden Arrow.** He was Jane Wyatt's wealthy father in **The Luckiest Girl in the World.** He played the harassed hotel detective in **Topper** (37), and he and Miss Brady were a wealthy husband and wife again, helping Deanna Durbin, in **One Hundred Men and a Girl.** He played yet another eccentric millionaire in **She Had to Eat,** and a playwright in **The Crime Nobody Saw.**

He was the perfect choice for the corpulent, gluttonous Friar Tuck in the fine adventure classic **The Adventures of Robin Hood** (38), starring Errol Flynn, and he played a dyspeptic newspaper editor in **There Goes My Heart,** bellowing at reporter Fredric March. In director Frank Capra's memorable populist political drama **Mr. Smith Goes to Washington** (39) he was one of the party hacks working for powerful boss Edward Arnold. He played his patented vulgar millionaire in **First Love,** with Miss Durbin as his niece, and was building contractor Warner Baxter's business partner in **Wife, Husband and Friend.** Having already played Friar Tuck, he was a good choice for the priest Father Felipe in **The Mark of Zorro** (40), and he played Loretta Young's father in **He Stayed for Breakfast.** He was a rail-road freight agent in **Young Tom Edison,** the governor in **It's a Date,** and a radio-station owner in **A Little Bit of Heaven.**

Now in his early fifties, Pallette had one of his best parts in the Barbara Stanwyck starrer **The Lady Eve** (41), as Henry Fonda's father, a brewery tycoon, howling for his dinner like a spoiled child and clashing the dish covers together like cymbals. He was the sheriff in **Swamp Water,** pursuing fugitive Walter Brennan, and played a blunt, uncouth butler in **Unfinished Business,** also portraying runaway heiress Bette Davis' oil-millionaire father in **The Bride Came C.O.D.,** which co-starred James Cagney.

The actor was getting to be known around the film capital as a deep-dyed right-winger in private life, and so he seemed appropriately cast as the ultra-reactionary college trustee clashing with liberal professor Henry Fonda in **The Male Animal** (42). He portrayed a comic mobster in **The Big Street,** and as Charles Boyer's valet he sold a tailcoat to Cesar Romero's butler (Roland Young) in the multi-episode drama **Tales of Manhattan.** He was Paulette Goddard's father in **The Forest Rangers.** In director Ernst Lubitsch's delightful comedy-drama **Heaven Can Wait** (43) he and Marjorie Main were comic hits as the parents of Gene Tierney. Film historian James Harvey has described the pair: "A gruff, portly couple locked into a marriage of pure and energizing hatred, seething grossly at each other in their Kansas mansion." Additionally that year, he was a newspaper tycoon in **Slightly Dangerous.**

Pallette played Jeanne Crain's wealthy father in **In the Meantime, Darling** (44), during the filming of which a startling and ugly incident took place, according to the director, Otto Preminger. In his autobiography Preminger reports: "...Eugene Pallette... was an admirer of Hitler and convinced that Germany would win the war. [One] scene took place in a kitchen where Pallette and a black actor [the veteran performer Clarence Muse] were to have a conversation. [Muse] was seated at a table and I told Pallette to make his entrance and then sit down beside him. 'You're out of your mind,' he said. 'I won't sit next to a nigger.' I went to [producer Darryl F.] Zanuck and had him fired. Most of his scenes had been shot. We wrote him out of what was left."

Also that year, he played Dennis O'Keefe's father in **Sensations of 1945** and several other forgettable films. But these had preceded **In the Meantime, Darling** into release. Now the word spread around Hollywood that the actor was a rabid fascist and an obnoxious racist. He was quickly blacklisted by the major studios, and for the next three years appeared in only four films, all done on Poverty Row by Republic or Monogram. He and Billie Burke were the heads of a family of wealthy snobs reformed by penniless actor Joseph Schildkraut in Republic's **The Cheaters,** and for the same studio he played Vera Hruba Ralston's gruff but kindly uncle in **Lake Placid Serenade,** both 1945 releases.

Whether it was because he had become a right-wing nut or because of the sharp decline in his film fortunes—or a combination of both—he now retired to a semi-reclusive life on an Oregon ranch, prepared, according to one source, "to stave off any anticipated attacks"—indicating that paranoia had set in. Report-edly tiring of the loneliness, he came back in 1948 to do one last film, working for Warner Bros. in the Errol Flynn starrer **Silver River,** in a part so small that his name doesn't appear in the published cast list. That was the end of his career, at age 59. One source says the reason for his retirement was a throat ailment that ultimately took his life. He died at 64 in 1954, not on the Oregon ranch but in Los Angeles.

Eugene Pallette's bulky figure can still be seen, and his incredibly deep, rasping voice can still be heard, on the numerous occasions when one of his films shows up on TV or at a revival house. He was truly inimitable.

THE FILMS OF EUGENE PALLETTE

NOTE: This filmography omits his four 1913 films because they were almost certainly not feature-length. The birth of the American feature-length film was in 1914; this list arbitrarily includes all five of his films released that year on the assumption that they were feature-length.

1914: The Horse Wranglers; The Burden; On the Border; The Peach Brand; The Sheriff's Prisoner.
1915: The Birth of a Nation; The Story of a Story; After 20 Years; The Death Doll; The Highbinders; The Penalty; When Love Is Mocked; Isle of Content; How Hazel Got Even; Spell of the Poppy; The Emerald Brooch; The Scarlet Lady; The Ever-Living Isles.
1916: Intolerance; Hell-to-Pay Austin; Gretchen the Greenhorn; The Children in the House; Whispering Smith; His Guardian Angel; Going Straight; Sunshine Dad; Runaway Freight; Diamond in the Rough.
1917: Lonesome Chap; The Bond Between; The Purple Scar; The Marcellini Millions; The Winning of Sally Temple; World Apart; The Victim; Each to His Kind; Heir of the Ages; A Man's Man; Ghost House.
1918: Tarzan of the Apes; Madame Who; No Man's Land; His Robe of Honor; The Turn of a Card; Breakers Ahead; Vivette.
1919: The Amateur Adventuress; Words and Music by...; Be a Little Sport; Fair and Warmer.
1920: Alias Jimmy Valentine; Twin Beds; Terror Island; Parlor, Bedroom and Bath.
1921: The Three Musketeers; Fine Feathers.
1922: Without Compromise; Two Kinds of Women.
1923: The Ten Commandments; North of Hudson Bay; To the Last Man; Hell's Hole; A Man's Man.
1924: The Wolf Man; The Cyclone Rider; Galloping Fish; Wandering Husbands.
1925: Wild Horse Mesa; The Light of Western Stars; Ranger of the Big Pines; Without Mercy.
1926: Mantrap; The Fighting Edge; Whispering Smith; Desert Valley; The Yankee Senor; Rocking Moon; Whispering Canyon.
1927: Chicago; Moulders of Men.
1928: Lights of New York; His Private Life; The Good-Bye Kiss; Out of the Ruins; The Red Mark.
1929: The Canary Murder Case; The Greene Murder Case; The Studio Murder Mystery; The Love Parade; The Virginian; Pointed Heels; The Dummy; The Kibitzer.
1930: The Benson Murder Case; Playboy of Paris; Paramount on Parade; Slightly Scarlet; Sea Legs; Let's Go Native; Follow Thru; The Sea God; The Border Legion; Men Are Like That; The Santa Fe Trail.
1931: Fighting Caravans; It Pays to Advertise; The Adventures of Huckleberry Finn; Girls About Town; Dude Ranch; Gun Smoke.
1932: Shanghai Express; The Half Naked Truth; Wild Girl; Thunder Below; Dancers in the Dark; The Night Mayor; Strangers of the Evening. *Credit uncertain:* Tom Brown of Culver.
1933: The Kennel Murder Case; Shanghai Madness; Hell Below; Storm at Daybreak; From Headquarters; Mr. Skitch; Made on Broadway.
1934: The Dragon Murder Case; Caravan; I've Got Your Number; Friends of Mr. Sweeney; Strictly Dynamite; Cross Country Cruise; One Exciting Adventure.
1935: Bordertown; Steamboat 'Round the Bend; All the King's Horses; Baby Face Harrington; Black Sheep.
1936: My Man Godfrey; The Ghost Goes West; The Golden Arrow; Stowaway; The Luckiest Girl in the World; Easy to Take.
1937: Topper; One Hundred Men and a Girl; She Had to Eat; The Crime Nobody Saw; Clarence. *Credit uncertain:* Song of the City.
1938: The Adventures of Robin Hood; There Goes My Heart.
1939: Mr. Smith Goes to Washington; First Love; Wife, Husband and Friend.
1940: The Mark of Zorro; He Stayed for Breakfast; Young Tom Edison; It's a Date; A Little Bit of Heaven; Sandy Is a Lady.
1941: The Lady Eve; Swamp Water; Appointment for Love; The Bride Came C.O.D.; Unfinished Business; World Premiere; Ride, Kelly, Ride.
1942: The Male Animal; The Big Street; Tales of Manhattan; Lady in a Jam; The Forest Rangers; Are Husbands Necessary?; Silver Queen; Almost Married.
1943: Heaven Can Wait; The Gang's All Here; Slightly Dangerous; The Kansan; It Ain't Hay.
1944: In the Meantime, Darling; Pin-Up Girl; Step Lively; Heavenly Days; The Laramie Trail; Sensations of 1945.
1945: The Cheaters; Lake Placid Serenade.
1946: Suspense; In Old Sacramento.
1948: Silver River.

Fussy, overwrought, epicene:
FRANKLIN PANGBORN

Probably no screen actor has ever cornered the market on one type of role so completely as Franklin Pangborn did.

Scores of performers could, and did, play Brooklyn-accented cab drivers, elegant butlers, cheap floozies, sinister spies or dumb cops. But when a certain character type was in the cast, there was only one possible choice, and it was Pangborn. That character was the fussy, flustered, hysterical and effeminate hotel clerk, store manager or department-store floorwalker, haughty, long-suffering and disdainful, usually in a stage of confusion or outrage brought on by the antics of hotel guests or store customers. One film historian has described him as "the movies' resident pansy."

With pursed lips, nose in the air, and a thin, unimpressive mustache, sometimes wearing a pincenez, he always looked as though he had just detected a bad smell, and invariably made it clear that whatever he was doing (and whomever he was addressing) was beneath him. Ultimately circumstances conspired to confound him, as the "prissy prune" (as one author has called him) came under pressure and dissolved into a state of collapse. The actor had that routine to perfection, and he must have played it in well over a hundred movies (his career total is impressive: more than 150 films).

Pangborn's role in a movie was almost always a small one, involving at best a few scenes. But he was one of the screen's most familiar figures in the Thirties and early Forties, and could always be counted on to reduce an audience to helpless laughter even in the midst of an otherwise lackluster film. His patented trademark scene was the one where, as a hotel clerk, his smile turns into a sick grin when he realizes that the people checking in are going to be nothing but trouble.

He was born January 23, 1893 (some sources say 1894), in Newark, New Jersey, and originally began as a dramatic stage actor. His career was interrupted by service in World War I, where he was wounded and shellshocked. After a period of recuperation, he resumed his stage work. He toured with the legendary actress Alla Nazimova, managing the company as well as acting in the plays, and at some point played the villain Messala in **Ben-Hur.** He had built a reputation as a fine dramatic performer when he began to appear in movies in the waning years of the silent era.

The actor made his screen debut in a supporting role in **Exit Smiling** (26), the only silent film to star comedienne Beatrice Lillie. In **The Cradle Snatchers** (27) he was one of the husbands of three wives who decide to cure the men of flirting with flappers by arranging for a trio of college boys to flirt with *them.* He was one of a gang of mail thieves in **Finger Prints,** played a doctor's patient with a nervous ailment in **The Girl in the Pullman,** and briefly achieved starring status in **My Friend from India,** as a young globetrotter who falls in love with Elinor Fair. He played Marie Prevost's father in **The Night Bride** (in real life he was 34 years old to her 28), and was in **The Rejuvenation of Aunt Mary,** starring character actress May Robson; he was the chum of one of her nephews.

He played an ex-suitor of the newlywed Miss Prevost, his occupation being owner of a dress shop, in **A Blonde for a Night** (28), and was in two other films that year. In director D.W. Griffith's **Lady of** the Pavements (29) he was a French dancing master, and in the Edward Everett Horton starrer **The Sap** he was Horton's wife's brother-in-law, joining Alan Hale in helping the star misappropriate bank funds for purposes of speculation (this was his first all-talkie). He supported Marion Davies in **Not So Dumb** (30), playing a smirking businessman in huge Harold Lloyd-style spectacles, and was a professor in **Cheer Up and Smile,** also being cast in **A Lady Surrenders.** At this point he was still appearing on screen clean-shaven, without the pencil-thin twitching mustache that would become one of his later trademarks.

Pangborn played a sailor in **Her Man,** and was in **A Woman of Experience** (31); both films starred Helen Twelvetrees. His first hotel-clerk role apparently came in **A Fool's Advice** (32), and he was a hotel manager in **The Half Naked Truth.** These roles launched his career-within-a-career of playing hotel functionaries.

That persona became fully developed in **Flying Down to Rio** (33), the first Fred Astaire-Ginger Rogers film, in which he was the irate hotel manager, declaiming, "I will dismiss, discharge and disqualify any employee who gets familiar with the guests!" (The mustache had now come into being.) And he was again a fastidious and effeminate hotel manager in **International House,** outraged when W.C. Fields makes a shambles of the registration desk; the actor's orderliness was an irresistible target for the anarchic Fields, and they would meet again on screen. His first role as a department-store floorwalker came in **Bed of Roses,** and he was also in such major productions as **Design for Living, Only Yesterday, Professional Sweetheart** and **Sweepings.**

The pace of the actor's filming increased now, with 11 movies in 1934. He played the town crier in **Cockeyed Cavaliers,** a secretary in **Many Happy Returns,** and a radio announcer in **Young and Beautiful.** In **Tomorrow's Youth** he was child star Dickie Moore's strict tutor. Several of his films that year were on Poverty Row, for Mascot, Majestic and Monogram. At the latter studio, he at least had a screen romance, playing an efficiency expert who falls in love with showgirl Joyce Compton. Most of his 1935 output—three out of four films—also consisted of low-budget cheapies.

He got right back into the swing of things as Gary Cooper's fussy tailor in director Frank Capra's smash hit **Mr. Deeds Goes to Town** (36), also getting good notices for his portrayal of the frantic master of ceremonies for the scavenger hunt in the classic screwball comedy **My Man Godfrey.** If the truth be told, Pangborn was probably in more screwball com-

edies—albeit in small roles—than any other performer. In film after film he makes himself the object of mockery, but never gives up his dignity. In fact, his comedy consists of the hysterical preservation of dignity in the face of an endlessly degrading and insulting reality.

Also that year, he was a prissy jeweler in Deanna Durbin's screen debut, **Three Smart Girls,** played a salesman in **Don't Gamble with Love,** and was in at least eight other films—again, many of them on Poverty Row.

If you were a film fan who preferred not to see Franklin Pangborn on the screen, your best bet in 1937 and 1938 would have been simply to stay home. The actor was in the amazing total of at least 39 films during that brief period—23 in the former year, 16 in the latter. He played Adolphe Menjou's effete butler in **Stage Door,** a hat salesman in a store in **Easy Living,** a theatrical agent in **Thrill of a Lifetime,** a Fuller Brush salesman in **Hotel Haywire,** a bartender in **We Have Our Moments,** a theatrical costumer in **All over Town,** and, inevitably, an apartment-hotel manager in **They Wanted to Marry,** all 1937 films. He also had small roles in such major productions as **A Star Is Born** and **Swing High, Swing Low.**

In the following year, he was a hotel manager, hotel clerk or apartment manager in at least five of his 16 films. As the hotel functionary in the Shirley Temple starrer **Just Around the Corner** he harassed Shirley and her father, Charles Farrell, and ended up getting dumped down a laundry chute. He also ran a hotel, or clerked in one, in **Vivacious Lady, Bluebeard's Eighth Wife, Three Blind Mice** and **Topper Takes a Trip,** and possibly played a (small) similar role, although uncredited, in **Mad About Music.** He was also the leader of a radio orchestra in **Joy of Living,** a bicycle salesman in **Always Goodbye,** and had parts in such films as **Carefree, Doctor Rhythm** and **Four's a Crowd.**

He played the butler in **Fifth Avenue Girl** (39), and was in **Broadway Serenade.** And now some fine comedy roles came his way. In the W.C. Fields starrer **The Bank Dick** (40) he was the fastidious bank examiner J. Pinkerton Snoopington—probably the role that provided his longest time on screen. There was a memorable scene in which Fields does everything possible to stop the examiner from checking over the bank's records, including breaking his glasses and crushing his hand in a letter press (earlier, he had had a bartender give Pangborn a Mickey Finn). He was also in director Preston Sturges' comedy **Christmas in July,** as a radio announcer on the verge of nervous collapse. Sturges, who liked to work with a "stock company" of offbeat and bizarre comedians, would use the actor in five more films. Pangborn played a bartender again in **The Villain Still Pursued Her** and also in **Elsa Maxwell's Public Deb No. 1,** and in **Hit Parade of 1941** he was the manager of a department store owned by Mary Boland. An interesting development came in **Turnabout,** when Joseph Breen, head of the Production Code enforcing agency, protested to Hal Roach and United Artists that the actor's characterization in the film was "too pansyish."

He worked with Fields again in **Never Give a Sucker an Even Break** (41), playing a glaring, twitching movie producer named...Franklin Pangborn! (Fields played a comedian named W.C. Fields.) Director Sturges cast him as a movie-studio functionary in the memorable comedy-drama **Sullivan's Travels,** and he and Mischa Auer were a pair of bar patrons in **The Flame of New Orleans.** Seven other films that year were routine or worse. He played the cruise official who introduces Bette Davis to Paul Henreid in **Now, Voyager** (42), and was once again an apartment manager in Sturges' **The Palm Beach Story.** In Sturges' **Hail the Conquering Hero,** a surprise comedy hit of 1944 starring Eddie Bracken, he almost walked off with the film as the harassed and desperately thwarted master of ceremonies, and he also appeared for Sturges in **The Great Moment,** as a physician in mutton chops. (It was hard to take him seriously as a doctor, but then it was difficult to take *anything* seriously in Sturges' films.)

Pangborn's screen appearances dropped off sharply as World War II ended. Now in his early fifties, he was a hotel clerk again in **Lover Come Back** (46), and worked for Sturges for the last time in **The Sin of Harold Diddlebock** (47), Harold Lloyd's last film (re-released in 1950 as **Mad Wednesday**). He was a barber in the Deanna Durbin outing **I'll Be Yours.** He supported Doris Day in her first two films, **Romance on the High Seas** (48) and **My Dream Is Yours** (49), and after one forgettable 1950 programmer he vanished from the screen for seven years.

Earlier, he had begun working on Jack Benny's radio show and had become a fixture there, repeating his patented screen characterization and adding a new trademark, an imperious one-word question, "Ya-a-ass?", in response to any inquiry. When Benny moved the show to television, Pangborn came along, and his visual impact in the part heightened its comedy appeal. He returned to the screen in 1957 for two last films, playing a bartender in **Oh, Men! Oh, Women!** and a French nobleman in the bizarre historical spoof **The Story of Mankind,** which also marked the final film appearance for both Ronald Colman and the Marx Brothers.

The actor died in 1958 at age 65, and with him died the era when films could cast a fussy, overwrought and effeminate hotel manager. Anybody essaying such a (politically incorrect) role today would only be compared unfavorably with the absolutely inimitable original, Franklin Pangborn.

THE FILMS OF FRANKLIN PANGBORN

1926: Exit Smiling.
1927: The Cradle Snatchers; Finger Prints; Getting Gertie's Garter; The Girl in the Pullman; My Friend from India; The Night Bride; The Rejuvenation of Aunt Mary.
1928: On Trial; A Blonde for a Night; The Rush Hour.
1929: Lady of the Pavements; The Sap; Watch Out.
1930: A Lady Surrenders; Not So Dumb; Her Man; Cheer Up and Smile.
1931: A Woman of Experience.
1932: A Fool's Advice; The Half Naked Truth; Midnight Patrol; Stepping Sisters.
1933: Flying Down to Rio; Only Yesterday; Design for Living; International House; Professional Sweetheart; Headline Shooter; Sweepings; Bed of Roses; The Important Witness.
1934: Imitation of Life; Cockeyed Cavaliers; Strictly Dynamite; Many Happy Returns; College Rhythm; That's Gratitude; Manhattan Love Song; Young and Beautiful; Unknown Blonde; Tomorrow's Youth; King Kelly of the U.S.A. *Credit uncertain:* Stand Up and Cheer.
1935: She Couldn't Take It; Eight Bells; The Headline Woman; $1,000 a Minute. *Credit uncertain:* Flirtation.
1936: Mr. Deeds Goes to Town; My Man Godfrey; Three Smart Girls; To Mary—with Love; The Luckiest Girl in the World; Don't Gamble with Love; The Mandarin Mystery; Hats Off; Tango; Doughnuts and Society. *Credit uncertain:* Give Us This Night; In His Steps.
1937: Stage Door; A Star Is Born; Easy Living; Swing High, Swing Low; Step Lively, Jeeves; Danger—Love at Work; I'll Take Romance; They Wanted to Marry; The Lady Escapes; She Had to Eat; It Happened in Hollywood; Turn Off the Moon; Thrill of a Lifetime; When Love Is Young; She's Dangerous; Hotel Haywire; The Life of the Party; Living on Love; High Hat; Rich Relations; We Have Our Moments; Dangerous Holiday; All Over Town. *Credit uncertain:* Dangerous Number.
1938: Carefree; Vivacious Lady; Joy of Living; Bluebeard's Eighth Wife; Rebecca of Sunnybrook Farm; Three Blind Mice; Always Goodbye; Just Around the Corner; Doctor Rhythm; Love on Toast; Four's a Crowd; It's All Yours; She Married an Artist; Topper Takes a Trip; Girls' School; The Girl Downstairs. *Credit uncertain:* Mad About Music.
1939: Fifth Avenue Girl; Broadway Serenade.
1940: The Bank Dick; Christmas in July; Spring Parade; Turnabout; The Villain Still Pursued Her; Elsa Maxwell's Public Deb No. 1; Hit Parade of 1941.
1941: Sullivan's Travels; Never Give a Sucker an Even Break; The Flame of New Orleans; Where Did You Get That Girl?; A Girl, a Guy and a Gob; Bachelor Daddy; Obliging Young Lady; Tillie the Toiler; Weekend for Three; Mr. District Attorney in the Carter Case.
1942: Now, Voyager; the Palm Beach Story; George Washington Slept Here; Call Out the Marines; Strictly in the Groove; What's Cookin'?; Moonlight Masquerade.

1943: His Butler's Sister; Holy Matrimony; Stage Door Canteen; Two Weeks to Live; Reveille with Beverly; Crazy House; Honeymoon Lodge.

1944: Hail the Conquering Hero; The Great Moment; The Reckless Age; Allergic to Love; My Best Gal.

1945: The Horn Blows at Midnight; You Came Along; See My Lawyer; Hollywood and Vine; Tell It to a Star.

1946: Two Guys from Milwaukee; Lover Come Back.

1947: The Sin of Harold Diddlebock (re-released in 1950 as Mad Wednesday); I'll Be Yours; Calendar Girl.

1948: Romance on the High Seas.

1949: My Dream Is Yours; Down Memory Lane.

1950: Her Wonderful Lie.

1957: Oh, Men! Oh, Women!; The Story of Mankind.

GAIL PATRICK

She was one of Hollywood's best "Other Women."

Cold, elegant, aloof and cynical, the beautiful Gail Patrick was always effective in a role that called for her to be aristocratically bitchy and snobbish. Occasionally she would play a nice type, but you remember this tall, willowy brunette best as a woman dripping with icy hauteur, forever finagling to snare some other woman's man.

Her typical role was as the "wrong woman," the languorous and worldly lady whom the leading man sometimes thinks he loves, but doesn't. Her characters exist to be disliked and feared, but in a delicious and enviable sort of way.

Miss Patrick was born (as Margaret Fitzpatrick) June 20, 1911, in Birmingham, Alabama (some sources give the date as 1915 or 1916, which seems highly unlikely). Educated at Howard College, she stayed at her alma mater briefly as assistant dean of women and then attended law school at the University of Alabama. She arrived in Hollywood in 1932 as a finalist in Paramount's "Panther Woman" contest, intended to select a starlet to play a key role in **Island of Lost Souls.** (The now-forgotten Kathleen Burke won the contest and played the part.) Miss Patrick stayed on, however, and signed on as a Paramount contract player; she would make 27 of her first 40 films for that studio.

She made her debut at age 21 in a bit part as a secretary in **If I Had a Million** (32). She had better parts in **Cradle Song** (33), as one of the young novice nuns, and in **Murders in the Zoo,** as the zookeeper's daughter romanced by Randolph Scott. And she played a radio singer in **The Phantom Broadcast.** She was noticed in **Death Takes a Holiday** (34), as one of the more calm and collected visitors to the castle where Death (Fredric March) makes an appearance (she flirts briefly with him), and she had a key part in **Murder at the Vanities** as the murdered private detective. She was in love with Scott again in **Wagon Wheels,** and in **One Hour Late** she returned to husband Conrad Nagel after having a fling with Ray Milland. She co-starred with Ralph Bellamy in **The Crime of Helen Stanley,** playing a movie star who is murdered on the set.

The raven-tressed actress was a fiery Southern coquette in the Bing Crosby starrer **Mississippi** (35), playing his ex-fiancée and losing him to Joan Ben-

nett. She played one of the women in Robert Montgomery's past, a husband-stealing intellectual, in **No More Ladies;** also involved with him is Joan Fontaine, making her screen debut under the name Joan Burfield, but in the end Joan Crawford wins him. She did romantic leads opposite Dean Jagger in **Wanderer of the Wasteland** and Lee Tracy in **Two Fisted,** and **Smart Girl** cast her and Ida Lupino (then still a little-known ingenue) as sisters who are rivals in love; Ida ultimately wins Kent Taylor from Gail.

Miss Patrick finally got a part she could sink her teeth into in the classic screwball comedy **My Man Godfrey** (36), and she made the most of it. As the frosty, bad-tempered, brattish Cornelia, she would have come close to stealing the picture from Carole Lombard, cast as her sister, except for the fact that William Powell and character actors Alice Brady, Mischa Auer and Eugene Pallette stole it instead. Miss Patrick tries to trap Powell by having him falsely accused of theft, as revenge for telling her off. She is so enjoyably mean-spirited that her reformation at the end comes as a distinct letdown (besides the fact that it does not ring true). This characterization was so notable that she became more or less permanently typecast in such roles.

Also that year, she was the heroine, opposite Melvyn Douglas, in **The Lone Wolf Returns,** the first of the talkie Lone Wolf series. She played a film star once again in **The Preview Murder Mystery;** in a plot similar to her 1934 movie **The Crime of Helen Stanley,** she is *nearly* murdered on the set. In **Murder with Pictures** she is a murder suspect, and falls in love with Lew Ayres. She played an old flame of Warner Baxter's in **White Hunter.**

Overshadowed by the likes of Katharine Hepburn and Ginger Rogers, the actress still scored as producer Adolphe Menjou's ex-mistress in the fine drama **Stage Door** (37), giving unsolicited advice and catty know-how to Miss Rogers. She sang two songs as the nightclub performer in **Her Husband Lies,** and was Edward Arnold's fiancée in **John Meade's Woman.** And she paired off with Jack Benny, of all people, in **Artists and Models.** Incredibly, at age 27, she was cast as 16-year-old Deanna Durbin's movie-star mother in **Mad About Music** (38), involved in a romance with Herbert Marshall. She played Warren William's wife, wrongly suspected by him of having an affair, in **Wives Under Suspicion,** and she was a nurse in **King of Alcatraz,** performing a critical operation (on Lloyd Nolan), guided only by wireless instructions from a surgeon; later she and Nolan are married. In **Dangerous to Know** she was the socialite with whom racketeer Akim Tamiroff becomes enamored.

Miss Patrick married Brown Derby restaurateur Bob Cobb in 1936, and they were divorced in 1940. She wed Navy officer Arnold White in 1944 and they split up in 1946. Her third marriage, to Thomas Cornwall Jackson, literary agent of popular mystery writer Erle Stanley Gardner, lasted from 1947 to 1969, and it also ended in divorce. She and Jackson adopted two children, Jennifer and Thomas; she had lost prematurely born twins in 1945 while married to White. In 1975, at age 64, she married businessman John E. Velde Jr.

The actress had a good role in **Disbarred** (39), as a lawyer whom disbarred mouthpiece Otto Kruger tries to use as a stooge, but she is won over by assistant district attorney Robert Preston. She played Richard Dix' socially ambitious wife in **Reno,** and also married him in **Man of Conquest,** after he (playing historical figure Sam Houston) has divorced his ill-tempered first wife, Joan Fontaine (still an unknown,

just before she became a star). Miss Patrick won critical praise for her patented silky elegance in **My Favorite Wife** (40), as Cary Grant's cold shrew of an extraneous wife (after Irene Dunne, believed dead, turns up again). But she was miscast as a simpering, baby-talking nincompoop in **The Doctor Takes a Wife,** engaged to Ray Milland but losing him to Loretta Young. **Gallant Sons** cast her as the mother of teen-ager Bonita Granville at a time when Miss Patrick was still just 29.

She played a home-wrecking seductress in the William Powell-Myrna Loy comedy **Love Crazy** (41), and was jilted by Herbert Marshall in the Shirley Temple vehicle **Kathleen.** As Melvyn Douglas' old flame, she complicated Norma Shearer's love life in **We Were Dancing** (42); it was Miss Shearer's next-to-last film. She caught Cesar Romero on the rebound when Ginger Rogers ran off with his best friend, Henry Fonda, in **Tales of Manhattan.** In **Quiet Please, Murder** she was the assistant and girlfriend of George Sanders, a murderous dealer in fake copies of valuable books; becoming afraid of him, she brings in a detective to put an end to his mad schemes. It was her last really good role.

Both her 1943 films were on Poverty Row, for Republic and Monogram. She was wasted in such farces as **Up in Mabel's Room** (44) and **Brewster's Millions** (45), both starring Dennis O'Keefe; in the latter she reprised her "old flame" characterization, but O'Keefe was no Melvyn Douglas. She was one of the victims of murderous artist Francis Lederer in **The Madonna's Secret** (46), and played a villainess helping Joseph Schildkraut stop the 1859-era Pony Express operation in **The Plainsman and the Lady.** She was a nightclub chanteuse in **Rendezvous with Annie.** Three of her four films that year were made for Republic. She had a standard romantic role opposite Preston Foster in **King of the Wild Horses** (47). Her last film, again for Republic, was a minor rural drama, **The Inside Story** (48). At age 37, Gail Patrick was to film no more.

Not as an actress, at any rate. But in 1957 she and third husband Jackson became the producers of a television series, "Perry Mason," which proved successful. (The series was based on Erle Stanley Gardner's popular stories, and Jackson was Gardner's literary agent.) It ran for 271 episodes and starred Raymond Burr. There was "The New Perry Mason Show" in 1973, with another actor, but meanwhile she and Jackson had divorced and the actress was just a consultant to the series now; in any case, she had more time for duties as board chairman of the American Diabetes Association and work on the advisory council of the National Institutes of Health.

(In the late Forties she had learned she was a diabetic, and for the rest of her life had to give herself insulin injections.)

In her sixties now, she retired, and in 1980 she died at age 69 after a three-year battle with leukemia. But audiences of today should not miss any chance they get to see a rerun of **My Man Godfrey,** where they can recapture the essential Gail Patrick—icily aloof, elegantly bitchy. It was a role that no one could have done better.

THE FILMS OF GAIL PATRICK

1932: If I Had a Million.

1933: Cradle Song; Murders in the Zoo; The Mysterious Rider; To the Last Man; The Phantom Broadcast. *Credit uncertain:* Mama Loves Papa; Pick-Up.

1934: Death Takes a Holiday; Murder at the Vanities; Wagon Wheels; One Hour Late; The Crime of Helen Stanley; Take the Stand.

1935: No More Ladies; Doubting Thomas; Rumba; Mississippi; The Big Broadcast of 1936; Smart Girls; Two Fisted; Wanderer of the Wasteland.

1936: My Man Godfrey; The Preview Murder Mystery; White Hunter; The Lone Wolf Returns; Two in the Dark; Early to Bed; Murder with Pictures.

1937: Stage Door; Artists and Models; Her Husband Lies; John Meade's Woman.

1938: Mad About Music; Wives Under Suspicion; King of Alcatraz; Dangerous to Know.

1939: Disbarred; Grand Jury Secrets; Reno; Man of Conquest; The Hunchback of Notre Dame (apparently in a very small, uncredited role, according to the American Film Institute Catalog).

1940: My Favorite Wife; The Doctor Takes a Wife; Gallant Sons.

1941: Love Crazy; Kathleen.

1942: We Were Dancing; Tales of Manhattan; Quiet Please, Murder.

1943: Hit Parade of 1943; Women in Bondage.

1944: Up in Mabel's Room.

1945: Brewster's Millions; Twice Blessed.

1946: Claudia and David; Rendezvous with Annie; The Madonna's Secret; The Plainsman and the Lady.

1947: King of the Wild Horses; Calendar Girl.

1948: The Inside Story.

Be nice to your aunt:
ELIZABETH PATTERSON

Most people have an ample supply of aging or elderly female relatives. Devoted mothers, doting aunts, crotchety grandmothers—they have all played their roles in your life. And in films of the Thirties, those roles frequently were played by Elizabeth Patterson.

Whether kindly, crabby or put-upon, she fussed her way through 59 films of the decade (with a career total of more than 100 from the silent era through 1960), playing the aunt or mother of many a major star in the process, and also frequently portraying a housekeeper or faithful family retainer.

Miss Patterson was the kind of actress who could be expected to say, "Land sakes alive! What won't they think of next?" or something similar. Fragile, scrawny and quavery-voiced, she seemed to have about her a touch of the small-town South (which was in fact where her roots lay). She tended a spotless kitchen, attired in an immaculate gingham dress and apron, and you expected to find her with wooden spoon in hand, smiling sweetly, fresh from making a batch of strawberry jam.

Mary Elizabeth Patterson was born November 22, 1874 (some sources say 1875 or 1876), in Savannah, Tennessee, the daughter of a judge. Educated at Martin College in nearby Pulaski and at Columbia Institute in Columbia, she then defied her parents and announced she was going on the stage. With an inheritance from her grandfather, she went to Chicago to study drama. First acting professionally with the Ben Greet Players, a touring Shakespearean company, she played 23 roles over three seasons. She then worked with New York's Washington Square Players and with Stuart Walker's stock companies in Cincinnati, Indianapolis, and on Broadway. Author Booth Tarkington saw her in Indianapolis and recommended her for a part in his play **Intimate Strangers,** starring Billie Burke; Miss Patterson appeared on Broadway in the role in 1920, at age 45.

In 1926 the actress left New York for Hollywood, and at the age of 52 made her screen debut in **The Boy Friend** (26), as the mother of the heroine (Marceline Day). She also had a part in **The Return of Peter Grimm.** But she went back to the stage for three more years, returning at the beginning of the sound era to take up a lengthy career in films.

She had a key role as the straitlaced dean of women in the college musical **Words and Music**

(29), was effective as a terrified woman in **The Cat Creeps** (30), and played a matchmaking mother who overdoes it in **Harmony at Home,** also appearing as Walter Catlett's wife in **The Big Party.** In Tallulah Bankhead's screen debut, **Tarnished Lady** (31), which was also George Cukor's first film as a solo director, she played Miss Bankhead's mother. She was a German baroness in **The Smiling Lieutenant,** the matron of the orphanage in **Daddy Long Legs,** a poor-white rural Mississippian (the mother of teen-age Anita Louise) in **Heaven on Earth,** and Clive Brook's icy-eyed mother-in-law in **Husband's Holiday.**

The early Thirties was the busiest period in Hollywood history for character actors, and Miss Patterson appeared in at least 13 films in 1932. She played Aunt Hester in Katharine Hepburn's debut film, **A Bill of Divorcement,** Carole Lombard's mother in **No Man of Her Own** (the only Gable-Lombard movie), and one of the chorus of three aunts

229

in the brilliantly innovative musical **Love Me To-night.** She was Robert Young's aunt in **New Morals for Old** and Loretta Young's mother in **They Call It Sin,** and played the murder victim in **Miss Pinkerton.**

Her roles continued to be relatively small ones in 1933, but some of the films were enduring classics. She was somebody's aunt in the Will Rogers vehicle **Doctor Bull** and also in the torrid shocker **The Story of Temple Drake,** and played a farmhand who marries fellow worker Roscoe Ates in **Golden Harvest;** there were also a few other aunt roles. Her only film in 1934 was **Hide-Out,** in which she played the mother of Maureen O'Sullivan and Mickey Rooney, and at this point in time she also appeared on the Broadway stage again, her plays including **Her Master's Voice** with Roland Young and Laura Hope Crews.

Now in her sixties, the actress returned to take a key part in the Civil War romance **So Red the Rose** (35), and was the cold-hearted proprietor of the boarding school attended by Anne Shirley in **Chasing Yesterday,** also playing a suspicious rural housewife in **Men Without Names.** She was seen to advantage in the Mae West starrer **Go West, Young Man** (36) as a flinty old aunt in Alice Brady's rural boarding-house menage, taking one look at Miss West and commenting, "In my time a woman with hair like that didn't come out in the daytime." She played Janet Gaynor's down-to-earth mother in **Small Town Girl,** Wallace Beery's long-suffering wife in **Old Hutch,** and a wealthy, timorous gem collector in **The Return of Sophie Lang.** In **Her Master's Voice,** as Edward Everett Horton's mother-in-law, she is hired as a maid by Grant Mitchell, who later proposes to her. She owned a bankrupt school for girls in **Three Cheers for Love,** and was actually top-billed in **Timothy's Quest** as a harsh rancher whose heart is softened by little Dickie Moore.

Miss Patterson was the archetypal small-town grandmother of Randolph Scott in **High, Wide and Handsome** (37), and was the murder victim, a paralyzed invalid slain by drug injection, in **Night of Mystery.** She had the key role of Claudette Colbert's aunt, the head of the family, in **Bluebeard's Eighth Wife** (38), and was the mother of Bing Crosby, Fred MacMurray and Donald O'Connor in **Sing, You Sinners** (hardly likely, because in real life she was 63 years old to O'Connor's 13). And she now appeared in the first of three Bulldog Drummond films, **Bulldog Drummond's Peril,** as one of the aunts, a regular character in the series. She was a town gossip in **Scandal Street.**

She reprised her **The Cat Creeps** role from 1930 as a terrified lady in the Bob Hope vehicle **The Cat and the Canary** (39), and did service in two more Bulldog Drummonds. Fred MacMurray had her for an aunt in **Remember the Night** (40) (she showed Barbara Stanwyck how to make popovers), and she had the title role as the murder victim in **Who Killed Aunt Maggie?** (Walter Abel was the killer.) She was fine as the eternally suffering wife of Jeeter Lester (Charley Grapewin) in director John Ford's drama of poor-white rural Southerners, **Tobacco Road** (41), played the grandmother in **The Vanishing Virginian,** and had a key role in **Belle Starr.**

The actress played Rosalind Russell's grandmother in **My Sister Eileen** (42), and was Norma Shearer's servant and confidante in the star's last film, **Her Cardboard Lover.** She also had a prominent part in **I Married a Witch.** She was a landlady in **The Sky's the Limit** (43), and there was a routine aunt role in **Hail the Conquering Hero** (44). She had a key part in **Together Again,** with Irene Dunne and Charles Boyer, and was seen in **Lady on a Train** (45) and **Colonel Effingham's Raid.** Now in her seventies, she supported Claudette Colbert and June Allyson in **The Secret Heart** (46). She was good as physician Barry Fitzgerald's housekeeper in the Bing Crosby starrer **Welcome Stranger** (47), and supported Betty Grable in **The Shocking Miss Pilgrim.** In 1948 she was in **Miss Tatlock's Millions,** and again she returned for a while to the Broadway stage.

At this point no one would have thought it unusual had the elderly actress gone into retirement after a career of half a century. Instead, she surprised all of Hollywood with a strong dramatic performance in an important film. Director Clarence Brown's **Intruder in the Dust** (49) was a powerful version of William Faulkner's novel about a Southern lynch mob pursuing a black man (Juano Hernandez) accused of murder. Miss Patterson, joining forces with teen-ager Claude Jarman Jr., was a moving symbol of delicacy and strength as the insignificant elderly lady who coolly defies the mob and doggedly finds the evidence that pins the guilt on the real murderer, who happens to be one of the leaders of the would-be lynchers. In this film, Elizabeth Patterson at age 74 gave the performance of her life, but it passed more or less unremarked and didn't even win her an Oscar nomination as best supporting actress. In that year she was also cast in **Little Women** and had a key role in **Song of Surrender.**

There was another prominent part in **Bright Leaf** (50), with Gary Cooper, Lauren Bacall and Patricia Neal, and a key role in **The Washington Story** (52). She then took a three-year vacation from the screen and returned to the stage, finally making her last Broadway appearance in **His and Hers** in 1954. She also did some work on television's "I Love Lucy" series.

In private life, the actress—who never married—lived the kind of existence that would have astonished those accustomed to her screen persona. She was an urban sophisticate who wore original dressmaker fashions, kept her hair an attractive red, maintained a swank apartment in one of Hollywood's best hotels, and was always ready to ride off in a limousine to the latest play or art-gallery opening.

In her eighties she continued to appear on the screen. She had an important part in **Las Vegas Shakedown** (55), and was also prominent in the Rita Hayworth-Frank Sinatra vehicle **Pal Joey** (57). She appeared in **The Oregon Trail** (59), and, at 85, closed out her film career with another key role in **Tall Story** (60), starring Jane Fonda (in her screen debut) and Anthony Perkins.

Elizabeth Patterson died in 1966 at the age of 91—one of the longest-lived performers in Hollywood history. But a quick twirl of the TV dial late at night will bring her back again. You can't miss her. In her freshly starched gingham apron, she smiles sweetly and, in a quavery voice, invites you to sample the strawberry jam she has just made. Land sakes alive! That jam is mighty good—and so was this delightful actress.

THE FILMS OF ELIZABETH PATTERSON

1926: The Boy Friend; The Return of Peter Grimm.
1929: South Sea Rose; Words and Music.
1930: The Cat Creeps; The Big Party; The Lone Star Ranger; Harmony at Home.
1931: Tarnished Lady; The Smiling Lieutenant; Daddy Long Legs; Heaven on Earth; Husband's Holiday.
1932: A Bill of Divorcement; No Man of her Own; So Big; Love Me Tonight; Man Wanted; Life Begins; Play Girl; Miss Pinkerton; New Morals for Old; The Expert; They Call It Sin; Guilty as Hell; Breach of Promise. *Credit uncertain:* The Conquerors; Two Against the World.
1933: Dinner at Eight; Hold Your Man; Ever in My Heart; The Story of Temple Drake; Doctor Bull; They Just Had to Get Married; Secret of the Blue Room; Infernal Machine; Golden Harvest.
1934: Hide-Out.
1935: So Red the Rose; Men Without Names; Chasing Yesterday.
1936: Go West, Young Man; Small Town Girl; Three Cheers for Love; Old Hutch; The Return of Sophie Lang; Her Master's Voice; Timothy's Quest. *Credit uncertain:* Poppy.
1937: High, Wide and Handsome; Night Club Scandal; Hold 'Em Navy!; Night of Mystery.
1938: Bluebeard's Eighth Wife; Sing, You Sinners; Bulldog Drummond's Peril; Scandal Street; Sons of the Legion.
1939: The Cat and the Canary; The Story of Alexander Graham Bell;

Our Leading Citizen; Bad Little Angel; Bulldog Drummond's Bride; Bulldog Drummond's Secret Police.
1940: Remember the Night; Who Killed Aunt Maggie?; Earthbound; Anne of Windy Poplars; Adventure in Diamonds; Michael Shayne, Private Detective.
1941: Tobacco Road; Belle Starr; The Vanishing Virginian; Kiss the Boys Goodbye.
1942: I Married a Witch; My Sister Eileen; Her Cardboard Lover; Beyond the Blue Horizon; Almost Married; Lucky Legs.
1943: The Sky's the Limit.
1944: Hail the Conquering Hero; Together Again; Follow the Boys.
1945: Lady on a Train; Colonel Effingham's Raid.
1946: The Secret Heart; I've Always Loved You.
1947: Welcome Stranger; The Shocking Miss Pilgrim; Out of the Blue.
1948: Miss Tatlock's Millions.
1949: Intruder in the Dust; Little Women; Song of Surrender.
1950: Bright Leaf.
1951: Katie Did It.
1952: The Washington Story.
1955: Las Vegas Shakedown.
1957: Pal Joey.
1959: The Oregon Trail.
1960: Tall Story.

With a trick eyebrow and a sardonic smile:
CLAUDE RAINS

One of the greatest character actors of the Golden Era—or any other Hollywood era—was Claude Rains, whose screen personality embodied a sardonic suavity. One writer has noted that he had as a trademark "a trick right eyebrow that could be raised to convey scorn, skepticism, mild amusement or total disbelief." His unique, quietly commanding voice, with its clipped tones, has been described as "honey with some gravel in it." Superbly controlled, he could be incisive, sophisticated, sarcastic, chilly, sympathetic or downright nasty.

A true actor's actor, with a piercing intelligence, he was fair-haired, stocky, slight (he wore elevator shoes on screen) and not handsome—not the type to be a leading man, but through most of his career he was either the star or led the supporting cast. He was charming even when playing a polished villain, which he did frequently.

He was a good enough actor to be nominated four times for an Academy Award as best supporting actor—and, incredibly, he lost every time. Perhaps his subtlety was lost on Oscar voters who preferred a more blatant acting style—but critics and audiences alike delighted in his portrayals.

William Claude Rains was born November 10, 1889, in London, a child of the slums, the son of a failed actor. His first appearance on the London stage came at the age of 10 or 11 when a choirmaster was asked to provide some boys for a crowd scene in **Nell of Old Drury** at the Haymarket. Queen Victoria was still on the throne, and the young thespian would still be acting 65 years hence. Shortly afterward he became a call-boy at His Majesty's Theatre (by this time Edward VII was king), and subsequently assistant stage manager, the latter position lasting seven years.

In 1911, at age 21, he got a small part in Lord Dunsany's **The Gods of the Mountain** (he first had to overcome a Cockney accent and a lisp), and then began an Australian tour as stage manager for Maurice Maeterlinck's **The Blue Bird,** also playing small parts. In 1914-15 he was stage manager in Australia for Sir Harley Granville-Barker, still playing occasional parts, and then returned to England for army service in World War I, serving with the London Scottish Regiment and then the Bedford Regiment and rising from private to captain. In 1919 he appeared in **Uncle Ned** in the industrial city of Sheffield, and then began to make a name for himself in London's West End.

The actor was liked by critics in **The Government Inspector,** and next was in a run of Bernard Shaw dramas at the Everyman Theatre: Louis Dubedat in **The Doctor's Dilemma,** Dick Dudgeon in **The Devil's Disciple,** Napoleon in **The Man of Destiny** (it would not be the last time he would portray the French ruler). Seldom out of work, he also taught acting by day at the Royal Academy of Dramatic Art, his pupils including Laurence Olivier, Charles Laughton and John Gielgud. (Gielgud later said, "His vitality and enthusiasm made him a delightful teacher, and most of the girls were in love with him.") Then, in 1926, he accompanied his third wife, actress Beatrix Thomson, to New York, where she was to star in a play.

Prior to Miss Thomson, he had been divorced from actresses Isabel Jeans (whom he married in 1913) and Marie Hemingway (a very brief liaison, beginning and ending in 1920); these three were among the most beautiful women on the London stage. Ultimately he would be divorced from Miss Thomson and would wed the much younger American stage actress Frances Propper in 1935; that marriage lasted 24 years and also gave him his only child, Jennifer, an actress now called Jessica Rains. In 1959 he married Hungarian pianist Agi Jambor, and she divorced him six months later; the following year he wed Rosemary Clark. All told, six marriages.

Rains took a small role in his wife's play, **The Constant Nymph,** but later played the male lead on a U.S. tour. Settling in America, he was soon a respected Broadway name in productions of the Theater Guild: starring as Samuel Pepys in **And So to Bed,** in the title role in **Volpone,** on tour in Eugene O'Neill's **Marco Millions,** back on Broadway in Shaw's **The Apple Cart.** In 1932 he appeared in **The Moon in the Yellow River** and **The Man Who Reclaimed His Head,** and co-starred opposite Alla Nazimova in the stage adaptation of Pearl Buck's **The Good Earth,** in the role Paul Muni would later play on the screen.

Hollywood now beckoned. He was screen-tested for the role John Barrymore ultimately played as the demented husband and father in **A Bill of Divorcement,** but was considered unlikely film material. Director James Whale saw that test and thought him suitable for his version of **The Invisible Man** (33), where only his voice would matter. That voice superbly conveyed the deranged character's agony and desperation, although the invisible man was never seen until he "materialized" as he died in the last few seconds of the film. The vocal performance (and the film's huge success) proved to be enough to make Claude Rains a leading movie actor at the age of 43.

Next, he was excellent in the offbeat drama **Crime Without Passion** (34), as a dissolute, coldly unscrupulous lawyer who becomes unhinged through his love for a socialite and tries to end his affair with a fiery Spanish dancer (the 17-year-old actress Margo) by killing her. It turns out that she lives, but while thinking her dead he learns he has killed someone else in trying to establish an alibi. Now he went back to Broadway to co-star with Ruth Gordon in **They Shall Not Die.**

He repeated his stage role on the screen in **The Man Who Reclaimed His Head** (35), as a writer who sells his talents to a newspaper publisher (Lionel Atwill) by ghostwriting pacifist editorials. But on the eve of a world war the publisher betrays him and sells out to the munitions makers; the writer goes insane and ends up reclaiming his professional integrity by cutting off the publisher's head, which he then carries around in a handbag. Joan Bennett portrayed his young wife. A fourth madman in a row

now followed: Rains was "brilliantly repellent" (the New York Times) as murderer John Jasper in the film adaptation of Dickens' unfinished last novel, **The Mystery of Edwin Drood.** In **The Clairvoyant (The Evil Mind)** he was a fake music-hall crystal gazer, a charlatan assisted by his wife (Fay Wray), who discovers he really can predict the future. **The Last Outpost** found him in a conventional love triangle with fellow British army officer Cary Grant; guess who wins the girl. His performance in this forgettable film was highly praised by critic Graham Greene, who said, "Mr. Rains' low husky voice, his power of investing even commonplace dialogue with smoldering conviction, is remarkable. He never rants, but one is always aware of what a superb ranter he could be in a part that did not call for modern restraint but only for superb diction."

In **Anthony Adverse** (36), the first film under what would be a long contract with Warner Bros., the actor was Anthony's (Fredric March's) domineering and vindictive stepfather, the gouty, irascible and wicked Don Luis, who marries his housekeeper (Gale Sondergaard in her film debut). Incredibly, Miss Sondergaard, in a mediocre performance, won an Oscar as best supporting actress (the first time this award was handed out), but Rains, in a much better performance, wasn't even nominated. Still, he showed that in his hands even a villain could be sympathetic. He next played Napoleon in the silly Marion Davies-Dick Powell outing **Hearts Divided.**

One of his best-remembered roles came in **They Won't Forget** (37), as the cold-bloodedly opportunistic Southern district attorney who exploits the murder of teen-ager Lana Turner and, in his attempt to win publicity for a run for governor, whips up prejudice against a man who may be innocent and railroads him (to a lynching, as it turns out) by means of circumstantial evidence despite the efforts of defense attorney Otto Kruger. Although the critics liked his performance, the truth is that in this film he overacted badly; his effectiveness depended on his response to his material, and he could ham it up when he felt like it.

Also that year, he was brilliant in **Stolen Holiday** as a big-time Russian financial swindler (based on the Stavisky case) who pays off top government officials and marries Kay Francis to achieve protection from the law, but he ends up shot dead by the police. He had a routine villain role in the Errol Flynn starrer **The Prince and the Pauper.** He was fine as the wily villain Prince John (later King John) in another Flynn film, the classic **The Adventures of Robin Hood** (38), and played Olivia de Havilland's father in the so-so **Gold Is Where You Find It.** He was married to (and well matched by) Fay Bainter in **White Banners,** as a small-town professor who is cheated out of a patent on his invention of a new kind of refrigerator; undaunted, he comes up with an even better one. In the fine drama **Four Daughters** he was the father of the Lane sisters (plus Gale Page), one of whom, Priscilla, was loved by John Garfield in his first credited screen role. Garfield was nominated for a supporting Oscar, but Rains wasn't.

He finally got his first Oscar nomination with a brilliant performance as the corrupt senator opposed to James Stewart in **Mr. Smith Goes to Washington** (39); he superbly created the tension of an elder statesman torn between duty and chicanery (the latter represented by political boss Edward Arnold), and gave his harangues with an eloquence and fervor that still stand out in revival showings or on video. This performance could well have won the Oscar, but he lost to Thomas Mitchell's equally fine portrayal of a whiskey-soaked doctor in **Stagecoach.** Also that year, he was a relentless detective pursuing Garfield in **They Made Me a Criminal,** and was somewhat hammy as the suavely scheming French emperor Napoleon III in **Juarez** (thus becoming the only film actor to play both Napoleons).

Then there was the matter of the sequels to **Four Daughters** (and this year would not even see the last of them). In **Daughters Courageous** virtually all of the original cast was reassembled, and Fay Bainter was brought in to play the wife he deserted 20 years earlier, now planning to marry Donald Crisp. Rains stole the show with his wry humor, his half-concealed contempt for Crisp, and the cunning with which he wins over his daughters. In **Four Wives** he had less to do, and the formula was now starting to wear thin.

It was an off year in 1940. He was a routine villain (and a Spanish grandee once again, as in **Anthony Adverse**), once more being nasty to Errol Flynn, in **The Sea Hawk,** and he was skillful as the flamboyant theatrical impresario David Belasco in **The Lady with Red Hair,** which starred Miriam Hopkins. He was Anne Shirley's father in the John Garfield starrer **Saturday's Children.**

It was back to psychopathology again for the fine melodrama **Kings Row** (41), in which he was excellent as the once idealistic Dr. Tower, so haunted by the fear of madness in his family that he kills his daughter (Betty Field) and himself. He was a bit hammy again as Mr. Jordan, the heavenly representative, in the fantasy **Here Comes Mr. Jordan,** and was utterly wasted in **The Wolf Man,** as the father of the title character, Lon Chaney Jr., whom he is finally forced to kill with a silver-tipped cane. Then there was the final sequel to **Four Daughters,** this one called **Four Mothers,** a completely routine film; fortunately, no one ever thought of making one called "Four Grandmothers."

Rains was Oscar-nominated again for his slippery, crafty police chief in the classic **Casablanca** (42), admonishing his underlings to "round up the usual suspects" and lending a hand to Humphrey Bogart at the finale. He was a charming and amiably immoral opportunist whom Bogie salutes in the film's curtain line: "Louis, I think this is the beginning of a beautiful friendship." It was a good performance, but lost out for the Oscar to Charles Coburn in **The More the Merrier,** who was equally good. Also that year, he was the psychiatrist who brings sheltered spinster Bette Davis out of her shell in **Now, Voyager,** a purely Forties creation, all-knowing, owlish and worldly-wise, every woman's dream of fatherly understanding; many a film fan wished that Miss Davis had ended up at the finale with him instead of the milksop Paul Henreid, and in two future films Rains would play her husband or her lover. To ring down the curtain on 1942, he was an intellectual bum, a mysterious, philosophical night prowler, in **Moontide,** starring Jean Gabin and Ida Lupino.

He was hardly the ideal choice to reprise Lon Chaney's old role as **The Phantom of the Opera** (43), and gave a mediocre performance as the obsessed man, albeit a more sympathetic one than Chaney's. In the all-star epic **Forever and a Day** he did one of the numerous cameos, as the villain in the opening historical episode. He won a third Oscar nomination as Miss Davis' stockbroker husband, in the title role, in **Mr. Skeffington** (44); the plot was that she married him for convenience and later discarded him, but years later, when she is old and her looks are gone, and he has become blind, they are reunited. He was good but not sensational in this glossy soap opera, and lost the Oscar to Barry Fitzgerald as the Irish priest in **Going My Way.** He and Vivien Leigh co-starred in the title roles of **Caesar and Cleopatra,** from the Bernard Shaw play, but the film was static and boring. In **Passage to Marseille** he was the Free French liaison officer who helps Humphrey Bogart and other Frenchmen, and he also narrated most of the film in flashback.

The weakest year of his prime time in Hollywood came in 1945. He stole the show as an old man in the Merle Oberon soap opera **This Love of Ours,** and starred in a forgettable programmer, **Strange Holiday.** Then came one of his most notable performances, as the Axis spy married to Ingrid Bergman (she is a pawn for American intelligence agent Cary Grant) in director Alfred Hitchcock's riveting drama **Notorious** (46). His shrewd and tense portrayal was the best thing in the film, but he lost the supporting Oscar (the last of his four nominations) to Harold Russell, the handless veteran in **The Best Years of Our Lives;** this was one Oscar that Rains really should have won. Co-starring with Bette Davis for the last time, in **Deception,** he played her lover, an egomaniacal composer, whom she murders; Paul Henreid was the third leg of the love triangle. In **Angel on My Shoulder** he played the Devil as a sly, humorous, cultured rogue, promising leniency to executed gangster Paul Muni if he will return to Earth and take over the body of a judge who is stamping out evil.

One of the actor's most enjoyable sympathetic villains came along in his only 1947 release, **The Unsuspected,** in which he is an elegant radio narrator of crime stories who turns to murder out of a consuming greed for possessions, and then is forced to follow the clues on the air until he is caught. He then played Ann Todd's cold, malevolent husband in **The Passionate Friends (One Woman's Story)** (48). In **Rope of Sand** (49) he supported Burt Lancaster, and in **Song of Surrender** he was an aging museum curator with a young wife, Wanda Hendrix (the actor in real life turned 60 that year). He was not especially noteworthy as an alcoholic in the mountain-climbing drama **The White Tower** (50). At this point he resumed stage work in addition to his filming; 1951 saw him star on Broadway in the anti-Communist drama **Darkness at Noon.**

Rains now appeared in **Where Danger Lives** (51), as an elderly man married to the psychopathic young Faith Domergue; she gets involved with Robert Mitchum and ends up murdering Rains. He was off the screen, appearing in stock, for a year, and returned to give one of his worst performances, in **The Man Who Watched Trains Go By (Paris Express),** as a clerk who steals money in order to fulfill his wish for world travel, which ends up in a murder. That 1953 film was his last for three years. He appeared on Broadway in T.S. Eliot's **The Confidential Clerk** in 1954, and then was back on the screen for **Lisbon** (56), stealing the film as an international thief who hires ship captain Ray Milland to rescue Maureen O'Hara's husband from imprisonment behind the Iron Curtain.

At age 69 he returned to appear in **This Earth Is Mine** (59), as Rock Hudson's grandfather, the patriarch of a winery-owning family, in this disjointed soap opera; once again he walked off with the film. But he failed to do even that in the remake of **The Lost World** (60), as Professor Challenger, the leader of the expedition. In 1961 he went to Italy for a film, and then was in a supporting role in the blockbuster **Lawrence of Arabia** (62). He was an elderly lawyer helping a younger one (Richard Chamberlain) win a murder case in **Twilight of Honor** (63), and had a cameo as Herod in his last film, **The Greatest Story Ever Told** (65), a life of Christ starring Max von Sydow.

His last appearance as an actor was at the Westport Country Playhouse in Connecticut in 1965, in the play **So Much of Earth, So Much of Heaven.** Two years later Claude Rains died at the age of 77. He was a colossus of his profession—not merely one of the greatest of character actors, but one of the finest actors the screen has ever seen.

THE FILMS OF CLAUDE RAINS

The shopworn floozy:
MARJORIE RAMBEAU

Under the harsh glare of a street light, she leans against the lamppost and sighs wearily. "I've been around, honey. I've seen it all."

We don't know whether Marjorie Rambeau ever played such a scene, but she *should* have, because it represents the essence of her screen persona. She portrayed an assortment of women of a certain age and a certain *kind:* blowsy aging harlots, fallen women, lusty grand dames, shopworn floozies and discarded mistresses. With a strong, brassy voice and a powerful acting attack, she could play high or low society, a good-hearted dame or a vicious slut; she also had some key roles as the mother of several star actors and actresses. And she was good enough to win two nominations for an Academy Award as best supporting actress.

Miss Rambeau was born July 15, 1889, in San Francisco, her father being a French-born business-man and her mother one of the first woman doctors in the West. After her parents separated, she went with her mother in 1899 to Alaska during the gold rush, where Mrs. Rambeau set up a clinic. On their return to California Marjorie made her stage debut in San Francisco at about age 12, and then spent a num-ber of years in stock companies. She is said to have starred in **Camille** while still in her teens. In 1913 she made her Broadway debut in **Kick In** with her husband, actor-playwright (and future screenwriter) Willard Mack, whom she had married the previous year. Within a few years she was a star.

The actress divorced Mack in 1917 (he later married an even bigger stage and screen star, Pauline Frederick), and two years later she wed actor Hugh Dillman, with a divorce in 1923. In 1931 she would marry Goldwyn film executive Francis A. Gudger, and would be widowed in 1967.

The attractive, strong-featured, brown-haired Miss Rambeau continued to be busy on the stage in the 1910s and '20s, playing elegant, refined women who were a far cry from her later screen persona. At the same time, she began in films in 1916, making eight movies through 1920. On Broadway she ap-peared in a number of popular plays, but was panned by critics when she essayed Shakespeare, playing Rosalind in **As You Like It** in 1923. She made an-other film, **Syncopating Sue,** in 1926 (playing *her-self*), just after starring in 1925 on Broadway in **Antonia,** directed by future film director George

Cukor. At the time, she was an active alcoholic and was causing problems for Cukor. The producer of the play finally threatened to sue her, so she sobered up when the play came to Broadway after its out-of-town tryouts.

The actress was already past 40 when, at the be-ginning of the sound era, she came to Hollywood for good. Her first talkie was **Her Man** (30), in which she got second billing as a Havana dance-hall girl. She followed this with a memorable performance as a vicious waterfront slut in the big hit **Min and Bill,** co-starring Wallace Beery and Marie Dressler; Miss Dressler (who won the best-actress Oscar for this film) has raised the other woman's daughter, and fi-nally kills Miss Rambeau to protect the girl's future.

She made 10 films in 1931, her busiest year by far on the screen. Four of them featured newcomer Clark Gable, who began the year as an unknown and ended it as a top star; in one of these, **The Se-cret Six,** she was a discarded moll of bootlegging czar Lewis Stone, and in another, **Laughing Sinners,** she played Joan Crawford's chorus-girl pal. As to the other two Gable films, she was Beery's girlfriend in **Hell Divers** and a model for an advertising agency in **The Easiest Way.** In other movies, she owned the beauty shop where Norma Shearer worked as a secretary in **Strangers May Kiss,** played an alcoholic former opera singer in **Leftover Ladies,** was the proprietor of a saloon in **Silence,** and supported Greta Garbo in **Inspiration,** as one of Stone's upper-crust pals.

She made no films the following year, but came back with a good role as the commanding (and Mae West-like) Queen of the Amazons in **The Warrior's Husband** (33). She was good as the heart-of-gold, alcoholic shantytown derelict in director Frank Borzage's fine drama **Man's Castle,** supporting Spencer Tracy and Loretta Young; she yearns for Tracy but he isn't interested, obviously preferring Miss Young. She and husband Edward Ellis ran a lonely-hearts club in **Strictly Personal.** In **A Modern Hero** (34) she was Richard Barthelmess' mother, a dissolute but shrewd circus performer with a drinking problem, and in **Palooka** (based on the comic strip "Joe Palooka," about a boxer) she gave an earthy performance as Joe's (Stuart Erwin's) countrified mother, an ex-burlesque queen. In **Ready for Love** she was Ida Lupino's actress mother.

She played the owner of a beer hall in **Under Pressure** (35), and ran a theatrical boarding house in **Dizzy Dames,** following which she took a year off from the screen, returning to play a Washington socialite in **First Lady** (37). She was Ann Dvorak's mother in **Merrily We Live** (38). In **Sudden Money** (39) she played Charlie Ruggles' wife, and in **Heaven With a Barbed Wire Fence** she was the old flame of hobo Raymond Walburn (this film marked the screen debuts of Glenn Ford and Richard Conte). In **Laugh It Off** she and three other old-time actresses (including Hedda Hopper) put on a nightclub show to avoid being sent to the poorhouse, and in **The Rains Came** she was one of the hoity-toity British colony in this film set in India.

The actress won the first of her two Oscar nominations for one of her finest characterizations, the raucous, blowsy, good-hearted mother of Ginger Rogers in **Primrose Path** (40); it seems that the female members of the family have always been employed in the world's oldest profession, and Miss Rambeau plans to pass on the street-walking tradition to her daughter—until Joel McCrea comes along to spoil those plans. In **Tugboat Annie Sails Again** she attempted unsuccessfully to bring to the charac-

ter the impact that Marie Dressler had several years earlier; as a footnote, the film's young leading man saves the day for her, and he is played by—Ronald Reagan! She was badly miscast in **East of the River** as John Garfield's mother, an Italian incredibly named Mama Raviola; she gave an exaggerated ethnic stereotype of a performance. In **Twenty-Mule Team,** starring Wallace Beery, she was a woebegone tavern owner, the mother of 17-year-old Anne Baxter, who was making her film debut.

She appeared for director John Ford in **Tobacco Road** (41), the adaptation of Erskine Caldwell's notorious novel about poor backwoods Southerners, playing the hymn-singing revival preacher Sister Bessie, and was a hearty godmother fixing up lovers' quarrels between John Wayne and Martha Scott in **In Old Oklahoma (War of the Wildcats)** (43). In her fifties now, she had a good role in the bizarre **Salome, Where She Danced** (45), stealing the show from newcomer Yvonne de Carlo by playing a broken-down trouper dressed in black tights and singing a gin-soaked version of "I Dreamt I Dwelt in Marble Halls." In that same year, 1945, she had a near-fatal car accident, followed by numerous operations, but returned in 1948 for a featured role in **The Walls of Jericho.** She played a dowager who is the front for an illegal adoption ring—a black-market baby racket—in **Abandoned** (49), and was the best thing in the film in a small part in the Clark Gable starrer **Any Number Can Play.** Then she was off the screen for four years.

She came back to win a second Oscar nomination with a touching performance as Joan Crawford's mother, a salty, reminiscing grand dame, in **Torch Song** (53). She was stern and stony as a pillar of the church in **A Man Called Peter** (55), and then was in **The View from Pompey's Head,** as the wife of aging author Sidney Blackmer, believing his royalties have been embezzled. She was once again the best thing in the movie in **Slander** (56), in support of Van Johnson, and then, at age 68, appeared in her last film, **Man of a Thousand Faces** (57), a biopic of Lon Chaney starring James Cagney, in which she had a cameo as an old trouper who is an acquaintance of the star; she and Cagney were the only things the critics liked.

The actress and husband Francis Gudger now retired to Palm Springs, California; he died in 1967 and she died in 1970 at age 81. But try turning on your TV set in the shank of the night when some of her old pictures come on. Nobody, but nobody, could play a shopworn floozy quite as well as Marjorie Rambeau.

THE FILMS OF MARJORIE RAMBEAU

1916: The Dazzling Miss Davison; Motherhood; The Greater Woman.
1917: Mary Moreland; The Mirror; The Debt.
1918: The Common Cause.
1920: The Fortune Teller.
1926: Syncopating Sue (as herself).
1930: Min and Bill; Her Man.
1931: Son of India; Inspiration; The Easiest Way; Silence; A Tailor Made Man; Strangers May Kiss; Leftover Ladies; Hell Divers; The Secret Six; Laughing Sinners.
1933: Man's Castle; The Warrior's Husband; Strictly Personal.
1934: A Modern Hero; Grand Canary; Ready for Love; Palooka.
1935: Under Pressure; Dizzy Dames.
1937: First Lady.
1938: Merrily We Live; Woman Against Woman.
1939: The Rains Came; Heaven with a Barbed Wire Fence; Sudden Money; Laugh It Off.
1940: Primrose Path; East of the River; Tugboat Annie Sails Again; 20-Mule Team; Santa Fe Marshal.
1941: Tobacco Road; So Ends Our Night; Three Sons o' Guns.
1942: Broadway.
1943: In Old Oklahoma (War of the Wildcats).
1944: Army Wives; Oh, What a Night!
1945: Salome, Where She Danced.
1948: The Walls of Jericho.
1949: Any Number Can Play; Abandoned; The Lucky Stiff.
1953: Torch Song; Bad for Each Other; Forever Female.
1955: A Man Called Peter; The View from Pompey's Head.
1956: Slander.
1957: Man of a Thousand Faces.

Hiss the villain:
BASIL RATHBONE

Loathsome. Vicious. Sinister. Evil. Sadistic. Murderous. He was all of these and more.

Basil Rathbone was the finest villain in the history of the cinema. He could, and did, portray anything from Pontius Pilate and Richard III to Nazis, psychopathic wife-killers, mad brain surgeons, and ruthless kings and palace advisers, with quite a few stops along the way for the classic villains of literature (such as the evil Mr. Murdstone in **David Copperfield**) and the sword-wielding enemies of Errol Flynn. Film historian William K. Everson has called him simply "the best all-around villain the movies ever had."

But he was far more versatile than that. Twice an Academy Award nominee as best supporting actor (once for a non-villainous role), he handled romantic leads (albeit early in his career only) and straight dramatic parts, and made a creditable detective. In fact, out of the detective genre he carved what amounted to a second career as the immortal Sherlock Holmes, a sleuth he played 14 times. (When you think of Holmes, inevitably it is Rathbone's face you see before you.)

Lean as a wolfhound, gaunt, saturnine, cerebral, incisive, sneering, and icily commanding, with precise and knifelike diction, the actor made an ideal arch-enemy for many of Hollywood's top stars, and could well have been the inheritor of Erich von Stroheim's old title, "The Man You Love to Hate." In fact, some thought him *too* villainous, but he seldom overdid his material. Still, if he had played his superb nasties on the boards in small-town theaters instead of on the screen, the air would have been filled with loud and vigorous boos and hisses.

Philip St. John Basil Rathbone was born June 13, 1892, in Johannesburg, South Africa, to English parents (his father was a prosperous mining engineer), and educated in England, where he made his stage debut with his cousin Sir Frank Benson's second-string company in 1911, following studies at Repton College and a brief job in an insurance office. That first role was Hortensio in Shakespeare's **The Taming of the Shrew.** In 1913 he went with the Benson troupe to America, still performing small parts. His London debut came in **The Sin of David** in 1914, and in that year he also played the Dauphin in **Henry V.** Called up in 1916 for World War I service, he was with the Liverpool Scottish Regiment and was

wounded, commissioned a lieutenant, and decorated. When he returned to the stage at Stratford-on-Avon, it was in lead roles in Shakespearean productions, such as Romeo, Cassius, Prince Hal and Iago, and he also co-starred with Constance Collier in **Peter Ibbetson** in London; he was now a matinee idol. He began working in British films in 1921, although for much of his life he would continue to appear on the stage, even after he had become a character star in the movies.

His first screen appearance was in **The Fruitful Vine** (21), in an unimpressive performance as a philanderer, but he was better as a selfish lover who discards the lady in **Innocent.** He made his Broadway stage debut in **The Czarina** and returned to London for the plays **East of Suez** and **R.U.R.** He co-starred in the British film version of **The School for Scandal,** as a scheming fortune-hunter; it was his last English film for some time. He returned to New York to co-star with Eva Le Gallienne in **The Swan.**

He now did his first Hollywood film, **Trouping with Ellen (Pity the Chorus Girl)** (24), playing a wealthy aristocrat who loses the girl to an orchestra leader, and then was successful starring in the play **Judas,** which he also co-wrote. He continued his work on Broadway, and also was on stage in London and San Francisco; the plays included **Love Is Like That, The Command to Love,** and **Julius Caesar** (as Cassius again; no one could look leaner or hungrier).

Rathbone's biggest film role to date came in **The Masked Bride** (25), as the leader of a ring of jewel thieves who sends Mae Murray to vamp Francis X. Bushman so they can rob him, but she falls in love with the potential victim instead. He was a German espionage agent in **The Great Deception** (26), and then went back on the stage for a couple of years, until MGM called him back to Hollywood to co-star with Norma Shearer in that old theatrical warhorse **The Last of Mrs. Cheyney** (29); she is a jewel thief, and they fall in love. The film was a big hit.

The actor was married in 1913 to his Shakespearean leading lady, Ethel Forman (or Foreman; sources differ), and later divorced; they had a son, Rodion, who had small roles in a few films under the name of John Rodion. In 1926 Rathbone married Ouida Bergere, a novelist, screenwriter and supporting actress in films of that era who had just divorced George Fitzmaurice, a prominent film director; she and Rathbone had a daughter, Barbara. She was six years his senior, and would outlive him by seven years. The couple became well known for the splendid parties they gave for the Hollywood set in the Thirties; Rathbone was also a prominent movie-colony wit (he was fond of answering his phone with "This is Razzle Bathbone speaking"), and while he may have been an unmitigated villain on the screen, he was one of the best-liked people in the film capital.

He starred as S.S. Van Dine's detective Philo Vance in **The Bishop Murder Case** (30) (he was the only actor to play both Vance and Sherlock Holmes), and in **A Notorious Affair** he was a violinist who almost gives up his wife (Billie Dove) for Kay Francis. In **The Lady of Scandal** he was a duke torn between two women, one of whom was Ruth Chatterton, and in **This Mad World** he was a wartime French spy attracted to the wife of a German general; she kills herself and he is executed by a firing squad. He displayed a flair for comedy in **The Flirting Widow,** as an army officer who is the recipient of love letters from a lady he has never met, and he romanced and then jilted a woman who had left her husband in **A Lady Surrenders.** He also romanced Constance Bennett in **Sin Takes a Holiday,** but eventually lost her.

He returned to Broadway for three plays (portraying a clergyman in one of them), and came back to film **A Woman Commands** (32), as a Ruritanian officer in love with Pola Negri (a queen whose king/husband is Roland Young); she had rejected Rathbone to marry the monarch, but gets him back when Young is killed. Then he did yet another Broadway play, and also two British films, in both cases playing a cad carrying on a flirtation or affair with a married woman. There was a good role in the English movie **Loyalties** (33), although he overplayed somewhat as a wealthy man who accuses a British officer of stealing. In 1934 he played Romeo to Katharine Cornell's Juliet in Shakespeare's drama on Broadway and in other locales. Then he went back to Hollywood, and at this point launched his career as the screen's master of villainy.

In a film filled with fine character actors, he was excellent as the loathsome, sadistic Mr. Murdstone in **David Copperfield** (35), the first and possibly the heaviest of his gallery of heavies. Murdstone cajoles David's (Freddie Bartholomew's) widowed mother into marriage and then proceeds to make the mother's and child's life a living hell. There is one almost unbearable scene where he whips David with gleeful intensity. This performance typed Rathbone for a decade, in a Hollywood that saw everything in metaphors of black and white, and he would be kept so busy as a movie nasty that he would not act on the stage again for 10 years.

Also that year, he played the supercilious, put-upon husband of Greta Garbo in **Anna Karenina,** whom she leaves for Fredric March, and was the evil Marquis de St. Evremonde in **A Tale of Two Cities,** unconcerned when his carriage runs over and kills a peasant. He was the chief villain in Errol Flynn's first starring film, **Captain Blood,** fighting the first of two memorable screen duels with that actor. He terrorized wealthy spinster recluse Aline MacMahon in **Kind Lady,** as an untalented but aggressive painter who appears to befriend her, moves himself and some associates into her home, drugs her, kills her maid, intercepts notes she tries to smuggle out, tells visitors she is demented, and plans to kill her after they have sold her valuable paintings. (She is saved at the end.) A disturbing mood of claustrophobic menace pervades this fine, half-forgotten melodrama.

And still more from 1935: He walked away with the film as the haunted Pontius Pilate in **The Last Days of Pompeii,** giving a compelling portrait of a clever, haughty man forever tortured by the memory of Jesus, the innocent religious leader he sentenced to death. Finally, he was seen in a straight role in **A Feather in Her Hat,** as a destitute, alcoholic aristocrat whom Pauline Lord asks to educate her son in the finer things of life. Meanwhile, in the fall of 1935 the previously mentioned gallery of five nasties was featured on first-run and neighborhood movie screens all across America, and Basil Rathbone had suddenly become a household word.

He was fine in **Romeo and Juliet** (36) as the fiery Tybalt, quick to draw his sword, an insolent flinger of challenges. (He won an Oscar nomination as best supporting actor—for the first of two times—but lost to Walter Brennan in **Come and Get It** in this first year of the supporting awards.) He played a jealous sheik attracted to Marlene Dietrich in **The Garden of Allah** (she prefers Charles Boyer), and a sinister butler who covets Loretta Young in **Private Number** (she was the housemaid, secretly married to the wealthy young scion, Robert Taylor). He was a polished psychopath trying to murder wife Ann Harding in **Love from a Stranger** (37), and then Kay Francis made a courtroom **Confession** that she killed him, her former lover, to protect her daughter (Jane Bryan) from his advances. In **Tovarich** he was the former arch-enemy (a murderer and torturer) encountered by ex-Russian royalists Claudette Colbert and Boyer after they have fled to America with the czarist treasury and taken jobs as servants. And, as a composer (non-villainous variety), he supported the absurd child star Bobby Breen in **Make a Wish.** Meanwhile, he was turning down roles in a vain effort to stop playing heavies.

There were in fact two more quintessential nasties, in 1938. As the evil Sir Guy of Gisbourne he matched wits (and swords) with Errol Flynn again in the rousing **The Adventures of Robin Hood,** and, as the would-be usurper of the throne of 13th-century Cathay, was dastardly toward Gary Cooper in **The Adventures of Marco Polo.** He also played the war-weary commanding officer in the remake of **The Dawn Patrol,** a superb characterization. But that year he also gave what was probably the greatest performance of his life, not as a villain but as the sly, hunchbacked Louis XI of France in the Ronald Colman starrer **If I Were King,** a reptilian, crotchety, doddering monarch who trusts no one. When seeing this film, it is hard at first to realize that this is Rathbone, for his voice, gait and mannerisms seem to be those of another man entirely. He received a second Academy Award nomination—and once again lost to Walter Brennan, in **Kentucky,** one of the latter's hammiest performances and one that was so far inferior to Rathbone's that it is pointless to compare them.

A momentary sea-change cast him as Sir Arthur Conan Doyle's great fictional detective Sherlock Holmes in **The Hound of the Baskervilles** (39), with Nigel Bruce as Watson. The film was just passable, but seven years and 14 movies would elapse before he was through playing Holmes. He did it again in **The Adventures of Sherlock Holmes,** an even better film, with Ida Lupino as the ingenue and George Zucco as a fine Professor Moriarty (the heavy). Three years would pass before he played Holmes again. Now he starred as the **Son of Frankenstein,** involved with Boris Karloff, Bela Lugosi and Lionel Atwill, and was Richard III in **Tower of London,** being at the same time particularly malevolent and credibly human. In **Rio** he led the cast as a crooked financier sweating it out in prison on Devil's Island, then escaping to join his wife, only to find she has been unfaithful; he ends up murdered by his aide, Victor McLaglen. And in **The Sun Never Sets** he and Douglas Fairbanks Jr. were two brothers in the African colonial service working to prevent a munitions baron (Lionel Atwill) from plunging the world into war.

Tyrone Power now replaced Errol Flynn as the swordsman/hero who kills him in a duel, in **The Mark of Zorro** (40), a film that also found Gale Sondergaard (who is already married) romancing him. The irony was that Rathbone—one of Hollywood's finest sword-wielders, who had long studied with top fencing instructors—had to content himself with the knowledge that off the screen he could have killed Flynn or Power with one thrust. In **Rhythm on the River** he was a pompous, neurotic, egotistical songwriter ghosted by budding musician Bing Crosby. In **The Mad Doctor** (41) he was a hypnotist who marries women and murders them for their money, and in **The Black Cat** he was definitely not one of the good guys in this family-summoned-to-the-spooky-house-of-an-old-recluse outing. He played a Scotland Yard man in **International Lady.**

Inevitably, like many another screen villain, he portrayed a Nazi in **Paris Calling** (42), and he was a Jack the Ripper type in **Fingers at the Window,** a maniac killer masterminding repeated ax murders. He and Claire Trevor were the conniving blackmailers who try to persuade William Powell that he is a thief and murderer (he isn't) in **Crossroads,** but they get their comeuppance at his trial. That year (in which he turned 50) also saw the beginning of Universal Studios' lengthy Sherlock Holmes series, in which he starred; the two earlier Holmes films had been for 20th Century-Fox. It kicked off with **Sherlock Holmes and the Voice of Terror,** in which he unmasks a Lord Haw Haw type in the war cabinet, and **Sherlock Holmes and the Secret Weapon,** in which he saves a stolen bombsight from the Nazis, with Lionel Atwill as Professor Moriarty. These films were programmers of uncertain quality, not "A" productions, and they deteriorated in quality as time went by.

He did two more in 1943: **Sherlock Holmes Faces Death** (weird murders in a convalescent home) and **Sherlock Holmes in Washington** (preventing Nazi spies, including George Zucco and Henry Daniell, from grabbing a secret document). But even while he was foiling Nazis, he was *playing* another Nazi: In **Above Suspicion** he was a Gestapo agent clashing with Joan Crawford and Fred MacMurray as amateur U.S. spies. And, in 1944, still more Sherlocking: **The Scarlet Claw** (grisly murders in Canada); **The Pearl of Death** (he traps "The Creeper" when a valuable pearl is stolen); and **The Spider Woman** (Gale Sondergaard, a female Moriarty, kills her victims with spiders so she can collect on their insurance policies). He was nasty again in **Frenchman's Creek,** as a lascivious nobleman pursuing Joan Fontaine, who finally hurls a suit of armor at him, knocking him down a flight of stairs and killing him. And he was the scheming publisher of songwriter Red Skelton in **Bathing Beauty.**

The Sherlock Holmes films ground on in 1945 with a trio of cheapies, and they concluded in 1946. A better role came along in **Heartbeat** (46), in which he was a modern-day Fagin, running a school for pickpockets, with Ginger Rogers as his star pupil. At this point, sick of Sherlock Holmes, he decided to return to the stage.

Rathbone was in the play **Obsession** on Broadway in 1946, and the following year played Wendy Hiller's suspicious, embittered father in the fine drama **The Heiress** (in the 1948 film, the parts were taken by Ralph Richardson and Olivia de Havilland). He provided the narration (but did not appear) in the Ichabod Crane sequence of the animated film **Ichabod and Mr. Toad** (49), his only screen work in an eight-year hiatus. In 1950 he toured in **The Winslow Boy** in summer stock, and later was in **The Gioconda Smile** and **Julius Caesar** on Broadway. Amazingly, in 1953 he starred in the play **Sherlock Holmes** in New York, but it was a flop. During this period he also made recordings of classics and toured college campuses giving readings.

In 1954 the actor was back in Hollywood, now in his sixties, once again being sinister—but in comedies; he supported Bob Hope in **Casanova's Big Night** that year. **We're No Angels** (55) cast him as a nasty businessman undone by three escapees from Devil's Island (Humphrey Bogart, Peter Ustinov and Aldo Ray); he ends up killed by a snake. He was the tyrannical would-be usurper of the throne who is overthrown by Danny Kaye in **The Court Jester** (56), and did a horror film, **The Black Sleep,** as a mad brain surgeon experimenting on humans and turning them into mutants—who eventually turn on him. His last decent film role came in **The Last Hurrah** (58), as an unpleasant banker opposing politician Spencer Tracy.

Meanwhile he had appeared on stage in **Hide and Seek** in 1957. He starred in Archibald MacLeish's play **JB** (i.e., Job) in 1959, and in the following year did his last stage work, touring Australia in **The Marriage-Go-Round.** He also worked in television, appearing in "Criminal at Large," "The Lark" and "Victoria Regina," the last two with Julie Harris. He then returned to the film capital for a final descent into a bunch of sorry cheapies to close out his screen career. Film historian David Shipman says he "gave them no more than they were worth; he traded on his reputation and collected his pay packet."

A quarter of a century after he had first done so, he played Pontius Pilate again in an Italian film, **Ponzio Pilato** (61). From here on it was nothing but horror schlock and junk as the actor turned 70. He, Vincent Price and Peter Lorre were in **Tales of Terror** (62), and he played an evil old sorcerer in **The Magic Sword.** In that year he also published his autobiography, "In and Out of Character." He joined Price, Lorre and Boris Karloff for **The Comedy of Terrors** (64), and was in **Planet of Blood** (66), about space vampires. His last four films, all done in 1967, bore titles that sound like the winners of a contest to pick the worst films of all time, and they were certainly contenders for the honor: **Dr. Rock and Mr. Roll, Gill Women, The Ghost in the Invisible Bikini** and **Hillbillys** [sic] **in a Haunted House.** Some of these movies are so bad that they don't even appear in a guide to 19,000 films that might turn up on TV.

In that year, 1967, Basil Rathbone died at 75. The best thing to do is to charitably forget the postwar years and the ultimate descent into junk. Just let your mind go back to the Thirties, to films such as **David Copperfield, Captain Blood** and **The Adventures of Robin Hood.** To the sadistic and sinister nasties so splendidly portrayed by the finest villain ever to appear on the screen.

THE FILMS OF RASIL RATHBONE

1921: The Fruitful Vine; Innocent.
1922: Loves of Mary Queen of Scots.
1923: The School for Scandal.
1924: Trouping with Ellen (Pity the Chorus Girl).
1925: The Masked Bride.
1926: The Great Deception.
1929: The Last of Mrs. Cheyney.
1930: The Bishop Murder Case; A Notorious Affair; Lady of Scandal; This Mad World; The Flirting Widow; A Lady Surrenders; Sin Takes a Holiday.
1932: A Woman Commands; One Precious Year; After the Ball.
1933: Loyalties; Just Smith.
1935: David Copperfield; Anna Karenina; A Tale of Two Cities; Captain Blood; Kind Lady; The Last Days of Pompeii; A Feather in Her Hat.
1936: Romeo and Juliet; The Garden of Allah; Private Number.
1937: Love from a Stranger; Confession; Tovarich; Make a Wish.
1938: The Adventures of Robin Hood; If I Were King; The Dawn Patrol; The Adventures of Marco Polo.
1939: The Adventures of Sherlock Holmes; The Hound of the Baskervilles; Son of Frankenstein; Tower of London; Rio; The Sun Never Sets.
1940: The Mark of Zorro; Rhythm on the River.
1941: The Mad Doctor; The Black Cat; International Lady.
1942: Paris Calling; Fingers at the Window; Crossroads; Sherlock Holmes and the Voice of Terror; Sherlock Holmes and the Secret Weapon.
1943: Above Suspicion; Sherlock Holmes Faces Death; Sherlock Holmes in Washington.
1944: The Spider Woman; Frenchman's Creek; The Scarlet Claw; Bathing Beauty; The Pearl of Death.
1945: The House of Fear; The Woman in Green; Pursuit to Algiers.
1946: Terror by Night; Heartbeat; Dressed to Kill.
1949: Ichabod and Mr. Toad (voice only).
1954: Casanova's Big Night.
1955: We're No Angels.
1956: The Court Jester; The Black Sleep.
1958: The Last Hurrah.
1961: Ponzio Pilato.
1962: Tales of Terror; Two Below Zero; The Magic Sword.
1964: The Comedy of Terrors.
1966: Planet of Blood (Queen of Blood).
1967: Dr. Rock and Mr. Roll; Gill Women; The Ghost in the Invisible Bikini; Hillbillys [sic] in a Haunted House.

NOTE: Some sources list him as having appeared in the 1927 Gloria Swanson starrer **The Love of Sunya.** However, he had refused that co-starring role, which was actually played in the film by John Boles.

Grand old granny:
MAY ROBSON

May Robson was just about everybody's favorite movie grandmother in the Thirties. Crusty and domineering, but with a heart of gold, she took no nonsense from anyone. Strong-willed, vigorous and tart-tongued, she huffed and puffed and pretended to be gruff, but she fooled nobody—deep down she was just an old pussycat. Rasping and sharp-featured, she was still basically kind-hearted.

She could, and did, play very human doyennes from both sides of the tracks, ranging from frowsy derelicts to society matrons. She usually took a firm hand with obstreperous juveniles, but was always good for a few tears in the audience by the end. This twinkly-eyed old curmudgeon was kept busy throughout the films' Golden Era as the mother, mother-in-law, aunt or grandmother of some of Hollywood's top stars, especially at MGM in the first half of the Thirties. Her specialty was a solid helping of horse sense that withered all cant and hypocrisy. And to top it off, she was so good a performer that she managed to win an Academy Award nomination as *best actress* when she was 75 years old.

She was born (as Mary Jeanette Robison) April 19, 1858, in Melbourne, Australia (making her by a full five years the oldest performer in this book), one of four children of a British navy captain. Educated in a London convent and in Brussels and Paris, she eloped at 16 to marry 18-year-old Charles L. Gore (one source gives his first name as Edward), and they emigrated to Fort Worth, Texas, to try ranching. After nearly a decade of struggle and failure, they went to New York, where Gore died, leaving her, at age 25, with three small children. She briefly tried to earn a living by teaching art and doing embroidering, but this ended when, on an impulse, she applied at a theatrical agency for a job; she was accepted, and began an acting career that was to last well over half a century.

Her first role (as an ingenue) was in **The Hoop of Gold** in 1884 (one source says 1883), and she performed on Broadway, in gaslit Bowery theaters and on the road, in leads and supporting roles, in a wide variety of productions. At some point during this period two of her children, a boy and a girl, died, of diphtheria and scarlet fever respectively; a son, Edward, survived. And in 1889 she remarried, to a doctor, A.H. Brown; this union was to endure until his death in 1922. Miss Robson continued to be very busy

on the stage in the Nineties. She performed some Shakespeare, and during 1893-96 was a member of Charles Frohman's Empire Theatre Company, one of her roles being Miss Prism in Oscar Wilde's **The Importance of Being Earnest** (in its American premiere). By the turn of the century (she was now in her forties) she had become a respected character player. Her first real acting triumph came in 1907 when she starred in **The Rejuvenation of Aunt Mary,** a role she played on and off for three years (and would repeat a generation later in a 1927 silent film).

The actress first appeared on the screen in 1915, at age 57, in **How Molly Made Good,** and was in five films by the end of 1919, then returning to the stage. She went back to Hollywood in 1926, when she was 68, launching a 16-year screen career that would involve more than 60 movies and would end only with her death while still filming. She and Rudolph Schildkraut (Joseph's father) played an elderly Jewish couple involved in gold mining in **Pals in Paradise** (26), and then she did seven movies in 1927. She was Schildkraut's landlady in **A Harp in Hock,** a hard-boiled nightclub hostess in **The Angel of Broadway,** and a violent and officious widow ruling a Near Eastern sultanate in **Turkish Delight.** In the film version of her own earlier stage hit **The Rejuvenation of Aunt Mary** she found a new lease on life and married a judge, and in the blockbuster **The King of Kings** she had a small part as the mother of Gestas, the unrepentant thief. There was a minuscule part in **The Blue Danube** (28), and then she was off the screen for two years.

She made her talkie debut in **Mother's Millions (The She-Wolf of Wall Street)** (31), in a role tailor-made for her now geriatric talents; she was sort of a Hetty Green type (with a similar name, Hattie Breen), a millionaire who alienates both her son and her daughter by interfering in their romances but relents when the son refuses a bribe of millions to betray her secrets, and her secretary, the daughter's beau, proves equally loyal. This film was produced by a Poverty Row studio, Liberty, but released by Universal.

Miss Robson was Norma Shearer's mother-in-law in the film adaptation of Eugene O'Neill's **Strange Interlude** (32), and played Joan Crawford's formidable, unsympathetic dowager mother in **Letty Lynton.** Her best role that year came in one of the episodes of **If I Had a Million:** A rebellious inmate in a grim home for old ladies, she uses her million to buy the home and convert it into a luxurious club, while the matron is paid to just sit and rock all day; there is even a hint of a geriatric romance between Miss Robson and the philanthropic millionaire (Richard Bennett). She played Jean Harlow's aunt in **Red Headed Woman,** and was a stubborn, wealthy woman who adopts an orphan boy in **Little Orphan Annie.**

Her greatest acting triumph came in director Frank Capra's big hit **Lady for a Day** (33), in which she played a drunken old Times Square derelict who has been secretly hoarding money (as an apple vendor) to keep her illegitimate daughter (Jean Parker) in a private school abroad. She is in despair when the girl and her titled fiancé announce they will visit New York, but in an elaborate hoax, gamblers, bookies and con men rally around to make Apple Annie's dream come true by having her pose as a wealthy woman. This white-haired Cinderella was unquestionably the star of this important film, hailed by critics as a new Marie Dressler (things didn't turn out that way, though), and was nominated for an Academy Award as *best actress,* at age 75, but lost to Katharine Hepburn in **Morning Glory.**

Continuing in an extremely busy year in which she made 11 films, she was featured in **Reunion in Vienna** as the rowdy, cigar-smoking Frau Lucher, who arranges and finances the whole forbidden reunion between John Barrymore and Diana Wynyard. She played Lewis Stone's wife in **Men Must Fight** (in real life she was old enough to be his mother), was the mother superior of a convent in **The White Sister,** and was cast as the Queen of Hearts in **Alice in Wonderland.** She was Franchot Tone's grandmother in **Dancing Lady,** Una Merkel's mother in **Beauty for Sale,** Lionel Barrymore's housekeeper in **One Man's Journey,** and a woman involved with Herbert Marshall in a jewel-theft ring in **The Solitaire Man.**

The actress rehashed her **Lady for a Day** performance in **Lady by Choice** (34), as the alcoholic old vagrant "adopted" by fan dancer Carole Lombard as her mother for publicity purposes, with happy results for both. **Straight Is the Way** had her badly miscast as Tone's Jewish mama, and in **You Can't Buy Everything** she was Hetty Green all over again, a miserly woman of vast wealth who looks on as her beloved but stingily reared son falls in love with the daughter (Jean Parker) of her most hated rival (Stone).

She starred as a high school teacher fired after 38 years on the job in **Grand Old Girl** (35); playing the film's young hero was Fred MacMurray, in his second credited screen appearance. She was good as the centenarian matriarch in the Helen Hayes starrer **Vanessa: Her Love Story,** and was Fredric March's mother in the Greta Garbo vehicle **Anna Karenina.** She starred in **Mills of the Gods** as an indomitable widow who, after running a plow factory for 40 years, comes out of retirement to summon her idle children home from the fleshpots of Europe to ask their financial help in keeping the Depression-stricken business running, but they refuse. One reactionary son (Raymond Walburn) even calls the police so the family can get away without facing the protesting workers, provoking a riot in which a grandson is killed by a stray police bullet. The old lady restores order with a stirring speech and a promise to reopen the plant at her own expense.

There was still more that year. She starred in **Strangers All,** a programmer, as the widowed mother of four grown children, all dependent on eldest son Preston Foster. One son is a radical, one a would-be actor, and the daughter is in college. The elderly mother has a suitor (Samuel S. Hinds), but the emphasis is on the selfish children's misuse of the money the eldest needs to buy a store. The radical is arrested and bailed out by the mother, and the actor ends as a

Hollywood extra. Next Miss Robson played a flinty millionaire regenerated by an encounter with three orphans in **Three Kids and a Queen.** She also played Jean Harlow's grandmother in **Reckless,** and in **Age of Indiscretion** she was a woman who lies and deceives to satisfy her selfish desire to possess a grandchild at any cost.

The actress played Clark Gable's mother, a gossipy old busybody forever hinting at naughty doings at the office, in **Wife vs. Secretary** (36), and was child star Bobby Breen's grandma in **Rainbow on the River.** In **The Captain's Kid** she was the star again, and there was a hint of geriatric romance with long-ago flame Guy Kibbee (who in real life was 54 that year to Miss Robson's 78!). She played the indomitable grandmother who gives Janet Gaynor the courage to go on after Fredric March's suicide in the classic drama **A Star Is Born** (37), starred in **Woman in Distress** as the owner of valuable paintings that Douglass Dumbrille's gang of thieves is after, and was Errol Flynn's eccentric granny in **The Perfect Specimen.** As she turned 80, she played the doughty aunt who keeps house for the family in the fine drama **Four Daughters** (38), was Aunt Polly in **The Adventures of Tom Sawyer,** and was seen to advantage in the classic screwball comedy **Bringing Up Baby** as the potential million-dollar donor to Cary Grant's museum; Katharine Hepburn was her niece.

She played Joan Bennett's grandmother in **The Texans.**

Her roles were getting smaller now. She was a patriotic French concierge given to histrionics in **Nurse Edith Cavell** (39), reprised her **Four Daughters** role in **Daughters Courageous** and **Four Wives,** had routine grandmother roles in **They Made Me a Criminal** and **Yes, My Darling Daughter,** and suffered the worst miscasting of her career in **The Kid from Kokomo,** as an offensive, gin-swilling, kleptomaniac old harridan. She played an indomitable old lady who becomes a sheriff to get her granddaughter freed of a murder charge in **Granny Get Your Gun** (40), was Anna Neagle's grandmother in **Irene,** and got into another senior-citizen romance, with Charley Grapewin, in **Texas Rangers Ride Again.**

Miss Robson concluded the **Four Daughters** series with **Four Mothers** (41), and was in John Barrymore's unbelievably bad final film, **Playmates.** She then had a good part in **Joan of Paris** (42), playing a British espionage agent—at the age of 84! It was to be her last role; before the year was over May Robson was dead, ending an acting career that had begun in an era of gaslights, bustles and horsehair sofas. Fortunately, she still lives on the TV screen— that crusty, no-nonsense, tart-tongued grandmother with the heart of gold, everybody's favorite old lady of Hollywood's Golden Era.

THE FILMS OF MAY ROBSON

1915: How Molly Made Good.
1916: A Night Out.
1919: A Broadway Saint; His Bridal Night; The Lost Battalion.
1926: Pals in Paradise.
1927: The Rejuvenation of Aunt Mary; A Harp in Hock; Rubber Tires; The Angel of Broadway; The King of Kings; Chicago; Turkish Delight.
1928: The Blue Danube.
1931: Mother's Millions (The She-Wolf of Wall Street).
1932: Strange Interlude; Red Headed Woman; Letty Lynton; Little Orphan Annie. *Credit uncertain:* Two Against the World.
1933: Lady for a Day; Reunion in Vienna; Dinner at Eight; Broadway to Hollywood; Dancing Lady; The Solitaire Man; Beauty for Sale; One Man's Journey; Alice in Wonderland; The White Sister; Men Must Fight.

1934: Lady by Choice; Straight Is the Way; You Can't Buy Everything.
1935: Grand Old Girl; Anna Karenina; Reckless; Age of Indiscretion; Vanessa: Her Love Story; Mills of the Gods; Strangers All; Three Kids and a Queen.
1936: Wife vs. Secretary; Rainbow on the River; The Captain's Kid.
1937: A Star Is Born; The Perfect Specimen; Woman in Distress. *Credit uncertain:* Top of the Town.
1938: Bringing Up Baby; Four Daughters; The Adventures of Tom Sawyer; The Texans.
1939: Yes, My Darling Daughter; The Kid from Kokomo; Daughters Courageous; Four Wives; Nurse Edith Cavell; They Made Me a Criminal; That's Right—You're Wrong.
1940: Granny Get Your Gun; Irene; Texas Rangers Ride Again.
1941: Four Mothers; Playmates; Million Dollar Baby.
1942: Joan of Paris.

Dithering, diffident, dilatory:
CHARLIE RUGGLES

Charlie Ruggles was one of the screen's best, most popular and most inimitable character comedians.

An amiable little rabbit of a man, he had a startled look, precise diction, and an apologetic cough. Genial, bumbling, disarming and quizzical, he chirped nasally and he huffled and snuffled. He played men who were timid and mischievously wistful, and who tended to be dithering, diffident and dilatory. With an acute sense of comedy timing, and with consummate charm and skill, he was kept busy for decades portraying henpecked husbands (often with his frequent co-star Mary Boland), friends of the hero, ineffective lovers, shy professors, newspapermen, music masters, and victims of predatory blondes. (It is difficult to think of a movie in which he got the girl, unless it was Miss Boland.)

With an amusingly offhand style, he was unfailingly right for his roles, and he could make lines sound funnier than they were. His talents kept him occupied for 37 years in the sound era alone, but all told he appeared on the screen for more than half a century.

Charles Ruggles was born February 8, 1886 (some sources say 1890 or 1892), in Los Angeles, the elder brother of future film director Wesley Ruggles, and made his acting debut as a teen-ager, portraying a schoolboy in a San Francisco stock-company production of **Nathan Hale.** Soon after this he appeared on the New York stage, and then returned to Los Angeles, where for six years he was with the Morosco Stock Company. In 1915, at age 29, he appeared in his first film, **Peer Gynt,** but continued to be busy on stage, primarily starring on Broadway, for many years. (Among other plays, he was featured in the musical **Battling Butler** in 1923.) He was in the movie **The Heart Raider** (23), directed by his brother, as an insurance agent who loses the girl he loves to another man.

At some point in time the actor married actress Adele Rowland, and they were divorced. He later married Marion La Barbe.

In 1929, at the beginning of the sound era, he more or less settled in Hollywood, and signed a contract with Paramount. In that year he was a newspaperman in **Gentlemen of the Press** and a genial drunk in **The Lady Lies,** both starring Walter Huston, and played a timid pickpocket in **The Battle of Paris.**

He was a reporter in **Roadhouse Nights** (30), and starred in the title role of **Charley's Aunt** as Lord Fancourt Babberley, disguised as the aunt and chewing up the scenery with a high-octane performance. He stole the show from Clara Bow in the spicy bedroom farce **Her Wedding Night,** and was a newsman again in **Young Man of Manhattan,** which marked the screen debut of Ginger Rogers. He and Frank Morgan were business partners in **Queen High.**

Appearing for the first time for director Ernst Lubitsch, he was a friend of Maurice Chevalier's in **The Smiling Lieutenant** (31), and he starred in **The Girl Habit** as a mild Lothario who gets himself arrested as protection from the gangster husband of a lady he has been dallying with. Other films that year were in routine friend-of-the-hero roles, usually with comic overtones.

In 1932 Ruggles began a screen teaming of about a dozen films with character comedienne Mary Boland (who in real life was six years his senior). In these domestic-comedy programmers he was the dapper, henpecked husband, timid and flustered; the physically substantial Miss Boland, a mistress of scatterbrained comedy who was every bit his match, was the genteel but dominant wife. They were married in all but one of the films, which would continue through 1939 (and they were the screen's most often paired male-female team, more than William Powell/Myrna Loy or Fred Astaire/Ginger Rogers, for example). Typically, they were a middle-class suburban couple with a marriageable daughter, and at some point Ruggles would unaccountably get into some hilarious trouble that was solved in the last reel. These highly successful comedies were Paramount's bread and butter in certain parts of the country for some time. And the critics' view? Here's the New York Times: "Miss Boland and Mr. Ruggles are unmatched on the screen as exponents of domestic comedy, and their work has the remarkable faculty for touching life."

There were three Ruggles-Boland teamings in 1932. **The Night of June 13** was a murder mystery featuring them in supporting roles, and in **Evenings for Sale**—the only movie in which they were not married—he was a headwaiter and she was a millionaire widow. She was his nagging spouse in **If I Had a Million,** in which he was a china-shop clerk who, upon winning his million, walks into the shop and casually smashes up the china, an episode that is a comic masterpiece. In director Lubitsch's **One Hour With You** he was a bachelor trying to court Jeanette MacDonald—who is already married to Maurice Chevalier—and in the brilliant musical comedy **Love Me Tonight** he played an impecunious viscount who owes tailor Chevalier for 20 suits. He was a friend of Cary Grant's in **Madame Butterfly,** had a key comedic role in Lubitsch's **Trouble in Paradise** as one of Kay Francis' suitors, and, amazingly enough, won the love of young Frances Dee in **This Reckless Age.** In **This Is the Night** he and Roland Young were both infatuated with Lili Damita, and commiserated by getting drunk together; this was Cary Grant's screen debut. He played an alcoholic reporter in **70,000 Witnesses.**

He was good as the March Hare in **Alice in Wonderland** (33), played a timid, alcoholic zoo press agent in **Murders in the Zoo,** was a comic womanizer in **Melody Cruise,** and co-starred with Miss Boland in **Mama Loves Papa.** He played a painter in **Girl Without a Room,** a butler in **Goodbye Love,** and a superstitious ship's steward in **Terror Aboard.** He starred in **Friends of Mr. Sweeney** (34) as the timid writer for a weekly paper whose meek personality undergoes a change when his friend Eugene

Pallette exposes the falseness at the core of his life. (This film is often cited as the screen debut of Fred MacMurray, but his name does not appear in the large cast list in the American Film Institute Catalog.) His other films that year were all with Miss Boland. They were the parents of Joan Bennett in **The Pursuit of Happiness;** got involved with W.C. Fields, Alison Skipworth, George Burns and Gracie Allen on a cross-country trip in **Six of a Kind;** and were in **Melody in Spring,** with Ann Sothern as their daughter (Ruggles was an eccentric dog-biscuit manufacturer).

Still married to Miss Boland, he played an English lord in **Ruggles of Red Gap** (35), and in **People Will Talk** they tried to patch up their daughter's faltering marriage. In **No More Ladies** (a Joan Crawford vehicle) Ruggles was out on a date with Gail Patrick, but Robert Montgomery came along and stole her away. There were more teamings with Miss Boland (the last for three years), in 1936: **Early to Bed** (they are married after a 20-year engagement) and **Wives Never Know** (Adolphe Menjou tries to talk him into philandering). In **Mind Your Own Business** he played a reporter again, married to Alice Brady. **Exclusive** (37) gave him a good dramatic role (fairly rare in the Ruggles canon) as yet another newsman, Frances Farmer's father, who rescues her from a killer and dies while on the job. He starred in **Turn Off the Moon** as a department-store owner persuaded by an astrologer to put on a big anniversary show.

The actor was a timid-soul big-game hunter in the classic screwball comedy **Bringing Up Baby** (38), suffered through a Bobby Breen vehicle, and in **Service de Luxe** was a bridge-building engineer who wants to write a cookbook (this film was Vincent Price's screen debut). He also starred in a mediocre farce, **His Exciting Night.** The last two of the Ruggles-Boland films came in 1939: **Boy Trouble** (they adopt a young orphan boy) and **Night Work** (another adoption, this time of Donald O'Connor). In **Sudden Money** he was married to Marjorie Rambeau, and in **Balalaika** he opened a Russian café in Paris. He stole the show from Rosalind Russell and James Stewart in **No Time for Comedy** (40), as a husband who has seen his wife's (Genevieve Tobin's) young male "protégés" come and go; with skill and great charm he showed his amused tolerance of her inane behavior. He played a Broadway theatrical promoter in **The Farmer's Daughter,** and was a soup manufacturer in **Elsa Maxwell's Public Deb No. 1.**

Ruggles, now in his mid-fifties, played a butler in **The Invisible Woman** (41). In **Friendly Enemies** (42) he and Charles Winninger had dramatic roles as lifelong friends who come into conflict during World War I because of their German heritage. The actor was one of the most active entertainers of servicemen during World War II, while continuing his film schedule—but in none of these films did he have a very good part. One exception, once the war was over, was **A Stolen Life** (46), in which he had a serious role as a friend of Bette Davis in one of her best pictures. In **Ramrod** (47) he clashed with daughter Veronica Lake over the ranch she owned. But after 1949 he chose to forsake filming for more than a decade, turning to the stage again and to television. He was on Broadway and toured in summer stock. On TV, he starred in some 150 episodes of "The Ruggles," followed by more than 100 episodes of "The World of Mr. Sweeney."

The highlight of his postwar stage work came in 1958, when at age 72 he won a Tony award as the father in **The Pleasure of His Company.** He soon returned to the screen, and played Lilli Palmer's witty father in the remake of that play in 1961. In that same year he was a wealthy executive who dies in **All in a Night's Work;** his nephew, Dean Martin, fears Shirley MacLaine will blackmail the company over what he suspects was her liaison with Ruggles. After a hiatus of many years he supported Maurice Chevalier again in **I'd Rather Be Rich** (64), and at age 80 he concluded his film career in 1966 with two Disney movies, **The Ugly Dachshund** and **Follow Me, Boys!**

His retirement was not to be long-lived; in 1970 he died at 84. But late-night television and theatrical revival showings assure that he can still be seen by lovers of classic comedy. The truly outstanding character comedians of Hollywood's golden age can be counted on your fingers, with plenty to spare. Charlie Ruggles was unquestionably one of them.

THE FILMS OF CHARLIE RUGGLES

1915: Peer Gynt.
1923: The Heart Raider.
1929: Gentlemen of the Press; The Lady Lies; The Battle of Paris.
1930: Roadhouse Nights; Young Man of Manhattan; Queen High; Her Wedding Night; Charley's Aunt.
1931: The Smiling Lieutenant; Honor Among Lovers; The Girl Habit; The Beloved Bachelor; Husband's Holiday.
1932: One Hour with You; If I Had a Million; Love Me Tonight; Madame Butterfly; This Reckless Age; This Is the Night; 70,000 Witnesses; The Night of June 13; Trouble in Paradise; Evenings for Sale; Make Me a Star.
1933: Alice in Wonderland; Murders in the Zoo; Melody Cruise; Mama Loves Papa; Girl Without a Room; Goodbye Love; Terror Aboard.
1934: Six of a Kind; The Pursuit of Happiness; Friends of Mr. Sweeney; Melody in Spring.
1935: Ruggles of Red Gap; No More Ladies; People Will Talk; The Big Broadcast of 1936.
1936: Anything Goes; Hearts Divided; Early to Bed; Wives Never Know; Mind Your Own Business.
1937: Exclusive; Turn Off the Moon.
1938: Bringing Up Baby; Breaking the Ice; His Exciting Night;

Service de Luxe.
1939: Invitation to Happiness; Balalaika; Boy Trouble; Night Work; Sudden Money.
1940: The Farmer's Daughter; Maryland; No Time for Comedy; Elsa Maxwell's Public Deb No. 1.
1941: The Invisible Woman; Honeymoon for Three; Model Wife; The Parson of Panamint; Go West, Young Lady; Opened by Mistake.
1942: Friendly Enemies.
1943: Dixie Dugan.
1944: The Doughgirls; Our Hearts Were Young and Gay; Three Is a Family.
1945: Incendiary Blonde; Bedside Manner.
1946: A Stolen Life; Gallant Journey.
1947: It Happened on Fifth Avenue; Ramrod; My Brother Talks to Horses.
1948: Give My Regards to Broadway.
1949: Look for the Silver Lining.
1961: All in a Night's Work; The Parent Trap; The Pleasure of His Company.
1963: Son of Flubber; Papa's Delicate Condition.
1964: I'd Rather Be Rich.
1966: The Ugly Dachshund; Follow Me, Boys!

Ach, himmel! Mein Gott!:
SIG RUMANN

There were two factors that made Sig Rumann a unique, instantly recognizable, and inimitable character comedian for many years in Hollywood. One was his on-screen demeanor: excitable, blustering, overbearing and spluttering. The other was his thick, guttural German accent.

He was typically an explosive, excited *dummkopf* or a caricature of Prussian pomposity. His pride was invariably injured, his dignity ruffled. With a furious look, popping eyes, a bulbous nose, bushy brows, a walrus mustache and a manic smile, he played many a comic psychiatrist, eccentric professor, idiot saboteur, moronic megalomaniac or befuddled foreigner (German, Russian, Hungarian, sometimes others). A splendid comedy actor, he made a fine foil for the Marx Brothers (in three films), Jack Benny, and Jerry Lewis, but his stern demeanor also stood out in dramatic roles, although he was seldom adequately showcased in worthwhile films.

In private life an eloquent anti-Nazi, he was cast as a Nazi on quite a few occasions—as were many Germanic actors in the World War II era. Of these, he is best remembered as "Concentration Camp" Ehrhardt in director Ernst Lubitsch's **To Be or Not to Be.**

Siegfried Albon Rumann (he was billed variously on screen as Siegfried Rumann, Sig Rumann or Sig Ruman) was, as one might expect, a native of Germany, born October 11, 1884, in Hamburg. He studied electro-technology for a year at a college in Ilmenau in Thuringia, but returned to Hamburg and studied for the stage instead. He performed in Bielefeld, Stettin and Kiel (in the latter city at the Kaiser's own theater), saw service in World War I, and went to the United States in 1924 at age 39. While doing German-language plays at New York's Irving Place Theatre he reportedly was discovered by actor George Jessel, playwright George S. Kaufman and critic Alexander Woollcott, who liked his style, and in 1928 he made his Broadway debut. Working steadily, he co-starred with Katharine Cornell and Ethel Barrymore, and had the key role of Preysing in **Grand Hotel** (played by Wallace Beery in the 1932 film version). During these stage years he married Claire Tuttleman.

There was one early film appearance, in a small part in 1929's **The Royal Box,** but apart from that he was busy on stage until 1934, when at age 49 he made

a permanent move to Hollywood. In director John Ford's **The World Moves On** (34) he was excellent as a cotton merchant, married to Louise Dresser, and they were also married in **Servants' Entrance,** in which he hires Janet Gaynor as a maid. In **Marie Galante** he was a saboteur plotting to blow up a Panama Canal power plant but thwarted by Spencer Tracy.

One of his best early roles came in **The Wedding Night** (35), as Anna Sten's father, a bitter, old-fashioned tobacco farmer who dominates her and tries to keep her away from married novelist Gary Cooper, preferring that she marry local lout Ralph Bellamy. The New York Times called his performance "brilliant." But the role that year that most film fans fondly remember was as the outraged opera impresario whose production is wrecked by the antics of the Marx Brothers in **A Night at the Opera.** He played a blacksmith in **The Farmer Takes a Wife,** with Henry Fonda (making his screen debut) and Miss

Gaynor, and he was a wild-animal trainer in **East of Java,** a moonshiner in **Spring Tonic,** and a doctor in **Under Pressure.**

Rumann was a German detective, murdered (along with a few others) by Douglass Dumbrille in **The Princess Comes Across** (36), and a tyrannical Mexican governor in **The Bold Caballero.** Then came a remarkably busy year, 1937, in which he was in 14 films. He was a police captain in the Shirley Temple vehicle **Heidi,** and was once again a victim of the Marx Brothers in **A Day at the Races.** He played a German espionage chief in **Lancer Spy,** was a Parisian in the remake of **Seventh Heaven,** a counterfeiter in **Midnight Taxi,** and one of the villains bested by Peter Lorre in two Mr. Moto outings. In **Nothing Sacred** he was the radium-poisoning expert who exposes the hoax (that Carole Lombard was dying), and he played a Spanish general in **Love Under Fire,** a European prime minister in **Thin Ice,** and a hospital superintendent in **The Great Hospital Mystery.**

Interestingly enough, during his Hollywood years the actor worked concurrently, between movie assignments, as a scientist in the bacteriology department at the University of Southern California.

He was French again in **Suez** (38), as a member of the Foreign Legion and the father of Annabella, and played a circus owner in **I'll Give a Million,** a hotel manager in **Paradise for Three,** a mobster in **The Saint in New York,** and the father of the ingenue (Jane Bryan) in **Girls on Probation.** In the Greta Garbo classic **Ninotchka** (39) he was one of the three Soviet functionaries who are sent to Paris and whose behavior she is dispatched to investigate. In **Only Angels Have Wings** he was intensely moving as Cary Grant's boss, the great-hearted but harassed owner of an airline operating over a dangerous mountain range in a banana republic. He was one of the Nazi agents in **Confessions of a Nazi Spy,** brought to justice by Edward G. Robinson, and played a comic psychiatrist in **Honolulu** and another doctor in **Remember?**

In the film adaptation of Joseph Conrad's novel **Victory** (40) he was the lecherous, put-upon hotel owner who first tries to seduce Betty Field and then sets Sir Cedric Hardwicke and his villainous underlings on the trail of recluse Fredric March. He was yet another Nazi, a journalist, in the Clark Gable starrer **Comrade X,** and was outstanding in **Dr. Ehrlich's Magic Bullet** as the doctor's (Robinson's) principal opposition. He played a Nazi again in **Four Sons,** and was the villain, a counterfeiter, in **Outside the 3-Mile Limit.** There was another Nazi role in **So Ends Our Night** (41), and he did another comic psychiatrist in **Love Crazy.** In the bizarre **World Premiere** he and Fritz Feld were comic subversives sent by Berlin to Hollywood to disrupt the movie industry, and he played John Jacob Astor in **This Woman Is Mine.**

The apotheosis of Sig Rumann was unquestionably as the Gestapo chief, Ehrhardt, in director Ernst Lubitsch's bitter, misunderstood and much maligned serio-comic classic **To Be or Not to Be** (42), starring Jack Benny and Carole Lombard (her last film). Delivering a richly comic performance, he appears one hour into the film and simply walks away with it as he keeps repeating, "So they call me 'Concentration Camp' Ehrhardt!" The two lines in the movie that came in for the most criticism were also spoken by him, the first being a reference to concentration camps, "We do the concentrating, and the Poles do the camping," and the most heavily criticized of all being "What he [Benny] did to Shakespeare, we are now doing to Poland." There were still more films that year. He was busy as a Nazi again in **Desperate Journey, Berlin Correspondent** and **Remember Pearl Harbor,** and in **Enemy Agents Meet Ellery Queen** you can be sure he didn't play Ellery Queen. In **They Came to Blow Up America** (43) he was one of the ones who did, and he was a Frenchman in **The Song of Bernadette.** He appeared as Von Hindenburg in **The Hitler Gang** (44), and was in a horror film, **House of Frankenstein.** He was part of the court of Catherine the Great (Tallulah Bankhead) in **A Royal Scandal** (45). Now in his early sixties, he was harassed once more by the Marx Brothers in **A Night in Casablanca** (46), and he was a member of the Emperor Franz Joseph's court in **The Emperor Waltz.**

Small parts were just about all he would get for the remainder of his career. He did get a good role in **Stalag 17** (53), as Schultz, the frustrated concentration-camp guard. At age 76 he provided comic support for Jerry Lewis in **The Errand Boy** (61), and three years later he was still playing a Nazi, in **36 Hours** (64). His last film work came in 1966.

Sig Rumann died the following year, 1967, at 82. But his films keep popping up at revival showings or on late-night TV. When you see a pompous, excited, explosive Teuton, you'll know who it is. It might even turn out to be "Concentration Camp" Ehrhardt.

THE FILMS OF SIG RUMANN

1929: The Royal Box.
1934: The World Moves On; Servants' Entrance; Marie Galante.
1935: A Night at the Opera; The Wedding Night; The Farmer Takes a Wife; East of Java; Under Pressure; Spring Tonic.
1936: The Princess Comes Across; The Bold Caballero.
1937: Nothing Sacred; Love Under Fire; Heidi; Maytime; Lancer Spy; Seventh Heaven; On the Avenue; This Is My Affair; A Day at the Races; Think Fast, Mr. Moto; Thank You, Mr. Moto; Thin Ice; Midnight Taxi; The Great Hospital Mystery.
1938: Suez; I'll Give a Million; The Great Waltz; Paradise for Three; The Saint in New York; Girls on Probation.
1939: Ninotchka; Only Angels Have Wings; Confessions of a Nazi Spy; Honolulu; Remember?; Never Say Die.
1940: Victory; Dr. Ehrlich's Magic Bullet; Bitter Sweet; Comrade X; Four Sons; Outside the 3-Mile Limit; I Was an Adventuress.
1941: So Ends Our Night; Love Crazy; Shining Victory; This Woman Is Mine; The Man Who Lost Himself; World Premiere; That Uncertain Feeling; The Wagons Roll at Night.
1942: To Be or Not to Be; Desperate Journey; Crossroads; China Girl; Berlin Correspondent; Remember Pearl Harbor; Enemy Agents Meet Ellery Queen.
1943: The Song of Bernadette; Government Girl; Sweet Rosie O'Grady; They Came to Blow Up America; Tarzan Triumphs.
1944: The Hitler Gang; It Happened Tomorrow; Summer Storm; House of Frankenstein.
1945: The Dolly Sisters; A Royal Scandal; The Men in Her Diary; She Went to the Races.
1946: Night and Day; A Night in Casablanca; Faithful in My Fashion.
1947: Mother Wore Tights.
1948: The Emperor Waltz; Give My Regards to Broadway; If You Knew Susie.
1949: Border Incident.
1950: Father Is a Bachelor.
1951: On the Riviera.
1952: The World in His Arms; O. Henry's Full House; Ma and Pa Kettle on Vacation.
1953: Stalag 17; The Glenn Miller Story; Houdini.
1954: White Christmas; Living It Up; Three-Ring Circus.
1955: Many Rivers to Cross; Spy Chasers; Carolina Cannonball.
1957: The Wings of Eagles.
1961: The Errand Boy.
1964: Robin and the Seven Hoods; 36 Hours.
1966: The Fortune Cookie; Way, Way Out; Last of the Secret Agents.

From a hero to a villain:

JOSEPH SCHILDKRAUT

A sea-change overtook Joseph Schildkraut in mid-career. In the silent era and the early Thirties he was playing suave, lithe, handsome heroes, but by 1934 he had become a smooth, irritable, even villainous character actor.

But not *always* villainous. One of his greatest dramatic roles earned him an Academy Award as best supporting actor, and there were some other good dramatic parts over the years.

Spending much of his career on the stage as well as on screen, he made film appearances for exactly half a century, but was in only some 60 movies. About half of these were in the Thirties, when he was especially busy in the last half of the decade.

Dashing, mustachioed, dark-haired, with a flashing (and sometimes sinister) smile, he played so many nationalities so convincingly that he earned a place in film history as one of Hollywood's finest character actors.

Schildkraut was born March 22, 1895 (some sources say 1896), in Vienna, the son of renowned stage actor Rudolph Schildkraut, and first trained for the stage, oddly enough, under his father's thespian rival, Albert Basserman, who was later to become a busy film character actor himself. (Father Rudolph also made some film appearances. Many years later Joseph would entitle his autobiography "My Father and I.") In any case, he joined his father on the latter's American tour in 1910, and enrolled at the American Academy of Dramatic Art. Returning to Germany in 1913, he joined the great Max Reinhardt's stage company, and soon became a star. He appeared in four German and Hungarian films between 1915 and 1920, and in the latter year settled in the United States. Within a year he was a leading matinee idol on Broadway. His first big role, in 1921, co-starred him with Eva Le Gallienne in Ferenc Mólnar's **Liliom** (which many years later became the hit Broadway musical **Carousel**) and won him the praise of critics.

He made an impressive American screen debut in 1922, at age 27, as the priggish nobleman lover of the harassed Lillian Gish in director D.W. Griffith's **Orphans of the Storm,** set in the days of the French Revolution. She hides him and barely escapes the guillotine. Apart from Miss Gish's performances and the fine crowd scenes, the film's only redeeming feature was Schildkraut as the feline Chevalier de Voudray, a characterization he would more or less

repeat in a famous film of the Thirties. Then he co-starred with Norma Talmadge in **Song of Love (Dust of Desire)** (23), as a French undercover agent trying to thwart an Arab uprising; to gain information, he romances Miss Talmadge, the rebel chieftain's daughter, and ultimately wins her. In this film his lurid makeup accentuated his somewhat effeminate appearance.

He starred on Broadway in Henrik Ibsen's play **Peer Gynt,** and won new laurels in 1924's **The Firebrand,** which also featured Edward G. Robinson. Back in Hollywood, he and William Boyd (the future Hopalong Cassidy) were romantic heroes involved in a love quadrangle and a train crash in **The Road to Yesterday** (25). He and his father played father and son in **Young April** (26), in which he is a crown prince who falls in love with Bessie Love, and there was another princely role in **Meet the Prince,** as a White Russian royal who fled after the 1917 revolution and now lives in a tenement on New York's

Lower East Side. In **Shipwrecked** he played a drifter, working as a ship's cook, who saves a woman stowaway (Seena Owen) from the lecherous captain and falls in love with her.

The actor had a fine villainous role as Judas in director Cecil B. DeMille's life of Christ, **The King of Kings** (27), and in **The Forbidden Woman** he played a violinist who falls in love with a spy, Jetta Goudal, but she is executed by a firing squad. He played a murderous gangster in **Tenth Avenue** (28), and in **The Blue Danube** he was a demented, villainous hunchback who cons Leatrice Joy into marriage although she really loves Nils Asther; ultimately he stabs himself in a fit of rage. He was the handsome hero (overacting badly) in the first screen version of the musical **Show Boat** (29), ardently in love with Laura La Plante, and that same year played a remarkably similar role, a riverboat gambler, in **Mississippi Gambler,** with 19-year-old Joan Bennett as the heroine.

He was in a German-language film made by MGM, **Die Sehnsucht jeder Frau** (30), the foreign version of **A Lady to Love,** based on the oft-filmed play **They Knew What They Wanted,** about an Italian winery owner in California who wins a mail-order wife by sending a photo of his hired man; he was the hired man, while Edward G. Robinson and Vilma Banky repeated their roles from the English-language version. He starred in **Night Ride** as a reporter who is the nemesis of racketeer Robinson (billed below him). Then he played a callous gigolo violinist opposite Myrna Loy (the *early* Myrna Loy) in the bizarre melodrama **Cock o' the Walk.** The plot goes like this: He saves her from suicide, then marries her, intending to collect on the life insurance when she *does* kill herself; meanwhile he chases other women. A wronged husband then tries to kill him, but she saves him, so he undergoes a change and realizes he loves her after all. Miss Loy is then maligned in a scandal, so Schildkraut kills the slanderer and goes to prison. Wait, that's not all. She tries suicide—again. He saves her—again. He returns to prison—again. Meanwhile, back at the ranch...

The actor was married three times. The first wife, at an unspecified date, was actress Elise (or Elsie) Bartlett, and they were divorced. His second marriage, to Mary McKay, also ended in divorce. In 1963, the year before his death, he married Lenora Rogers.

He was in two films in 1931 (both somehow unrecorded in the comprehensive American Film Institute Catalog, so possibly they were foreign films), and then returned to the stage for three years. One of his roles during this time was (once again) the starring part in **Liliom** on Broadway. When he returned to the film capital at age 39, it was to begin a fairly busy decade at the peak of Hollywood's Golden Era, with good character roles, often in top-budget classics.

Schildkraut played Herod in the Claudette Colbert starrer **Cleopatra** (34), and in **Viva Villa** there was another good villain role as a treacherous Mexican general who ends up staked out on the ground next to an anthill. In **Sisters Under the Skin** he was a bohemian composer who steals the young mistress (Elissa Landi) of Frank Morgan; six years later he would play the seducer of Morgan's wife in a better film. He was a Saracen leader in **The Crusades** (35), and a jaunty desert guide in support of Marlene Dietrich and Charles Boyer in **The Garden of Allah** (36).

He won the Oscar for best supporting actor (in the second year of that award) as the hapless Captain Alfred Dreyfus in the classic biographical drama **The Life of Emile Zola** (37), as the French army officer wrongly convicted as a spy and imprisoned on Devil's Island, but ultimately freed, in this story of one of the most famous cases in the history of jurisprudence; Paul Muni starred as his defender, Zola, and Gale Sondergaard played Schildkraut's wife. This superb film was the most honored movie of the year, and his taut performance as the wretched Dreyfus was every bit the equal of Muni's. In that year he also was good as a fatuous weakling of a German prince in **Lancer Spy,** and played a murderous slave dealer in **Slave Ship** and a gigolo in **Lady Behave!**

The actor fairly reeked of decadence in **Marie Antoinette** (38), as the unctuous, treacherous and poisonously diverse Duc d'Orleans, also known as Philippe Egalité, his face painted like a courtesan's; this performance reminded some critics of the one he gave in **Orphans of the Storm** years earlier. He was also a French nobleman in **Suez,** and yet another nobleman, this time Hungarian, in **The Baroness and the Butler,** losing his wife, Annabella, to William Powell. He was excellent in **The Man in the Iron Mask** (39), as Fouquet, the power behind the throne, ultimately dying at swordpoint in a carriage. He was ideally cast as a native of India, the over-Anglicized Mr. Bannerjee, in **The Rains Came,** and in **Lady of the Tropics** he played a villainous Asiatic pursuing Hedy Lamarr. He portrayed a much older man in **Mr. Moto Takes a Vacation,** a thief who steals the English crown jewels and is revealed at the end as the murderer as well. He was an agitated European army officer in **Idiot's Delight,** the king of France in **The Three Musketeers,** and played Jane Withers' father, a French army officer engaged in spying in Germany, in **Pack Up Your Troubles.**

Schildkraut was again involved in stealing a woman from Frank Morgan, this time in **The Shop Around the Corner** (40); the unctuous seducer was Morgan's employee and had an affair with the boss' (unseen) wife, ending up by being not merely fired but hurled bodily from the shop by manager James Stewart. In the programmer **Phantom Raiders** he was the suave villain, a gangster who sets off bombs on ships by means of a radio. He was the chief villain in **Rangers of Fortune,** committing two murders before being killed in a gunfight with Fred MacMurray, Albert Dekker and Gilbert Roland. In **Meet the Wildcat** he played an international art thief brought to justice by Ralph Bellamy. He was one of the baddies in **The Parson of Panamint** (41), and then was off the screen during all of World War II, returning to the stage. Three starring roles on Broadway were in **Clash by Night** with Tallulah Bankhead and Robert Ryan in 1941 and two plays with his long-ago co-star Eva Le Gallienne: **Uncle Harry** in 1942 and Chekhov's **The Cherry Orchard** in 1944.

He returned to filming at the war's end, at age 50. In **Flame of the Barbary Coast** (45) he was back in the kind of suave romantic role that had once made him a matinee idol, only this time he was a San Francisco scion turned gambling impresario, competing against hick rancher John Wayne for saloon singer Ann Dvorak, and there are no prizes for guessing who wins. A far more interesting film, and a far better role, came along in **The Cheaters,** in which, as a downtrodden actor invited for Christmas dinner by a wealthy, snobbish family (including Billie Burke and Eugene Pallette), he ends up by humanizing them, capped by a fireside reading of Dickens' "A Christmas Carol." He was the top-billed star of this film.

The actor's performances at this point in time were mainly for Republic Pictures, the biggest name on Poverty Row, which was a long step down from his work of a decade earlier. He played a supercilious courtier, engaging in a sword duel with Bob Hope, in **Monsieur Beaucaire** (46), but that year he was also in a cheapie, **The Plainsman and the Lady,** in which he and Gail Patrick were the villains trying to stop the Pony Express. A few more forgettable programmers in the next two years, and then he left the screen in disgust for a long stretch of 11 years, stepping up the pace of his stage work and also ultimately going into television, where he was the host on "Joseph Schildkraut Presents."

During the Fifties he won plaudits on Broadway for his role in **The Diary of Anne Frank,** as Anne's father, and in 1959 he accepted a call to return to Hollywood for the film version; he was now 64. The actor's feeling and skill for this performance could not have been bettered; he was moving and magnificent as the lone survivor of the tragedy. Remarkably, while he did not receive a second Oscar nomination as best supporting actor, two other character players in the film, Shelley Winters and Ed Wynn, did get nominations, and Miss Winters actually won.

He was well down the cast list in **King of the Roaring Twenties** (61), and then after three more years played his last screen role, a cameo (as were virtually all the roles in the film) in **The Greatest Story Ever Told,** a life of Christ starring Max von Sydow; he portrayed Nicodemus. By the time it was released in 1965, Joseph Schildkraut had died the previous year at the age of 69. His was a talent often misused and even wasted on the screen, but time cannot erase his moment of glory as the tortured Captain Dreyfus in the classic **The Life of Emile Zola,** with a gold statuette to verify his splendid skills as an actor.

THE FILMS OF JOSEPH SCHILDKRAUT

1915: Arpad Szomory Schlemihl.
1916: Schweigepflich.
1918: Die Leben von Theodore Herzl.
1920: Der Roman der Komtesse Orth.
1922: Orphans of the Storm.
1923: Song of Love (Dust of Desire).
1925: The Road to Yesterday.
1926: Young April; Meet the Prince; Shipwrecked.
1927: The King of Kings; the Forbidden Woman; The Heart Thief; His Dog.
1928: Tenth Avenue; The Blue Danube.
1929: Show Boat; Mississippi Gambler.
1930: Night Ride; Cock o' the Walk; Die Sehnsucht jeder Frau (German-language version of A Lady to Love).
1931: Venetian Nights (Carnival); The Blue Danube (remake).
1934: Cleopatra; Viva Villa; Sisters Under the Skin.
1935: The Crusades.

1936: The Garden of Allah.
1937: The Life of Emile Zola; Souls at Sea; Lancer Spy; Slave Ship; Lady Behave!
1938: Marie Antoinette; Suez; The Baroness and the Butler.
1939: The Man in the Iron Mask; The Rains Came; Idiot's Delight; The Three Musketeers; Lady of the Tropics; Pack Up Your Troubles; Mr. Moto Takes a Vacation.
1940: The Shop Around the Corner; Phantom Raiders; Rangers of Fortune; Meet the Wildcat.
1941: The Parson of Panamint.
1945: Flame of the Barbary Coast; The Cheaters.
1946: Monsieur Beaucaire; The Plainsman and the Lady.
1947: Northwest Outpost.
1948: Gallant Legion; Old Los Angeles.
1959: The Diary of Anne Frank.
1961: King of the Roaring Twenties.
1965: The Greatest Story Ever Told.

Meet the duchess:
ALISON SKIPWORTH

Lofty matrons, grand dames, dowagers, duchesses and shady ladies were the stock in trade of the stately, imposing and formidable Alison Skipworth.

Physically on the hefty side, with a slightly menacing look to her features, she was a highly engaging character actress, frequently hammy and theatrical, who looked like she was cut out for serious drama but actually scored more often in comedy. (She was in three films the co-star and foil for W.C. Fields.)

Called by one writer "Paramount's answer to Marie Dressler," she looked two decades younger than her real age (she was in her seventies when playing fiftyish women in films of the Thirties), and people were always amazed to find out when she was born.

As a matter of fact, that occurred July 25, 1863, in London. (Some sources, probably including studio publicity, list dates of 1870, 1875 and even 1883!) A regal beauty in her youth, Alison Groom was educated privately by tutors from Oxford. She was married early to artist Frank M. Skipworth (and widowed at an unspecified date), and with her duchess-like beauty and masses of auburn hair she was his favorite model. She made her London stage debut in 1894, at age 31, in **A Gaiety Girl;** she said it was to supplement her husband's meager income. The following year she traveled to the United States and appeared on Broadway in a play called, appropriately, **The Artist's Model,** returned to London briefly, went back to New York, and in 1897 joined Daniel Frohman's stage company.

She appeared in numerous plays, first in leads, then, as she grew older, in supporting roles. In 1907 she led the supporting cast in D.W. Griffith's play **A Fool and a Girl.** Her other stage work included Shakespeare, **The Prisoner of Zenda, The Torch Bearers** (co-starring with Mary Boland and scoring a notable success as the harassed drama coach), and **The Grand Duchess and the Waiter.** By the mid-Twenties, when she had turned 60, she had an impressive reputation. But between 1925 and 1930, she said, she was in 21 straight failures, so she was glad to accept film offers. (There had been just one movie, **Handcuffs or Kisses,** in 1921.) In 1930, at age 66, she moved to Hollywood to begin a brief but busy career in films.

In **Outward Bound** (30), starring Leslie Howard, she was a haughty woman of wealth, and in **Raffles**

she played Lady Melrose, whose jewels are stolen. She supported Norma Talmadge (in the latter's last film) in **Du Barry, Woman of Passion,** and Jeanette MacDonald in **Oh! for a Man,** and played Lewis Stone's mother in **Strictly Unconventional.** In **Night Angel** (31) she was an impoverished countess who has become a brothel keeper (she calls it a cabaret, but the police know better) and ends up sent to prison by lawyer Fredric March, who then falls for her daughter, Nancy Carroll. She played Jean Arthur's mother in **The Virtuous Husband,** and in **Tonight or Never** (starring Gloria Swanson) she was an Italian noblewoman, a former opera diva with a notorious past (the film marked the screen debut of Melvyn Douglas). She also played upper-class ladies in **Devotion** and **The Road to Singapore** (no relation to the later Bing Crosby-Bob Hope vehicle).

Miss Skipworth was the star of **Madame Racketeer** (32) as a lifelong larcenous con woman who, released from prison, returns to the town where she left her husband (Richard Bennett, the father of Joan and Constance), but remains only long enough to straighten out the affairs of her two daughters before being taken back to the big house for plotting a new extortion scheme. She played Carole Lombard's mother in **Sinners in the Sun,** and was especially good in **Night After Night** as Miss Jellyman, the grand dame who gives lessons in deportment and speech to speakeasy owner George Raft (meanwhile, making her screen debut, a lady named Mae West walked off with the picture). In **Unexpected Father** she was a bootlegger, making her deliveries in a baby carriage—with a baby in it. But her best-remembered role that year marked the first of her three teamings with W.C. Fields, in one of the segments of the multi-episode film **If I Had a Million;** they were a couple whose car has been wrecked by a road hog, so after winning their million they get their revenge, of sorts, by going on a joyous spree with a fleet of old cars, smashing each one in turn (driven by a hired chauffeur) into the car of every road hog they encounter. For comedy, she and Fields were an even more effective teaming than Wallace Beery and Marie Dressler, without a bit of sentimentality, and the public responded favorably.

They were together again in **Tillie and Gus** (33), this time the stars of the film, a pair of artful card sharps who must win a race between two decrepit ferryboats to regain her niece's rightful inheritance (naturally, they do). She was properly unpleasant as Marlene Dietrich's rum-guzzling old aunt in **The Song of Songs,** and played the Duchess in **Alice in Wonderland** and a *grand* duchess (from a Balkan country) in **Tonight Is Ours.** She and Roland Young co-starred in **A Lady's Profession** as a titled, aristocratic English brother and sister who run a New York speakeasy where they serve only non-alcoholic beverages and thus run afoul of the booze-pushing mob. **He Learned About Women** cast her as "Mme. Pompadour," a retired stage actress, and in **Midnight Club** she was yet another titled Englishwoman.

Her final teaming with Fields (in real life she was nearly old enough to be his mother) came in the wacky comedy **Six of a Kind** (34); the other four were (a) Charlie Ruggles and Mary Boland and (b) George Burns and Gracie Allen, and they all drove across the country together. She was a ruthless "social adviser," arranging fashionable society events such as debuts, in **Coming-Out Party,** and supported Victor McLaglen in **Wharf Angel** as "Mother Bright," a lady with a purple past operating an unsavory waterfront saloon. She was a millionairess in **The Captain Hates the Sea** (the last film of John Gilbert), and the accomplice of jewel thief Gertrude Michael in **The Notorious Sophie Lang,** also playing a carnival ticket-taker in **Shoot the Works.**

Miss Skipworth, now in her seventies, played Franchot Tone's disapproving housekeeper, trying to keep Bette Davis from drinking, in **Dangerous** (35), and in **The Girl from 10th Avenue** she was Miss Davis' landlady, a former Floradora Girl. **The Casino Murder Case** cast her as a foolish dowager (Rosalind Russell was her secretary), and she was Marlene Dietrich's scheming guardian in **The Devil Is a Woman.** In **Doubting Thomas** she was fine as the self-important dramatic coach Madame Pampinelli, hired to tutor Will Rogers' wife, Billie Burke, but the amateur theatrical that results, directed by Madame, is a community disaster. (The actress had previously played this role on Broadway.) She was Alan Mowbray's mother in **Becky Sharp** and Loretta Young's aunt in **Shanghai.**

In the bizarre **Satan Met a Lady** (36), a very peculiar remake of 1931's **The Maltese Falcon** and a sort of forerunner to the 1941 classic, she took what was in effect the later Sydney Greenstreet role with a sex change, as Madame Barabbas; playing what amounted to the Mary Astor and Humphrey Bogart roles were Bette Davis and Warren William. She was Carole Lombard's traveling companion on an ocean voyage in **The Princess Comes Across,** and starred in a Poverty Row film, **Hitch Hike Lady,** as an Englishwoman undergoing misadventures in the American West. **Two in a Crowd** cast her as Joel McCrea's landlady.

The actress played an employee of a swank Parisian dress shop in **Stolen Holiday** (37), and it was her last major film. She also starred in another Poverty Row outing, **Two Wise Maids,** as a schoolteacher. She played Lew Ayres' foster mother in **King of the Newsboys** (38), starred as a rural mayor in **Ladies in Distress,** and was Jane Wyman's aunt in **Wide Open Faces.** And at that point she retired from the screen, at 75.

She returned after a while to Broadway, where she appeared in several plays, and then retired from acting in 1942 after working in **Lady of the Valley.** And in 1952 Alison Skipworth died at the age of 89. But on television screens in the small hours of the morning she lives on in the dowagers, duchesses and dastardly dames she portrayed to perfection for all too brief a moment in Hollywood's Golden Era.

THE FILMS OF ALISON SKIPWORTH

1921: Handcuffs or Kisses.
1930: Outward Bound; Raffles; Du Barry, Woman of Passion; Oh! for a Man; Strictly Unconventional.
1931: Tonight or Never; Night Angel; Devotion; The Virtuous Husband; The Road to Singapore.
1932: Madame Racketeer; If I Had a Million; Sinners in the Sun; High Pressure; Unexpected Father; Night After Night.
1933: Tillie and Gus; The Song of Songs; Alice in Wonderland; Tonight Is Ours; A Lady's Profession; He Learned About Women; Midnight Club.
1934: Six of a Kind; Wharf Angel; The Captain Hates the Sea; The Notorious Sophie Lang; Here Is My Heart; Shoot the Works; Coming Out Party.
1935: Dangerous; The Devil Is a Woman; Becky Sharp; Shanghai; The Girl from 10th Avenue; Doubting Thomas; The Casino Murder Case.
1936: Satan Met a Lady; The Gorgeous Hussy; The Princess Comes Across; White Hunter; Two in a Crowd; Hitch Hike Lady. *Credit uncertain:* Follow Your Heart.
1937: Stolen Holiday; Two Wise Maids.
1938: King of the Newsboys; Ladies in Distress; Wide Open Faces.

The sun never sets on the British Empire:
SIR C. AUBREY SMITH

The scene: a British army outpost on India's northwest frontier, late in the 19th century. Enter, stage right, a gung-ho young lieutenant. He approaches the desk of the colonel, a distinguished-looking old gentleman with a bristling mustache and a no-nonsense bearing.

"Sir, the natives are restless tonight, and there's trouble brewing at the Khyber Pass."

"Mmmm," says the colonel. "Can't have that, you know." He quietly issues an instruction to another subaltern. Then he turns back to the young lieutenant. "Nothing to worry about, my boy. I've dealt with these things before. Now get a good night's sleep." And so another crisis ends.

For any mischief that might be afoot among restless natives, in whatever far-flung outpost of the British Empire, would unfailingly be firmly suppressed by Sir C. Aubrey Smith, the grand old Englishman of Hollywood's Golden Era. And when not in uniform he could usually be found in a tweedy suit, with a lit pipe. Tall, stately and imposing, with craggy, patrician features, a Roman nose, jutting eyebrows and a mustache he frequently fussed with, he invariably played crusty, benevolent or authoritarian old gentlemen, giving orders or advice with a quiet gentility and confidence. For two decades he stole many a scene from some of Hollywood's major stars, and he usually appeared in top-budget productions.

Charles Aubrey Smith was born July 21, 1863, in London, the son of a doctor, and he really did have the old school tie (from Charterhouse and Cambridge). A member of England's national cricket team (his love of that sport persisted throughout his life), he made his stage debut in 1893 at age 30. He worked with such stars as Ellen Terry and Mrs. Patrick Campbell, made his first New York stage appearance in 1896 (one source says 1903), and continued in a long career on the boards on both sides of the Atlantic.

In 1915 he was in his first film, **Builder of Bridges,** in the United States, and appeared in a total of 11 English and American movies through 1924, continuing his stage work at the same time. He is said to have been the star or co-star in some of these films, but in at least several his roles were small.

The actor married Isobel Wood in 1896. They had a daughter, Honor.

It was not until 1931, at the fairly late age of 68 (after making two British films in 1930), that Smith

moved to Hollywood to embark on a serious film career. And in the years that remained to him he would make nearly 100 movies, keeping very busy at an age when many actors have already retired.

He played a general in the Austrian imperial court in **Daybreak** (31), and in **Bachelor Father** he repeated his 1928 stage hit as a rakish British nobleman who rounds up his three illegitimate children by different mothers and then finds that the one he prefers (Marion Davies) isn't his after all. He was Leslie Howard's father in **Never the Twain Shall Meet,** a clergyman in **Guilty Hands,** and Robert Montgomery's father in **The Man in Possession.** He played a Prussian general in **Surrender,** and was a murder victim in **The Phantom of Paris.**

Smith was excellent as the crusty old duke, the lord of the chateau, in the innovative musical comedy **Love Me Tonight** (32), and in **Trouble in Paradise** he played the biggest crook of all, systematically manipulating the books of Kay Francis' perfume company, of which he is chairman of the board. He was Montgomery's father again in **But the Flesh Is Weak** (as was typical of movie casting in that era, in real life he was old enough to be the star's grandfather). He played Maureen O'Sullivan's old dad in **Tarzan the Ape Man,** and was the villain, an irascible curmudgeon, Walter Connolly's father-in-law, in **No More Orchids.** In **Polly of the Circus** he was the stern old bishop who disapproves when clergyman Clark Gable falls for trapeze performer Marion Davies.

The actor played Greta Garbo's elderly servant in **Queen Christina** (33), and was the veteran stage performer whom Katharine Hepburn seeks out for elocution lessons in **Morning Glory.** He was Mary Pickford's unsympathetic father in **Secrets** (her last film), and portrayed the unfortunate father in **The Monkey's Paw.** He played a Mittel-European prime minister in **Adorable** and an elderly detective in **Curtain at Eight.**

Now in his seventies, he let his interest in the game of cricket continue unabated, and as the doyen of Hollywood's English colony he invariably organized its cricket matches and served as captain of the team manned by many of the numerous Britishers appearing in American films during that Anglophile era in the film capital.

Smith played the Duke of Wellington in the George Arliss vehicle **The House of Rothschild** (34), and was the cruel czarist judge in **We Live Again.** He was the Roman general Enobarbus in **Cleopatra** and a Russian prince in the Marlene Dietrich starrer **The Scarlet Empress. One More River** cast him as yet another general, and he was a police inspector in **The Firebird,** Joel McCrea's father in **Gambling Lady,** and a Hungarian baron, Phillips Holmes' father, in **Caravan.** He was a Scotland Yard inspector (not for the last time) in **Bulldog Drummond Strikes Back.**

He played his patented colonel-on-the-Indian-frontier in **Lives of a Bengal Lancer** (35), dispensing advice to Gary Cooper and Franchot Tone, and was the British prime minister in **Clive of India.** In **Jalna** he was the septuagenarian son of centenarian Jessie Ralph—but in real life the actress was a year younger than he was. He was one of the ship's passengers in **China Seas,** the hermit in **The Crusades,** a doctor in **The Florentine Dagger,** and Ray Milland's father in **The Gilded Lily.**

The actor was good as Freddie Bartholomew's crusty old grandfather in **Little Lord Fauntleroy** (36), played Norma Shearer's father in **Romeo and Juliet,** and was a priest in **The Garden of Allah.** He was fine as yet another priest, Father Paul, in direc-

tor John Ford's **The Hurricane** (37), praying with his congregation in the church on a South Seas island just before the hurricane destroys the edifice. Once again he played a colonel on the Indian frontier in the Shirley Temple starrer **Wee Willie Winkie,** and was Colonel Zapt in the splendid production of **The Prisoner of Zenda.** During the filming of the latter, Raymond Massey asked Smith for advice on how to interpret his (Massey's) part, the villain, Black Michael. The veteran actor, who by this time had become rather deaf and had to read lips on the set, switched on his hearing aid, listened thoughtfully, and said, "Ray, in my time I've played every part in **Zenda** except [Princess] Flavia, and I've always had trouble with Black Michael." He then switched off his hearing aid and resumed reading The Times of London.

In **Four Men and a Prayer** (38), once again directed by Ford, he was an unjustly cashiered British army officer murdered by crooked businessmen; his four sons (including George Sanders and David Niven) proceed to track down the killers. He was the stern Duke of Argyle in **Kidnapped,** and once again portrayed the Duke of Wellington, this time in **Sixty Glorious Years (Queen of Destiny).** He was fine in a small role in **The Four Feathers** (39) as an old military bore, forever demonstrating on a dining-room table how the "Thin Red Line" fought off the Fuzzy-Wuzzies. He was the murder victim of Virginia Grey in **Another Thin Man,** and played Loretta Young's grandfather, a bishop, in **Eternally Yours.** He gave Bing Crosby a job crooning at a radio station in **East Side of Heaven,** met death in a South American jungle after a plane crash in **Five Came Back,** and played a czarist Russian general in **Balalaika.** He was the father of Douglas Fairbanks Jr. and Basil Rathbone in **The Sun Never Sets** and Gloria Jean's grandfather in **The Underpup.**

Smith was one of the visitors to Manderley in **Rebecca** (40), and played Robert Taylor's father, a duke, in **Waterloo Bridge.** In **Beyond Tomorrow** he and Charles Winninger were two elderly ghosts who return at Christmas to help a pair of young lovers, and in **City of Chance** he ran an illegal casino. He played Gloria Jean's grandfather for the second time in **A Little Bit of Heaven.** He was yet another bishop in the remake (starring Spencer Tracy) of **Dr. Jekyll and Mr. Hyde** (41), and was back on the stage briefly. He was cast in the historical role of Lord Kelvin in **Madame Curie** (43), and was a clergyman who tries to help Edward G. Robinson in **Flesh and Fantasy.** At the age of 81 he was knighted, becoming *Sir* C. Aubrey Smith, in 1944, and he was once again a colonel in **The White Cliffs of Dover,** also appearing in a cameo as the chancellor of Oxford University in **The Adventures of Mark Twain.** He was back as a Scotland Yard investigator in **Secrets of Scotland Yard.**

The actor was one of the numerous murder victims (of Barry Fitzgerald) in the fine mystery-comedy **And Then There Were None** (45), and then played still another **Scotland Yard Investigator,** with Erich von Stroheim as the baddie. He was another colonel in **Cluny Brown** (46), and was the Lord Chief Justice in **Unconquered** (47) and an English nobleman in **An Ideal Husband.** In 1948 he was busy working on the remake of **Little Women,** as the stern old Mr. Laurence, his best moment coming when he is kissed by Margaret O'Brien, but that year he died at age 85 before the 1949 film could be released.

In the years since then Hollywood has filmed many another epic of troubles along the Indian frontier, with the natives restless somewhere near the Khyber Pass, but whatever innocuous colonels may have tried to put them down, you don't remember them at all. Whenever you recall such a film, in your mind's eye you see grand old Sir C. Aubrey Smith, confidently and firmly taking the situation well in hand. He was what they call a class act.

THE FILMS OF SIR C. AUBREY SMITH

1915: Builder of Bridges.
1916: The Witching Hour.
1918: Red Pottage.
1920: The Face at the Window; Castles in Spain; The Shuttle of Life.
1922: Flames of Passion; The Bohemian Girl.
1923: The Temptation of Carlton Earlye.
1924: The Unwanted; The Rejected Woman.
1930: The Perfect Alibi (Birds of Prey); Such Is the Law.
1931: Daybreak; Bachelor Father; Never the Twain Shall Meet; Guilty Hands; The Man in Possession; Son of India; Surrender; The Phantom of Paris; Just a Gigolo.
1932: Love Me Tonight; Trouble in Paradise; Polly of the Circus; But the Flesh Is Weak; Tarzan the Ape Man; No More Orchids; They Just Had to Get Married.
1933: Queen Christina; Morning Glory; Bombshell; The Barbarian; Secrets; Curtain at Eight; Adorable; Luxury Liner; The Monkey's Paw.
1934: Cleopatra; The House of Rothschild; The Scarlet Empress; One More River; We Live Again; The Firebird; Gambling Lady; Caravan; Bulldog Drummond Strikes Back. *Credit uncertain:* Riptide; Madame Du Barry.
1935: The Lives of a Bengal Lancer; The Crusades; China Seas; Clive of India; Jalna; The Gilded Lily; The Florentine Dagger; The Right to Live; Transatlantic Tunnel (The Tunnel).
1936: Romeo and Juliet; Little Lord Fauntleroy; The Garden of Allah; Lloyd's of London.
1937: The Hurricane; The Prisoner of Zenda; Wee Willie Winkie; Thoroughbreds Don't Cry.
1938: Four Men and a Prayer; Kidnapped; Sixty Glorious Years (Queen of Destiny).
1939: The Four Feathers; Another Thin Man; Eternally Yours; The Sun Never Sets; East Side of Heaven; Five Came Back; Balalaika; The Underpup.
1940: Rebecca; Waterloo Bridge; A Bill of Divorcement; Beyond Tomorrow; City of Chance; A Little Bit of Heaven.
1941: Dr. Jekyll and Mr. Hyde; Free and Easy; Maisie Was a Lady.
1943: Madame Curie; Flesh and Fantasy; Forever and a Day; Two Tickets to London.
1944: The White Cliffs of Dover; The Adventures of Mark Twain; Secrets of Scotland Yard; They Shall Have Faith; Sensations of 1945.
1945: And Then There Were None; Scotland Yard Investigator.
1946: Cluny Brown; Rendezvous with Annie.
1947: Unconquered; An Ideal Husband; High Conquest.
1949: Little Women.

The sinister smile:
GALE SONDERGAARD

Villainy on the screen has largely been the province of men, but occasionally an actress has emerged to take such roles. Hollywood's best female villain during the period 1939-47 was unquestionably Gale Sondergaard, who started off in 1936 playing mainly nice roles but quickly found her niche in nasty ones.

Tall, dark and stern-looking, with high cheekbones, a commanding voice and impeccable diction, she had a faintly reptilian quality and a sinister smile that was almost a sneer, enabling her to successfully convey an elegant malevolence. Typically catty, cunning or vicious, and invariably humorless, she cornered the market in sinister housekeepers, and she threatened comedians such as Bob Hope, was the Spider Woman opposed to Basil Rathbone's Sherlock Holmes, and played several Nazi spies. Her wicked women were often the brains behind evil plots, but sometimes they had cruel accomplices or loaned their services to evil governments.

The winner of an Academy Award as best supporting actress for her very first film, and later nominated for another one, she saw her screen career abruptly cut short in the postwar period as a result of Hollywood's anti-Communist witch hunt. But she survived, returning to films again years later as an elderly woman.

Edith Holm Sondergaard, of Danish descent, was born February 15, 1899 (one source says 1900), in Litchfield, Minnesota. Her father was a college professor, her mother a pianist and suffragette. Educated at the University of Minnesota and also a graduate of the Minneapolis School of Dramatic Art, she first toured as Jessica in **The Merchant of Venice** with a Shakespeare company, then joined Jessie Bonstelle's stock company in Detroit, tackling any part that came her way—"hags and ingenues, mothers and daughters, wantons and nuns," as she later related. Moving to Broadway in the late 1920s, she signed a five-year contract with the Theater Guild, and played leading roles in such plays as **Red Rust, American Dream, Doctor Monica** and, most notably, Eugene O'Neill's **Strange Interlude** (taking over from Judith Anderson in the starring role of Nina, later done on the screen by Norma Shearer).

The actress was first married to Neill O'Malley in 1922, and they were divorced in 1930. In that year she married Herbert Biberman, a future screen director who was to become well known later as one of

the "Hollywood Ten." They adopted two children, Daniel and Joan. About 1935 the couple moved to Hollywood, where they both began screen careers.

Few performers could have had a more auspicious beginning in the movies than did Gale Sondergaard, winning the Oscar as best supporting actress for her first film (and in the first year the supporting Oscars were handed out). The movie was **Anthony Adverse** (36), and the 37-year-old actress played Faith Paleologue, the scheming housekeeper to the villain, Claude Rains, who later marries him. The Academy Award was an odd judgment, though, for her performance was somewhat absurd, consisting mainly of flashing teeth. (For the record, her four competitors for the award all delivered performances that were at least its equal, if not its superior: Beulah Bondi in **The Gorgeous Hussy,** Alice Brady in **My Man Godfrey,** Bonita Granville in **These Three** and Maria Ouspenskaya in **Dodsworth.**)

She was sympathetic as the wife of the unfortunate Captain Alfred Dreyfus (Joseph Schildkraut) in the fine biographical classic **The Life of Emile Zola,** starring Paul Muni as Zola. She played one of the put-upon villagers involved in the 1692 witch ruckus in **Maid of Salem,** and stole the show from James Stewart and Simone Simon as the latter's malevolent sister in the absurd remake of **Seventh Heaven;** this was her first real villainess role. She also outdid the star, recent double Oscar winner Luise Rainer, in **Dramatic School** (38), playing with great panache the aging actress, a former stage star, jealous and resentful of the young actresses she now trains (other students included Lana Turner and Paulette Goddard). In **Lord Jeff** she and George Zucco were professional thieves and swindlers who recruit Freddie Bartholomew to work for them—but he reforms and turns them in.

Miss Sondergaard was married to Claude Rains again in **Juarez** (39), another Paul Muni vehicle; they were Napoleon III and the slyly reptilian Empress Eugenie, coldly spurning Bette Davis when she (as Carlotta, wife of the Emperor Maximilian of Mexico) asks for their help. She played her first sinister housekeeper in the Bob Hope outing **The Cat and the Canary,** appearing entirely in black and with a cat to match—only she was really a red herring, merely appearing to be a baddie but later turning out to be one of the few nice people in the film. In another Hope film, **Never Say Die,** she was a murderous adventuress who tries to marry Hope (a millionaire), but he prefers Martha Raye, and Miss Sondergaard ends up with...Andy Devine! These two roles pretty well established her screen persona.

Having refused to help Miss Davis in **Juarez,** she now proceeded to have her murdered in the classic drama **The Letter** (40); she played the Oriental wife of Bette's lover and murder victim, getting her revenge in the contrived ending (not in Somerset Maugham's original story), in which the star had to receive retribution under the Production Code (having been acquitted at her murder trial), so Miss Sondergaard has a henchman knife her to death. She was the malevolent cat, Tylette, frightening Shirley Temple in **The Blue Bird,** and was one of several nasties in the Tyrone Power starrer **The Mark of Zorro** (Linda Darnell was her daughter, J. Edward Bromberg her husband, and Basil Rathbone was in love with her). In **The Llano Kid** she and husband Alan Mowbray were corrupt ranch managers. She played yet another sinister housekeeper in the spooky-old-house mystery **The Black Cat** (41).

The actress was a seductive Nazi agent pursuing Bob Hope and Madeleine Carroll in **My Favorite Blonde** (42), and in **Enemy Agents Meet Ellery Queen** you can be sure she was one of the enemy agents. Continuing in this vein, she was one of a group of Nazi broadcasters in **Appointment in Berlin** (43), and was still on the German side in **The Strange Death of Adolf Hitler.** In the Poverty Row cheapie **Isle of Forgotten Sins** she played a South Seas cabaret owner.

She had her busiest year on the screen in 1944, with seven films. The most unusual role of her career came in the bizzarre drama **Christmas Holiday,** as the sinister mother of the equally sinister (and badly miscast) murderer Gene Kelly, who leads wife Deanna Durbin astray; there are even incestuous overtones between mother and son in this adaptation of a Somerset Maugham novel. She was a baddie in **The Invisible Man's Revenge,** and she and Basil Rathbone had the lead roles in **The Spider Woman (Sherlock Holmes and the Spider Woman);** she runs a murder ring involving loaning money to men, killing them (with poisonous spiders) and collecting on the insurance policies (which had made her the beneficiary in return for the loans). In that film the New York Times called her "very sinister in a soporific way." She was (of course) one of the villains in **Enter Arsene Lupin,** played yet another sinister housekeeper in **The Climax,** and was a gypsy in the Maria Montez vehicle **Gypsy Wildcat.**

Miss Sondergaard made no films in 1945, and then won a second supporting-Oscar nomination for the fairly routine role of the king's (Rex Harrison's) aging first wife in **Anna and the King of Siam** (46), with Irene Dunne starring as Anna, but this time the statuette went to Anne Baxter for **The Razor's Edge.** In **A Night in Paradise** she was overwrought and campy as a sorceress seeking revenge on Merle Oberon, and once more she played a sinister housekeeper, menacing Abbott and Costello on a haunted estate, in **The Time of Their Lives.** Then there was **The Spider Woman Strikes Back,** a pitiful waste of her talents that had nothing to do with Sherlock Holmes.

She was heiress Dorothy Lamour's sinister aunt in **The Road to Rio** (47), with Bing Crosby and Bob Hope trying to wrest the young lady from her control, and was in another Maria Montez cheapie, **Pirates of Monterey.** She was good as Barbara Stanwyck's mother in the soap opera **East Side, West Side** (49). And then the curtain came crashing down abruptly on the screen career of Gale Sondergaard.

Her husband, director Herbert Biberman, was one of the "Hollywood Ten," the group of directors and screenwriters accused in the 1950 investigations by the witch-hunting House Committee on Un-American Activities in Washington. Neither he nor she would testify about their affiliations, but took the protection of the Fifth Amendment instead. (She was called for further interrogation in 1956, and was still an articulate defender of her political rights.) Biberman, along with others, was sent to prison for a short term, and Miss Sondergaard's filming (she was now 51 years old) was stopped dead in its tracks by a blacklist that would last two decades.

It wasn't until 1965, after a long hiatus, that she was back at any kind of acting. She worked on television, and did a one-woman Off-Broadway show, **Woman,** which she scripted herself. During 1967-68 she was a member of the Minnesota Theatre Company of Minneapolis' Tyrone Guthrie Theatre, a repertory group; she played the Lynn Fontanne role in **The Guardsman** and had other parts. In 1968 her alma mater, the University of Minnesota, gave her an award for outstanding achievement. In the following year she was on stage in Arthur Miller's **The Crucible** (interestingly, about witch hunts), starring Charlton Heston.

That same year, 1969, she finally returned to the screen, at age 70, in **Slaves,** written and directed by her husband, but her role was a minor one. In 1970 she was in a cheapie called **The Comeback** (later retitled **Savage Intruder);** she also starred for six months in the TV series "The Best of Everything." On stage again, she did **A Family and a Fortune** with Sylvia Sidney in Seattle, and was in the TV series "Medical Center." In 1973 she was in a made-for-TV movie, **The Cat Creature,** a horror tale featuring her as a cat goddess. Meanwhile, her husband had died in 1971. At the time of his death he had completed a film script about their blacklist experience, "Over the Carnage," that his wife had been showing to Hollywood producers; apparently it was never filmed. She was to say that her philosophy of life, which had helped her survive such upheavals, was: "Follow the bends in the river."

The actress had a key role as an American Indian in **The Return of a Man Called Horse** (76), also appearing in **Pleasantville,** and was in **Hollywood on Trial** (77), which was probably a documentary about the witch hunts. Her last film, made when she was 81, was **Echoes** (80) (another source says 1983), in a minor role as a clairvoyant. She now retired to the Motion Picture Country House and Hospital near the film capital, where she died in 1985, aged 86. Near the end, friends said, she had come to terms with her life without bitterness, but there was a sense of loss about performances that might have been.

When she died, it had been nearly half a century since Gale Sondergaard's heyday as the screen's supreme female villain, a time when she was enjoyably nasty to Bette Davis, caused plenty of problems for Sherlock Holmes, and scared the daylights out of Bob Hope. She was definitely an actress you loved to hate.

THE FILMS OF GALE SONDERGAARD

1936: Anthony Adverse.
1937: The Life of Emile Zola; Maid of Salem; Seventh Heaven.
1938: Dramatic School; Lord Jeff.
1939: Juarez; The Cat and the Canary; Never Say Die.
1940: The Letter; The Mark of Zorro; The Blue Bird; The Llano Kid.
1941: The Black Cat.
1942: My Favorite Blonde; A Night to Remember; Enemy Agents Meet Ellery Queen; Paris Calling.
1943: Isle of Forgotten Sins; Appointment in Berlin; The Strange Death of Adolf Hitler.
1944: Christmas Holiday; The Invisible Man's Revenge; The Spider Woman (Sherlock Holmes and the Spider Woman); Enter Arsene Lupin; The Climax; Gypsy Wildcat; Follow the Boys.
1946: Anna and the King of Siam; A Night in Paradise; The Time of Their Lives; The Spider Woman Strikes Back.
1947: The Road to Rio; Pirates of Monterey.
1949: East Side, West Side.
1969: Slaves.
1970: The Comeback (later titled Savage Intruder).
1976: The Return of a Man Called Horse; Pleasantville.
1977: Hollywood on Trial (probably a documentary).
1980: Echoes.

Here come de judge:
LEWIS STONE

Most filmgoers still living are likely to remember Lewis Stone only as the wise paterfamilias Judge Hardy, father of Mickey Rooney in the Hardy Family films of the late Thirties and early Forties.

But the actor's very substantial film career (144 feature-length movies), going back to before World War I, encompassed far more than that. He was originally a popular leading man of the silents, playing dignified, gentlemanly romantic heroes, with occasional forays into silky villainy. In the sound era, he gradually and gracefully eased into solid character portrayals, ultimately ending up by playing genial senior citizens.

Tall, lean, handsome and straight-backed, he was a sturdy, versatile and dependable performer. More at home in a drawing room than in a uniform (although he was an expert horseman, fencer and boxer), he had an innate dignity that didn't suggest a man of action. A master of the subtle glance or gesture, he half-concealed, in his earlier years, a slightly sinister personality that later took on an attitude of concern. (When Andy Hardy came along, there was much reason for concern.)

Stone was born November 15, 1879 (one source says 1878), in Worcester, Massachusetts. At age 18 he was a soldier in the Spanish-American War. He was only 20 when his hair turned prematurely gray, and he was already taking on the distinguished look that he put to good use in his later career. An early interest in writing changed to an interest in acting, and around the turn of the century he began a stage career. By 1904 he was, at 24, a highly regarded leading man in San Francisco. D.W. Griffith (at that point still a stage actor) used to drop in and watch him perform. Before long Stone had become a matinee idol.

Sometime during the period 1911-14 he appeared in his first movies, "Indian Westerns" for the Bison studio (part of the Ince organization), starring Princess Red Wing, an authentic Indian who in 1914 would be the co-star of Cecil B. DeMille's first film, **The Squaw Man.** These Bison films were shorts of one or two reels. In 1915 he made his first feature-length movie, **Honor's Altar,** co-starring with Bessie Barriscale, and also two other films. Then he saw service in World War I as a major in the cavalry. He returned to films in 1918, but in the meantime he had appeared in several Broadway plays, co-starring with Laurette Taylor in **The Bird of Paradise** in 1912 and

with Marjorie Rambeau in **Where Poppies Bloom** in 1918. In Hollywood, he made one film each in 1918 and 1919, and then four in 1920, the beginning of a busy schedule that would continue for a third of a century.

He soon developed into a popular leading man on the screen. In films of the Twenties he was one of the era's foremost proponents of the gallant, loyal, sportsmanlike hero. Often this gallantry did him little good when it came to romantic involvements, and he frequently stood aside, concealing his feelings, while the heroine left him for a younger man.

Stone had a dual role as a Canadian Mountie and the criminal he is hunting in **The River's End** (20), a film later remade with Charles Bickford. In **The Concert** (21) he was a married man who strays temporarily, and in **The Child Thou Gavest Me** he had a powerful dramatic role as a man who wants to kill the unidentified soldier who attacked, and fathered a child by, the man's fiancée several years earlier; he soon realizes that he himself was that man. He was once again a Mountie in **The Golden Snare,** on the trail of murderer Wallace Beery, and in **Beau Revel** he starred as a man who falls in love with his son's fiancée (Florence Vidor) and later kills himself. He loved another man's wife in **Don't Neglect Your Wife,** and, leaving his career, became an alcoholic recluse, but the woman left her husband and reclaimed Stone. In most of these films he was billed as "Lewis S. Stone."

Now in his early forties, he starred in **The Prisoner of Zenda** (22) (the part Ronald Colman would play in the remake) as Rudolf Rassendyll, winning the heroine (Alice Terry) and dueling with Rupert of Hentzau (Ramon Novarro, at that point still appearing under his real name, Ramon Samaniegos). In **Trifling Women** he killed Novarro in a duel, and in **The Rosary** he was a priest, narrowly escaping being killed by the villain (Beery again). He was a married man who fell prey to a vamp in **A Fool There Was.** He played a villainous marquis in **Scaramouche** (23), hated by Novarro but later revealed as his secret father. (Interestingly, in 1952, as an elderly man, he would appear in the remakes of both **The Prisoner of Zenda** and **Scaramouche,** but in different, smaller roles.) Once again he played a temporary philanderer in **The Dangerous Age,** and the plot was similar in **You Can't Fool Your Wife,** in which he got involved with Nita Naldi while married to Leatrice Joy. As a Broadway producer, he fell in love with Bebe Daniels in **The World's Applause,** and won her despite the attentions paid to her by Adolphe Menjou.

He was still straying from the hearth in **Why Men Leave Home** (24), in which he did just that, and there was more of the same in **Cytherea.** The shoe was on the other foot in **Husbands and Lovers,** in which his wife (Florence Vidor) nearly left him. In **Inez from Hollywood** he won the love of Mary Astor. But he could also lose the heroine, as he did in **The Lost World** (25), as a member of Wallace Beery's expedition, losing Bessie Love to Lloyd Hughes. Meanwhile, he had become one of MGM's original contract players when that studio was formed in 1924. (He worked for MGM longer than any other performer in its history—29 years, up to 1953—a mark that even Lionel Barrymore failed to match; however, most of his 1925-27 films were made for First National.)

In other 1925 films, he was a prominent lawyer who fell for a gold-digger and ended up killing himself in **Cheaper to Marry,** and in **Confessions of a Queen** he was a philandering monarch. His wife (Anna Q. Nilsson) left him but later came back in

The Talker, and again he was rescued from an alcoholic oblivion in **What Fools Men.** He won Barbara La Marr in **The Girl from Montmartre** (26) (it was that doomed actress' last film), and he was wed to Miss Nilsson again in **Midnight Lovers.** He lost the girl, though, in **Don Juan's Three Nights,** as a concert pianist falling for a 16-year-old girl (Shirley Mason).

The actor was Menelaus, king of ancient Troy, in **The Private Life of Helen of Troy** (27), temporarily losing his queen (Maria Corda) to Ricardo Cortez, and in **An Affair of the Follies** he became infatuated with showgirl Billie Dove, but she decided to stay with her husband. He was at this point typecast in romantic triangles, where sometimes he would win the lady and sometimes lose her; if he did win, there were often many vicissitudes to work through before all came out well. But in **Lonesome Ladies** there were no fewer than three of them competing for him; one was his wife (Miss Nilsson again), and he stuck by her. He played a headwaiter in **The Prince of Headwaiters** and a British army officer in **The Notorious Lady.**

A major acting triumph for Stone came in director Ernst Lubitsch's late silent film **The Patriot** (28), in which he portrayed the scheming Count Pahlen, the adviser to a mad Russian czar (Emil Jannings), killing him for the good of the state but then being killed in turn by the crown prince (Neil Hamilton); in this movie Florence Vidor was his mistress. This performance won him, in the second year of the Academy Awards, an Oscar nomination as *best actor,* the only time he would be in such a competition; he lost to Warner Baxter in **In Old Arizona.** He played a French Foreign Legion commandant in **The Foreign Legion** and a corrupt politician exposed by a newspaper in **Freedom of the Press.** In that year he signed another MGM contract, one that would result in his making nearly all of his films in the sound era for that studio (only 12 out of 93 would be for other studios).

Stone married stage actress Margaret Langham in 1909; she later died. He then married actress Florence Oakley in 1920; she made one screen appearance, in a small part in **A Most Immoral Lady** in 1929. They had two daughters, Virginia and Barbara, but were divorced in 1929. In 1930 he married Hazel Wolf (whose name is given by some sources as Hazel Wolf Hood); one source says the daughters were by her, not Miss Oakley.

With his fine, well modulated voice, the actor made an easy change-over to talkies, and the most significant aspect of his work in the period 1929-33 was his seven appearances with Greta Garbo (in two instances she played his wife or mistress); no other performer ever made as many films with Garbo as he did. However, in Garbo's case the transition to sound took a little longer than was the case with most other stars, and both their 1929 teamings were still silent. In that year, he was a plantation owner and she was his young wife in **Wild Orchids;** she returns to him after having an affair with Nils Asther. In this year in which he turned 50, he played a sexless, avuncular old husband to the young Garbo (who turned 24 that year). In **A Woman of Affairs** he was merely one of her friends. While both these movies were silent, his other three films in 1929 were either talkies or part-talkies. In **Wonder of Women** he played an adulterous concert pianist, and in **Madame X** he cast out his philandering wife (Ruth Chatterton), leading to her ultimate downfall. Things got pretty complicated in **The Trial of Mary Dugan;** here he was Norma Shearer's defense attorney at her murder trial, but he withdraws from the case, only to be revealed as the murderer himself.

In **Romance** (30), his first sound film with Garbo, the actor was a wealthy industrialist and she was his mistress, an opera star who wants to leave him for a young clergyman. In **The Office Wife** he played the older man on whom young secretary Dorothy Mackaill sets her sights, and she wins him away from his wife. **Passion Flower** cast him as an invalid married to Kay Francis, who almost steals the husband (Charles Bickford) of her cousin. He was the warden in the archetypal prison drama **The Big House,** and played Miss Shearer's philandering father in **Their Own Desire.** He was a puritanical husband who loses his wife to a younger man in **Strictly Unconventional;** Alison Skipworth played his mother.

Stone was a friend of Garbo's in **Inspiration** (31), and in **The Secret Six** played a dignified but corrupt and alcoholic lawyer who is actually the criminal mastermind helping murderous Wallace Beery to the top of the underworld; eventually Beery kills him. **The Sin of Madelon Claudet** cast him as a wealthy man who takes young Helen Hayes for a mistress; he is then arrested as a jewel thief and commits suicide, and Miss Hayes is tried as his accomplice (although she is not) and goes to prison for 10 years. In **Strictly Dishonorable**—in what was apparently his first role as a judge—he stole the film from Paul Lukas. He played a soap manufacturer in **The Bargain,** a frustrated man who had originally wanted to be an artist and is so disappointed when his son makes the same choice that he retires and tries to paint, too late—but then the son goes off to study art after all (yeah, sure). He was a millionaire involved with young Elissa Landi in **Always Goodbye,** and gave up Bebe Daniels to Ben Lyon in **My Past (Ex-Mistress).** In **The Phantom of Paris** he played the police chief suspecting John Gilbert of murder, and in **Father's Son** he was an overly strict father.

The actor was good as the callous spymaster dealing with his agent, Garbo, in **Mata Hari** (32), and they were both in the classic drama **Grand Hotel,** but in that film he had no scenes with her, instead playing the cynical house physician, Dr. Otternschlag, who keeps asking for messages that never come— and who is the one who says, "People come, people go, but nothing ever happens at the Grand Hotel!" (Oh no, not much.) He had a strong dramatic role in **The Wet Parade,** as a courtly Southern aristocrat and hopeless drunk who, after a two-day binge, kills himself in a pigpen. In **The Mask of Fu Manchu** he was Sir Nayland Smith, battling the Yellow Peril in the form of Boris Karloff, and he was the murdered judge in **Night Court** (Walter Huston was the other judge, a corrupt and villainous one). He played the district attorney prosecuting Joan Crawford for murder in **Letty Lynton,** and was Jean Harlow's father-in-law in **Red Headed Woman.** In **New Morals for Old,** which had a plot that was the reverse of **The Bargain,** he was a wallpaper manufacturer who discourages the artistic ambitions of his son (Robert Young). He played Young's defense attorney at his murder trial in **Unashamed** and was Jackie Cooper's father in **Divorce in the Family.**

Stone had his last part in a Greta Garbo film in **Queen Christina** (33), as her adviser, Oxenstierna, and then played Helen Hayes' father twice: as a stern Italian in **The White Sister,** opposed to her romance with Clark Gable, and as a Chinese in **The Son-Daughter,** in which he and Ramon Novarro are killed by the evil Warner Oland before the latter is finally dispatched by Miss Hayes. He was a police official in **Bureau of Missing Persons,** and was fine as the secretary of state in **Men Must Fight.** He played the owner of an old London department store with a faithless wife and ungrateful children in **Looking Forward (The New Deal);** the store is ultimately saved from ruin by the venerable bookkeeper (Lionel Barrymore).

He was an aging admirer of young Jean Harlow in **The Girl from Missouri** (34), committing suicide because she doesn't reciprocate, and he played Captain Smollett in **Treasure Island.** He was cast as a police inspector in **The Mystery of Mr. X,** and in **You Can't Buy Everything** he was a banker revealed as the man who, many years before, had left May Robson at the altar (the actress in real life was old enough to be Stone's *mother*). He was lost in an avalanche of character actors in the classic **David**

Copperfield (35), as the alcoholic Mr. Wickfield, the father of Madge Evans, who plays Agnes. Then he had one of his best roles in the Clark Gable-Harlow vehicle **China Seas,** as the aging former third officer of a ship, branded a coward, who becomes a hero in death when he grabs an armful of bombs and deliberately falls, an exploding human arsenal, into the pirate vessel. He played an Army general in **West Point of the Air,** and in **Vanessa: Her Love Story** he was once again Helen Hayes' father; this time Miss Robson, the actress old enough to be his mother, *was* his mother. He was a prison warden in **Public Hero No. 1,** a Navy admiral (and Dick Powell's father) in **Shipmates Forever,** and the district attorney in **Woman Wanted.**

The actor played Cary Grant's father in **Suzy** (36), and was one of the **Three Godfathers,** along with Chester Morris and Walter Brennan, in this oft-filmed Western story about three bank robbers fleeing across the trackless desert. He was a small-town high-school principal serving on a parole board in **Don't Turn 'Em Loose,** ending up by killing his murderous criminal son (Bruce Cabot), and he was Robert Taylor's father in **Small Town Girl.** He played a Scotland Yard official in **The Unguarded Hour.** In the interesting film **The Man Who Cried Wolf** (37) he starred as a hammy actor who repeatedly "confesses" to murders he didn't commit, so that when he does kill the man who took away his wife and child his confession won't be believed. However, when his own son is convicted of the murder, he must convince the police he really is guilty this time. He played another Scotland Yard inspector in **The Thirteenth Chair.**

The most significant casting in his later career came in 1938. In the previous year MGM had launched what turned out to be the long-running Hardy Family series, featuring Mickey Rooney as the teen-age son of a small-town judge. In the 1937 film his parents had been Lionel Barrymore and Spring Byington, but in 1938 Stone and Fay Holden were given the roles in **You're Only Young Once.** For the next eight years the veteran actor would portray Judge Hardy again and again, ending up with a total of 14 films (all the remaining ones would have either "Andy Hardy," "Judge Hardy" or "The Hardys" in the title). In noting that he made 14 Hardy films in this period, it should be noted that he did only 10 others at the same time.

The immensely popular Hardy Family series usu-ally had as the plot the rambunctious Rooney getting into some kind of amusing scrape and going to his father, the stern but understanding judge, for advice about it. Individually none of the films is particularly memorable, but taken as a whole they are a key part of screen history for this period. In some respects they date badly. One exchange between the judge and Andy is typical. Andy: "You can say that again!" Judge: "Why should I say it again? Didn't you understand me the first time?"

Of course, Stone continued to do other films throughout this period. Besides four Hardys, in 1938 he was one of the senior Army officers in **Yellow Jack,** and was excellent in **Stolen Heaven,** as a once-great pianist living in a secluded cottage and dreaming of a comeback; jewel thieves Gene Raymond and Olympe Bradna stumble on the place and use it as a hideout, pretending to arrange for Stone's return to the concert stage, but end up making good on the promise—and reforming into the bargain. He was a film-studio head in **Ice Follies of 1939** (39), and did two more Hardys that year, in which he turned 60. He played the president of the United States in the programmer **Joe and Ethel Turp Call on the President** (40), and was a cavalry officer in **The Bugle Sounds** (42), but in 1941, 1943 and 1944 he appeared in nothing but Hardys.

In 1946, the year the Hardy Family series ended (except for a 1958 sequel with Rooney), the actor was one of the **Three Wise Fools** (along with Lionel Barrymore and Edward Arnold) won over by little Margaret O'Brien. He was a senior politician in **State of the Union** (48). During the next several years he had parts of modest size in some major and not-so-major films, but the 1952 remakes of both **The Prisoner of Zenda** and **Scaramouche,** in which he had been the star in the early Twenties, cast the 72-year-old actor in supporting roles. He played his last part in **All the Brothers Were Valiant** (53).

His continuing career was cut short in 1953 when he ran out of his Beverly Hills home to chase some young vandals from his property. In the excitement he suffered a heart attack, and within hours Lewis Stone was dead. Probably he would have liked to be remembered for some of his fine dramatic roles of the Twenties and early Thirties, but that just isn't in the cards. If you recall him, it's almost certainly as the wise and dignified Judge Hardy, patiently doling out advice to a troubled Mickey Rooney.

THE FILMS OF LEWIS STONE

1915: Honor's Altar; The Man Who Found Out; The Havoc.
1918: Man of Bronze.
1919: Man's Desire.
1920: The River's End; Nomads of the North; Milestones; Held by the Enemy.
1921: The Concert; The Child Thou Gavest Me; The Golden Snare; Beau Revel; Don't Neglect Your Wife; Pilgrims of the Night; The Northern Trail (this film not listed in the American Film Institute Catalog).
1922: The Prisoner of Zenda; Trifling Women; The Rosary; A Fool There Was.
1923: Scaramouche; The Dangerous Age; You Can't Fool Your Wife; The World's Applause.
1924: The Stranger; Why Men Leave Home; Cytherea; Husbands and Lovers; Inez from Hollywood.
1925: The Lost World; Cheaper to Marry; Confessions of a Queen; The Talker; The Lady Who Lied; What Fools Men; Fine Clothes.
1926: The Girl from Montmartre; Too Much Money; Old Loves and New; Midnight Lovers; The Blonde Saint; Don Juan's Three Nights.
1927: The Private Life of Helen of Troy; An Affair of the Follies; The Notorious Lady; The Prince of Headwaiters; Lonesome Ladies.
1928: The Patriot; The Foreign Legion; Freedom of the Press.
1929: A Woman of Affairs; Wild Orchids; Madame X; The Trial of Mary Dugan; Wonder of Women.
1930: Romance; The Big House; Their Own Desire; The Office Wife; Passion Flower; Strictly Unconventional.
1931: Inspiration; The Sin of Madelon Claudet; The Secret Six; Always Goodbye; My Past (Ex-Mistress); Father's Son; The Bargain (You and I); Strictly Dishonorable; The Phantom of Paris.
1932: Grand Hotel; Mata Hari; The Wet Parade; Letty Lynton; The Mask of Fu Manchu; Night Court; New Morals for Old; Red Headed Woman; Unashamed; Divorce in the Family.
1933: Queen Christina; The White Sister; The Son-Daughter; Bureau of Missing Persons; Men Must Fight; Looking Forward (The New Deal). *Credit uncertain:* Christopher Bean.
1934: Treasure Island; The Girl from Missouri; The Mystery of Mr. X; You Can't Buy Everything.
1935: David Copperfield; China Seas; West Point of the Air; Vanessa: Her Love Story; Public Hero No. 1; Shipmates Forever; Woman Wanted.
1936: The Three Godfathers; The Unguarded Hour; Small Town Girl; Suzy; Sworn Enemy; Don't Turn 'Em Loose.
1937: Outcast; The Thirteenth Chair; The Man Who Cried Wolf.
1938: You're Only Young Once; Judge Hardy's Children; Love Finds Andy Hardy; Out West with the Hardys; Stolen Heaven; Yellow Jack; The Bad Man of Brimstone; The Chaser.
1939: Andy Hardy Gets Spring Fever; The Hardys Ride High; Ice Follies of 1939.
1940: Judge Hardy and Son; Andy Hardy Meets a Debutante; Sporting Blood; Joe and Ethel Turp Call on the President.
1941: Andy Hardy's Private Secretary; Life Begins for Andy Hardy.
1942: The Courtship of Andy Hardy; The Bugle Sounds.
1943: Andy Hardy's Double Life.
1944: Andy Hardy's Blonde Trouble.
1946: Love Laughs at Andy Hardy; The Hoodlum Saint; Three Wise Fools.
1948: State of the Union.
1949: Any Number Can Play; The Sun Comes Up.
1950: Key to the City; Stars in My Crown.
1951: Grounds for Marriage; Night into Morning; Angels in the Outfield; The Unknown Man.
1952: It's a Big Country; Just This Once; Scaramouche; The Prisoner of Zenda.
1953: All the Brothers Were Valiant.

NOTE: His first film appearances were in "Indian Westerns" made by Bison/Ince during the period 1911-14. These were short films of one or two reels. See text for details.

Sweaty and swarthy:
AKIM TAMIROFF

"He steals so many scenes that he should be arrested for kleptomania." Thus did a New York Times reviewer assess the flamboyant screen presence of Akim Tamiroff, an actor who was extremely active in Hollywood in the Golden Era, playing sinister or eccentric character leads with a heavy Slavic accent and winning two Academy Award nominations as best supporting actor.

"One can still see him in that white trilby [hat]," writes film historian David Quinlan, "mustache glistening with sweat, white handkerchief mopping the brow, cooking up some new double-deal. Nearly all the characters he created were disreputable, whether in filthy sweater or lurking beneath semi-respectable clothes."

Unshaven, swarthy, sweaty, dark and hairy, he was also squat and round, a beetle of a man. He played unsavory and mysterious foreigners and many a petulant and dangerous gangster boss, but beneath the grease and grime, and beneath the prodigious eating and wine-guzzling, there often lurked a fellow whose heart was really in the right place. And he could be equally effective in broad comedy.

Some of his quirky characters are virtuous, but others are shiftless, untrustworthy, unsavory or even ruthless. Many of his immigrants are mobsters or crooked political bosses. But even his worst scoundrels are hard to dislike, because he supplied them with a loud, flustered, humorous delivery and accent; his hurt expression when he isn't trusted, and his teddy-bear body, add to the effect. He convinces us that his authority figures are underdogs who have little chance of staying on top.

Oddly enough, out of a 37-year screen career, he was an important character actor for only a decade. In his first four years in the movies (1932-35) he passed absolutely unnoticed, although he had roles (relatively small ones) in well over a dozen important film classics. And by the end of World War II he had ceased to be given parts of any importance. No matter; in the period 1936-45 he more than made up for that.

Tamiroff was born October 29, 1899 (one source says 1898), in Baku, the Caspian Sea port of the Russian Caucasus. (But one source says it was in Tiflis, an inland city.) Trained for the stage at the drama school of the famed Moscow Art Theatre, he came to the United States in 1923 with a touring troupe from

that organization and decided to stay. He also appeared with Nikita Balieff's Chauve-Souris repertory company, and on Broadway in a number of productions of the Theater Guild. But it wasn't until several years into the sound era that he made his film debut.

At an unspecified date the actor was married to actress Tamara Shayne. She had a fairly active screen career, but always in small parts.

In 1932, at age 32, he came to Hollywood, and is said by some sources to have made his movie debut in **Okay America,** although this credit is uncertain. (In many of his films of the early Thirties he does not even appear in the published cast list.) From 1933 through 1935 he was in a substantial number of major films—including **Queen Christina, The Merry Widow, Now and Forever, Chained, Black Fury, Naughty Marietta, China Seas** and **The Big Broadcast of 1936**—but you can hardly remember him in any of them; he played such small parts as a restaurant manager, a coal miner, or a general in a banana republic. He was a little more prominent, though, in 1934's **Sadie McKee,** as a coarse maitre d' with a hyena-like laugh in a seedy nightclub where Joan Crawford works, and he played an Indian emir in 1935's **The Lives of a Bengal Lancer.**

Strangely, his stature took a sudden quantum leap in 1936, with an important role and an Oscar nomination. That was in **The General Died at Dawn,** starring Gary Cooper, in which Tamiroff was nothing short of brilliant as an evil Chinese warlord (in fact, the title role). He walked off with the film and was nominated as best supporting actor (in this first year in which that award was given), but lost to Walter Brennan, whose performance in **Come and Get It** was certainly not the equal of Tamiroff's. Before the movie was released the actor had small parts in more classics: **The Story of Louis Pasteur** (as one of the skeptical doctors), **Anthony Adverse,** and **Desire** (as a police official).

Unquestionably, **The General Died at Dawn** turned Tamiroff into a major name in Hollywood. For in 1937 he was being *starred* in films, albeit programmers that usually showed up on double bills. **King of Gamblers** cast him as a villainous crime boss, the czar of a big slot-machine racket, in love with a nightclub singer (Claire Trevor) who in turn loves a reporter (Lloyd Nolan) out to expose the gangster. And he was top-billed again in **The Great Gambini,** in a semi-sympathetic role as a mysterious mind-reader who predicts deaths and ends up dead himself. He had a supporting part as an eccentric town boss in **High, Wide and Handsome,** and played what one writer calls "the ogreish Ogaroff, the terrible Tatar torturer," in **The Soldier and the Lady.** He was the head of a gambling ring in **Her Husband Lies.**

There were more starring roles—still in "B" programmers—in 1938. He played a suave rackets king who loves classical music and aspires to the hand of socialite Gail Patrick in **Dangerous to Know;** everything backfires when his Chinese mistress (Anna May Wong) finds out about it. In the unusual ending, he ecstatically pumps out Tchaikovsky on an organ, oblivious to the fact that Miss Wong is committing hara-kiri right behind him. Newspaper ads said, "He wouldn't stop at murder to win the woman he wants! He holds a city in his grasp and defies the law to stop his rackets!"

Equally bizarre that year was another Tamiroff starrer, **Ride a Crooked Mile,** in which he is a former Russian Cossack running a Western cattle-rustling ring and is disappointed when his son won't help him escape from jail. This time the newspaper ads minced no words as to the actor's star status: "They chained a rebel heart that was born to be free! [He is] defying

man and manmade laws. You'll thrill to Tamiroff in his new role as you've never thrilled before! You'll call him great...exciting...unforgettable!" This was the kind of ad copy usually reserved for luminaries at the lofty level of, say, Clark Gable, but the truth was that the stardom of Akim Tamiroff had just two more years to run. Meanwhile, in that same year, he was in support in **Spawn of the North** (as the head of Russian pirates harassing Alaskan fishermen) and also in **The Buccaneer,** in which he stole the film from Fredric March as he played the pirate Dominique You, erstwhile cannoneer to Napoleon. And in the Bing Crosby vehicle **Paris Honeymoon** he gave a deft comic performance as a buffoonish European peasant who runs a village tavern.

The actor—and his agent—probably realized at this point that appropriate star roles to suit his off-beat image would likely be few and far between, and that he would do better to switch to colorful supporting characters. If the money were right, and his name known to audiences, billing should be a secondary consideration. But in 1939 one more year of stardom still remained. He impersonated a murdered South American president in **The Magnificent Fraud,** and the ads trumpeted, "Now cheer him in his greatest role!" Other ads were now calling him by Lon Chaney's old title "Man of a Thousand Faces." But of this film, the trade publication Variety ominously commented, "No marquee names; filler fodder for duals."

Also that year, he starred in **King of Chinatown** as an underworld racketeer trying to become just that but double-crossed by henchman J. Carrol Naish. The ad copywriters were busy again: "This king can do no right! Top boss of a city of shadows with the power of life and death over a million terrified subjects!" But his best role in 1939 was in **Disputed Passage,** which starred Dorothy Lamour but which Tamiroff walked away with as a great neurosurgeon (with a beard), a medical cynic who in the end is forced to admit that science cannot solve everything. He also played a mule-driving boss for the railroad in **Union Pacific** and a window washer(!) in **Honeymoon in Bali.**

The critics at this point had pretty well figured out what the actor was up to on the screen. Reviewing **The Magnificent Fraud,** the New York Times commented: "Magnificently [playing several roles], tearing off and chewing...the scenery...Give him a putty nose and he will strut like Cyrano; [give him] a drooping forelock and he [is] Napoleon. But through all these changes, alas, he continues to talk like Tamiroff...in a formidably mongreloid accent which is neither Provençal nor Corsican nor Latin American, but purely and simply Akim."

Incidentally, moviegoers must have been surprised to learn that the actor had turned 40 that year; for years he had been playing men who were considerably older than himself.

He finally got a chance (his first and last one) to star in what was basically an "A" production in **The Way of All Flesh** (40), the remake of the 1927 film that had (along with **The Last Command**) won Emil Jannings the very first best-actor Oscar. The protagonist is a middle-aged bank cashier, the paragon of bourgeois virtue, who falls under the spell of a dubious blonde and is robbed of a large amount of the bank's cash. Through a mistake in identity the body of one of his captors is identified as his; realizing he can never go back, he spends the rest of his life friendless, alone and broken.

That wasn't really his best part that year, though. In Preston Sturges' brilliant directorial debut film, **The Great McGinty,** he was surprisingly restrained and incisive as the political boss who maneuvers ward heeler Brian Donlevy into the governorship. In an improbable climax, both men find themselves in prison, and they break out, ultimately ending up in a banana republic where Tamiroff owns a bar and Donlevy is the bartender. Also that year, the actor was hammy as a north woods guide in **Untamed,** played a French-Canadian in **North West Mounted Police,** and was in **Texas Rangers Ride Again.** He was a refugee Polish painter in **New York Town** (41), and hammed it up unmercifully in **The Corsican Brothers** as the villain who steals Douglas Fairbanks Jr.'s parents' estate and rules Corsica with an iron hand.

Tamiroff won his second and final Oscar nomination in 1943 with a surly and subtle characterization of the brutish, unpredictable Spanish partisan leader Pablo in the filmization of Ernest Hemingway's novel **For Whom the Bell Tolls,** starring Gary Cooper and Ingrid Bergman. His performance was a masterpiece of dark and devious moods, as fine an expression of animal treachery and human pride as has ever been put on the screen. (When someone tries to stir him to anger, he keeps repeating, "I don' provoke!") But while Katina Paxinou won the best-supporting-actress Oscar for this film, he lost, to Charles Coburn in **The More the Merrier.** That year he was also in support in **Five Graves to Cairo** (as an Egyptian innkeeper) and **His Butler's Sister.**

The actor was blatantly miscast as the Chinese quisling in **Dragon Seed** (44), poisoned (along with a banquet hall full of Japanese officers) by Katharine Hepburn. The New York Times critic minced no words: "[His] speech falls upon the ear as resonantly as the sound of a gefilte fish banged against a temple gong." He was also a Peruvian in **The Bridge of San Luis Rey.** There was a role in **Pardon My Past** (45), and in **A Scandal in Paris** (46) he was the former cellmate and later the assistant to thief George Sanders.

As he matured into the real age of the characters he played on the screen, Tamiroff suddenly became much less interesting as an actor. He almost seemed to work at making his always heavy Russian accent *less intelligible* now. From here on, Hollywood threw little his way, and his appearances declined substantially. He was atrociously bad as a soda-shop proprietor in **The Gangster** (47), and his performance as Lilli Palmer's immigrant father in **My Girl Tisa** (48) was one of the worst in the film. He was a member of the French Foreign Legion in **Outpost in Morocco** (49), and made an important friendship with actor-director Orson Welles when they both appeared in the mediocre **Black Magic;** Welles was the magician Cagliostro and Tamiroff his faithful gypsy friend. In the years to come he would have roles in four of Welles' best and most important films.

He did not appear on screen for four years now, emerging in 1953 as a Legionnaire again in **Desert Legion.** He was in **They Who Dare** (54), and in **Cartouche** played a pseudo-nobleman who attains his title through pure rascality. Now in his mid-fifties, he worked under Welles' direction for the first time in **Mr. Arkadin (Confidential Report)** (55), playing a dying derelict with a lust for one last taste of *paté de foie gras.* He was good as a shady banker in the Ingrid Bergman starrer **Anastasia** (56), but that year also dipped into the horror genre, as the man who supplies mad surgeon Basil Rathbone with victims for his experiments on mutants in **The Black Sleep.** The following year he played Sancho Panza to Welles' **Don Quixote,** a film that unfortunately was never finished.

The actor had a good role in Welles' fine **Touch of Evil** (58), as the terrified Uncle Joe Grandi, whom Welles murders, and he supported Danny Kaye in **Me and the Colonel.** In **Desert Desperadoes (The Sinner)** (59) he was a scheming, avaricious merchant who tries to betray the Judeans to Herod for the reward money; that year, as he turned 60, he also made a return to the stage, playing one of the leads in an adaptation of the film **Rashomon** on Broadway. From this point on he would primarily drift around Europe, playing minor roles, often in Italian films, and frequently forming part of Orson Welles' somewhat eclectic entourage.

In **Ocean's Eleven** (60) he was part of Frank Sinatra's gang that robs five Las Vegas casinos in one night. He was good as the Russian ambassador in **Romanoff and Juliet** (61), and was in a veritable avalanche of Italian epics that year. He had a part in Welles' **The Trial** (62), and was one of the gang of robbers in **Topkapi** (64). His last film for Welles was **Chimes at Midnight (Falstaff)** (65), and he appeared in **Lord Jim** and several others, including two French films. In director Jean-Luc Godard's **Alphaville** (66) he played a bewildered senior citizen, and he was in eight other films that year. He was in **Great Catherine** (67), and had one last key role in an Ameri-can film in **The Great Bank Robbery** (69), as a Mexican gang leader. Then he made his last film, **Sabra**, a French-Italian production, in the lead role as an Arab police inspector who pretends to befriend a young Israeli spy in order to gain his confidence. And at age 70 he retired from the screen.

Akim Tamiroff died in 1972, having largely dissipated his talents for a quarter of a century. But in the late Thirties he stood in the top rank of Hollywood's performers, a character actor who was brilliant, versatile and always a pleasure to watch.

THE FILMS OF AKIM TAMIROFF

1932: *Credit uncertain:* Okay America.
1933: Queen Christina; The Devil's in Love; Fugitive Lovers; The Barbarian. *Credit uncertain:* Gabriel over the White House; Storm at Daybreak.
1934: The Merry Widow (and French version); Now and Forever; Sadie McKee; Chained; Lady by Choice; The Great Flirtation; Here Is My Heart; The Winning Ticket; Whom the Gods Destroy; The Captain Hates the Sea; Murder in the Private Car; Wonder Bar. *Credit uncertain:* The Scarlet Empress.
1935: The Lives of a Bengal Lancer; Black Fury; Naughty Marietta; China Seas; The Big Broadcast of 1936; Rumba; Paris in Spring; The Winning Ticket; The Gay Deception; Go into Your Dance; Two Fisted; The Last Outpost; Black Sheep; Ladies Love Danger. *Credit uncertain:* Reckless; Chasing Yesterday.
1936: The General Died at Dawn; The Story of Louis Pasteur; Anthony Adverse; Desire; The Jungle Princess; Woman Trap.
1937: King of Gamblers; The Great Gambini; High, Wide and Handsome; The Soldier and the Lady; Her Husband Lies; This Way Please.
1938: Dangerous to Know; Ride a Crooked Mile; Spawn of the North; The Buccaneer; Paris Honeymoon.
1939: The Magnificent Fraud; King of Chinatown; Disputed Passage; Union Pacific; Honeymoon in Bali. *Credit uncertain:* Geronimo.
1940: The Great McGinty; The Way of All Flesh; North West Mounted Police; Texas Rangers Ride Again; Untamed.
1941: The Corsican Brothers; New York Town.
1942: Tortilla Flat; Are Husbands Necessary?
1943: For Whom the Bell Tolls; Five Graves to Cairo; His Butler's Sister.
1944: Dragon Seed; The Bridge of San Luis Rey; Can't Help Singing; The Miracle of Morgan's Creek (brief "surprise" cameo reprising his character from The Great McGinty).
1945: Pardon My Past.
1946: A Scandal in Paris.
1947: The Gangster; Fiesta.
1948: My Girl Tisa; Relentless; Tenth Avenue Angel.
1949: Black Magic; Outpost in Morocco.
1953: Desert Legion; You Know What Sailors Are.
1954: They Who Dare; Cartouche.
1955: Mr. Arkadin (Confidential Report); The Black Forest; The Widow (La vedova).
1956: Anastasia; The Black Sleep.
1957: Battle Hell. *Unfinished film:* Don Quixote.
1958: Touch of Evil; Me and the Colonel.
1959: Desert Desperadoes (The Sinner).
1960: Ocean's Eleven; Les bacchantes (Le baccanti).
1961: Romanoff and Juliet; Seduction of the South (I briganti italiani); With Fire and Sword; The Last Judgment (Il giudizio universale); Tartar Invasion (Ursus e la ragazza tartara); La moglie di mio marito.
1962: The Trial; The Reluctant Saint; A Queen for Caesar.
1963: The Black Tulip; Panic Button.
1964: Topkapi; Four Kinds of Love (La bambole); Spirit Elf; The Fabulous Adventures of Marco Polo.
1965: Chimes at Midnight (Falstaff); Lord Jim; The Blue Panther; Crime on a Summer Morning (Par un beau matin d'ete); The Liquidator; Marie-Chantal contre le docteur Kah.
1966: Alphaville; After the Fox; Hotel Paradiso; The Happening; Lt. Robin Crusoe USN; Adultery Italian Style; The Vulture; Every Man's Woman (A Rose for Everyone); I nostri mariti.
1967: Great Catherine.
1968: Justine and Juliet (Marquis de Sade: Justine); The Girl Who Couldn't Say No (Tenderly).
1969: The Great Bank Robbery; Sabra.

Hello, sweetheart, get me rewrite:
LEE TRACY

Few major screen actors have ever been so stereotyped as to *occupation or line of work* as was Lee Tracy. Most of the roles he played in his prime were newspaper reporters—wisecracking, fast-talking, irrepressible, hard-drinking journalists.

With an inimitable nasal delivery of dialogue that was as fast as a machine gun, he played a newsman far too many times, quickly becoming stereotyped in the part. Neither sexy nor handsome, but ingratiating, the stocky, bouncy, light-haired actor in private life shared one characteristic often attributed to reporters—his thirst for alcohol was legendary. He lived at a pace that defied a publicist's dream, and seemed to approach life with a perpetual thumb to his nose—which led to an incident that virtually destroyed his career when he was only in his mid-thirties. Known as the "bad boy of Hollywood," he had an unconcealed contempt for many of the film capital's pretensions of genius.

The bizarre episode that more or less ended his career as a film actor after two brief years of considerable popularity occurred simultaneously with the situation of his appeal having dated and fading, so that after the 1930s he was seldom seen on the screen. (All told, he made only 36 movies.) But, amazingly, after being away from Hollywood and on the stage for 17 years he came back to the screen at age 66 to win an Academy Award nomination as best supporting actor—for his very last movie role.

William Lee Tracy was born April 14, 1898, in Atlanta, Georgia, the son of a railroad official. He attended a military academy and then Union College in Schenectady, New York. He is said to have worked briefly for a railroad, served in World War I, made a 1921 stage debut in stock (some sources say 1919), and served as a U.S. Treasury agent for two years before entering vaudeville with a partner, Harry Horton, working the Loew's circuit in a sketch called "The Old Homestead." Then he bought the playlet **Bonded Stock** and toured in it briefly. He toured for stock companies in St. Louis, Dallas and Baltimore, and then in **Whispering Wires.** In 1924 he made his Broadway debut, starring in **The Show Off.**

Tracy was kept busy on the New York stage, appearing in **The Book of Charm, The Wisdom Tooth** and **Glory, Hallelujah.** He attained stardom in 1926 as a hoofer in the play **Broadway,** and won the New York critics' award for best performance; the play

ran for 603 performances. He next did a vaudeville sketch at the Palace, and then, in 1928, took the role that would lead to his screen stereotyping: reporter Hildy Johnson in **The Front Page,** which was later filmed three times—but never with him. (Hildy ended up being portrayed at various times by Pat O'Brien, Jack Lemmon, and—in a sex change—Rosalind Russell.) Tracy made his first film, **Big Time,** in 1929, co-starring with Mae Clarke in the story of a husband-and-wife vaudeville team who break up; his act goes from bad to worse, while she becomes a movie star; he gets a job as an extra in one of her films, and they are reunited. He did a few more plays, and then went back to Hollywood.

In **Liliom** (30), which later became the stage musical and film **Carousel,** he was "the Buzzard," a petty criminal who tempts Charles Farrell into a bungled robbery and then to suicide. In **Born Reckless,** a gangster film, he played a reporter for the first time, and in **She Got What She Wanted** he was an old flame of the married Betty Compson, trying vainly to get her back. After that he returned to Broadway for two years.

When the actor went back to Hollywood, he was a star. In **The Strange Love of Molly Louvain** (32) he gave an unsparing portrait of a disenchanted yellow journalist, a tabloid reporter, romancing femme fatale Ann Dvorak and then walking out on her. He was an alcoholic news-hound in **Love Is a Racket,** and gave one of his best performances in the horror film **Doctor X,** as a reporter investigating a series of strange murders (Lionel Atwill was the too-obvious red herring, and Preston Foster was the killer). He starred as a Walter Winchell-like columnist in **Blessed Event,** building the paper's circulation with his unscrupulous scoops and again delivering an expert performance. (Dick Powell made his screen debut here, as an insipid crooner whom Tracy loathes.)

In that same year, in a brief respite from this onslaught of journalists, he starred in **Washington Merry-Go-Round** as an idealistic, crusading young congressman whose battle against corruption leads to his being unseated by a phony recount. And he was again a politician in **Night Mayor,** a dapper playboy mayor (obviously based on New York City's Jimmy Walker) who loves sports, the theater, and especially an actress, even while his administration is being investigated for corruption (as Walker's was at this precise point in time). To avoid scandal he has the actress married off to a writer, and is last seen leading a "Bring Back Beer" parade. And he was good in **The Half Naked Truth** as a preposterous press agent who starts out as a carnival shill, trying to make Lupe Velez an instant celebrity; he becomes a top New York advertising man, but ends up as… a carnival shill again. Thus in 1932, in seven films, he played five reporters or press agents.

Tracy was in support in the classic comedy-drama **Dinner at Eight** (33), giving a good performance as the theatrical agent who verbally attacks over-the-hill actor John Barrymore, leading to the latter's suicide. And he was fine opposite Jean Harlow in **Bombshell,** as the incredibly unscrupulous, fast-talking studio publicity man who continually battles with her but ends up with her in his arms at the fadeout. In **Clear All Wires** he was the fast-talking head of a Chicago newspaper's foreign bureau, posted to Moscow, who constantly out-scoops the New York Times, and he was a soldier in **Private Jones,** rebelling against the military system. This was a biting satire on war in which reluctant draftee Jones cannot understand the motivations that lead a man to kill in battle.

And more films that year: **The Nuisance** cast him as an ambulance-chasing lawyer, an irresistible rogue who works hand in glove with a drunken doctor (Frank Morgan) and a professional "accident victim" (Charles Butterworth). In **Advice to the Lovelorn** he parlayed a newspaper's lonely-hearts column, to which he was assigned as a demotion, into a successful business enterprise. And in **Turn Back the Clock** he played a dissatisfied cigar-store owner who is transported under anesthesia back to his youth, but with a full memory of all that has happened in the interim, so he can make the right decisions, avoid the military draft, amass a fortune, and marry the woman whom in real life he had lost to his rich rival (Otto Kruger)—but he finds himself so unhappy that he is glad to awake to his real existence and real wife (Mae Clarke).

By this point in time the actor had developed quite a reputation as a hard drinker, and as time passed it just got worse. Ultimately it would lead to the incident that would wreck his career.

He played a drunken vaudeville comic in **You Belong to Me** (34), and appeared in **The Lemon Drop Kid** as a "horse medium" who knows what the ponies are going to do at the track before *they* know it; the plot veered toward **Liliom** when, although he has been trying to go straight for the sake of his wife, he turns to robbery to get medical help for her. In **I'll Tell the World** he was back as a reporter again, working for a news syndicate and falling in love with a Ruritanian princess (Gloria Stuart).

And now came the incident that proved to be the self-inflicted fatal turning point in the film career of Lee Tracy. He had accepted the role of guess what— a newspaperman—in the Wallace Beery starrer **Viva Villa,** and journeyed to Mexico for location shooting. He was standing on a balcony, drunk, when, as part of a parade, a group of military-academy cadets passed by; the actor made insulting remarks and then reportedly urinated on the marching cadets. After loud protests by the Mexican government, he was taken off the film, replaced in the part by Stuart Erwin, and fired by MGM.

His movie career never really recovered after this episode. He had fewer and poorer parts, and when he starred it was strictly in programmer fare to fill double bills. From here on he would freelance, primarily with RKO. In **Carnival** (35) he played a widowed puppeteer who takes custody of his child, sought by the maternal grandfather, and seeks anonymity in a circus; he also romances Sally Eilers. In **Two Fisted** he was a prizefighter; he and his manager (Roscoe Karns) join a socialite's household as bodyguards. He was Edward Arnold's friend in **Sutter's Gold** (36), and appeared in **Wanted: Jane Turner** as a postal inspector rounding up a gang that robbed a mail truck and killed the driver.

It was back to journalism in **Behind the Headlines** (37), as the indefatigable reporter for a radio station, and in **Criminal Lawyer** he was back to his old form as the attorney for racketeer Eduardo Ciannelli, having a change of heart and going straight when elected district attorney.

Tracy often appeared in weak vehicles that were unworthy of his talents. The New York Times at one point commented: "[He] continues to be an excellent performer even if his pictures have a habit of getting in his way." One of the ones that did was **Crashing Hollywood** (38), in which he played an aspiring screenwriter getting tangled up with crooks. He was still another mouthpiece lawyer in **The Spellbinder** (39), posing as a pillar of respectability but sowing the seeds of his own comeuppance by defending men he knows are guilty; he ends up standing trial for murder. His high-energy performance was the only good thing in this weak programmer. **Fixer Dugan** cast him as the troubleshooter for a circus. He played a convict in **Millionaires in Prison** (40). And then his screen work came to a dead stop for three years.

In 1938 the actor married Helen Thoms Wyse. Sources give no further details.

Now in his early forties, he worked on the stage again, and was back on the screen in 1943 in **Power of the Press** as a managing editor tangling with unscrupulous publisher Otto Kruger, who doesn't hesitate to commit murder to achieve his ends. In **Betrayal from the East** (45) he was a ne'er-do-well carnival showman employed by Japanese agents to get hold of plans for the defense of the Panama Canal, but of course he is really working for U.S. Army intelligence. In **I'll Tell the World** he remade his own 1933 film **Advice to the Lovelorn,** starring as a small-town sports announcer who saves Raymond Walburn's failing radio station by starting a popular lonely-hearts program. (Oddly, the film had no connection with his 1934 film also titled **I'll Tell The World.**) And he starred in one last programmer, **High Tide** (47), about a newspaper's attempts to prevent racketeers from taking over a city. (The New York Times said, "Mr. Tracy hasn't forgotten how to make a role sparkle.")

The actor at this point presumably thought he would never go back to filming—although he did nearly a generation later. He now worked exclusively on the stage and in television for 17 years. He co-starred on Broadway in **The Traitor** in 1949 and—after a quarter of a century—repeated his Broadway role in **The Show Off** in 1950. He starred in the TV series "Martin Kane—Private Eye" and was in many other TV programs. In the early 1960s he was a standout on Broadway in Gore Vidal's play **The Best Man,** playing the dying ex-president of the United States while his potential heirs jockey for power at a political convention. When the drama was brought to the screen in 1964 it was one of the year's most important films, starring Henry Fonda and Cliff Robertson as rival candidates, and with Tracy repeating his stage role and giving an extraordinary performance, the greatest of his career—in his last role. The movie received only one Academy Award nomination: Lee Tracy as best supporting actor. (But he lost to Peter Ustinov in **Topkapi.**)

Tracy died in 1968 at age 70. His character stardom had been an all-too-brief meteor flashing across the sky in 1932 and 1933, a time early in Hollywood's Golden Era, when if a producer wanted to cast a brash, fast-talking newspaper reporter, there was no question about who was the first choice for the role: Lee Tracy.

THE FILMS OF LEE TRACY

1929: Big Time.
1930: Liliom; Born Reckless; She Got What She Wanted.
1932: The Strange Love of Molly Louvain; Love Is a Racket; Doctor X; Blessed Event; Washington Merry-Go-Round; The Night Mayor; The Half Naked Truth.
1933: Bombshell; Dinner at Eight; Clear All Wires; Private Jones; The Nuisance; Turn Back the Clock; Advice to the Lovelorn.
1934: You Belong to Me; The Lemon Drop Kid; I'll Tell the World.
1935: Carnival; Two Fisted.
1936: Sutter's Gold; Wanted: Jane Turner.
1937: Criminal Lawyer; Behind the Headlines.

1938: Crashing Hollywood.
1939: Fixer Dugan; The Spellbinder.
1940: Millionaires in Prison.
1943: Power of the Press.
1945: Betrayal from the East; I'll Tell the World.
1947: High Tide.
1964: The Best Man.

NOTE: Except for having the same title, his 1934 and 1945 films titled **I'll Tell the World** are unrelated and do not have the same plots.

Bewitching bitchery:
HELEN VINSON

Three young actresses cornered the market on the role known as "The Other Woman" in Hollywood's Golden Era—Helen Vinson, Claire Dodd and Gail Patrick. And some film buffs insist that Miss Vinson was the best of these.

Cool, aristocratic, sophisticated and aloof, she usually either played a designing ex-wife or catty fiancée determined to wrest the hero away from the heroine or else was a faithless philanderer or husband-stealer. And occasionally she was a rather uninteresting kittenish good girl—but far more often engaged in bewitching bitchery.

She was stylishly prim, with fluffy, severely arranged dark blonde hair, long penciled eyebrows, and a small upturned mouth with mean lips. One writer has noted some catlike characteristics: "Behind that pussycat smile were claws. At her best, she was decidedly feline—but a very upper-class cat indeed." Meow!

Miss Vinson was born (as Helen Rulfs) September 17, 1907, in Beaumont, Texas, the daughter of an oil-company executive. After two years at the University of Texas she went on stage in 1927 in a Houston stock-company production of **The Charm School,** and in that same year made her Broadway bow in a play called **Los Angeles.** After five years on the stage she left for Hollywood.

She played a shallow socialite who toys with and then drops attorney William Powell in **Lawyer Man** (32); Claire Dodd had a bigger role and harassed Powell even more notably. There was a key part in the classic drama I Am a **Fugitive from a Chain Gang,** one of her few good-girl parts, as the society girl who falls in love with Paul Muni. In the sensational ending, she calls out to him, "But what do you do? How do you live?" From the darkness he replies, "I steal." That year she also played Ralph Bellamy's faithless **Second-Hand Wife.**

Possibly the actress' nastiest bad-girl role came in **The Power and the Glory** (33). She begins by breaking up railroad tycoon Spencer Tracy's marriage to Colleen Moore, causing Miss Moore to kill herself. Miss Vinson and Tracy are married, but she proceeds to betray him with his own son, whereupon Tracy too commits suicide. It would be hard for Miss Vinson to be more evil than this on the screen in the years to come—but it wouldn't be for lack of trying. She now turned her attention to the hapless Warner

Baxter, playing his bitchy wife (for the first of three times) in **As Husbands Go,** having an affair with Warner Oland but finally returning to the fold.

Also that year, she tangled with Edward G. Robinson in **The Little Giant,** as a con woman posing as a society girl, getting engaged to him, and trying to sell him phony stocks—but he gets wise and walks out. She played one of the suspects in **The Kennel Murder Case** (she didn't do it), and in **Midnight Club** she was one of a gang of jewel thieves, trying to fend off detective George Raft by romancing him (it didn't work). She was a chilly socialite unhappily married to Baxter (again) in **Broadway Bill** (34), but he throws her over for her sister, Myrna Loy. And she was the cold, selfish wife of John Boles in **The Life of Vergie Winters;** he really loves Ann Harding (as Vergie), by whom he has a child, and before long Miss Vinson kills Boles, but Miss Harding takes the blame and serves time for the murder; later Miss Vinson makes a deathbed confession. She was a crook in John Gilbert's last film, **The Captain Hates the Sea,** and played a nurse in **Gift of Gab.**

She had another "nasty" role in **Private Worlds** (35), as an acquitted murderess, the unstable, philandering, predatory sister of the new head doctor (Charles Boyer) of a mental hospital; her brazen pursuit of young doctor Joel McCrea soon drives his wife (Joan Bennett) insane. Miss Vinson was married to high-minded Paul Lukas in **Age of Indiscretion;** she sleeps around and later deserts him. The New York Times commented: "It is unfortunate that the part of the evil wife is performed by the most charming player in the film...Miss Vinson's clear and cool-eyed intelligence, even when it is enlisted on the side of the Devil, has an unhappy way of winning our sympathy."

But neither of those performances was her best one that year. Cast against type in a "good" role, she was sympathetic as Gary Cooper's wife in **The Wedding Night.** It seems that novelist Cooper, wed to the somewhat possessive Miss Vinson, becomes interested in Anna Sten, the daughter of Sig Rumann, who prefers to see her married off to Ralph Bellamy. At the climax, Miss Sten is killed in a fall, and Cooper is reconciled with his wife. Miss Vinson played the part with intelligence and contributed strongly to the film's power.

In **A Notorious Gentleman,** Charles Bickford plans to murder Sidney Blackmer and incriminate the man's fiancée, Miss Vinson, but it doesn't work. The British film **King of the Damned** involved her with Conrad Veidt in a mutiny at a South Seas convict settlement. She had fled to England briefly that year, tired of the "bad girl" typecasting and unsuccessfully seeking a wider range.

The actress' first husband was Harry N. Vickerman, a manufacturer, whom she married in 1925 at age 18 and divorced in 1934. In 1935 there was a brief marriage to English tennis star Fred Perry, also ending in divorce. In 1946 she wed stockbroker Donald Hardenbrook, a union that would endure for many years until his death in 1976. She had no children.

Warner Baxter, who had already been unhappily married to her twice before on screen, tried it one last time in **Vogues of 1938** (37). She was the selfish wife whose avant-garde theatrical ventures are driving him to ruin; after a while he gets rid of her and falls in love with Joan Bennett. Miss Vinson was back to attempted husband-stealing in **Live, Love and Learn,** but can't pinch nonconformist artist Robert Montgomery from wife Rosalind Russell. She played a friend of Carole Lombard's in **In Name Only** (39); in the past you might have expected her to have the "bad girl" part of Cary Grant's nasty wife who refuses to give him a divorce, but that role went to an over-the-hill Kay Francis.

There were really almost no good parts left. She did manage to be delightfully nasty as Jerome Cowan's bored, faithless wife in the James Cagney starrer **Torrid Zone** (40), and she played a temperamental stage star in **Curtain Call,** with two Broadway producers buying an absolutely awful play for her as a form of revenge—but she *likes* it. She was also in a few cheesy programmers. In 1941 she supported Bob Hope in **Nothing But the Truth.**

There was a three-year hiatus from films, and she returned in 1944. Billed seventh, she was in **The Thin Man Goes Home** (44), and then she must have felt that she had hit rock bottom in the horror film **The Lady and the Monster,** starring Erich von Stroheim, because "the lady" was played not by her but by the notoriously mediocre actress Vera Hruba Ralston. She was Ann Blyth's mother in **Chip Off the Old Block,** and starred as a neglectful mother in a bad programmer, **Are These Our Parents?** At this point she was ready to quit the movies in disgust, but she came back two years later for a last role in a forgotten cheapie called **The Lady and the Doctor.** That was the end of her screen career, at age 38.

With third husband Donald Hardenbrook, and later after his death, Miss Vinson was for years a figure on the New York social scene; later she moved to Chapel Hill, North Carolina. Still living as this is written, and in her late eighties, she is one of the few remaining survivors (among prominent performers) of Hollywood's Golden Era. And during that era, when it came to cheating on a husband or stealing somebody else's, no one could do it on the screen with more sophisticated, calculating bitchery than Helen Vinson.

THE FILMS OF HELEN VINSON

1932: Lawyer Man; Jewel Robbery; I Am a Fugitive from a Chain Gang; They Call It Sin; The Crash; Two Against the World; Second Hand Wife.
1933: The Power and the Glory; The Little Giant; Grand Slam; The Kennel Murder Case; As Husbands Go; Midnight Club.

1934: Broadway Bill; The Life of Vergie Winters; The Captain Hates the Sea; Gift of Gab; Let's Try Again. *Credit uncertain:* Their Big Moment.
1935: The Wedding Night; Private Worlds; Age of Indiscretion; A Notorious Gentleman; King of the Damned; Transatlantic

Tunnel (The Tunnel).
1936: Love in Exile; Reunion.
1937: Walter Wanger's Vogues of 1938; Live, Love and Learn.
1939: In Name Only.
1940: Torrid Zone; Beyond Tomorrow; Married and in Love; Curtain

Call; Enemy Agent; Bowery Boy.
1941: Nothing But the Truth.
1944: The Thin Man Goes Home; The Lady and the Monster; Chip Off the Old Block; Are These Our Parents?; They Are Guilty.
1946: The Lady and the Doctor.

The pompous blusterer:
RAYMOND WALBURN

Have you ever seen "Esky," the pop-eyed little man who for many years graced the cover of Esquire magazine? That was Raymond Walburn to the life. He was ideally cast as a blustering, pompous, lovable rogue.

Ever the cheeky braggart, he played bumbling idiots, crafty con men, Kentucky colonels and phony military types. Rotund, round-eyed and round-faced, with an often haughty manner, he was an amiable rascal, constantly surprised when someone pricked his pomposity or bogusness. He also played a couple of choice villains.

With these skills, he had a busy screen career in the Thirties and Forties, but altogether his acting career on both stage and screen encompassed at least half a century.

Walburn was born September 9, 1887, in Plymouth, Indiana, and is said to have left home at age 16 to join a stock company, although one source says he didn't start acting until he was 25. He reportedly made his debut in Oakland, California, and worked steadily in stock and theaters all over the country, with his first Broadway appearance coming in **Mary Jane's Pa.** He also saw World War I service, just after making an early film appearance in a serial, **The Scarlet Runner,** in 1916. But he had been on the stage for many years before he briefly went to Hollywood in 1929 to play Ruth Chatterton's philandering husband in **The Laughing Lady** (29). He returned to the stage, and came back to the film capital permanently five years later, at age 46.

The actor was the phony racetrack habitué Colonel Pettigrew in **Broadway Bill** (34), a role he would repeat years later in 1950's **Riding High,** the remake by the same director, Frank Capra. In a swift change of pace, he played the treacherous villain Danglars in **The Count of Monte Cristo,** one of those involved in sending Robert Donat to prison; he escapes and inveigles Walburn into financial speculations, leading him to bankruptcy and gibbering insanity. In **Lady by Choice** he was the press agent for fan dancer Carole Lombard, coming up with the brilliant idea of having her "adopt" elderly derelict May Robson as her mother.

He was villainous again in **Mills of the Gods** (35), as the reactionary son of Miss Robson (she was a factory owner), calling the police so the family can flee the shut-down plant without facing the protest-

ing workers. He was a confused, blustering, alcoholic politician in **Thanks a Million,** a doctor in **Society Doctor,** and Melvyn Douglas' tipsy butler in **She Married Her Boss,** in which at one point the two get riotously drunk together. He was a small-town sheriff in **It's a Small World,** and played the theatrical "angel" who backs a musical film after falling for its co-star in **Redheads on Parade.**

Walburn was good as the unctuous butler assigned to newly made millionaire Gary Cooper in **Mr. Deeds Goes to Town** (36), played a doctor turned con man in **Three Wise Guys,** and was a society reporter who plays detective in **They Met in a Taxi.** Once again he was Douglas' servant, this time his valet, in **The Lone Wolf Returns,** and he played a submarine commander in **Born to Dance.** He was one of a planeload of strangers involved in a murder plot after being forced down on a ranch in **Absolute Quiet.** He played Irene Dunne's father, the hawker of "Wizard Oil," in **High, Wide and Handsome** (37), and he was a horse-farm owner, once again involved with racetrack betting, in **Breezing Home.** He was a soothsayer with a crystal ball in **It Can't Last Forever.**

At an unidentified date the actor was married to Gertrude Steinman, and later was widowed. Some sources say her death didn't come until the early 1960s, while others report that it happened earlier; in any event, he was married a second time, to Jane Davis, with one source saying that occurred in 1955.

As a steel magnate, he proved more attractive to Gypsy Rose Lee than did either of the stars, Victor McLaglen and Brian Donlevy, in **The Battle of Broadway** (38), and in **Gateway** he was a lecherous masher attempting to molest a young Irish immigrant on an ocean liner. He was a kindly judge helping Harold Lloyd in **Professor Beware,** and a college dean in **Start Cheering.** He played a venal newspaper editor in **Let Freedom Ring** (39), and a twittery tycoon married to ZaSu Pitts in **Eternally Yours,** also portraying the head of an advertising agency in **It Could Happen to You** and "The Professor," the head of a hobo camp, in **Heaven with a Barbed Wire Fence,** renewing an old love with Marjorie Rambeau.

In **Christmas in July** (40) he was Dick Powell's boss, the head of a coffee company, and he played Myrna Loy's father in **Third Finger, Left Hand,** as well as Frances Farmer's dad, an oil-well speculator, in **Flowing Gold.** He and Lee Tracy were a couple of the convicts in **Millionaires in Prison.** He was the ghost of a murdered bookmaker in **The Man in the Trunk** (42). One of his best parts came in the fine comedy **Hail the Conquering Hero** (44), as the corrupt, fraudulent small-town mayor put to rout by

a homecoming Marine, Eddie Bracken; he gave a splendid portrayal of a fatuous political windbag. In **And the Angels Sing** he was the father of Dorothy Lamour and Betty Hutton.

Walburn was one of the wealthy, snobbish family humanized by down-and-out actor Joseph Schildkraut in **The Cheaters** (45), and in **I'll Tell the World** his failing radio station was revitalized when Lee Tracy introduced a lonely-hearts program. He was Harold Lloyd's boss in that star's last film, **The Sin of Harold Diddlebock (Mad Wednesday)** (46), and played Billie Burke's philandering husband in **Breakfast in Hollywood.** Now past 60, he had a small part in **State of the Union** (48), and was once again the phony racetrack tout from 1934's **Broadway Bill** in the remake, **Riding High** (50). He now proceeded to star for Monogram, a Poverty Row studio, in a series of comedies about a man named Henry, involving five films from 1949 through 1951. Meanwhile, he was in small supporting roles in several major productions.

The actor had his last screen role in the fourth remake of the oft-filmed **The Spoilers** (55). After a while, in the 1960s, he returned to the stage (he was now in his seventies), and appeared in **A Funny Thing Happened on the Way to the Forum** in 1962, and with Ruth Gordon in **A Very Rich Woman** in 1965. That was his last acting, after an extremely long career.

Raymond Walburn died in 1969 at age 81. His pompous, blustering rogues, whether crafty or bumbling, were done with inimitable style, and remain among the highlights of the films of Hollywood's Golden Era.

THE FILMS OF RAYMOND WALBURN

1916: The Scarlet Runner (serial).
1929: The Laughing Lady.
1934: The Count of Monte Cristo; Broadway Bill; Lady by Choice; The Great Flirtation; Jealousy; The Defense Rests.
1935: Mills of the Gods; Thanks a Million; It's a Small World; She Married Her Boss; Society Doctor; Death Flies East; I'll Love You Always; Welcome Home; Redheads on Parade.
1936: The Great Ziegfeld; Mr. Deeds Goes to Town; Born to Dance; Craig's Wife; The King Steps Out; The Lone Wolf Returns; They Met in a Taxi; Absolute Quiet; Three Wise Guys; Mister Cinderella.
1937: High, Wide and Handsome; Thin Ice; Broadway Melody of 1938; Breezing Home; Murder in Greenwich Village; Let's Get Married; It Can't Last Forever.
1938: Sweethearts; The Battle of Broadway; Professor Beware; Gateway; Start Cheering.
1939: Eternally Yours; Let Freedom Ring; The Underpup; It Could Happen to You; Heaven with a Barbed Wire Fence.
1940: Christmas in July; Flowing Gold; Third Finger, Left Hand; Dark Command; San Francisco Docks; Millionaires in Prison.

1941: Confirm or Deny; Kiss the Boys Goodbye; Rise and Shine; Louisiana Purchase; Bachelor Daddy; Puddin' Head.
1942: The Man in the Trunk.
1943: Let's Face It; Dixie; Lady Bodyguard; The Desperadoes; Dixie Dugan.
1944: Hail the Conquering Hero; And the Angels Sing; Music in Manhattan; Heavenly Days.
1945: The Cheaters; I'll Tell the World; Honeymoon Ahead.
1946: The Sin of Harold Diddlebock (Mad Wednesday); Rendezvous with Annie; Lover Come Back; The Plainsman and the Lady; Breakfast in Hollywood; The Affairs of Geraldine.
1948: State of the Union.
1949: Riding High; Red, Hot and Blue; Leave It to Henry; Henry the Rainmaker.
1950: Key to the City; Father Makes Good; Short Grass; Father's Wild Game.
1951: Golden Girl; Excuse My Dust; Father Takes the Air.
1953: She Couldn't Say No.
1955: The Spoilers.

Dignified versatility:
H.B. WARNER

If you were a Hollywood casting director, you might say that actor John Jones would be the perfect type to portray Jesus Christ in a film, or that William Smith might be ideally cast as a murderer. But turning up an actor who could handle *both* those roles might be tough. Casting directors in the movies' Golden Era had no such problem. The prolific and versatile H.B. Warner, for example, could and did play Jesus, as well as a couple of murderers—not to mention an ascetic Chinese mandarin, a shellshocked Army deserter, a priest, a druggist, a banker, a gambling-hall croupier, and quite a few judges and Scotland Yard inspectors, among many other roles, in a long film career that encompassed some 140 movies.

Tall, stately and dignified, with chiseled features and a trim mustache, and thin to the point of appearing almost emaciated, he spent more than 40 years playing men whose opinion had to be respected, even when (as was often the case) they were under pressure. Although his roles were usually modest in scope for much of his career, his performances were gems of style. And one of them was good enough to win an Academy Award nomination.

Henry Byron Warner (one source gives his last name as Warner-Lickford) was born October 26, 1876, in London, the son of a prominent stage actor, Charles Warner. He made his debut at age 7 in his father's theater, later studied medicine at London's University College, but finally settled on an acting career. He came to the United States in 1905 with a touring troupe, and appeared in many stage plays. He first began filming in this country in 1913 or 1914, although he had reportedly appeared in a very early English film (obviously a one-reeler, about 10 minutes long), **English Nell,** with the date given as 1900, at the very dawn of the cinema. He co-starred on stage with Laurette Taylor in **Alias Jimmy Valentine** in 1910, and became a matinee idol in **The Ghost Breaker** in 1913, the film version of which he made the following year. In that movie he is an amateur sleuth who goes to a haunted Spanish castle to investigate the disappearance of various heirs to a fortune. He also made two other films that year.

The actor was fairly busy in films during the World War I era, but during the Twenties appeared in them only sporadically while continuing an active stage career. (Among other stage roles, he toured as the star of **Bulldog Drummond.**) He starred at age

44 in **When We Were Twenty-One** (21) as a middle-aged man who marries a much younger woman, and played a detective in **Below the Dead Line,** falling in love with the wife of the murderer he brings to justice. Gloria Swanson loved him in **Zaza** (23), and in **Is Love Everything?** (24) he yielded up wife Alma Rubens to an old flame of hers. He was saved from hanging as a convicted murderer at the last minute in **Silence** (26), and starred in **Whispering Smith,** killing the villain and—does this sound familiar?—falling in love with the bad guy's wife.

Warner came to Hollywood permanently in 1927, and in that year, at age 50, played one of his most famous roles, starring as Jesus in director Cecil B. DeMille's **The King of Kings,** depicting the life of Christ as seen more or less from the viewpoint of Mary Magdalene. The advertising for the film called the actor "the reverent genius of great players," but the New York Times reviewer had mixed feelings. While admitting that he had portrayed Jesus "with admirable dignity and sympathy," he added that "his face is not the general conception of Jesus; his expression is a little severe, and his smile, despite his obvious earnestness and sincerity, is more mundane than spiritual; it is not a smile of sympathy or pity." Interestingly, it has been reported that playing Jesus sparked an old drinking problem of Warner's.

In that same year he starred in **Sorrell and Son** (which he would also remake a few years later), as a soldier who returns from the war to find his wife about to leave with another man; with a young son to bring up, he is forced to take a job as a hotel porter. The son grows up to be a famous surgeon (Nils Asther) who ultimately gives his father an extra dose of morphine to save him from pain in his last illness. In **French Dressing** he nearly lost wife Lois Wilson to Clive Brook.

In **Conquest** (28) he left his friend Monte Blue to die when their plane crashed, and then married Miss Wilson, whom both had courted; but Blue hasn't died, and comes seeking revenge. He was the English nobleman whose wife, Emma Hamilton (Corinne Griffith), falls in love with Lord Nelson in **The Divine Lady** (29), and in **The Trial of Mary Dugan** he was the district attorney prosecuting Norma Shearer for murder. He was married to Ruth Chatterton in **The Doctor's Secret,** and to Miss Wilson once again in **The Gamblers.** He played a murderer in **The Argyle Case,** and in **Tiger Rose** he was a maddened physician obsessed with young Lupe Velez and killed in a fight with her lover.

He played the supernatural guide in **Liliom** (30), the forerunner of the stage and film musical **Carousel,** was one of a group of Britishers held prisoner by Indian maharajah George Arliss in **The Green Goddess,** and portrayed a police inspector who turns out to be the murderer in **The Second Floor Mystery.** In **Wedding Rings** he marries the shallow Olive Borden, but eventually realizes he prefers her sister (Lois Wilson again), and he was Maureen O'Sullivan's father in **The Princess and the Plumber.** He loved Miss Wilson again in **The Furies,** but she is married, so he kills her husband and ends up committing suicide.

In **Five Star Final** (31) he and his wife both kill themselves after her unsavory past is exposed by sensation-peddling newspaper editor Edward G. Robinson, causing the latter to leave journalism in disgust after the tragedy. He played the father of Joan Blondell and Dorothy Mackaill in **The Reckless Hour,** and was a lawyer successfully defending Dolores Costello from a murder charge in **Expensive Women.** He played a Scotland Yard inspector in both **The Menace** (32) and **Charlie Chan's Chance,** a Chinese in **The Son-Daughter,** a shrewd defense lawyer in

Cross-Examination, and the young hero's supposedly dead father, turning up later as a shellshocked war deserter, in **Tom Brown of Culver.** In **The Phantom of Crestwood** his wife (Pauline Frederick) murdered his ex-lover (Karen Morley), and he played a Serbian military man, Basil Rathbone's commanding officer, in **A Woman Commands.** He was a police inspector in **The Menace.**

The actor played Sylvia Sidney's hot-headed father in **Jennie Gerhardt** (33), was an art critic in **Christopher Bean,** and a psychologist who believes in transubstantiation and other mystical doings in **Supernatural.** He repeated his 1927 role in the remake of **Sorrell and Son** (34), and he and Laura Hope Crews were Gene Raymond's snobbish parents in **Behold My Wife,** distressed because he has married an American Indian (Miss Sidney). He was a city's political boss in **Night Alarm.** He had a small part as an old tutor in the classic **A Tale of Two Cities** (35). Then he took the key role of the judge at Gary Cooper's trial in director Frank Capra's **Mr. Deeds Goes to Town** (36), and in **The Garden Murder Case** he was the Hindu fakir who plots the murders. He played a symphony conductor in **Moonlight Murder,** and was Gladys Swarthout's elderly Hispanic father in **Rose of the Rancho.**

Warner's Academy Award nomination came in 1937 for his portrayal of the spiritual, refined, philosophic Chang, a Tibetan lama (priest), in director Capra's superb classic **Lost Horizon** (37). Out of the outstanding cast, headed by Ronald Colman, he was the only one to receive an acting nomination for the film, but he lost the supporting-actor Oscar to Joseph Schildkraut in **The Life of Emile Zola.** Also that year, he played Lord Melbourne in the historical drama **Victoria the Great.**

The actor was married at an unspecified date to Mrs. F.R. Hamlin, and later divorced. He then married actress Marguerite (or Rita) Stanwood, and this union also ended in divorce, in 1933.

He had a key role in Capra's **You Can't Take It with You** (38), as ruthless tycoon Edward Arnold's desperately ill, utterly destroyed former business partner, who bitterly confronts him and gasps, "You can't shut out every decent impulse—and survive!", then collapses and dies. He was a 13th-century Chinese scientist working to develop gunpowder in **The Adventures of Marco Polo, and** was a priest, the spiritual adviser to Jeanette MacDonald, in **The Girl of the Golden West.** He was in a small part as an attorney in **Kidnapped,** was Luise Rainer's father in **The Toy Wife,** and played the commander of an Army tank regiment in **Army Girl.** And for two years he succeeded John Barrymore as the Scotland Yard inspector (a part he was familiar with) in the Bulldog Drummond series, starring (if that is the right word) the forgettable John Howard; Warner was in four of the Drummonds in 1938-39.

For the fourth time, he worked for director Capra in **Mr. Smith Goes to Washington** (39), playing the Senate majority leader, and he was the dignified old maharajah in **The Rains Came,** with Maria Ouspenskaya as his wife. He was a gambling-hall croupier in **Let Freedom Ring.** Now in his mid-sixties, he was a priest again (and helping Jeanette MacDonald again) in **New Moon.** He had two good parts in 1941: as the fanatical Justice Hathorne in **All That Money Can Buy (The Devil and Daniel Webster),** ultimately won over by Webster's (Edward Arnold's) persuasive courtroom oratory, and as the invalid who turns out to be the surprise masked murderer of Joan Blondell in **Topper Returns.** He was also seen in **The Corsican Brothers** and in several programmers.

Increasingly, Warner's roles were getting smaller as he grew older; where he had been the top-billed star in the Twenties, now he would typically find himself eighth or ninth on the cast list. During World War II he was seen in such fare as **Hitler's Children** (43), solemnly dignified as an anti-Nazi bishop, and

Crossroads (42), as the prosecuting attorney at William Powell's trial. He had his last role for Frank Capra in the fine classic **It's a Wonderful Life** (46), starring James Stewart; in the early scenes, as a pharmacist, he accidentally gets a prescription confused and is about to send out a dose of deadly poison to a customer when delivery boy Stewart (or to be more precise, the young actor playing him as a boy) catches the error just in time. He was in several forgettable movies (including one more Bulldog Drummond) until his cameo appearance in **Sunset Boulevard** (50) as one of "the waxworks," Gloria Swanson's bridge partners from her silent-screen days (the other two were Buster Keaton and Anna Q. Nilsson).

In **The First Legion** (51) he played a paralyzed old priest who gets up and walks in what many believe to be a miracle, and there was a small part as an uncle in **Here Comes the Groom,** starring Bing Crosby. Then there was a five-year hiatus from the screen, and he returned for a very small role in **The Ten Commandments** (56). At age 80, he played his last role in **Darby's Rangers** (57). He died the following year, one of the few people ever to be able to look back on three-quarters of a century on stage and screen. And few performers ever matched the acting versatility of H.B. Warner.

THE FILMS OF H.B. WARNER

1914: The Ghost Breaker; Your Ghost and Mine; Lost Paradise.
1915: The Beggar of Cawnpore; The Raiders.
1916: The Vagabond Prince; The Market of Vain Desire; The House of a Thousand Candles; Shell 43; A Wife's Sacrifice.
1917: The Danger Trail; The Seven Deadly Sins; God's Man.
1919: The Man Who Turned White; A Fugitive from Matrimony; Haunting Shadows; For a Woman's Honor; The Pagan God; Maruja.
1920: Grey Wolf's Ghost; Once a Plumber; Dice of Destiny; The White Dove; One Hour Before Dawn; Uncharted Channels; Felix O'Day.
1921: When We Were Twenty-One; Below the Dead Line.
1923: Zaza.
1924: Is Love Everything? *Credit uncertain:* The Dark Swan.
1926: Silence; Whispering Smith. *Credit uncertain:* The Temptress.
1927: The King of Kings; Sorrell and Son; French Dressing.
1928: Conquest; Romance of a Rogue; The Naughty Duchess; Man-Made Women.
1929: The Divine Lady; The Trial of Mary Dugan; The Doctor's Secret; The Gamblers; The Show of Shows; The Argyle Case; Stark Mad; Tiger Rose.
1930: Liliom; The Green Goddess; The Second Floor Mystery; Wedding Rings; On Your Back; The Princess and the Plumber; The Furies; Wild Company.
1931: Five Star Final; The Reckless Hour; A Woman of Experience; The Prodigal; Expensive Women.
1932: A Woman Commands; The Menace; The Son-Daughter; The Phantom of Crestwood; Tom Brown of Culver; Charlie Chan's Chance; The Crusader; Cross-Examination; Unholy Love.
1933: Jennie Gerhardt; Christopher Bean; Supernatural; Justice Takes a Holiday.

1934: Behold My Wife; Grand Canary; Sorrell and Son (remake); Night Alarm; In Old Santa Fe.
1935: A Tale of Two Cities; Born to Gamble.
1936: Mr. Deeds Goes to Town; The Garden Murder Case; Moonlight Murder; The Blackmailer; Rose of the Rancho; Along Came Love.
1937: Lost Horizon; Victoria the Great; Torpedoed! (Our Fighting Navy).
1938: You Can't Take It with You; Kidnapped; The Adventures of Marco Polo; The Toy Wife; The Girl of the Golden West; Army Girl; Bulldog Drummond in Africa.
1939: Mr. Smith Goes to Washington; The Rains Came; Let Freedom Ring; The Gracie Allen Murder Case; Nurse Edith Cavell; Arrest Bulldog Drummond!; Bulldog Drummond's Secret Police; Bulldog Drummond's Bride. *Credit uncertain:* Tell No Tales.
1940: New Moon. *Credit uncertain:* The Man from Dakota.
1941: All That Money Can Buy (The Devil and Daniel Webster); Topper Returns; The Corsican Brothers; City of Missing Girls; South of Tahiti; Ellery Queen and the Perfect Crime.
1942: Crossroads; A Yank in Libya; Boss of Big Town.
1943: Hitler's Children; Woman in Bondage.
1944: Faces in the Fog; Action in Arabia; Enemy of Women.
1945: Captain Tugboat Annie; Rogues' Gallery.
1946: It's a Wonderful Life; Strange Impersonation; Gentleman Joe Palooka.
1947: High Wall; Driftwood; Bulldog Drummond Strikes Back.
1948: The Judge Steps Out; Prince of Thieves.
1949: Hellfire; El Paso.
1950: Sunset Boulevard.
1951: The First Legion; Here Comes the Groom; Journey into Light; Savage Drums.
1956: The Ten Commandments.
1957: Darby's Rangers.

The acidulous dowager:
HELEN WESTLEY

The specialized niche carved out by Helen Westley in films of the Thirties was the crusty, crotchety and acidulous matron or dowager, domineering but kind-hearted. Owlish and imposing, with aquiline features, she portrayed ladies in advanced middle age who were gruff and supercilious, with a quick eye for the proprieties.

There were plenty of sweet old grandmothers in Hollywood films of her era, but she debunked that tradition with a sharp and scathing tongue. You are likely to remember her in these roles whether her part was good or not (often it was not), whether she was in a classic or just playing stooge for Shirley Temple or Jane Withers. Coming to the screen at a late date (just before she turned 60), she had a short hour in the sun, making only 37 films in the nine years before her death, but she made good use of it.

Her name at birth is given by various sources as Henrietta Meserole Manney, Henrietta Remsen Meserole Manney, or Henrietta Conroy. The actress was born March 28, 1875 (some sources say 1879), in Brooklyn, New York, the descendant of famous old Dutch families. (Remsen and Meserole are the names of streets in that borough of New York City.) The younger of two children of a druggist, she aimed to be an actress from the start, and studied at the Brooklyn School of Oratory, Boston's Emerson College of Oratory, and the American Academy of Dramatic Art. At age 22 she made her New York stage debut in **The Captain of the Nonesuch,** and then worked in vaudeville and stock before marrying actor John (Jack) Westley in 1900. (They had a daughter, Ethel, and separated in 1912.)

Miss Westley became a leading spirit in the Bohemian and creative life of Greenwich Village at the peak of its great days in the World War I era. She helped organize the Washington Square Players in 1915; the Players became the Theater Guild in 1918. Continuing to be busy on the stage, she appeared in many of the Guild's productions and acted in at least one of its plays in every season (also serving on its board of directors) until 1934, when at age 59 she settled in Hollywood to work as a character actress in films.

She immediately got good parts in major movies. She was good in her debut as a retired actress helping Constance Bennett to stage stardom in **Moulin Rouge** (34), and was a duchess in **Death Takes a**

Holiday. She was fine as the matriarch of the Rothschilds and the mother of George Arliss in **House of Rothschild,** and was "splendid as the mellow dowager" (New York Times), the indomitable grandmother of both Irene Dunne and John Boles' wife (Boles loved Miss Dunne hopelessly) in the first film version of Edith Wharton's novel **The Age of Innocence.** And she played the bitter spinster Marilla Cuthbert who, with her brother (O.P. Heggie), expected a boy from the orphanage but got Anne Shirley instead, and ended up softened by her, in the children's classic **Anne of Green Gables.**

The actress had the title role in **Roberta** (35), nominally a Fred Astaire-Ginger Rogers film, playing a famous couturier who leaves her Parisian dress salon to nephew Randolph Scott, who falls in love with her assistant, Miss Dunne. In **Splendor** she was poisonously effective as Joel McCrea's embittered dowager mother, trying to break up his marriage to Miriam Hopkins. She, Miss Shirley and Heggie were reunited for **Chasing Yesterday,** a sentimental romance like the earlier film. In **Captain Hurricane** she was a Cape Cod spinster who has been pursued for years by crusty old fisherman James Barton.

Show Boat (36) cast her as the captain's wife, Parthy Ann Hawks (a wonderfully tart performance), and she was Shirley Temple's eagle-eyed grandmother in **Stowaway,** also appearing as the wealthy society woman who offers Frank Morgan money to let her adopt his granddaughter (little Miss Temple) in **Dimples.** In **Half Angel** she was a wealthy woman murdered by her husband (Henry Stephenson), and she had a grandmother role in **Banjo on My Knee.** At this point in time she was working under a long-term contract with 20th Century-Fox.

Miss Westley was Shirley Temple's blind grandmother in **Heidi** (37), and Loretta Young's mother in **Cafe Metropole,** also portraying Grace Moore's tough mother in **I'll Take Romance.** It was back to little Miss Temple (for the last time) in **Rebecca of Sunnybrook Farm** (38), this time as her watchful aunt, trying to keep her away from (horrors!) show-business people. She played Tyrone Power's aunt in **Alexander's Ragtime Band,** ran a school attended by Jane Withers in **Keep Smiling,** and played a Hungarian countess, the wife of Henry Stephenson (butler William Powell's employer) in **The Baroness and the Butler.** She was cast as John Boles' housekeeper in **She Married an Artist.**

She had one of the top supporting roles in the Claudette Colbert starrer **Zaza** (39), and for the second time played Miss Young's mother in **Wife, Husband and Friend.** In that year she also reappeared on the Broadway stage, in **Primrose Path.** She was quite involved with show-business-on-film in 1940, running a theatrical boarding house in the Miriam Hopkins vehicle **The Lady with Red Hair** and playing Alice Faye's hawk-eyed grandmother in **Lillian Russell.** She was near the top of the supporting cast in the Bette Davis starrer **All This, and Heaven Too,** and played the director of a retirement home for elderly ladies in **The Captain Is a Lady.**

She was the wise old Cousin Philippa in **Adam Had Four Sons** (41), and played to the hilt the harridan aunt of John Carroll in the musical **Sunny,** appearing to be the only one in the cast having a good time. And she supported John Wayne in **Lady from Louisiana** and appeared in a couple of programmers. She was a friend of married couple Fredric March and Loretta Young in **Bedtime Story** (42), and supported comedian/bandleader Kay Kyser in a silly "B" picture, **My Favorite Spy.** That was her last work as an actress, for she died that year, 1942, at age 67. Helen Westley survives, though, on late-night television, her sharp-tongued dowagers counterbalancing those sweet old aunts and grandmothers, a bottle of vinegar among the marshmallows.

THE FILMS OF HELEN WESTLEY

1934: Death Takes a Holiday; The Age of Innocence; House of Rothschild; Anne of Green Gables; Moulin Rouge.
1935: Roberta; Splendor; Chasing Yesterday; The Melody Lingers On; Captain Hurricane.
1936: Show Boat; Half Angel; Stowaway; Dimples; Banjo on My Knee.
1937: Heidi; Cafe Metropole; I'll Take Romance; Sing and Be Happy.
1938: Rebecca of Sunnybrook Farm; Alexander's Ragtime Band; She Married an Artist; Keep Smiling; The Baroness and the Butler.
1939: Zaza; Wife, Husband and Friend.
1940: Lillian Russell; All This, and Heaven Too; Lady with Red Hair; The Captain Is a Lady.
1941: Adam Had Four Sons; Lady from Louisiana; Sunny; Million Dollar Baby; The Smiling Ghost.
1942: Bedtime Story; My Favorite Spy.

Bemused and quizzical:
ROLAND YOUNG

Whimsy, done well, is not easy to achieve. But Roland Young was Hollywood's acknowledged king of whimsy in the Golden Era.

He was by turns—or simultaneously—bemused, quizzical, ineffectual, distracted, vague, apologetic, bewildered and wistful, and he adhered to these characteristics throughout a 30-year screen career. Ever the urbane bourgeois, he underplayed with skill and charm in some of the screen's best comedies, often screwball comedies.

He had a number of trademarks that were absolutely inimitable. These included a wispy smile, eyes twitching at the corners, faint unfinished gestures, a stammer, talking through tightly pursed lips, crinkling his face to avoid chuckling, and jamming his hands into the pocket of his jacket (which was usually a tuxedo). Short and balding, he had only two or three facial expressions, but the way he employed them made him a more interesting and enjoyable actor than many who had 20 or 30. And, in the mad world of film comedy, he was never surprised at the madness of others.

The critic James Agee, who was never easy to please, once said Young "is able to make anything he appears in seem much more intelligent, human and amusing than it has any intrinsic right to do." And years after his death the film star Catherine Deneuve declared that the best piece of acting she had ever seen was his supporting performance as a nobleman in the 1935 movie **Ruggles of Red Gap.**

Roland Young was born November 11, 1887, in London, the son of an architect. He was educated at Sherborne College and London University, and trained for the stage at the Royal Academy of Dramatic Art. He made his London debut in 1908 in **Find the Woman,** and in 1912 traveled to America and opened on Broadway in **Hindle Wakes.** When World War I broke out it was in the U.S. Army that he served. Returning to Broadway after the war, he became an established name, appearing in the first plays of the newly formed Theater Guild and also in three comedies written for him by Clare Kummer: **Good Gracious Annabelle!, A Successful Calamity** and **Rollo's Wild Oat.** He also appeared in **Luck in Pawn.**

He made one early film appearance, at age 34, playing Dr. Watson to John Barrymore's **Sherlock Holmes** (22). When Barrymore saw the completed

film, he was stunned to find that Young had stolen numerous scenes from him, and he said to a friend, "...That quiet, agreeable bastard had stolen, not one, but every damned scene!...He is such a splendid gentleman in real life, but what a cunning, larcenous demon when on the boards!"

The actor married playwright Kummer's daughter Marjorie (some sources give her name as Frances) in 1921, and they would be divorced in 1940. In 1948 he married Patience DuCroz, an actress whose stage name was Dorothy Patience.

Continuing to be busy on the stage, he played General Burgoyne in Bernard Shaw's **The Devil's Disciple** in London in 1923, starred on Broadway in **Beggar on Horseback** with Spring Byington in 1924 (Edward Everett Horton took the role in the film version), and co-starred with Ina Claire in **The Last of Mrs. Cheyney** in 1925. Many other plays followed. In 1929 he answered Hollywood's call for stage-trained actors at the birth of talkies, and at age 41 signed a contract with MGM. His debut was in **The Unholy Night** (29), a thriller directed by Lionel Barrymore, in which he played a British nobleman. In **The Bishop Murder Case** (30) he was an innocent murder suspect, and he played an amorous bachelor in the bizarre comedy **Madam Satan.**

Young played Grace Moore's father, a Russian count, in **New Moon** (31), and in **Don't Bet on Women** he was the overly trusting husband of Jeanette MacDonald, betting Edmund Lowe that he (Lowe) won't be able to kiss her. He reprised his stage role in **Good Gracious Annabelle!,** now called **Annabelle's Affairs,** in which he and Victor McLaglen are tycoons battling for control of a mine; he falls for Miss MacDonald, but later accuses her of theft. He was inimitable as a drama critic in **The Guardsman,** played a drunken doctor in **The Pagan Lady,** and was Eleanor Boardman's brother in **The Squaw Man.** He played a hobo in **The Prodigal.**

In director Ernst Lubitsch's **One Hour with You** (32) he was the odd man out in a romantic quadrangle, as his wife (Genevieve Tobin) dallies with Maurice Chevalier even as Chevalier's wife (Miss MacDonald) is being wooed by Charlie Ruggles. And as a careless, happy-go-lucky Ruritanian king he stole **A Woman Commands** from Pola Negri (his wife, the queen) and Basil Rathbone (her lover). In **This Is the Night** he was splendidly droll as a man who hires Lili Damita to pose as his wife to help cover up his amorous pursuit of Thelma Todd, the wife of an Olympic javelin thrower (Cary Grant in his screen debut). He stole the film in the Kay Francis vehicle **Street of Women,** as her unsuccessful suitor.

The actor was highly praised for **His Double Life** (33), an offbeat but felicitous teaming with Lillian Gish, in which he was a shy artist who impersonates his own valet and marries the latter's potential mail-order bride (Miss Gish) after the valet dies. In **A Lady's Profession** he and Alison Skipworth were a harebrained, titled English brother and sister who operate a New York speakeasy where they serve only non-alcoholic beverages and so run afoul of booze-pushing mobsters. He played a rakish burglar in **Blind Adventure,** and secretly went aboard to spy on wife Genevieve Tobin when she went on a **Pleasure Cruise.** Then he was married to the flirtatious Verree Teasdale in **They Just Had to Get Married**—but the "they" was not them, but ZaSu Pitts and Slim Summerville. Meanwhile, back on the Broadway stage, he co-starred with Laura Hope Crews in **Her Master's Voice.**

He was an impoverished member of the exiled Russian royal family, and involved in running a racket, in **Here Is My Heart** (34). He was superb as the slimy and villainous Uriah Heep in the classic **David Copperfield** (35), undone by W.C. Fields as Mr. Micawber; he was cast against type, and he would say later that it was his favorite role. And he was fine in **Ruggles of Red Gap** as an English nobleman out West, playing "Pretty Baby" on drums in a duet with Leila Hyams. He stole the show as Kay Francis' novelist confidant in **Give Me Your Heart** (36), a *deus ex machina* who helps solve her problems; was a friend of Loretta Young's in **The Unguarded Hour,** and played a theatrical producer in **One Rainy Afternoon.**

His most memorable screen portrayal, with the possible exception of Uriah Heep, was in the title role of **Topper** (37), as a stuffy, timorous, henpecked suburban banker at the mercy of his wife (Billie Burke) and butler (Alan Mowbray) and beset by a couple of squabbling ghosts (Cary Grant and Constance Bennett), the nominal stars). He was the worm long overdue to turn, the downtrodden millionaire neglected by a selfish wife and family. His talent for being harassed found exquisite expression here, and in addition to stealing the film from the stars he won an Oscar nomination as best supporting actor, but lost to Joseph Schildkraut in **The Life of Emile Zola.** In that year he also starred in the comedy **The Man Who Could Work Miracles,** as a store clerk chosen by the gods who discovers he can turn objects upside down, materialize animals, send people to Hell, and so on. He nearly causes the end of the world, but when he tries to do good he comes up against human nature, and fails. In **Call It a Day** he was a pixyish bachelor pursuing Frieda Inescort, and in the Eddie Cantor vehicle **Ali Baba Goes to Town** he played a sultan in Bagdad in the year A.D. 937, having trouble with 365 wives and also defeated in a bid for re-election.

The **Topper** series continued with **Topper Takes a Trip** (38), which lacked Grant but featured Miss Bennett as a ghost who helps Young save his wife (Miss Burke again) from Riviera philanderer Mowbray, who had been their butler in the previous outing. Far better, though, was **The Young in Heart,** in which he was again married to Miss Burke and the father of Janet Gaynor and Douglas Fairbanks Jr.; the whole family are con artists on the run, they call Young "Sahib," and they end up reformed by a rich little old lady they had tried to fleece. In **Yes, My Darling Daughter** (39) he was married to Fay Bainter and the father of Priscilla Lane, and **Here I Am a Stranger** cast him as a Mr. Chips-like English professor. He and Pat O'Brien played two actors in **The Night of Nights.**

Young was fine as Katharine Hepburn's whimsical, irrepressible, scapegrace Uncle Willie in the classic **The Philadelphia Story** (40), and was a dress-shop owner in **Irene** and a talent scout in **Star Dust.** He played Joel McCrea's lawyer in **He Married His Wife,** and was married to Billie Burke again in **Dulcy.** His last really important part came in **Topper Returns** (41), the conclusion of the series, in which the ghost of Joan Blondell helps him solve her own murder (H.B. Warner did it). In **The Flame of New Orleans** he talked Marlene Dietrich into marrying him, but while they are standing at the altar and about to recite their vows another admirer of hers suddenly appears, the man she really loves (Bruce Cabot); she faints, the wedding never comes off, and soon after she departs with Cabot.

The actor was an acquaintance of Greta Garbo's in her last film, **Two Faced Woman** (42), and a business associate of Joan Crawford's in **They All Kissed the Bride.** In **Tales of Manhattan** he was cast as Cesar Romero's butler. In the multi-episode film **Forever and a Day** (43) he was in a real tear-jerking sequence, as he and wife Gladys Cooper are told of their son's death in action in World War I. He was one of the numerous murder victims (of Barry Fitzgerald) in **And Then There Were None** (45), and then was off the screen for two years. Astonishingly, he was a mass murderer, a strangler, in the Bob Hope outing **The Great Lover** (49). He had a key role in the Fred Astaire musical **Let's Dance** (50), and then was in the bizarre **St. Benny the Dip** (51), in which he, Lionel Stander and Dick Haymes (a popular crooner who made a few films) played con men on the run who hide out by disguising themselves as priests and running a Bowery mission; inevitably, they are converted to good works.

His last film was **The Man from Tangier** (53), a weak programmer starring Nils Asther (a long-over-the-hill actor whose career had peaked a generation earlier). In that year, 1953, Roland Young died at 65. He was truly one of Hollywood's greatest character actors, a master of comedy, the bemused and quizzical king of whimsy, an irreplaceable talent.

THE FILMS OF ROLAND YOUNG

1922: Sherlock Holmes.
1929: The Unholy Night; Her Private Life; Wise Girls.
1930: Madam Satan; The Bishop Murder Case.
1931: New Moon; Don't Bet on Women; The Prodigal; Annabelle's Affairs; The Guardsman; The Squaw Man; The Pagan Lady.
1932: One Hour with You; A Woman Commands; This Is the Night; Lovers Courageous; Street of Women; Wedding Rehearsal.
1933: His Double Life; They Just Had to Get Married; A Lady's Profession; Pleasure Cruise; Blind Adventure.
1934: Here Is My Heart.
1935: David Copperfield; Ruggles of Red Gap.
1936: The Unguarded Hour; One Rainy Afternoon; Give Me Your Heart.
1937: Topper; The Man Who Could Work Miracles; Ali Baba Goes to Town; Call It a Day; King Solomon's Mines.

1938: Topper Takes a Trip; The Young in Heart; Sailing Along.
1939: Yes, My Darling Daughter; The Night of Nights; Here I Am a Stranger.
1940: The Philadelphia Story; He Married His Wife; Star Dust; Irene; Dulcy; Private Affairs; No, No, Nanette.
1941: Topper Returns; The Flame of New Orleans.
1942: Two Faced Woman; Tales of Manhattan; The Lady Has Plans; They All Kissed the Bride.
1943: Forever and a Day.
1944: Standing Room Only.
1945: And Then There Were None.
1948: You Gotta Stay Happy; Bond Street.
1949: The Great Lover.
1950: Let's Dance.
1951: St. Benny the Dip.
1953: The Man from Tangier.

A villain for connoisseurs:
GEORGE ZUCCO

Hollywood's master of villainy in the top-budget, or "A," picture may have been Basil Rathbone, but the great venomous villain of cheap programmers was George Zucco, who has been called by one writer "the Karloff of 'B' features." Actually, he was a rather more complex and interesting villain than most. Film historian Doug McClelland puts it this way:

"Who is your favorite villain from the movies' golden age? Mad Lionel Atwill? Suave Henry Daniell? Decadent George Macready? Sadistic Arthur Hohl? Scheming Robert Douglas? Foreign Eduardo Ciannelli? Ruthless Walter Slezak? Diabolical Charles Middleton? Crooked Marc Lawrence? Deadly Barton MacLane? Spying Conrad Veidt? Desperate George Coulouris? Lascivious Jack Elam? Inescapable Douglass Dumbrille? Mine is mad, suave, decadent, sadistic, scheming, foreign, ruthless, diabolical, crooked, deadly, spying, desperate, lascivious, inescapable George Zucco."

The sepulchral-toned, tight-lipped, staring-eyed actor, who gave off an aura of faintly seedy, unctuous upper-class menace, played many a mad scientist, arch-fiend and master criminal, especially in grade "B" horror films of the World War II era that were far beneath his talents (although he started out in the Thirties in more conventional, even non-villainous, roles). As one writer has put it, he "lent his Manchester lip-roll and marbly eyeballs to many a creepy cameo." Smooth and quiet-spoken, when he came on the scene you knew there was treachery afoot.

He played his mad scientists and unredeemable scoundrels with a supercilious condescension, and his eyes would light up with satanic glee at his own perfidy whenever he thought of something particularly revolting. Clearly, he enjoyed villainy for its own sake. No wonder that he is the favorite screen nasty of some of the connoisseurs of cinema.

Zucco was born January 11, 1886, in Manchester, a large industrial city in the English Midlands, the son of an importer who died when George was an infant. At school, he earned honors in mathematics and played on the cricket and soccer teams. Adventure-minded, he journeyed to Manitoba, Canada, where for a time he worked on a wheat farm, then went to Winnipeg to clerk in a grain exchange. He appeared in a number of plays presented by his club, then abandoned the business world to join a touring

stock company. He made his stage debut in 1908 in Regina, Saskatchewan, as the bishop in **What Happened to Jones,** then toured both coasts of the United States in vaudeville and in stock, ultimately winding up in New York in a vaudeville sketch, "The Suffragette." Following World War I service as a lieutenant in the British army (during which he was wounded in France), he enrolled in the Royal Academy of Dramatic Art and then played roles on the London stage. He did Shakespeare and was seen in **Lightnin', They Knew What They Wanted,** Ibsen's **Hedda Gabler** and **Ghosts, Autumn Crocus, Reunion in Vienna** and **Journey's End.** He was a prominent actor in both London and New York by the time he began working in British films in 1931 at the age of 45.

At an unspecified date the actor married Frances Hawke, and they had a daughter, also named Frances.

His first film, made in London, was **The Dreyfus Case** (31), called simply **Dreyfus** in Britain. He was in a few 1932 programmers starring Jessie Matthews, and was far down the cast list in **The Good Companions** (33). He repeated his stage role as a clergyman in **Autumn Crocus** (34), and was in several forgettable films before moving to Hollywood early in 1936. Meanwhile, he was featured as Disraeli with Helen Hayes in **Victoria Regina** on Broadway in 1935, a performance that got mixed reviews; newspaper critic Percy Hammond had good things to say ("...A vivid study...a triumph of florid reticence...he bends the pregnant hinges of a showy sycophant"), while on the other side of the ledger Robert Garland commented, "[He] puts you in mind of Dracula pretending to be George Arliss."

Zucco was cast as a psychologist in **After the Thin Man** (36), supported Roland Young in **The Man Who Could Work Miracles,** and was a Uriah Heeplike lawyer, a murder suspect, in **Sinner Take All.** In the Joan Crawford starrer **The Bride Wore Red** (37) he played Count Armalia, a bon vivant who enjoys playing ironic games on what he calls "the wheel of life" at a cabaret; he proceeds to finance Miss Crawford's trip to a Tyrol resort, where she meets Franchot Tone and Robert Young. Some sources indicate that he played a Polish senator who asks Greta Garbo to give herself to Napoleon in **Conquest;** however, his name does not appear in the large, detailed cast list that appears in the American Film Institute Catalog. He was a Secret Service chief in **The Firefly,** a Scotland Yard inspector in **London by Night,** the shrewd defense attorney at Clark Gable's murder trial in **Parnell,** the doctor who examines Jean Harlow in **Saratoga** (her last film), and the queen's agent who, in flashback, tells the story of imprisoned sailor Gary Cooper in **Souls at Sea.** He was merely a family friend in **Madame X,** and in **Rosalie** he played the European general who breaks up (temporarily) student-princess Eleanor Powell's romance with football hero Nelson Eddy.

He played the prefect of police in **Arsene Lupin Returns** in 1938, the last year in which he played entirely conventional roles before his villainous period began, and was a doctor helping **Charlie Chan in Honolulu.** He was the reactionary British prime minister opposed by Disraeli in **Suez,** Margaret Sullavan's sanatorium doctor in **Three Comrades,** the governor of the Conciergerie in **Marie Antoinette,** and the murder victim, a rare-book collector, in **Fast Company.** In **Lord Jeff** he and Gale Sondergaard were a pair of crooks using young Freddie Bartholomew to swindle jewelry stores; later the youngster turns them over to the cops.

The actor really came into his own as a first-class villain in 1939. He was excellent as the evil Professor Moriarty opposite Basil Rathbone's Sherlock Holmes in **The Adventures of Sherlock Holmes,** walking away with the film as he gloats from under his elegant top hat while plotting to steal England's crown jewels. In **Captain Fury** he was a cruel, slave-owning Australian sheep rancher, ultimately undone by Brian Aherne. And he was the chief villain, stealing a death-ray machine, in **Arrest Bulldog Drummond.** He played the grim-faced prosecutor in **The Hunchback of Notre Dame,** trying to have the unjustly imprisoned Maureen O'Hara tortured and hanged, and he was a lawyer who is one of the murder victims in the Bob Hope vehicle **The Cat and the Canary.** He played a lawyer in **Here I Am a Stranger** and was cast as a politician in a Central American banana republic in **The Magnificent Fraud.**

He was the murderous leader of a gang of jewel thieves in **Dark Streets of Cairo** (40), the French police commissioner trailing Nelson Eddy in **New Moon,** and had a nice cameo in **Arise, My Love** as the governor of a Spanish prison, tricked into releasing Ray Milland when Claudette Colbert poses as the latter's wife. But, in retrospect, what was far more significant in his overall career was his appearance in a "B" horror film for Universal, **The Mummy's Hand.**

In that film, he was introduced as the villainous High Priest of Karnak, head of an evil ancient Egyptian sect. Attired in a smart fez, he revivifies a mummy and uses it to kill off members of an archaeological expedition and to abduct one of them, pretty Peggy Moran. The film starts off as a comedy, but the last half hour is one of the most frightening sequences in movie history. As he prepares to make the captive beauty "immortal by administering a secret formula of tana leaves," she is saved by other members of the expedition; Zucco is shot, and falls down an incredibly long flight of steps, where he is presumed dead (but just wait until the sequel!).

The actor was a fine red herring (i.e., he was not the murderer) in **Topper Returns** (41), playing a sinister doctor with roving eyes, giving an ambivalent edge to such lines as "Are the young ladies comfortable?", which as said by him sound like a definite threat. He played a Nazi agent (and not for the last time) in **International Lady,** and then a mad scientist (his first such role) in **The Monster and the Girl,** a piece of Grand Guignol in which he transplants a dead man's brain into a gorilla's body. Over the next seven years a number of his characters would dabble in things best left alone, and frequently he would be involved in doomed medical ventures. In a more normal role, he was Joan Crawford's defense attorney in **A Woman's Face,** but in **Ellery Queen and the Murder Ring** he was the maniacally zany chief physician of a hospital.

He played Maureen O'Hara's father, the corrupt governor of Jamaica, in **The Black Swan** (42), was a villainous Nazi in **My Favorite Blonde,** and appeared in three of his best-remembered cheapie horror films. In **The Mummy's Tomb,** the sequel to **The Mummy's Hand,** he comes back from the dead ("The bullet he fired into me [in the previous film] only crushed my arm") as the palsied old high priest, once again unleashing the mummy—and once again dying (don't bet on it). **Dr. Renault's Secret** found him as a mad scientist again, transforming an ape into a semi-human (J. Carrol Naish). And for the PRC studio, the lowest of the low on Poverty Row, he effortlessly stole the show as a crazed doctor who changes a man into a beast—a wolf man—in **The Mad Monster;** this film was banned for 12 years in Great Britain.

The actor starred in a dual role in the horror cheapie **Dead Men Walk** (43), underplaying (for a change) as a good doctor and his evil vampire brother; the former finally kills the latter (but the good brother then turns vampire). Okay, how about another mad scientist? In **The Mad Ghoul** he needs fresh hearts to keep alive the victims of his experiments with a poison vapor, so he has a "ghoul" dig up some new graves to obtain them. In this film, as in others of this genre, his suave manner and cultivated accent hardly concealed his lustful designs on the heroine (in this case Evelyn Ankers). He was a Nazi spy, opposing Basil Rathbone again, in **Sherlock Holmes in Washington,** and played a crooked nightclub owner in **Never a Dull Moment.**

He finished off the Mummy series with **The Mummy's Ghost** (44), in which once again he returned from the dead; John Carradine played the mummy. In **Shadows in the Night** he was a drug-company chemist whose mistake causes the deaths of 15 people, and in **Voodoo Man** he was a gas-station manager(!) detouring young women to a mad doctor (Bela Lugosi). He played the Nazi concentration-camp commandant in the Spencer Tracy starrer **The Seventh Cross,** and was the proprietor of a traveling chamber of horrors in **House of Frankenstein,** ending up murdered by Boris Karloff and J. Carrol Naish.

He gave one of his more florid performances in **Sudan** (45), cocking an evil eye and plotting the murder of rightful ruler Maria Montez, and played a police inspector in **Confidential Agent.** He and Lionel Atwill co-starred in **Fog Island,** with a bunch of people gathered at his eerie mansion, where he plans vengeance on them, and in **Having Wonderful Crime** he was a magician whose act ends up in a real murder. He played a sheet-shrouded Near Eastern potentate in **Weekend at the Waldorf.** In **The Flying Serpent** (46) he was a doctor protecting an Aztec treasure with a prehistoric bird (maybe he couldn't afford a watchdog).

Zucco played a Scotland Yard detective in **Moss Rose** (47), and, in a similar role, was Lucille Ball's Scotland Yard bodyguard in **Lured.** He was a French priest in **Desire Me,** and played a member of a secret society plotting to overthrow a European country in **Where There's Life.** In **Captain from Castile** he was a family "friend" who refuses to help Tyrone Power when the latter's parents and sister are arrested by the Spanish Inquisition. There was one last mad scientist, in **Who Killed "Doc" Robbin?** (48), and in **The Pirate** he was the Caribbean viceroy who wants to execute Gene Kelly for piracy. He played a constable warning Ingrid Bergman of danger ahead in **Joan of Arc,** and was a treacherous high priest in **Tarzan and the Mermaids.**

He had a cameo as a judge in **The Barkleys of Broadway** (49), the last Fred Astaire-Ginger Rogers film, and played a lawyer who sternly warns his clerk to stay away from the married Jennifer Jones in **Madame Bovary.** He was in **Let's Dance** (50), played the Egyptian ambassador in **David and Bathsheba** (51) and a priest in **The First Legion,** and wound up his screen career in **Flame of Stamboul,** as a high-powered international crook, "The Voice," trying to obtain documents about the future of the Suez Canal.

That was the end of George Zucco's film career, at age 65. But it was hardly the end of the drama connected with him. When he died at 74 in 1960, according to the not always reliable Kenneth Anger in one of his "Hollywood Babylon" books, it was in a mental institution, and, Anger relates, his wife and daughter thereupon committed suicide. However, a check of obituaries on file at the library of the Academy of Motion Picture Arts and Sciences shows that the actor's death occurred in a "sanitarium"—an ambiguous term—and the cause of death is not given. These reports also say that the wife and daughter attended the funeral two days later—which still does not offer any conclusive evidence one way or the other regarding any suicide. But a magazine article by film historian Doug McClelland later said that the daughter died in 1962. So for a man whose acting was so often meshed in mysteries, the ending of the story remains shrouded in doubt.

But there is no doubt at all about the skill of George Zucco in portraying some of the most interesting and unusual nasties ever to appear on the screen. He was, indeed, a villain for connoisseurs.

THE FILMS OF GEORGE ZUCCO

1931: The Dreyfus Case (Dreyfus).

1932: There Goes the Bride; The Midshipmaid (Midshipmaid Gob); The Man from Toronto.

1933: The Good Companions. *Credit uncertain:* The Roof.

1934: Autumn Crocus; What Happened Then?; The Lady Is Willing. *Credit uncertain:* What's in a Name?

1935: It's a Bet; Abdul the Damned.

1936: After the Thin Man; The Man Who Could Work Miracles; Sinner Take All

1937: Saratoga; Parnell; Souls at Sea; The Bride Wore Red; Rosalie; Madame X; The Firefly; London by Night. *Credit uncertain:* Conquest (see text).

1938: Marie Antoinette; Suez; Three Comrades; Charlie Chan in Honolulu; Lord Jeff; Fast Company; Vacation from Love; Arsene Lupin Returns.

1939: The Adventures of Sherlock Holmes; The Hunchback of Notre Dame; The Cat and the Canary; Captain Fury; Here I Am a Stranger; The Magnificent Fraud; Arrest Bulldog Drummond.

1940: Arise, My Love; New Moon; The Mummy's Hand; The Dark Streets of Cairo.

1941: A Woman's Face; Topper Returns; International Lady; The Monster and the Girl; Ellery Queen and the Murder Ring.

1942: The Black Swan; My Favorite Blonde; The Mummy's Tomb; The Mad Monster; Dr. Renault's Secret; Halfway to Shanghai.

1943: Never a Dull Moment; The Mad Ghoul; The Black Raven; Dead Men Walk; Sherlock Holmes in Washington; Holy Matrimony; Song of Russia (voice only, dubbing for actor Kurt Katch).

1944: The Seventh Cross; House of Frankenstein; The Mummy's Ghost; Shadows in the Night; Voodoo Man; One Body Too Many. *Credit uncertain:* The Devil's Brood.

1945: Weekend at the Waldorf; Confidential Agent; Sudan; Hold That Blonde; Midnight Manhunt; Having Wonderful Crime; Fog Island; One Exciting Night.

1946: The Flying Serpent.

1947: Captain from Castile; Lured; Desire Me; Moss Rose; Where There's Life; Scared to Death; The Imperfect Lady.

1948: Joan of Arc; The Pirate; Tarzan and the Mermaids; Who Killed "Doc" Robbin?; Secret Service Investigator.

1949: Madame Bovary; the Barkleys of Broadway; The Secret Garden.

1950: Let's Dance; Harbor of Missing Men.

1951: David and Bathsheba; The First Legion; Flame of Stamboul.

BIBLIOGRAPHY

Academy Awards. New York: Frederick Ungar, 1978.

The American Film Institute Catalog: Feature Films 1921-30. 2 volumes. New York: R.R. Bowker, 1971.

The American Film Institute Catalog: Feature Films 1931-40. 3 volumes. Berkeley: University of California Press, 1993.

Anger, Kenneth. *Hollywood Babylon.* New York: Delta/Dell, 1975.

_____. *Hollywood Babylon II.* New York: E.P. Dutton, 1984.

Barbour, Alan G. *Humphrey Bogart.* New York: Pyramid, 1973.

_____. *John Wayne.* New York: Pyramid, 1974.

Basinger, Jeanine. *Lana Turner.* New York: Pyramid, 1976.

_____. *Shirley Temple.* New York: Pyramid, 1975.

Bauer, Barbara. *Bing Crosby.* New York: Pyramid, 1977.

Bavar, Michael. *Mae West.* New York: Pyramid, 1975.

Baxter, John. *Hollywood in the Thirties.* New York: Paperback Library, 1970.

Belafonte, Dennis, and Alvin H. Marill. *The Films of Tyrone Power.* Secaucus, N.J.: Citadel, 1979.

Bergan, Ronald. *The United Artists Story.* New York: Crown, 1986.

Bergman, Andrew. *James Cagney.* New York: Pyramid, 1973.

_____. *We're in the Money: Depression America and Its Films.* New York: Harper Colophon, 1972.

Blum, Daniel. *A Pictorial History of the American Theater, 1900-1950.* New York: Greenberg, 1950.

_____. *A Pictorial History of the Silent Screen.* New York: Grosset & Dunlap, 1972.

Bojarski, Richard. *The Films of Bela Lugosi.* Secaucus, N.J.: Citadel, 1980.

_____, and Kenneth Beale. *The Films of Boris Karloff.* Secaucus, N.J.: Citadel, 1974.

Bookbinder, Robert. *The Films of Bing Crosby.* Secaucus, N.J.: Citadel, 1977.

Brown, Curtis F. *Ingrid Bergman.* New York: Pyramid, 1973.

_____. *Jean Harlow.* New York: Pyramid, 1977.

Burdick, Loraine. *The Shirley Temple Scrapbook.* Middle Village, N.Y.: Jonathan David Publisher, 1975.

Capra, Frank. *The Name Above the Title.* New York: Macmillan, 1971; Bantam, 1972.

Chierichetti, David. *Hollywood Director: The Career of Mitchell Leisen.* New York: Curtis, 1973.

Conway, Michael, Dion MacGregor and Mark Ricci. *The Films of Greta Garbo.* Secaucus, N.J.: Citadel, 1973.

_____, and Mark Ricci. *The Films of Jean Harlow.* Secaucus, N.J.: Citadel, 1974.

Corliss, Richard. *Greta Garbo.* New York: Pyramid, 1974.

Deschner, Donald. *The Films of Cary Grant.* Secaucus, N.J.: Citadel, 1973.

_____. *The Films of Spencer Tracy.* Secaucus, N.J.: Citadel, 1973.

Dickens, Homer. *The Films of Barbara Stanwyck.* Secaucus, N.J.: Citadel, 1984.

_____. *The Films of Gary Cooper.* Secaucus, N.J.: Citadel, 1974.

_____. *The Films of Ginger Rogers.* Secaucus, N.J.: Citadel, 1975.

_____. *The Films of James Cagney.* Secaucus, N.J.: Citadel, 1974.

_____. *The Films of Katharine Hepburn.* Secaucus, N.J.: Citadel, 1974.

_____. *The Films of Marlene Dietrich.* Secaucus, N.J.: Citadel, 1974.

Dooley, Roger. *From Scarface to Scarlett: American Films in the 1930s.* New York: Harcourt Brace Jovanovich, 1979.

Druxman, Michael B. *Basil Rathbone: His Life and His Films.* South Brunswick, N.J.: A.S. Barnes, 1975.

_____. *Paul Muni: His Life and His Films.* South Brunswick, N.J.: A.S. Barnes, 1974.

Eames, John Douglas. *The MGM Story.* New York: Crown, 1975.

_____. *The Paramount Story.* New York: Crown, 1985.

Edwards, Anne. *Shirley Temple: American Princess.* New York: William Morrow, 1988.

Essoe, Gabe. *The Films of Clark Gable.* Secaucus, N.J.: Citadel, 1970.

Everson, William K. *The Bad Guys: A Pictorial History of the Movie Villain.* New York: Cadillac/Citadel, 1964.

_____. *Classics of the Horror Film.* Secaucus, N.J.: Citadel, 1974.

_____. *Claudette Colbert.* New York: Pyramid, 1976.

_____. *The Detective in Film.* Secaucus, N.J.: Citadel, 1972.

Eyles, Allen. *The Marx Brothers: Their World of Comedy.* New York: Paperback Library, 1971.

Fields, Ronald J. *W.C. Fields: A Life on Film.* New York: St. Martin's Press, 1984.

Gabree, John. *Gangsters: From Little Caesar to the Godfather.* New York: Pyramid, 1973.

Garnett, Tay. *Light Your Torches and Pull Up Your Tights.* New Rochelle, N.Y.: Arlington House, 1973.

Gelman, Howard. *The Films of John Garfield.* New York: Jove/Harvest/HBJ, 1975.

Gifford, Denis. *Karloff: The Man, the Monster, the Movies.* New York: Curtis, 1973.

_____. *A Pictorial History of Horror Movies.* London: Hamlyn, 1973.

Golden, Eve. *Platinum Girl: The Life and Legends of Jean Harlow.* New York: Abbeville Press, 1991.

Green, Stanley, and Burt Goldblatt. *Starring Fred Astaire.* New York: Dodd, Mead, 1973.

Halliwell, Leslie. *Halliwell's Filmgoer's Companion.* 9th ed. New York: Scribner's, 1988.

_____. *Halliwell's Harvest: A Further Choice of Entertainment Movies of the Golden Age.* New York: Scribner's, 1986.

_____. *Halliwell's Hundred: A Nostalgic Choice of Films of the Golden Age.* New York: Scribner's, 1982.

Harvey, James. *Romantic Comedy in Hollywood, from Lubitsch to Sturges.* New York: Alfred A. Knopf, 1987.

Harvey, Stephen. *Fred Astaire.* New York: Pyramid, 1975.

_____. *Joan Crawford.* New York: Pyramid, 1974.

Higham, Charles. *The Art of the American Film, 1900-1971.* Garden City, N.Y.: Doubleday, 1973.

Hirsch, Foster. *Edward G. Robinson.* New York: Pyramid, 1975.

Hirschhorn, Clive. *The Columbia Story.* New York: Crown, 1990.

_____. *The Hollywood Musical.* New York: Crown, 1981.

_____. *The Universal Story.* New York: Crown, 1983.

_____. *The Warner Bros. Story.* New York: Crown, 1979.

Jacobs, Jack, and Myron Braum. *The Films of Norma Shearer.* Secaucus, N.J.: Citadel, 1977.

Jewell, Richard B., and Vernon Harbin. *The RKO Story.* New York: Arlington House/Crown, 1982.

Jordan, Rene. *Clark Gable.* New York: Pyramid, 1973.

_____. *Gary Cooper.* New York: Pyramid, 1974.

Juneau, James. *Judy Garland.* New York: Pyramid, 1974.

Kass, Judith M. *Olivia de Havilland.* New York: Pyramid, 1976.

Katz, Ephraim. *The Film Encyclopedia.* New York: Harper Perennial/HarperCollins, 1994.

Kay, Karyn. *Myrna Loy.* New York: Pyramid, 1977.

Kendall, Elizabeth. *The Runaway Bride: Hollywood Romantic Comedy of the 1930s.* New York: Alfred A. Knopf, 1990.

Kerbel, Michael. *Henry Fonda.* New York: Pyramid, 1975.

Kobler, John. *Damned in Paradise: The Life of John Barrymore.* New York: Atheneum, 1977.

Kotsilibas-Davis, James. *The Barrymores: The Royal Family in Hollywood.* New York: Crown, 1981.

_____, and Myrna Loy. *Myrna Loy: Being and Becoming.* New York: Alfred A. Knopf, 1987.

Madsen, Axel. *Stanwyck.* New York: HarperCollins, 1994.

Maltin, Leonard. *Carole Lombard.* New York: Pyramid, 1976.

_____, ed. *Leonard Maltin's Movie and Video Guide.* New York: Signet, 1994.

_____, ed. *The Real Stars: Articles and Interviews on Hollywood's Great Character Actors.* New York: Curtis, 1973.

_____, ed. *The Real Stars* [Vol. 2]. New York: Popular Library, 1979.

Marill, Alvin H. *The Complete Films of Edward G. Robinson.* Secaucus, N.J.: Carol Publishing/Citadel, 1990.

_____. *Katharine Hepburn.* New York: Pyramid, 1973.

_____. *Samuel Goldwyn Presents.* South Brunswick, N.J.: A.S. Barnes, 1976.

McBride, Joseph. *Frank Capra: The Catastrophe of Success.* New York: Simon & Schuster, 1982.

_____. *Orson Welles.* New York: Jove/Harcourt Brace Jovanovich, 1977.

McCarty, Clifford. *Bogey: The Films of Humphrey Bogart.* Secaucus, N.J.: Citadel, 1974.

McGilligan, Patrick. *George Cukor: A Double Life.* New York: St. Martin's Press, 1991.

_____. *Ginger Rogers.* New York: Pyramid, 1975.

Miller, Don. *B Movies.* New York: Ballantine Books, 1988.

Morris, George. *Errol Flynn.* New York: Pyramid, 1975.

_____. *John Garfield.* New York: Jove/Harcourt Brace Jovanovich, 1977.

Nemcek, Paul L. *The Films of Nancy Carroll.* New York: Lyle Stuart, 1969.

The New York Times Film Reviews. 7 volumes. New York: New York Times/Arno Press, 1970.

Ott, Frederick W. *The Films of Carole Lombard.* Secaucus, N.J.: Citadel, 1974.

Parish, James Robert. *The Fox Girls.* New York: Castle Books, 1971.

_____. *Hollywood Character Actors.* New Rochelle, N.Y.: Arlington House, 1978.

_____. *Hollywood Players: The Thirties.* New Rochelle, N.Y.: Arlington House, 1976.

_____. *Hollywood's Great Love Teams.* New Rochelle, N.Y.: Arlington House, 1974.

_____. *The Paramount Pretties.* New Rochelle, N.Y.: Arlington House, 1972.

_____. *The RKO Gals.* New Rochelle, N.Y.: Arlington House, 1974.

_____. *The Tough Guys.* Carlstadt, N.J.: Rainbow Books, 1977.

_____, and Don E. Stanke. *The Glamour Girls.* New Rochelle, N.Y.: Arlington House, 1975.

_____, and Don E. Stanke. *The Leading Ladies.* New Rochelle, N.Y.: Arlington House, 1977.

Peary, Danny. *Cult Movie Stars.* New York: Simon & Schuster/Fireside, 1991.

Peters, Margot. *The House of Barrymore.* New York: Simon & Schuster/Touchstone, 1990.

Quinlan, David. *The Illustrated Encyclopedia of Movie Character Actors.* New York: Harmony Books/Crown, 1986.

_____. *The Illustrated Directory of Film Stars.* New York: Hippocrene Books, 1981.

_____. *Wicked Women of the Screen.* New York: St. Martin's Press, 1987.

Quirk, Lawrence J. *The Complete Films of William Powell.* Secaucus, N.J.: Citadel, 1986.

_____. *The Films of Fredric March.* Secaucus, N.J.: Citadel, 1971.

_____. *The Films of Ingrid Bergman.* Secaucus, N.J.: Citadel, 1974.

_____. *The Films of Joan Crawford.* Secaucus, N.J.: Citadel, 1968.

_____. *The Films of Myrna Loy.* Secaucus, N.J.: Citadel, 1980.

_____. *The Films of Robert Taylor.* Secaucus, N.J.: Citadel, 1975.

_____. *The Films of Ronald Colman.* Secaucus, N.J.: Citadel, 1977.

_____. *The Great Romantic Films.* Secaucus, N.J.: Citadel, 1974.

Ragan, David. *Who Was Who in Hollywood.* 2 volumes. New York: Facts on File, 1992.

Ringgold, Gene. *The Films of Bette Davis.* Secaucus, N.J.: Citadel, 1974.

_____, and DeWitt Bodeen. *The Films of Cecil B. DeMille.* Secaucus, N.J.: Citadel, 1974.

Robinson, Edward G. *All My Yesterdays: An Autobiography.* New York: Hawthorn, 1973.

Rogers, Ginger. *Ginger: My Story.* New York: HarperCollins, 1991.

Scherle, Victor, and William Turner Levy. *The Films of Frank Capra.* Secaucus, N.J.: Citadel, 1977.

Sennett, Ted. *Lunatics and Lovers.* New Rochelle, N.Y.: Arlington House, 1973.

_____. *The Movie Buff's Book.* New York: Pyramid, 1975.

_____. *The Movie Buff's Book 2.* New York: Pyramid, 1977.

Shipman, David. *The Great Movie Stars: The Golden Years.* New York: Crown, 1970.

_____. *The Story of Cinema.* New York: St. Martin's Press, 1982.

Sikov, Ed. *Screwball: Hollywood's Madcap Romantic Comedies.* New York: Crown, 1989.

Silver, Alain, and Elizabeth Ward, eds. *Film Noir.* Woodstock, N.Y.: Overlook Press, 1979.

Silver, Charles. *Marlene Dietrich.* New York: Pyramid, 1974.

Smith, Ella. *Starring Miss Barbara Stanwyck.* New York: Crown, 1974.

Springer, John. *Forgotten Films to Remember.* Secaucus, N.J.: Citadel, 1980.

_____, and Jack Hamilton. *They Had Faces Then: Superstars, Stars and Starlets of the 1930s.* Secaucus, N.J.: Citadel, 1974.

Stern, Lee Edward. *Jeanette MacDonald.* New York: Jove/Harvest/HBJ, 1977.

_____. *The Movie Musical.* New York: Pyramid, 1974.

Swanson, Gloria. *Swanson on Swanson: An Autobiography.* New York: Random House, 1980; Pocket Books, 1981.

Thomas, Tony. *The Complete Films of Henry Fonda.* Secaucus, N.J.: Citadel, 1983.

_____. *The Films of Olivia de Havilland.* Secaucus, N.J.: Citadel, 1983.

_____. *The Great Adventure Films.* Secaucus, N.J.: Citadel, 1980.

_____. *A Wonderful Life: The Films and Career of James Stewart.* Secaucus, N.J.: Citadel, 1988.

_____, Rudy Behlmer and Clifford McCarty. *The Films of Errol Flynn.* Secaucus, N.J.: Citadel, 1969.

_____, and Aubrey Solomon. *The Films of 20th Century-Fox.* Secaucus, N.J.: Citadel, 1979.

Thompson, Howard. *James Stewart.* New York: Citadel, 1974.

Tozzi, Romano. *Spencer Tracy.* New York: Pyramid, 1973.

Truitt, Evelyn Mack, [ed.]. *Who Was Who on Screen.* New York: R.R. Bowker, 1984.

Tuska, Jon. *The Detective in Hollywood.* Garden City, N.Y.: Doubleday, 1978.

_____. *The Films of Mae West.* Secaucus, N.J.: Citadel, 1973.

Vermilye, Jerry. *Barbara Stanwyck.* New York: Pyramid, 1975.

_____. *Bette Davis.* New York: Pyramid, 1973.

_____. *Cary Grant.* New York: Pyramid, 1973.

_____. *The Films of the Thirties.* Secaucus, N.J.: Citadel, 1982.

_____. *Ida Lupino.* New York. Pyramid, 1977.

_____. *More Films of the Thirties.* Secaucus, N.J.: Citadel, 1989.

Wolf, William. *The Marx Brothers.* New York: Pyramid, 1975.

Yanni, Nicholas. *Rosalind Russell.* New York: Pyramid, 1975.

_____. *W.C. Fields.* New York: Pyramid, 1974.

Youngkin, Stephen D., James Bigwood and Raymond C. Cabana Jr. *The Films of Peter Lorre.* Secaucus, N.J.: Citadel, 1982.

INDEX